This house, believed to have been built by Nathaniel Bunnell, younger son of the immigrant William Bunnell, is not only the oldest standing structure we can associate with the Bunnell/ Bonnell family, it is the oldest surviving house in Elizabeth, NJ. It stands at 1045 East Jersey Street, Elizabeth. It is owned and operated by the Elizabethtown Historical Foundation as "The Nathaniel Bunnell Homestead" and is open to the public. For some time it served as the New Jersey State Headquarters of the Sons of the American Revolution.

Nathaniel and his bride Susannah moved to Elizabethtown from New Haven, CT, in 1665. He was granted a lot of six acres, 15 by 4 chains, bounded, E., by Thomas Price; W. and N., by Isaac Whitehead, Sen. (his father-in-law), and S., by a highway. The first documentary reference to the house occurs in a deed in 1682, but it must have been built before 1677 when Nathaniel sold the property to Benjamin Price.

The photograph was taken by Guilbert Gates, New York, NY, and sent to me on 25 August 2003.

The Bunnell/Bonnell Family in America

Second Edition

Consisting of
Volume I Revised and Volume II

William Bunnell
of
Massachusetts Bay and
New Haven Colonies

Comprising Full Accounts of the First Six Generations,
Vital Records of the Seventh Generation, and the
Names and Relationships of the Eighth Generation

Compiled by
William R. Austin

HERITAGE BOOKS
2007

HERITAGE BOOKS
AN IMPRINT OF HERITAGE BOOKS, INC.

Books, CDs, and more—Worldwide

For our listing of thousands of titles see our website
at
www.HeritageBooks.com

Published 2007 by
HERITAGE BOOKS, INC.
Publishing Division
65 East Main Street
Westminster, Maryland 21157-5026

International Standard Book Number: 978-0-7884-4493-7

TABLE OF CONTENTS

INTRODUCTION to Volume I

I was 15 years old when I first became interested in genealogy, and for many years it has been my principal hobby. In the late 1950's my father-in-law showed me several pages of his father's papers briefly outlining the ancestry of his great grandmother, Amanda (Bunnell) Chamberlain. The Bunnell name was new to me. Apparently it was a relatively small family, and we decided that it would be fun to put together a more complete genealogy of the Bunnell family.

More than 40 years have elapsed, and I have learned that the Bunnell/Bonnell family extends in the thousands across the United States and, in fact, across the English-speaking world. More than 550 people have corresponded with me about their connections to the family. For ten years, from 1987 to 1996 I published the quarterly *Bunnell/Bonnell Newsletter*. Now it is time to put all the data I have accumulated into permanent form.

There are still a tremendous number of loose ends I would like to tie together, but it is clear that if I wait to do so, the history will never be published. Many people have contributed the results of their own research, and it is only fair that their work be made available to others. Therefore, with this volume, the first five generations of the family of William Bunnell, we begin the history of the Bunnell/Bonnell family in America, leaving until later, or to other researchers, the discovery of the missing links.

Essentially, the following history is a compilation of the work of many people. I have not had the time nor the opportunity to do exhaustive basic genealogical research across the country. Where primary records have been available to me I have used them. But the principal purpose of my work has been to bring together in one place the research that has been done piece by piece by many people over the years. An extensive correspondence, with occasional visits to some of the major libraries in the Northeast, has been the modus operandi. Where I have found discrepancies or conflicting data, I have tried diligently to analyze, compare and clarify the information in order to present in these pages a story that is as close to factual as possible.

The preparation of this material was actually begun well before 1900 by John Addison Biles of Homets Ferry, Bradford co, PA. Through the generosity of his granddaughter, Miss Marian E. Biles of Greene, NY, I was able to secure a copy of his manuscript and to make copies of hundreds of letters that Mr. Biles received from Bunnells and Bonnells all over the United States. They range in date from 1895 to 1925. Together with the manuscript they have been an invaluable resource, frequently providing answers that were unavailable from any other source. I am very pleased that through this means the results of John Biles' effort will finally be published.

Homer E. Baldwin of Greensburg, PA, also contributed very heavily to this work. We wrote back and forth for years, and in the process he sent me copies of hundreds of pages of genealogical data that he had accumulated in his life-long study of the family, particularly the Bonnell side. Homer was also the source of contact with many many others who subsequently made contributions large or small.

In the late 1970's I learned that Ruth Cost Duncan of West Simsbury, CT, was also working on a genealogy of the family. We corresponded at length, sharing information. I am greatly indebted to her for giving me the benefit of her extensive research in the original records of Connecticut. In 1986 she published her work under the title, *William Bunnell and His Descendants*, the first comprehensive study of this family to appear in print. Then she boxed up all her correspondence and research papers and sent them to me to help me continue the work.

Claude Mitchell of Muskegon, MI, also turned over to me his many years of correspondence with family members all over the country. Ruth and Mitch both continue to pass along whatever new information they come across.

One of the most significant contributors to my research, in terms of sheer volume of useful data, is Claude A. Bunnell of Ocean City, NJ, and Longboat Key, FL. Years ago Claude began to accumulate family records in a computer database comprising vital records of every person he could find with any variant of the name of Bunnell, Bonnell, Burnell, etc. Among the many sources he has entered in his database are most of the U.S. Federal Census records through 1920. He is constantly seeking additional primary records to include. His database already contains data on some 38,000 people born with the name. Their spouses add thousands more.

In January 1987 I began publishing the quarterly *Bunnell/Bonnell Newsletter*. The response was very gratifying, and I continued it for ten years. During that time, and continuing to the present, it has generated for me hundreds of new correspondents. The most recent new letter was from correspondent #557. While some of the files include an exchange of only one or two letters, many comprise a years-long sharing of intensive research. I am deeply grateful for all their help, and will try to acknowledge their specific contributions in the References on the following pages.

The Bunnell/Bonnell Newsletter continues, with Carole Bonnell as editor and publisher, at P. O. Box 4282, Spanaway WA 98387.

I am aware that in recent years a growing chorus of reviewers and other genealogy experts have pushed the idea that every fact must be proved by reference to original, primary and contemporary documents. The implication is that, without that proof, a genealogy has no value.

In my view, that is a goal to be strived for, recognizing that the goal is not attainable much of the time. Very few genealogists have the time, money or opportunity to live up to that ideal. Data is not false just because it does not come from a primary document. Conversely, it is not always true just because it does.

In compiling this work I have been able to correct a number of published errors. Most errors result from unsupported family traditions, wishful thinking on the part of the genealogist, or misinterpretation of the available data. Sometimes, however, it comes from incorrect information recorded in original primary documents. (My own sister's birth certificate was recorded with the wrong year of birth.)

The point is not that all records are equally valuable. It is that one must use all the information available, from whatever source, examine it critically, and compile a finished result that is reasonable, logical and consistent with the data. I have tried to do that. While I have corrected a number of errors, I have probably missed others, and may even have inadvertently introduced some new ones of my own. Future genealogists, with access to better information, will have to correct them.

In what follows I have tried to identify my source for each statement, where possible quoting contemporary records. Where these were not available to me I have identified the earliest source or what I deemed to be probably the most reliable source. Abbreviated references are listed at the end of each article. Full references can be found in the Key to References beginning on page 475. In a very few cases I was unable to determine where I found the information originally. In those cases I used the statements without identifying a source, recognizing that their value is principally as clues for further research.

This history is as complete and accurate as I have been able to make it. In here there are instances of substantial disagreement with the work of earlier researchers. I have tried to make clear the reasons for my conclusions which differ from those of others. Readers may feel that I was wrong in some instances, and they will inevitably find errors and omissions. I hope they will feel free to write to me immediately when they do.

INTRODUCTION to the Second Edition

Almost before the ink dried on the printing of Volume I, new information was discovered which radically changed some of the family relationships I had compiled. Almost all of these corrections and additions are found in the descendants of William Bunnell's second son Nathaniel Bonnell.

Accept the accounts in these pages for what they are, my best judgement of the facts, based on the tools and sources available to me, applying whatever skill I have as a genealogist. If you find your ancestors here, you will surely want to learn more about them than I have been able to provide. I encourage you to search specifically for that information. I have tried to include all the clues for further research that have come to me. The answers you find will give you a more complete picture of your ancestor's life, and they may correct mistakes in my account.

I am a great believer in serendipity. So many instances have come to my attention in which knotty, "insoluble" problems have been overcome by the chance discovery of some unlooked for record.

The new role of technology opens many genealogical doors. The internet gives us access to huge amounts of information previously available, if at all, in far away libraries, court houses, cemeteries, etc. There are a number of websites now on the internet which can usefully connect Bunnell/Bonnell seekers. The most important is that of Claude A. Bunnell's huge Database. Since I published Volume I, Claude has posted the entire Database on the internet for free use of anyone interested, at *http://bunnellbonnellburnellfamily.com*. He is continually adding new information and corrections. I have made liberal use of his material in this second edition.

Carole Bonnell, of Spanaway, WA, the second publisher of *The Bunnell/Bonnell Newsletter*, issued the Newsletter quarterly for seven years. Then she passed the baton to Charles E. Bunnell, P. O. Box 1507, Fairfield Glade, TN 38558, phone (931) 707-1444, e-mail *www.bunnellfamily.com*, who continues the publication, now in its 21st year. Charles has introduced a fascinating new aspect to our research, that of DNA testing to check the validity of suggested relationships. Steven Bonnell, 1523 Good Shepherd Road, Montoursville, PA 17754, has volunteered to become the DNA Group Administrator. His e-mail address is *BNL_dna@kbsb.com*. If you are a male in the direct Bunnel/Bonnell/Burnell/etc. line, your participation in the DNA testing program would be very helpful in proving (or disproving) the results of our research.

It has been fifty years since I made my first inquiries regarding the Bunnell family. With the publication of this edition I plan to retire. Others will have to carry on the work. I will make sure that my files are placed where they will be available for study.

THE NAME

In common with most surnames, this name has been subject to many variations in spelling and several variations in pronunciation over the years. Several origins for the name have also been proposed.

In his *Directory of the Ancestral Heads of New England Families 1620-1700*, Frank R. Holmes called BUNNELL "A corruption of Bonhill, a parish in County of Dumbarton, Scotland." It should be noted that almost every other statement Mr. Holmes includes about this family is false. However, there is a parish of Bonhill in the county of Dumbarton. It appears just south of Loch Lomond on my copy of *Ordnance Survey Motoring Atlas of Great Britain* by Temple Press, 1983. So far, at least, I have not found any Bunnells or Bonnells originating in Scotland to give credence to this suggestion.

A similar, but much more likely, derivation appears in Bardsley's *A Dictionary of English and Welsh Surnames, With Special American Instances:*
- p. 117. "BONEHILL, BONHILL, BONELL, BONNELL, - Local, 'of Bonehill,' a township in the parish of Tamworth, co. Stafford. The variants are well known in the country."
- p. 118. "BONNELL, v. BONEHILL."
- p. 147. "BUNNELL, - Local, "of Bonehill,' co. Staff.; v. Bonehill; cf. Buckle and Buckell for Buckhill."

Mrs. Clarence Bunnell, Winsted, CT, sent me a newspaper clipping in 1961 entitled, "Is Your Name Bunnell?" It was printed in *The Eagle Bulletin*, a local newspaper in the New Haven, CT, area. Here are a couple of relevant excerpts:

> "Bunnell, an old and honored surname, is principally of English origin. It is a local name, and, according to most authorities on nomenclature, is obtained from Bonehill, a community in Staffordshire, England. It signifies literally 'bonny or fair hill' and is sometimes spelled as 'Bunnel'."
>
> . . .
>
> "Bunnell is a beverage that is made from crushed apples or pears after they have been used to make cider or perry. It is popular in England."

Bonehill, near Birmingham in Staffordshire, seems a more likely local name site for this family when you consider the many early members of the family who lived in the immediate area. See the chapter on Family Origins for more about that.

While my personal opinion is that William Bunnell's ancestry was probably pure English, many people have suggested a Huguenot ancestry for him and attempted to trace his ancestry back to France. It is certainly true that many Bonnells are descended from Huguenot forebears even if

William was not. If we look for place names in France that might have given a name to the family, there are several possibilities:

Bonnelles, a little southwest of Paris.
Bonneuil-sur-Marne, just outside of Paris on the east.
Bonneuil-en-Valois, northeast of Paris near Soissons.
and Bonneuil-Matours, just east of Poitiers.

As in Scotland, I do not know of any Bonnells or Bunnells who can be connected to any of these places. However, also as in Scotland, I haven't done any research on the family in France.

Every once in a while in your ancestor hunt you find someone who asserts strongly that the name is correctly spelled one way and no other. That is true here also. For example:

In a letter dated 22 April 1941 from Homer Deats, of Hunterdon co, NJ, to Margaret Fletcher, Minneapolis, MN: "I note that you spell the name B<u>u</u>nnell. It is frequently pronounced that way here, but is properly B<u>o</u>nnell."

Carolyn Syron Valentine, in her manuscript, *Syron-Searing Wills, Deeds and Ways*, 1925, said (erroneously), "There were two William Bonnels, or Bunnels, as the records persisted in making them, in New England."

In *American Families of Historic Lineage - Long Island*, we find: "The original spelling of the name was distinctly Bonnell. In the New Jersey records the latter 'l' was dropped, and the fact that Nathaniel Bonnel, the Elizabethtown settler, and his children, including Joseph Bonnel, all spelled their names Bonnel instead of Bunnell, shows that this was the original spelling of the name, and in nearly every English record the spelling is Bonnell. The emigrant ancestor's name was spelled Bunnil and Bunnill, this being a corruption, and due to the writers of the early colonial records."

It would be just as logical to say that "the fact that Benjamin Bunnell, the elder son of the immigrant, and all his children spelled their names Bunnell instead of Bonnell shows that this was the original spelling of the name."

The fact of the matter is that there was no "original" spelling of the name any more than there is today a "correct" spelling.

For many generations prior to the nineteenth century, and even later, spelling was extremely haphazard, and names were no exception. Writers spelled them the way they heard them. It is not at all unusual to find a given person's name spelled in more than one way in the same document.

So far in my research I have found 70 spellings which apparently applied to members of this family. It would be absurd to say that one is original or correct and that the other 69 are "corruptions":

Banel	Bonhole	Bonneul	Bounell	Bunneel
Bennel	Bonieul	Bonney	Bouniolle	Bunneell
Boinel	Bonill	Bonnill	Boynel	Bunnel
Boinell	Bonle	Bonnille	Boynell	Bunnell
Bonall	Bonnall	Bonnioles	Bundle	Bunnelle
Bonay	Bonnay	Bonnoel	Bunel	Bunnells
Boneal	Bonneel	Bonnoual	Bunell	Bunniel
Boneale	Bonnel	Bonoel	Bunells	Bunniell
Boneall	Bonnele	Bonoeul	Bunhall	Bunnil
Bonehill	Bonnell	Bonuile	Bunhill	Bunnill
Bonel	Bonnelle	Bonuill	Buniel	Bunwell
Bonele	Bonneuall	Bonyll	Bunill	Burnell
Bonell	Bonneuil	Boonall	Bunle	Burwell
Bonhall	Bonneuill	Boonel	Bunles	Buynall

Generally speaking, by 1850 and after, spelling conventions had settled down and the different branches of the family had chosen, or accepted, a spelling which has endured. Most branches today use either Bunnell or Bonnell. But a few branches use Bunnel, Bonnel, Burnell, Bundle, Bunnells or Bunnelle, all of which can be found among present descendants of the immigrant William.

What these spellings can do is give us a clue as to the early pronunciation of the name in this country. The most common spellings in the colonies were Bunnel and Bonnel, which leads one to believe that the accent was on the first syllable. All documents in Connecticut spelled with a "u". In New Jersey the earliest records referring to Nathaniel also used the "u". Only later in life did his name appear as Bonnel or Bonnell. Many of Nathaniel's descendants reverted to the Bunnell spelling in later generations, I suppose because that is the way it sounded to them.

When you consider that the vagaries of the English language provide the same pronunciation for sun and son, tun and ton, funny and honey, thunder and wonder, it is easy to see that Bunnel and Bonnel can represent the same sound. Even Homer Deats, quoted above, said that the name was frequently pronounced Bunnell in his area of New Jersey, although there it was usually spelled Bonnell in his time.

Clearly, the early generations in this country said "Bun´l," and many still do. Here in northeast Pennsylvania that is the usual pronunciation. But Merton Bunnell, a prominent local auctioneer, told me once that he is Bun´l here at home, but when he goes to Florida in the winter he is Merton Bun nell´. In several cases families who preferred the latter pronunciation have added a final "e", Bunnelle, to encourage people to speak it that way. Those who spell it Bonnell usually put the emphasis equally on both syllables.

The fact remains that you can spell your name and pronounce it any way you wish, and that is the correct way for you. No one who spells or pronounces his name differently has any reason to say that you are wrong.

In the following text I have generally tried to use the "u" or "o" spelling as the individual in question did, but I have not tried to keep track of the number of "l"s or "n"s. Bunnell or Bonnell appears here as the usual standard, although all documents quoted appear with the original spelling.

FAMILY ORIGINS

The majority of Bunnells and Bonnells in America are descendants of William Bunnell, the immigrant whose history is covered in the first generation in this volume.

In the contemporary records, made in his lifetime, there are three items which make clear that William's home was in England, but nowhere is the location pinpointed to a specific place in England. Two different origins have been presented for him in twentieth century literature, but neither has been supported by any sort of evidence.

First - It has been asserted by a number of writers that he was a farmer and tanner from Cheshire, England. (Ref. *The Compendium of American Genealogy*, Vol. IV, p. 128; Snell's *History of Sussex and Warren Counties, New Jersey*, pp. 225 and 226; *Boston Transcript* query No. 8895, May 31, 1921; *Genealogy of the Bonnell Family as it Pertains to Edgar Marsh Gibby and His Descendants*, p. 3; manuscript history on *The Bunnell Family* from the files of the Institute of American Genealogy; *William Bonnell*, by Hubert Baum.) This statement cannot be confirmed from any contemporary record that has come to light. Mr. Baum actually cites Vol. I, page 21, of the *New Haven Vital Records*, as his source, but I cannot find the reference on that page or any other page of the *New Haven Vital Records*. The records of New England do not give any indication that he worked as a tanner during his residence here.

Second - Several of William Bunnell's descendants have become members of the Huguenot Society on the strength of his supposed descent from Thomas Bonnell, a Huguenot refugee who settled in Norwich, England, where he died in 1607. Thomas's son Benjamin is supposed to have been the father of William, the American immigrant.

The earliest published reference to this suggested origin that I have found is in *History of Union County, New Jersey*, edited by F. W. Ricord, 1897. On page 599 a biographical account of Jonathan Crane Bonnel begins,

> "He comes of one of the early families of the State. Early in the 17th century, the first ancestors, supposed to have been French Huguenots, settled on Long Island, and from there, Nathaniel Bonnel, the great grandfather of our subject, removed to Elizabethtown, New Jersey, becoming one of the first company of Elizabethtown associates."

Although a great many of the Elizabethtown Associates came from Long Island, Nathaniel Bonnel did not. He, like his father-in-law, was one of a smaller group of the Associates who came from New Haven, CT.

Another *History of Union County, New Jersey*, edited by A. Van Doren Honeyman and published by Lewis Historical Publishing Company in 1923, in an article on Jonathan Crane Bonnel in Vol. III, p. 184, expands on the earlier statement:

"The family of Bonnel is believed to have been of French Huguenot origin, its early members having been among those who left France after the revocation of the Edict of Nantes. The first ancestor of record is Thomas Bonnell, of Ypres, France, who fled to England to escape the persecutions of the Duke of Alva, and the patronymic has been variously spelled, Bonal, Bonnail, Bonnel, Bonel, and Bonnell, members of the family being referred to as Seigneurs de Bonal, and the coat-of-arms: Azure, three mullets or. Supporters--Two lions. Some of the family came to this country and settled in Long Island. Thence came Nathaniel Bonnell, who settled in Elizabethtown, New Jersey, and there became a member of the first company of Elizabethtown Associates. Later he moved to Chatham, New Jersey. His son, Nathaniel Bonnell, who was a soldier of the Revolution and bore the military title of captain, was born in 1731, and died in July, 1809. He married Elizabeth Allen, . . ."

I included this lengthy paragraph to show the inaccuracy of the data that can be proved. For example, the first Nathaniel Bonnel did not come from Long Island and he did not move to Chatham. The Nathaniel who married Elizabeth Allen was not his son, but rather his great grandson. With false "history" like this where evidence was readily available to supply the true facts, we have no reason to be confident about the earlier vague connection to a presumed Huguenot source.

It fell to Carolyn Syron Valentine, a Bonnell descendant, to fill in the blanks to show us how Nathaniel Bonnell was supposed to be descended from the Huguenot Thomas. About 1925 she compiled a lengthy manuscript entitled, *Syron-Searing Wills, Deeds and Ways.* Copies are filed in the New York Public Library, the Library of Congress, and perhaps others. Mrs. Valentine first provides some background on Thomas Bonnell and his sons. It should be noted that her account frequently conflicts with that of other published accounts of this family. On page 103 of her manuscript, she goes on to say:

> "With a family so stable, and so well recorded, we might expect it to be very easy
> to show William Bonnel's immediate ancestor. Yet, if he had veritably sprung from
> the sea, his parentage could scarcely be harder to prove. There is no William
> recorded as a Bonnel in England at the required period, who could possibly have
> been he."

It is hard to understand how her conclusions could have won such wide-spread acceptance when she began by saying she had no evidence to support them. With the resources available today, it is clear that the last sentence in that paragraph is false. Bunnells and Bonnells were living in many of the counties of England at the end of the sixteenth century.

In her next paragraph Mrs. Valentine continues:

> "Moreover, there was only one Bonnel of this group in England, previous to his
> birth, whose story is not known. The logic of the <u>known</u> facts affirms that

10

William must be the son of that one--namely Benjamin, son of Thomas the English founder. But we know so very little of the personal life of Benjamin Bonnel that proof, in the absence of records, appears impossible. There are, however, numerous pointers which may serve to convince us, even in the absence of records."

The first sentence in this paragraph is also not true, even if it refers only to the family of Thomas Bonnell. A great deal of information about Thomas Bonnell and his family is available in *"The Perverse Widow,"* compiled by Arthur W. Crawley-Boevey, and published by Longmans, Green, and Co., London, 1898. Thomas had seven sons, four by his first wife and three by the second. Daniel and David, the second and third sons, married and had large families and many descendants. There were five sons of Thomas "whose story is not known." Benjamin and his oldest brother Thomas, Jr., were specifically mentioned in their father's will in November 1607. The three half-brothers, John, Abraham and Isaac, appear only in the baptismal records. They were not named in Thomas Sr.'s, will and probably were not living at the time. I have found no further record of any of the five after 1607. Benjamin was 18 years old that year when he disappeared from history. Why Mrs. Valentine chose Benjamin instead of Thomas, Jr., for William's father is not clear. Thomas, Jr., would at least have been old enough to have had a son about 1600 if he had been married by then.

Mrs. Valentine then states:

"All that we certainly know of William Bonnel's life before his marriage is told in the brief news item which announces his arrival. But enough of Benjamin Bonnel's business life is known to permit us to follow his activities fairly well. Capt. Richard Lord, who carried some of Benjamin's dispatches, was very closely connected with Hartford activities. William Bunnel or Bonnel's life was connected with New Haven solely, as far as extant records found show. I shall therefore consider Benjamin Bonnell, son of Thomas, the English Founder, as the immediate ancestor of William, the American Founder, so long as no proof appears to the contrary."

With that astonishing leap of faith, Mrs. Valentine grafted the American Bunnell/Bonnell family to the Huguenot family of Thomas Bonnell. This line has been accepted for membership in the Huguenot Society in the past, but it is no longer eligible. I offer as evidence to the contrary the following: Ben Bonnell, male child of Tho Bonnell, was christened on 7 January 1589 at the church of Saint Martin at Palace, Norwich, England. Since christening at the period normally took place in the first few days after birth, Benjamin would have been too young to have been the father of William, assuming as I have, that William was born in or before the year 1600.

It would have been helpful if Mrs. Valentine had quoted "the brief news item which announces his arrival," or at least told us where to find it. Her manuscript includes many similar vague references that can't be identified or confirmed.

Mrs. Valentine identifies Benjamin Bonnell, son of Thomas, with the Benjamin Bonnell who was in the service of Sweden or various Swedish companies from 1625 until 1660 or later. Prior to moving to Sweden this man resided in Spain and Portugal for about twenty years. He also seems to have been a merchant in Amsterdam for a time. There is no evidence to show that he ever married. He appears to have visited England at very rare intervals. (ref: *The Swedish Settlements on the Delaware 1638-1664*, by Amandus Johnson, Vol. II, pp. 676 and 677.) This may have been the same Benjamin Bonnell, but I see no evidence for it and find it highly unlikely.

I submitted my conclusions and the reasons for them to Arthur Louis Finnell, CGRS, Registrar General of The National Huguenot Society. I asked his opinion on the evidence for the supposed descent of William Bunnell from the Huguenot Thomas Bonnell of Norwich, England. His reply, dated 14 December 1991, is as follows:

"As Registrar General I must state that from all the records we have on the family of Thomas Bonnell (the Huguenot Ancestor), I find NO evidence or primary documents to FIRST indicate that Benjamin Bonnell had a family or that he was a resident of England long enough at the right time to sire and raise a family. No creditable evidence is presented or found to establish that he had any heirs. SECONDLY the Society files contain nothing to establish beyond a reasonable doubt that William Bonnell had a father Benjamin. In fact no evidence has been presented to even establish the name or identity of a father for William. The use of Virkus' book The Compendium of American Genealogy is not an acceptable source for statements of this nature and is totally undocumented as a publication and is unusable as a source for Lineage Society applications. No National Society will accept materials from this unless they are verified and documented.

"I totally agree with your position that it is an astonishing leap of faith to graft the American Bonnell family as a branch of the Huguenot family of Thomas Bonnell. I would have to, after a complete review, state that NO new applications for membership in the National Huguenot Society will be accepted through the line of William Bonnell, the immigrant, until these questions can be completely and thoroughly researched and resolved.

"I hope this will not be too strong a statement, but I feel the statement you have made regarding this has merit and the line should be closed until further research has been done to prove who William's father is. I do look forward to a continued healthy exchange of ideas and notes in the hope that some where a new grain of truth is uncovered and we find the missing link."

In the pages of the Newsletter and in correspondence, I have frequently invited debate from any person who feels he has evidence to support the Huguenot ancestry. No one has ever taken me up on it, but the false ancestry continues to appear from time to time in new accounts.

So much for the Huguenot connection. In an effort to find some evidence of William's origin in England, I extracted the Bunnell/Bonnell entries in all the counties of England from the International Genealogical Index update of April 1984. Judith Osborne, St. Petersburg, FL, told me that these records included only some 3% of all the parish records in England, but even that small sample gives us food for thought. It suggests the need for an exhaustive search of the original parish records, when time or money can be made available for it.

In the meantime, here is what I found in 1984. There were 193 entries for marriages or christenings which took place prior to 1631. They included eleven Williams (underlined once on the list below), any one of which could have been the man we are looking for. If further research in the English records proves that none of these is the right one, I found some thirty Bunnell/ Bonnell men (underlined twice on the list below), who could have been the father of William without recording his christening in a record which has survived. All this with only 3% of the parish records available in the IGI!

Here is the list, by parish and county: The first column shows the name of the individual; second, the name of the father/mother if a christening, or the spouse if a marriage; third, F or M for sex of child and H or W for husband or wife in a marriage; fourth, C for christening and M for marriage; fifth, the date of the event.

♦Wantage parish, BERKSHIRE

Bonle, Jone	John Bonle/Margrett	FC	09 Jun 1590

♦Chester, Saint John the Baptist, CHESHIRE

Bunnel, Anne	Raph Bunnel/	FC	14 Dec 1630
Bunnell, Henrie	Richard Bunnell/	MC	15 Mar 1599
Bunnell, Roger	Richard Bunnell/	MC	20 Dec 1598

♦Chester, Holy Trinity, CHESHIRE

Bunell, Edward	Rafe Bunell/	MC	15 Jan 1626
Bunell, Elizabeth	James Lawton (or Langton?)	WM	16 Jun 1600

♦Gawsworth, CHESHIRE

Bunnell, Ales	Jhois. Bunnell/	FC	12 Feb 1626
Bunnel, Ann	Jhis. Bunnel/	FC	23 Jul 1618
Bunnell, Catheren	Jhis. Bunnell/	FC	16 Mar 1624
Bunnell, Ellen	Georg Brearton	WM	15 Jul 1607
Bunnell, Isabell	Johis. Bunnell/	FC	13 Jan 1620
Bunnell, Jho.	Jhis. Bunnell/	MC	26 May 1622
Bunnell, John	Alice Stubbs	HM	24 Nov 1583
Bunnell, Tho.	Jh. Bunnell/	MC	21 May 1629

◆Saint Gluvias, CORNWALL

Bonnall, Robart	Henry Bonnall/Grace	MC	01 Jun 1630

◆Saint Mabyn, CORNWALL

Bonnell, Richard	Joan Myner	HM	28 Nov 1584

◆Plymouth, Saint Andrew, DEVONSHIRE

Bunnell, Mary	Philip Rawlyn	WM	02 Feb 1601
Bunell, Nicholas	John Bunell	MC	14 Jan 1593

◆Netherbury, DORSET

Bonnell, Joana	Petrus Clark	WM	16 Jan 1611

◆Jarrow, DURHAM

Bonell, Isabel	Bonell/	FC	18 Nov 1577

◆Ryton, DURHAM

Bunle, Jane	Robert Bunle/	FC	21 Jul 1616

◆Colchester, Saint Botolph, ESSEX

Bonell, Ellsebeth	Thomas Baker	WM	23 Oct 1616

◆Elmore, GLOUCESTER

Boneall, William	Elizabeth Haile	HM	01 Aug 1604

◆Tewkesbury, GLOUCESTER

Bonnell, Anne	Richd Bonnell/	FC	25 Jun 1599
Bonnell, Anne	Richard Bonnell/	FC	25 Aug 1599
Bonnell, Elizabeth	Wm Griffin	WM	04 Nov 1610
Bonnell, Will	Richard Bonnell/	MC	22 Jun 1601
Bonnell, William	Elizabethe Vnderwoode	HM	30 Jul 1620

♦Carisbrooke, HAMPSHIRE

Bonell, Ana	Mathias Hills	WM	11 Feb 1604

♦Little Hormead, HERTFORD

Bonel, William	Luce Newman	HM	16 Oct 1609

♦Canterbury, KENT

Bonnelle, Marguerite	Jean Caudrelie	WM	31 Jan 1619
Bonnelle, Marie	Bastien Fremeneux	WM	19 Jan 1612

♦Greenwich, Saint Alphage, KENT

Bunnell, Hester	John Strire	WM	03 Dec 1629

♦Farnworth near Prescot, LANCASTER

Bonell, Eduardus	Johannis Bonell/	MC	11 Nov 1615

♦Ormskirk, LANCASTER

Bonnell, Anne	John Bonnell/	FC	09 Sep 1622
Bonell, Catherine	John Bonell/	FC	18 Oct 1618

♦Warrington, LANCASTER

Bunnell, Elizabeth	Richard Thomason or Richersone	WM	05 Jul 1612
Bunnell, Ellen	Randle Bunnell/	FC	09 Aug 1629
Bunnell, Ellen	Peeter Bunnell/	FC	04 Apr 1630
Bunell, John	Alis Burscoue	HM	13 Feb 1614
Bunell, Mary	John Bunell/	FC	24 Aug 1601
Bunnell, Peeter	Jane Sankey	HM	27 May 1629
Bunell, Peter	John Bunell/	MC	09 Nov 1606
Bunnell, Randall	Keteren Birkett	HM	08 Jul 1624
Bunell, Thomas	John Bunell/	MC	16 May 1592
Bunell, Thomas	John Bunell/	MC	29 Jan 1604
Bunnell, Thomas	Joane Croft	HM	19 Aug 1629

♦Claybrook, LEICESTER

Boonall or Bognall, Joane	John Boonall or Bognall/Sessell	FA	25 Jul 1598

◆Epworth, LINCOLN

| Bunell, Robert | Ane Clarke | HM | 07 May 1592 |

◆Sibsey, LINCOLN

Bonell, Alse		FC	17 Apr 1595
Bonell, John		MC	06 Oct 1597
Bonell, Willm		MC	03 Feb 1588

◆Tattershall, LINCOLN

| Bonnel, Katherine | Thomas Warde | WM | 20 Jul 1609 |

◆All Hallows The Less, LONDON

Bunnell, Dorothie	Thomas Bunnell/	FC	23 Mar 1599
Bunhill, Robert	Thomas Bunhill/	MC	22 Nov 1607
Bunnell, Suzan	Thomas Bunnell/	FC	01 Jan 1592
Bunhill, William	Thomas Bunhill/	MC	05 Dec 1602

◆Saint Augustine Watling Street, LONDON

| Bunnell, Elizabeth | Hierome Fisher | WM | 29 Jan 1609 |

◆Saint Botolph Bishopsgate, LONDON

| Bonle, John | John Bonle/ | MC | 20 Feb 1592 |

◆Saint Giles Cripplegate, LONDON

Bunhill, Fortune		FC	28 Feb 1588
Bunnell, Richard	Thomas Bunnell/	MC	10 Jan 1562
Bynnell, Walter	Mabell Sherburne	HM	17 Oct 1596

◆Saint Gregory by Saint Paul, LONDON

| Bonell, Richard | Bonell/ | MC | 28 Nov 1585 |

◆Saint Lawrence Jewry and Saint Mary Magdalene Milk Street, LONDON

| Bonel, Margerie | Anthonie Humfrey | WM | 04 May 1561 |

16

◆Saint Mary at Hill, LONDON

Bunnel, Jhon		MC	17 Apr 1605
Bonnell, Katherine		FC	07 Oct 1564

◆Saint Mary Colechurch, LONDON

Bunneell or Bunnell, Anna	David Bunneell or Bunnell/	FC	26 May 1611
Bunneel, Catherina	David Bunneel/	FC	26 Dec 1605
Bunneel or Bunnell, David	David Bunneel or Bunnell/	MC	07 Aug 1608
Bvnnell, Elizabethe	David Bvnnell/	FC	10 Jul 1625
Bonnell, Esther	David Bonnell	FC	13 Mar 1613
Bunneell or Bunnell, Jacob	David Bunneell or Bunnell/	MC	26 Nov 1609
Bunnell, Jeremii	David Bunnell/	MC	08 Oct 1615
Bunnell, Marie	David Bunnell/Catheryne	FC	11 Nov 1621
Bonnell, Nathaniell	David Bonnell/Katherine	MC	27 Jul 1617
Bunnell, Paule	David Bunnell/Katharyne	MC	08 Feb 1623
Bunnell, Samuell	David Bunnell/	MC	25 Oct 1612
Bunnell, Sarah	David Bunnell/Katheryne	FC	01 Nov 1618
Bonnell, Simeon	David Bonnell/Catherine	MC	09 Apr 1620
Bunneell or Bunnell, Susanna	David Bunneell or Bunnell/	FC	15 Feb 1606

◆Saint Mary Somerset, LONDON

Bonnell, Margaret	John Owen	WM	23 May 1574

◆Saint Peter Cornhill, LONDON

Bonnell Richard	Bonnell/	MC	12 Feb 1556

◆Saint Peter-le-Poer, LONDON

Bonnell, Dorathe		FC	01 Dec 1588
Bonnell, Jacobus	Richardi Bonnell/	MC	25 Apr 1585
Bonell, Richard	Richard Bonell/	MC	08 Dec 1583

◆Stepney, Saint Dunstan, MIDDLESEX

Bunnell, Cicely	Michaell Dorch	WM	11 Sep 1580

♦Westminster, Saint Martin in the Fields, MIDDLESEX

Bunnell, Gualterus	Elisabetam Cowper	HM	14 May 1607
Bonhall, Sarah	John Bonhall/Sarah	FC	21 Jul 1628

♦Great Yarmouth, NORFOLK

Bonell, Agnes	Nycholas Gybbs	WM	21 Sep 1579
Bonell, John	Thos Bonell/Agnes	MC	18 Jul 1604

♦North Walsham, NORFOLK

Bunwell, Marye	Wm. Pearson/	FS	18 Jun 1575

♦Norwich, NORFOLK

Bonnel, Abraham	Thomas Bonnel/	MC	15 Apr 1599
Bonnel, Abygaell	Dannel Bonnel/	FC	06 Jul 1606
Bonnel, Anne	Daniel Bonnel/Rebecca	FC	13 Feb 1614
Bonel, Daniel	Daniel Bonel/	MC	15 Nov 1601
Bonnel, Danyel	Daniel Bonnel/	MC	26 Oct 1600
Bonnell, Elyzabette	Thomas Bonnel/	FC	10 Aug 1595
Bonnel, Isac	Thomas Bonnel/	MC	01 Jan 1604
Bonnel, Judye	Thomas Bonnel/Jaquemaine Bygote	FC	16 Mar 1606
Bonnel, Sara	Daniel Bonnel	FC	01 Sep 1611

♦Norwich, All Saints, NORFOLK

Bunell, Elizabeth	Robert Bunell/	FC	24 Jan 1601

♦Norwich, Saint George Tombland, NORFOLK

Bonnell, Tobias	Danielis Bonnell/	MC	26 Apr 1618

♦Norwich, Saint John Timberhill, NORFOLK

Bvnnell, Anne	Robert Bvnnell/Ann	FC	08 Apr 1604
Bvnnell, Ann	William Thwanborowe/	FS	26 Apr 1607
Bunell, Elizabeth	Willim Baldinge	WM	15 Nov 1629

♦Norwich, Saint Martin at Palace, NORFOLK

Bonnell, Ben	Tho Bonnell/	MC	07 Jan 1589
Bunnell, Jn.	Tho Bunnell/	MC	19 Aug 1593
Bunnell, Judith	Jn. Marshall	WM	20 May 1594
Bunnell, Sus	Tho Bunnell/	FC	15 Jul 1591

♦Norwich, Saint Stephen, NORFOLK

Bonnell, Maria	Richard Anderson	WM	13 Aug 1575

♦Norwich, Walloon Church, NORFOLK

Bonnel, Samuel	Dannel Bonnel/	MC	13 Sep 1608

♦Winkburn, NOTTINGHAM

Bunnell, Catherine	William Richardson	WM	12 Oct 1584

♦Much Wenlock, SHROPSHIRE

Bunnell, Edward	John Bunnell/Elizabeth	MC	16 Mar 1630

♦Rowley Regis, STAFFORD

Bunnell,	Willm Bunnell/	MC	20 Aug 1626
Bunnell, Margaret	Wm Bunnell/	FC	28 Sep 1623

♦Walsall, Saint Matthew, STAFFORD

Bonill, Eustace	Agnes Cassmore	HM	25 Jul 1593
Bonell, John	Humfery Greene	WM	16 Aug 1615
Bonyll, Jone		FC	16 Jul 1572

♦Weeford, STAFFORD

Bunnill, Agnes	John Clarke	WM	27 Oct 1571

♦Ipswich, Saint Mary Stoke, SUFFOLK

Bunnell, Rose	Richard Payne	WM	01 Jul 1617

◆Sotherton, SUFFOLK

| Bunell, Robert | Susan Chapman | HM | 1590 |

◆Weybridge, SURREY

| Bonall, Kathrin | John Bonall/Sarah | FC | 1626 |
| Bonall, Margaret | John Bonall/Sarah | FC | Jul 1625 |

◆Aston Juxta Birmingham, WARWICK

| Bunnell, Marie | Thomas Peat | WM | 07 Jun 1621 |

◆Fillongley, WARWICK

| Bonell, Elizabetha | Davidus Alline | WM | 17 Oct 1614 |

◆Sheldon, WARWICK

Bonell, Agnes	Eustace Bonell/	FC	21 Aug 1603
Bonell, Anne	Edward Callowe	WM	29 Jan 1575
Bonell, Dorothie	Thoms Bonell/	FC	13 May 1568
Bonell, Dorothie	Eustace Bonell/	FC	16 Mar 1605
Bonell, Eustache		MC	14 Oct 1571
Bonell, Grace	Edward Bragge	WM	07 Jul 1578
Bonell, Henrie	Thoms Bonell/	MC	16 Nov 1565
Bonell, John	Thomas Bonell/	MC	24 Mar 1560
Bonell, John	Eustise/	MC	11 Mar 1609
Bonell, Jone	Edward Gryffyn	WM	30 Nov 1561
Bonell, Jone	Thomas Bonell/	FC	28 Nov 1564
Bonell, Jone	Willm/	FC	22 Apr 1593
Bonell, Jone	Eustace Bonell/	FC	13 Jul 1595
Bonell, Sara	Eustace Bonell	FC	19 Feb 1597
Bonell, Thomas	Jone	HM	10 Jun 1559
Bonell, Thomas	Eustace Bonell/	MC	26 Jul 1601
Bonell, William	Anne Burbagge	HM	02 Jun 1565
Bonell, Willm	Thomas Bonell/	MC	11 Oct 1562

◆Southam, WARWICK

| Bonnell, Feles | Harrie Nurse | WM | 09 Oct 1551 |

♦Tanworth, WARWICK

Bunnell, Richus	Elizabetha Dixson	HM	14 Oct 1587
Bonnell, Willms	Elizabetha Robbias	HM	27 Oct 1630

♦Trowbridge, WILTSHIRE

Bonell, Agnes	John Cheman	WM	28 Nov 1544

♦Alvechurch, WORCESTER

Bonell, Ales	Nicholas Bonnell/Margaret	FC	10 Apr 1590
Bonell, Ales	John Dauis	WM	12 Oct 1617
Bvnnell, Elleno	Walter Bvnnell/Maryon	FC	13 Apr 1585
Bonnell, Henry	George Bonnell/	MC	23 Jan 1555
Bvnnell, Henry	Walter Bvnnell/Maryon	MC	05 May 1577
Bunhill, Henry	Nicles Bunhill	MC	19 Dec 1601
Bonnell, Jane	George Bonnell/	FC	12 Oct 1553
Bonnell, Jane	Rychard Bonnell/	FC	27 Aug 1559
Bvnnell, John	Walter Bvnnell/Maryon	MC	03 Apr 1580
Bonnell, Mary	Nicholes Bonnell/Margaret	FC	18 Apr 1593
Bonnell, Nicholas	Rychard Bonnell/	MC	22 Jan 1557
Bunnell, Nicholas	Margaret Boulton	HM	18 Aug 1588
Bvnnell, Rychard	Walter Bvnnell/Maryon	MC	03 Apr 1580
Bonnell, Thomas	Walter Bonnell/Maryon	MC	15 Oct 1581
Bonnell, Walter	George Bonnell/	MC	04 Mar 1557
Bunnell, Walter	Maryon Horton	HM	14 Feb 1575
Bonnell, Wyllm	Nicholas Bonnell/	MC	18 Mar 1597

♦Chaceley, WORCESTER

Bonnell, Richard	Mergerie Cowpy	HM	06 Nov 1592

♦Dudley, Saint Thomas, WORCESTER

Bunles, Willm	Willm Bunles/	MC	24 Jan 1572

♦Elmbridge, WORCESTER

Bonell, Elizabeth	Henry Onnion	WM	24 Sep 1610

♦Hanley Castle, Saint Marys, WORCESTER

Bonell, Agneta		FC	04 May 1554

◆Kings Norton, WORCESTER

Bunnell, Elizabeth	John Fields	WM	07 Aug 1551

◆Pedmore, WORCESTER

Bonell, John	George Bonell/	MC	20 Oct 1622

◆Hutton Bushel, YORKSHIRE

Bonell, Anna	Francesci Bonell/	FC	14 Jun 1573
Bonell, Anna	Giulielmi Bonell/	FC	24 Apr 1576
Bonell, Anna	Francesci Bonell/	FC	07 Jun 1584
Bonell, Anna	Gualteri Bonell/	FC	03 Dec 1587
Bonell, Elizabetha	Antonii Bonell/	FC	04 Sep 1572
Bonell, Elizabetha	Francisci Bonell/	FC	20 Feb 1580
Bonell, Elizabetha	Willmi Bonell/	FC	26 Apr 1610
Bonell, Helena	Mathaei Bonell'	FC	16 Sep 1599
Bonell, Ingeram	Antonii Bonell/	MC	21 Feb 1577
Bonell, Isabella	Francisci Bonell/	FC	20 Apr 1583
Bonell, Jane	Guilielmi Bonell/	FC	20 Apr 1583
Bonell, Joannes	Francisci Bonell/	MC	13 Jan 1579
Bonell, Joannes	Willmi Bonell	MC	27 Dec 1607
Bonell, Joshua	Antonii Bonell/	MC	13 Nov 1585
Bonell, Margareta	Antonii Bonell/	FC	09 Jun 1583
Bonell, Rachell	Matthaei Bonell/	FC	05 Mar 1600
Bonell, Radulphus	Matthaei Bonell/	MC	09 Mar 1605
Bonell, Rogerus	Guallteri Bonell/	M	02 Feb 1592
Bonell, Sarah	Antonii Bonell/	FC	21 Aug 1575
Bonell, Thomas	Antonii Bonell/	MC	20 Feb 1580
Bonell, Willmus	Matthea Bonell/	MC	15 Feb 1607

◆Whitby, YORKSHIRE

Bonuill, Isabell	Wm. Bonuill/	FC	25 Oct 1624
Bonuile, Jane	Georgie Bonuile/	FC	03 Oct 1608

I plotted these records on a map of the counties of England. (See page 24.) In this small sample five concentrations showed up.

1. 23 records in two parishes in the North Riding, Yorkshire, 21 of them in the parish of Hutton Bushel. What I can't tell from this record is whether this parish is unusual in Yorkshire for the number of Bonells, or whether it is an indication that examination of the records of nearby parishes would show that Bonells were common throughout the area.

2. 20 records in the city of Norwich, Norfolk. These are all accounted for as children and grandchildren of the Huguenot immigrant, Thomas Bonnell. A copy of the PEDIGREE OF BONNELL, page 198 in *"The Perverse Widow"* follows the map. It shows that this branch of the family has been researched probably more thoroughly than any other English branch.

3. 35 records in London and vicinity. 14 of these are the baptisms of the children of David Bonnell, son of the Huguenot Thomas of Norwich.

4. The fourth grouping is intriguing. The village of Bonehill is in the southeast corner of Staffordshire. Within a range of twenty or so miles of Bonehill we find 47 Bunnells, Bonnells, etc., in 11 parishes in Staffordshire, Leicestershire, Warwickshire and Worcestershire. Extending the range for another 15 or 20 miles encloses several other parishes where the family appears. This adds weight to the theory that the Bunnell/Bonnell name was derived from the village of Bonehill.

5. 27 individual records in 6 parishes in Cheshire and Lancaster. William Bunnell is said to have come from Cheshire, on what authority I can't discover. But this shows that some of the family were living there during his lifetime. I haven't been able to make the connection, but further research in English records is indicated.

Charles Edward Banks, in his study, *The Winthrop Fleet of 1630*, first published in 1930, was able to identify, at least tentatively, the county of origin of 455 of the 700 passengers in the fleet. A third of those were from Suffolk co, another third were from London and vicinity, and one sixth from Essex co. The remaining sixth were scattered in 16 other counties, mostly in the eastern half of England. Lancashire accounted for 6 passengers, Cheshire for one, and Warwickshire for one. None were identified from any other county in the west of England. In this study, Banks listed William Burnell(Bunnell) as "origin undetermined."

Unfortunately, none of this brings us closer to the English origin of William Bunnell. I include it only as a possible aid to others researching this matter. My personal preference is for the region near Bonehill, Staffordshire, where so many Bunnell and Bonnell families were recorded. That is purely a guess at this stage, and may well turn out to be totally wrong if and when the true origin is discovered.

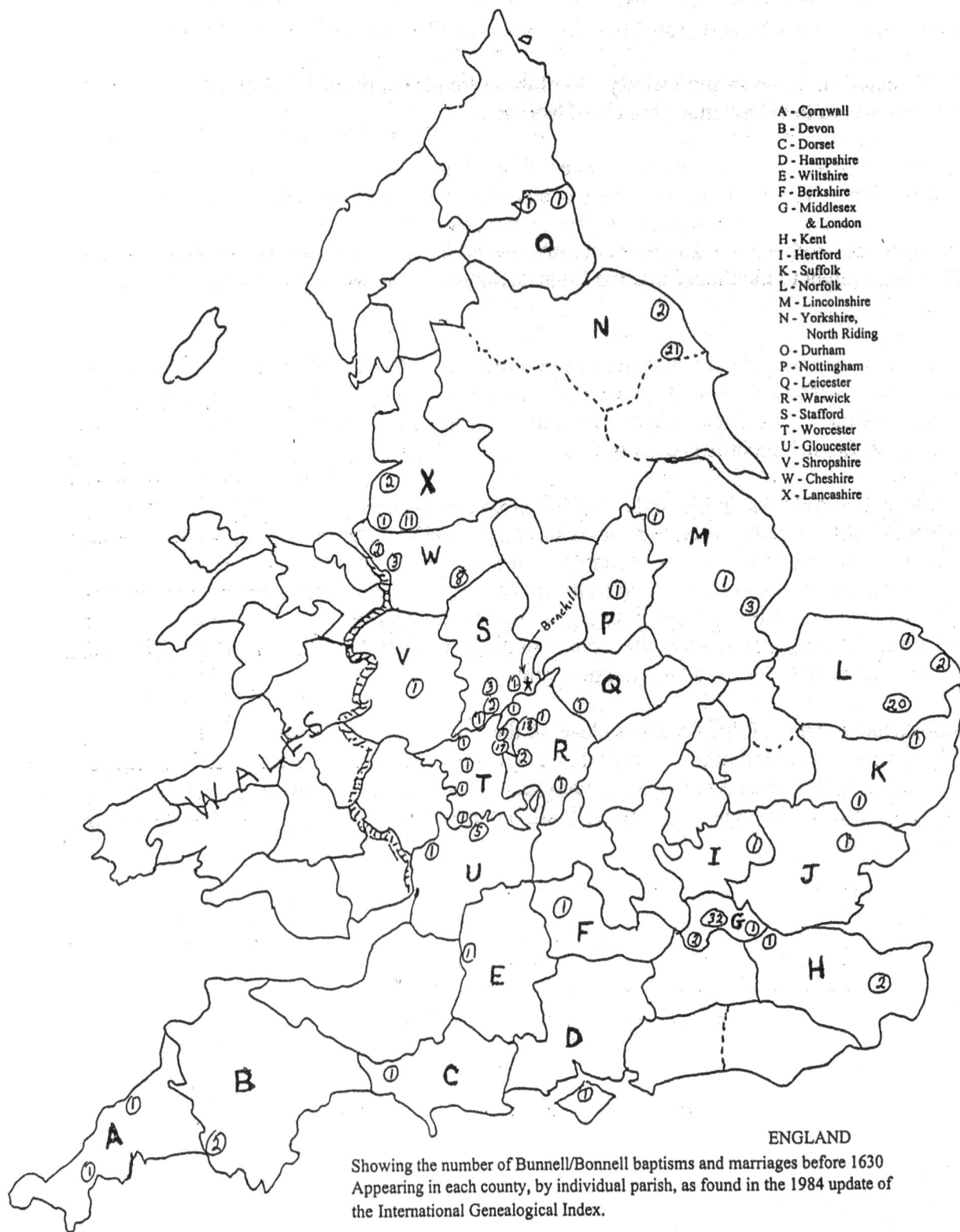

County key (right side of map):

A - Cornwall
B - Devon
C - Dorset
D - Hampshire
E - Wiltshire
F - Berkshire
G - Middlesex
& London
H - Kent
I - Hertford
K - Suffolk
L - Norfolk
M - Lincolnshire
N - Yorkshire,
North Riding
O - Durham
P - Nottingham
Q - Leicester
R - Warwick
S - Stafford
T - Worcester
U - Gloucester
V - Shropshire
W - Cheshire
X - Lancashire

ENGLAND

Showing the number of Bunnell/Bonnell baptisms and marriages before 1630
Appearing in each county, by individual parish, as found in the 1984 update of
the International Genealogical Index.

THE "PERVERSE WIDOW", Being Passages from the Life of
CATHARINA, WIFE OF WILLIAM BOEVEY, ESQ., of Flaxley Abbey in the County of Gloucester,
with Genealogical Notes on that Family and others Connected Therewith.
Compiled by Arthur W. Crawley-Boevey, M.A., Bombay Civil Service (Ret.), Barrister-at-Law of
Lincoln's Inn - Fellow of the Huguenot Society of London.
Published by Longmans, Green, and Co., 39 Paternoster Row, London; New York and Bombay.
1898

PART I.—PEDIGREE OF BONNELL.

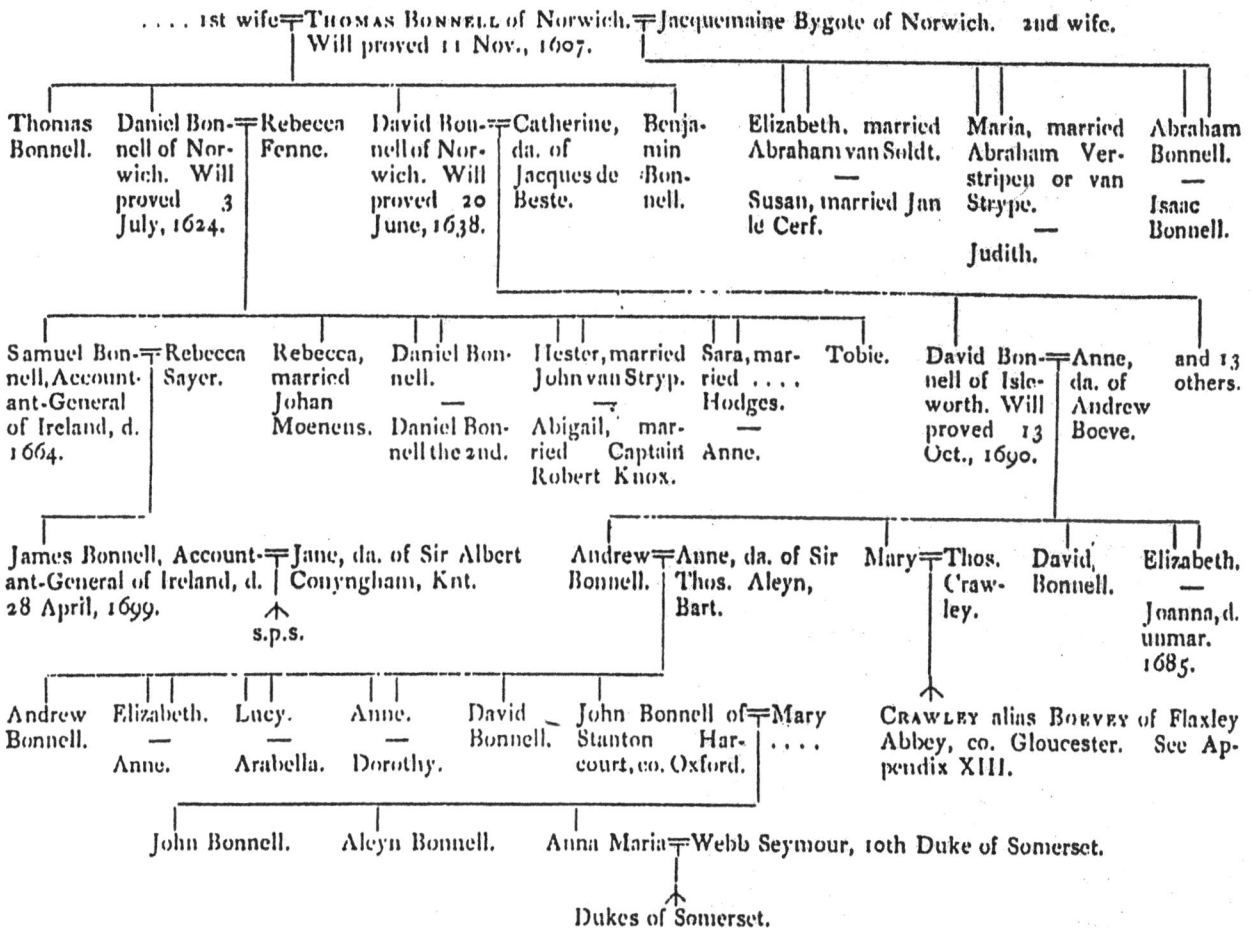

.... 1st wife═THOMAS BONNELL of Norwich.═Jacquemaine Bygote of Norwich.   2nd wife.
Will proved 11 Nov., 1607.

Thomas | Daniel Bon-═Rebecca | David Bon-═Catherine, | Benja- | Elizabeth, married | Maria, married | Abraham
Bonnell. | nell of Nor- Fenne. | nell of Nor- da. of | min | Abraham van Soldt. | Abraham Ver- | Bonnell.
| wich. Will | wich. Will Jacques de | Bon- | — | stripen or van | —
| proved 3 | proved 20 Beste. | nell. | Susan, married Jan | Strype. | Isaac
| July, 1624. | June, 1638. | | le Cerf. | — | Bonnell.
| | | | | Judith.

Samuel Bon-═Rebecca | Rebecca, | Daniel Bon- | Hester, married | Sara, mar- | Tobie. | David Bon-═Anne, | and 13
nell, Account- | Sayer. | married | nell. | John van Stryp. | ried .... | | nell of Isle- | da. of | others.
ant-General | | Johan | — | | Hodges. | | worth. Will | Andrew
of Ireland, d. | | Moenens. | Daniel Bon- | Abigail, mar- | — | | proved 13 | Boeve.
1664. | | | nell the 2nd. | ried Captain | Anne. | | Oct., 1690.
| | | | Robert Knox. | | |

James Bonnell, Account-═Jane, da. of Sir Albert | Andrew═Anne, da. of Sir | Mary═Thos. | David, | Elizabeth,
ant-General of Ireland, d. | Conyngham, Knt. | Bonnell. | Thos. Aleyn, | Craw- | Bonnell. | —
28 April, 1699. | | | Bart. | ley. | | Joanna, d.
s.p.s. | | | | unmar.
| | | | | 1685.

Andrew | Elizabeth. | Lucy. | Anne. | David | John Bonnell of═Mary | CRAWLEY alias BOEVEY of Flaxley
Bonnell. | — | — | — | Bonnell. | Stanton Har- .... | Abbey, co. Gloucester. See Ap-
| Anne. | Arabella. | Dorothy. | | court, co. Oxford. | pendix XIII.

John Bonnell.   Aleyn Bonnell.   Anna Maria═Webb Seymour, 10th Duke of Somerset.

Dukes of Somerset.

Vide "Complete Peerage," G.E.C., vol. vii., p. 182.

FIRST GENERATION

1   D1   CB260001

WILLIAM BUNNELL

[Note that three numbers are used to identify each subject individual. The first is a number I have assigned to reflect both the generation number and the placement in each family. The second is the number assigned by Ruth C. Duncan, for the benefit of those who have or use her book, *William Bunnell and His Descendants*, published in 1986. The third is the number assigned in the massive Database created and maintained by Claude A. Bunnell, Ocean City, NJ, and Longboat Key, FL.]

WILLIAM[1] BUNNELL was certainly born in England, although no evidence showing the date or place of his birth has been found. From circumstantial evidence, I have concluded that he was born "about 1600." His birthdate has been given in various family histories as 1605, 1610, between 1610 and 1620, 1610-1612-1617, and most frequently 1617 (many references in *The Compendium of American Genealogy*). None of these accounts provide any basis for the statement, and so far as I know there is no contemporary record that states his age or date of birth.

The earliest record in which William Bunnell appears is dated 1630[1], when he was old enough to serve on a jury to inquire into the death of Austin Bratcher at Watertown, MA. This certainly excludes a birthdate as late as 1617. He must have been an adult in 1630 and could not have been born after 1610.

About 1650, at New Haven, there are several records which mention "old Bunill,"[7,13, 14, 15,16, 19] and refer to tax exemptions based on "his age, poverty and weakness." Granted that people aged faster in those days, this is strange language to use if he were only 40 at the time. If we assign a date of birth of 1600 he would have been only 50. This is possible, but just within the range of credibility.

I am inclined, until other evidence becomes available, to conclude that he was born "about 1600" in England.

William Bunnell appears first in the Massachusetts Bay Colony[1], where he was selected on 28 September 1630 to be a juror in an inquiry concerning the death of one Austen Bratcher. Therefore, we can suppose that he was one of the settlers who arrived in New England in the great Winthrop fleet of 1630. (Charles Edward Banks, in his book *The Winthrop Fleet of 1630*, identified this juror with the William Burnell who died at Boston in 1660/1. However, the name is clearly Bunell in the record, and there seems to be no reason to question it.)

William Bunnell does not appear in the records again for the next ten years and it is not certain that the later records refer to the same person. For the purposes of this account, I assume that they do, and I believe that his marriage strengthens the likelihood. He married ANN WILMOT, daughter of Benjamin and Ann Wilmot.[12, 21, 22, 24] Presumably they were married at Massachusetts Bay in 1635 or before, although I have found no record of the Wilmot family in Massachusetts. Benjamin Wilmot was one of the early settlers of New Haven Colony, where he signed the covenant some time after June 1639.[23] No earlier record of him has turned up anywhere in the colonies, but it can be shown that most, if not all, the early settlers of New Haven first came to the Massachusetts Bay Colony, where they lived anywhere from nine months to ten years before moving to New Haven in 1638-43. I will assume that the Wilmots followed this pattern unless conflicting evidence can be found.

The first three children of William and Ann Bunnell must have been born at Massachusetts Bay. The order of birth followed by Donald Lines Jacobus in *Families of Ancient New Haven* places Lydia first, followed by Benjamin and Nathaniel. No record seems to exist which mentions the age at any time of any of the three. Based on the date of her marriage and the dates of birth of her nine children, I am inclined to consider Lydia somewhat younger, and have tentatively suggested that she was born between Benjamin and Nathaniel.

In 1640 we find the first of the numerous records of the public assistance provided to William Bunnell and his family, when the General Court of the Colony requested the town of Watertown to provide William Bunnell with a lot, which the Colony would pay for if William could not.[2] If the lot was actually provided, no record of it has been found.

In 1645 the General Court appointed a committee with power to dispose of the children of Goodman Bunnell, "if their grandfather will not take care of them."[3] (The grandfather, Benjamin Wilmot, had moved to New Haven Colony several years before.) On the same day the Court provided that certain goods be delivered to the same committee "to be disposed of to Goodman Bunnell & his use."[4] Six months later, in May 1646, William Bunnell returned to England, and the Court agreed to pay for 30 shillings worth of clothing for him when he arrived there.[5]

There is nothing to show why William went back to England or where in England he went, but he seems to have simply abandoned his family. In a court action in New Haven several years later his wife testified that "he left little or nothing to maintain them, and she asked him what she should do with them; he said they were hers as well as his, and he left them with her."[12] One of the sons, presumably Benjamin, testified that "he remembers his father did say so to his mother." With no alternative, Ann Bunnell took the three children and moved to New Haven to live with her parents. Her father could not support such a large addition to his family, and they decided "to put forth the children." Nicholas Elsy took one of the boys, presumably the elder (Benjamin, in the traditional order), and Samuel Whitehead took Lydia.

By the middle of 1649, or earlier, William Bunnell returned from England and followed his family to New Haven. On 3 April 1650 he makes his first appearance in the New Haven records, when

"The Court freed old Goodman Bunill from paying his poll money to the town, because of his poverty, age and weaknes."[7] This is the only reference to William's age in any record.

On 4 May 1650 Ann Bunnell gave birth to another daughter, Mary,[8] and in August of that year William was fined 5 shillings for failure to report the birth within three months.[9] A few months later he was in trouble again. On 7 January 1650/51 John Tompson sought the help of the Court to make William Bunnell move out of Tompson's house.[10] Tompson said he was willing to give him a year's rent if he would move peacably out. This probably means that the Bunnells were at least a year behind in their rent payments, which Tompson would forgive if they would simply vacate. The Court ordered William to move, and gave him two or three weeks to do so. A month later John Tompson was back in Court again asking that William Bunnell be put out of his house.[11] This time Stephen Goodyear undertook to guarantee the move if Tompson would let the Bunnells stay for another week. John Tompson expressed himself satisfied with that arrangement, and apparently it was successful, since the issue did not come before the Court again.

In October 1651 it was William's turn to sue, when he asked the Court to revoke the apprentice agreements Ann and her father had made with Nicholas Elsy and Samuel Whitehead. The Court refused to do so.[12]

During the next six or eight months the Town authorities had to "consider of the charge which old Bunill hath been to the Town, and how it might be lessened."[13] The first step was to give him an allowance of two shillings a week, "provided that hee and his family doe what they can towards their maintaynance."[14] Then they took up the problem of the son who was still at home (presumably Nathaniel). The Townsmen felt that the boy should be put out to apprenticeship, both to reduce the charge to the Town, and for the good of the boy, "who now for want of due nurture growes rude and offensive."[15] William Judson's son offered the Bunnells a cow if he could take the boy for "such a number of years as might answer it." When William Bunnell refused to accept this arrangement, the Townsmen retaliated by withdrawing the weekly allowance.[16]

On 28 August 1653 another son, Ebenezer, was born to the Bunnells.[17] He seems to have died very soon.[19] The following February it was reported that Ann Bunnell was sick, and the authorities were still concerned about how much public support was proper and how to make sure that the two remaining children (Nathaniel and Mary) were put out "both for the good of the chilldren (who are not educated as they should) & for the easing ye Towne of charge."[18]

Ann Bunnell died soon after, and on the first of May 1654 William told the Town he wanted to go to old England where "he hath some frends to take care of him."[19] The Townsmen and Treasurer were authorized to negotiate his passage on a ship bound from Milford to Newfoundland (and from there to old England). Their conclusion was that this "might free the Towne from some charge, though they made some prsent disburssmt for his passage and other necessaries for him."

That is William Bunnell's last appearance in the records of New Haven. We can assume that he boarded the ship and returned to England. He left his four children in New Haven. No record has been found to show whether the two younger children were "put out", or if so to whom. Perhaps their grandparents or their maternal uncles assumed responsibility for them. Benjamin Wilmot, in his will dated 7 August 1669, left 20 shillings to each of his Bunnell grandchildren.[21]

William Bunnell probably died in England, if he ever arrived there. It is sometimes asserted that he died on the island of Barbadoes in the West Indies, since a man of that name was buried in the parish of St. Michaels, Barbadoes, 5 August 1678.[20] This seems very unlikely, since William would have been around 80 years old and would have made at least five crossings of the Atlantic Ocean.

Children:
1. 270004. Benjamin,[21, 24] b. about 1636.
2. 270003. Lydia,[21, 24] b. about 1638?, m. 10 Apr. 1661, Francis French;[24] d. 1 Apr. 1708.[24]
     Children (surname French):[24]
     1. Lydia.   4. Mary.   7. Susannah.
     2. Elizabeth.   5. Lydia.   8. Francis.
     3. Anna.   6. Samuel.   9. Jane.
3. 270005. Nathaniel,[21, 24] b. about 1640-42.
4. 270006. Mary, b. 4 May 1650;[8, 21, 24] m. 31 Oct. 1671 Eleazer Peck;[24, 25] d. 20 July 1724.[24]
     Children (surname Peck):[24]
     1. Samuel.   4. Martha.   7. Eleazer.
     2. Abigail.   5. Stephen.   8. Nathaniel.
     3. Mary.   6. Eleazer.   9. Elizabeth.
5. 270007. Ebenezer, b. 28 Aug. 1653;[17, 24] d. before 1 May 1654.[19, 24]

REFERENCES:

Here, verbatim, is every contemporary record which I have found referring to William Bunnell and his wife:

The first five entries are from the *Records of The Governor and Company of Massachusetts Bay,* edited by N. B. Shurtleff, 6 vols., 1853.

   1. Vol. 1, page 77.

        28 Sept. 1630. A jury (of fifteen names, "Willm Bunell" being seventh on the list) was impaneled to inquire concerning the death of Austen Bratcher.

                "The Juryes Verdict:--
        Wee finde that the strookes giuen by Walter Palmer were occationally the meanes of the death of Austin Bratcher, & soe to be manslaughtr./"

2. Vol. 1, page 307.

      7 Oct. 1640. "A Genrall Cort, held at Boston"
"The country desires Watertowne to graunt Willi: Bunnell a lot, & if hee do ᵽve chargable, the country to beare it./"

3. Vol. 2, page 134.

      1 Oct. 1645. "At a Session of the Generall Court"
"Mr Sparhauke & Leift Mason are appointed a committee wth all powr to dispose of ye childrn of Goodman Bunnell, if their grandfathr will not take care of ym."

4. Vol. 2, Page 139.

      1 Oct. 1645. "It is thought meet yt those things, viz, cotton woole, canvas, or else, whch returnes wn Capt Bridges returnes, should be delivred to Mr Sparhauke & Leift Mason to be disposed of to Goodman Bunnell & his use."

5. Vol. 2, Page 149.

      6 May 1646. "At a Generall Courte, at Boston, for Election"
"It is ordred yt if Mr Maverick & Mr Manning shall please to lay out 30 s in cloathing in England for Wm Bunnell at his arrivall, on their receit undr his hand for so much delivred by them to ye said Wm Bunnell in England this Corte determines it shalbe repaid them againe here."

That is the last reference to William Bunnell in the Massachusetts records. The next entry is from *Records of the Colony and Plantation of New Haven, from 1638 to 1649,* by Charles J. Hoadly, M.A., 1857.

6. Vol. I, page 478.

      "At a Court Held at Newhaven the 7th of August, 1649
. . . . Jeremiah Osborne informed the court that Henry Pecke reported that their maide (Sarah Ollard,) was wth child by him ye said Jeremiah. Henry Pecke answered that such a report of ye maid was brought into his house as he tooke it vp, but vpon examination it proved to be but a supposition, and he reported that it was so, but he sees that it was his mistake and his sinn & is sorry that he was so foolish to speake so, and for Jeremiah being the father of it, it was his mistake also, for he hearing some a talking of Jeremiah and the maide, tooke it vp that they spake of that matter and him to be ye father, but vpon examination it appeared they spake of no such thing, but that Jeremiah was to haue her, but vpon this mistake he reported it. He was asked whoe brought it to his house, he said goodwife Bunill. Goodwife Bunill said that she had said to goodwife Pecke that goodwife Charles wished ther was no more in ye towne in Rebecka Turners case, for ther was a maide that satt neere her at meeting that did barnish apace, but she named nobody, nor could she tell who it was, and she said to goodwife Charles, if that be yor thoughts yow were best speake of it wher yow best may. Goodwife Charles, that she and Thomas Marshall (whoe was at worke at her house,) being speaking about Rebecka Turner, what a sad thing it was, she said it is well if ther be no more in her case, she remembers no more that she saide. Henry Pecke was asked if he had any witnes that could cleare it that either of these women was ye auther of this report, he said he had none. The plantifs hauing also spoken what they would in ye case, the court proceeded to sentence, and ordered that Henry Pecke paye to Jeremiah Osborne & Sarah Ollard for ye wrong he hath done them 5 l, wch is to be devided betwixt them."

FIRST GENERATION

The following entries are taken from the *Ancient Records Series* of the New Haven Historical Society, edited by Franklin Bowditch Dexter, Volume 1, *New Haven Town Records, 1649-1662*, identified as "Dexter," and from *Vital Records of New Haven, Conn., to 1850,* identified as "NHVR".

7. Dexter, Vol. 1, page 20.

"At a Generall Court Held at Newhauen Aprill 3th 1650."

"The Court freed old Goodman Bunill from paying his poll money to ye towne, because of his poverty, age and weaknes."

8. NHVR, page 5.

"Mary Bunill the Daughter of William Bunill was borne the 4th of may 1650."

9. Dexter, Vol. 1, page 44.

"At a Court Held at Newhaven August 6th 1650."

"Mr Tuttill, Jno Wakefeild, William Bunill was Ordered to paye 5 s a peece because ye names of each of them a child was not brought in wthin three monethes after they were borne:/"

10. Dexter, Vol. 1, page 55.

"At a Court Held at Newhaven January 7th 1650."
"John Tompson declared that he lett William Bunill his house, & he is willing to give him a yeeres rent, if he would goe peacably out: Bunill said he is willing to goe out but cannot tell where to haue another house, he hath inquired but cannot yet here of any, he hath sent to Thomas Barnes aboute his house, but yet hath no Answer from him. Jno Tompson desired ye help of ye Court that William Bunill might goe out of his house: William Bunill was told he must not live in another mans house against his will, but must provide for himselfe elswhere: he said he would doe what he could:/
John Tompson was asked if he would lett him be in it a while till he may speake wth Thomas barnes: Jno Tompson said he cared not if he staid in it a fortnight, or three weekes, so he may then haue his house free, and not be troubled to come to ye Court any more. The Court told Goodman Bunill he must hasten to gett out, he hath libbertie but for a fortnight or three weekes: if he be not out by that time he must be warned to ye next Court, when the Court will doe as they see cause, though John Tompson be not here, for ye charges of ye Court it is at prsent forborne:/"

11. Dexter, Vol. 1, page 60.

"At a Court Held at Newhaven February Ye 4th 1650."

"John Tompson desired William Bunill might be put out of his house. Mr Goodyeare desired he might staye in one weeke more & he would vndertake he should then goe out, wth wch Jno Tompson was satisfied at present:/"

12. Dexter, Vol. 1, page 89.

"At a Court Held at Newhaven the 7th of October, 1651."

"William Bunill declareth that while he was gone for England, his wife and her father put forth his sonn to Nico Elsy and his daughter to Sam: Whithead, to prentice wthout his consent. wch when hee came he disallowed of; onely was willing they should keepe them a while, but now desires that he may haue them againe for his help.

Nicolas Elsy said that the Grandfather of the boy came to him, and desired him to take him, and he did. Goodman Willmot, the Grandfather of the boy was asked the ground therof; hee said his sonn Bunill was in the Bay, and was a charge to the country there, after went to England, left his wife and children but no meanes to maintayne them: after hee was gone shee & her children came vp heither to him, but hee was not able to keepe them: therfore they did advise together, and agreed to put forth the children, and did put the boy to Nico Elsy:

Samuel Whithead said for the girle he sought her not; but Goodwife Bunill came to his house, declared her condition, wch was to be pittyed, hauing diuers small children and no meanes to maintayne them, and desired him to take her daughter, wch they did vpon the termes they agreed. Goodwife Bunill was asked what direction her husband left for providing for the chilldren; she said he left little or nothing to maintayne them, and she asked him what she should doe wth them; hee said they were hers as well as his, and he left them wth her. And the boy saith he remembers his father did say so to his mother:

William Pecke said that his wife heard Goodman Bunill say after hee came here from England, that he was well satisfyed wth the chilldren where they were; and Luke Atkinson said he heard Goodman Bunill say he was well satisfyed in ye placing of ye chilldren. Goodman Bunill said hee ment for the present, a yeere or two, or so. Goodman Bunill was told hee must not thinke that they will take chilldren small and keepe them till now and let him haue them againe, but he must allow what is just for keeping them; wch he is not able to doe, and the case was such it seemes that if they had not placed them, the Magistrate must haue taken care to dispose of them.
Wherefore, all things considered, the Court cannot but confirme the placeing of them: but if they finde the time too longe, they will consider that some of it be abated, or some thing allowed to them:/"

13. Dexter, Vol. 1, page 108.

"At a Generall Court for Newhaven, February 9th 1651."

"The Townesmen were desired to consider of the charge wch old Bunill hath bine to ye Towne, and how it may be lessened, and setle a weekely allowance to him, as they see cause, that hee may not runn out in vnnecessary charges:/"

14. Dexter, Vol. 1, page 116.

"At a Meeting of the Townesmen, February 21th, 1651."

"The case of old Bunill was taken into consideration, and for the present it is agreed that hee should haue 2 s a weeke alowed him, provided that hee and his family doe what they can towards their maintaynance."

33

15. Dexter, Vol. 1, page 112.

"At a Generall Court for Newhaven the 11th of March, 1651-52."

"The Townesmen were desired to speake wth old Bunill aboute putting forth his boy, that his famylie may be lessened, that the Towne may be at as litle charge as may bee. It was saide that Goodman Judsons sonn offered him a cow for the boy, so he might haue him such a number of yeares as might answer it. It was answered if any in the Towne would haue him vpon the termes that another would give, they might: if not, then the Townesmen must put him out as they can; for it was said that the boy is not onely a charge, but he will be spoyled for want of gouermt:/"

16. Dexter, Vol. 1, page 129.

"At a Generall Court for Newhaven the 10th of May, 1652."

"The Towne was acquainted that old Bunill refuseth to let his sonn be put forth as an Apprentize, according as they gave Order he should: where vpon ye Towne declared that his weekely allowance should be wthdrawne, for they are not willing to maintayne the boy at home, when he may be put out so as will be both an advantage to ye family in a cow that is proffered for him, wch will be a good help to keepe them, and for the good of ye boy, who now for want of due nurture growes rude and   offensive:/"

17. NHVR, page 9.

"Ebenezer Bunill the sonn of William Bunill was borne the 28th of August 1653."

18. Dexter, Vol. 1, page 200.

"At a Generall Court for New Haven, February 27th, 1653."

"The Gouernor informed that one cause of this meeting is aboute Goodwife Bunill who is sicke, vpon whom the Towne hath bine at some charge, but whether as much be done as her case requireth is a question; and is by some reported they are neglected; others say they are at two much charge wth them. The Towne was desired now to speake their minds, and not privately in a complaining way. Also, there is two chilldren to be put out, both for the good of the chilldren (who are not educated as they should) & for the easing ye Towne of charge. Concerning what hath bine done for Goodwife Bunill, none spake against it; but for ye chilldren, ye Towne desired they might be put out, and reffered it to ye Townesmen to doe it speedily:/"

19. Dexter, Vol. 1, page 208.

"At a Generall Court for Newhaven, May ye First, 1654."

"The Towne was informed that old Bunill (whose wife and child is dead) is desirous to goe to old England, wch if it could be attayned might free the Towne from some charge, though they made some prsent disburssmt for his passage and other necessaries for him, and vnderstanding a vessell at Milford is bound for Newfoundland, it was Ordered that the Townsmen and Treasurer should treate wth them for his passage theither, and Agree of some course how he may be sent from thence to old England, where he saith he hath some frends to take care of him:/"

That is the last reference to William Bunnell in New England that has come to light.

20. Hotten, p. 428.
21. Bassette, p. 183, quotes from the will of Benjamin Wilmot, William's father-in-law. The will, dated 7 Aug 1669, includes, "Item twenty shillings to each of the foure children of my daughter Anne Bunnell, vizt: Benjamin & Nathan[ll] Bunnill & Lydia ffrench & Mary Bunnill, the which I will to be payd them at or before ye terme of two years from ye date hereof."
22. NEHGR, Vol. 59, *"The Wilmot Family of New Haven, Conn."*
23. NEHGR, Vol 44, *"Lieutenant William French and His Descendants."*
24. New Haven - Jacobus, Vol. 1, p. 358.
25. NHVR, page 31.

1-1   D2   CB270004

BENJAMIN[2] BUNNELL (William[1]) was born about 1636, probably in one of the towns of the Massachusetts Bay Colony. After his father returned to England in 1646, his mother took her children to the New Haven Colony to join her father there. Benjamin was soon apprenticed to Nicholas Elsy to relieve the strain on the family budget. In October 1651 his father, who had returned from England several years before, sued for the return of Benjamin and his sister Lydia, who had also been apprenticed. Benjamin testified in court that he heard his father tell his mother in 1646 that the children were hers as well as his when he left them without support.[2]

The next notice of Benjamin Bunnell in the public records occurs on 23 March 1652 when he, along with five other boys, was found guilty of committing "much wickedness in a filthy corrupting way one with another." They were sentenced to be publicly whipped.[3]

He apparently outgrew his youthful "wickedness," because we find that he took the oath of fidelity at New Haven on 7 April 1657.[12] On the first of February in the following year, he was called to testify concerning a debt alleged to be owed by John Tompson to Thomas Morris. ". . . it was desired yt the testimony of Benjamine Bunnell might be taken, who being called affirmed yt Rich. Johnson desireing him to mow for him he told him he would, if he would pay him wheat, . . . "[4]

About 1665 or 1666 Benjamin Bunnell married as his first wife REBECCA MALLORY,[14] daughter of Peter and Mary (Preston) Mallory.[14] She was born 18 March 1649 at New Haven[1]. Benjamin and Rebecca began their married life in a home rented from John Wakefield on the west side of the West Creek.[6] During the next several years Benjamin appeared before the Town Court for various reasons.[5, 6, 8, 9] A couple of times he was fined 5 or 10 shillings for his transgressions.[6,9]

In March 1676 he was appointed one of the fence viewers in the suburbs quarter in the West Side Farms area.[10] This is the only record I have found of his public service.

Benjamin received 25 ½ acres of land in the Third Division in 1680[11] (the so-called West Side Farms, now West Haven, CT). In 1684, Peter Mallory, his father-in-law, gave him an additional ten acres of land in the West Side Farms section.[13] Several other deeds are extant showing that Benjamin Bunnell, "husbandman" bought and sold various properties in and around New Haven between 1685 and 1691. In 1691 he bought 60 acres of land from Thomas Trowbridge, "abbutting on ye sound or sea, between Malbone's Cove, or Oyster River, and is bounded on ye north-west by commons or towne lands, on ye south-west by lands belonging to s'd Benjamin Bunnell, on ye south-east by ye sound or sea, and on ye north-east by lands belonging to ye s'd Thomas Trowbridge."[17]

On 7 February 1667/8 the Committee appointed for the new seating in the meeting house assigned "Benja: Bunnill" a seat in the fourth row of the Gallery,[7] although he did not become a member of the church until near the end of his life. He was baptized in the First Congregational Society of

New Haven on 12 January 1690[19] and was admitted to church membership on 23 April 1690[19]. His six youngest children were baptized in that church four days later[14]. He was No. 412 on the First Church membership roll.[15]

Rebecca (Mallory) Bunnell died at New Haven 12 March 1691[1]. Benjamin married (second) ELIZABETH POST,[14] daughter of John and Hester (Hyde) Post,[14] and widow of John Sperry.[14] She was born 22 February 1655 at Saybrook, CT.[14] She had joined the First Congregational Society of New Haven in 1687, and was No. 358 on the membership roll.[15]

Benjamin Bunnell died at New Haven in 1696[14] (12 March 1696?[18]). On 8 September 1696 the inventory of his estate was taken as follows: £278.8.10. 65 acres of land, house, barn and orchards, £200.[17] Samuel Burwell, husband of Benjamin's oldest daughter Rebecca, was administrator of the estate. Burwell (incorrectly called Samuel Bunnell in the transcription of the following document) made a settlement with the widow on behalf of the children by Benjamin's first wife, most of whom were still under age:[17]

"Concerning the Estate of Benjamin Bunnell.\
    Elizabeth Bunnell:
    Samuel Bunnell: Whereas, upon a contract of marriage intended by and between Benjamin Bunnell, late of New Haven, and Elizabeth Sperry, relict of John Sperry, late of New Haven, deceased, which s'd marriage was after consumated. The s'd Benjamin and Elizabeth discourst and determined to make and conclude on a settlement of their estates respectively, but the s'd settlement according to their intentions being prevented by ye speedy death of s'd Benjamin.
    "Therefore, know all who it may concern that by the allowance of the Honorable Court, in ye County of New Haven, and in presence of ye s'd Elizabeth now relict of s'd Benjamin Bunnell on ye one party, and Sam'l Bunnell son-in-law and administrator to ye s'd Benjamin Bunnell on ye other party, and for each of ye s'd children of s'd Benjamin by his first wife, Do covenant, agree, and conclude as followeth, vis't.
    "1. That ye s'd Elizabeth may and shall receive unto her possession and unto her use and disposal as before s'd marriage all such estate, real or personal, as before s'd marriage to s'd Bunnell she was possessed of, free from all dues and demands whatsoever.
    "2. That ye s'd Samuel as administrator shall pay, or cause to be paid, out of the personal estate of s'd Bunnell according to inventory appraised, ye full sum of ten pounds unto s'd Elizabeth or her order on demand made, in consideration of her care and charge in bringing up a certain child (Anna) left by s'd Benjamin born of ye s'd Elizabeth. In witness whereof ye parties above named have this thirteenth of November, One thousand six hundred ninety and six, set to their hands and seals, signed, sealed and delivered in ye presence of us

      (Samuel Beles   Elizabeth Bunnell
      (John Stevens   her X mark   (Seal)
      (John Miles   Samuel Bunnell (Seal)

    "Acknowledged by ye parties in Court, November 13, 1696, and approved for record. Test   Wm. Jones, Clerk. (Seal)"[17]

The widow Elizabeth was married, for the third time, on 19 September 1700[1] to Edmund Dorman. She died in 1715[14].

Children (by first wife), born in New Haven:
    1. 280001. Rebecca, b. 19 Jan. 1667[1]; d. 26 Jan. 1667[1].

2. 280002. Rebecca, b. 11 Feb. 1668[1]; m. 27 Nov. 1684 Samuel Burwell.[14]
        Children (surname Burwell):[14]

1. Ann.	5. Dinah.	9. John.
2. Ann.	6. Stephen.	10. Nathan.
3. Ann.	7. Elizabeth.	11. Mary.
4. Rebecca.	8. Bathsheba.	12. Gideon.

3. 280004. Judith, b. 13 April 1672[1]; m. (first) after 1690 Thomas Hodge;[14] m. (second) Daniel Bristol;[14] d. 21 July 1746.[14]
        Child (illegitimate, by John Eels):[14]
        1.
        Children (surname Hodge):[14]

2. Daniel.	5. Thomas.	8. Mary.
3. Jesse.	6. Miriam	9. Martha.
4. Judith.	7. Susanna.	10. Miriam.

4. 280005. Benjamin, b. 4 Jan. 1675[1]; d. 8 Jan. 1675[1].
5. 280008. Anna, b. 8 Jan. 1677[1]; d. 23 Feb. 1690/1[1].
6. 280006. Benjamin, b. 29 Nov. 1679[1].
7. 280009. Hezekiah, b. 23 Mar. 1681/2[1].
8. 280010. Rachel, b. 16 Dec. 1683[1]; m. John Plumb, Jr.;[14] d. 21 July 1728.[14]
        Children (Surname Plumb):[14]

1. John.	4. Zuriel.	6. Benjamin.
2. Samuel.	5. Seth.	7. Rachel.
3. Jemima.		

9. 280011. Nathaniel, b. May 1686[1].
10. 280012. Israel, b. 12 Mar. 1689/90[1].

Child (by second wife), born in New Haven:
11. 280013. Anna, b. 11 Oct. 1695[1]; m. 2 Jan. 1723/4 Nathaniel Mix, Jr.;[14] d. 15 Sept. 1731.[14]
        Children (surname Mix):[14]

1. Nathaniel.	2. Stephen.	3. Jabez.

REFERENCES:

1. NHVR.
2. Dexter, Vol. 1, p. 89.
3. Dexter, Vol. 1, p. 179.

"A MEETING OF YE COURT EXTRAORDINARY, MARCH 23TH, 1652
    March 23th, 1652

"Vpon a complaint made to yᵉ Gouernoʳ of sundrie youthes in yᵉ Towne that had committed much wickedness in a filthy corrupting way one wᵗʰ another, they were called before the Gouernor & Magistrats, vizᵈ; Benjamin Bunill, Joshua Bradly, Joseph Benham, William Trobridg, Thomas Tuttill & Thomas

Kimberly; they were examined in a private way, and their examinations taken in wrighting, wch were of such a filthy nature as is not fitt to be made known in a publique way; after wch the Court were called together, and ye youthes before them; their examinations were read and vpon their severall confessions the Court, being mett at the meeting house vpon the day aboue written, sentenced the youthes aboue named to bee whipt publiquly; and whereas Jn° Clarke, servant to Jeremiah Whitnell, was questioned and charged by one of them for some filthy cariag, he denyed it, and another of the company in some measure cleered him from that the other charged him w^th, wherevpon he was not sentenced to be corrected publiquly, but the Court left it wth his master to giue him that correction in the family wch he should see meete, warning John Clarke that if euer any such cariag came forth against him hereafter, the Court would call these miscariages charged vpon him to minde againe:/"

4. Dexter, Vol. 1, p. 388.

"AT A COURT HELD AT NEWHAVEN THE FIRST OF FEBRUARY 1658

"Benjamine Bunnell" was called to testify concerning a debt alleged to be owed by John Tompson to Tho. Morris.

". . . it was desired y^t the testimony of Benjamine Bunnell might be taken, who being called affirmed y^t Rich. Johnson desireing him to mow for him, he told hime he would, if he would pay him wheat; . . . "

5. Dexter, Vol. 2, p. 152.

"AT A COURT HELD AT NEW HAVEN OCTOB: 3^d 1665:

The jury	
Lt Tho: Munson	The jury were acquainted with what
Mr Henry Rotherford	was proper worke in Cases p^rsented,
John Gibbs	& they all tooke oath; and Lt Tho:
John Cooper senior	Munson apointed foreman of the jury.
Wm Andrewes	
Henry Glover	

Jonathan Lampson Plaintiffe   }   In an action of slaunder & Defamation to ye Value of twenty pounds:
Cornelius Williamson Defendant}   The Plaint: Declared, That Cornelius hath reported, That Benjamin Bunill sd, that Jonathan Lampson Lay wth an indian squaw, & that Jn° Thomas junio^r saw it: The Defend^t answered y^t he could not have his witnesses, some were sicke & others were out of ye towne, & desired y^t ye Plaint: might prove w^t he declared:

"The Plaint: produced his testimonies: And first, The Wife of John Thomas senior testified That Cornelius Williamson sd at their house That Benjamin Bunnill had told Jonathan Lampson that he Lay ^wth an indian squaw & that John Thomas junio^r see it, and she told Jonathan of it & y^t it Concerned him to looke to it.

"Roger Alling testified y^t Cornelius W^mson, the 5th day of ye last weeke sd, that there was some differance between Benjamin Bunnill & Jonathan Lampson about a gun, & Benjamin Bunnill told Jonathan Lampson, that he Lay wth an jndian squaw & Jn° Thomas junio^r saw it:

"John Alling testified ye same onely saith y^t upon a question put if he could make it out he sd Jn° Thomas saw it.

"Mary Browne was called to speake in the Case, whoe testified That Jn° Gold, Jn° Thomas junio^r, & Jonathan Lampson being at their house, she sd to ye sd Jonathan Lampson y^t there was falling out on their side ye towne, then Jonathan answ^rd That Benjamin Bunnill was ye basest ffellow, & hath sd y^t he knockt

an Jndian squaw & that Jn° Thomas would say it, but Mary Browne replied y^t shee understood it worse:

I, saith Jonathan Lampson, Benjamin Bunnill is ye basest ffellow, & turnes it another way; then she told him y^t it was a base disgrace to him; if she was as he, she would have him to ye Co^rt; soe sd alsoe Jno Gold; I, sd Jonathan, if it went further abroad soe he would: Jno Gold being Called testified the same in substance with goodw: Browne & was accepted wth out oath:

"Benjamin Bunnill was Called to speake w^t he knew in ye Case, And declared that he knew noe such thing of Jonathan as was Charged nor ever sd soe; he had heard y^t Cornelius had sd soe, both of him & Jonathan. The Plaint & Defend^t haveing noe more to say The jury haveing Considered of ye Case brought this as their Verdict: That they find for ye Plaintiffe twenty shillings & Costs of Court: And the Court ordered Judgem^t to be Entred accordingly."

6. Dexter, Vol. 2, p. 179.

AT A COURT HELD AT NEW HAVEN JULY. 3^d 1666:.

"Jno Alling & Ephraim Pennington being upon ye Watch June 2^d 66: were Called to relate how they found matters y^t night? Jno Alling declared y^t they goeing over the Creeke about ten of ye Clock in ye night & as they was against Hitchcockes house, they heard a great noyse in Wakefields house;* & comeing nearer they saw some run out into ye quarter, &c. The busines being examined, it appeared that there was Jno Tharpe, Sam^ll Tharpe, Dan^ll Thomas, Elisabeth Thomas & Zubah Lampson, (Benjamin Bunnill & his Wife being gone from home whoe lived there), the sd Zubah being left by ye sd Bunnill & his wife to look after things in ye house. Benjamin Bunnill & his wife Called & told y^t he had heard what was sd about night-meetings at his house, He sd That they Left Zubah Lampson to looke after things in the day, & to ly at some neighbo^rs house & mentioned goodman Thomas his house & her mother Lampsons: But he was told of his slightnes herein in Leaveing things with her, & not take Care himselfe, whom he knew to have been soe faulty formerly, &c. The Co^rt haveing Considered of the Case p^rsented, & upon Consideration of their acknowledgements, though they had thought of a higher fine, yet hopeing it may be a warneing to them for the future, did only Sentence them to pay five shillings a person viz, Benjamin Bunnill, Jno Tharpe, Sam^ll Tharpe & Dan^ll Thomas: Elisabeth Thomas was onely past wth a serious admonition to take warneing for ye future, or else this would be brought as an aggravation against her:

"Zubah Lampson Called three times but answered not, though it was sd she had notice of it, for which Contempt & her oth^r miscarriage shee was fined ten shillings the ninth of this moneth."

"*The lots occupied by Mathias Hitchcock and John Wakefield were on the west side of the west creek."

7. Dexter, Vol. 2, page 221.
8. Dexter, Vol. 2, page 246.

AT A COURT HELD AT NEWHAVEN MARCH 2^d 1668/9:

"Mr Sam^ll Hopkins made complaint to ye Court that he had sustained great dammage by severall persons imbeizling of his goods: viz, Thomas Wilson, Edward Bunce & some others, and declared that he had lost a great quantity of strong Liquo^rs, & wine, & other goods, as Linnen and sugar & Ribband, &c, for when he went from home he left two Barrills of Rumm & there was not above a 3^d of each at his returne, besides a 3^d part of barr^ll of wine, wanting two or three gallons, two whole pieces of Ribband, 4 handkerchiefes, 4 neckcloathes, a razor, a bottle & sugars of both sorts, both white & muscovado.

"Tho: Wilson was asked what he had to say? He answered that what he had Confest hee should owne, & must leave himselfe to his Master and ye Court: He was asked how much Liquo^rs? He answered y^t he carried some of it into the woods, he could not tell how often, with a quart bottle, he sold none of it, sometimes there was Benjamill Bunnill & sometimes Jonathan Lampson & Edward Bunce, they work^t about two moneths together.

"Thomas Wilson was asked how much wine & Liquo^{rs} he thought he had?

"Hee answrd that he had not anything to say, but that there might bee as much as Mr Hopkins Charges, for he had tooke of the wine severall times as well as the Liquors, he knowes not how often, & he knowes not anything, but that is ye truth which his master saith.

"He was asked if he had any way to satisfy the dammage? Hee answered, noe, onely his body. The Court Concerneing him declared That they transmitt ye business to ye County Court, & he to be secured until ye sd Court, except bayle be given.

"And for Edward Bunce The Court by way of sentence declared That for ye gallon of liquo^{rs} which he confessed hee tooke with Thomas Wilson he pay to Mr Sam^{ll} Hopkins shillings, and for the Criminall part & fellowship in ye imbeizlement, that he pay 4^{lb} fine to ye publike treasury, or bee severely whipt: Edward Bunce y^t he should pay ye fine to-morrow, & sam^{ll} miles ingaged on his behalfe./--"

9. Dexter, Vol. 2, page 247.

AT A SPECIALL COURT HELD AT NEWHAVEN MARCH. 8th 1668/9:--

"Upon ye desire of Mr Hopkins that this Co^{rt} would issue ye matter left ye last Court Concerneing Thomas Wilson, informeing the Court that he had compounded with him about ye Restitution: Thomas Wilson was called & reminded of what past ye last Court in his oweneing of what M^r hopkins Charged him withall, saying that he thought it might bee soe: He was wished to relate whoe partaked with him in the drinke: He sd y^t he could not say y^t. Benjamin Bunnill ever bid him bring any, but twice he asked him where the bottle was, &c.

"Benjamin Bunnill sd he would relate the truth of the matter, That they being at worke in his Corne Thomas would aske him if hee had a bottle, he sd he could have some wine or Liquo^{rs} of a friend y^t had none to sell, And the first time was at Chesnut hill when they went to worke there he brought a small bottle of wine, and ye 2^d time ye same with wine, & a 3^d time the same bottle almost full of Liquo^{rs}, then after at Henry Bristowes he had a bottle of about 3 pints, & they dranke round, & burnt ye rest, and once he was at his house & brought a halfe a bottle, & Thomas Drawwater was there,; he knew not of anymore, onely he dranke at Mr Eeles his house with y^m some y^t Thomas brought out to them.

"Thomas Drawwater confessed that he was one night at Benjamin Bunnills house drinking Liquo^{rs} with Thomas Wilson, alsoe once at Mr Hopkins his house & twice in ye barne.

"Thomas Wilson was told the greatnes of his evil with the aggravations of it, y^t it was to his master whoe intrusted him with his estate, &c. But seeing his master & he had Compounded about ye restitution they should not medle with that; But for the Criminall part they must beare due witnes against, And therefore did sentence the sd Thomas Wilson to pay 4^{lb} fine to ye publike treasury, or bee severely whipt. The Court allowed him liberty until ye Court in Aprill next for ye paym^t of the sd fine, or else then to appeare to bee dealt with as ye Court shall see cause.

"Benjamin Bunnill for his entertainem^t of other mens servants tipling at his house unseasonably contrary to law, was fined Ten shillings.

"Thomas Drawwater alsoe for his dissorder was fined Ten shillings."

10. Dexter, Vol. 2, page 352.

In March 1676 "Jno Alling & Beniamin Bunnell" were appointed fence viewers in the suburbs quarter by the Townsmen.

11. Dexter, Vol. 2, page 408.

ATT A TOWNE MEETING HELD IN NEWHAUEN Y[e] 20th OF DECEMBER 1680

In the third division of town lands "Beniamin: Bunnell" drew the ninth lot on the Western side of the town. He received 25½ acres based on his family of six and his "estate" of £5.

12. New Haven Colony Records, Vol. 1, page 140.
13. New Haven Deeds.
14. New Haven - Jacobus, pp. 358, 359.
15. Bassette.
16. Gillen.
17. Biles Manuscript.
18. CB Database - no source.
19. CB Database - Records of the First Congregational Church of New Haven.

1-3 D3 CB270005

NATHANIEL[2] BUNNELL or BONNELL (William[1]) was probably born in one of the towns of the Massachusetts Bay Colony. At the time of the move to the New Haven Colony in 1646 Ann (Wilmot) Bunnell had "divers small children."[2] Benjamin and Lydia were apparently the two who were put out to other families. The births of Mary and Ebenezer were recorded in New Haven in 1650 and 1653 respectively[1]. Nathaniel was therefore probably the youngest of three brought from Massachusetts Bay. He was probably born between 1640 and 1642. The will of his grandfather Benjamin Wilmot, dated 7 August 1669 in New Haven, bequeathed 20 shillings to Nathaniel, specifically identified as one of the four children of "my daughter Anne Bunnell."[4]

In 1652 and 1653 there was considerable agitation in New Haven for this boy to be put out as an apprentice[2]. The town was paying for the family's upkeep and resented paying for a hungry child when alternatives were available. One of the neighbors had offered a cow for the boy, but the Bunnells had refused. It was asserted that the boy was becoming wild through lack of management and training. After his mother died and his father went back to England, Nathaniel may well have been apprenticed. If so, however, no evidence has been found of it.

With one exception, the events of Nathaniel's youth went unrecorded. At a Court held at New Haven 1 December 1663 his name came up in an inquiry by the Court into alleged misconduct by Isaac Melyn and Hester Clark:

. . .

"Then Hester was questioned about some persons being at their house in y[e] night after the last Thanksgiving? But she was slow of giveing answer to this, & had many guilefull turneings of speech: as y[t] there was some in y[e] streete, & y[t] John Gold crossed from theyr Barne through the yard, they haveing been about Sidar &c but at last Confessed y[t] they was in the house; & being asked who? She named Elizabeth and Bathshua How, Isaack Melijen, Nath: Bunnill, John y[e] Dutchman & John Gold:

"Then Sam: Hall was asked if he knew not of this? He answered, that he came out of his Chamber & saw them there, And being asked, what they did there? He sd he saw nothing but smoake Tobacco."[3]　　. . .

We next see him on his wedding day, 3 January 1665/6[1], when he was married by Mr. William Jones at New Haven to SUSANNAH WHITEHEAD[1], daughter of Isaac Whitehead[5]. She was born at New Haven 5 August 1650[1]. Almost immediately after their wedding, Nathaniel and Susannah, with her father and his family, joined the party about to settle Elizabethtown, NJ. Both Nathaniel Bunnell and Isaac Whitehead are listed among the 65 persons who took this oath of allegiance at Elizabethtown 19 February 1665/6: "You doe Sweare upon the Holy Evangelist Contained in this Book to bare true faith and Allegeance to our Soveraine Lord King Charles the Second and his Lawfull Successors and to be true and faithfull to the Lords Proprietors their successors and the Governem' of this Province of New Jarsey as Long as you shall Continue an Inhabitant vnder the Same without any Equivocation or Mentall Reservation whatsoever and so help you God."[12]

At a Court held at New Haven on 6 March 1665/6 this deed was recorded:

"Mr Jnº Davenport junior doth alienate to Isaack Whitehead two acres of land in yᵉ quarter next goodm Tods lot & against yᵉ spring; And the said Isaack giveing a small parcell of this Land, to his sonne in Law Nathaniell Bunnill, The sd Nathanˡˡ Bunnill doth alienate this small parcell of Land with the house now sett upon it, to Willm Payne for ever."[3]

The Elizabethtown Associates, originally 65 in number, were mostly from Long Island (Jamaica and "the East End"), with a few families from New Haven. In October 1664 the Associates purchased from the Indians a tract of land running 17 miles north from the mouth of the Raritan River and west for 34 miles from the river which separates Staten Island from the mainland of New Jersey. In December of that year the Associates obtained a charter for their settlement from Col. Robert Nicolls, deputy governor of New York, under the Duke of York. Unknown to the Associates at the time, the Duke of York had granted New Jersey to Lord John Berkeley and Sir George Carteret, as proprietors, in June 1664. This was to spark years of contention between the settlers and the Proprietors[6].

In Elizabethtown, basing their claims on the Indian purchase and Col. Nicolls' charter, each of the Associates was assigned a six-acre home lot, plus additional acres for a farm. Nathaniel had a house lot of 15 chains by 4 chains, bounded east by Thomas Price, west and north by his father-in-law Isaac Whitehead, Sr., and south by the highway[7]. The house which he built here, some time before 1677, still stands at 1045 East Jersey Street, the oldest surviving house in the city of Elizabeth[7]. In recent years it was for a while the home of the New Jersey Sons of the American Revolution and is now the headquarters of the Elizabethtown Historical Foundation[7]. It is open to the public.

Nathaniel also had an original allotment of 120 acres, "Lying upon the south branch of Elizabethtown Creek and by ye plaine which said above creek passeth through," and 12 acres of meadow "lying in the greate meadows upon John Woodruffe's Creek."[14] On 11 March 1669 he was No. 90 in the list of 170 freeholders at Elizabeth who drew a first lot right of 100 acres[14]. He had 180 acres surveyed to him on 10 April 1676, and his lands bounded on lands of Matthias Hatfield, Joseph Osborne and Isaac Whitehead[14].

He sold his six-acre home lot in Elizabethtown to Benjamin Price on 15 June 1677[9]. Where he lived from then on is not clear, but presumably it was on one of his farm properties. A good guess might be that he settled in the part of Elizabethtown called "Connecticut Farms" (now Union, NJ). Certainly, his wife Susannah was living there towards the end of her life.

In addition to being a large landowner, Nathaniel was involved in community affairs. He served on a jury, 6 May 1671, by order of Gov. Carteret, for the trial of William Hackett, captain of the sloop "Indeavor," of Massachusetts, for illegal trading in the Province[14]. "Nathaniel Bunnel" was one of the executors of his father-in-law's estate under the terms of Isaac Whitehead's will, which was dated 31 January 1690/1 and proved 26 February 1690/1[11]. In 1692 and 1694 he was a member of the General Assembly from Elizabethtown[14].

In 1694 "Nathaniel Bunnell" was among the 124 members of the First Presbyterian Church of Elizabethtown who subscribed to the support of Rev. John Harriman, his contribution being £1 10s[14]. His son "Nathaniel Bunnell, Jr.," was also one of the subscribers, and his son Isaac subscribed a few years later.

He, like many others, was opposed to "constituting courts," etc.,[14] instituted by the Proprietors of New Jersey, to force the settlers to pay annual quitrents to the Proprietors for their land or lose their title to it. He was one of the Elizabethtown Associates[11] who petitioned the Crown in 1696 for relief from this oppression by the Lords Proprietors. They closed their petition with a request that the government of the colony be transferred from the Proprietors to the Crown, a move which finally took place in 1702[12].

This seems to be the last public mention of his name. He probably died not long afterward without leaving a will[11]. Duncan gives a death date of "about 1696", although I do not see the source.

His widow outlived him for many years. At the time of her death she resided at Connecticut Farms (now Union, NJ) where her son Joseph was living[11]. Her gravestone in the Presbyterian churchyard at Connecticut Farms read:[10,16,17]

> "Here lyes y[e] Body of
> Susannah, wife of Nath[ll]
> Bonnel Dec[d] Feb[ry] y[e]
> 12th : 173[3/4] in y[e] 84th
> year of her Age." [17]

Children (all born at Elizabethtown):
1. 280015. Nathaniel, b. about 1670[11].
2. 280014. Isaac[11], b. early 1670s.

3. 280017. Samuel[11], b. about 1675.
4. 280018. Lydia, b. about 1680[11]; m. Samuel Littell[13].
   Children (surname Littell):[13]

1. Elizabeth.	7. Benjamin.	12. Abigail.
2. Martha.	8. Daniel.	13. Catherine.
3. John.	9. David.	14. Nathaniel.
4. Samuel.	10. Jonathan.	15. child, d. y.
5. Joseph.	11. Sarah.	16. child, d. y.
6. James.		

5. 280019. Jane[11], b. about 1680; m. Ephraim Price[11].
   Children (surname Price):[8]

1. Jane.	4. Isaac.	7. Nathaniel.
2. Lydia.	5. James.	8. Ebenezer.
3. Ephraim.	6. Samuel.	9. Daniel.

6. 280020. Benjamin, b. about 1682[11].
7. 280016. Joseph, b. about 1685[11].

REFERENCES:

1. NHVR.
2. Dexter, Vol. I.
3. Dexter, Vol. II.
4. Bassette.
5. New Haven - Jacobus, p. 359.
6. Monnette, pp. 53, 58, 101.
7. Bunnell Homestead.
8. NJ Wills - Vol. II, p. 387
9. NJ Conveyances.
10. CT Farms Cem Inscriptions. p. 171.
11. NJ Genesis, July 1961, pp. 331, 332.
12. Thayer.
13. Littell, p. 215.
14. Amer Fam - Long Island, pp. 57, 58.
15. *Documents Relating to the Colonial History of New Jersey*, Vol. 1, 1631-1684,
    edited by William A. Whitehead, 1880, pp. 49, 50, sent to me by John C. Bonnell, Jr..
16. CT Farms Cem Inscriptions, p. 171.
17. CT Farms Cem - 2.
18. Gibby.
19. Duncan, p. 11.
20. CB Database.

THIRD GENERATION

1-1-6   D4   CB280006

BENJAMIN[3] BUNNELL (Benjamin[2], William[1]) was born 29 November 1679[1] at New Haven, CT. He was baptized 27 April 1690[2], four days after his father, in the First Congregational Society of New Haven. He married (first), at New Haven, HANNAH PLUMB[2], daughter of John and Elizabeth (Norton) Plumb[2]. She was born 15 April 1677[2] at Milford, CT.

Benjamin was listed as a freeman in New Haven in March 1702/3. While he was living in New Haven various deeds list his occupation as cordwainer (shoemaker)[4]. He owned land in the New Haven area at Oyster River, Long Hill and Ridge Hill[4]. In 1714 Benjamin and his cousin, Caleb Mallory, purchased land in New Milford, CT[5], and soon after Benjamin and his family moved to New Milford. There are a few hints in the records that this may not have been Benjamin's first move. A deed dated 15 April 1707 indicates that "Benjamin Bunnel, *late* of New Haven," sold to Samuel Burwell, his brother-in-law, 16 acres of land at Oyster River being part of his farm or third division lot[4]. A few weeks later, on 1 May 1707, Benjamin and Hannah's fifth child, Gershom, was born "at Elizabethtown in east Jersey," according to the New Haven Vital Records[1]. It appears that Benjamin spent some time with his cousins in New Jersey, and he may have intended to move there permanently. If so, he changed his mind, because a deed dated 24 March 1713 shows him back in New Haven purchasing land from his brother Nathaniel[4], and Hannah's last child, Isaac, was born there in August of that year[1].

The following year the move to New Milford took place, and there he resided for the rest of his life. (It should be noted that the births of all the children of Benjamin and Hannah were then rerecorded in the vital records of New Milford, a circumstance which has led many chroniclers to believe they were born there.) On 20 May 1714 he and Caleb Mallory bought from Richard Bryan of Milford for 15 pounds a right to a whole share in the purchase of New Milford[5]. On 25 May 1714 John Noble, Sr., and John Bostwick, Sr., laid out for Caleb Mallory and Benjamin Bunnell 40 acres of upland, 100 rods long and 64 rods wide, on the east side of the Great River, also a home lot and a ten-acre division for a pasture lot[5]. A year later Benjamin traded his share in the home lot to Mallory for another home lot next north of Benoni Stebbins[5]. Then on 20 June 1715 Benjamin sold the last of his property in New Haven to John Merwin, Jr., for £76. It consisted of 15 acres at Oyster River, including his home, barn and orchard[4].

Hannah (Plumb) Bunnell died in New Milford 16 November 1716[2]. Benjamin did not long remain a widower. On 27 August 1717[2] he married, at New Milford, PATIENCE (WHEELER) MILES[2], daughter of Joseph and Patience (Holbrook) Wheeler[2], and widow of Stephen Miles[2]. She was born 7 June 1679 at Milford, CT[2]. Benjamin and Patience joined the First Congregational Church of New Milford in 1721, he on faith and she received by letter. "Patience Bunnel" was listed as one of the heirs in the will of her father Joseph Wheeler when it was probated on 15 September 1727[3]. He had removed from Milford, CT to Newark, Essex co, NJ, and died there.

Benjamin Bunnell was never prominent in the affairs of New Milford, but from time to time he was chosen at Town meeting to collect the meeting house rate, to serve on a committee to raise money for a school, and similar civic duties[7]. Occasionally his name appears in the land records of the Town as he bought or sold various parcels of land[5]. Since he is sometimes referred to as Sergeant Benjamin Bunnell, he must have been active in the military forces of the Town[2].

When old age began to overtake them, Benjamin and Patience deeded their real property to their son-in-law Nathan Hawley in consideration of his maintenance and support of them during the rest of their natural lives. This deed was dated 30 November 1747[5]. A little over a year later, on 17 February 1748/9, they gave a quit claim deed to "Nathaniel Hawley, son and Keziah Hawley, daughter, all the movable estate that we are now possessed of or shall be at our decease both in the house and abroad."[5]

Benjamin Bunnell died at New Milford 20 August 1749[2] in his seventieth year. His widow died in 1761[8].

Children (by first wife), all but Gershom born at New Haven:
    1. 290001. Rebecca, b. 8 Mar. 1701[1]; m. 11 Apr. 1717 Ebenezer Bostwick[2]; d. 16 Nov. 1761[6].
        Children (surname Bostwick)[6]:

1. Ebenezer.	4. Abigail.	7. Hannah.
2. Robert.	5. Gershom.	8. Isaac.
3. Rebecca.	6. Edmund.	

    2. 290002. Hannah, b. 11 Apr. 1702[1]; m. 10 Aug. 1738 Nathan Barnum[2].
    3. 290003. Benjamin, b. 30 Apr. 1704[1].
    4. 290004. Solomon, b. 27 Oct. 1705[1].
    5. 290005. Gershom, b. 1 May 1707[1].
    6. 290006. Isaac, b. 30 Aug. 1713[1].

Children (by second wife), born at New Milford:
    7. 290007. Keziah, b. 17 Oct. 1718[6]; m. 8 Nov. 1733 Nathan Hawley[2].
        Children (surname Hawley)[6]:

1. Keziah.	4. Benjamin.	7. Jabez.
2. Eunice.	5. Nathan.	8. Abijah.
3. Patience.	6. Ira.	

REFERENCES:
    1. NHVR.
    2. New Haven - Jacobus, pp. 358, 359, 360.
    3. NJ Wills - Vol. I, p. 501.
    4. New Haven Deeds
    5. New Milford Deeds.
    6. Duncan, p. 13.
    7. New Milford History.
    8. CB Database

THIRD GENERATION

1-1-7 D5 280009

HEZEKIAH[3] BUNNELL (Benjamin[2], William[1]) was born at New Haven, CT, 23 March 1681/2[1]. On 27 Apri l 1690[2] he was baptized in the First Congregational Church of New Haven. He married RUTH PLUMB[2], daughter of John and Elizabeth (Norton) Plumb[2]. She was born 29 November 1685[2,8] and died about 1744[2]. In 1707 he deserted his wife and removed to Hopewell, Hunterdon (now Mercer) co, NJ[2]. There he joined the party of Jonathan Stout and his associates who had made the first settlement in Hopewell the year before.[7]

Ruth Bunnel, of Milford, filed for divorce from her husband Hezekiah Bunnel, at New Jersey, in New Haven Superior Court on 13 March 1711/12, citing desertion for five years. A letter was sent to her father with a copy of the court order[5]. The voters of the Town were unwilling to take on the charge of supporting the imbecile child, saying they would defray the cost of a lawsuit instead. In 1719 John Plumb made provision to the Town for the sale of some land for the care of his granddaughter Ruth Bunnell[6].

In 1722 Hezekiah was witness to the will of Jonathan Stout in Hopewell, NJ[3]. He died before 1729, when Deliverance Bunnell sold his portion of his deceased father's "home lot at Oyster River" to his brother Hezekiah[4].

Children:
1. 290012. Hezekiah, b. about 1702[2].
2. 290013. Deliverance, b. about 1705[2].
3. 290014. Ruth, b. about 1706[2]; d. after 1719[6]; imbecile[2].

REFERENCES:
1. NHVR.
2. New Haven - Jacobus, pp. 358, 359, 360, 361.
3. NJ Wills - Vol. I, p. 445.
4. Duncan, p. 14.
5. New Haven Superior Court.
6. New Haven Historical Society, Vol. II.
7. NJ Collections.
8. CB Database

1-1-9 D6 CB280011

NATHANIEL[3] BUNNELL (Benjamin[2], William[1]) was born in May 1686[1] at New Haven, CT. On 27 April 1690[2] he was baptized, with his brothers and sisters, in the First Congregational Church of New Haven. On 29 July 1702 he chose Ebenezer Sperry to be his guardian[5]. He was married (first) at New Haven by Abraham Bradley, justice of the peace, on 10 May 1709[1] to DESIRE PECK[1], daughter of Benjamin and Mary (Sperry) Peck[2]. She was born at New Haven 26 August 1687[1]. In the will of Benjamin Peck in April 1730, he devised "one eighth part to ye children of my daughter Desire Bunnell".[5]

On 2 September 1709 Nathaniel purchased, from Samuel and William Andrews, 65 acres of land with the buildings thereon in the western part of the Town of Wallingford, the part that was later set off as the Town of Cheshire.[5] It lay west of Mill River, bounded south by Stephen Hotchkiss, east by a four-rod road from Hartford to New Haven, north by Ebenezer Doolittle, west by town lands.[5] Since the birth of their first child was recorded at New Haven, it is likely that the move to Wallingford occurred about the year 1712. Nathaniel bought more land of Matthias Hitchcock, "four or five acres more or less, nere Hoppers Meadow; bounded north to a poynt west on on Decon Hull, his land; Eastward on Stephen Hodgkis' land:: South on John Hitchcock his land."[3] Later he paid £10 to Ebenezer Doolittle for 2 ½ acres near Stephen Clark, a triangle bounded southwest and west by the highway, probably as a building lot for his son Ebenezer.[5]

By 1718 the "West Farmers" in Wallingford began to agitate for a meeting house and parish of their own, "by reason of the distance from the town and difficulty in the way."[4] At that time the General Assembly denied their request. The question of separation was not dropped, however, and in 1723 the district was constituted as the "West" or "New Cheshire" society.[4] At the second meeting of the society on 16 September 1723 Timothy Tuttle was chosen moderator, and Thomas Brooks, Nathaniel Bunnil and John Hitchcock "a Com[tee] to manage ye affairs of the society for the year insuing."[3] In December they decided to build a 30 by 40 foot meeting house, and Nathaniel Bunnil was one of the committee chosen to "manage ye work of ye meeting house."[3] Nathaniel also carried out military responsibilities, for the records call him Sergeant, and later Ensign, Nathaniel Bunnell.[4]

Desire (Peck) Bunnell died in 1724[2] at Wallingford. Nathaniel married for the second time 17 February 1725/6[2] at Wallingford MARY BROOKS[2], daughter of Thomas and Martha (Hotchkiss) Brooks[2]. She was born at Wallingford 14 May 1704[2].

"The number of ye names of the Freemen in Wallingford which was taken as they appeared at a Freemans meeting Aprill the last day 1730--are as followeth--"[3] The list which followed included Nathaniel Bunel, his nephew Hezekiah Bunel, and two of his sons, Ebenezer Bunel and Parmenius Bunel. Parmineas was only 13 years old at this time.

Two years later, on 4 May 1732[2], Nathaniel died of small pox at Wallingford at the age of 46. He was buried in the Hillside Cemetery in Cheshire[6]. His will read: "In the name of God, Amen. The 25th day of April, 1732. I, Nathaniel Bunnell, of Chesire in Wallingford, in New Haven Co., being of sound mind and memory, thanks be given to God for the same, do make this my last will and testament. I first recommend my soul unto ye hand of God, in and through the Lord Jesus Christ, and my body to Christian buryall, and at the discretion of my executors hereafter mentioned, hoping to receive it again at the resurrection of the Just, a glorious Body; and my worldly estate I dispose of as follows; I will and bequeath to my beloved wife Mary, ye one third of my movable estate to be at her absolute Disposall and use and improvements of one third part of my real estate, During her continuing my widow and no longer. It is my Will, that all the remainder of my Estate both Reall and personal be equally divided among my children, Ebenezer, Benjamin, Parmenus, Jeras, Abner, Joseph, Desire, Patience, Rachel and Rebecca, and Stephen C., except Ebenezer my eldest son in consideration of that into heirs(?) a Double portion out of it. My wife Mary and son Ebenezer to be executors."[5] The will was probated 7 May

THIRD GENERATION

1732 at New Haven by Mary Bunnell, executrix. She was appointed guardian to her minor children, Patience, Rachel, Rebecca and Stephen Bunnell. Benjamin Hitchcock was appointed guardian to Ebenezer, Benjamin, Parmineas, [and?] three minor children of Nathaniel by his first wife[5].

His widow married (second) at Wallingford, 3 August 1735[2], Joseph Benham[2]. She died 11 January 1743/4[2] at Farmington, Hartford co, CT.

Children (by first wife), all but Desire born at Wallingford:
    1. 290019. Desire, b. 16 Mar. 1711[1]; m. 9 May 1733 William Sanford[1].
        Children (surname Sanford)[2]:

1. Miriam.	4. Thomas.	7. Titus.
2. Lois.	5. William.	8. Miriam.
3. Lois.	6. Hannah.	

    2. 290020. Ebenezer, b. 21 May 1713[2].
    3. 290015. Benjamin, b. 16 April 1715[2].
    4. 290016. Parmineas, b. 1 Mar. 1717[2].
    5. 290017. Jairus, b. 25 June 1719[2].
    6. 290021. Abner, b. 24 Mar. 1721[2].
    7. 290018. Joseph, b. 17 Jan. 1723[2].

Children (by second wife), all born at Wallingford:
    8. 290039. Patience, b. 28 Nov. 1726[2]; m. 27 Nov. 1745 Caleb Grannis[2]; d. 26 Aug. 1788[2].
        Children (surname Grannis)[2]:

1. Rachel.	5. Caleb.	8. Medad.
2. Mary.	6. Simeon.	9. Mary.
3. Patience.	7. Eldad.	10. Beda.
4. Esther.		11. Parmineas Bunnell.

    9. 290040. Hezekiah, b. 21 Nov. 1727[2]; d. 21 Nov. 1727[2].
   10. 290041. Rachel, b. 15 Nov. 1728[2]; m. 2 June 1747 Samuel Thompson[2]; d. 1 Nov. 1800[2].
        Children (surname Thompson)[2]:

1. John.	4. Rachel.	7. Jesse.
2. Samuel.	5. Samuel.	8. John.
3. Phebe.	6. Asa.	9. Jairus.

   11. 290042. Rebecca, b. 6 Jan. 1730[2]; m. 7 Feb. 1745/6 Joseph Burr[2].
        Children (surname Burr)[2]:

1. child.	4. Andrew.	7. Jared.
2. Sarah.	5. Hannah.	8. Samuel.
3. Joseph.	6. Andrew.	

   12. 290043. Stephen, b. 6 July 1731[2].

THIRD GENERATION

REFERENCES:
1. NHVR.
2. New Haven - Jacobus, pp. 359, 361, 362, 363 364.
3. Cheshire.
4. Wallingford.
5. Biles Manuscript, pp. 270, 271, 271A, 273..
6. Duncan, pp. 14, 15.
7. Lines.

1-1-10 D7 CB280012

ISRAEL[3] BUNNELL (Benjamin[2], William[1]) was born 12 March 1689/90[1] at New Haven, New Haven co, CT, where he was baptized in the First Congregational Society on 27 April 1690[2]. He married HOPE SMITH[2], daughter of John and Grace (Winston) Smith[2]. She was baptized in the First Congregational Society of New Haven 13 December 1685[2]. Israel was a cordwainer (shoemaker) and lived in the West Farms section of New Haven[3]. He was a member of the First Congregational Church in West Haven and was a Captain in the militia[3]. His name appears frequently in the New Haven Town Records between 1719, when he took the oath of freeman[3], and 1756, when he was chosen for a fourth term as sealer of leather[3]. Over the years he served at various times as fence viewer, constable, selectman, tithingman, grandjuryman, and other town offices[3]. He died in 1757 at West Haven, CT[2]. His estate was probated in New Haven in 1757[4].

Children (born at New Haven):
1. 290022. Israel, b. 7 Nov. 1715[1].
2. 290023. John, b. 4 Sept. 1717[2].

REFERENCES:
1. NHVR.
2. New Haven - Jacobus, pp. 359, 364, 365.
3. Duncan, pp. 15, 16.
4. CB Database.

1-3-1 D8 CB280015

NATHANIEL[3] BONNELL (Nathaniel[2], William[1]) was born about 1670[3] at Elizabethtown, NJ. His wife was MARY SEARING, daughter of John and Susanna (Pine) Searing. For Mary's maiden name and the names of her parents, I am indebted to Miss Gladys Ingram, of Stillwater, OK, and her exhaustive research in the records of Hempstead, Long Island, NY. Although her chain of evidence is circumstantial, it goes a long way toward proving Mary's identity. The

THIRD GENERATION

National Society of Colonial Dames XVII Century found it persuasive enough to grant Miss Ingram a supplementary membership. I also find it persuasive, and unless and until some conflicting data turns up I will consider Miss Ingram's identification of Mary Searing as correct. Here is her analysis of the data as I published it in *The Bunnell/Bonnell Newsletter,* Vol. I, No. 3:

> Miss Ingram was unable to locate the will of John Searing. It was either not recorded or it was lost. However, in the division of some of his lands by his sons in 1713, as recorded in <u>Town Records of North and South Hempstead,</u> Vol. II, pp. 334-5, it is plainly stated that there <u>was</u> a will. This entry names John, "Jeams" (James), Simon and Jonathan Searing as sons of John Searing. A later entry, Vol. II, page 27, adds to these the name of "Samuel Serring of elisabeth Town in ye County of essex in east jersey." No daughters are mentioned in these documents.
>
> In the 1920's a librarian in the Queens Borough Public Library in Jamaica, Long Island, began a collection of records of some of the early families of Long Island. This collection lists the sons of John Searing as named in the town records and adds the names of his three daughters, <u>Mary,</u> Hannah, and Sarah.
>
> Mary Searing is believed to have married Nathaniel Bonnell, Jr., and the names of her children lend strong support to that belief. The children named in Nathaniel's 1736 will are Nathaniel and Mary, named for their parents; Isaac, the name of Nathaniel's grandfather Isaac Whitehead, and also of his brother Isaac Bonnell; Sarah, Hannah and James, names found on the list of John Searing's children; and Abigail, the name of Mary Searing's aunt, a sister of her mother. The names of all the children are thus accounted for, the last four having no previous occurrence in the Bonnell family.
>
> That the name "Mary" was a favorite among the five brothers of Mary Searing is shown by the records of their wills: three of the five each named a daughter Mary; one, Jonathan, named his only daughter Mary. Samuel Searing, who died in Elizabethtown, NJ, honored all three of his sisters by naming daughters for them.
>
> Miss Ingram adds, "Another major item of circumstantial evidence is the involvement of the family of Nathaniel Bonnell in the execution of the wills of Simon and Samuel Searing in Elizabethtown, New Jersey. In 1735, Benjamin Bonnell, brother of Nathaniel, was called to witness the will of Simon Searing, as was his first cousin, Timothy Whitehead. In 1738 Timothy Whitehead served with Simon Searing, Jr. as executor of the will of Samuel Searing, with Nathaniel Bonnell, Jr. as witness. Both Benjamin and Joseph Bonnell, another brother of Nathaniel, appear with Samuel Searing earlier in witnessing the will of Jeremiah Peck.[7]

Nathaniel Bonnell was a carpenter who lived all his life at Elizabethtown. In 1694, as a member of the First Presbyterian Church there, he contributed six shillings to the support of Rev. John Harriman[4,5]. He was named as one of the "Rabbell of Elizabethtowne" who took part in the roughing up of the judges at Newark on 10 September 1700[8]. Why the men of Elizabethtown were so concerned about the arrest of Samuel Burwell is no longer apparent, but it seems clear that it was triggered by the continuing resentment of the Elizabethtown Associates toward the corrupt government of the Proprietors[9].

THIRD GENERATION

In addition to following his trade of carpenter or joiner, Nathaniel was a prosperous yeoman as well, the owner of large tracts of land[5]. From 1724 to 1726 he was county collector for Essex co[5]. He joined the Elizabethtown Associates, and signed his name in the Elizabethtown Book B, in 1729[5]. On 2 August 1720 he and his brother Joseph and five others were chosen by the freeholders as a committee for the disposal of the common lands of the town[5].

Nathaniel Bonnell, with others, bought land from the East New Jersey Society on 4 November 1708[5]. This was the large tract of land known as the New Britain Grant, in Essex co, northwest of Elizabethtown[5]. This is the land which Nathaniel mentions in his will, "My lands above the mountains west from Elizabethtown," which he gave to his son Nathaniel[5].

He died at Elizabethtown 4 September 1736[1] and was buried in the First Presbyterian Churchyard. His gravestone reads "Here lieth ye Body of Nathaniel Bonnel who Died Sept. ye 4 1736 in ye 67 year of his Age."[1] His will can be found at Trenton in East Jersey Will Book C, page 141[5]. It was dated 19 June 1736 and proved 13 September 1736[5]. It reads as follows:

"I, Nathan Bonnel of Elizabeth Town, N.J., carpenter, give to my wife, Mary, one-third part of all my moveable estate to be her sole disposal forever and the use and improvement of the other   two equal parts thereof during the time she shall continue my widow, and if it so happens that she never marries after my decease, the whole part shall be at her disposal.

"My three daughters, Abigal Morris, Sarah Thompson and Mary Chandler and the children of my daughter Hannah Broadwell deceased, shall have the two-thirds part of my movable estate.

"My wife Mary, the one third part of the rents or income of my Plantation where I now live, together with which room she shall choose of my new dwelling-house to be at her sole disposal during the time she continues my widow and no longer.

"I give my beloved sons Nathaniel Bonnel and Isaac Bonnell, to be equally divided between them, all the several tracts or parcels of land situated in the bounds of Elizabeth Town hereafter described, viz: all that my Plantation where I now live, also all that tract of land lying for 30 acres and is bounded on the southeast by land of John Crane, east and north by land not surveyed and westerly by land belonging to John Clark deceased.

"Also all that tract of land called the Flag Swamp lying for 12 acres and is bounded on the northwest by the land of William Broadwell, westerly and southerly by the highway and easterly by the land of William Jones, and to my son Nathaniel Bunnell all my right of lands lying above the mountains westward of Elizabethtown.

"I give to my son James Bonnell all that tract of land layed out to me by the Freeholders of Elizabeth town lying by the Scotch Plains containing 140 acres and is bounded northeasterly by land of Richard Beech, southerly by land in the possession of John Shadwell and southeast and northwest by land left for highways.

"To my three sons Nathaniel, James and Isaac - to be equally divided, all my salt meadow together with all my reversions or right of land in the meadow (not above disposed) throughout the whole bounds of Elizabethtown aforesaid.

"My will is (anything above expressed to the contrary and not withstanding) that my son Isaac shall not live in any part of my now dwelling house during the time of his mother's remaining my widow without the consent, good liking and approbation of my other sons, viz: Nathaniel and James. Signed: Nathaniel Bonnel. 1736."[6]

Mary was made executrix and Nathaniel executor of the will. The witnesses were Jesse Moffard, William Jones and Benjamin Bunnell. Inventory of the personal estate was valued at 80 pounds, 15 shillings and 2 pence.[6]

THIRD GENERATION

Children (all born in Elizabethtown):
1. 290034. Hannah, b. about 1694[3]; m. Richard Broadwell[3]; d. before 19 June 1736[3].
   Children (surname Broadwell):

1. John.	3. Lydia.	5. Rachel.
2. David.	4. Sarah.	6. Margaret.

2. 290025. Nathaniel, b. about 1696[3].
3. 290030. Abigail, b. about 1699[3]; m. _____ Morris[3] (Norris[2]).
4. 290027. Isaac, b. about 1702[3].
5. 290026. Sarah, b. about 1704[3]; m. _____ Thompson[3].
6. 290031. Mary, b. about 1706[3]; m. Samuel Chandler[3]; d. 4 Nov. 1763[1].
   Children (surname Chandler):

1. Phebe.	4. Abigail.	7. Stephen.
2. Mary.	5. Benjamin.	8. Sarah.
3. Samuel.	6. David.	9. Lydia.

7. 290029. James[3], b. about 1710.

REFERENCES:

1. Elizabeth, NJ, Cemeteries, pp. 47, 75.
2. NJ Wills - Vol. II, p. 51.
3. NJ Genesis, July 1961.
4. Union & Middlesex Co NJ Hist.
5. Amer Fam - Long Island, pp. 69, 70.
6. Duncan, pp. 16, 17.
7. Bunnell/Bonnell Newsletter, Vol. I, No. 3, pp. 6, 7.
8. NJ Colonial Documents, Vol. I, 1631-1687, pp. 333-335:
   "At a Court of Sessions or County Court held at Newark for ye County of Essex on
   Tuesday ye Tenth day of September 1700
         Prsent Mr Wm Sandford P'sidt
         Capt John Curtis   }
         Mr Elias McKeilson & } Juts
         Mr Theophilus Pearson}
   The Court according to adjourmt being opened, Samll Carter appeared & demanded of the Court
   by virtue of what authority they Satt. The P'sident made answer by the Kings. The Court then
   proceeding in bissnese as lay before them, called one Samll Burwell who was bound over to this
   Court by Recognizance to answer for his misdemeanor being for begetting a bastard child
   Whereupon the Court demanded security of the sd Samll for the maintanance of the Child, who
   Refused to give the same Upon which the Court Required the Constable to take the sd Samll into
   Cusstody The Constable in the Execution of his office was sett upon by Thomas Johnson,
   Samll Carter & Jos: Burwell & Severall others, The P'sident Wm Sandford pulled of the bench
   by Abra: Hettfield & Daniel Craine & his hatt & wigg halled of his head by the sd Hattfield the
   Clerke of the Court all soe grosely abused in P'ticuquler by John Luker who struck him with
   great vilence with his fist, Wm Luker Junr with a Stick & John Clerke tore his wiff from of his
   head, The P'sident allsoe having had his Sword Taken from him by Daniel Craine & broak in
   peices by him the sd Daniel The Rest of the Justices grosely abused, some their clothes torn of
   their backs with many other abusefull words & actions Recieved from the Rabbell of
   ElizabethTowne, The prissoner Samll Burwell Resshewed out of the Constable hands made
   his Escape, the Constable alsoe grosely abused pulled by the haire & his staff Taken from him &

Thrown out of doore, the P'sident allsoe being struck Three blows, Two of which ponches in the brest & one in the face, The Rabble Consisted of neere 60 horse, the Names of most of them are as followeth

[Here a list of 50 names was inserted, including Natt Bunell Junr., his brother Isaac Bunell, their brothers-in-law, Ephram Price and Sam'll Little, and several Whitehead cousins.- WRA]

"All which and many more were present in the disturbing the said Court, The Sheriffe of The County Robert Smith allsoe at the same time grosely abused, after all which dissturbance soe done and acted by them, The Court adjourned themselves to the house of M[r] Theophilus Pearson the next day at 6 a Clock in the morning."

   9. Thayer, pp. 59, 60.
  10. CB Database.

1-3-2 D9 CB280014

ISAAC BONNELL (Nathaniel[2], William[1]) was born at Elizabethtown, NJ, in the early 1670s[1]. He married ELIZABETH _____. Her maiden name is unknown, but Ellen Dorn, Alhambra, CA, suggests that she might have been Elizabeth Hatfield, daughter of Matthias and Maria (Melyn) Hatfield, one of the original Elizabethtown Associates[4]. If so, she married as her second husband Maxmilian LaLour, whose wife she was in 1725. Elizabeth LaLour died 18 December 1742 in the 68th year of her age, and was buried in the First Presbyterian Church Cemetery in Elizabethtown[3]. The grave next to hers was that of Isaac Bonnell, Jr., who died 15 February 1736 (her son?)[3]. The next grave was that of her brother Cornelius Hatfield[3]. Cornelius Hatfield was one of the witnesses to the will of Isaac Bonnell, Sr. (his brother-in-law?)[2].

Elizabeth LaLour was in her 68th year when she died in 1742. She was born about 1675 if we can assume that her gravestone is correct. I believe this strengthens the case that she was Isaac Bonnell's wife. Isaac's wife Elizabeth is usually said to have been born about 1666, although I am unaware of any evidence to support it. There is no reason Isaac could not have married a woman a few years older than he, but it would have been more usual for him to have taken a bride somewhat younger. A small point, but an additional indicator. Then, too, a birthdate of 1675 fits better with the dates of birth of the children, beginning about 1697 when Elizabeth would have been 22 rather than 33. The more I consider the matter, the more likely it seems that Isaac's wife was Elizabeth Hatfield, who later married Maximilian LaLour.

Isaac, like his brother Nathaniel, was named as one of the "Rabbell of Elizabethtowne" who took part in the roughing up of the judges in Newark on 10 September 1700[5]. The same year he was one of the signers of the remonstrance to the king[8]. He served on the Essex co Grand Jury on 9 February 1703/4[8]. On 8 January 1709/10 he was one of the witnesses to the will of Thomas Clarke of Elizabethtown[2].

His death occurred on 17 January 1711/12. His will names his wife Elizabeth and the seven children, all under age. He willed land "derived from my father Nathaniel" as well as land known as New Britain bought from his brothers Samuel and Joseph Bonnell[2]. His widow Elizabeth died several years later, in 1716[7] or 1720[6] (or 17 December 1742 as Elizabeth LaLour?).

Children:

> There is some question as to the order of birth of the children since we have little or no contemporary evidence regarding their ages. Isaac's will listed them by name, sons first, then daughters. It would have been normal to have named them in order by age, and I assume that is the case, making Isaac, Jr., the oldest son and Lydia the older daughter. We know from his gravestone that Isaac, Jr., was born about 1697. No information on the ages of the other sons has turned up and the suggested birth dates simply recognize that they were younger than Isaac, Jr. For sister Lydia, however, we know that her first child was born in 1718, which means that she could not have been born as late as 1708. I suggest about 1699. Except that Sarah was younger than Lydia, we don't know where in the line up she was born.

1. 290053. Isaac, b. about 1697[6].
2. 290024. Abraham, b. about 1700[6].
3. 290054. Jacob, b. about 1702[6].
4. 290055. John, b. about 1704[6].
5. 290056. William, b. about 1706[6].
6. 290057. Lydia, b. perhaps about 1699; m. about 1717 Joseph Thompson[7]; d. 24 Mar. 1749.
   Children (surname Thompson):
   1. Phebe.   4. Mary.   7. Desire.
   2. Stephen.   5. Aaron.   8. Rachel.
   3. Hannah.   6. Daniel   9. David.
7. 290058. Sarah.

REFERENCES:
1. New Haven - Jacobus, p. 359.
2. NJ Wills - Vol. I, pp. 47, 48, also 95.
3. Elizabeth, N.J. Cemeteries, p. 264.
4. Ltr. 10 Apr. 1990 from Ellen Dorn, Alhambra, CA.
5. NJ Colonial Documents, Vol. I, 1631-1687, pp. 333-335, Vol. III, 1703-1709, pp. 495, 496.
6. Pedigree Chart and Family Group Sheet: Isaac[3] Bonnell, compiled by H. Russell Bonnell, Logan, UT, 12 Mar. 1961, citing N.J. Archives, Vol. 1, pp. 21, 23, 48, 184.
7. CB Database.
8. Deats, citing New Jersey Archives, Vol. II, p. 324, and Vol. III, p. 496.
9. Bible of Joseph and Lydia (Bonnell) Thompson, photocopy sent to me by R. Craig Kammerer, Basking Ridge, NJ.

1-3-3   D3iii   CB280017

SAMUEL[3] BONNELL (Nathaniel[2], William[1]) was born at Elizabethtown, NJ[1], about 1675. His wife was ABIGAIL[1,2] _____, called "daughter-in-law" by Samuel Rose of Newark, in his will, written 31 May 1698[4,8]. She may have been the widow of a son of Samuel Rose when she married Samuel Bonnell, or the term may also have been used to mean a step-daughter, that is, daughter of the wife of Samuel Rose by a previous marriage. It would appear that her antecedents should be sought among the early settlers of Newark, Essex co.

I have found very few references to Samuel Bonnell. He was one of the witnesses to the will of Benoni Lee, tailor, of Elizabethtown, on 19 July 1705[3]. He seems to have inherited part of his father's home farm in Elizabethtown and sold it to his brother Isaac[3]. Samuel Bunall (Bonnell) appears on a list of the first settlers of Woodbridge, Middlesex co, NJ, about 1707[6]. In 1715 there was an indictment in Woodbridge against Samuel Bonnell[6] and he was fined £15 early the next year[6].

Perhaps Samuel and Abigail were divorced. While we find references to Samuel and Susanna Bunall in Woodbridge after 1707[6], Abigail may have returned to Newark. On 3 February 1712/13 Abigail Bonnel witnessed the will of Samuel Dod in Newark[3].

Samuel and Abigail are not known to have had any children. However, Ellen Dorn brought to my attention an indenture of apprenticeship which suggests that there may have been a son Benjamin[7]. Although it is undated, it is written on the same sheet as the recording of the will of Edward Osborne, probated 14 June 1714: "Benjamin Bunhill of Elizabeth Town binds himself, with the consent of his mother Abegell Bunhill, as apprentice to Anthony Ollife and wife."[3] Anthony Olife was listed in 1697 as the owner of 60 acres in Newark. His name is mentioned in wills in Newark in 1713 and 1715[3]. I know of no other Abigail Bunhill or Bonnell in this area and time except the ex-wife of Samuel Bonnell.

Samuel Bonnell is said to have died in 1715[1,2].

Children: (tentative)
    1. 290008. Benjamin, b. between 1700 and 1705.

REFERENCES:
    1. New Haven - Jacobus, p. 359.
    2. NJ Genesis, July 1961, p. 332.
    3. NJ Wills, Vol. I, pp. 47, 139, 288, 348, 394.
    4. NJ Wills, Vol. II, p. 564.
    5. Ltr. 11 Sept. 1987 from Ellen Dorn, Alhambra, CA.
    6. Monnette, pp. 97, 253, 540.
    7. Duncan, p. 11.
    8. CB Database, citing New Jersey Patents and Deeds 1664-1703, by William Nelson, 1899.

1-3-6   D3vi   CB280020

BENJAMIN[3] BONNELL (Nathaniel[2], William[1]) was born about 1682[13] in Elizabethtown, NJ, and lived there all his life. The earliest reference I have found for him is a notation that he sold land in New Brittan to Joseph Meeker, Jr., on 14 April 1711[11]. In January 1711/12 he was one of the executors of the estate of his brother Isaac[6]. He seems to have been well respected by his neighbors in Elizabethtown. Between 1715 and 1758 he was asked at least 17 times to witness their wills[6,7,8]. In 1731 he was High Sheriff of Essex co, NJ[10]. This seems to have embroiled him in the disputes between the East Jersey Proprietors and the people of Elizabethtown, whom he would naturally support. He was accused by one Edward Vaughan of sundry maladministrations in his office as Sheriff. At a Council held at Perth Amboy on 31 July 1731, in the presence of Lewis Morris, President of the Council, and seven Council members:

> "Likewise this Board haveing heard the Memorial of M[r] Edward Vaughan Clerk [Note-Clergyman] against Benjamin Bonnel Esq[r] high Sheriff of the County of Essex in the presence of the said Sheriff and finding that the said Sheriff has Exacted Exorbiant fees for poundage Contrary to Law which he Confessed but pretended he did it Ignorantly and it further appearing that he was a person too much concerned in Interest on one Side in Disputes that have happened in that County and has Summoned Jurys accordingly And that disputes of that Kind have been and are likely to be very frequent in that County, think him a person very unfitt to be Continued in that Station of high Sherriff of the said County and Advise the President to appoint some other in his Stead and place."[10]

I have not found a record to show what action, if any, was taken about this matter.

In February 1734 he appears as one of the many debtors to the estate of John Morris of Elizabethtown[7]. He married SARAH POTTER[13], daughter of Deacon Samuel Potter[13]. She was born about 1696[13]. Since she was 14 years younger than he, it is possible that this was a second marriage. (a quit-claim deed of Benjamin Bonnell to Joseph Bonnell of Elizabethtown dated 13 March 1734/5 was signed by Benjamin and Margaret (x) Bonnell[12]. I have found no other Benjamin Bonnell at Elizabethtown at this time. Is this the first marriage?) He witnessed his brother Nathaniel's will on 13 September 1736[7], and was one of those responsible for taking an inventory of the personal estate of his nephew Nathaniel, son of Joseph Bonnell, on 2 April 1745[7].

Benjamin's brother Joseph, in his will dated 6 October 1746 and proved 14 March 1747/8, gave "unto my brother Benjamin Bonnell, my weavers loom together with all the weavers tackling to me belonging which are now in his possession."[7]

He and his wife Sarah both died in the year 1760, he on 27 May in his 78th year[2,3,4] and she on 17 December in her 64th year[2,3,4]. They were buried in the Presbyterian Cemetery at Connecticut Farms, NJ[2,3,4]. Apparently he left no will. Sarah's will, dated 3 April 1760 and proved 19 January 1760/1, made bequests of a cow to her husband Benjamin, her Bible and wearing apparel to her sister Hannah, and the remainder of her possessions to be given to the children of her brothers and sisters[9]. It would seem to be a safe assumption that Benjamin and Sarah had no children. If Benjamin had been married to a first wife, Margaret, it is possible that they had children, ancestors of some of the unplaced Bonnells in the next several generations. However, no evidence has come to hand to suggest any children for Benjamin.

REFERENCES:
1. New Haven - Jacobus, p. 359.
2. Tombstone inscriptions from the Connecticut Farms, NJ, Presbyterian Cemetery, in a letter from Mrs. Helen P. Alleman, 5 Sept. 1961.
3. CT Farms Cem Inscriptions, p. 170.
4. CT Farms Church records.
5. NJ Genesis, July 1961, p. 332.
6. NJ Wills - Vol. I, pp. 7, 47, 48, 68, 95, 348, 371.

7. NJ Wills - Vol. II, pp. 34. 51, 52, 97, 347, 387, 423, 538.
8. NJ Wills - Vol. III, pp. 20, 21, 54, 106, 215, 359, 360.
9. NJ Wills - Vol. IV, pp. 49, 50.
10. NJ Colonial Documents, Vol. XIV, Journal of the Governor and Council, Vol. II, 1715-1738, pp. 457, 458.
11. NJ Conveyances.
12. Ltr. 11 Sept. 1987 from Ellen Dorn, Alhambra, CA: "From N.J. Vit. Gardiner Mormon Film 0848922 Quit Claim 3-13-1734/5 of Benjamin Bonnell to Joseph Bonnell of Elizabethtown. Sam Headly, Sr., grantee. wit: Joseph & Nathaniel Bonnell. Signed Benjamin and Margaret (X) Bonnell. She not mentioned in Quit Claim."
13. Duncan, p. 11.
14. CB Database.

Note: In a ltr 29 June 1991 Mrs. Frederick F. Kellogg, Jr., New York, NY, speculates on a possible daughter Phoebe, b. about 1719, d. 1794, who married (1) _____ Dickerson, (2) Stephen Lindsley, & (3) David Bruen. It is not known that Phoebe was a Bonnell, but location of gravestones and other circumstantial details suggest the possibility.

1-3-7 D10 CB280016

JOSEPH[3] BONNELL (Nathaniel[2], William[1]) was born at Elizabethtown, NJ, about 1685[1]. Little is known of his early life, although his will suggests that he may have learned and carried on the trade of a weaver. It would seem that he must have had a first wife, name unknown, if the approximate birth dates for his first three children are correct. In that case, he married (second) REBECCA DODD[1], daughter of Samuel and Martha Dodd[3], and widow of Samuel Riggs[3]. Samuel Riggs was still living when he wrote his will on 31 January 1709/10. The will was proved on 16 May 1711, with widow Rebecca as executrix. By that time she was already the wife of Joseph Bonnell[3]. However, she died very soon, probably about 1712, and he married (third) MARTHA FRAZEE[1,7], daughter of Joseph and Mary (Osborne) Frazee[1,7], and widow of John Clark[2,3]. In January 1711/12 Joseph Bonnell served as co-executor of the will of his brother Isaac[3], and in May 1716 he was appointed co-executor of the will of Martha's brother, Samuel Frazee[3].

Joseph Bonnell became very prominent in the civil and military affairs of Elizabethtown. He was a captain of militia from 1718 to 1725, receiving his commission from Gov. Carteret[2]. On 2 August 1720 Capt. Joseph Bonnel, with six others, was chosen a committee of freeholders to dispose of the common lands of the town and for the systematic and organized defense of the people's title to their inheritance[2]. From 1727 to 1730 he held the commission of major[2]. For seven years he was a justice of the peace for Essex co, and in 1724 he was one of the justices of the court of common pleas at Elizabethtown[2]. He was repeatedly chosen, from 1716 to 1743, to represent the town in the General Assembly[2]. In 1738 he was chosen Speaker, and the same year was appointed Judge of the Supreme Court, which office he held until his death[2].

Throughout his adult life his name appeared in the wills of the citizens of Elizabethtown, as witness, executor, debtor or creditor[3,4]. In 1739 Joseph Bonnel's name is first among seventeen on a petition praying Gov. Morris to procure from the King a charter of incorporation for the town as a free town and borough[2]. It is quite likely that he himself prepared and presented the petition, as he was chosen the first mayor of the Borough in February of that year[2]. On 19 April 1745 he acted as administrator of the estate of his son Nathaniel, following Nathaniel's tragic death by accident[4].

He died at the close of the winter of 1747/8. His home was in the neighborhood of Connecticut Farms[2]. In the graveyard of the Presbyterian Church there his remains were buried[2]. Over his grave a monument was erected with this inscription:

> "Who knew him living must lament him dead,
> Whose corpse beneath this verdant Turf is laid.
> Bonnel in Private Life, & Public Trust,
> Was wise & kind, was Generous & Just.
> In Vertues rigid path Unmoved he Trod,
> To Self impartial, pious To his God.
> Religion's patron & a Patriot True,
>
> A General Good & private Blessing too,
> What Bonnel was, & what his Vertues were,
> The Resurrection day will best declare.
> Joseph Bonnel, Esq., Dec[d] march y[e] 14, 1747/8
> In y[e] 63[d] year of his Age." [6]

His widow survived him for many years. Her gravestone at Connecticut Farms read:

> "Here lies the Body of Martha, Widow of Joseph Bounel, Esq., who died Aug. ye 3d
> A.D. 1759. In the 81st Year of her Age."[6]

His will, proved 22 March 1747/8, gives us much valuable family information. Although it is too long to print in entirety, the following extracts will be of interest:

Will of Joseph Bonnell.   Liber E, Folio 154.

In the name of God Amen. The sixth day of October in the twentieth year of the Reign of Our Sovereign Lord George the Second by the Grace of God King of Great Britain, France and Ireland, etc., and in the year of our Lord Christ one thousand seven hundred and forty-six.

I, Joseph Bonnell of the Borough of Elizabeth in Essex County within the province of New Jersey, yeoman, being advanced in years and considering the uncertainty of this present life and also being of sound and perfect mind, memory and understanding (thanks be to Almighty God Therefor) Do make this my last will and testament in manner and form following, that is to say.

-First, I bequeath my Immortal Soul to the care of Almighty God.

-my body I commit to the Earth to receive a decent Christian burial.

-my debts to be well and truly paid out of my moveable estate.

-To my loving wife Martha one hundred pounds to be at her sole dispose.

-To said beloved wife Martha the use, benefit and improvement of which room she shall chuse in my new Dwelling House and one acre of land adjoining to the same during the whole term of her natural life.

-My son David Bonnell shall provide for, keep and maintain one cow winter and summer for my said wife

Martha (his mother) during the whole term of her natural life, she first providing the cow.

-To my son Joseph Bonnell four tracts of land, all part of my Plantation whereon I now live.

-To my brother Benjamin Bonnell my weaver's loom together with all the weaver's tackling to me belonging which are now in his possession.

-To my son David Bonnell a Tract of land containing twenty acres, being a part of my Plantation whereon I now live. Together with my Dwelling House and all the remaining part of my plantation not about disposed of.

-To each of my sons Joseph and David the sum of twenty pounds.

-To each of the Daughters of my son Nathaniel Bonnel, late of the Borough of Elizabeth, deceased, the sum of fifty pounds to be put out at Interest for them at the rate of six per cent per annum, viz. Temperance Bonnel, Joanna Bonnel, Mary Bonnel, Nancy Bonnel, Phebe Bonnel, to be paid to them when they reach age 21 or on their wedding day, if before 21.

-To my daughter-in-law Martha Lyon, wife of Benjamin Lyon, one silver spoon.

-To my three daughters, viz. Phebe, wife of Noadiah Potter, Keziah, wife of Ebenezer Sturgis, Martha, wife of John Dickinson, all my moveable estate not above disposed of to be equally divided between them.

-My sons-in-law Noadiah Potter and Ebenezer Sturgis and my son David Bonnel to be Executors.[2]

Children (by which wife?)[2]:
1. 290035. Joseph, b. about 1706.
2. 290036. Phebe, b. about 1708; m. Noadiah Potter[2,5].
    Children (surname Potter):[5]
    1. Noadiah. 3. David. 5. Phebe.
    2. Nathaniel. 4. Joseph. 6. Sarah.
3. 290037. Keziah, b. 1710 (or 1709); m. Ebenezer Sturgis[2,5]; d. 18 Aug. 1759[5].
    Children (surname Sturgis)[7]:
    1. Margaret.
4. 290038. Nathaniel, b. about 1712.
5. 008365. Samuel. (?) q.v.
6. 290033. Martha, b. about 1719; m. John Dickinson[2] (or Dickerson)[7]; d. 5 Oct. 1793[7].
    Children (surname Dickinson or Dickerson):
    1. Nathaniel. 2. John.
7. 290047. David, b. 1721.

REFERENCES:
1. NJ Genesis, July 1961, p. 332.
2. Amer Fam - Long Island, pp. 58 - 61.
3. NJ Wills - Vol. I, pp. 93, 139, 175, 386.
4. NJ Wills - Vol. II, p. 51.
5. NJ Wills - Vol. III, p. 256.
6. CT Farms Cem Inscriptions - 2.
7. Banta.
8. Conkling.
9. Union & Middlesex Co NJ Hist.
10. Thayer, p. 64.
11. Fern Bonnell.
12. Virkus, Vol. VI, p. 30, Vol. VII, p. 27.
13. Duncan, pp. 18, 19.
14. CB Database.

NOTE: The "daughter-in-law" Martha Lyon, mentioned in Joseph's will, was probably the widow of his deceased son Nathaniel, who had married (second) Benjamin Lyon[14].

1-1-6-3   D11   CB290003

BENJAMIN[4] BUNNELL (Benjamin[3], Benjamin[2], William[1]) was born 30 April 1704[1] at New Haven, CT. In 1714 his parents took their family to settle in New Milford, CT. As a young man he removed to Milford, CT, where he was married to MEHITABLE BALDWIN[2] on 13 April 1726[2] by Jonathan Law, Deputy Governor[8]. She was born 25 February 1702/3[8], the daughter of Obadiah and Abigail Baldwin[8], and was baptized 10 March 1736 in the Derby Congregational Church[8].

Apparently Benjamin was a coppersmith by trade, for on 6 January 1728 we find that "Jonathan Buck a copper-non apprentice to Benjamin Bunnell of Milford" asked the town of New Milford for a contribution of land if he would settle there "as soon as his time is out with his Master Bunnell, which will be perhaps in Nov., 1729; and he will also be obliged to supply the town with needful copper ware, viz: set-work and Rhine work at a reasonable price . . ."[3]

The births of his first six children are recorded in the vital records of Milford, and his oldest child was buried there[2]. Her tombstone read "Abigail Bunnel aged 1 year 5 mo. & 11 days died March ye 12, 1728."[4] It would appear that some time around the year 1735 Benjamin and his family moved from Milford to Derby, CT. Benjamin's wife Mehitable and their two-week-old son Luke were baptized in the Derby Congregational Church on 3 October 1736[2]. Benjamin and Mehitable and some of their children are included among the genealogies in *The History of the Old Town of Derby, Connecticut, 1642-1880.*[7]

Benjamin and his father were two of the 64 individuals who purchased land in New Milford called the "North Purchase"[8]. Lolita Bunnell Gillen researched the land records of Milford and Derby, CT, and compiled a list of 27 real estate transactions in which Benjamin and Mehitable bought or sold land. In several of these she indicated references to his occupation as "cooper" and to his "cooper's shop." Was he a coppersmith or a cooper, or both? Among the transactions she cites:

--Benjamin bought an acre of land with a house and barn in Milford on 17 December 1725. This seems to place the time of his move to Milford. In 1735 he sold this land and bought 10 acres of land known as Hogs Meadow (apparently in Derby).
--On 10 February 1747 Benjamin and Mehitable sold to Thomas Baldwin for £50 land which had belonged to her father, Obadiah Baldwin, and his grandfather, John Plumb.
--On 22 November 1754 Benjamin bought the right of land which his mother, Hannah Bunnell, late of New Milford, had left to his brothers Solomon Bunnell of Kingwood, NJ, and Gershom Bunnell of Danbury, CT.
--On 22 March 1757 Benjamin, ". . . in consideration of the parental love and regard I have for my dutiful son, Isaac Bunnell, I give to my son 20 acres of land in Derby containing upland and meadow land and part of the farm in Quaker Farms where I now live."
           and finally,
--On 13 September 1762 Benjamin and Mehitable sold for £150, land in Derby with a dwelling house and cooper's shop.[6]

In the *"Papers of the New Haven Colony Historical Society,"* Vol. V, published in 1894, we find the Inscriptions on Tombstones in Milford. No. 94 reads, "Here lyes ye body of Benjn Bunnell Died June ye . . . 1753 aged 21." A foot-note at the bottom of the page indicates, "94 Son of Benjamin and Mehetable (Baldwin) Bunnel."[4] This identification is incorrect, since the son Benjamin is abundantly documented as surviving to marry and raise a family. His death did not occur until 1770. This grave should be that of Benjamin, the subject of this article. The stone was obviously badly worn at the time it was copied since the complete date could not be read. The age and year must have been incorrectly copied, but it would seem that Benjamin's body was returned to Milford to lie with that of his infant daughter. In any case Benjamin was still alive in late 1762[6]. The death of Mehitable at age 60 on 14 February 1765 is found in the records of the Congregational Society of Oxford, CT[8]. Was she buried in Milford with her husband? If not, where?

Children:
1. 300001. Abigail, b. 3 Dec. 1726[2] ;bapt. 19 Mar. 1726[9] ;d. 12 Mar. 1728[2,4].
2. 300002. Mehitabel, b. 20 Feb. 1728[2]; bapt. 25 Feb. 1728[9]; d. 22 Oct. 1753[2].
3. 300003. Mercy, b. 30 Aug. 1729[2]; bapt. 7 Sept. 1729[9]; m. 16 Mar. 1748, Titus Tyler[2].
4. 300004. Benjamin, b. 7 Mar. 1731[2]; bapt. 12 Mar. 1731[9].
5. 300005. Abigail, b. 12 June 1734[2]; bapt. 16 June 1734[9]; d. 12 Mar. 1765[8].
6. 300006. Isaac, b. 12 June 1734[2]; bapt. 16 June 1734[9].
7. 300007. Luke, b. 20 Sept. 1736[2]; bapt. 3 Oct. 1736[9].
8. 300008. Charles, b. 15 Sept. 1738[2]; bapt. 22 Oct. 1738[9].
9. 300009. Lois, b. 18 Sept. 1740[2]; bapt. 14 Dec. 1740[9]; m. 17 Aug. 1769 Jeremiah Peck[5]; d. 24 Feb. 1813[2].
   Children (surname Peck)[8]:
   1. Lois.   2. Content.

REFERENCES:
1. NHVR.
2. New Haven - Jacobus, pp. 359, 360.
3. New Milford History.
4. New Haven Hist Society, Vol. V, 1894.
5. Nutmegger, Vol. 27, No. 2, p. 264, Marriages - Town of Waterbury, CT, from the Barbour Collection.
6. Gillen.
7. Derby.
8. Duncan, p. 20.
9. CB Database.

1-1-6-4   D12   CB290004

SOLOMON[4] BUNNELL (Benjamin[3], Benjamin[2], William[1]) was born 27 October 1705[1] in New Haven, New Haven co, CT. In 1714 he moved with his parents to their new home in New Milford, Litchfield co, CT. About 1737[5] he married MARY HOLDREN[2,5,7], who was born in 1707[5]. The DAR Lineage Book lists her name as Elizabeth Mary Holdren[6], and Joan England Murray has theorized that she may have been the same person as the Elizabeth Haldron, baptized 5 October 1709, daughter of John and Cornelia (Van Tienhoven)(Holst) Haldron[10]. However, note that "The Kakiat Patent" states specifically that this Elizabeth Haldron, baptized 5 October 1709, died young[11]. I think it more likely that Mary was the daughter of John's brother, Henry Haldren, whose residence in Hunterdon co is attested as early as 1699. This is only guesswork, however, based on proximity.

Where Solomon and Mary were married is not clear. New Haven, CT, New Milford, CT, Elizabethtown, NJ, and Kingwood, NJ, have all been suggested. Kingwood, Hunterdon co, NJ, may be most likely, since Solomon's name is found on a record dated 19 February 1732/3, when he was ordered to appear in Hunterdon co court[16].They appear early in their married life in Kingwood, and Solomon may have spent a short time in Elizabethtown visiting his cousins there before moving on to Kingwood. (Contrary to statements in *Bunnell and Allied Families*, by Joan England Murray[10], none of Solomon's brothers or sisters ever moved to New Jersey or Pennsylvania.)

They remained at Kingwood until 1755 and all, or most, of their children were born there. In 1755, according to a family tradition told to John Biles in 1881 by Solomon's granddaughter, Catherine (Bunnell) Crawford, when she was 84 years old, Solomon and his family decided to move to a new home in the Susquehanna valley in Pennsylvania. While on the way they met near the Delaware Water Gap the refugees fleeing from the first Indian massacres on the Susquehanna River following Braddock's defeat in July 1755. Turning aside, Solomon settled in a hunter's cabin in "The Hollow" in Smithfield twp, Northampton (now Monroe) co, PA, on the farm afterwards occupied by his son Isaac. He brought with him young apple trees which they planted and which lasted for many years as a flourishing orchard[5]. On 18 June 1765 he bought 244 acres from John Jennings[5]. Solomon Bunnel, farmer, appears on the 1772 tax list in Lower Smithfield twp, Northampton co[12]. He seems to have joined, or at least attended, the Smithfield Dutch Reformed Church, where he served as reader of the English service[12]. He signed the Oath of Allegiance in Northampton co and remained there until he died in 1779[5]. It is said that he was buried in Kingwood, NJ. His widow died in 1804[5], according to her granddaughter who was 7 years old in 1804, or 1784[12].

Children (order uncertain):
  1. 300044. Isaac, b. 13 July 1738[2].
  2. 300047. Rachel, b. 1740[5]; m. James Brink[8]; d. 8 Mar. 1830[5].
         Children (surname Brink)[8]:
         1. Benjamin.   2. Mary.

3. 300045. Benjamin[2], b. 10 Nov. 1742[5].

4. 300046. Solomon[2].

5. 300130. Martha[5], m. (first) Robert Hanna[5]; m. (second) John Tock[5].
    Children (surname Hanna):
    1. Robert.
    Children (surname Tock):
    2. Benjamin.   3. John.   4. Hannah.

6. 300128. Mary[5], b. 1746[16]; m. about 1776 Elias Daley[13, 14, 15]; d. 15 Sept. 1836[14].
    Children (surname Daley)[14, 15]:
    1. Abram.   2. Rachel.   3. Eleanor.

7. 300131. Elizabeth[5], m. Benjamin Drake.

8. 300129. ?Rebecca Hannah?[12].

REFERENCES:

1. NHVR.
2. New Haven - Jacobus, P. 360.
3. Minisink, p. 34.
4. Pennsylvania Archives, 3rd Series, Vol. XIX, pt. 1, p. 67.
5. Biles Manuscript, pp. 9 and 12.
6. DAR, Vol. 99, page 265.
7. Snell.
8. Hoagland, CCXX, Timothy Culver.
9. Jayne History.
10. Murray, Chapter Nine,   pp. 64 et seq.
11. Durie.
12. CB Database.
13. Affidavit of James Winans, 31 May 1852, sent to me by James Raywalt, Washington, DC.
    (See 1-1-6-4-4 Solomon[5] Bunnell.)
14. Affidavit of Rachel (Daley) Gilson, 30 June 1852, sent to me by James Raywalt.
15. Affidavit of John Cox, 4 June 1852, sent to me by James Raywalt.
16. Raywalt.

1-1-6-5 D13 CB290005

GERSHOM[4] BUNNELL (Benjamin[3], Benjamin[2], William[1]) was born 1 May 1707, "at Elizabethtown in east Jersey,"[1] according to the birth records of New Haven, CT. Apparently his parents spent considerable time with their Bonnell cousins in New Jersey during which Gershom was born. At least by 1713 the family was back in New Haven, and made a final move to New Milford, CT, in 1714. No other record with respect to Gershom Bunnell has been found until his marriage to MARGARET JOHNSON[6], daughter of George and Hannah (Dorman) Johnson[6] on 1 January 1728/9[6] at Stratford, CT. She was born at Stratford 22 September 1706[6].

During their thirty years of married life Gershom and Margaret moved a number of times. Stratford, Milford, Redding, Huntingdon, and finally Danbury were all home to them for varying periods[9]. The births of their first four children are recorded in Stratford[9], those of the first six children are recorded in the vital records of Milford[6], while the next five were baptized at Redding[7]. Gershom is listed in the Parish Register of the First Congregational Church at Redding as "Gershom Burril."[9] He and his wife were members #62 and 63 in the Congregational Church at Redding[5], when they were admitted on 22 October 1738. He was recommended by Rev. Whittlesey and she by Rev. Gold[11]. The church record at Stratford shows that Margaret Bunnel was a member in 1737, but no record of her death or dismissal appears there[9].

Gershom died at Danbury 8 July 1758[8]. The Danbury probate records indicate that he died insolvent[2]. An inventory of his estate is dated 18 December 1758[2]. His widow Margaret was appointed guardian of their two youngest children John and Job, who were not yet of an age to select their own guardians[2]. She died 28 December 1769[10].

Children:
1. 300010. Margaret[3] (Margot,[6,7, 8, 9]), b. 15 June 1729[3]; d. 2 July 1729[3].
2. 300011. Hannah, b. 15 June 1729[3,6]; m. Francis Boughton[6].
3. 300012. Rebecca, b. 28 Dec. 1730[6].
4. 300013. Gershom, bapt. 30 April 1732[6].
5. 300014. Joseph, b. 3 Dec. 1733[8]; bapt. 16 Dec. 1733[6].
6. 300015. Margaret, bapt. 16 Nov. 1735[6]; m. 4 Aug. 1755 Benjamin Warner[6]; d. without issue[6].
7. 300016. Elizabeth, b. about 1737[7]; d. 29 Jan. 1740[7].
8. 300017. Solomon, bapt. 5 Aug. 1739[7].
9. 300018. Noah, b. 18 Jan. 1741/2[8]; bapt. 31 Jan. 1742[7].
10. 300019. Nathaniel, bapt. 17 Oct. 1743[7].
11. 300020. Isaac, bapt. 21 July 1745[7].
12. 300021. John[6], b. 11 Nov. 1746[10].
13. 300022. Job[6], b. 15 Jan. 1750/1[8].

REFERENCES:
1. NHVR.
2. Danbury.
3. New Haven Hist Society, Vol. V, 1894 - Inscriptions on Tombstones in Milford, CT.
4. Nutmegger, Vol. 27, No. 2, p. 264, Marriages - Town of Waterbury, CT, from the Barbour Collection.
5. Redding.
6. New Haven - Jacobus, Vol. 2, p. 260.
7. Fairfield - Jacobus, Vol. II, p. 180.
8. Duncan, p. 21.
9. Andrews, pp. 59, 60.
10. Biles Manuscript, pp. 191, 192.
11. CB Database.

FOURTH GENERATION

1-1-6-6   D4vi   CB290006

ISAAC[4] BUNNELL (Benjamin[3], Benjamin[2], William[1]) was born 30 August 1713[1] at New Haven, CT. (When the births of Benjamin's children were reentered in the Vital Records of New Milford after the move there, Isaac's birthdate was listed as 29 August 1713.)[2] He died 14 June 1734[3] in the twenty-first year of his age and was buried in Milford Center Cemetery, Milford, CT.[3]

No other reference to this Isaac has been found, with one possible exception. Parson Hall's records, as printed in the *"History of Cheshire, Connecticut From 1694 to 1840,"* include the following notation under "Burials": "May 22, 1741. Son of Isak Bunnil."[4] At that time there was no other Isaac Bunnell in Connecticut who could have been father of this child. This may, therefore, indicate a family for Isaac.

However, every other reference to Bunnells in Cheshire, and there are many, refer to Nathaniel[3] Bunnell, No. 1-1-9, or Hezekiah[4] Bunnell, No. 1-1-7-1, or their descendants. It is more likely that in transcribing Parson Hall's handwritten record "Hezek" was misread as "Isak." See No. 1-1-7-1 for further discussion of this record.

REFERENCES:
1. NHVR, p. 121.
2. New Haven - Jacobus, p. 360.
3. Nutmegger, Vol. 5, p. 368, Hall's Collection of Cemetery Records in the Connecticut State Library.
4. Cheshire.

1-1-7-1   D14   CB290012

HEZEKIAH[4] BUNNELL (Hezekiah[3], Benjamin[2], William[1]) was born about 1702[1] at New Haven, CT. On 6 July 1726[1] at New Haven he was married by the Rev. Mr. Jonathan Arnold to ESTHER BRISTOL[1], daughter of Daniel and Esther (Sperry) Bristol[3]. She was born 6 February 1697[1] at New Haven. For several years they remained in New Haven, and their first three children were born there. As early as 30 April 1730, however, "Hezekiah Bunel" is listed as one of the freemen of the Town of Wallingford[4]. They resided in the western portion of the town known as the New Cheshire Society, later set off as the Town of Cheshire. Hezekiah Bunnell was admitted to the Cheshire church in September 1733[7], and the first three sons were baptized there at the same time[3].

The rest of their children were all born in Cheshire[3], and there the eldest son Hezekiah died and was buried[3]. Parson Hall records two burials which might apply to this boy. "December, 1743. Ch. of Hez. Bunnil."[4] Donald Lines Jacobus interpreted this entry to refer to Hezekiah's oldest son Hezekiah, and therefore indicated in *"Families of Ancient New Haven"*: "i Hezekiah, b. 11 Mar 1726/7 NHV, bp Sep 1733 CC, 'child' d Dec 1743 CC."[3] However, Parson Hall also lists another burial: "May 22, 1741. son of Isak Bunnil."[4] There is no possible Isaac Bunnell, with the very unlikely

68

exception of Isaac No. 1-1-6-6, q.v., to whom this could refer. I suggest that Isak is a misreading for Hezek. and that both of these burial records refer to children of Hezekiah and Esther. Assuming that to be true, it would appear more likely that "son" of Hezekiah Bunnell would refer to the teenage boy and that "ch." of Hezekiah Bunnell refers to an otherwise unidentified child who probably died at birth since no other record appears.

On 5 February 1744/5 Hezekiah purchased 3 acres of land with a house in Cheshire from Joseph and Jemima Morgan for £47[6]. Then in the late 1740's or early 1750's Hezekiah moved his family to Farmington, CT, in that part of the town which later became Bristol. He died there 25 May 1764[2] and Esther died 20 December 1768[5]. They were both buried in the Bridge Street Cemetery in Bristol[5].

Hezekiah's will, probated in Farmington in 1764[7], reads as follows: "I, Hezekiah Bunnell give to my wife Esther Bunnell, one third part of my moveable and inmoveable estate such as: house, barn and lands with the profits from orcharding, to be hers as long as she remains my widow. One exception is the land I hereafter give to my daughter Esther in which my wife is not to have a third.
    "I give to my son Daniel Bunnell all my land in Harwinton which I bought of Nathaniel Hatch, containing 130 acres.
    "I give to my grandchildren: Susanna, Nathaniel and Thankful, children of Nathaniel, deceased, 90 acres of land at the west end of the farm I now live on. Nathaniel is to have one half and the other half to be divided between Susanna and Thankful.
    "I give to my sons Jesse and Titus all the rest of my land in Farmington to be divided equally between them. I also give to my sons Jesse and Titus two thirds of my moveable estate after my debts are paid and my wife's thirds taken out, to be divided equally between them.
    "I give to my daughter Esther Royce about 27 acres of land in Harwinton that I bought of David Wilcox. I also give her the remaining third part of my moveable estate.
    "I appoint my son Titus, Executor. Signed: Hezekiah Bunnel. 28 Jan. 1761. Witnesses: Stephen Rosseter, Mary Rosseter and Andrew Bartholomew."[5]

The estate of Hezekiah's widow Esther was probated in 1769, with her son Jesse as administrator[7].

Children:
    1. 300048. Hezekiah, b. 11 Mar. 1726/7[1]; bapt. Sept. 1733[3]; d. 22 May 1741[4] (?)
    2. 300049. Daniel, b. 3 Nov. 1729[1]; bapt. Sept. 1733[3]..
    3. 300050. Jesse, b. 26 Jan. 1731/2[1]; bapt. Sept. 1733[3].
    4. 300051. Nathaniel, b. 23 Jan. 1734[3].
    5. 300052. Titus, b. 9 Nov. 1735[3]; bapt. Nov. 1735[3].
    6. 300053. Esther, b. 30 Nov. 1737[3]; bapt. 4 Dec. 1737[3]; m. (first) Benedict Royce[3]; m. (second) about 1772 John Spencer[5]; d. 1808[5].
        Children (surname Royce)[5]:

1. Silas.	3. Amy.	5. John.
2. Esther.	4. Dimon.	

        Children (surname Spencer)[5]:

6. Hezekiah.	8. Nathaniel.	10. Betsey.
7. John.	9. Matilda.	

7.   (?) child, d. Dec. 1743[4].

REFERENCES:
1. NHVR.
2. Barbour, Farmington, CT.
3. New Haven - Jacobus, pp. 360, 361, 511.
4. Cheshire.
5. Duncan, pp. 22, 23.
6. Lines.
7. CB Database.

1-1-7-2   D15   CB290013

DELIVERANCE[4] BUNNELL (Hezekiah[3], Benjamin[2], William[1]) was born about 1705[1] at New Haven, New Haven co, CT. In 1729 he sold his portion of his deceased father's home lot at "Oyster River" to his brother Hezekiah[3]. On 25 December 1730, in Branford, New Haven co, CT, he was married by Rev. Jonathan Merrick[5] to JOHANNA BARNES[1], who was baptized 4 November 1705[2] in East Hampton, Suffolk co, Long Island, NY. She was the daughter of Thomas Barnes and his second wife Mindwell Dibble[2]. Deliverance and Johanna resided in Branford, and all of their children were born there[1]. (Note: *William Bunnell and His Descendants,* by Duncan, misreads Jacobus's article on the Barnes Families of Eastern Long Island and Branford, Conn., and states that East Hampton, where Johanna was baptized, was in Connecticut, and that her mother was the first wife of Thomas Barnes.)

No other record of Deliverance Bunnell has come to the attention of the compiler except that of his death, which occurred at North Branford, New Haven co, CT, in January 1789[1].

Children:
1. 300055. Martha, b. 9 Mar. 1732[1].
2. 300056. Jacob, b. 6 Apr. 1734[1].
3. 300057. Joseph, b. 24 Aug. 1736[1].

REFERENCES:
1. New Haven - Jacobus, p. 361.
2. NEHGR, Vol. 124, pp. 184-186, Barnes Families of Eastern Long Island and Branford, Conn., by Donald Lines Jacobus.
3. Connecticut vital records and land records researched by Ruth Duncan, West Simsbury, CT.
4. Duncan, p. 22.
5. CB Database.

FOURTH GENERATION

1-1-9-2   D16   CB290020

EBENEZER[4] BUNNELL (Nathaniel[3], Benjamin[2], William[1]) was born 21 May 1713[1] in the Cheshire section of Wallingford, CT. Still in his teens he was included in a list of freemen of the Town of Wallingford on 30 April 1730[6]. Parson Hall recorded that Ebenezer was admitted to the Congregational Church at Cheshire in August 1736[6].

Ebenezer was married at Cheshire 6 March 1738[1,6] to LYDIA CLARK[1,6], daughter of Stephen and Lydia (Hotchkiss) Clark[1]. Her birth was recorded at Wallingford 25 November 1718[1]. They lived all their lives in Cheshire where Ebenezer became a man of some substance. He was a shoemaker[7]. In 1732 Ebenezer had inherited a double portion of his father's estate[8]. Later he purchased the rights of his brothers Jairus, Abner and Joseph and his sister Desire to their father's farm[8,9]. During the 1740's he purchased a number of other parcels of land adjoining his farm to increase his acreage[9]. On 19 January 1740 Ebenezer was appointed guardian of his sister Rachel[10]. On 8 October 1745, after his mother's death, he was appointed guardian of his sister Rebecca[10]. Between 1747 and 1759 he was several times chosen by the church to serve on the committee to manage the affairs of the Society for the ensuing year[9]. In a tax list dated 1762 he was assessed on 91 pounds[6].

In May 1755 he was appointed Ensign of the North Company, New Cheshire, and in May 1757 was made Lieutenant of the same company[8]. He served for 18 days as a Lieutenant in Capt. Samuel Hull's Company, Benjamin Hall's Regiment in August 1757 on the Alarm for Relief of Fort William Henry[7], but no evidence has been found to support the statement in Vol. I of the *Abridged Compendium of American Genealogy* that he served as a lieutenant in the American Revolution. He died 14 December 1786[1,6] and his widow 4 May 1802[1,6] at Cheshire. Both were buried in the Hillside Cemetery in Cheshire[7].

Ebenezer's will, probated in Cheshire in 1787, reads as follows: "I, Ebenezer Bunnel of Wallingford, New Cheshire Parish, give to my wife, Lydia, one third of my real and personal estate during the time she remains my widow.

"I give to my two sons, Nathaniel and Israel all my land to be divided between them (my widow holding the one third mentioned above) and the whole of my moveable estate except the widows dowry and except one oxen which I give to my son Israel.

"I give to my daughter Lydia, wife of Abner Johnson, 15 pounds, this with what she has already been given is to be her portion.

"I give to my daughter, Hannah, 20 pounds.

"I give to my daughter, Desire, 20 pounds.

"I give to my daughter, Merriam, 20 pounds to be paid to her when she reaches lawful age.

"I give to my two grandchildren, Ebenezer Bunnel Brooks and David Brooks, sons of my daughter, Sarah deceased, 28 pounds to be divided equally between them. If either should die before they arrive at lawful age then the other will receive the whole amount. Also a note against Jonathan Brooks for 28 pounds 3 shillings 2 pence and a note against Samuel Brooks for 5 pounds.

"I appoint my two sons, Nathaniel and Israel, Executors. Signed: Ebenezer Bunnel. 27 March 1775. Witnesses: John Foot, William Clark and Samuel Abernathy."[7]

Children (all born at Cheshire):
1. 300063. Nathaniel, b. 4 June 1739[1].

2. 300064. Sarah, b. 6 Oct. 1741[1]; m. 8 Mar. 1759 David Brooks[1,6]; d. 1 Jan. 1763[1].
          Children (surname Brooks)[1]:
          1. Ebenezer Bunnel.   2. David.

3. 300065. Lydia, b. 19 May 1744[1]; d. 22 July 1746[1,6].

4. 300040. Israel, b. 17 Mar. 1746/7[1].

5. 300066. Ebenezer, b. 15 Feb. 1750[1]; d. 1 Mar. 1756[1] (He fell into a tub of boiling
          beer and died with 5 ½ hours.[2])

6. 300067. Lydia, b. 26 Jan. 1753[1]; m. 30 June 1773 Abner Johnson[1,3].
          Children (surname Johnson)[1]:
          1. Van Julius.   3. Narcissa.   4. Chloe.
          2. Fanny.

7. 300068. Hannah, b. 11 Apr. 1756[1]; m. 11 July 1776 Samuel Parker[1,6].
          Children (surname Parker)[1]:
          1. Jared.   2. (?) Hannah.   3. (?) Jared.

8. 300069. Desire, b. 7 June 1759[1]; m. 24 Feb. 1778 Ichabod Merriam[1,6].

9. 300070. Miriam, b. 20 Mar. 1762[1]; m. 16 May 1781 Ebenezer Hale[1,4,6]; d. 14 Sept.
          1805[1,4].
          Children (surname Hale)[4]:
          1. Thomas.   3. Amanda.   5. Elias.
          2. Ruth.   4. Ebenezer.

REFERENCES:
1. New Haven - Jacobus, pp. 361, 362.
2. New Haven Newspapers, pp. 24, 76.
3. Nutmegger, Vol. 27, No. 2, p. 264, Marriages - Town of Waterbury, CT, from the Barbour Collection.
4. Hale, House, pp. 121, 122.
5. Wallingford.
6. Cheshire.
7. Duncan, pp. 22, 23, 24.
8. Biles Manuscript.
9. Lines.
10. CB Database.
11. Virkus, Vol. I

1-1-9-3 D17 CB290015

BENJAMIN[4] BUNNELL (Nathaniel[3], Benjamin[2], William[1]) was born 16 April 1715[1] in the Cheshire section of Wallingford, New Haven co, CT. On 22 December 1743[1] at Wallingford he married LYDIA JACOBS[1], born at New Haven, New Haven co, CT, in October 1708[1], daughter of Samuel and Margaret (Olds) Jacobs[1]. She was a widow with three small children, having previously been married to Ebenezer Fox[1]. The following year, in June 1744, Benjamin was admitted to the Congregational Church of Cheshire[2]. He died there in 1758[1]. His widow Lydia was appointed guardian of their only surviving child, Benjamin[3]. She survived him for many years, until 1 August 1790[1,2], when she died in Cheshire.

Children (all born in Cheshire):
1. 300023. Joseph, bapt. Jan. 1742/3[1,2]; d. Oct. 1744[1,2].
2. 300024. Susannah, bapt. Nov. 1744[1,2]; d. 1746[1,2].
3. 300025. Lydia, bapt. Apr. 1746[1,2]; d. 1746[2].
4. 300026. Benjamin, b. 15 July 1747[1]; bapt. July 1747[1].
5. 300027. Samuel, b. 7 Jan. 1749/50[1]; bapt. Feb. 1749/50[2]; d. 18 Aug. 1750.[1]

REFERENCES:
1. New Haven - D. L. Jacobus, p. 362.
2. Cheshire.
3. CB Database.
4. Duncan, p. 24.

1-1-9-4   D18   CB290016

PARMINEAS[4] BUNNELL (Nathaniel[3], Benjamin[2], William[1]) was born 1 March 1717[1] in the Cheshire section of Wallingford, New Haven co, CT. Although only 13 years old at the time, he was listed as one of the freemen of Wallingford on 30 April 1730[2]. He married at Cheshire, 20 September 1739[1], RACHEL CURTIS[1], daughter of Thomas and Mary Curtis[1]. She was born 14 October 1715[1], according to the Vital Records of Wallingford. Parmineas and Rachel were admitted together as members of the Congregational Church at Cheshire in December 1741[2].

Parmineas Bunnell and his oldest son Parmineas, Jr., were both casualties of the French and Indian Wars. In the campaign of 1755, Connecticut authorized the enlistment of Connecticut troops in a regiment to be paid by the Colony of New York as long as it was officered by Connecticut men. Parmineas was one of 97 men who enlisted on 30 May 1755 in a company commanded by Capt. Street Hall of Wallingford. He served until 1 July 1755 and again from 1 November to 2 December 1755. The following year he served in Capt. Israel Woodward's 6th Company, Col. David Wooster's 2nd Connecticut Regiment in the expedition against Crown Point from 2 April to 5 December 1756, and in the campaign of 1757 he served   in Capt. Ephraim Preston's 13th Company, Col. Phineas Lyman's Connecticut Regiment from 4 March to 23 November[5]. He enlisted again for the campaign of 1758 in Capt. Eldad Lewis' 7th Company, Col. Nathan Whiting's 2nd Regiment from 29 March to 10 November 1758. His son Parmineas, Jr., served in the same company with him until his death in August, only 16 years old. On 26 March 1759 Parmineas and his brother Joseph enlisted together in Captain Joel Clark's Fourth Company, Col. Nathan Whiting's 2nd Regiment[6]. This time his luck ran out and he died while in service on 25 November 1759[1,6], leaving his wife with five minor children.

His estate was probated in New Haven in 1760, and Rachel was appointed guardian of her children[7]. Davis's *"History of Wallingford"* erroneously states that she married (second) Samuel Thompson. It was Parmineas's sister Rachel Bunnell who married Samuel Thompson on 2 June 1747, twelve years before Parmineas died[1]. "Rachel Bunnel," widow of Parmineas, was included on a list of the Cheshire town poor 17 April 1780 when Wallingford and Cheshire divided up their responsibilities[2]. She died 30 June 1803 at Cheshire[1].

Children:
1. 300030. Desire, b. 19 May 1740[1]; d. 5 Oct. 1749[1].
2. 300031. Parmineas, b. 1 Jan. 1742[1].
3. 300032. Mary, b. 6 Jan. 1744/5[1]; m. 15 Jan. 1778, Jared Newton[1].
4. 300033. John, b. 18 Apr. 1746[1]; d. Nov. 1753[1].
5. 300034. Rachel, b. 2 July 1748[1]; d. after 1792[1].
6. 300035. Desire, b. 7 Nov. 1750[1]; m. 25 Feb. 1779 William Parker[1]; d. 24 Sept. 1836[1].
      Children (surname Parker)[1]:
      1. William.   2. Nancy.
7. 300036. Damaris, b. 30 June 1752[1]; m. 14 Nov. 1771 Charles Jones[1].
      Children (surname Jones):
      1. John[1].   3. Phebe[4].   4. Charles[4].
      2. Lucy[4].
8. 300037. John, b. 25 July 1754[1].

REFERENCES:
1. New Haven - Jacobus, p. 362.
2. Cheshire.
3. Wallingford.
4. Duncan, pp. 24, 25.
5. CT Historical Society - Vol. IX.
6. CT Historical Society - Vol. X.
7. CB Database.

1-1-9-5   D19   CB290017

JAIRUS[4] BUNNELL (Nathaniel[3], Benjamin[2], William[1]) was born 25 June 1719[1] in the Cheshire section of Wallingford, New Haven co, CT. On 13 October 1741[1,2], at Wallingford, he married ABIGAIL PAGE[1,2], daughter of Nathaniel and Abigail (Wheaton) Page[1]. She was born 29 March[5] 1722[1]. Jairus and Abigail removed to the North Branford section of Branford, New Haven co, CT. He was 58 years old when he enlisted in Capt. James Wadsworth, Jr.'s 9th Company, Col. Nathan Whiting's 2nd Regiment, where he served as a drummer[4]. He died in service on 29 July 1758 before the end of his enlistment[1,4]. His estate was probated in Branford in 1759[5]. His widow died 7 August 1806[1] at North Branford.

Children (born in Branford, CT)[3]:
1. 300071. Lucy, b. about 1743[1]; m. 23 Mar. 1768 Jacob Foote[1]; d. 12 Jan. 1838[1].
   Children (surname Foote)[3]:
   1. Lucy.   3. Hannah.   4. Joseph.
   2. Jacob.
2. 300072. Abigail, b. about 1742[5]; m. 27 Jan. 1763 Asa Jones[1].
   Children (surname Jones)[3]:
   1. Jerusha.
3. 300073. Jairus[1], b. about 1744[5].
4. 300074. Nathaniel[1], b. about 1753[5].
5. 300075. John, b. about 1753[1], or 1751[5].
6. 300076. Abraham[1], b. 175x[5].
7. 300077. Desire, b. 176x[5]; m. 23 Nov. 1780 Michael Taintor[1].

REFERENCES:
1. New Haven - Jacobus, pp. 362, 363.
2. Cheshire.
3. Duncan, p. 25.
4. CT Historical Society - Vol. X.
5. CB Database.

1-1-9-6   D20   CB290021

ABNER[4] BUNNELL (Nathaniel[3], Benjamin[2], William[1]) was born 24 March 1721[1] in the Cheshire section of Wallingford, New Haven co, CT. He lived in Cheshire all his life. On 28 March 1743 Abner purchased 52 acres of land in Cheshire from Jonathan Atwater[6]. On 30 March 1743 he sold his right in his father's farm to his brother Ebenezer for £80[6]. On 19 February 1745/6[1], at Wallingford, he married (first) ELIZABETH PRESTON[1], daughter of Eliasaph and Deborah (Merwin) Preston[1]. She was born in Wallingford 28 December 1727[1]. In November 1746 the records show that Elizabeth was admitted to the Congregational Church at Cheshire[2]. Abner was also a member and served the church in various offices beginning in 1748[2]. Abner's name appears on a tax list for the minister's rate in Cheshire in 1762, when he was assessed on 85 pounds[2].

They had a family of twelve children, all born in Cheshire, and raised ten of them. Also, in September 1768 he was appointed legal guardian of John Bunnell, the 14-year-old son of his deceased brother Parmineas[5]. By the time of the first United States census in 1790, all of the children had left home and only Abner and Elizabeth were left. (1790 census Cheshire, CT: 1-0-1-0-0[3].) Four years later, on 23 March 1794[1], after forty-eight years of married life Elizabeth (Preston) Bunnell died.

FOURTH GENERATION

Abner married again. His second wife was THANKFUL BEACH[1], daughter of William and Martha (Clark) Beach[1]. She was born in Wallingford 25 September 1747[1]. Abner died at Cheshire 13 February 1810[1]. His widow Thankful appears in the 1810 census in Cheshire: 0-00001. On 19 August 1817 she sold 3 acres of land to Burrage Beach for $135[6]. She died 27 January 1818[1]. Abner and his wives were buried in the Old Cheshire Cemetery[5].

Children (by first wife):
1. 300080. David, bapt. Apr. 1746[1]; d. Oct. 1746[1].
2. 300081. David, b. 2 Dec. 1747[1].
3. 300041. Abner, b. 18 Nov. 1749[1].
4. 300082. Elizabeth, b. 20 Nov. 1751[1]; m. 2 Jan. 1772 Joseph Benham[1]; d. 7 Feb. 1832[1].
    Children (surname Benham)[1]:
    1. George.   4. Betsey.   7. Isaac.
    2. Amos.   5. Ransom.
    3. Jared.   6. Adah.
5. 300083. Enos, b. 15 May 1753[1].
6. 300084. Reuben, b. 22 Feb. 1755[1].
7. 300085. Samuel, b. 12 May 1757[1].
8. 300086. Esther, b. 26 Mar. 1759[1]; m. 19 June 1780 Thomas Benham[1].
    Children (surname Benham)[1]:
    1. Samuel.   3. Mary Ann.   5. Thomas.
    2. Adna.   4. child.
9. 300087. Jehiel, b. 29 Oct. 1763[1].
10. 300088. Thankful, b. 17 July 1765[1]; m. 31 Jan. 1788 Reuben Doolittle[1].
    Children (surname Doolittle)[1,4]:
    1. Reuben.   4. David.   7. child.
    2. Ormus.   5. Chauncey.   8. child.
    3. Munson.   6. Araminta.
11. 300089. Lucy, b. 27 Jan. 1768[1]; m. 18 Jan. 1787 Zuriel Lewis[1]; d. 3 Feb. 1843[1].
    Children (surname Lewis)[4]:
    1. Eunice.   5. Thankful.   9. Samantha.
    2. Chauncey.   6. Rebecca.   10. Marcus.
    3. Jerusha.   7. Amarillis.   11. Aravilla.
    4. Lucy.   8. Zuriel.   12. Adeline.
12. 300090. Chloe, b. 22 June 1770[1]; d. 3 Feb. 1773[1].

REFERENCES:
1. New Haven - Jacobus, p. 363.
2. Cheshire.
3. Census 1790 - Cheshire, CT.
4. Letters to John A. Biles dated 10 Nov. 1907 and 15 Dec. 1907 from Harry W. Lewis, Erie, PA.
5. Biles Manuscript.
6. Lines.
7. Duncan, p. 26.
8. CB Database.   76

FOURTH GENERATION

1-1-9-7   D21   CB290018

JOSEPH[4] BUNNELL (Nathaniel[3], Benjamin[2], William[1]) was born 17 January 1723[1] in the Cheshire section of Wallingford, New Haven co, CT. On 28 February 1744/5[1], in Wallingford, he married HANNAH HOTCHKISS[1], daughter of John and Miriam (Wood) Hotchkiss[1], who was born 3 July 1726[1] at Wallingford. They lived near Broad Swamp Brook in Cheshire[2,10]. Their first two children were born there[1]. He tanned leather and made shoes[10]. In November 1746 Hannah was admitted to the Cheshire Congregational Church[11].

In the early 1750's they removed to Farmington, Hartford co, CT, where the rest of their children were born[1]. Joseph served in Capt. Israel Woodward's 6th Company, Col. David Wooster's 2nd Regiment, in the campaign against Crown Point from 3 April to 12 November 1756[6]; in Capt. Joel Clark's 4th Company, Col. Nathan Whiting's 2nd Regiment, from 26 March to 7 December 1759[7]; and in Capt. John Pattison's 4th Company, Major-General Phineas Lyman's 1st Regiment, from 3 September to 3 December 1762, during which time he joined Capt. Ledlie's Company at Crown Point[7]. (Presumably all these periods of service were by the same Joseph Bunnell. However, it is not easy to determine which Joseph is referred to in the military records, and other candidates are available.)

According to Ruth Duncan[5], he was the Joseph Bunnell who served in the Revolution as a private in Capt. Hooker's Company, Col. Erastus Wolcot's Regiment, from January to March in 1776[8]. However, this service was credited to Joseph Bunnell 1-1-6-5-5 D35 CB300014 by the DAR application of Fannie L. Bunnell #84166, in the DAR Lineage Book, Vol. 85, p. 66.

By 1790, when the first Federal census was conducted (2-0-1-0-0)[3], they were living at Southington, Hartford co, CT, where both Joseph and Hannah died, she on 13 March 1798[1] and he on 1 October 1799[1].

Children:
1. 300094. Eunice, b. 23 Aug. 1745[1]; bapt. Aug. 1747[1]; m. 19 Nov. 1767 George
    Dickinson[1,9].
    Children (surname Dickinson)[9]:
    1. Levi Dwight.   3. Florinda.   5. Noadiah.
    2. Jemima.   4. James.
2. 300095. Miriam, b. 31 May 1747[1]; bapt. Aug. 1747[1]; d. Nov. 1749[1].
3. 300096. Miriam, b. 20 Mar. 1753[1]; bapt. 6 May 1753[1]; d. 23 Apr. 1757[1].
4. 300101. Hannah, bapt. 28 Mar. 1756[4]; d. 13 Apr. 1758[4].
5. 300097. Joel, b. 12 Nov. 1758[1].
6. 300098. Amos, b. 9 May 1761[1].
7. 300099. Hannah Miriam, b. 25 Sept. 1765[1].
8. 300100. Hull, b. 2 Oct. 1768[1].

REFERENCES:
1. New Haven - Jacobus, pp. 363, 364.
2. Cheshire.
3. Census 1790 - Southington, CT.
4. Biles Manuscript.
5. Duncan, p. 27.
6. CT Historical Society - IX, pp. 120, 238.
7. CT Historical Society - X, pp. 132, 305, 317.
8. CT Historical Society - XII, p. 382.
9. FGS, George & Eunice (Bunnell) Dickinson, sent to me by Gertrude Corey 8 Nov. 1988.
10. Lines.
11. CB Database.

1-1-9-12   D22   CB290043

STEPHEN[4] BUNNELL (Nathaniel[3], Benjamin[2], William[1]) was born 6 July 1731[1] in the Cheshire section of Wallingford, New Haven co, CT, and was baptized 11 July 1731[1] in the Cheshire Congregational Church. Following his father's death in May 1732, his mother was appointed his guardian[6]. When his mother died in January 1744, Thomas Brooks was appointed his guardian[6]. He married 26 September 1752[1], at Wallingford, MARY HENDRICK[1], daughter of William and Elizabeth (McKay) Hendrick[1]. She was born at Wallingford 30 March 1730[1]. Beginning in 1752 Stephen served the Parish of New Cheshire in various official positions[2]. During the French & Indian War, Stephen served in Capt. Eldad Lewis's 7th Company, Col. Nathan Whiting's 2nd Regiment, from 16 March to 3 December 1762[3]. He appears on a tax list in the Parish of New Cheshire in 1774 with an assessment of £16[2]. He died in 1779[1] in Wallingford (Cheshire). His widow Mary joined the First Congregational Church in Waterbury, New Haven co[6]. In 1791 she transferred her membership to the First Congregational Church in Bethlehem, Litchfield co[6], and in 1797 to the First Congregational Church in Middlebury, New Haven co[6]. There she died 13 September 1811 at the age of 82[6].

Children (all born at Cheshire):
1. 300104. Lois, b. 7 July 1754[1]; m. 10 Mar. 1778 Elijah Bronson[1].
     Children (surname Bronson)[4]:
     1. Lucy.   2. Giles.
2. 300105. Mary, b. 27 Mar. 1756[1]; d. June 1757[1,2].
3. 300106. Levi, b. 11 July 1759[1].
4. 300107. Eunice, b. 10 Jan. 1761[1]; m. 19 Feb. 1784 James Harvey Coburn[1,5].
     Children (surname Coburn)[4]:
     1. Rebecca.   2. Chester.
5. 300108. Ann, b. 21 Sept. 1769[1]; d. 4 Apr. 1771[1].
6. 300109. Lucinda Ann, b. 19 Nov. 1773[1]; m. Jesse Wilmot[1].

REFERENCES:
1. New Haven - Jacobus, p. 364.
2. Cheshire.
3. CT Historical Society - X, p. 335.
4. Duncan, p. 27.
5. Nutmegger, Vol. 27, No. 2, p. 263, Marriages - Town of Waterbury, CT, from the Barbour Collection.
6. CB Database.

1-1-10-1   D23   CB290022

ISRAEL[4] BUNNELL (Israel[3], Benjamin[2], William[1]) was born 7 November 1715[1] at New Haven, New Haven co, CT. He studied theology at Yale College[4] and graduated in 1743[3], then became a teacher in New Haven[4]. Several items relating to his teaching appeared in the *Connecticut Gazette* and the *Connecticut Journal,* published in New Haven:

> 29 Nov. 1765 - Jonathan Lyman, Richard Woodhull, Noah Williston, John Whiting, Thomas Clap, John Rhode, Joshua Chandler, Philip Daggett, Solomon Palmer, Chauncy Whittelsey Timothy Mix, John Noyes, Stephen Hawley, Leverit Hubbard, Thomas Darling, and Ebenezer R. White attest to the efficacy of Israel Bunnel, the New Haven schoolmaster's new methods of instruction.
>
> 16 May 1767 - Israel Bunnel informs the public that he can best educate the children of the citizens of New Haven.
>
> 3 Mar. 1769 - Israel Bunnel, in King St., New Haven, teaches navigation and has oakum for sale.[5]

His wife was SARAH MALLORY[2], daughter of Daniel and Abigail (Trowbridge) Mallory[2]. Israel took the oath and was admitted as a freeman in New Haven on 11 April 1768[4]. He died in January 1781[2]. His widow was dead by 1795[4].

Children (born in New Haven):
1. 300112. Anna, bapt. 27 Feb. 1763[2].
2. 300113. Abigail, bapt. 27 Feb. 1763[2].
3. 300114. Sarah, b. about 1760[2]; bapt. 27 Feb. 1763[2]; d. 10 Mar. 1778[2].
4. 300115. Israel, bapt. 5 Feb. 1764[2]; d. 6[3] or 14 Dec. 1765[2].
5. 300118. Frederick[4].
6. 300116. Joseph[2] J[4].
7. 300117. William, bapt. 23 Aug. 1772[2].

REFERENCES:
1. NHVR.
2. New Haven - Jacobus, pp. 364, 365.
3. New Haven Hist Society, Vol. III, Inscriptions on Tombstones in New Haven, Erected Prior to 1800.
4. Duncan, p. 28.
5. New Haven Newspapers, pp. 169, 193, 241.

FOURTH GENERATION

1-1-10-2   D7ii   CB290023

JOHN[4] BUNNELL, (Israel[3], Benjamin[2], William[1]) was born 4 September 1717[1] at New Haven, New Haven co, CT. He took the oath of freeman in New Haven on 7 April 1760[3]. John studied theology at Yale College[3] and was licensed to preach in 1738[3]. He was employed as a preacher and was a teacher in Haddam, Middlesex co, CT[3]. On 29 May 1768 he was admitted to the church at Middle Haddam from Christ Church, West Haven, CT[4]. Later that year he was admitted to membership in the Haddam Neck Congregational Church in East Hampton, Middlesex co[4], where he was confirmed on 3 December 1769[4]. His death, recorded in the Haddam Neck Church, occurred on 7 July 1773[3].

REFERENCES:
1. NHVR.
2. New Haven - Jacobus, p. 365.
3. Duncan, p. 16.
4. CB Database.

1-3-1-2   D24   CB290025

NATHANIEL[4] BONNELL (Nathaniel[3], Nathaniel[2], William[1]) was born about 1696[5] at Elizabeth, NJ. In August 1719[15] he married JOANNA MILLER[3,6], daughter of Samuel and Elizabeth (Riggs) Miller[3,6] of Westfield, NJ. (Joanna's mother is sometimes given as Elizabeth *Thompson*, but she was the daughter of Joseph Riggs and step-daughter of Aaron Thompson.[6]) Joanna was born about 1702[8] at Westfield, NJ.

Nathaniel and Joanna spent the first twelve or fifteen years of their life together in Elizabeth. Their daughter Jane, who died when almost ten years old, was buried in the cemetery of the Presbyterian Church there[1]. In 1736 Nathaniel, with his mother Mary, acted as administrator of his father's estate[2]. In 1739 he was one of the signers of a petition to Governor Morris to procure from the King a charter of incorporation for the town of Elizabeth as a free town or borough[7]. The charter was granted, and on 8 February 1739/40 Nathaniel was appointed assistant alderman and a member of the Common Council for the free borough and town of Elizabethtown[7]. He was a freeholder of the Borough of Elizabethtown in 1755[5]. In some of the records he is called Capt., a military title which he probably earned in the militia[5].

Nathaniel and his family removed to Turkey (now New Providence), NJ[5,7]. Possibly this was "my land above the mountains west from Elizabethtown," which he inherited under the terms of his father's will[2]. Nathaniel was a wheelwright[13]. He bought land along the Passaic River in Chatham, NJ. The area was then called "Bonnelltown[13]." His house, still (1991) standing at 32 Watchung Avenue, Chatham, is being restored and has been open to the public from time to time[12].

FOURTH GENERATION

Nathaniel Bonnell died 18 November 1763 in his 67th year, and was buried in the Bottle Hill Presbyterian Cemetery at Madison, NJ[8]. His gravestone read "Here lies the Body of Capt. Nathaniel Bonnel, who departed this life, November ye 18 Anno Domini, 1763 In the 67th year of his age."[7] His widow married (second) Deacon Timothy Whitehead[5,8]. She died 1 February 1793 at age 91 and was buried in the Bottle Hill Presbyterian cemetery at Madison[8].

Children:

1.   daughter, b. 1720 or 1722[7]; m. Samuel Crane[3,7].
           Children (surname Crane)[3]:
           1. Nathaniel.   2. Samuel.   3. Jane.
2. 300043. Benjamin[7], b. 23 Nov. 1723[10].
3. 300175. Jane[1,7], b. Oct. 1725[1]; d. 2 Aug. 1735[1].
4. 300180. Mary[7], b. 3 Apr. 1730; m. 13 June 1751 Elijah Woodruff; d. 19 May 1811.
           Children (surname Woodruff):
           1. Joanna.
5. 300178. Nathaniel[7], b. 29 Dec. 1731[15]
6. 300176. Abigail[7], b. 17 Nov. 1735[7]; m. (first) 28 Nov. 1750 Aaron Allen[4,7];
           m. (second) 1765 Thomas Gardner[7]; d. 10 June 1824[7].
           Children (surname Allen):
           1. Samuel.   3. Uriah.   5. David.
           2. Abigail.   4. Nathaniel Bonnel.   perhaps others.
7. 300181. John[7], b. 26 Sept. 1737[7].
8. 300179. Elizabeth[7], b. 1737/8[11]; m. Capt. Israel Ward[11]; d. Aug. 1809[11].
           Children (surname Ward)[11]:
           1. Mary.   3. Elizabeth.   5. Johanna.
           2. Sarah.   4. Aaron Montgomery.
9. 300177. Sarah, b. 1741[8]; m. 28 Sept. 1761 Samuel Roberts[14]; d. 24 Oct. 1822[8].

REFERENCES:
1. Elizabeth, N.J., Cemeteries.
2. NJ Wills - II, p. 51.
3. NJ Wills - III, pp. 80, 222.
4. Morristown Church Records.
5. NJ Genesis, July 1961, p. 332.
6. NJ Genesis, October 1961, p. 349.
7. Amer Fam - Long Island, pp. 70, 71.
8. Madison Church Records, pp. 26, 267.
9. Littell, pp. 46, 505.
10. Duncan, p. 28.
11. Gibby.
12. Bunnell/Bonnell Newsletter, Vol. VII, No. 1, Jan. 1993.
13. Ltr. 23 Feb. 1988 from Florence H. Gibby, Short Hills, NJ.
14. NJ Marriages.
15. CB Database.

NOTE: Did they also have a daughter Phoebe, b. about 1719, who m. (first) _____ Dickerson, (second) Stephen Lindsley, and (third) David Bruen? Or was she a daughter of his uncle Benjamin by an unknown first wife? Or perhaps Phoebe was not a Bonnell at all. See ltr. 29 June 1991 from Mrs. Frederick F. Kellogg, Jr., New York, NY.

1-3-1-4   D8iv   CB290027

ISAAC[4] BONNELL (Nathaniel[3], Nathaniel[2], William[1]) was born at Elizabeth, NJ, about 1702[2]. In 1736 he inherited land in Elizabeth left to him by his father[1,2]. He is apparently the Isaac Bonnel, householder, who was listed among the rateables in Elizabeth township, Town Ward, Essex co, NJ, in January 1779 and February 1780[4]. He is listed as exempt from military service[4]. He was probably the Isaac Bonnel who owed a bond to the estate of John Hendricks of Elizabeth Town in 1733[1]. It is also likely that he was the Isaac Bonnell who received payment from the administrators of the estate of John Carrington of Newark some time between Carrington's death in late 1732 and the settlement of the administrators' account on 22 May 1746[1]. His cousin Isaac 1-3-2-1, CB290053, who died in 1736, is the only other possibility for either of these two records.

Nothing further has been learned about this man except for an old family Bible which lists the births of the children of Isaac Bonnell, whom I believe to be identical with this Isaac[3]. The two youngest children were baptized 19 August 1755 in St. John's Episcopal Church in Elizabeth[5].

Children:
1. 300190. Hannah, b. 19 Oct. 1735[3].
2. 300191. David, b. 24 Feb. 1739[3].
3. 300192. William, b. 28 Nov. 1740[3].
4. 300193. Sarah, b. 26 July 1740[3] (sic)(Probably should be 1741): m. Nathaniel Crane[3]; d. 15 May 1832[3].
5. 300194. Isaac, b. 8 Dec. 1743[3].
6. 300195. Susan, b. 12 July 1745[3].
7. 300196. Mary, b. 25 Sept. 1748[3]; bapt. 19 Aug. 1755[5].
8. 300197. Samuel, b. 1 Oct. 1750[3]; bapt. 19 Aug. 1755[5].

REFERENCES:
1. NJ Wills - II, pp. 51, 84, 230, 231.
2. NJ Genesis, July 1961, p. 332.
3. Records from a Bible owned by Helen Bertha Crane, 220 South Broad St., Elizabeth, NJ, copied by Evelyn Leary Ogden. Copied and sent to me by Homer E. Baldwin, 2 Nov. 1959.
    "Bible Records & Wills Boudinot Chap. DAR Elizabeth N.J.
    Births of children of Isaac Bonnell.

1. Hannah Bonnell		b Oct. 19 1735
2. David	"	b Feb. 24 1739
3. William	"	b Nov. 28 1740
4. Sarah	"	b July 26 1740 ?
5. Isaac	"	b Dec. 8 1743

    6. Susan   "   b July 12 1745
    7. Mary   "   b Sept. 25 1748
    8. Samuel   "   b Oct. 1   1750.
                Deaths.
    Sarah wife of Nathaniel Crane d May 15 1832
    David E. Wade d Nov. 26 1832
    Isaac Bonnell d Mar. 1833."
4. Gen Mag of NJ, Vol. 43, No. 1, p. 30.
5. IGI - New Jersey.

1-3-1-7 D25 CB290029

JAMES[4] BONNELL (Nathaniel[3], Nathaniel[2], William[1]) was born about 1710[4] at Elizabeth, Essex (now Union) co, NJ. His wife SARAH _____ was born about 1716[4]. (Several correspondents say she was SARAH BROADWELL, born about 1712 at Elizabeth[5,6], daughter of Richard and Hannah (Bonnell) Broadwell[9] and granddaughter of Nathaniel and Mary (Searing) Bonnell[9]. No source is given.) (M.P. Welch gives SARAH BROWNELL[11]. Again no source.) They removed to Scotch Plains, Essex (now Union) co, NJ, before their first child was born. On his father's death in 1736 James inherited 140 acres in Scotch Plains[2]. He appears in the March 1779 tax list in Elizabeth twp, Westfield Ward, Essex co, with 80 acres, 4 horses, 6 cattle, 4 pigs, 1 slave and a riding chair; he was exempt from military service[12]. In February 1780 he was also taxed on £300 at interest[12].

James Bonnell died 27 September 1788 at the age of 78[4]. The abstract of his will published in the *New Jersey Calendar of Wills--1786-1790* reads:

"**1788, May 28. Bonnell, James,** of Essex Co., yeoman: will of. Wife, Sarah, household goods and riding chair, and use of my negro. Sons, Stephen, Abraham and Daniel, plantation where I live: Stephen's part to be along land of John Smith Shotwell, of 80 acres; Abraham is to come next, and then Daniel. Grandson, Jonathan Price, land I bought of my son, Abraham, April 29, 1760. Grandson, Jacob Hearty, a note I have against David Broadwell, dated April 17, 1781. Granddaughter, Joanna Price, £10. Daughters, Jemima Hearty, Sarah Wilson, Abigail Blackford and Mary Blackford, £20 each. Residue to my said children. Executors--friend, William Darby, and my son, Abraham. Witnesses--William Elstun, John Marsh, William Coles. Proved Oct. 16, 1788.

1788, Oct. 1. Inventory, £289.18.5, made by John Darby and William Elstun.   Lib. 36, p. 482."[3]

His wife Sarah died 14 March 1791[1,4] "in the 76th year of her age"[14] (or at the age of 78[5]). They were both buried in the Baptist cemetery at Scotch Plains[1].

Children (order uncertain):
    1. 300135. Stephen, b. 1731[5].
    2. 300137. Joanna[6] (or Susan[5] 300028, b. 1746[14]), m. Jonathan Price[5].
            Children (surname Price)[5]:
            1. Jonathan.   2. Joanna.
    3. 300134. Abraham, b. 3 Sept. 1736[5,13].

4. 300138. Jemima[5], b. 1737 (or about 1744[7]); m. about 1763[7] or 1764[13] Dennis Harty; d. by 20 Feb. 1811[7].
Children (surname Harty)[7]:

1. Anne.	4. Joseph.	7. Rebecca.
2. Jacob.	5. Lydia.	8. Jane.
3. Phoebe.	6. Daniel.	

5. 300139. Sarah[5], b. 1739; m. 18 Feb. 1768 Joshua Wilson[5,13].
6. 300140. Abigail[5], b. 2 Oct. 1741[14] (or 2 Oct. 1754[8,9]); m. 1771[9] Isaiah Blackford[8]; d. 7 Apr. 1839[9].
Children (surname Blackford):

1. Mary Bonnell.	3. Isaiah Martin	5. Zephaniah.
2. Susanna.	4. Sarah.	6. Abigail.

7. 300141. Mary[5], b. 3 Oct. 1743[14]; m. 21 Nov. 1773[10, 13] Benjamin Blackford[5,10,13].
Children (surname Blackford)[10]:
1. Mary Elizabeth.
8. 300136. Daniel, b. 30 Mar. 1751[5].

REFERENCES:
1. NJ Genesis, July 1961, p. 332.
2. NJ Wills - II, p. 51.
3. NJ Wills - VII, p. 25.
4. Gravestones in the Baptist Cemetery at Scotch Plains, NJ, copied by Frederick Conkling, East Orange, NJ. Copied and sent to me by Homer E. Baldwin, 2 Nov. 1959.
5. Duncan, p. 29.
6. Family Group Sheet: James Bonnell, prepared by Nona Bassett, Merced, CA.
7. Family Group Sheet: Dennis Harty, prepared by Anne Coker, Carmichael, CA.
8. Family Group Sheet: Isaiah Blackford, prepared by Marian Burnett, Bakersfield, CA.
9. Ancestral Chart: Mary Bunnell Blackford, prepared by Maria Roseberry, New Albany, IN.
10. Ltr 6 July 1993 from Robert E. Dils, Dolores, CO.
11. Ltr 10 Feb. 1987 from Mrs. M. P. Welch, Dallas, TX.
12. Gen Mag of NJ, Vol. 43, No. 3, p. 132.
13. IGI, New Jersey.
14. CB Database.

1-3-2-1   D9i   CB290053

ISAAC[4] BONNELL (Isaac[3], Nathaniel[2], William[1]) was born about 1697[11] at Elizabethtown, Essex co (now Union co), NJ. He was the first child named in his father's will of January 1711/12, all the children called "under age"[2]. On 2 January 1729 he gave his beloved friend William Robinson power of attorney over all his houses, lands, tenements and plantations that are within the bounds of Elizabethtown[4]. He may have been the Isaac Bonnel who owed a bond to the estate of John Hendricks of Elizabeth Town in 1733[3], or the Isaac Bonnell who received payment from the administrators of the estate of John Carrington of Newark some time between Carrington's death in late 1732 and the settlement of the administrators' account on 22 May

1746[3]. I think it more likely that these records applied to his cousin Isaac, 1-3-1-4, CB290027. Isaac died 15 February 1736 and was buried in the burying ground of the First Presbyterian Church, Elizabeth, NJ, where his gravestone read:

> "Hear Lyeth y[e] Bod
> y. of Isaac Bonn
> el who Dep[d] this
> Life Feby y[e] 15th
> Anno Dom : 1736
> in ye 38th year of
> his age"[1]

REFERENCES:
1. Elizabeth, NJ, Cemeteries, p. 264.
2. NJ Wills - I, p. 47.
3. NJ Wills - II, pp. 84, 231.
4. CB Database.

1-3-2-2   D26   CB290024

ABRAHAM[4] BONNELL (Isaac[3], Nathaniel[2], William[1]) was born about 1700[10] at Elizabethtown, Essex (now Union) co, NJ. He was "underage" when listed as an heir in his father's will in January 1711/12[3]. On 23 November 1731, in Chesterfield, Burlington co, NJ, he married MARY SHINN[1,2], daughter of John and Ellen (Stacey) Shinn[9,11]. She was born about 1711[10] in Burlington co, NJ. Before his marriage he had removed to Burlington co, since his marriage license reads, "Nov. 23, 1731, Abraham Bonnel, Chesterfield, Burlington co, cordwainer, and Mary Shinn, same, spinster."[2]

It would seem that they continued to live for several years in Chesterfield twp in the northwest corner of Burlington co, and perhaps the first two sons were born there. In December 1732 the inventory of the estate of Henry Clothier, in the adjacent twp of Upper Freehold, Monmouth co, mentions a note of "William Thorne (granted to Abraham Bonnel)".[4]

In 1737 Abraham purchased property in Gloucester (now Atlantic) co, NJ, as evidenced by the deed by which his grandchildren sold the property in 1811, which reads in part as follows:

> All that certain tract of land formerly surveyed to Abraham Bonnel on or about the year of our Lord one thousand seven hundred & thirty seven 1737. Situate lying and being at or near Great Eggharbour River in the County of Gloucester in the State of New Jersey aforesaid duly recorded in the Surveyor Generals Office at Burlington in Lib. M. folio 333. bounded as followeth. Beginning at a maple tree by a branch of sd. River called Myery run on the South side of the said branch thence extending North sixteen degrees West thirty one chains and a half to a stake and thence North seventy three degrees East thirty five chains to a white oak - thence South eleven degrees East thirty two chains to the aforesaid run thence bounding by the several courses of the same to the place of beginning. Containing one hundred acres of Land and allowance for Highways be the same contained in the reputed bounds more or less. Which tract of Land was left by Will of said Abraham Bonnel dated the eighth day of January 1768 to his son John Bonnel . . ."[7]

Abraham and his family removed to Hunterdon co, NJ, perhaps as early as 1740. The first reference I have found for him there is a record of 25 September 1744, when he made the inventory of the estate of John Stevenson, Esq., of Bethlehem[4]. (They may have lived for a time in Kingston, Somerset co, since the will of Leonard Thomas, Esq., of Princeton, along with the bequests of dozens of properties around the state, left to one of his heirs, "my house and about one acre of land in Kingstown, which I bought of Abraham Bonnell."[5] The will was dated 6 December 1755, but there was nothing in the will abstract to indicate when he bought the land from Abraham.)

Abraham's name appears in various roles in the probate records of Hunterdon county in 1747,[4] 1751, 1755 and 1756[5].

On 16 December 1752 he purchased 262 ½ acres of land along Capalong, Capoolong, or Cakopoulin Brook and Kings Road, Amwell twp, Hunterdon co, from the West Jersey Society[8,9]. In his later years he was an innkeeper at Kingwood, Hunterdon co, where he died early in the year 1768. The abstract of his will in *Calendar of New Jersey Wills* reads: "**1768, Jan. 28. Bonnel, Abraham,** of Kingwood Twsp., Hunterdon Co., innholder; will of. Son, Abraham, £5, and the same amount to my other three sons, Isaac, Jacob and John. Son, John, to have a tract of land in Gloucester Co., at Great Egg Harbor, of 100 acres. Rest of real and personal I give to my wife, Mary. Executors--my wife, and my son, Isaac. Witnesses--Isaac Leet, Lazarus Adams. Proved April 1, 1768.

  1768, March 31. Inventory, £217.2.1, made by Daniel Lake and Tunis Aike. Lib. 12, p. 520."[6]

Children:
1. 300042. Abraham, b. 4 Aug. 1732[9,10].
2. 300162. Jacob, b. about 1735[10].
3. 300164. Isaac, b. about 1743[10].
4. 300163. John, b. about 1745[10].

REFERENCES:
1. NJ Marriages, p. 28.
2. Gen Mag of NJ, Vol. 15, p. 96.
3. NJ Wills - I, p. 47.
4. NJ Wills - II, pp. 100, 228, 398, 456.
5. NJ Wills - III, pp. 11, 108, 111, 197.
6. NJ Wills - IV, p. 49.
7. Deed 6 July 1881, John & Jemima Bonnel and Andrew & Rachel (Bonnel) Fleming to George West, copy sent to me by Paula Sacco, Pittsburgh, PA.
8. NJ Conveyances, p. 47.
9. Deats.
10. Duncan, p. 29.
11. Letter to John A. Biles dated 1 Sept. 1919 from Mrs. Addie W. Crawford, Canton, PA.

FOURTH GENERATION

1-3-2-3 D9iii CB290054

JACOB[4] (Isaac[3], Nathaniel[2], William[1]) was born at Elizabeth, NJ, about 1702[3]. In his father's will of 15 January 1711/12 he was listed as "underage."[1] Nothing positive has been learned about the later life of this man. On 18 January1734 a Jacob Bonel was one of the many debtors to the estate of John Morris of Elizabethtown[2]. I know of no other Jacob Bonnell to whom this could apply. In 1759 there was a Jacob Bonnell who served as an ensign in a New Jersey regiment in the French and Indian War[4], but at age 57 or thereabouts this was probably not the person.

REFERENCES:
1. NJ Wills - I, p. 47.
2. NJ Wills - II, pp. 347, 518.
3. Family Group Sheet: Isaac Bonnell, compiled by H. Russell Bonnell, Logan, UT.
    Ref: N. J. Archives Vol. 1 pp. 23 & 48, 21, 184.
4. Deats.

1-3-2-4 D9iv CB290055

JOHN[4] BONNELL (Isaac[3], Nathaniel[2], William[1]) was born at Elizabeth, NJ, about 1704[3]. In his father's will of 15 January 1711/12 he was listed as "underage."[1] On 24 January 1731/2 a John Bonnel was listed as a debtor to the estate of Benjamin Spinning of Elizabeth Town and on 18 January 1734/5 to the estate of John Morris of Elizabeth Town[2]. These references apparently indicate that this John was still living in the 1730s, since I find no other candidate.

REFERENCES:
1. NJ Wills - I, p. 47.
2. NJ Wills - II, pp. 347, 450.
3. Family Group Sheet: Isaac Bonnell, compiled by H. Russell Bonnell, Logan, UT.
    Ref: N. J. Archives Vol. 1 pp 23 & 48, 21, 184.

1-3-2-5 D9v CB290056

WILLIAM[4] BONNELL (Isaac[3], Nathaniel[2], William[1]) was born at Elizabeth, NJ, about 1706[2]. In his father's will of 15 January 1711/12 he was listed as "underage."[1] I have found no other record of this person.

REFERENCES:
1. NJ Wills - I, p. 47.
2. Family Group Sheet: Isaac Bonnell, compiled by H. Russell Bonnell, Logan, UT.
    Ref: N. J. Archives Vol. 1 pp 23 & 48, 21, 184.

FOURTH GENERATION

1-3-3-1 CB290008

BENJAMIN[4] BONNELL (?Samuel[3], Nathaniel[2], William[1]) was born between 1700 and 1705 in Elizabeth Town, Essex (now Union) co, NJ. His parents were divorced, and he seems to have remained with his mother. Around the year 1714 she gave her consent to his apprenticing himself to Anthony Ollife and wife of Newark, Essex co, NJ[1]. How long Benjamin remained with him hasn't been discovered.

Anthony Olef (or Olive) was not one of the original settlers of Newark in 1666. He appeared in 1678 when he took up land, apparently as a squatter, on Watchung Mountain in the western part of the town and began farming there[2]. On 13 February 1678/9 he was called up before a Newark Town Meeting where he "doth confess his Fault, in taking up land and Meadow, contrary to the Town Order; and doth freely submit it to the Town's Dispose. And upon his Desire he is admitted a Planter." [3] At the same time the Town granted him 40 acres of land at the Mountain[3]. This land, located in what is now Llewellyn Park, West Orange, NJ,[2] became Benjamin Bonnell's home in 1714. Nothing has been learned about Benjamin's life for a number of years after that. A thorough review of the history of Anthony Olive might be useful. He died in the early 1730s[4].

The next mention of Benjamin which has turned up places him in Mendham twp, Morris co, NJ, in the 1770s, **if this is the same person. No evidence indicates a connection other than a complete lack of any other candidates.** In the meantime (under this assumption), Benjamin has moved west, married twice and raised a family[5]. He was listed as one of the bondsmen on the marriage license of his son Aaron on 13 April 1772[6]. He appears on the June 1778 tax list of rateables in Mendham twp as Benjamin Bunnel Householder, with 8 acres of improved land and 1 horse. He was exempt from military duty[7], probably because of age. He does not appear on the tax list for June 1780[7], suggesting that he had died in the meantime.

All else that we know of this Benjamin is included in the letter written by Richard Brotherton of Dover, Morris co, NJ, to his cousin Charles Bonnell of Waterloo, Seneca co, NY[5]. From this letter we learn that Benjamin had one son Jacob by his first wife and five sons, Aaron, David, Nathaniel, Simeon and Benjamin by his second wife. (The Hatfield family Bible gives us "Eleanor" as the name of the second wife, mother of Aaron[8]). He may well have had daughters also, not mentioned in the Brotherton letter.

Children (by first wife):
    1. 300039. Jacob, b. about 1735.

Children (by second wife):
    2. 300054. Benjamin, b. about 1744.
    3. 300058. Aaron, b. 30 Mar. 1749[8].
    4. 300059. Nathaniel, b. about 1755.
    5. 300060. Simeon.
    6. 300061. David, b. about 1762.

FOURTH GENERATION

REFERENCES:

1. NJ Wills - Vol. I, p. 348.
2. *This is West Orange, A Community Handbook*, Revised 1967, published by the League of Women Voters of West Orange, NJ, p. 9.
3. *Records of the Town of Newark 1666--1836*, in *Collections of the New Jersey Historical Society, Vol. VI*, published by the Society, 1864, p. 74.
4. *The History of Newark, New Jersey*, by Joseph Atkinson, 1878, reprint 2001 by Heritage Books, Inc., p. 58.
5. Letter 28 Nov. 1855 from Richard Brotherton, Dover, NJ, to Charles Bonnell CB331672, Waterloo, NY. Typed copy, notarized on 2 Jan. 1920, on file in DAR Library, Washington, DC, submitted by Mrs. Grace (Gridley) Roscoe with her application for membership:

> "Dover, 11th mo, 28th, 1855.
>
> Cousin Charles
>
> Thine of the 10th instant came duly to hand, as touching the object of thy inquiry. Benjamin Bonnell lived in this neighborhood, Jacob was a son he had by his first wife. Henry was Jacob's only son. Benjamin had a second wife. By her he had five sons, namely Aaron, David, Nathaniel, Simeon, and Benjamin. Simeon died when a young man,, Benjamin I never knew, - therefore, I suppose he died before my time. Aaron remove'ed to Redstone, Pennsylvania, about sixty six 66' years ago. His two oldest sons Moses and Henry, each came back and spent one year   Moses returned to Redstone and I had a letter informing me of his decease near 38 years ago. Henry went from here to upper Canada and settled at Pickering, a younger one by the name of William was afterwards out here. That was all that I ever knew of that family, David removed with a view of going to Redstone but settled in the upper part of Virginia   When he left here he had two sons, Thomas and John. Nathaniel settled at Waterloo. He had four sons Simeon and William are both deceased. Darius Nathaniel both went with their father to York State. The personal property of Elizabeth Vail is not yet settled, but they expect to have it settled soon, which when done I will attend to,   I should like to know if thy Mother is yet living, if so, of her welfare.
>
>   to Charles Bonnel   Richard Brotherton"

6. Marriage License in the vault of the Secretary of State, State House, Trenton, NJ. Typed copy sent to me by Marilyn Lynch, Sayre, OK.
7. *New Jersey Rateables 1778-1780*, by Kenn Stryker-Rodda. Morris County, Mendham Township, June 1778 and June 1780, published in Gen Mag of NJ, Vol. 45, No. 3.
8. Hatfield Family Bible, family record sent to me by Mrs. Floyd Nielsen, Ashland, OR

1-3-7-1 D28 CB290035

JOSEPH[4] BONNELL (Joseph[3], Nathaniel[2], William[1]) was born about 1706[4] at Elizabethtown, Essex (now Union) co, NJ. His wife was SARAH _____ [2,3]. From his father he inherited in

1747 four tracts of land in Elizabeth and the sum of twenty pounds[1]. He lived all his life at Elizabeth and died there in November 1761[2]. His will dated 3 November 1761, proved 5 December 1761, provided that his wife Sarah should have all his goods, hogs, corn, etc., his daughter Keziah to have £25 when she reached 18 years of age, his son John to be supported until his death after which all lands were to be sold and the money divided between the two remaining sons, Synesy Bonnell and Dr. Watts Bonnell[2]. (His son Joseph had died earlier the same year.[2]) The inventory of his estate amounted to £354.19.17[2]. He was buried in the Connecticut Farms Presbyterian Church Cemetery next to his sons Joseph and Synesy[5]. His widow was still living in 1777 when she was mentioned in her son Synesy's will[3].

Children[2]:
1. 300172. John.
2. 300170. Doctor Watts.
3. 300168. Joseph, b. 1735.
4. 300171. Keziah, b. after 1743.
5. 300169. Synesy, b. 1747.

REFERENCES:
1. NJ Wills - II, p. 51.
2. NJ Wills - IV, p. 49.
3. NJ Wills - V, p. 52.
4. Family Group Sheet: Joseph Bonnell CB280016, compiled by Iva Bunnell Adams, Midway, UT.
5. CB Database.
6. Records copied from a Bible published in Philadelphia, 1830, by Tower & Hogan at 255 Market St.
   In the possession of Mrs. A. P. Hopler of Brookside, NJ. Copied by Mabel Day Parker, Morristown, NJ, 25 August 1951. Copy sent to me by W. Jerome Hatch, Chicago, IL.
   Extract: "David Thompson born October 4, 1737, died December 28, 1824, married
   Rachel Bonnel born October 15, 1737, died March 27, 1766.
   Their children   Joseph born 20th June 1759   died 6th May 1773
                     Lydia born 29th July 1761   died 1st March 1791
                     Lois born 2d March 1763   died 30th July 1808
                     Phebe born 29th December 1764 died 7th October 1773"
NOTE: Did he also have a daughter Rachel, b. 15 Oct. 1737; m. David Thompson; d. 27 March   1766?[6] His brother David m. David Thompson's older sister Hannah. I don't see any other likely placement for Rachel.

1-3-7-4 D27 CB290038

NATHANIEL[4] BONNELL (Joseph[3], Nathaniel[2], William[1]) was born about 1712[2] at Elizabethtown, Essex (now Union) co, NJ. His wife was PHEBE[2] THOMPSON[7]. She died before 1740, and he married (second) MARTHA DAY[7]. Nathaniel died accidentally 22 March 1744/45 in his 32nd year[2], and was buried in the Presbyterian graveyard at Connecticut Farms, NJ[2]. *The New Jersey Archives, Newspaper Extracts*, Vol. XII, has the following article regarding the death of Nathaniel:

New York Evening Post, 1 April 1745: "New York, April 1st. We have the Malencholy News from the Borough of Elizabeth, in New Jersey, that Mr. Nathaniel Bunnel, son to Joseph Bunnel, Esq.; one of his Majesty's

Judges of the Supreme Court of that Province, died some Time last week, whose Death was occasion'd by an unhappy Blow on the back part of his Head; which he receiv'd from a Rail, that lay in the Cart-rut which the Wheel of the Cart flung up as it went over; t'is said he lived a Week after this sad Accident happen'd but never came to his perfect Sences, nor spoke but a few Words. He was a very Hopeful Gentleman, useful to the Church he belong'd to, helpful in publick Affairs, charitable to the Poor, a dutiful Son, a kind and loving Husband, and a tender Father, and liv'd in good Repute among his Neighbors, was respected by his Acquaintance and Friends, was belov'd and is much lamented by his Parents and Family, he has left a wife and six Children the youngest about a Fortnight old."[3]

His father Joseph Bonnell gave bond as administrator of his estate which amounted to £230.15.10 ½, inventory made by Benjamin Bonnel and John Cooke[1]. In his will of 6 October 1746 Joseph Bonnell made generous provision for the five daughters of his son Nathaniel to be paid to them when they reach age 21 or on their wedding day, if before 21[1].

Children (by first wife)(all born at Elizabeth):
1. 300156. Temperance, b. 1733; d. 14 May 1749[2].
2. 300157. Joanna. (H.T. Smutz asks if this could be the Hannah Bonnell who married David Samson, acc. to Littell's *Genealogies of the Passaic Valley.*[4,5] The time and place are right, but no evidence has been found to support or reject the hypothesis.) CB Database says she married Moses Lune, but gives no source[7].
3. 300158. Mary.
4. 300159. Nancy.

Children (by second wife):
5. 300155. Eleazer, b. 1742; d. 26 Aug. 1746[2].
6. 300160. Phebe, b. March 1744/45[3]. (Is this the Phebe Bonnell who m. John Townley? Cf. Littell, p. 434; Notes, p. 120[4]. Probably not, *Genealogical Magazine of New Jersey*, Vol. 3, p. 53, says Townley's wife was born in 1754. More likely she was the Phebe Bunnel, CB010218, b. 174_ in Elizabethtown, NJ, who married Richard Clarck on 7 July 1766 in the Dutch Reformed Church in Greenwich Village, New York co, NY.[7])

REFERENCES:
1. NJ Wills - II, pp. 51, 52.
2. CT Farms Church Records.
3. Duncan, p. 30.
4. Littell, p. 434.
5. Letters dated 30 April 1960, 18 June 1962 and 28 July 1970 from Harold Turk Smutz, Webster Groves, MO.
6. Amer Fam of - Long Island, p. 61.
7. CB Database.

1-3-7-5   CB008365

SAMUEL[4] BONNELL (Joseph[3], Nathaniel[2], William[1]) was born at Elizabeth, NJ. His wife was PHEBE _____. The only authority I have found for the existence of this son of Joseph[3], is *"American Families of Historic Lineage - Long Island"*, p. 61. It was issued under the editorial supervision of William S. Pelletreau and John Howard Brown, and published by National Americana Society, New York[1]. It seems to have been based on considerable original research, and many specific references are included. However, no sources are cited for the information about Samuel and his family. If Samuel Bonnell actually existed he and his family were probably all dead by 1746 since they are not mentioned in his father's very detailed will.

However, the probate of the estate of John Bahm of Elizabeth Town and Rahway in November 1739 lists among the payments made by the administrator a payment to *Samuel Bonnel*[2]. I find no other Samuel Bonnell to whom this could refer.

Children:
    1. Eleazer, b. 1736; d. 1740[1]. [This is apparently the same child as Eleazer, son of Nathaniel and Phebe, although the dates are slightly different.]

REFERENCES:
    1. Amer Fam - Long Island, p. 61.
    2. NJ Wills - II, p. 35.

1-3-7-7   D29   CB290047

DAVID[4] BONNELL (Joseph[3], Nathaniel[2], William[1]) was born about 1719[3] at Elizabethtown, Essex (now Union) co, NJ. He was a well-to-do yeoman, and prominent in the affairs of Elizabeth[5]. His first wife was HANNAH THOMPSON[5], daughter of Joseph and Lydia Thompson[7]. She was born 3 December 1721[5]. When his father died in 1746 David was one of the executors of his father's will[1]. He inherited that portion of his father's "plantation" at Connecticut Farms (now Union twp, Union co, NJ) which included the dwelling house[1]. In 1748 David Bonnel and Mr. Jacob Green made the inventory of the estate of Nathaniel Tucker, Minister of the Gospel at Connecticut Farms[1].

David's wife Hannah died 28 April 1749[3,5], and he married (second) about 1752 ELIZABETH JONES[2,5], who was born in May 1729. David was elected one of the freeholders or selectmen of Elizabethtown in 1755[5]. In June 1780, during the American Revolution, the British forces on Staten Island made a sortie through Elizabethtown in an abortive attempt to capture the village of Chatham on the Passaic River and ultimately the American military stores at Morristown[4]. The British were turned back at a sharply fought engagement at Connecticut Farms[4]. Before retreating they set fire to the little village, destroying some thirty buildings, including even the

Presbyterian church[4]. David Bonnell's house and barn were burnt, whatever wouldn't burn was stolen, and even his orchard was destroyed[4]. In 1789 he submitted an appraisal of the loss to the State Legislature, but never received any compensation[4]. This list can be read in great detail in *New Jersey in the Revolution 1763-1783*[4].

He died 24 March 1811[3] at Union twp, Essex (now Union) co, NJ. He and his wives were buried in the Presbyterian burial ground at Connecticut Farms, NJ[3]. His gravestone, no longer standing, read as follows:

> "D.B. In memory of David Bonnel, who died March 24, 1811, in the 92nd year of his
> age."

> "Mortals a Saviours love secure, before the mournful days
> When youth and mirth are known no more and life and strength decays,
> Old age with all his dismal train,
> Invades your golden years, with sighs and groans and raging pains,
> And Death that never spares."[3]

> "Here lies ye body of Hannah, wife of David Bonnel, d. April 28, 1749, in the 28th year of her age."[3]

His will dated 28 August 1809 and proved 4 April 1811, appears in Will Book A, page 287, as follows:

> "In the name of God, Amen: I, David Bonnel, of the Township of Union, in the county of Essex, State of New Jersey, being weak in body but of sound mind and memory, do make and publish this my last will and testament in manner and form following, that is to say:

> "First, my will is and I do give and bequeath to my beloved son William and to his heirs and assigns forever, all my real and personal estate of whatever nature or kind soever which is Bequeathed to him on the following conditions, and no other: in the first place he shall pay or cause to be paid all my just debts and funeral charges, and to pay to each of my surviving children, the sum of five shillings each and second, that the said William shall keep, maintain and support in a Decent and Comfortable manner, my wife, Elizabeth, during her natural life, free from any charge whatever, to the residence(sic) of my said children or any part of them, and lastly, I do hereby appoint my beloved son Joseph and William executors, to this my last will and testament, hereby revoking all former wills by me made, in witness whereof, the said David Bonnel hath hereunto set his hand and seal this twenty-eighth day of August, in the year of our Lord, One Thousand Eight Hundred and Nine.

> Witnesses (John Woodruff
> (David Wade
> (John Smith"[5]

His widow Elizabeth died 18 October 1819 at age 90[3].

I believe the following list of David's children is correct, but it is by no means proven. Of particular concern, because of the number of his descendants, is the question of whether Nathaniel, b. 1746, was David's son. For an analysis in some depth of this question, see *The Bunnell/Bonnell Newsletter,* Vol. 8, No. 3, pp. 36-39[6].

Children (by first wife)[7]:
1. 300147. David, b. 1739-40[3] (or about 1748[5]).
2. 300154. Nathaniel, b. 1746[6].
3. 300148. Stephen, b. 28 Apr. 1749; d. 28 Apr. 1749[3].

Children (by second wife)[7]:
    4. 300149. Stephen, b. about 1755; d. 7 Sept. 1757[3].
    5. 300153. Oliver, b. about 1759 (or about 1767)[3].
    6. 300150. Joseph, b. about 1760 (or 21 Apr. 1761)[3].
    7. 300151. Jerusha, b. 17 Jan. 1764; m. (first) before 1782 John Beach[2]; m. (second) 22 Apr. 1804 David Muchmore[2]; m. (third) 14 Oct. 1805 Joseph Tomkins[2]; d. 19 July 1843[2].
            Children (surname Beach)[2]:

1. James.	4. William.	7. Samuel.
2. Joanna.	5. Joseph.	8. John.
3. Susan.	6. Jabez.	9. Abigail.

            Children (surname Tomkins)[2]:
            10. Ashbel Allen.
    8. 300152. William, b. about 1765[3].

REFERENCES:
    1. NJ Wills - II, pp. 51, 489.
    2. Littell, pp. 35, 36, 428.
    3. CT Farms Cem Inscriptions, pp. 170, 171.
    4. Rev War - NJ -2, 1975, pp. 322-324, and Chatham at War, chapter 15.
    5. Amer Fam - Long Island, pp. 61, 62.
    6. Bunnell/Bonnell Newsletter, Vol. VIII, No. 3, pp. 36-39.
    7. Family Group Sheet: David Bonnell, compiled by Iva Bunnell Adams, Midway, UT.

1-1-6-3-4 D30 CB300004

BENJAMIN[5] (Benjamin[4], Benjamin[3], Benjamin[2], William[1]) was born 7 March 1731[1] at Milford, New Haven co, CT. He was baptized 12 March 1731 in the Milford Congregational Church[6]. He was married 10 October 1752[1] by Rev. Jonathan Lyman at Derby, New Haven co, CT[6], to RUTH SMITH, daughter of Joseph and Elizabeth Smith[1]. She was born about 1737[1]. Benjamin and Ruth were admitted to full communion in the Congregational Church of Oxford, New Haven co, CT, on 5 April 1753[4,5]. In June 1761 Benjamin advertised in the Connecticut Gazette offering a reward for the apprehension of a runaway named Daniel Wording, aged about 25 years, who was apprenticed to him after he paid to save Wording from jail[3].

Benjamin and his family became members of the Episcopal Church in the parish of Oxford when it was established in 1764 by the labors of Rev. Richard Mansfield[2]. On 22 December 1766 Joseph Davis, of Derby, in the parish of Oxford, granted to the parishioners of the Church of England in Oxford, a meeting-house lot of about five acres "to have and to hold to the said Abel Gunn, Benjamin Bunnell, and to all the rest of the professors of the Church of England, in said Oxford."[2] Benjamin died 5 November 1770 at Waterbury[3,6] (or Derby[1]), New Haven co, CT. His estate was probated in Waterbury in 1771[3,6]. His widow Ruth served as administratrix[3], and she was appointed guardian of the children[6]. Ruth appears in the 1800 census in Oxford, CT, living alone[5]. She died in 1809 at Oxford, CT, at the age of 72[5].

Children:
1. 310099. Charles, b. 19 Jan. 1759[1]; bapt. 22 Jan. 1759[1].
2. 310100. Benjamin[1] B.[5], b. 19 July 1763[1].
3. 310101. Reuben, b. 24 Dec. 1765[1].
4. 310102. Elizabeth Ann, b. 12 Apr. 1771[1]; bapt. 14 Apr. 1771[1]; m. 1 May 1794 Isaac Hill[1].
   Children (surname Hill):
   1. Charlotte.   2. Sarah.

REFERENCES:
1. New Haven - Jacobus, pp. 359, 365.
2. Derby, pp. 233, 705.
3. New Haven Newspapers, pp. 99, 106, 291.
4. Biles Manuscript, p. 6.
5. Duncan, pp. 33, 34.
6. CB Database.

1-1-6-3-6 D31 CB300006

ISAAC[5] BUNNELL (Benjamin[4], Benjamin[3], Benjamin[2], William[1]) was born 12 June 1734[1] at Milford, New Haven co, CT, and was baptized in the First Congregational Church there on 16 June 1734[5]. While he was still an infant his parents moved to Derby, New Haven co, CT, probably in that part of the town which fell in the parish of Oxford[4]. About 1755 he married ANN COLLINS[1], daughter of Joseph and Hannah (Clark) Collins[1]. She was born 26 August 1737[1] at New Haven, CT. On 22 March 1757, Isaac's father Benjamin, "... in consideration of the parental love and regard I have for my dutiful son, Isaac Bunnell, I give to my son 20 acres of land in Derby containing upland and meadow land and part of the farm in Quaker Farms where I now live."[4] During the Revolution he enlisted as a private in Capt. Jesse Curtis's company, Col. Noadiah Hooker's regiment, serving from 5 April to 21 May 1777[3]. He appears in the 1790 census of Derby: 1-1-2-0-0, and in the 1800 census of Oxford, CT: 00101-01001. (The town of Oxford was set off from the towns of Derby and Southbury in 1798.) He died 4 May 1808[1,5] at Oxford, New Haven co, CT. His estate was probated the same year, with his son Luke as administrator[5]. Isaac's widow Ann was living in Oxford with her son Truman when the 1820 census was taken[5]. She died 14[5] or 15[2] January[2,5] 1822[1], also at Oxford. Both were buried in the Oxford Cemetery[2].

Children:
1. 310001. Luke, b. 28 Feb. 1758[1].
2. 310002. Isaac, b. 11 May 1759[1].
3. 310003. William, b. 16 Dec. 1761[1].
4. 310004. Mehitabel, b. 6 Feb. 1765[1]; m. Peter Osborn[2].
5. 310005. Philemon B., b. 27 Sept. 1767[1].
6. 310006. Truman, b. about 1770[1].
7. 310007. David[1?,2], b. about 1775.
8. 310008. Anna[1] (or Hannah[5]), bapt. 17 May 1778[1]; m. 25 Dec. 1799 Elijah Wooster[1].
9. 310052. Nathan, b. about 1782[2,4].

REFERENCES:
1. New Haven - Jacobus, pp. 359, 360, 365, 366.
2. Duncan, p. 34.
3. Rev War - CT, p. 500.
4. Gillen.
5. CB Database.

1-1-6-3-7   D11vii   CB300007

LUKE[5] BUNNELL (Benjamin[4], Benjamin[3], Benjamin[2], William[1]) was born 20 September 1736[1] in Derby, New Haven co, CT. He was baptized in the Derby Congregational Church on 3 October 1736[1]. He died at Canaan[2], Litchfield co, CT, 23 October 1756[1] in service in the French and Indian War. He served in the campaign of 1756 in the Seventh Company, commanded by Capt. David Baldwin of Milford, CT, in the First Regiment under Major General Phineas Lyman of Suffield, CT[3]. This company sailed from Milford to New York and Albany, proceeded to the

Half Moon, and worked at Fort George[1]. There was much sickness and death from dysentery[1]. In a muster roll of Capt. Baldwin's company in 1756 Luke Bunnel was listed as "sick at Fort Edward."[3] (See the Journal of Peter Pond, a member of this company, published in The Connecticut Magazine, Vol. 10, p. 239.[1])

REFERENCES:
1. New Haven - Jacobus, pp. 360, 491.
2. Derby, p. 705.
3. CT Historical Society - IX, p. 105.

1-1-6-3-8   D11viii   CB300008

CHARLES[5] BUNNELL (Benjamin[4], Benjamin[3], Benjamin[2], William[1]) was born 15 September 1738[1] in Derby or Milford, New Haven co, CT. He was baptized 22 October 1738 in the Milford First Congregational Church[3]. Jacobus states, quoting the Vital Records of Derby, that he was killed by the enemy between Fort Edward and Lake George on 26 July 1758 while in service in the French and Indian War[1]. A Char[s] Bunnel was one of the soldiers who was admitted to his Majesty's Hospital at Fort Edward in the period between July 3 and August 24, 1758[2]. If he died in the hospital as the result of wounds received, this is consistent with the above statement.

However, a Ca[s] Bunnell from Col. Whiting's Regiment of Provincials was sent to the hospital at Albany some time between 2 June and 31 October 1759[2]. The abbreviation has to stand for Charles, and I know of no other likely candidate. If this is the same person, and it probably is, it means that he survived his hospitalization in 1758, enlisted again for the 1759 campaign, and died in the hospital that year instead. Like his brother Luke, Charles left no descendants.

REFERENCES:
1. New Haven - Jacobus, p. 360.
2. CT Historical Society - X, pp. 94, 175.
3. CB Database.

1-1-6-4-1   D32   CB300044

ISAAC[5] BUNNELL (Solomon[4], Benjamin[3], Benjamin[2], William[1]) was born 13 July 1738[1] in Kingwood, Hunterdon co, NJ[7]. When he was about 17 years old he moved with his parents to "The Hollow", now in Middle Smithfield, Monroe co, PA[7]. There, in 1766, he married ELEANOR (LENA, LANAH) BARKALOW, daughter of Jacques and Jane Barkalow[13]. She was born 17 June 1741[2] in Hunterdon co, NJ, and was baptized 12 July 1741 in Readington twp, Hunterdon co, NJ[13]. Isaac obtained a patent from the state for the land in "The Hollow" upon which his father settled where he cleared up the farm and resided until his death[7]. His children were all born and reared on this homestead[7]. Isaac Bunnel, farmer, appears on the 1772 tax list in

Lower Smithfield twp, Northampton co, PA[11], and again on the 1785 tax list there as the owner of 100 acres, 2 horses and 4 cattle[11]. He took the Test Oath in 1775 in Hunterdon co, NJ[4]. He appears in the 1790 census in Lower Smithfield, Northampton co, PA: 4-4-3-0-0. In 1791 he and his wife filed several suits against her brother Herman Barkalow for money he owed them[14]. He died in September 1812[12] in Middle Smithfield twp, Northampton (now Monroe) co, PA.

Children:
1. 310250. James, b. 16 Feb. 1767[7].
2. 310251. Mary, b. 7 Oct. 1768[7] ; m. 28 Aug. 1791 William Rushton Bensley[6]; d. 6 Dec. 1828[7].
    Children (surname Bensley)[3,6]:

1. Gershom.	4. Henry.	7. Anna.
2. John.	5. Eleanor.	8. Mary Ann.
3. Daniel.	6. Elizabeth.	9. Sarah.

3. 310252. Gershom, b. 12 July 1770[7].
4. 310253. John, b. 11 Aug. 1772[7].
5. 310255. Henry, b. 3 July 1778[7].
6. 310256. William, b. 2 Oct. 1780[7].
7. 310257. David, b. 23 Apr. 1783[7].
8. 310259. Barnett, b. 16 (or 26[9]) Feb. 1789[7]; baptized 19 Apr. 1789[9].

REFERENCES:
1. New Haven - Jacobus, p. 360.
2. CBR NE PA, p. 407.
3. Tioga Gazetteer, p. 79.
4. DAR, Book 99, p. 265.
5. Jayne, p. 25.
6. NEHGR, Vol. 93, pp. 204, 205.
7. Biles Manuscript.
8. Snell, p. 226.
9. NYGBR, Vol. 57, p. 150, Records of the Reformed Dutch Church at Smithfield, PA.
10. Family Group Sheet - Isaac Bunnell - prepared by Joan Murray, Palatine, IL.
11. Pennsylvania Archives, 3rd Series, Vol. XIX, part 1, pp. 67, 171, copied and sent by Monty Peden, Rochester, IN.
12. Duncan, p. 34.
13. *Bunnell and Allied Families*, by Joan England Murray, 1990, p. 101.

1-1-6-4-3   D33   CB300045

BENJAMIN[5] BUNNELL (Solomon[4], Benjamin[3], Benjamin[2], William[1]) was born 10 November 1742[1] in Kingwood, Hunterdon co, NJ. When about eleven years of age he came with his parents to "The Hollow", now in Middle Smithfield twp, Monroe co, PA[1]. About 1777[1] he married CATHERINE BARRY[1], the daughter of James and Hester (Bryant) Barry[1] of Bucks co, PA. She was born 26 November 1759[1] in Kingwood twp, Hunterdon co, NJ[8].

On 4 April 1777[1] Solomon deeded the homestead farm (or part of it) to Benjamin. The following year, after his father's health failed, Benjamin entered the military service himself and continued to serve till the close of the war[1]. In 1778 he served as a private in Capt. Timothy Jayne's 7th Company of the 6th Battalion, Northampton co, PA, militia, and in 1780, 1781 and 1782 under Capt. Henry Shoemaker in the 5th Battalion, Northampton co, militia[2]. Benjamin Bunnel appears in the 1785, 1786 and 1788 tax lists in Lower Smithfield twp, Northampton co, PA, where he was the owner of 120 acres[3]. He appears in the 1790 census in Lower Smithfield, Northampton co: 2-1-7-0-0[8], in the 1800 census in Middle Smithfield twp, Wayne co: 32001-02202[8], and in the 1810 census in Middle Smithfield twp, Wayne co: 10201-11011[8].

Benjamin's health was much impaired by his military service[1]. He died on the homestead farm in Middle Smithfield twp on 24 March 1814 and was buried in the Coolbaugh Presbyterian Churchyard in Middle Smithfield. The widow Catherine appears on the tax lists in Middle Smithfield, Pike (now Monroe) co, PA in 1816, 1817 and 1818[8] About 1820 his widow and ten of their twelve children, most with families of their own, removed to the Susquehanna River valley in what is now Wyoming co, PA[1]. She appears in the 1820 census in Tunkhannock twp, Luzerne (now Wyoming) co, PA: 02000-10101[8]. Catherine (Barry) Bunnell died 5 September 1843 in Washington twp, Wyoming co, PA, and was buried in the Bunnell Cemetery at Vosburgh on "The Neck" in Washington twp, where her gravestone reads "Catharine wife of Benj. Bunnel died Sept. 5, 1843 Aged 83 years 9 months & 9 days."[4]

(John Addison Biles, Benjamin's great-grandson, was born 16 February 1858 and died 13 September 1929. As early as 1880 he began compiling a Bunnell genealogy, a project which he pursued to the end of his life. At that time he was able to speak personally to a great many family members whose recollection of the entire nineteenth century was still clear and dependable. I have relied on his manuscript for much information, particularly regarding the descendants of Solomon Bunnell, 1-1-6-4. In his manuscript he reported some early incidents which can only be described as "family traditions." Some of these are demonstrably not true, and others cannot be validated through other documentation. However, rather than ignoring these traditions as unproven, I include them here for what they are worth:

"The following is a copy of the notes taken by the author [J. A. Biles] in the spring of 1881 while on a visit to his great aunt Katharine Bunnell (Carney) Crawford's, at the home of Katherine and her husband, Benjamin Crawford, then residing about two miles north of Meshoppen, Pa. near the home of Rebecca Bunnell Davis.

"She was then 84 years of age, in good health and sound mind with a clear recollection of the events of her early childhood. She possessed numerous antique articles which she showed with apparent pride. Among them my notes show the following: An old fashioned stand which had been in the family 74 years; an old bedstead for 63 years; a very large heavy pewter plate that she could trace to 1797; her great grandmother's flat irons with a date as early as 1775; a pair of shears that had belonged to her great great grandmother.

"Her husband, Benjamin Crawford, aged 87, was cutting his summer's wood when this visit was made in the month of March and preparing for garden work, while his wife performed all the necessary duties of the household.

"In speaking of her grandfather, Solomon Bunnell, she said he was a Yankee from Rhode Island, she thought, born in 1705, and died in 1779. When a young man he came from New Haven, Conn., with his brother Nathaniel,

FIFTH GENERATION

stopping for a time at Elizabethtown, N.J., with relatives, an uncle, I think she mentioned. Nathaniel remained there and changed the spelling of his name to Bonnell instead of Bunnell as before. Solomon came on to Kingwood, Hunterdon Co., N.J., where he remained until the beginning of the French and Indian War, when he started for the valley of the "Sisquehannah", as she called it. Near the Wind Gap [Water Gap?-wra], near Stroudsburg, Pa., they met the refugees fleeing from the first Indian massacre in the valley after Braddock's defeat at Fort Pitt. They turned off into "The Hollow" and settled. He brought with him young apple trees which they planted. Her grandmother's maiden name, she said, was Mary Holdren, a low Dutch girl, born in 1707, and lived till 1804."

"Benjamin, the third child of Solomon and Mary (Holdren) Bunnell, was born Nov. 10, 1742, in Kingwood, Hunterdon Co., N.J. When about eleven years of age he came with his parents to "The Hollow" now in Middle Smithfield Twp., Monroe County, Pa., where he later became possessed with a portion of his father's farm. At the beginning of the Revolutionary War, Benjamin was induced by his father to remain at home and care for the family and attend the farm while he entered the service.

"Solomon's jovial nature is shown by a little occurrence which proved rather romantic. About the commencement of the Revolutionary War he employed Katie Barry to assist in his household. She was an expert spinner of wool and flax. Money then being scarce, he offered to pay her for her labor in either wool, tow, or "Ben", if she chose. Katy was a girl of some 16 years, while "Ben" was about 30. Here Caty proved her native ability or wit, saying "I'll take wool and tow for my work', and after she had a goodly stock of these then necessary commodities, she also "took" Ben, which proved to be a happy joke on Solomon.

"Katy's mother, Hester Bryant, also had a romantic incident. She was bound out in Ireland to a master so cruel that she could not endure the torture, so she fled to America as a stowaway in a ship bound for Philadelphia. The Captain, according to custom, offered for sale the time (enough to pay passage charges) of all who could not furnish cash, and all but Hester were soon disposed of. She being small of her age, none would bid on her. She pled in vain, stating her ability to spin all kinds of wool, flax, and tow. At last a young man whose parents were well-to-do was touched by her distress and came forward and paid the passage money and took Hester home to his mother as a servant girl. She proved to be so expert in all spinning and weaving, and at only sixteen years of age, that she was finally retained permanently, for the young man who paid her ship fare took her as a wife and she became Mrs. James Barry."

"After his father's health failed, Benjamin entered the service in 1778, and continued to serve till the close of the war, as the records show. When he entered, he took his newly wedded wife to a fort in New Jersey, where their eldest child, Polly or Mary, was born. Benjamin's health was much impaired by his military service."[1])

Children:
1. 310245. Mary, b. 5 Aug. 1779[1]; m. 1817, John Jayne[1]; d. 24 Jan. 1838[4].
    Children (surname Jayne)[1]:
    1. Benjamin.   2. David.   3. Aaron.
2. 310246. Elizabeth, b. 13 Feb. 1780; baptized 11 June 1780; m. 23 Sept. 1797[9]
    William Jayne[1]; d. 30 Dec. 1842[5].
    Children (surname Jayne)[1]:

1. Timothy.	5. Benjamin Bunnell.	9. Norton.
2. Catherine.	6. Polly.	10. John.
3. Anna.	7. Allan.	11. Experience.
4. Elizabeth.	8. David.	12. William.

3. 310248. Rebecca, b. 17 Oct. 1782[1]; m. 1805 Moses Bartron[1]; d. 7 July 1850[4].
       Children (surname Bartron)[1]:

1. Esther.	4. Moses.	7. Daniel.
2. Benjamin Bunnell.	5. Mary.	8. Ann.
3. Sarah.	6. Aaron.	9. Elizabeth.

4. 310247. Esther, b. 17 May 1784[1] or 20 June 1783[6]; m. Moses Washington
       Kennedy[1]; d. 20 Feb. 1865[6].
       Children (surname Kennedy)[7]:

1. Katherine.	3. Obediah.	5. Margaret.
2. Mariah.	4. Benjamin Franklin.	6. Hetty.

5. 310243. Martha, b. 12 Oct. 1787[1]; m. 10 July 1809 John Bowden Place[1];
       d. 16 Mar. 1876[1].
       Children (surname Place)[1]:

1. Esther.	3. Benjamin.	4. Mary.
2. Rebecca.		

6. 310242. Benjamin, b. 29 Oct. 1788[1].

7. 310241. John, b. 13 Aug. 1790[1].

8. 310249. Solomon, b. 21 July 1792[1].

9. 310244. Isaac, b. 18 Feb. 1795[1].

10. 310260. Catherine, b. 13 Mar. 1797[1]; m. (first) 1818 Dr. Elijah Carney[1];
       m. (second) 1832 Benjamin C. Crawford[1]; d. 20 Feb. 1892[1].
       Children (surname Carney)[1]:
       1. Benjamin.
       Children (surname Crawford)[1]:

2. Esther Mary.	4. Charles T.	5. Gershom Bunnell.
3. Alpheus B.		

11. 310261. James, b. 27 May 1799[1].

12. 310262. Gershom, b. 15 Dec. 1803[1].

REFERENCES:
1. Biles Manuscript, pp. 9, 71, 72, et seq.
2. Pennsylvania Archives, 5th Series, Vol. 8, pp. 379, 417, 420, 435.
3. Pennsylvania Archives, 3rd Series, Vol. XIX, part 1, pp. 171, 278, 390.
4. Gravestone Inscriptions, Bunnell Cemetery, Washington twp, Wyoming co, PA,
   copied by William R. Austin.
5. Gravestone Inscriptions, North Mehoopany Cemetery, Wyoming co, PA, copied by William R. Austin.
6. Ltr. 11 April 1962 from John R. Shaw, Barrington, IL.
7. *Pioneer Families of Northwestern New Jersey*, by William C. Armstrong, 1979, pp. 454, 455.
8. CB Database.
9. Duncan, p. 35.

FIFTH GENERATION

1-1-6-4-4 D12iii CB300046

SOLOMON[5] BUNNELL (Solomon[4], Benjamin[3], Benjamin[2], William[1]) was born about 1745 at Kingwood, Hunterdon co, NJ. He moved with his parents to Middle Smithfield twp, now Monroe co, PA. Solomon Bunnel, single man, appears in the 1772 tax list in Lower Smithfield twp, Northampton co, PA[3]. He married ELEANOR FOX[1], daughter of Jacob Fox[1]. A. F. Bonnell, in his *Genealogy of the Bonnell Family*, has a single reference to this Solomon when he is listed in the family of his father, Solomon, Sr.: "Solomon Bunnell married _ had three children, was crazy - killed the negroes."[5]. John A. Biles, in his Bunnell manuscript, refers to Solomon as "crazy" without elaboration[1].

Children:
1. 310208. Hannah, b. July 1772[1] Stroudsburg, PA; m. May[2] (or 1 Mar.[4]) 1791[1]
   James Winans[6]; d. 13 Sept. 1838[1] Ohio.
   Children (surname Winans)[4]:

1. Jacob James.	4. Mary (Polly).	7. James Isaac.
2. Jemima.	5. Henry Stringer.	8. Anna.
3. Isaac.	6. Susannah.	9. Hannah Bunnell.

   Was there also a son Clark?
2. 310209. Sarah, b. 1776[1]; m. Henry Stringer[1]; d. 29 Dec. 1829[1].
   Children (surname Stringer)[1]:

1. James.	2. Sarah.	3. Hannah.

others?

REFERENCES:
1. Biles Manuscript.
2. Ltr. 1 Feb. 1969 from Grace Petersen, Provo, UT.
3. Pennsylvania Archives, 3rd Series, Vol. XIX, part 1, p. 69.
4. Winans, pp. 23, 24.
5. Bonnell.
6. Affidavit of James Winans 31 May 1852, sent to me by James Raywalt.
   Note: Because this affidavit is the only contemporary evidence I have seen linking Hannah Bunnell to her husband James Winans, as well as making a firm connection with Polly (Mary) Bunnell, daughter of Solomon, Sr., I feel it will be valuable to quote the affidavit in full here:

"The State of Ohio, Trumbull County. Personally appeared before me a Justice of the Peace in and for said County, James Winans a resident of Milton in the County of Mahoning and State aforesaid who after being first duly sworn according to law deposeth and saith. That he was eighty five (85) years of age on the seventeenth day of February last, and establishes his age as such by a family record in his possession which was many years since copied into his Bible from an old original record in the handwriting of his father. That he was born in Smithfield township Northampton County, Penn[a]. That from his earliest recollection he was acquainted with Elias Dalley late of Bristol in the County of Trumbull, now, and for many years deceased. That though quite young at the time not to exceed eight or nine years, he recollects distinctly hearing it talked that 'Elias Dalley and Polly Bunnel were going to get married,' and that they were so married. That he was equally well acquainted with the said Polly Bunnell as her parents resided in the same neighborhood as his father. That the said Dalley and wife the said Polly, lived together as husband and wife in the said town of Smithfield, for a number of years, and then removed

to Mount Bethel a few miles distant where they continued to live and raised a family, till they removed to the West. That his, deponents, acquaintance with the said Dalley and family may have been more intimate from the fact of his, deponents, marrying a niece of the said Polly Bunnell, afterward Dalley. This deponent believes from his positive knowledge of his own age and his best recollection of the age of the said Dalleys oldest child a son, that the marriage of the said Elias Dalley and Polly Bunnell took place as early as 1775 or 1776. That the acquaintance of deponent continued intimate with the said Dalley till they removed to the west many years since. Subsequently, he, deponent, also removed to the said County of Trumbull, and saw the said Dalley once only previous to his death.
"Sworn to and subscribed Before me U. D. Kellogg a Justice of the Peace in and for the County aforesaid, this 31st day of May AD 1852."

1-1-6-5-4   D34   CB300013

GERSHOM[5] BUNNELL (Gershom[4], Benjamin[3], Benjamin[2], William[1]) was baptized 30 April 1732[1,2] at Milford, New Haven co, CT. On 3 April 1758 he enlisted in the First Company, Fourth Regiment of Connecticut troops under Col. David Wooster for service in the French and Indian War. He served until his discharge on 15 November 1758[6]. He was apparently living in Danbury, Fairfield co, CT, in 1790, when the census listed him as head of household, with one male over 16 years, one male under 16 years, and one female[1]. No other contemporary references have come to my attention, and it is difficult to form a picture of his life. See my discussion of this problem in *The Bunnell/Bonnell* Newsletter[3]. Several references state that he was a loyalist who removed to Nova Scotia during the Revolution, but it is clear that the loyalist Gershom was a younger person[3], who might perhaps have been his son. No children have been identified, although Duncan thinks he could have been the father of Joseph and Gershom[4]. Although I have seen no evidence to support this relationship, and Duncan offers none, I am aware of no conflicting evidence either. Duncan says that Gershom's wife was MARGARET TOMER[4]. However, Claude Bunnell informed me that Margaret was of Westfield, Essex (now Union) co, NJ. She was probably the wife of the Garshom Bounell who was taxed in March 1779 on land valued at £3 and in February 1780 on 6 acres of improved land, 1 cattle and 2 hogs in Elizabeth twp, Westfield Ward, Essex co, NJ[5]. This is clearly not the same person as the subject of this article.

Possible? Children??:
1. 010506. Gershom, b. about 1757.
2. 013196. Joseph, b. about 1763.

REFERENCES:
1. New Haven - Jacobus, p. 360.
2. Fairfield - Jacobus, Vol. 2, p. 180.
3. Bunnell/Bonnell Newsletter, Vol. VII, No. 1, pp. 10-13.
4. Duncan, pp. 35, 36.
5. Gen Mag of NJ, Vol. 43, No. 3, p. 132, New Jersey Rateables, 1778-1780, by Kenn Stryker-Rodda.
6. CT Historical Society - X, p. 75.
7. CB Database.

FIFTH GENERATION

1-1-6-5-5   D35   CB300014

JOSEPH[5] BUNNELL (Gershom[4], Benjamin[3], Benjamin[2], William[1]) was born 3 December 1733[4] in Stratford[4], Fairfield co, CT, and baptized 16 December 1733[1] at Milford[1], New Haven co, CT. He was a soldier in the French and Indian War. Although it is difficult to identify the various Josephs who appear on the military rolls, I believe that he was the Joseph Bunnel who served for 18 days in the campaign of 1757 in Capt. John Barnum's Company, Col. Andrew Burr's Regiment at the time of the alarm for relief of Fort William Henry and places adjacent[2]. All of the officers of this company were from Danbury and Newtown[2], and Joseph was probably living with his parents in Danbury at the time the company was raised.

On 10 March 1762, "Joseph Bunnil of Woodbury" was chosen by his brother John as his guardian in the recognizance of £100 that Joseph will faithfully discharge his guardianship and return an account thereof[6]. About 1767 he married ABIAH KIRBY[10], daughter of Roger and Martha Kirby[10] of Woodbury, Litchfield co, CT. She was born 7 July 1732[8] at Woodbury.

Joseph also served in the Revolutionary War. Again, it is very hard to match the right Joseph with the names in the extant service records. According to DAR lineage records[3], and also *New England Families*,[10], this is the Joseph who enlisted 9 July 1775 as private in the 3rd company of Colonel Huntingdon's 8th Connecticut regulars, discharged 18 December 1775[5], and in 1776 in Captain Hooker's company, Colonel Erastus Wolcott's regiment, marching to Boston in January 1776, serving for six weeks[5]. Duncan[4], on the other hand, ascribes the service in Captain Hooker's company in 1776 to a different Joseph Bunnell (1-1-9-7, D21, CB290018). Solely on the basis that Joseph 1-1-9-7 was 53 years old in 1776, while Joseph 1-1-6-5-5 was 43, I am inclined to agree with the DAR record. Further investigation may help to resolve the question. However, the 1782 service Duncan assigns to this Joseph belongs instead to Joseph[6], grandson of Gershom[4], and possibly son of Gershom[5]. The pension application of Joseph[6] of Weston, CT, makes this clear. *New England Families*[10] also credits him with service in Capt. Daniel Sloper's company, Major Elisha Sheldon's regiment of Light Horse, which accompanied Washington in his retreat across New Jersey in December 1776 (Joseph marched with the company on 26 October and was discharged on 24 December 1776[5]), and in Capt. Charles Smith's company, in the state brigade raised by General David Waterbury for the defense of the Connecticut coast line in 1781[5]. Joseph was hired by the town of Danbury on 20 April 1781 for this service.

It is said that Abiah (Kirby) Bunnell was one of the patriot women of Litchfield, CT, who melted the leaden statue of King George III and moulded it into bullets for American soldiers[10]. During her husband's absence in the army, an Indian attack seemed so imminent that for several nights she carried her young children to a nearby field of rye, deeming them safer there[10].

Margaret Behme, Flushing, MI, sent me transcripts of four deeds from Berkshire co, MA, which appear to refer to this Joseph Bunnell. If so, they throw more doubt on some of the Revolutionary War service outlined above.

On 29 December 1778 Roger Kirby of New Ashford, Berkshire co, MA, sold to Joseph Bunnell 8 acres in Lot 47, 2nd Division, Lanesborough, Berkshire co, adjoining land already owned by Joseph Bunnell.
On 8 April 1782 Joseph Bunnell sold to Nathan Stuart of Lanesborough 60 acres in Lot 47.
On 8 July 1782 Salmon Holburt, Jr., of Lanesborough sold to Joseph Bunnell (of same place) 11+ acres in Lot 8, 2nd Division, in Lanesborough.
On 10 May 1784 Joseph Bunnell, now of Stockbridge, Berkshire co, MA, sold to Jacob Bacon of Lanesborough the 11+ acres he bought in 1782.[13]

If these deeds do refer to Joseph 1-1-6-5-5 (and I know of no other likely candidate), it shows that he lived in Massachusetts for some years before returning to Connecticut, where he spent the rest of his life, in Cornwall, Litchfield co. He appears in the 1800 census in Cornwall: 00101-00101[12].

He died at East Cornwall[3], Litchfield co, on 12 May 1807[9]. His gravestone, in the cemetery at Cornwall, with a Revolutionary War marker, reads, "In memory of Joseph Bunnell who died May 12, 1807 age 73."[9] His will, dated 20 April 1804, was probated in Cornwall and left everything to his wife, Abiah Bunnell[4]. She died in 7 May 1835[4] (or 7 May 1825[7]), and was buried with her husband[4].

Children:
1. 310009. James, b. 12[7] (or 21[4]) Dec. 1768.
2. 310010. Joel, b. 1770, twin[7, 11].
3. 310013. Joseph, b. 1770, twin[7,11].
4. 310011. Elijah, b. 2 June 1771[4] (or 12 Aug. 1770[7]).
5. 310040. Emmonds[11].

Duncan[4] also includes a son Wesley, but omits Joseph and Emmonds.

REFERENCES:
1. New Haven - Jacobus, p. 360.
2. CT Historical Society - IX, p. 238.
3. DAR, Vol. 85, p. 66.
4. Duncan, p. 36.
5. Rev War - CT, p. 572.
6. Danbury, Probate records, Vol. 2, p. 126.
7. Biles Manuscript.
8. Woodbury, Part B, p. 24.
9. Cornwall Cem.
10. Cutter - NE, Vol. II, p. 652.
11. Ltr. 31 Jan. 1969 from Mrs. Jacques Johnson, Vallejo, CA.
12. CB Database.
13. Ltr 24 Jan. 1990 from Margaret Behme, Flushing, MI.

1-1-6-5-8   D13viii   CB300017

SOLOMON[5] BUNNELL (Gershom[4], Benjamin[3], Benjamin[2], William[1]) was baptized 5 August 1739[1] at Redding, Fairfield co, CT. During the campaign of 1759 in the French and Indian War he served as a private from 16 April to 3 December in Capt. Samuel Hubbel's Fifth Company, Col. David Wooster's Third Regiment of Connecticut troops[2].

On 8 November 1761 Solomon married ANNA BEARDSLEY in New Fairfield, Fairfield co, CT[3]. She was apparently the sister of Mary Beardsley who married Solomon's brother Noah. They are thought to have been the daughters of Obadiah and Mercy (Jackson) Beardsley of New Fairfield[4]. Although Adele Andrews' identification is expressed only tentatively, the six "suggestive facts" she cites strike me as conclusive[4]. Anna was born 5 November 1741[4]. Solomon's residence at the time of his marriage was listed as "Philipi" in the records of the South Church, New Fairfield[3].

No other information has come to my attention which can definitely be attributed to this Solomon Bunnell.

However, he _may_ have been the same person as the Solomon Bunnell who served as a Loyalist in General Burgoyne's army in 1777. (Note that Solomon's brother Isaac was a Loyalist soldier who fled to New Brunswick after the Revolution.) This Solomon was taken prisoner by the patriot forces at the battle of Bennington on 16 August 1777[5]. He was accused of shooting two of his neighbors, Lt. Abel Prindle and Lt. Isaac Nash, and was sent to jail in Northampton, VT(sic)(probably Northampton, MA-wra)[3]. Solomon escaped to New York and later went to Digby, Nova Scotia[3]. There he had lot #24 on the north side of the Sissibou River. In 1784 he built a sawmill on his lot, but in 1794 he sold his property in Digby and left with his family for an unknown destination[3].

I do not find the name of the wife of the Loyalist Solomon nor a complete list of his children. Harold Bonnell, in a visit to the library in Digby, NS, in 1986 found the following: "There were three Loyalist Bonnells who came in to Annapolis and were shown on the original Botsford Grant of Digby (then Conway) Isaac, David and Solomon. . . .Solomon Bonnell had Lot 24 on north side of Sissiboo River and was in the Sawmill business. On the Original "Muster" at Weymouth, it shows a Family of 7. Solomon was of Lanesborough, Conn.(sic). Had at least one son, Solomon (see Jane Fitzrandolph Story) Had at least one dau. Anne Bonnell, m. Jonathan Bedford, rem. to Hope Township, Durham Co. Ont."[8]

Margaret Behme's letter of 28 September 1987 refers to land records for "Anne (Bunnell) Bedford in Hope Twp., New Castle District, Ont. (now Durham Co.) . . . Jonathan Bedford petitioned in Hope Twp. for 1200 acres of land on 17 Aug. 1796 - stated had come from Nova Scotia - married a dau. of a Loyalist. . . . Proof of her ancestry was provided in affidavit by Sam Adams, Captain of the Kings Regiment, who certified she was a dau. of Solomon Bunnel, a Loyalist. . . . Jonathan was a res. of N.Y. at outbreak of war and joined Royal Standard at White Plains, N.Y. in 1776. . . . Stephen Bedford, eldest of Jonathan & Anne's fam. was born N.Y. 25 May 1769 so Anne was born latest 1754, more likely ca 1735 to 1752."[6]

Paul Bunnell lists Polly, Sally and Solomon, Jr. as Solomon's children, adding that Solomon was possibly born in Lanesboro, MA[5]. He seems to have owned land in Lanesboro, which was confiscated after he joined the British cause[3].

If Anne (Bunnell) Bedford was the daughter of this Loyalist Solomon, then he could not have been the same person as 1-1-6-5-8, the subject of this sketch. He could not have had a grandchild (Stephen Bedford) born in 1769 before he was 30 years old. If there was another Loyalist Solomon who was the father of Anne Bedford, then it would still be possible for Solomon Bunnell, born in Redding, CT, in 1739, to have moved to Lanesboro, Berkshire co, MA, before the Revolution and thence to Nova Scotia afterwards.

Another set of records which should also be considered concern a Solomon Bunnell who appears in Chittenden co, VT. The 1790 census of Chittenden co lists a Solomon Burnel with 2 males over 16 and 4 females (2-0-4-0-0)[3]. Vol. 3 of the land records of South Hero, Chittenden co, shows that on 26 June 1792 Timothy Pearl of South Hero, for £36, sold to Solomon Bunnel of the same place 64 acres in the First Division, Lot 82 (the original rights formerly owned by William Ward)[7].

The 1800 census of South Hero, Franklin co, VT, lists Solomon Bunnel: 10111-01101[3]. That is, 1 male under 10, 1 male between 16 and 26, 1 male between 26 and 45, 1 male over 45; 1 female between 10 and 16, 1 female between 16 and 26, and 1 female over 45.

Vol. 5 of the South Hero land records indicate that on 29 November 1802 Solomon Bunnel of South Hero, for $700, sold to Albert Bunnel of the same place the whole of the First Division (original rights of William Ward)[7]. Vol. 4 records that on the same day Albert Bunnel of South Hero, for $700, sold and transferred rights to the same lands in the First Division (original rights of William Ward) plus 34 acres off the east end of First Division (original rights of Parmalee Allen) to Solomon Bunnel during the lifetime of Solomon Bunnel and wife[7]. It would appear that a will bequeathing the property to Albert (a son?) would have accomplished the same purpose, but a will would have been revocable by Solomon, while this arrangement would not.

Note that South Hero was in Chittenden co in 1790, in Franklin co in 1800 and in Grand Isle co after 1802.

Margaret Behme suggested that it is possible the Albert above was the Albertus Bunnell, son of Solomon Bunnell, who was baptized as an adult on 15 August 1786 at the Trinity Anglican Church in Sissiboo Falls, Nova Scotia[7].

Much further research is necessary to determine whether all or any of these records refer to Solomon Bunnell 1-1-6-5-8.

FIFTH GENERATION

REFERENCES:

1. Fairfield - Jacobus, Vol. II, p. 180.
2. CT Historical Society - X.
3. CB Database.
4. Andrews.
5. *Bunnell/Bonnell Newsletter*, Vol. II, No. 1, p. 5, The Loyalist Bunnells and Bonnells, by Paul J. Bunnell, F.A.C.G., U.E.
6. Ltr. 28 Sept. 1987 from Margaret Behme, Flushing, MI.
7. Ltr. 24 Jan. 1990 from Margaret Behme, Flushing, MI.
8. Ltr. 25 Nov. 1986 from Harold Bonnell, Woodstock, New Brunswick, to Margaret Behme.

1-1-6-5-9   D36   CB300018

NOAH[5] BUNNELL (Gershom[4], Benjamin[3], Benjamin[2], William[1]) was born 18 January 1741[4] and baptized 31 January 1741[4] (or 1742[3]) at Redding, Fairfield co, CT. [The most thorough research into the history of Noah Bunnell was made by his great great great granddaughter Adele Andrews[1].] On 9 January (or 9 June[4]) 1763[5] he married MARY BEARDSLEY[5], daughter of Obadiah and Mercy (Jackson) Beardsley[1,6] of New Fairfield, Fairfield co, CT. She was born 30 March 1743[1]. In 1765 Noah Bunnel signed a petition of the Society of Southbury in Woodbury, and in 1774 a petition to the assembly of the township of Derby[1].

During the Revolutionary War he served as a private[2] (or sergeant[1]) in Capt. John Hinman's company, 13th Regiment of Connecticut Militia in 1776[1,2]. His name appears on a pay abstract of that company dated Litchfield co, Woodbury, 18 June 1777[1]. He was discharged 14 August 1777[2]. The company served at New York that year[2] and he may have been with it. At various times he lived at Derby, New Haven co, CT, Fairfield, Fairfield co, CT, and New Milford, Litchfield co, CT. His name first appears in the land records of New Milford in 1785[1].

He died 11 December 1790 from heart disease while helping his son Noah in Hyde Park, Clinton twp, Dutchess co, NY[9]. His body was not returned to his home in New Milford, CT, but was buried in the Reformed Dutch Churchyard in Hyde Park[1]. From the inventory of his estate in the New Milford probate records it would appear that Noah Bunnell was a cooper by trade[1]. His son Salmon acted as administrator of his estate[1]. Noah's widow Mary died 2 May 1793[1]. She was buried in the Gallows Hill Burying Ground, New Milford, CT, where her gravestone reads: 'In Memory of Mrs. Mary, wife to Mr. Noah Bunnel who died May 2nd 1793 in the 50th year of her age."[1] Her brother Gideon Beardsley was appointed guardian of her daughter Polly Esther[7]: "Capt. Gideon Beardsley of New Fairfield is appointed Guardian to Polly Bunnil minor of about nine years old, Daughter of Noah Bunnil, late of New Milford deceased, and gave bond according to the Law which is lodged on file. Test Joseph T. Cooke, Junr., Clerk."[7]

Children:
1. 310041. Lucy, b. 5 Mar. 1766[4]; m. 19 June 1786 Ebenezer Keeler[10]; d. after 1838[10].
    Children (surname Keeler)[10]:
    1. Clora H.   4. Billy C.   7. Sally.
    2. Salmon Bunnel.   5. Lucy H.   8. Nehemiah.
    3. Noah B.   6. Levi.
2. 310042. Noah, b. 9 Oct. 1767[4].
3. 310043. Salmon Beardsley, b. 9 May 1769[4].
4. 310044. Havilah, b. 18 Apr. 1772[4].
5. 310045. Sebah, b. 25 Feb. 1774[4,5]; bapt. 29 May 1774[1].
6. 310046. Zethan, b. 19 Apr. 1776[4].
7. 310047. Sarah, b. 12 Jan. 1779[4].
8. 310048. Rebecca, b. 12 Feb. 1781[4].
9. 310049. Polly Esther, b. 22 Nov. 1784[4]; m. _____ _____; 5 children[5];
    d. Meredith, NY[5].
10. 310050. Elizabeth, b. 17 Apr. 1787[4]; m. _____ _____; 3 children[5]; d. Ohio[5].

REFERENCES:
1. Andrews.
2. Rev War - CT, p. 466.
3. Fairfield - Jacobus, Vol. II, p. 180.
4. Biles Manuscript.
5. Bunnell Sketch.
6. Beardsley.
7. Danbury..
8. Duncan, p. 36.
9. CB Database.
10. From the National Archives, the pension applications of Ebenezer Keeler and his widow Lucy (Bunnell) Keeler, photocopies sent to me by Alice D. Gedge, Riverton, UT.

1-1-6-5-10   D37   CB300019

NATHANIEL[5] BUNNELL (Gershom[4], Benjamin[3], Benjamin[2], William[1]) was born 11 October 1743[6] and baptized 17 October 1743[2] at Redding, Fairfield co, CT. He removed to Newtown, Fairfield co, CT, where he married SARAH PARSONS[1] of North Stratford[3], Fairfield co, on 18 September 1768[1]. She was born in 1744[5]. They lived in Newtown.

He was apparently dead by October 1777, when Sarah Bunnell "of Newtown" bought 14 acres of land in Danbury, Fairfield co, CT from Ebenezer Ferry for £40[4]. Several years later this land was surveyed and recorded in Danbury land records, Book 2, p. 253: "Surveyed to the widow Sarah Bunnill the acres of Land lying in Danbury at Ferry's field, so called, beginning at the NE corner at a large Rock with Stones on it, runing a Southwesterly course to a Rock, with stones on it, then Easterly to a heap of stones, then Southerly to a heap of stones near a Ledge of Rocks, then Easterly to a red ash _____mark and stone by it, then Easterly to a heap of stones, then Northerly to a heap of stones then Northerly to the place begun at, bounded Easterly by highway or common Land, Northerly by Eben Hickoks Land & by Eben. Ferry Land, Westerly by Collins Chapman's Land, Southerly by Jonas Weed, Jr. Land and Eben. Ferry's Land. Danbury, April 29th 1783, recorded 305th Aug. 1786."[4]

Children (born in Newtown[1]):
1. 310053. Nathaniel, b. 7 Dec. 1769[1].
2. 310054. Hannah, b. 9 Feb. 1773[1] (not the Hannah who m. Jesse Wilmot)[1].
3. 310055. Patience, b. 12 July 1775[1]; m. (first) David Lynes[1]; m. (second) Elijah Seeley[1].

REFERENCES:
1. New Haven - Jacobus, p. 360.
2. Fairfield - Jacobus, Vol. II, p. 180.
3. Duncan, p. 37.
4. Danbury.
5. CB Database.
6. Biles Manuscript.

1-1-6-5-11   D38   CB300020

ISAAC[5] BUNNELL (Gershom[4], Benjamin[3], Benjamin[2], William[1]) was born 13 July[3] and baptized 21 July 1745[2] at Redding, CT. Although he was not yet 16 years old, he may have been the Isaac Bunnel who enlisted on 10 April 1761 in the 2nd Company, 2nd Connecticut Regiment under Lt. Col. Smedley, to serve in the French and Indian War[4]. He was discharged 6 December 1761[4]. He removed to Newtown, CT[1]. In 1771, in Newtown, Fairfield co, CT, he married JERUSHA SHERWOOD[2], daughter of John and Hannah (Parruck)[8] Sherwood[2]. She was born 1 March 1751[4] in Newtown, CT.

He was a Tory during the American Revolution and fled Connecticut to New York on 15 November 1776[7]. He joined the Prince of Wales American Regiment, in which he served as a captain, and was credited with capturing Capt. Sillivan and with enlisting men for the Regiment[7]. In 1777 his regiment was stationed at Kingsbridge, NY, and in June 1778 it was moved to Conanicut, RI. It went to South Carolina in 1780 for two years, ending at James Island.

In 1783 he moved to New Brunswick, arriving at St. John on the "Hope."[4] Muster on the "Hope" shows 4 children over 10 years, but muster at St. John shows only 3 over 10[4]. Perhaps Daniel, the eldest son, was declared a single immigrant in order to draw a full share of the King's Bounty. "Esaac Bunill" was granted Lot No. 6 (200 acres) on Kennebecassis Bay at Clifton, Hawser's Survey, NB, on 14 July 1784[4], but in only a few years he moved up the Bellisle to better ground at Collina where he had lot No. 5 of 306 acres[4]. On 25 February 1786 he applied for reimbursement of expenses he incurred while in the British service, but the expenses did not fall within the meaning of the Act[7].

He died intestate in 1791[4] at Collina[4], Studholm Parish, Kings co, NB. Administration of his estate was granted to Jerusha Bonnell, widow, of Sussex, on 5 September 1791 at Westfield, NB[5]. The inventory of his estate on 24 September 1791 amounted to £46[5]. After his death his widow married (second) widower James Dugan, who had lot No. 4 next door[4]. Jerusha and her son "David"(Daniel) sold the original grant at Clifton in 1799 to William Frost (Book G-1, p. 91[4]. (For some legal reason, this deed was re-registered at Hampton on 27 July 1814 as No. 3010 in Book V-1, page 418. It has the signatures of all of Daniel's brothers and sisters and recites in part: "and whereas our said brother Daniel at the time he conveyed the said Lot to William Frost, had the care and charge of our Father's family upon him and did what was in his power towards the support and maintenance of the same, and did convert the purchase money for the said lot to our use and benefit")[4]

Jerusha died in 1817 at the home of her son Justus Bonnell who lived between Snyder Mountain and Marrtown, NB, on the Bonnell Road[4].

Children (first 6 born in Newtown, CT):
1. 310201. Daniel, b. 1772[4].
2. 310202. Jemima, b. 1773[4]; m. 16 June 1793[4] (13 Jan. 1790[9]) Benjamin Keirstead[4].
   Children (surname Keirstead)[4]:

1. Isaac.	5. Bethia.	9. Daniel.
2. John Bonnell.	6. Lydia.	10. Leonard.
3. David.	7. Gershom.	11. Sarah.
4. Thomas.	8. Justus.	12. Deborah.

   (One source lists also Samuel, but not Daniel or Leonard.)
3. 310203. Mary, b. 1775[4]; m. Ezekiel Foster[4]; d. 1852[4].
   Children (surname Foster)[4]:

1. Lydia.	3. Sarah.	5. Clarisse.
2. Hannah.	4. Elizabeth.	

4. 310207. Jerusha, b. 1777[4]; m. John McLeod[4]; d. soon.
5. 310205. John, b. 1779[4].
6. 310204. Isaac, b. about 1780[4].
7. 310206. Justus, b. about 1790[4] (or about 1786[9]) in Collina, NB.

NOTE: Isaac came from the Bunnell side of the family, and the land grants made to him in New Brunswick were to Isaac Bunnell. However, many of his descendants seem to have spelled the name Bonnell, the only descendants of William's son Benjamin that have made this change, so far as I have learned.

REFERENCES:
1. New Haven - Jacobus, p. 360.
2. Fairfield - Jacobus, Vol. II, p. 180.
3. CT Historical Society - X, p. 261.
4. Ltr. 17 Feb. 1992 from Harold Bonnell, Woodstock, NB, containing extensive research on Isaac Bunnell.
5. Early New Brunswick Probate Records 1785-1835, by R. Wallace Hale, p. 40., sent to me by Carole Bonnell.

6. Gravestones in Kierstead Mountain United Baptist Cemetery, Kings co, NB,
    copied and sent to me by Carole Bonnell.
7. American Loyalist Claims, p. 65, sent to me by Carole Bonnell.
8. Family Group Sheet, Isaac Bonnell, prepared by Harold Bonnell, Woodstock, NB.
9. Duncan, p. 37.

1-1-6-5-12   D13xi   CB300021

JOHN[5] BUNNELL (Gershom[4], Benjamin[3], Benjamin[2], William[1]) was born in Connecticut (probably Redding, Litchfield co) on 11 November 1746[2]. "Att a Court of probate held in Danbury for the district of Danbury October 8th 1759 widow margarit Bunnil is appointed gardain to John Bunnil son to Gershom Bunnil late of Danbury Decd: he being in his non age for the choice of a Gardain and the said margerit Bunnil & Joseph Bunnil of Woodbury acknowledge themselves jointly and severally bound to the treasurer of the said county of Fairfield in a recognizance of £20 lawful money that the said margerit shall faithfully discharge his gardainship for the said John and render an account thereof as the law directs."[3]   On 10 March 1762 John, son of Gershom Bunnil, being of age for the choice of a guardian, made choice of Joseph Bunnil of Woodbury[3]. John removed to Woodbury, Litchfield co, CT[1]. Is he the John Bunnel CB010974 in the 1790 census of Milford, New Haven co, CT: 1-5-1-0-0[4]?

REFERENCES:
1. New Haven - Jacobus, p. 360.
2. Biles Manuscript.
3. Danbury, probate records, Vol. 2, pp. 87, 126.
4. CB Database.

1-1-6-5-13   D39   CB300022

JOB[5] BUNNELL (Gershom[4], Benjamin[3], Benjamin[2], William[1]) was born 15 January 1750[2] at Redding, Fairfield co, CT. "Att a Court of Probate held in Danbury for the District of Danbury December the first AD 1758 widw margerit Bunnill widow and Relict to Gershom Bunnill Late of Danbury aforsd Decd is appointed gardian to Job Bunnill son to sd Gershom Dec. he being in his non age for a choice of a gardian, and the sd margaret Bunnell and Garshom Bunnill of sd Danbury acknowledged themselves Joyntly & Severally bound to the Treasurers of the County of Fairfield in the Recognizance of one hundered Pounds Lawful money that the sd margarit shall faithfully Discharge her Gardainship for the sd Job according to Law."[3]   Job married 10 September 1772[1], at Newtown, Fairfield co, CT, RACHEL BRADLEY[1], daughter of Griffin and Mabel (Thompson) Bradley. She was born 25 December 1751. In 1790 they were living at Brookfield, CT, where he appears in the census there: 1-3-4-0-0[1]. In 1791 he was an appraiser for his brother Noah's estate in New Milford, CT[10]. They later removed to the town of Windsor (now Colesville), Broome co, NY, where he died[4]. Job Bunnell appears in the 1820 census in the town of Windsor, Broome co, NY: 000001-00001[10] The first school in Colesville was taught by Job Bunnell[5] (in 1803?[2]). John A. Biles found the graves and copied the gravestones of Job's three youngest children in the cemetery in Colesville[2]. However, there are at least 10 cemeteries in the town of Colesville. Biles did not identify the location. The Index of Deeds in Broome co courthouse, NY, lists Job Bunnell as a grantee on 3 September 1827[7].

Children:
1. 310058. Hannah, b. 14 July 1773[1]; d. 5 Aug. 1775.
2. 310059. Hannah, b. 10 June 1776[1]; m. (first) 14 Oct. 1795[8] Jesse Wilmot[6] of Colesville; m. (second) Stephen Franklin[8]; d. 18 Sept. 1854[8].
       Children (surname Wilmot)[6]:
       1. Stephen Bunnell.　　3. Amos.　　　5. Lyman.
       2. Lowly.　　　　　　 4. Asahel.　　　6. Jesse.
3. 310060. Stephen, b. 22 Nov. 1778[1].
4. 310017. Rebecca, b. 5 May 1781[1]; m. 16 Jan. 1803 Amasa S. Bird[8]; d. 31 Dec. 1851[8].
       Children (surname Bird)[9]:
       1. John L.
5. 310061. Bradley, b. 26 Jan. 1784[1].
6. 310018. Loderna (Ludema?), b. 27 May 1786[8].
7. 310037. Billy, b. 17 June 1789[2].
8. 310062. Aurelia, b. Oct. 1791[2] (28 Oct. 1780[8]); d. 26 Feb. 1812, age 20 yrs. 4 mos.[2]
9. 310038. Rachel, b. June 1794[2] (20 Sept. 1794[8]); d. 6 Feb. 1809, age 14 yrs. 8 mo.[2]

NOTE: Biles found a conveyance of land to a Job Bunnell at Hammondsport, Steuben co, NY, in 1827.

REFERENCES:
1. New Haven - Jacobus, p. 360.
2. Biles Manuscript, pp. 191, 238.
3. Danbury, probate records, Vol. 2, p. 74.
4. Bunnell Sketch, p. 3.
5. NY Gazetteer, p. 182 note.
6. History of Deerfield, IL, by Marie Ward Reichelt, Glenview Press, 1929, p. 113, quoting The Portrait and Biographical Album of Lake County, IL, 1891.
7. Broome co, NY, Index of Deeds: Book 10, p. 327.
8. Chart No. X-212, Descendants of Benjamin & Rebecca (Mallory) Bunnell, prepared by Claude B. Mitchell, Jr., Muskegon, MI, citing James R. Bird, Medford, NJ.
9. Ltr. 18 Oct. 1961 from James R. Bird, Medford, NJ.
10. CB Database.

1-1-7-1-2 D40 CB300049

DANIEL[5] BUNNELL (Hezekiah[4], Hezekiah[3], Benjamin[2], William[1]) was born 3 November 1729[1] at New Haven, New Haven co, CT, and was baptized in September 1733[1,2] in the Congregational Church at Cheshire, New Haven co, CT. On 13 November 1755[5], in Harwinton, Litchfield co, CT, he married ESTHER YALE[1], daughter of Asa and Esther (Manross) Yale[1] of Farmington, Hartford co, CT. She was born 11 March 1737[1] in Wallingford, New Haven co, CT. They lived at Harwinton, Litchfield co, CT[1]. Daniel was one of the heirs of his mother's estate in 1769[6].

Sometime around the year 1770 they seem to have moved from Harwinton to Bristol, Hartford co, CT, where the last two children were born[4]. Daniel appears in the 1790 census in Bristol, Hartford co, CT: 2-1-4-0-0[1]. He died in 1792 in Bristol[5]. His estate in Bristol was probated in Farmington District in 1792[6].

Children (first 5 born in Harwinton, CT):
1. 310104. Esther, b. 29 Apr. 1756[1].
2. 310105. Hezekiah, b. 21 Mar. 1758[1].
3. 310106. Sarah, b. 2 Oct. 1760[1]; m. Diamond Clark[1]; d. 23 Nov. 1830[1].
   Children (surname Clark)[5]:
   1. Wooster.
4. 310107. Daniel, b. 11 Apr. 1763[1].
5. 310108. Lemuel L., b. about 1767[5].
6. 310051. Phebe[4], b. 1774[3] (or 1777[3]); m. Nehemiah Maine[3]; d. 1846/7[3]..
   Children (surname Maine)[3]:

1. Nehemiah.	4. Seth.	7. Henry.
2. Belinda.	5. Daniel.	8. Solomon.
3. Esther.	6. John.	

7. 310039. Miles, b. about 1775[4].

REFERENCES:
1. New Haven - Jacobus, pp. 360, 361, 366.
2. Cheshire, Parson Hall's Record of Baptisms.
3. Ltrs. 9 Dec. 1989 & 22 Jan. 1990 from John S. Butler, Stillwater, OK.
4. Bunnell/Bonnell Newsletter, Vol. IV, No. 1, p. 14, No. 2, pp. 18, 19, No. 3, pp. 39, 40.
5. Duncan, p. 38.
6. CB Database.

1-1-7-1-3   D41   CB300050

JESSE[5] BUNNELL (Hezekiah[4], Hezekiah[3], Benjamin[2], William[1]) was born 26 January 1731/2[1] at New Haven, New Haven co, CT, and was baptized in September 1733[1] in the Congregational Church in Cheshire, New Haven co, CT. On 19 April 1757[1,6], at Farmington, Hartford co, CT, he married MEHITABEL ROYCE[1,6], daughter of Abel and Joanna (Beach) Royce[1]. She was born 1 April 1737[1] in Wallingford, New Haven co, CT. The births of the first 6 children were recorded in the Farmington Vital Records, and the last 3 were baptized in St. Matthew Episcopal Church in East Plymouth, Litchfield co, CT[2]. In 1769 Jesse was an heir and administrator of his mother's estate[9]. Jesse died in 1782[1] (or 1786[9]). Jesse's will, dated 7 June 1782[2], was probated in 1786 in Farmington[9]. He left his estate to his wife Mehitable and children, Abel, Jesse, Bela, Seth, Levi and Ruth Gaylord, wife of Chauncey Gaylord[2]. On 11 August 1786 his widow was appointed guardian of her daughter Mehitabel and son Levi, minors[9]. On 1 July 1798 she was admitted to the First Congregational Church in Plymouth, Litchfield, CT[9]. Mehitabel married (second) Henry Brooks[1]. She died 23 February 1813[1] at Claremont, NH. Her gravestone in the Old Village Cemetery calls her Mehitable Bunnell, "wife of Jesse then relict of Henry Brooks," d. 23 Feb. 1813, 77 yr.[8].

Children:
1. 310111. Abel, b. 29 Apr. 1758[1,6]; bapt. 9 July 1785[1].
2. 310112. Ruth, b. 19 Mar. 1760[1,6]; bapt. 1 June 1760[1]; m. Chauncey Gaylord[2]; d. 1835[2].
   Children (surname Gaylord)[2]:
   1. Hannah.   4. Chauncey.   7. Asaph.
   2. Jesse.   5. Orrin.   8. Levi.
   3. Eber.   6. Royce.   9. Chloe.
3. 310113. Jesse, b. 19 June 1763[1,6]; bapt. 7 Aug. 1763[1].
4. 310114. Bela, b. 27 Aug. 1765[1,6]; bapt. 20 Oct. 1765[1].
5. 310115. Levi, b. 14 Sept. 1768[1,6]; d. soon[1].
6. 310116. Seth, bapt. 9 Dec. 1770[1].
7. 310117. Mehitabel, bapt. 17 Oct. 1773[1]; m. Bela Rice[4,5]; d. about 1847[4].
   Children (surname Rice)[4,5]:
   1. Bela Fitch.
8. 310119. Jessie[7], b. 1775[7]. Only one reference to this person. Very doubtful.
9. 310118. Levi, bapt. 21 Dec. 1777[1].

REFERENCES:
1. New Haven - Jacobus, pp. 361, 366.
2. Duncan, pp. 38, 39.
3. Cheshire, Parson Hall's Record of Baptisms.
4. Ltr. 2 Dec. 1914 from Mrs. Kate M. Rice to John A. Biles.
5. Ltr. Nov. 1917 from Mrs. Kate M. Rice to John A. Biles.
6. Barbour.
7. Family Group Sheet, Jesse Bunnell, prepared & sent to me by Doris M. Denton, Pleasant Hill, CA.
8. *Grave Stone Records from the Ancient Cemeteries in the Town of Claremont, New Hampshire*, by Charles B. Spofford, 1896.
9. CB Database.

1-1-7-1-4 D42 CB300051

NATHANIEL[5] BUNNELL (Hezekiah[4], Hezekiah[3], Benjamin[2], William[1]) was born 23 January 1733[9] at Wallingford, New Haven co, CT. On 8 September 1755[1,5], at Farmington, Hartford co, CT, he married THANKFUL SPENCER[1,5]. She was born in 1735[8]. They lived in Burlington, then part of the town of Farmington, Hartford co, CT. He died 15 December 1759[1] at

Burlington. He was found frozen to death while hunting deer within a mile of his home[2,3,6]. He was buried in the Bridge Street Cemetery in Bristol[2,8]. His widow married (second) Moses Wilcox[2,4] of Harwinton, CT, on 30 March 1762[4]. In 1769 Nathaniel's brother Titus was appointed guardian of the two youngest children, Nathaniel and Thankful[9]. Thankful (Spencer) (Bunnell) Wilcox died 25 January 1817[2,3,8] and was buried in the Wilcox Cemetery[8] in Harwinton, Litchfield co, CT.

Children (born in Farmington, CT):
    1. 310120. Susanna, b. 4 Aug. 1756[1,5]; m. Joseph Gaylord[1].
           Children (surname Gaylord)[7]:

1. Nathaniel.	4. Joel.	7. Ruth.
2. Linus	5. Lydia.	
3. Allen.	6. Lydia.	

    2. 310121. Nathaniel, b. 9 May 1758[1,5].
    3. 310122. Thankful, b. 1760[1] (posthumously).

REFERENCES:
    1. New Haven - Jacobus, p. 366.
    2. Ltrs. 18 Nov. 1909 and 24 Nov. 1909 from Mae Bunnell Cook, Terryville, CT, to John A. Biles.
    3. Ltr. 11 Nov. 1907 from Charles Rollin Bunnell, Bristol, CT, to John A. Biles.
    4. Ltr. 5 May 1975 from Raymond J. Bentley, Harwinton, CT, to Jean Brewer,
          Tunkhannock, PA: Vital Statistics, Town of Harwinton, CT.
    5. Barbour.
    6. Genealogical Data from New York Post, 1693-1773, p. 78, copied and sent to me by
          Nona Bassett, Merced, CA.
    7. Ltr. 3 March 1992 from James P. Brewton, Magalia, CA.
    8. Duncan, p. 39.
    9. CB Database.

1-1-7-1-5   D43   CB300052

TITUS[5] BUNNELL (Hezekiah[4], Hezekiah[3], Benjamin[2], William[1]) was born 9 November 1735[1] at Wallingford, New Haven co, CT, and was baptized in November 1735[1,3] in the Cheshire Congregational Church there. During the French and Indian War Titus served for 16 days under Capt. William Pitkin, Jr., of Hartford, in Col. Joseph Pitkin's Regiment at the time of the alarm for the relief of Fort William Henry and parts adjacent in August 1757[6]. He served in Capt. Josiah Lee's 10th Company, Gen. Phineas Lyman's 1st Regiment from 26 May to 14 November 1758[6].

About 1764[8] he married SYBIL YALE[1], daughter of Asa and Esther (Manross) Yale[1]. She was born 31 March 1743[1] at Wallingford. They lived in the town of Farmington, Hartford co, CT, in the northwest part of the town. In 1769 Titus was appointed guardian of his niece and nephew Thankful and Nathaniel Bunnell[8]. In May 1770 Titus Bunnell and others submitted a church petition asking to be annexed to Harwinton in Litchfield co, since they lived ten miles from the meeting house in Farmington, but only four miles from Harwinton[4]. This was apparently unsuccessful, since he was named in the petition of 1774 which sought to have that part of Farmington incorporated as an Ecclesiastical Society, the parish of West Britain, an effort which succeeded[7].

During the Revolution he was an ensign in Capt. Gad Stanley's First Company, Col. Fisher Gay's Second Battalion, Wadsworth's Brigade[2] which was raised in June 1776 to reinforce Washington at New York[4]. The company served at the Brooklyn front, just before and during the battle of Long Island on 27 August and retreated to New York on the 29th and 30th[4]. By 15 September they were in retreat from New York and were with the main army at the battle of White Plains on 28 October[4]. Titus's enlistment expired on 25 December 1776[4]. Lt. Titus Bunnell served in the 12th Company in Farmington in Col. Heart's 15th Regiment, chosen by order of Col. Heart[2]. In various records he is called "Capt."[1] and "of Farmington, Conn."[2]

In 1785 the western part of the town of Farmington, including the parish of West Britain, was set off as the town of Bristol[7], and Titus Bunnell appears in the 1790 census in Bristol, Hartford co, CT: 2-1-2-0-0[1]. The parish of West Britain, where Titus lived, was eventually (1806) set off as the town of Burlington[7]. However, by 1795 Titus had moved his family to Litchfield co, where he was one of the incorporators of the town of Plymouth in 1795[5]. He appears in Plymouth in the 1800 census: 00011-00201[8] and the 1810 census: 00001-00011[8]. He died 29 November 1820[1] and his wife died 30 January 1822[1], both at Plymouth, Litchfield co, CT. They were buried in the Old Cemetery in Plymouth[9].

Children:
1. 310130. Ambrose,[1] b. 22 Mar. 1765[4].
2. 310128. Solomon,[1] b. 29 Dec. 1766[4].
3. 310125. Oliver, b. 29 Dec. 1768[1,10] (sic).
4. 310126. Titus Jefferson, b. 19 July 1769[1,10] (sic).
5. 310127. Sybil, b. 20[1] (or 26[8,10]) June 1771[1,8,10].
6. 310129. Allen,[1] b. 11 Dec. 1772[4] (or 11 Dec. 1773[8]).
7. 310131. Asa, b. 24 May 1776[4,10,11].
8. 310132. Rhoda, b. 2 Aug. 1778[4,10].

REFERENCES:
1. New Haven - Jacobus, pp. 361, 366.
2. Rev War - CT, pp. 395, 629.
3. Cheshire, Parson Hall's Record of Baptisms.
4. Biles Manuscript, p. 258.
5. Ltr. 24 Nov. 1909 from Mae Bunnell Cook, Terryville, CT, to John A. Biles.
6. CT Historical Society - IX, p. 230, - X, p. 25.
7. Ltr. 5 May 1775 from Mrs. Stanley J. Humphrey, Burlington, CT, to Jean Brewer, Tunkhannock, PA.
8. CB Database.
9. Duncan, pp. 39, 40.
10. Barbour.
11. Photocopy of original record of births in Farmington, CT, showing birth of Asa Bunnel, sent to me by Bess R. Hubbard, Fuquay-Varina, NC.

FIFTH GENERATION

1-1-7-2-2 D44 CB300056

JACOB[5] BUNNELL (Deliverance[4], Hezekiah[3], Benjamin[2], William[1]) was born 6 April 1734[1] at Branford, New Haven co, CT. On 17 May 1756[1], in Branford, he married MARY KIMBERLY[1], daughter of Abraham and Mary (Sherman) Kimberly[1]. She was born 14 August 1735[1] in Guilford, New Haven co, CT. In May 1776 he was Lieutenant of the 14th Company, 2nd Connecticut Regiment[3].He was probably the Jacob Bunnell who was 2nd Lieutenant in Capt. Samuel Ellis' company of 57 volunteers raised in the town of Branford, 13 January 1777[2]. He appears in the 1790 census: 4-0-2-0-0[1], in the 1800 census: 00001-00101[5] and in the 1810 census: 00001-00001[5] in Branford. His wife died 6 December 1810[1], and he died 19 January 1828[4], both at North Branford, New Haven co, CT. (The Northford Congregational Church records state he died 18 December 1827 age 90.[4])

Children:
1. 310133. Joseph, b. 23 July 1757[1].
2. 310134. Mary, b. 26 Apr. 1759[1]; m. Elihu Grannis[1]; d. 10 Feb. 1834[1].
   Children (surname Grannis)[1]:
   1. Polly..   4. Polly.   6. Amy.
   2. Olive.   5. Sarah.   7. Wealthy.
   3. Eunice.
3. 310135. Jacob, b. 12 Dec. 1761[1].
4. 310136. Hannah (Sally), b. 25 Feb. 1764[1]; m. Apr. 1790 Jacob Foote[4]; d. 1843[5].
5. 310137. Sherman, b. 3 Apr. 1766[1].
6. 310138. Samuel[1], b. about 1768[4].
7. 310139. Stephen, b. about 1776[1].

REFERENCES:
1. New Haven - Jacobus, pp. 361, 366, 367.
2. Rev War - CT, p. 613.
3. Biles Manuscript, p. 240.
4. Duncan, p. 40.
5. CB Database.

1-1-7-2-3 D15iii CB300057

JOSEPH[5] BUNNELL (Deliverance[4], Hezekiah[3], Benjamin[2], William[1]) was born 24 August 1736[1] in Branford, New Haven co, CT. He appears in the 1790 census: 2-1-6-0-0[2] and in the 1800 census: 00001-00301[2].

NOTE: From the census records it would appear that Joseph had a wife and children. This may provide placement for some of our unattached branches.

REFERENCES:
1. New Haven - Jacobus, p. 361.
2. CB Database: 1790 and 1800 census.

1-1-9-2-1   D16i   CB300063

NATHANIEL[5] BUNNELL (Ebenezer[4], Nathaniel[3], Benjamin[2], William[1]) was born 4 June 1739[1] at Wallingford, New Haven co, CT. On 17 January 1759[1,3], at Wallingford, he married LOIS ROYCE[1,3], daughter of Evan and Rachel (Parker) Royce[1]. She was born 4 November 1740[1] at Wallingford. They lived in the section of Wallingford later set off as the town of Cheshire. In 1762 Nathaniel was taxed on £43 for the minister's rate in the Society of New Cheshire in Wallingford[3].

He served at length as an officer in almost constant service during the Revolution. Biles says he was appointed lieutenant of the 17th company, 10th Connecticut regiment, on 4 October 1774[8]. He was commissioned 1 May 1775 as 2nd Lieutenant in the 9th Company, 1st Connecticut Regiment of General Wooster's Continentals[2]. This regiment was on the first call for troops by the Legislature[8]. It marched to New York in the latter part of June and encamped at Harlem[8]. On 18 September it was sent to the northern department under General Schuyler[8]. They took part in the operations along Lake George and Champlain, assisted in the reduction of St. John in October, and were afterwards stationed at Montreal[8]. He was discharged in December 1775[2]. The next year he was a Captain in the 7th Company of th 5th Battalion under Col. William Douglas of Northford, CT, General James Wadsworth's State Brigade[3]. This battalion was raised in June 1776 to reinforce Washington's army at New York[3]. It served in the city and on the Brooklyn front[3]. It was at the battle of Long Island on 27 August 1776 and retreated to New York on 29 and 30 August 1776[3]. It was with the militia at Kips Bay, 34th Street, East River at the attack on New York 15 September 1776, and took part in the battle of White Plains on 28 October 1776[3]. Subsequently he served as Captain in a regiment of militia commanded by Colonel Roger Enos in June 1777 and then in a regiment commanded by Colonel Jonathan Baldwin of Waterbury, serving at Fishkill, NY, where in October 1777 he received a bounty payment of £14[2]. He was Captain of a company in Col. Thaddeus Cook's 10th Regiment, which turned out to repel the enemy at New Haven on 5 July 1779 in Tryon's invasion of Connecticut[2] .

On 26 June 1780 Nathaniel was chosen a member of a committee for hiring the soldiers to fill up the Continental Army for 3 years or during the war[3]. He died 29 December 1787[1,5] without issue. (Note that several published records state his death date erroneously as 20 December 1767.) His gravestone said:

> "In Memory of Capt
> Nathaniel Bunnell
> who died Decb[r] 29th
> AD 1787 in the 49th
> Year of his age

From death scourge nor great
nor small for death at
Last will blast them all
the Hero brave & Infant age
when death does call do quit the
Stage"[6]

His widow appears in the 1790 census in Cheshire: 0-0-1-0-0[1]. She died 15 September 1792[1,5] at Cheshire. Their negro man Phillip was set free after her death[7]. Parson Foot's records, under the heading "Burials" lists "Negro Philip Bunnel (frozen to death) --December 26, 1811."[5]

REFERENCES:
1. New Haven - Jacobus, p. 361.
2. Rev War - CT, pp. 43, 396, 547, 614.
3. Cheshire, pp. 140, 175, 180, 186, 189, 202, 204, 209, 214, 505, 543.
4. Cheshire, Parson Hall's Records.
5. Cheshire, Parson Foot's Records.
6. Lines.
7. CB Database.
8. Biles Manuscript, p. 274.

1-1-9-2-4   D45   CB300040

ISRAEL[5] BUNNELL (Ebenezer[4], Nathaniel[3], Benjamin[2], William[1]) was born 17 March 1746/7[1] and was baptized in February? [1,3] in the Congregational Church in the parish of New Cheshire at Wallingford, New Haven co, CT. He was admitted to membership in the Cheshire Church on 19 August 1770[2]. On 12 December 1770[1], in Wallingford, he married JERUSHA (not Jemima) DOWD[1,2], daughter of Benjamin and Azuba (Hildridge) Dowd[1,2]. She was born about 1749[1] in Middletown, Middlesex co, CT. Jerusha became a member of the Cheshire Church on 22 May 1774[2].

Israel was prominent in the affairs of Cheshire, both before and after its incorporation as a separate town in New Haven co in 1780. He had a 400-acre grant in Cheshire which extended through the town to the hills. In 1774 he was taxed on £58 for the minister's rate[2]. His property included a house and a tavern in Cheshire. Bishop Lines recorded in his notebook that,

"Deacon Israel Bunnell lived at the corner of the Bunnell lane, in a house that stood in front of the present High School. here he lived and kept a tavern for several years. he was an extensive land owner. he owned about 400 acres running from his house on the turnpike, west to the West mountains. the road now known as the Bunnell lane. was opened first by him, for the convenience of reaching his own land and took its name from his ownership. This house was removed down the Bunnell lane to the corner of Bunnell land and Horton Ave.. & is now owned by A.S.Bennett. The roof of the house was slightly altered by Dr. Horton who formerly owned it & sold it to Mr Bennett. otherwise the house is as it was built. The Tan Vats owned by Dea Israel Bunnell & can still be seen, are at the foot of the Mountain in the Meadow, owned by Benj[n] F. Munson."[8]

He took the oath of fidelity in Wallingford in 1777[2]. At the first Town Meeting of the new town of Cheshire on 7 June 1780 Israel Bunnel was chosen one of the surveyors of highways and as sealer of leather[2]. He was also chosen as a member of a committee to inspect provision and to supply provisions to the families of soldiers[2]. John Biles, in his manuscript, says of him,

> "Israel Bunnell was deacon, captain, justice, member of the Legislature, and president of the first State Agricultural Society. He was prominent in business and public affairs. His farm contained nearly three hundred acres of land. He carried on the tanning and shoe making business also, was assistant commisary in the Revolutionary War, butchered and packed meat for the army. He was a thick set man of medium height, and a giant in strength, being able to load a barrel of cider by the chines over the end of an ox cart. No bully or violent man ever desidered a second tussle or scrap with him, hence he was retained in offices to moderate and keep the peace."[6]

Israel served in the 15th Company, 10th Regiment, during the Revolution[7]. He appears in the 1790 census: 2-5-3-0-0, 1800 census: 23101-00202, and 1810 census: 00301-01001 in Cheshire, CT[9]. The land records of Wallingford and Cheshire show that he was active in buying and selling real estate[8]. In 1794 Israel petitioned for, and received approval of, the right to set free his negro maid servant Katie, about 30 years of age[8]. In 1810 he served as administrator of the will of his uncle Abner Bunnell[9].

Israel died of apoplexy [2] 21 May 1813[1,2] at Cheshire, and his wife died 24 July 1829[1,2]. They were buried in the old Hillside Cemetery at Cheshire[7]. The inventory of his estate June 1813 was $16,383[6]. Governor Samuel A. Foote composed[6] the epitaph engraved on his tombstone:

"Sacred   In memory of
to the memory of   Jerusha, wife of
Israel Bunnell, Esq.   Israel Bunnell, Esq.
who died May 21, 1813.   who died July 24, 1829.
ae 66.   ae 80.

The various public offices which he held
As selectman, magistrate, deacon of the church,
And his liberal charity to the poor
Are monuments of his worth.
The sons of want can n'er forget
The liberal hand that gave them meat,
The church, the town have lost a friend,
Whose memory but with life can end." [6,8]

Children:
1. 310019. Hannah, b. 4 Dec. 1771[1]; m. 16 Oct. 1790 John Smith[1,4]; d. 9 May 1827[6].
   Children (surname Smith):
   1. Horace[5,6].   3. Frances[5,6].   5. Lola[5,6].
   2. Andrew[5,6].   4. Julia[5,6]   6. Henry[6].
2. 310020. Nathaniel, b. 21 Jan. 1775[1]; bapt. 29 June 1775[1,4].
3. 310014. Rufus, b. 19 Mar. 1777[1]; bapt. 4 May 1777[1,4].

4. 310021. Jerusha, b. 9 Dec. 1779[1]; bapt. 12 Dec. 1779[1,4]; m. 2 May 1802 Dr. Pierre
Elizabeth Brandin[1,2]; d. 5 Mar. 1854[6].
Children (surname Brandin)[2]:

| 1. Jane Elizabeth. | 3. Mary Jerusha. | 5. Antoinette Amelia. |
| 2. Henry Pierre. | 4. Mary Jerusha. | |

5. 310022. Israel, b. 14 Aug. 1782[6]; bapt. 18 Aug. 1782[1,4]; d. 20 Mar. 1785[1,4].
6. 310023. Virgil, b. 21 Sept. 1784[6]; bapt. 7 Nov. 1784[1,4].
7. 310024. Israel, b. 25 Apr. 1787[6]; bapt. 17 June 1787[1,4].
8. 310142. Jairus, b. 21 July 1789[6]; bapt. 6 Sept. 1789[1,4].
9. 310143. Ebenezer, b. 29 Jan. 1792[6]; bapt. 18 Mar. 1792[1,4].
10. 310144. Dennis Dowd, b. 6 Aug. 1794[6]; bapt. 28 Sept. 1794[1,4].

REFERENCES:
1. New Haven - Jacobus, pp. 361, 367.
2. Cheshire, pp. 152, 175, 178, 214, 233, 448, 471, 505, 543.
3. Cheshire, Parson Hall's Records.
4. Cheshire, Parson Foot's Records.
5. Ltr. 11 Dec. 1907, from A. J. Bunnell, North Judson, IN, to John A. Biles.
6. Biles Manuscript, pp. 275, 276, 280.
7. Duncan, p. 41.
8. Lines.
9. CB Database: 1790, 1800, 1810 census.

1-1-9-3-4   D17iv   CB300026

BENJAMIN[5] BUNNELL (Benjamin[4], Nathaniel[3], Benjamin[2], William[1]) was born 15 July 1747[1] at Cheshire, New Haven co, CT, and was baptized there in 1747[1] (21 Aug. 1747[3]). He is apparently the Benjamin Bunnel who is assessed on £2 on the tax list in Cheshire in 1774[2].

REFERENCES:
1. New Haven - Jacobus, p. 362.
2. Cheshire, p. 52.
3. CB Database.

1-1-9-4-2   D18ii   CB300031

PARMINEAS[5] BUNNELL (Parmineas[4], Nathaniel[3], Benjamin[2], William[1]) was born 1 January 1742[1] at Cheshire, New Haven co, CT. He died 23 August 1758 as a soldier in the French and Indian Wars. He served with his father in Capt. Eldad Lewis's Seventh Company, Col. Nathan

Whiting's Second Regiment from 3 April 1758 until his death in August[2]. The death date and the military service listed in Duncan, pp. 24 and 25, were those of his father, rather than of this Parmineas[3].

REFERENCES:
1. New Haven - Jacobus, p. 362.
2. CT Historical Society - X, p, 43.
3. Duncan, pp. 24, 25.

1-1-9-4-8   D46   CB300037

JOHN[5] BUNNELL, (Parmineas[4], Nathaniel[3], Benjamin[2], William[1]) was born 26[2] (25[1]) July 1754[1,2] in the Cheshire section of Wallingford, New Haven co, CT. In 1760, following the death of his father, his mother was appointed his guardian[7]. When he was old enough, in 1768, John chose his uncle Abner Bunnell as his guardian[7].

In August 1776 John was a private in a militia company in Cheshire commanded by Capt. Hull and Lt. Newton. About the middle of the month the company was ordered to New York City where they camped for several weeks. Following the evacuation of Brooklyn Heights at the end of September, the American troops, John included, were marched north to Harlem and on to Kings Bridge at the northern tip of Manhattan Island. After about two months of service he was discharged[2]. In June 1779 he was drafted into Capt. Divan Berry's company. He served until the last of August, keeping guard at Byram's and Sherwood's bridges. Early in July his company sustained an attack by the British, part of Gen. Tryon's descent on New Haven, Fairfield and Norwalk[2]. Then early in September 1779 he hired as a substitute for Asa Thompson, serving for six weeks or two months in New Haven under Capt. Isaac Bronson[2].

About this time he married DESIRE _____ [1]. They were admitted to membership in the Cheshire Congregational Church on 24 September 1780[7]. In June 1780 (according to his pension application) he was drafted for three months to go to the Hudson River in a company commanded by Capt. Starr of Middletown. He said this was the summer after he was married, which suggests that his marriage took place in late 1779 or early 1780[2]. (Note, however, that a return of Connecticut troops under Col. Samuel Canfield at West Point, 15 September 1781, included John Bunnell of Cheshire[3]. Did John make a mistake in the year of his last service when he applied for his pension 50 years later?).

John was listed as a Freeman in Cheshire in April 1806[3]. He appears in the 1790 census: 1-0-5-0-0, in the 1800 census: 00001-01401, in the 1810 census: 10001-00011, and in the 1820 census: 000001-00011, all in Cheshire, CT[7]. On 17 August 1832 he appeared in the Probate Court of Cheshire to apply for a pension under the act of Congress passed 7 June 1832. He stated that he was born in the town of Cheshire and lived there all his life except for about seven years' residence in Wolcott, New Haven co, CT[2]. The application (S12382) was approved, and he was inscribed on the pension roll at the rate of $28.33 per annum to commence on the 4th day of March, 1831[2]. He died 16 January 1841[1] at Cheshire. A Cheshire tombstone in the Hillside Cemetery reads, "John Bunnell died Jan. 16, 1841 ae 84."[5]

Children:
1. 310146. Lydia Ann, b. 20 Oct. 1780[1]; bapt. 17 Dec. 1780[1].
2. 310147. Mary, b. 19 Oct. 1782[1]; bapt. 26 Jan. 1783[1]; m. Andrew Bradley[6].
    Children (surname Bradley)[6]:
    1. John Andrew.
3. 310148. Lowly, b. 13 Dec. 1783[1]; bapt. 21 Dec. 1783[1]; m. 1 Dec. 1808 Jared Hitchcock[1].
4. 310149. Desire, b. 26 Oct. 1785[1].

REFERENCES:
1. New Haven - Jacobus, pp. 362, 367.
2. Revolutionary War Pension File S12382, obtained from the National Archives and sent to me by Claude A. Bunnell.
3. Cheshire, pp. 203, 448, 505.
4. Cheshire, Parson Foot's Records, p. 349.
5. Biles Manuscript, p. 289.
6. Duncan, p. 41.
7. CB Database.

1-1-9-5-3   D47   CB300073

JAIRUS[5] BUNNELL (Jairus[4], Nathaniel[3], Benjamin[2], William[1]) was born about 1745 at Branford, New Haven co, CT. On 14 March 1770[1], in the Northford, New Haven co, Congregational Church, he was married by Rev. Williams[6] to LYDIA BALDWIN[1], daughter of John and Margery (Tyler) Baldwin[1]. They lived in Branford, New Haven co, CT, from which town he marched for the relief of Boston in the Lexington Alarm, April 1775. He served six days[2]. Jairus appears in the 1790 census: 3-1-6-0-0[1], in the 1800 census: 0-0-1-0-1:0-2-2-0-1[5], in the 1810 census: 10002-00212[6] and in the 1820 census: 010001-01110[6], all in Branford, CT. He died 22 (or 2[4]) November 1822[3,6] at Branford at the age of 78. Lydia died in Branford 5 February 1823[4] at the age of 77[4]. Both were buried in the North Branford Cemetery[4].

Children (born in Branford, CT):
1. 310403. Jairus[3] B.[4], b. 1772?[3] or 1771[6].
2. 310408. Phoebe[3,4], b. 1774[3] or 1785[6]; d. unmarried 1866[4].
    Her will probated in North Branford reads as follows:

"I, Phebe Bunnell, give to my nephew, Lewis Bunnell all my right and share in the dwelling house & barn and all the lands that I own in North Branford. He is to pay all my just debts.

"I give to my two sisters, Lydia Palmer, wife of Jonathan Palmer and Rebecca Barns, wife of Martin Barns all my personal estate to be divided equally between them.

"I appoint my nephew, Lewis Bunnell, Executor. Signed: Phebe Bunnell, 9 Oct. 1839. Witnesses: Benjamin Page, Mary Page and Zebulon Page."[4]

3. 310409. Lydia[3,4], b. 1776[3] or 1787[6]; m. Jonathan Palmer[4].

4. 310410. Rebecca[3,4], b. 1779[3] or 1789[6]; m. Martin Barnes[4].

5. 310404. Betsey[3], b. 31 Dec. 1781[3]; m. 5 Apr. 1805 Fosdick Harrison[3]; d. 31 Mar. 1816[3].

6. 310405. Abigail[3], b. 1783[3]; m. _____ Palmer[3]; d. 1822?[3]

7. 310406. Anna[3], b. 1785[3]; m. William R. Harrison of Bethlehem, CT[3].

8. 310407. Philema[4]; b. 1783[6]; m. about 1804 _____ Harrison[4]
   Children (surname Harrison)[4]:
   1. Betsy.   2. Mary.   3. Fosdick.

NOTE: The list of children is confusing and is probably not correct. Biles lists the first seven. Duncan lists only five children, the first four plus number eight. One wonders if there are not too many Harrison and/or Palmer marriages. Probably at least two of the brides should be combined into one person and one marriage.

REFERENCES:
1. New Haven - Jacobus, p. 362.
2. Rev War - CT, p. 6.
3. Biles Manuscript, p. 290.
4. Duncan, pp, 41, 42.
5. 1800 census data copied and sent to me by Claude Mitchell, Muskegon, MI.
6. CB Database.

1-1-9-5-4   D48   CB300074

NATHANIEL[5] BUNNELL (Jairus[4], Nathaniel[3], Benjamin[2], William[1]) was born about 1748/50[5] or 1753[3] in Branford, New Haven co, CT. He married ABIGAIL ABERNATHY[1], daughter of Enos and Beulah (Beach) Abernathy[1], who was born 27 November 1748[1] in Wallingford, New Haven co, CT. They lived in Farmington, Hartford co, CT. He died in October 1776 in the Northern Army during the Revolution[1]. His estate was probated in Farmington with his wife Abigail as administratrix[3]. In 1778 she was appointed guardian of their minor son[3]. His widow married (second) 12 November 1778[1], in Avon, Hartford co, CT, Elisha Miller[1].

Children:
   1. 310063. Nathaniel, b. 26 June 1776[2]; bapt. 26 June 1776[1].

NOTE: *The Connecticut Journal*, published in New Haven, CT, 26 February 1768, reported that Nathaniel Bunnell and three others were sentenced at Fairfield and were cropped and branded with C for counterfeiting New York bills[4]. Is this the Nathaniel?

REFERENCES:
1. New Haven - Jacobus, p. 362.
2. Barbour.
3. CB Database.
4. New Haven Newspapers, p. 214.
5. Duncan, p. 42.

1-1-9-5-5   D49   CB300075

JOHN[5] BUNNELL (Jairus[4], Nathaniel[3], Benjamin[2], William[1]) was born about 1753[1] at Branford, New Haven co, CT. During the Revolution he served as a drummer in Sixth Company, First Regiment, 1775, commanded by Capt. William Douglas, under General Wooster. He served for five months and one day and was discharged 23 September 1775 in the Northern Department[2,3]. The privates each received 52 shillings bounty money, and the majority of them were credited with mileage for 253 miles[3]. His name appears in a volume of "Sick Bills", 1775, being itemized accounts of the expenses of individual soldiers during sickness[3]. His brother Abraham served in the same company[2,3].

About 1776 he married PUAH (or PURE) AUGUR[1], daughter of John and Rachel (Barnes) Augur[1]. She was born 1 May 1755[1]. She was admitted to membership in the Northford Church in Branford on 18 June 1780[6].

John appears in the 1790 census: 1-3-3-0-0, in the 1800 census: 21310-11110, in the 1810 census: 02101-00201, and in the 1820 census: 000111-00001, all in the town of Branford[6]. He is also found in the tax list in the town of Branford in November 1817: List $140.94, tax $3.82[4]. He died 9 December 1826[1] (or 1825[6]) at North Branford, New Haven co, CT, at the age of 74. John's probate record in Northford contains the following distribution: "We, Anna, Luther & Elizur Bunnell, all of Branford, being the lawful heirs of our father, John Bunnell who died intestate, mutually agree to divide the real estate equally between ourselves with the exception of the widow's dower. Signed: Ann Bunniel, Luther Buniel & Elizur Bennel. 8 Dec. 1827. Witnesses: Benjamin Page & Jesse Buniel."[5]

After the passage of the act of Congress on 7 June 1832 his widow applied for a pension based on his Revolutionary War service. It was approved, and her name was still on the pension list (Pension #W20825) in 1840[2]. She died 16 February 1842[1] in North Branford. They were both buried in the Old Northford Cemetery in North Branford[5]. Puah's probate record in Northford contains the following distribution: "Estate distributed to Anna, Augustus, Luther, Elizur, Nathaniel, Jesse Bunnell, Lucy Tyler, wife of Malichi S. Tyler and Betsey Rose, wife of Amariah Rose. 10 April 1850 signed: Eliukim Linsley & Timothy Bartholomew, Distributors."[5]

Children:
1. 310153. Anna, b. 28 Sept. 1777[1]; bapt. 25 June 1780[6]; d. 31 Jan. 1864[1].
2. 310154. John, b. 29 Dec. 1779[1].
3. 310155. Luther, b. 20 Mar. 1782[1].
4. 310156. Jesse, b. 12 June 1784[1].
5. 310157. Nathaniel, b. 6 Feb. 1787[1].
6. 310158. Lucy, b. 22 Nov. 1789[1]; m. Malachi Stent Tyler[1]; d. 17 Aug. 1877[1].
    Children (surname Tyler)[5]:
    1. Henry.
7. 310159. Betsey, b. 24 Oct. 1792[1]; bapt. 1 Dec. 1792[6]; m. Amariah Rose[1]; d. 1871[6].
8. 310160. Augustus[1] Barnes[7], b. 16 May 1795[1].
9. 310161. Elizur, b. 4 May 1798[1].

REFERENCES:
1. New Haven - Jacobus, pp. 362, 367, 368.
2. Rev War - CT, pp. 42, 659.
3. CT Historical Society - VIII, pp. 9, 25.
4. Nutmegger, Vol. 26, No. 3, Dec. 1993, p. 384, Tax List, Town of Branford, CT, November 1817.
5. Duncan, pp. 42, 43.
6. CB Database.
7. Ltr. 6 Aug. 1987 from Harry A. Stowell, St. Augustine, FL.

1-1-9-5-6   D50   CB300076

ABRAHAM[5] BUNNELL, (Jairus[4], Nathaniel[3], Benjamin[2], William[1]) was born in 1754[7] at Branford, New Haven co, CT. With his brother John he served in the Revolution in the Sixth Company, First Regiment, 1775, commanded by Capt. William Douglas, under General Wooster. He served for seven months and was discharged 20 November 1775 in the Northern Department[2,3]. His name appears in a volume of "Sick Bills", 1775, being itemized accounts of the expenses of individual soldiers during sickness[3]. He served as a corporal in Capt. Elisha Ely's Company, Col. William Douglas's 6th Regiment, Connecticut Line, from 24 April 1777 until he transferred 10 April 1782 to the Invalid Corps[5]. From 1 January 1781 until 31 December 1781 he was a corporal in Capt. Theophilus Munson's Company, Col. Zebulon Butler's 4th Regiment, Connecticut Line[2].

On 14 April 1779[1], at Wallingford, New Haven co, CT, he was married by Oliver Stanley, J.P.[6], to ADAH MUNSON[1], daughter of Abel and Sarah (Peck) Munson[1]. She was baptized 19 November 1758[1] in the Northford Congregational Society in Northford, town of Branford, New Haven co, CT. They moved to New York state, and Abraham appears in the 1790 census: 1-1-3-0-0[6] in Freehold, Albany (now Greene) co, NY, in the 1800 census: 00101:12010[6] at Rensselaerville, Albany co, NY, and in the 1810 census: 10011-01001[6] in Norway, Herkimer co, NY.

Children:
1. 310068. Nathaniel, d. young[1].
2. 310069. Lydia B.[1], b. 1788[6]; m. William Morse[1]; d. 1 Dec. 1823[6].
3. 310070. Orilla[1] (or Orvilla[5]), m. Harry Morse[1].
4. 310071. Rebecca[1]; m. 3 Oct. 1817 William Wendover[4] (or m. Harry Windover[1]).
5. 310072. James Munson, b. 1 Aug. 1802[1].
6.   Desire[1]. It is possible, though not likely that this is the Desire Bunnel CB010358 who was listed as a member of the Congregational Church in Wolcott, New Haven co, CT, on 5 March 1830[6].

REFERENCES:
1. New Haven - Jacobus, pp. 362, 363.
2. Rev War - CT, pp. 42, 319.
3. CT Historical Society - VIII, pp. 10, 16.
4. Marriage Index of New York, compiled by Nancie Davis, West Columbia, SC.
5. Duncan, p. 43.
6. CB Database: 1790, 1800 and 1810 census.
7. Biles Manuscript, p. 290.

1-1-9-6-2 D51 CB300081

DAVID[5] BUNNELL (Abner[4], Nathaniel[3], Benjamin[2], William[1]) was born 2 December 1747[1] at Cheshire, town of Wallingford, New Haven co, CT, and was baptized in December 1747 in the Cheshire Congregational Church[1,2]. On 25 December 1766[1], in Wallingford, New Haven co, CT, he married RACHEL GRANNIS[1], daughter of Caleb and Patience (Bunnell, 1-1-9-8, CB290039) Grannis[1]. She was born 20 August 1746[1] in New Haven, New Haven co, CT. She was admitted to the church in Cheshire in 1774.[8] Rachel died 30 November 1796[1,3] in Cheshire, and David married (second) 24 May 1797[1], in the Cheshire Congregational Church, PATIENCE[1,3] _____, widow of Ephraim Smith[1,3]. David appears in the 1790 census: 2-2-6-0-0, the 1800 census: 0-0-0-0-1:0-1-0-0-1, and the 1810 census: 00001-01001, all in Cheshire, CT[8]. On 6 May 1805 and again on 15 May 1810 David sold small parcels of land on the west side of his property in Cheshire to Asa Peck[7].

David died 2 September 1810[1,3] at Cheshire. On 22 September 1810 Patience Bunnell sold her right in the estate, including the land with the home and barn standing on it[7]. (To whom?, her children?) The executors of his estate were the widow Patience Bunnell and son-in-law Obed Moss[7]. On 13 November 1811 the executors sold 2 acres and 13 rods of the land to neighbor Jesse Thompson for $100.

The widow Patience Bunnell appears in the 1820 census: 0-00001 and in the 1830 census: 0-00000000001 in Cheshire[8]. I have not found a record of her death.

Children (by first wife):

1. 310164. Sarah, b. 6 July 1767[1]; m. 22 Jan. 1786 Obed Moss[1,3]; d. 2 May 1814[1].
    Children (surname Moss):
    1. Jesse[5]. 2. Chloe[6]. 3. Anson[6].
2. 310165. Ebenezer, b. 25 July 1769[1]; baptized 30 July 1769[1,3].
3. 310166. Amarinda Lovisa, b. 20 Apr. 1771[1]; d. 29 July 1777[1,3].
4. 310172. Lucinda, b. 19 Nov. 1772[5].
5. 310167. Rachel, b. 30 Mar. 1774[1]; bapt. 3 Apr. 1774[1,3]; m. Feb. 1798 Jonathan Doolittle[1,4]; d. 25 Apr. 1808[1].
    Children (surname Doolittle)[6]:
    1. Lines. 2. Miles. 3. Beede.
6. 310168. Chloe, b. 2 Mar. 1776[1]; bapt. 3 Mar. 1776[3]; d. 23 May 1794[1,3].
7. 310169. Amarinda Lovisa, b. 26 Nov. 1777[1]; bapt. 30 Nov. 1777[1,3]; m. Theophilus Nettleton[1].
8. 310170. Roxanna, b. 13 Aug. 1779[1]; bapt. 15 Aug. 1779[1,3]; m. (first) 8 Feb. 1801 Moses Blakeslee[1,3]; m. (second) 15 Jan. 1820 Abel Andrews, Jr.[1]; d. 22 Sept. 1849[1].
9. 310171. Achsah[1], b. 1781[5]; m. 1806 Humphrey Avery, Esq.[1,5]; d. 1814[5].
    Children (surname Avery)[5]:
    1. Harriet Currance. 2. Anson D.

REFERENCES:
1. New Haven - Jacobus, pp. 363, 368.
2. Cheshire, Parson Hall's Records.
3. Cheshire, Parson Foot's Records.
4. Cheshire, Town Records of Cheshire.
5. Biles Manuscript, pp. 293, 294.
6. Duncan, p. 44.
7. Lines.
8. CB Database.

1-1-9-6-3   D52   CB300041

ABNER[5] BUNNELL (Abner[4], Nathaniel[3], Benjamin[2], William[1]) was born 18 November 1749[1] and baptized 25 December 1749[1,2] by Parson Hall at Cheshire, New Haven co, CT. On 10 February 1774[1,4], at Cheshire, he married SARAH ATWATER[1,4], daughter of Moses and Eunice (Newton) Atwater[1], who was born 16 November 1755[1] at Wallingford, New Haven co, CT. The tax list for the minister's rate for the Society of New Cheshire in Wallingford in 1774 lists Abner Bunnell, Jr., assessed on £20[2]. His wife Sarah was admitted to membership in the Church on 30 July 1775[9]. In 1777 he was an officer of the Cheshire Congregational Church[2]. The land records of Cheshire include a number of deeds by which Abner bought or sold land in the town[8]. Abner appears in the 1790 census: 2-2-4-0-0, in the 1800 census: 11101-31110, and in the 1810 census: 00101-01101 in Cheshire, CT[9].

FIFTH GENERATION

Abner died in Cheshire; his wife Sarah and son Reuben were administrators of his estate, for which they took out a bond on 19 December 1814[7]. Deeds show they sold several small parcels of the land in 1815 and 1816[7,8]. His wife died 27 January 1818 in Cheshire[10].

Children:

1. 310025. Moses Atwater, b. 18 Nov. 1774[1]; bapt. 20 Aug. 1775[1,4].
2. 310015. Eunice, b. 14 Mar. 1776[1,6]; bapt. 5 May 1776[1,4]; m. 11 Mar. 1801 Abel Ives Hall[1,4,6]; d. 4 Mar. 1852[5,6].
   Children (surname Hall)[5,6]:
   1. Lois Ives.   3. Abner Bunnell.   5. Sarah.
   2. Dency Hull.   4. Eunice Atwater.   6. Lucy.
3. 310026. Chester, b. 16 Mar. 1778[1]; bapt. 3 May 1778[1,4].
4. 310176. Abner, b. 24 Sept. 1780[1,2]; bapt. 12 Nov. 1780[1,4].
5. 310027. Sarah Lecta, b. 14 Dec. 1782[1,2]; bapt. 2 Mar. 1783[1,4]; m. 23 Aug. 1802 Harvey Thompson[1].
6. 310028. Elizabeth, b. 1784; d. 26 May 1785[1,4].
7. 310029. Reuben, b. 17 July 1786[1,2]; bapt. 23 July 1786[1,4].
8. 310030. Susa, b. 17 Dec. 1789[1,2]; bapt. 28 Mar. 1790[1,4]; probably the "Susanna" who d. 1 Aug. 1804[1].
9. 310031. Esther, b. 25 (or 21[2]) Sept. 1792[1]; bapt. 2 Dec. 1792[1,4].
10. 310174. Elias, b. 4 Oct. 1795[1,2]; bapt. 17 Jan. 1796[1,4].
11. 310175. Clara, b. 9 Dec. 1798[1,2]; bapt. 17 Mar. 1799[1,4].

NOTE: Jacobus[1], p. 66, gives correctly the parents of Abner's wife, Sarah (Atwater) Bunnell. They are listed incorrectly on page 363 in the same work.

REFERENCES:

1. New Haven - Jacobus, pp. 66, 363, 368.
2. Cheshire, pp. 52, 448.
3. Cheshire, Parson Hall's records.
4. Cheshire, Parson Foot's records.
5. Biles Manuscript, pp. 296, 296A.
6. Ltr. 16 Mar. 1912, from Florence Maddox, Wauseon, OH (great granddaughter of Eunice (Bunnell) Hall), to John A. Biles.
7. Cheshire, CT, deed book, Vol. 12, pp. 309, 409, extracted and sent to me by Nona Bassett, Merced, CA.
8. Lines.
9. CB Database.
10. Duncan, pp. 44, 45.

1-1-9-6-5   D53   300083

ENOS[5] BUNNELL (Abner[4], Nathaniel[3], Benjamin[2], William[1]) was born 15 May 1753[1,3] at Cheshire, then in the town of Wallingford, New Haven co, CT. In April or May 1775 he enlisted as a private in Capt. James Arnold's 9th company, Col. David Wooster's 1st regiment[2,3]. This company spent most of the summer camped in Harlem, NY. During this time they made a short tour in Long Island. In September they were carried up the Hudson River to Albany and marched to Ticonderoga and Crown Point. They took part in the capture of St. John's after a three or four week siege. From there Enos went with the army to Laprairie and Montreal, where he was discharged on 28 December 1775[2,3]. Almost immediately after arriving home in January 1776 he enlisted as orderly sergeant in a company formed in Cheshire under Capt. Stephen Rowe Bradley[3]. They were marched to New York City, where they remained through part of the spring of 1776. The company was discharged after a tour of three or four months[3]. Later during the war he was called out several times on alarms for a few days at a time[3].

On 20 January 1777[1,6], in Wallingford, New Haven co, CT, he married (first) FREELOVE TUTTLE[1,6], daughter of Moses and Sybil (Thomas) Tuttle[1], who was born 8 April 1756[1] in Wallingford. She died 7 May 1777[1,6] in Wallingford, and he married (second) 1 June 1780[1,3,6], in Cheshire, CT, NAOMI ATWATER[1,3,6], daughter of Stephen and Hannah (Hotchkiss) Atwater[1]. She was born 17 August 1756[1] in Wallingford.

Enos appears in the 1790 census: 1-2-4-0-0, the 1800 census: 11101-21101, and the 1810 census: 01001-00001, all in Cheshire, CT[8]. On 11 June 1810 he sold his right to the estate of his father Abner Bunnell to his son Wareham for $75[4]. On 10 August 1832 Enos Bunnell, residence Cheshire, applied for a pension based on his service in the Revolution. It was approved (W17385) on 19 October 1832 at the rate of $41.66 per annum to commence as of 4 March 1831[3]. Enos does not appear in the 1820 census in Cheshire, but his wife Naomi does: 000000-00011. In his pension application Enos stated that he had lived all his life in Cheshire except for a period of four months when he visited his son in Canada[3]. (Enos, Jr., son of his first wife, had moved to Brantford, Ontario, Canada, in 1806.) Perhaps the visit was made in 1820 when the census was taken.

Enos died 19 March 1834[1,3] (or 22 January 1834 in Kensington or Berlin[8]), Hartford co, CT. On 11 November 1837 Naomi Bunnell applied for a widow's pension. She was then living in Berlin, Hartford co, CT. Her application stated in part: "She further declares that she was married to said Enos Bunnell (her maiden name having been Naomi Atwater) on the first day of June A.D. 1780 as appears by the Town Records of the aforesaid Town of Cheshire in which Town she was married, that her husband the said Enos Bunnell, died on the 19th day of March A.D. 1834; and that she has remained a widow ever since that period, . . ."[3] She appears in the 1840 census in Berlin, CT, as a pensioner[7,8], living with her son-in-law Luther Stocking and daughter Ann[8]. She died 16 January 1843[1].

Children (by first wife):
    1. 310179. Enos, b. 25 Apr. 1777[1,5].

Children (by second wife):

2. 310180. Warham, b. 25 Apr. 1781[1,5]; bapt.24 June 1781[1,6].
3. 310181. Freelove, b. 25[1] (or 21[5]) Feb. 1783[1,5]; bapt. 20 Apr. 1783[1,6]; m. 13 Apr. 1806 Abel Hine[1,6].
4. 310182. Naomi, b. 7 Dec. 1784[1,5]; bapt. 13 Feb. 1785[1,6]; d. 18 Dec. 1827[1].
5. 310183. Lucy, b. 7 Feb. 1787[1,5]; bapt. 27 May 1787[1,6]; m. 10 Dec. 1806 Jesse Barnes[1].
6. 310184. Anna, b. 23 Mar. 1790[1,5]; m. 23 Jan. 1817 Luther Stocking[8].
7. 310185. Hannah, b. 25 Mar. 1792[1,5]; bapt. 1 July 1792[1,6]; m. Luther Stocking[1].
     (Is this one marriage for Luther Stocking or two? Did he marry Hannah first, then Anna after Hannah's death? Or did Anna die in infancy - note that I find no record of a baptism for her - ? The names Anna and Hannah were frequently used interchangeably.)
8. 310186. William, b. 20 Sept. 1794[1,5]; bapt. 7 June 1795[1,6].
9. 310187. Elizabeth, b. 20 Aug. 1796[1,5]; bapt. 28 May 1797[1,6]; m. 1815 George J. Bridge[7].
     Children (surname Bridge)[7]:
     1. George A.   2. S. Dickerson.

REFERENCES:

1. New Haven - Jacobus, pp. 363, 368, 369.
2. Rev War - CT, p. 43.
3. Pension record W17385, National Archives, photocopy sent to me by Claude A. Bunnell.
4. Lines.
5. Cheshire, pp. 54, 56, 448.
6. Cheshire, Parson Foot's records.
7. Duncan, p. 45.
8. CB Database: 1790, 1800, 1810, 1820 and 1840 census.

1-1-9-6-6   D54   CB300084

REUBEN[5] BUNNELL (Abner[4], Nathaniel[3], Benjamin[2], William[1]) was born 22 February 1755[1] at Cheshire, town of Wallingford, New Haven co, CT. On 2 November 1775[1,3] in Cheshire, he married EUNICE ROWE[1,3], daughter of Joseph and Abigail (Beecher) Rowe[1]. She was born 29 June 1755[1] in New Haven, New Haven co, CT. Reuben served as a teamster in Capt. Thomas Gilbert's Company in 1777[6]. On 25 June 1780 Eunice (Rowe) Bunnell was admitted to membership in the Cheshire Congregational Church[3].

Reuben died 18 June 1786[1] at Cheshire. His gravestone there reads "In memory of Mr. Reuben Bunnell, died June 18, 1786, ae. 32. Time how short, Eternity how long."[4] Eunice (Rowe) Bunnell appears in the 1790 census: 0-1-4-0-0[1] and in the 1800 census: 00000-01001[7] in Cheshire, CT. One of the many Bunnell transactions copied by Bishop Lines from the Cheshire land records into his notebook reads as follows: "Know yᵉ that one Joseph Hotchkiss & Nabby Hotchkiss of Cheshire, for the consideration of Sixteen pounds, two shillings & eight pence. lawfull money. Received to our satisfaction from Eunice Bunnell, do assign a certain piece of land in the estate of her father Reuben Bunnell of Sd Cheshire deceased and lies on the East Side of land set out to Eliab from said estate & is two rods and four feet and one inch & one half in width at the South end & 2 rods 1 ft & ½ inch on the North end. Bounds as follows   North on Abner Bunnells land East on Ruth Bunnells land south on highway & West on Eliab Bunnells land. and we do hereby convey to the said Eunice Bunnell all the property that was set out to Sd Nabby in the dwelling home of Sd Reuben Bunnell Deceased Standing near the premises. April 30ᵗʰ 1798. Witnessed by Ruth Amy Bunnell, Andrew Hull."[5]

On 17 January 1809 Eunice was living in Plymouth, Litchfield co, CT, when she sold land in Cheshire[5]. She married (second) 14 April 1813, in Wallingford, New Haven co, CT, David Moss[6].

Children:
1. 310190. Nabby, b. 16 Mar. 1776[1]; bapt. 6 Aug. 1780[1,3]; m. 10 May 1797 Joseph Hotchkiss[1,3].
2. 310191. Ruth Amy[1] (or Ruth Anna[3], or Guetherma[2]), b. 16 Jan. 1779[1]; bapt. 6 Aug. 1780[1,3]; m. 25 Nov. 1804 Isaac Peck[1].
3. 310192. Freeman, b. 27 Jan. 1781[1]; bapt. 18 Mar. 1781[1,3]; d. 26 May 1792[1].
4. 310193. Eliab[1] (or Elias[2]), b. 6 Apr. 1783[1].
5. 310194. Abbacinda[1] (or Alice Cecelia[2]), b. 20 Apr. 1785[1]; m. 1810 Joel Parker[1] of Augusta, NY.

REFERENCES:
1. New Haven - Jacobus, pp. 363, 369.
2. Cheshire, pp. 448, 505.
3. Cheshire, Parson Foot's records.
4. Biles Manuscript, p. 305.
5. Lines.
6. Duncan, pp. 45, 46.
7. CB Database.

1-1-9-6-7   D55   CB300085

SAMUEL⁵ BUNNELL (Abner⁴, Nathaniel³, Benjamin², William¹) was born 12 May 1757[1] at Cheshire, in the town of Wallingford, New Haven co, CT. During the Revolution he served at Boston as a private in Capt. Street Hall's Second Company, Col. Charles Webb's Seventh Regiment, second call, from 14 July 1775 to 19 January 1776[2,3]. He was stationed on Long Island Sound until 14 September 1775 when, at the request of General Washington, the regiment was ordered to Boston until expiration of its service in December 1775[4].

On 10 June 1790[1,5] at Cheshire, he married MARY HITCHCOCK[1,5], daughter of Jotham and Mary (Hull) Hitchcock[1]. She was born 4 December 1752[1] at Wallingford, New Haven co, CT. Samuel appears in the 1790 census: 1-1-1-0-0[1,8] and in the 1800 census: 10010-10002[8] in

Cheshire, CT. He died 29 March 1808[1,4] at Cheshire and was buried in Hillside Cemetery there[7]. His widow survived him. On 27 February 1809 she sold 23 acres with the building thereon to Leverett Bradley for $1200[6], on 4 February 1812 she sold 15+ acres to Joseph Benham and Jedediah Moss for $387.50[6], and on 6 September 1812 "Mary Bunnell of Cheshire as guardian to Samuel P. Bunnell a Minor, Sells land to Burrage Beach. 3 acres & 102 rods and bounds South on Highway. West on lands set to the heirs of Reuben Bunnell North on Thankfull Bunnell and East on land set to Jehiel Bunnell & interest in the old house & Barn, and also a piece of land that was set to the widow of Abner Bunnell deceased containing 4 acres & 106 rods Situated North & East on Abner Bunnells deceased land. for $149.25."[6]

In 1818 widow Mary Bunnell had been receiving a Revolutionary War pension since 1813 of $48.00 per year[8].

Children:
1. 310076. Mary, d. Sept. 14, 1791, age 0[1,5].
2. 310077. Samuel Preston, b. 12 July 1796[1]; bapt. 9 Oct. 1796[1,5].

REFERENCES:
1. New Haven - Jacobus, p. 363.
2. Rev War - CT, pp. 80, 462.
3. CT Historical Society - XII, p. 14.
4. Cheshire, pp. 186, 448, 505.
5. Cheshire, Parson Foot's records.
6. Lines.
7. Duncan, p. 46.
8, CB Database: 1790, 1800 census.

1-1-9-6-9   D56   CB300087

JEHIEL[5] BUNNELL (Abner[4], Nathaniel[3], Benjamin[2], William[1]) was born 29 October 1763[1] at Cheshire, in the town of Wallingford, New Haven co, CT. In June 1780 he joined the company of Capt. Amos Hotchkiss in the regiment of Col. Waterbury of the Connecticut Militia as a substitute for Titus Morse. During a tour of three months he was stationed at various points in New London co, CT, including Winthrops Point opposite New London, Poquetanuck and Mohegan[5].

In February 1781 he enlisted for one year as a teamster in a company commanded by Capt. Zenas Andrews. His service took him to Newburgh, the Highlands, Peekskill, and White Plains, all along the Hudson River in New York State. He was discharged in February 1782 at Newburgh by Major John I. Skidmore, Deputy Wagon Master[5].

He married (first) 21 November 1784[1], in Waterbury, New Haven co, CT, TEMPERANCE HOTCHKISS[1], daughter of Jesse and Charity (Mallory) Hotchkiss[1]. She was born 3 December 1767[1] in Waterbury, and died 3 May 1787[1,3] in Cheshire, CT. On 23 December 1788[5], by Rev. John Foote at Cheshire, he was married (second) to STATIRA HOTCHKISS[1,5], daughter of Benjamin and Martha (Brooks) Hotchkiss[1]. She was born 16 November 1765[1] at New Haven, New Haven co, CT.

Jehiel appears in the 1790 census in Cheshire, CT: 1-1-2-0-0[8]. He took the oath of fidelity in Cheshire in 1794[2]. He removed from Cheshire to Whitehall, Washington co, NY, before 1800 where he appears in the 1800 census: 12001-01001[8] and in the 1810 census: 21301-00001. His youngest child Dennis was born there. On 25 December 1811 Jehiel sold his right in the real estate of his father Abner Bunnell deceased to Burrage Beech for $75.00[6]. In his pension application Jehiel stated that he lived in Whitehall about twenty years and then moved to Lima, Livingston co, NY. However, a letter from his son Bellostee sent from Canandaigua, NY, 4 November 1815, was sent to Jehiel Bunnell, Poultney, Rutland co, VT. The letter told his parents about the sickness and impending death of their son Rodney[7]. It would seem that Jehiel had moved across the state line to Vermont for some period before his move to Lima.

Jehiel and Statira appear in the 1830 census in Lima, Livingston co, NY: 00000001-00000001[8]. On 28 May 1833, he applied for a pension as a Revolutionary War veteran (R1434)[5]. The pension was approved at the rate of $50 per annum to commence as of 4 March 1831[5]. When the 1840 census was taken Jehiel and Statira were living in the household of their son Dennis in Lima[8]. Jehiel died 8 April 1844 at Lima[5]. On 15 August 1844 Statira Bunnell applied for a pension under the act of Congress passed 17 June 1844[5]. She died 17 August 1846[5] at South Livonia, Livingston co, NY.

Children (by first wife):
1. 310216. Lovina, b. 15 Apr. 1785[5]; m. 1819 Shuball Pierce[8]; d. 19 Feb. 1852[4].
2. 310218. "child of Jehiel", d. 30 Dec. 1786[3].

Children (by second wife):
3. 310219. Miles, b. 17 Nov. 1789[5].
4. 310220. Bellostee, b. 29 Dec. 1791[5].
5. 310221. Rodney, b. 30 Dec. 1793[5].
6. 310222. Asahel, b. 29 Aug. 1796[5].
7. 310217. Zuriel, b. 24 Sept. 1801[5].
8. 310224, Dennis, b. 15 Sept. 1806[5].

NOTE: Asael O. Bunnell, son of Dennis, in his history, *Dansville, 1789-1902*, included a statement that his father Dennis was the youngest of the seven sons of Jehiel Bunnell of Cheshire, Conn. Unless the child who died in December 1786 was counted as one of the sons, I can't find seven sons in any of the records, including the Bible record submitted with the pension application. However, Claude Bunnell found a Daniel Bunnell in the 1840 census in Lima, Livingston co, NY, who was between 30 and 40 years of age. Although he appears to have had a wife and family, no other reference to him has been found so far. Claude assumes that Daniel was the seventh son and assigned number 310223 to him. If Daniel were the son of Jehiel, which seems doubtful, he was certainly dead by 1 January 1855, when the pension papers state that Dennis, Bellostee and Miles were the only surviving children[5].

REFERENCE:

1. New Haven - Jacobus, p. 363.
2. Cheshire, pp. 214, 233.
3. Cheshire, Parson Foot's records.
4. Biles Manuscript.
5. Pension record R1434, National Archives, photocopy sent to me by Claude A. Bunnell.
6. Lines.
7. Ltr. 4 Nov. 1815 from Bellostee Bunnell to Jehiel Bunnell.
8. CB Database: 1790, 1800, 1810, 1830 and 1840 census.

1-1-9-7-5   D57   CB300097

JOEL[5] BUNNELL (Joseph[4], Nathaniel[3], Benjamin[2], William[1]) was born 12 November 1758[1,6] at Farmington, Hartford co, CT, and baptized 31 December 1758 in the Congregational Church at Southington, Hartford co, CT.

He served as a private in Capt. Selah Heart's 3rd company, Col. Erastus Wolcott's State Regt., in service at Boston, January to March 1776[2,3]. He was stationed at Roxbury carrying dirt to build the fort on Dorchester Hill[3]. He witnessed the departure of the British ships from Boston Harbor[3]. In late 1776 he enlisted again in the Connecticut State Troops under Capt. Asa Bray. His company marched to Westchester co, NY, and was stationed for most of their four-month tour of duty near the house of John Jay in East Chester. He was discharged with the rest of the company about 22 March 1777. It was during this tour, he said: "I was on guard at Byrams Bridge one night and took one of the British and brought him into camp and delivered him to General Wooster, & received his hearty thanks, & he wished me to take another."[2]

In 1777 he was drafted in June as a private in Capt. Porter (Peter?) Curtiss' company of Farmington. He served for two months on this tour, but was drafted again for two months later that year, this time into Capt. Ambrose Sloper's company, Col. Ichabod Norton's regiment. Service in both tours was in New York State along the Hudson River. It was during the second tour that he learned of the taking of Burgoyne and his army in October 1777[2].

Over the next several years Joel was in and out of the army half a dozen times. In 1778 he was drafted into Capt. Sloper's company. In May 1779 he volunteered under Capt. Mathew Cole of Farmington. He was drafted in August 1779, again under Capt. Sloper. Each of these two-month tours of duty took him to Westchester co, NY. He served for 32 days in 1780 as a substitute in the Continental Army for Reuben Peck, mainly as a guard at Dobbs Ferry, Westchester co. Then finally in September 1781 he was drafted into Capt. Lemuel Hotchkiss' company for six weeks' service at New Haven. He said they kept a day of rejoicing on hearing of the surrender of Cornwallis. His pension application also states that he volunteered for seven days at the New Haven Alarm and for 14 days at the Danbury Alarm[2].

He married (first) MARTHA (PATTY) _____. They lived in Cromwell parish in the town of Middletown, Middlesex co, CT. On 20 February 1785 Joel and Martha were admitted to membership in the Cromwell First Congregational Church in Middletown[9]. Their first four children were baptized in the Cromwell church[7,8]. Joel appears in the 1790 census: 1-2-4-0-0 in Middletown, Middlesex co, CT.

Soon after, they moved to Kensington parish, town of Berlin, Hartford co, CT. They joined the Kensington Congregational Church in Berlin, Hartford co, CT, by letter from the Cromwell church in Middletown in May 1791[9]. The rest of his children were baptized in the Kensington church. Joel appears in the 1800 census: 30010-12011[9] and in the 1810 census: 20001-00110[9], both in the town of Berlin. His wife Martha died 5 December 1811 at Kensington at the age of 54[8] (or 18 December 1811 at the age of 46[5]). She was buried in the Ledge Cemetery in Berlin[8]. He married a second time.

He appears in the 1820 census in Berlin: 200011-01110[9]. In 1828 he got in some kind of difficulty with the Kensington Congregational Church, for the church records show that he was disciplined on 31 January and was excommunicated by the church on 14 February 1828[9].

On 4 August 1832 he applied for a pension in order to obtain the benefit of the Act of Congress passed 7 June 1832[2]. A Certificate of Pension was issued 4 October 1833 at the rate of $66.66 per annum to commence on 4 March 1831[2]. He appears in the 1840 census of Revolutionary pensioners in Berlin[8]. He died 2 September 1840 at the Alms House at Kensington, CT[8].

Children (by first wife):
1. 310080. Joel, bapt. 13 Mar. 1785[8].
2. 310081. Sarah (Sally), bapt. 2 July 1786[8]; m. 2 Aug. 1801 Levi Lewis[8].
3. 310082. Raphael, b. 20 Feb. 1789[4,8]; bapt. 17 Oct. 1790[7].
4. 310083. Sybil, bapt. 17 Oct. 1790[7,8].
5. 310091. Zenas[1], bapt. 6 Nov. 1791[5,8].
6. 310084. John[1], bapt. Feb. 1797[5,8].
7. 310087. Lucy[1], bapt. 12 Oct. 1808[5,8]; m. 31 July 1822 Nelson Sperry[8].
8. 310085. Martha[1], bapt. 12 Oct. 1808[5,8]; d. Dec. 1816[8].
9. 310086. Edmund[1], bapt. 12 Oct. 1808[5,8].
10. 310088. Russell[1], bapt. 12 Oct. 1808[5,8].

Children (by second wife):
11. 310090. Cyrus[8] Robinson[1,8], b. 1814[8]; bapt. Sept. 1814[1,5,8].

REFERENCES:
1. New Haven - Jacobus, p. 364.
2. Pension record S15334, National Archives, photocopy sent to me by Claude A. Bunnell.
3. Rev War - CT, p. 383.
4. Ltr. 7 Dec. 1907 from Mrs. Charles Bunnell, Spencer, NY, daughter-in-law of Raphael Bunnell, to John A. Biles.

5. Biles Manuscript.
6. Farmington vital records in The Barbour Collection, Connecticut State Library, copied and sent to me by Mrs. Clarence H. Bunnell.
7. Ltr. 2 Oct. 1983 from Frances Davenport, Head, History & Genealogy Section, Connecticut State Library, to Mrs. Richard W. Bunnell, Fullerton, CA.
8. Duncan, pp. 46, 47, with additional information on Cyrus Robinson Bunnell from the Springfield, MA, vital records sent to me by Mrs. Duncan in January 1989.
9. CB Database: 1790, 1800 and 1810 census.

1-1-9-7-6 D58 CB300098

AMOS[5] BUNNELL (Joseph[4], Nathaniel[3], Benjamin[2], William[1]) was born 9 May 1761[1,5] at Farmington, Hartford co, CT. He served in the Revolutionary War, enlisting in April 1777 as a private in Capt. Asa Bray's company, Col. Noadiah Hooker's Regiment and Col. Roger Enos's Regiment of Connecticut State troops[2]. He was discharged 15 May 1777[2] and then served for three months in the same company in 1778[2]. He enlisted again in 1780 for the duration of the War, serving under Capt. Lemuel Clift in Col. John Durkee's Regiment of Connecticut Troops[2,3]. He engaged in the battles of White Plains, Trenton and Princeton[7]. He was discharged in 1783 on account of a rupture[3].

On 16 March 1780[1,4,6], in Southington, Hartford co, CT, he married KATHERINE MERRIMAN[1,4,6], daughter of Lent and Katherine (Wright) Merriman[1], who was born 23 May 1760[1] in Wallingford, New Haven co, CT. Amos appears in the 1790 census: 1-1-3-0-0, in the 1800 census: 10010-21010, in the 1810 census: 00001-20001, and in the 1820 census: 200001-00100, all in Southington, Hartford co, CT[9]. On 10 April 1818 he applied for a military pension under the provisions of the Act of Congress passed 18 March 1818[3]. His residence at that time was Southington. A Certificate of Pension was issued 30 June 1818 at the rate of $8.00 per month, commencing on 10 April 1818. He died 5 November 1834[8,9] in Farmington, CT. Katherine died the same year[9].

Children:
      1. 310226. Samuel, b. 29 Nov. 1780[6].
      2. 310227. Amos[8], b. about 1790[9].
  ?? 3. 004688. William, b. 7 Nov. 1792. [see 1-1-9-7-6-3 for discussion]
      4. 310225. Julia Katherine, b. 1 Feb. 1796[7]; m. (first 1817 or 1818 Stephen Grannis[7];
            m. (second) Simeon Stedman[7]; m. (third) Russell Grannis[7]; d. July
            1870[7].
            Children (surname Grannis, by first husband)[7,8]:
            1. Henry Horace.   2. Charles Stephen.

REFERENCES:
    1. New Haven - Jacobus, p. 364.
    2. Rev War - CT, pp. 319, 499, 632, 666.
    3. Pension record S36 460, National Archives, photocopy obtained by William R. Austin.

4. Cheshire, p. 385, Parson Foot's records.
5. Farmington vital records in The Barbour Collection, Connecticut State Library, copied and sent to me by Mrs. Clarence H. Bunnell.
6. Southington vital records, from Kathy Lark, Town Clerk's office, Southington, to Stephen E. Baylor, Arlington, WA, December 1992.
7. Copy of DAR application by Esther E. (Grannis) Kennedy, daughter of Charles Stephen Grannis, sent to John A. Biles, 1913.
8. Duncan, p. 47.
9. CB Database.

1-1-9-7-8   D59   CB300100

HULL[5] BUNNELL (Joseph[4], Nathaniel[3], Benjamin[2], William[1]) was born 2 October 1768[1] at Farmington, Hartford co, CT, and was baptized 8 June[2] (or January[5])1769[2,5] in the Congregational Church at Southington, Hartford co, CT. He appears in the 1800 census with a wife, two sons and three daughters: 20010-21010 and in the 1810 census: 01010-41111, both in Southington[5], and in the 1820 census: 100001-02101[5] in Berlin, Hartford co, CT. He married MARY R. _____[2], who was born about 1776[2]. Hull served as a private under Nathan Johnson in the 15th Regiment for 11 days during the War of 1812, from 18 to 29 August 1814[2,3]. He died 28 December 1825[2]. His widow died 18 December 1845 at the age of 69[2], and was buried in Indian Hill Cemetery[2] in Middletown, Middlesex co, CT.

Children:
1. 310421. Polly[4] or Mary, b. 1794[5]; m. 7 Feb. 1815 Horace Bailey[4,5].
2.   George[4].
3.   Jesse[4].
4.   Eunice[4].
5. 310422. Laura[2,4,5], b. 1797[5];m. (first) Wyllis Bradley[2,4]; m. (second) Amzi I. Barnes[2,4].
6.   Leva[4].
7.   Betsy[4].

NOTE: The list of children given above was reported thus in the John A. Biles Manuscript[4]. Ruth Duncan[2] lists Laura as the first child, with her marriages, omits the other six on the above list, and adds the following four children not given by Biles. Claude Bunnell[5] found a church record and a Bible record for the marriage of Mary (Polly). No other source I have yet seen names any of Hull's children.

8. 310423. Henry[2], b. about 1802[2].
9. 310426. Harriet, b. about 1807[2].
10. 310428. Marcus, b. 1810[2].
11. 310427. Amelia, b. about 1812[2].

FIFTH GENERATION

REFERENCES:
1. New Haven - Jacobus, p. 364.
2. Duncan, p. 48.
3. War of 1812, p. 25.
4. Biles Manuscript.
5. CB Database.

1-1-9-12-3   D22iii   CB300106

LEVI[5] BUNNELL (Stephen[4], Nathaniel[3], Benjamin[2], William[1]) was born 11[1] (or 19[4,5]) July 1759[1,4,5]. During the Revolutionary War he enlisted as a private in Kimball's company, Col. John Chandler's Eighth Regiment of the "Connecticut Line," on 28 May 1777[2]. He died in camp 21 August 1777[1,2].

REFERENCES:
1. New Haven - Jacobus, p. 364.
2. Rev War - CT, p. 232.
3. Cheshire, pp. 206, 209, 407.
4. Wallingford.
5. CB Database.

1-1-10-1-5   D60   CB300118

FREDERICK[5] BUNNELL (Israel[4], Israel[3], Benjamin[2], William[1]) was born about 1758[2] in New Haven, New Haven co, CT. During the Revolution he served as a private in 1775 in Capt. Eli Leavenworth's 10th Company, Col. Charles Webb's 7th Regiment[1]; served as a matrosse in Capt. John Bigelow's Artillery Company in 1776 at Fort Ticonderoga, NY[1]; and in 1779 he served at Horseneck in Capt. David Leavenworth's Company, Col. Mosley's Regiment of Militia[1].

He married (first) 25 August 1785[3], in Livingston Manor, Albany co (now town of Livingston, Columbia co), NY, RUTH FRANCIS[3]. Frederick appears in the 1790 census: 2-1-2-0-0 in Litchfield co, CT[4]. He was a tailor by trade[2]. Ruth divorced him on 18 August 1800[3] in Litchfield co, CT. Ruth appears in the 1800 census: 0001-1101 in Goshen, Litchfield co, CT[4], and again in Goshen, apparently living with her daughter Janette, in the 1820 census: 0-00101[4].

Frederick married (second) ANN _____[3]. They appear in the 1820 census: 001101-00101[4] in Fishkill, Dutchess co, NY. He was a resident of Fishkill when he applied for a pension on 23 April 1818 based on his service in the Revolution. On 26 June 1820, in a court appearance regarding his pension, he referred to his wife, aged about 55 years, one daughter aged 17 and a son aged 15[2]. He had no real estate, and his personal estate was valued at $7.50[2]. Frederick died 10 April 1825 at the age of 67[4] in Fishkill. His widow Ann appears in the 1830 census: 00001-000010001[4] in Fishkill. She died 3 May 1838 at the age of 70[3]. They were buried in the churchyard of the First Reformed Dutch Church of Fishkill Village[3].

Children (by first wife):
    1. 319432. Sally[3]; b. about 1787[4]; m. _____ Porter[3].
    2. 310433. Janette[3,4], b. about 1796[4].

Children (by second wife):
    3. 310434. Charlotte[3], b. about 1803[2]; m. _____ Berget[3].
    4.   son, b. about 1805[2].

NOTE: Regarding Frederick's dates of birth and death:
    The papers collected by Ruth Duncan in preparing her book include two different transcriptions of Frederick's gravestone: 1. Copied by Mrs. H. Tolivaisa, Stamford, CT, from *Tombstone Inscriptions From The Churchyard of the First Reformed Dutch Church of Fishkill Village, Dutchess Co., N.Y.,* compiled by Elias W. VanVoorhis, 1882:
    "p. 19 Frederick Bunnel, died April 10, 1828, age 67 yrs."

    2. A typed sheet labeled Old Gravestones of Dutchess County New York, source unknown to me.

    "Town of Fishkill "Frederick died 1825, April 10, age 82 years 2 mo. Dutch Churchyard."

Claude A. Bunnell in CB Database 1996 cites Vol 1, p. 139 of *Pension Roll of 1835,* by the U. S. Government: "Was on pension roll - died 10 Apr/1825 - age 67."

Frederick's pension application states that on 26 June 1820 Frederick Bunnell aged sixty-two appeared in the court of Common Pleas of Dutchess co, NY.

I conclude that if he was age 62 in 1820 and was 67 when he died, that his death occurred in 1825 and that he was born in 1758.

REFERENCES:
    1. Rev War - CT, pp. 84, 86, 615, 641.
    2. Pension record S44716, National Archives, photocopy sent to me by Claude A. Bunnell.
    3. Duncan, p. 48.
    4. CB Database: 1790, 1800, 1820 and 1830 census.

1-1-10-1-6   D61   CB300116

JOSEPH J.[5] BUNNELL (Israel[4], Israel[3], Benjamin[2], William[1]) was born about 1755?[2] in New Haven, New Haven co, CT. He removed to Simsbury, Hartford co, CT[1]. On 24 August 1777[3], in Southington, Hartford co, CT, he married SYBIL THORPE[1,3]. Joseph was admitted to the

First Congregational Church in Southington from the Wallingford church on 5 November 1780[5]. Joseph and Sybil transferred their membership to the Avon, Hartford co, CT, Congregational Church on 25 May 1788[4] from the Southington Congregational Church. Joseph appears in the 1790 census: 1-0-3-0-0[1] in Farmington, Hartford co, CT. He died about 1794[4]. The same year some of their property in Farmington was attached for debt[5]. Sybil appears in the 1800 census: 10000-01001[5] in Simsbury and in the 1810 census: 01000-00101[5] in Farmington, CT.

Children:
1. 310095. Sybil, b. 5 Sept. 1778[3].
2. 310093. Sarah Mallory, b. 31 Jan. 1789[4]; bapt. 26 Apr. 1789[1].
3. 310094. William, b. 28 Oct. 1795[5]; bapt. 22 July 1796[1].

REFERENCES:
1. New Haven - Jacobus, pp. 364, 365.
2. Biles Manuscript.
3. Southington vital records from Kathy Lark, Town Clerk's office, Southington, to Stephen E. Baylor, Arlington, WA, December 1992.
4. Duncan, pp. 48, 49.
5. CB Database.

1-1-10-1-7   D62   CB300117

WILLIAM[5] BUNNELL (Israel[4], Israel[3], Benjamin[2], William[1]) was baptized 23 August 1772[1] in the 2nd Congregational Church at New Haven, New Haven co, CT. By 1795 he had removed to Simsbury, Hartford co, CT[1]. On 29 May 1796[2], in Simsbury, he was married by Dudley Pettibone, J.P., to RUTH TULLER[2], who was born about 1775[2]. William served in the War of 1812 as a Captain in the 25th Regiment[2]. He appears in the 1800 census: 00010-00100[3], and in the 1810 census: 0101-0001[3] in Winchester, Litchfield co, CT. He was a blacksmith[2]. He died 27 July 1820[2] at age 46 in Winchester and was buried there in Winchester Center Cemetery[2]. His will, dated 26 July 1820[3] and probated in Winchester, left everything to his wife, including his house, a large piece of land and many books[2]. His widow Ruth appears in the 1820 census: 0001-00101[3] in Winchester.

REFERENCES:
1. New Haven - Jacobus, p. 365.
2. Duncan, p. 49, with additional information on Ruth Tuller sent to me by Ruth Duncan.
3. CB Database.

1-3-1-2-2   D63   CB300043

BENJAMIN[5] BONNELL, Esq. (Nathaniel[4], Nathaniel[3], Nathaniel[2], William[1]) was born 23 November 1723[1] in Elizabethtown, Essex (now Union) co, NJ. (This date of birth seems to be generally accepted, but I have not found it in any primary record or any record prior to the 1950s.) About 1745 he married RACHEL VAN WINKLE[1], daughter of Johannes and Magdalene (Speer) Van Winkle[17]. She was born 18 December 1727.[18]

Benjamin Bonnell was prominent in the affairs of Elizabeth Township for many years. His home was in the Springfield Ward, in what is now Summit, NJ, along the Passaic River.[9] He owned a sawmill[6,9] and was part owner, with his brother John, of a gristmill.[9]

His title of "Captain," which appears in documents at least as early as 1765, would indicate leadership service in the Essex co militia. William Parson, Sr., in 1765,[3] Benjamin Pettit in 1769,[4] and Josiah Broadwell in 1774[4] each appointed "my friend Capt. Benjamin Bonnel" to serve as executor of his estate. On 28 October 1765 Benjamin paid £650 for a messuage along the opposite side of the Passaic River in what is now the village of Chatham, Morris co.[10] Tax records for 1778 and 1780 for Morris twp, Morris co, show that he owned about 40 acres of unimproved land and a sawmill there.[6]

He continued to reside in Springfield Ward, however, for the rest of his life. "Capt[n]. Benjamin Bonnell" was taxed in Springfield in February 1779 on 170 acres of land, 4 horses, 9 cattle and 4 pigs, as well as on £1036 loaned out at interest.[5] Because of his age (about 55) he was exempt from military service. On the tax list for February 1780, his livestock was reduced to 2 horses, 8 cattle and 2 pigs, but money at interest had increased to £1636.[5] His name appears on the Springfield tax lists at least through 1796.[7]

From 1780 to 1785, and perhaps earlier, he served as Justice of the Peace in Elizabeth Town.[9]

In some accounts, DAR Lineages, etc., Benjamin is credited with considerable service in the Continental Army during the Revolutionary War. However, in light of his age and exemption from service in 1779 and 1780, it is far more likely that his son Benjamin, Jr., or one or more of the other Benjamin Bonnells in the area was the soldier listed in the records. It is said that Benjamin and six of his sons all took part in the battle of Springfield in June 1780. This is a reasonable assertion, since all able-bodied men were called out to defend their homes from the attack by the British. In the first attack 5000 British soldiers under Lieutenant General Baron von Knyphausen crossed from Staten Island to Elizabethtown Point on June 7 and marched as far as Connecticut Farms, where they burnt most of the homes and other buildings before retreating to Staten Island. A second attempt on June 23 was led by Sir Henry Clinton in an effort to destroy the American base at Morristown. A spirited defense by Continental troops and the local militia halted the British advance at the battle of Springfield. The village of Springfield was put to the torch by the invaders, but General Greene's American troops forced them to give up their mission, putting an end to the last British effort to control any territory in New Jersey.[9,12] This probably represents Benjamin's only service as a soldier during the Revolution. His principal contribution to the war effort was in furnishing supplies, chiefly flour and grain from the gristmill, to the American troops.[9]

Benjamin was a member of the Presbyterian church and served his church as an elder.[11] He was a member of session in the New Providence Church in 1768.[15] He was listed as a contributor in the records of the Madison (Bottle Hill) Presbyterian Church in 1793, 1794 and 1795.[8] His wife Rachel became a member of the Bottle Hill church in 1801, after Benjamin's death.[8] In all probability, their membership was retained in the Presbyterian church at New Providence during his lifetime.

He was drowned in the East River, near New York, with ten others, on 10 November 1798 on a boat crossing from the city to Brooklyn, upon which a number of casks of rum rolled to one side and overturned the vessel[14] (or "in New York Bay"[1,11] or "crossing Hudson River"[9] or "through the overturn of a ferry boat of the Bergen Ferry to Staten Island"). His tombstone read

> "Here lies deposited the remains
> of Benjamin Bonnel, Esq.
> who was by an awful
> dispensation of Providence drowned
> together with 10 others on the
> 10th Nov. 1798
> in the 75th year of his age
> Sudden was the word which call'd his soul away:
> But found him watching, ready to obey."[17]

He was buried in Hillside Cemetery, Madison (Bottle Hill), Morris co, NJ.[17] He did not leave a will, and after his death his widow Rachel declined to take Letters of Administration. She asked that her two sons be appointed, and her sons Benjamin and John were named Administrators.[16] Rachel married (second) Albert Ackerman. She died 18 December 1813[18] (or in 1812 at the age of 85.[14])

Children:
1. 310307. Joanna, b. 4 Dec. 1746[13]; m. 2 Jan. 1764 Matthias Woodruff[11,19]; d. Dec. 1778.
2. 310306. Jane, b. 25 Mar. 1748[13]; m 21 July 1763 Abner Brown.[11,19]
3. 310239. Benjamin, b. 4 Mar. 1751.[8]
4. 310308. Nathaniel, b. 20 Mar. 1753.[13]
5. 310238. Samuel, b. 10 Feb. 1755.[13]
6. 310240. John, b. 18[12] Mar. 1757.[20]
7. 310236. Aaron, b. 4 Mar. 1759.[20]

8. 310312. Rachel, b. 28 Oct. 1760[13]; m. 13 Mar. 1783 Luke Miller[11]; d. 19 Nov. 1797, age 38.
   Children (surname Miller):
   2 sons and 6 daughters.

9. 310311. Paul, b. 7 Nov. 1762.[20]

10. 310237. Sarah, b. 20 Feb. 1765[13]; bapt. 14 Apr. 1765[19]; m. 21 Mar. 1785 Jacob Searing Parsons.[11]
    Children (surname Parsons):[11]

1. William.	3. Nancy.	5. Mariah.
2. Benjamin.	4. James Hervey.	6. Electa.

11. 310313. Rhoda, b. 30 May 1767[13]; bapt. 28 June 1767[19]; m. 17 May 1787 Calvin Morrell.[11,19]

12. 310309. Abigail, b. 9 Aug. 1769[13]; bapt. 17 Sept. 1769[19]; m. 9 May 1790 Jonathan Johnson[19];d. 1859[13].

13. 310310. Mary (Polly), b. 28 Sept. 1772[13]; m. 2 May 1790 Stephen Day.[8,11]
    Children (surname Day):

1. Jane.[11]	4. Barna.[11]	6. Edwin Sayre.[8,11]
2. Elias.[11]	5. Damaris.[8]	7. Lewis.[8,11]
3. Mary.[11]		

REFERENCES:

1. Duncan, pp. 49, 50.
2. DAR
3. NJ Wills - IV, p. 321.
4. NJ Wills - V, pp. 66, 392, 441.
5. Gen Mag of NJ, Vol. 43, No. 2, p. 79.
6. Gen Mag of NJ, Vol. 46, No. 1, p. 35.
7. NJ Tax Lists, pp. 296, 300.
8. Madison Church Records, p. 23.
9. Chatham at War.
10. Morris co, NJ, Deeds, Book A., p. 17.
11. Littell.
12. NJ Collections.
13. CB Database.
14. Hamilton co, OH, - biographical sketch on Mr. and Mrs. Marcus Seneca Bonnell.
15. Amer Fam - Long Island, p. 71.
16. Ltr. 12 May 1969 to Mrs. Russell S. Cooke, Springfield, IL, from Carl M. Williams, editor & publisher of *The New Jersey Genesis Quarterly*, citing File 9068-9071G, New Jersey State Library, the probate record for Benjamin's estate.
17. Lynch, pp. 21, 22.
18. Ancestral line of Gladys Marcella Fenton (b. 9 Feb. 1892, m. 24 Apr. 1920 Edward Shepherd Steebe), sent to me by Homer E. Baldwin, Greensburg, PA, on 2 Nov. 1959. The information was sent to him by Mrs. E. J. Spang, Lakewood, OH.
19. Gen Mag of NJ, Vol. 18, pp. 4, 6, 33, 87, Vol. 19, pp. 19, 21, records of the New Providence Presbyterian Church, in a typed extract sent to me by Claude Bunnell.
20. Rev War pension appl., John Bonnell, Aaron Bonnell, Paul Bonnell.

FIFTH GENERATION

1-3-1-2-5   D64   CB300178

NATHANIEL[5] BONNELL (Nathaniel[4], Nathaniel[3], Nathaniel[2], William[1]) was born in 29 December[14] 1731[9] in Elizabethtown, Essex (now Union) co, NJ. He married (first) 28 Nov. 1750[1], in Morristown, Morris co, NJ, ELIZABETH ALLEN[1], daughter of Jacob Allen[10] of South Hanover, Morris co, NJ. She was born about 1736[2] and died 20 April 1774[2,3]. For his second wife he married, on 24[9] (or14[3]) November 1775[3,9] at New Providence, Essex (now Union) co, NJ, MARY SIMPSON[3], daughter of Alexander Simpson[9].

The census of Morris twp, Morris co, NJ, taken in July 1771 to July 1772, lists "Nathaniel Bunnel" with 3 males under 16, 2 males 16 to 50, 3 females under 16 and 2 females 16 to 50, which exactly corresponds to this family as we know it. At that time Chatham was included in Morris twp.[21]

Nathaniel served in the New Jersey militia, apparently with the rank of captain, since that title was applied to him occasionally in church[3] and tax[6] records as early as April 1774[3]. It is alleged that, when the Revolution began, he enlisted in November 1775 as a private in the 2nd Regiment of the Essex co militia under Capt. Josiah Pierson, and served into January 1776[12]. D. W. White cites "Revolutionary War Records" as the source of this statement. However, sources available to me identify the enlistee only as Nathaniel Bonnell[5]. Unless White found a source that was more specific, I think it is far more likely that this was the son Nathaniel, Jr., age 23, than the father at age 44. Determining which Nathaniel is referred to in a record is frequently very difficult.

Nathaniel's home was the house built, it is said, in 1750 by his father, and still standing (1991) at 32 Watchung Avenue, Chatham, NJ[13]. He lived there as a prominent citizen of the town until his death. He, like his brothers Benjamin and John, engaged in milling operations using water power created by dams built on the Passaic River. Tax records and the deed and mortgage books in Essex and Morris counties show that Nathaniel was the owner, or part owner of the grist mill known as the "Chatham Old Mill" and of a sawmill as well. The New Jersey Journal, Vol. 1, No. 34, 5 October 1779, has the following notice:[14]

> "The subscriber desires to inform the public that a Fulling Mill is erecting at Chatham in Morris Co.
> which will be ready to go in 10 to 15 days. Those people who are pleased to favor him with their
> custom, may depend on being served as soon as possible.   Nathaniel Bonnell"

He took an active part in the political life of the community, serving as Overseer of the Roads in 1771, 1785 and 1786, and as Overseer of the Poor in 1778, 1779 and 1780[12]. In May 1776 he cast his vote as a Whig for Morris co delegates to the New Jersey Provincial Congress, "an essentially revolutionary assembly, separate and distinct from the colonial legislature.[12].

He was a member and a ruling elder[15] of the Presbyterian Church of New Providence (Turkey), NJ, and his children were baptized there[3]. The records of the Presbyterian Church of Bottle Hill, Madison, NJ, show that he was a contributor in 1793[2], and he and both of his wives were buried in the churchyard there[2].

Nathaniel died in Chatham 23 July 1809[2]. He was buried with his first wife in the Presbyterian Churchyard at Madison, Morris co, NJ[2]. In his will dated 10 October 1808, proved 27 July 1809[4], he provided for his wife to have a comfortable living as long as she remained his widow; left £20 each to his son Nathaniel and daughter Elizabeth; divided 58 acres of land in the Great Swamp equally among his sons Gilbert, William, Jacob and Enoch; divided the residue of the estate among all his children except Nathaniel "to whom I have given heretofore what I think proper". "If Jonathan should not be living and had no lawful heirs, the £20 given to my daughter Elizabeth should be paid out of the estate which would have fallen to him." The inventory of his estate, made 9 August 1809, amounted to $518.27[4]. His widow died 16 September 1813 and was buried at Madison[2].

Children (by first wife):
1. 310357. Abigail, b. July 1754[9]; m. 24 Sept. 1775[3], Jacob Minturn (or Minthorn)[3]; d. 3 Sept. 1835[16].
   Children (surname Minturn)[16]:
   1. Barton.
   2. Allen.
   3. Phebe.
   4. Jane.
   5. Bunnel.
   6. George.
   7. Sarah.
2. 310358. Nathaniel, b. 15 June 1756[9].
3. 310359. Caleb Gilbert, b. Nov. 1758[9].
4. 310360. Phebe, b. May 1761[9]; m. William Johnson[9].
   Children (surname Johnson)[19]:
   1. Wickliff.   probably others.
   (Littell[9] lists Theodocia and Abigail Johnson as her children, but no sons.)
5. 310361. Jane, b. 23 Apr. 1763[9,17]; bapt. 5 June 1763[3]; m. 16 Jan. 1782 Samuel Crane[9,17]; d. 26 Mar. 1848[17].
   Children (surname Crane)[17]:
   1. Smith.
   2. Isaac Miller.
   3. Jacob Bonnel.
   4. Joseph Crane.
   5. Elizabeth.
   6. Jonathan.
   7. Samuel.
   8. John.
   9. John.
   10. Jacob Bonnel.
   11. Calvin.
6. 310363. Jonathan, b. Mar. 1765[9]; bapt. 23 June 1765[3].
7. 310365. Jacob, b. May 1767[9]; bapt. 14 June 1767[3].
8. 310368. Elizabeth, b. Aug. 1769[9]; bapt. 15 Oct. 1769[3]; m. 29 July 1787[3] Gabriel Friend[3].
   Children (surname Friend)[18]:
   1. John.
   2. daughter.
   3. Elizabeth.
   4. Jacob.
   5. John.
   6. Jonathan.
   7. Joseph.
   8. Keziah.
   9. Anna.
   10. Rebecca.
   11. Sarah Anne.

Children (by second wife):
9. 310369. William, d. young[9].

10. 310371. Nancy, b. July 1778[9]; m. 28 Feb. 1808[2] Sylvanus Bonnell[9] (1-3-1-2-7-7); d. 4 July 1851.[2]

11. 310370. Chloe, b. Dec. 1779[9], m. about 1798 Abraham Samson[9]; d. 23 May 1866[2,20].

    Children (surname Samson)[2,9]:

1. Julia.	5. Zebra (Sabra).	9. Enoch Nelson.
2. Sally.	6. Aminda (Amanda)	10. Anne Mariah.
3. Aaron Smith.	7. Elizabeth Shaver.	11. Wickliff Condit.
4. Nancy Bonnel.	8. Mary Malvina.	

12. 310372. William, b. Jan. 1783[9]; bapt. 9 Mar. 1783[3].
13. 310373. Enoch, b. 5 Oct. 1784(5 Oct. 1785)[9]; bapt. 28 Nov. 1784[3].

REFERENCES:

1. Morristown, Church Records, The Combined Registers.
2. Madison , Church Records, pp. 26, 275.
3. Gen Mag of NJ, Vol. 17, p. 12, Vol. 18, pp. 3, 4, 6, 33, 37, 38, 91, 92, Vol. 19, pp. 19, 44, records of the New Providence Presbyterian Church, in a typed extract set to me by Claude Bunnell.
4. NJ Wills - Vol. XI, Morris co, NJ, File 1386N.
5. Rev War - NJ - 1, p. 513.
6. Gen Mag of NJ, Vol. 43, No. 2, New Jersey Rateables, 1778-1780, by Kenn Stryker Rodda.
7. New Jersey Tax Lists.
8. Morris co, NJ, Deeds, Book R, p. 341.
9. Littell, pp. 47, 193, 368, 369.
10. Gen Mag of NJ, Vol. 17, No. 1, p. 12.
11. Gen Mag of NJ, Vol. 43, No. 2, p. 80.
12. Chatham at War.
13. Article in the *Sunday Star-Ledger*, Newark, NJ, 15 December 1991, copies sent to me by Clement M. Bonnell III, Richard Lesser and Claude Bunnell. See *Bunnell/Bonnell Newsletter*, Vol. III, No. 1, p. 3.
14. CB Database.
15. Union & Middlesex co, NJ, Hist, p. 348.
16. Champaign co, OH, Deed Book F, p. 298, copy sent to me by Mrs. Charles Gardiner, Morton, IL.
17. *My Father's People*, by Becky Hardin, Mooresville, IN, Library of Congress No. 81-84053, including a photo of Jane (Bonnel) Crane's gravestone, and a transcript of widow Jane Crane's application for Revolutionary War Pension - File No. 4822, Vol. A, p. 153.
18. *Indian Blood*, by Evelyn Guard Olsen, McClain Publishing Co., Parson, WV, pp. 77, 78, sent to me by Bernard V. Mayhle, Seattle, WA.
19. Ltr. 12 April 1965 from J. Clinton Johnson, Lancaster, OH.
20. Duncan, p. 51.
21. NJ Hist Soc, Vol. 63, No. 1, Jan. 1945, p. 27.

1-3-1-2-7 D65 CB300181

JOHN[5] BONNELL (Nathaniel[4], Nathaniel[3], Nathaniel[2], William[1]) was born 26 September 1737[1,9] at New Providence, Elizabethtown, Essex (now Union) co, NJ. He married SARAH CARTER[1] about 1756[10]. She was born about 1737[1,8], daughter of Benjamin Carter[10]. "In the early 1740's

FIFTH GENERATION

James Carter and Benjamin Carter, Sarah's father, purchased large tracts of land from the proprietors on the east side of the Passaic opposite Chatham, with the result that the Carters owned practically the entire valley in which is now the city of Summit, from Morris Avenue to the Morris Turnpike. All the Carter land acquired about 1740 subsequently came to be owned by John Bonnell. John and Sarah lived in the Carter homestead on River Road."[10]

Some DAR records assert that during the Revolution John served as a private in the New Jersey Line[14]. One source refers to him as a captain of militia[12]. *American Families of Historic Lineage* says "From the best authority he was the John Bonnel who served as a private in the Morris county troops during the Revolution."[9] D. W. White also referred to him as a private in the militia and stated that when he died in 1817 he was the last survivor of the Revolutionary veterans from the Chatham area.[11] On the other hand, Stryker lists only one John Bonnell in service during the Revolution.[2] We know from his pension application that John's nephew, known as John, Jr., served in 1775 and in several one-month tours of duty during the war. Another John Bonnell, from Hunterdon co, also left evidence of his service with a pension application. While it is possible, and even likely, that our subject took part in the defense against the British attacks on New Providence and Connecticut Farms, I have seen no evidence to support these assertions of his military service. His principal service to the Revolutionary cause was undoubtedly as a mill operator providing necessary supplies to the army.

He was a prominent and well-to-do farmer and businessman, owner of a sawmill and, with his brother Benjamin, a one-third interest in the grist mill known as the "old Chatham mill", and later as the "Franklin Mill".[4,9,11] He also had a forge for the conversion of iron into bars of metal.[9,11] He dealt largely in land in both Essex and Morris counties,[3,4] as well as in Luzerne and Wayne counties in Pennsylvania.[9,10] He loaned money out at interest secured by mortgages.[6,7] From a reference in his will it would appear that, with his son Israel, he also conducted a retail merchandise operation out of Israel's home in Chatham, a piece of property he had given to Israel in November 1808.[5]

John Bonnell, like most of his family, was Presbyterian, apparently a member of the church at Springfield. In 1793 and in the years following he appears as a contributor on the records of the Presbyterian Church at Madison (Bottle Hill), and his wife Sarah was entered on the rolls there about 1810.[1]

He died 15 December 1817[1,9] at his home in Springfield[9], Essex (now Union) co, NJ, just across the Passaic River from Chatham in Morris co. His widow died 2 September 1824[1,9] at Turkey, Essex co (now New Providence, Union co), NJ. They were buried in the Presbyterian Church graveyard in Madison, Morris co, NJ[1]. John's will, dated 7 September 1811, was probated 3 January 1818. It is lengthy, but it reveals much about his manner of life. Two copies of the will are in my files, one printed in *American Families of Historic Lineage-Long Island*[9], and another printed in *Day Unto Day*[10]. The two versions vary somewhat. I use the former copy for the following, with variants from the latter enclosed in brackets only when the differences are significant:

"In the name of God Amen! I John Bonnel of the Township of Springfield, County of Essex, State of New Jersey, being of sound mind and memory, do make and publish this my Last will and Testament.

1st. It is my will and I do order that all my just debts and funeral expenses be duly paid and satisfied as soon as conveniently be after my decease.

2nd. I give to My Dear Wife Sarah Bonnel my mansion house together with all my Homestead Barns Buildings Tenements and Privileges upon or unto the same belonging and one third of the grist mill [that is to say-the use and profits ariseing therefor I give & bequeath to my aforesaid wife as long as she lives]. One horse and riding chair, three cows, and as much furniture as she wants for her own use. My negro woman Sucke [Luck] and Five hundred dollars in cash to be paid her as follows, one half in three months and the other half in six months after my decease which bequests I give in lieu of Dower out of my estate.

3rd. [I order and direct my Executors herein after named as soon as convenient after my decease to dispose of my moveable property by way of Vendue and likewise to collect in all debts and moneys at Interest in order that it may be immediately disposed of as hereafter directed--excepting only so much as may be sufficient to defray their expenses as nearly as can be ascertained.]

4th. To son Israel all the Land I bought of Dr. Peter Smith lying between lands of Jacob Marrel [Morrell] and Wm. Spencer and also a small piece of land opposite my dwelling house across the river adjoining land of Jacob Marrel [Morrell] at the West end, the River on the south side, the mill pond on the east, and Land of Israel Bonnel on the north. Likewise I give and bequeath to my son Israel all my right in and to the store of goods at his house and all the debts due for goods sold out of the same.

5th. I give and devise to my son Silvanus his heirs and assigns forever all the remainder of my Lands in the village of Chatham. Likewise a small piece of land adjoining the forge Lott and the river that I bought of Thomas Parsal [Parcel] together with the Houses, mills, privileges, and appurtenances to the same belonging.

6th. I give and bequeath to my daughter Johannah the use of the Land which I bought of Israel Day adjoining Lands of Peter and Caleb Dickinson as long as she lives and at her decease my will is that the Land be sold and the money be equally divided among her children and I give to my said daughter Johannah the use of two pair of oxen and waggon. I also give to my said daughter Johannah one hundred dollars yearly and every year during her life the first hundred to be paid in three months after my decease which annuity my will is and I direct the same to be paid by my son Silvanus. I also give and bequeath to my said daughter Johannah's children after her decease each one fifty dollars to be paid to them as they shall respectively arrive to the age of twenty one years and I direct and it is my will that this also be paid by my son Silvanus and his heirs and I do charge the payment of the same and the above annuity which I have given to my daughter Johannah upon and out of the land houses and mills which I have given to my Silvanus in fee.

7th. I give and bequeath to my daughters, Nancy, Elenor, and Salle, their heirs and to my grandchildren Matilda, Joel, Alvea, and John Bonnel all the plantation where my son Jonathan lived except about 23 acres which I heretofore gave to my son Jonathan (now deceased) by Deed which plantation my will is and I direct shall be sold and the money divided among my above said children and grandchildren as follows viz: Two thirds be equally divided between my said daughters Nancy, Elenor, and Salle and the other third to be equally divided between my said grandchildren Matilda, Joel, Alvea, and John Bonnel.

8th. I give and bequeath to my son James' children, Stephen, Elias, Hannah, Nancy, David and Mahlon all the wood land that I bought of Stanberry and Morse adjoining the river by Nathaniel Bonnel's saw mill my will is and I direct the said land be sold and the money to be equally divided between them.

9th. I give and bequeath to all my children and their heirs viz: Nancy, Israel, Silvanus, Johannah, Eleanor [Elenor], and Salle all my lands in Wayne County and Luzerne County in the State of Pennsylvania. The said lands I will to be sold when they shall think it advisable and the money to be divided equally between them.

10th. I give and bequeath to my son James [James' children] and my son Jonathan's children Ichabod excepted my land in the Great Swamp which I bought of Samuel Allen which said land I direct to be sold and the money to be equally divided between my said grandchildren viz: Stephen, Elias, Hannah, Nancy, David, and Mahlon and Matilds [Metilda], Joel, Alvea, and John Bonnel.

11th. I give and bequeath to my grandson Ichabod $25 to be paid in 6 months after my decease.

12th. I give and bequeath to my daughters Nancy, Elenor, and Salle, and my son Israel their heirs and assigns all my Homestead Lands, Buildings, and Tenements lying between Major Israel Days and Matthias Bonnels they to have it at my wife's decease and not before and I will and direct the said Homestead Lands, Buildings, etc., to

150

be sold at my wife's decease and the money to be equally divided between said Nancy Elenor, Salle, and Israel.

13th. All the residue of my estate together with my right and interest in the Morris Turnpike road, which I authorize my executors to sell if it shall appear to them most expedient I give to my daughter Nancy, Elenor, and Salle and my son Israel their heirs and assigns to be equally divided among them excepting out of the same $200 which I give and bequeath to my daughter Johannah.

I appoint my sons Israel and Silvanus and my son-in-law Wm. Day executors of this my testament and last will.

Witnesses: Jacob Potter, Ichabod Potter, Jacob Bonnel.

The inventory of his estate was made by Jacob Potter and Linus Burnet on 31 December 1817[10]:

His wearing apparel	22.00
Horses & horned cattle	334.00
Hay, , & Manure	158.12 ½
Farming Utensils	88.18 ½
Grain in Sheaf & otherwise	423.93 ½
Turnpike Stock	57.62 ½
Chair, Sulkey & Sleigh	59.50
Set of Blacksmith Tools	20.00
One Male Slave	100.00
Cyder, and cyder Spirits	51.50
Potatoes, Turnips, Cabbage	8.62 ½
Beef, Pork, & Poultry	71.25
Household goods	250.00
Rent in arrear	1300.00
	$2943.74 ½

Note that the inventory did not include any of the land.. Also that it mentions a male slave, but not the female slave bequeathed in the will.

The will of the widow Sarah Bonnell, of the township of Springfield, was made 9 August 1824 and filed 21 September 1824. She left bequests to two sons, Israel and Silvanus, and to four daughters, widow Nancy Day, widow Joanna Day, Ellenor Ward, wife of Matthias, and Sally Sayer, wife of Ezekial.[16]

Children:
1. 310316. James, b. 10 Oct. 1758[8,9,10].
2. 310317. Nancy, b. 4 Sept. 1760[8,9,10]; m. 12 Mar. 1780[9] William Day[8,9]; d. 24 Aug. 1853[1,10].
   Children (surname Day)[8,9]:
   1. Foster.   3. Charlotte.   5. Calvin.
   2. Sarah.   4. Lewis.   6. Joanna.
3. 310318. Jonathan, b. 12 May 1763[8,9,10].
4. 310319. Israel, b. 24 May 1765[8,9,10].
5. 310320. Joanna, b. 20 Oct. 1767[8,9,10]; m. Jan. 1785[10] Moses Day[1,10]; d. 23 May 1848[10].

Children (surname Day)[10]:

1. Betsey (Elizabeth).	5. Sylvanus B.	9. Jenette.
2. Charles.	6. William.	10. Emulous Horton.
3. Matthias.	7. Nancy.	11. Thaddeus.
4. James Harvey.	8. Benjamin Franklin.	

6. 310321. Hannah, b. 9 Sept. 1770[8,9,10], d. young[8,9].

7. 310322. Sylvanus, b. 28 Feb. 1773[8,9,10].

8. 310323. Eleanor, b. 21 Jan. 1776[8,9,10]; m. Matthias Ward[1,8,9].

Children (surname Ward)[8,9]:

1. Philip.	4. Mahetabel.	7. Laura.
2. Mahlon.	5. Harriet.	8. Enos.
3. Sarah.	6. Louise.	9. Juliette.

9. 310324. David, b. 5 Sept. 1778[8,9,10].

10. 310325. Sally (Sarah), b. 28 July 1781[8,9,10]; m. 7 Feb. 1808[1] Ezekiel Sayre[1,8]; d. 13 June 1855[15] (or 20 Jan. 1850?[9]).

Children (surname Sayre)[8]:

1. Sally Day.	3. Catherine.	5. John Edgar.
2. Electa.	4. David B.	6. Lewis.

11. 310326. Caty[8] (Catherine[10]), b. 1 Feb. 1784[8,9,10]; d. young[8].

REFERENCES:

1. Madison Church Records, pp. 23, 24, 25, 26, 102, 103, 279, 325.
2. Rev War - NJ - 1, p. 513.
3. NJ Tax Lists.
4. Gen Mag of NJ, Vol. 43, p. 80, and Vol. 45, p. 20, *New Jersey Rateables*, by Kenn Stryker-Rodda.
5. Morris co Deeds, Book P, p. 109; Book R, p. 359.
6. Morris co Mortgages, Book F, p. 346.
7. Essex co Mortgages, Book G, p. 309; Book I, p. 63.
8. Littell, pp. 50, 118, 120, 122, 372, 462, 463.
9. Amer Fam - Long Island.
10. Day.
11. Chatham at War.
12. Fern Bonnell.
13. Duncan, pp. 51, 52.
14. DAR, Vol. 88, p. 280, Vol. 97, p. 79.
15. CB Database.
16. NJ Wills to 1900, in Trenton State Library, 11551G, abstract sent to me by Claude Bunnell.

1-3-1-4-2 CB300191

DAVID[5] BONNELL (Isaac[4], Nathaniel[3], Nathaniel[2], William[1]) was born 24 February 1739[1] in New Jersey, probably in Elizabethtown, Essex (now Union) co.

REFERENCES:

1. Bible Records and Wills, Boudinot Chapter DAR, Elizabeth, NJ. Wade, Bonnell & Crane Bible. Records from Bible owned by Helen Bertha Crane, 220 South Broad St., Elizabeth, NJ. Copied by Evelyn Leary Ogden. Copied and sent to me by Homer Baldwin in 1959.

NOTE: See 1-3-7-7-1, CB300147. It is entirely possible that this is the David Bonnell who and lived and died in Mendham twp, Morris co, NJ. No contemporary evidence I have seen makes either identification more likely than the other.

1-3-1-4-3   CB300192

WILLIAM[5] BONNELL (Isaac[4], Nathaniel[3], Nathaniel[2], William[1]) was born 28 November 1740[1] in New Jersey, probably in Elizabethtown, Essex (now Union) co.

REFERENCES:

1. Bible Records and Wills, Boudinot Chapter DAR, Elizabeth, NJ. Wade, Bonnell & Crane Bible. Records from Bible owned by Helen Bertha Crane, 220 South Broad St., Elizabeth, NJ. Copied by Evelyn Leary Ogden. Copied and sent to me by Homer Baldwin in 1959.

1-3-1-4-5   CB300194

ISAAC[5] BONNELL (Isaac[4], Nathaniel[3], Nathaniel[2], William[1]) was born 8 December 1743[1] at Elizabeth, Essex (now Union) co, NJ. He married PUAH ABIGAIL WOODRUFF[2], daughter of Timothy and Elizabeth (Parsons) Woodruff[2]. She was born about 1745[2] and died 13 June 1777[3]. Isaac is apparently the Isaac Bonnel, Jr., householder, who was listed among the rateables in Elizabeth twp, Town Ward, Essex co, NJ, in January 1779 and February 1780[4]. He appears in the 1830 census in Elizabeth: one male between 40 and 50 and one male between 80 and 90[5]. He died 12 March 1833 in the 90th year of his age[6]. He was buried in the cemetery of the First Presbyterian Church of Elizabeth[6]. His gravestone read, "The Grave of NOAH BONNELL who died April 3rd 1856 In the 86th Year of his age   Also His Father ISAAC BONNELL died March 12th 1833 In the 90th Year of his age."[6]

Children:
1. 310341. David[7], b. about 1769[9].
2. 310343. Noah[7], b. about Oct. 1770[9].
3. 310342. Seth[7], b. 9 Nov. 1775[9].
4. 310344. Betsy[7].

REFERENCES:

1. Bible Records and Wills, Boudinot Chapter DAR, Elizabeth, NJ. Wade, Bonnell & Crane Bible. Records from Bible owned by Helen Bertha Crane, 220 South Broad St., Elizabeth, NJ. Copied by Evelyn Leary Ogden. Copied and sent to me by Homer Baldwin in 1959.
2. Woodruff. See *Bunnell/Bonnell Newsletter*, Vol. III, No. 3, p. 6.

3. NEHGR, Vol. 44, p. 357.
4. Gen Mag of NJ, Vol. 43, p. 30, *New Jersey Rateables, 1778-1780*, by Kenn Stryker-Rodda.
5. 1830 Federal Census, Elizabethtown, Union co, NJ, in the records compiled by Ruth C. Duncan.
6. Elizabeth, NJ, Cemeteries. Grave #1734 in the First Presbyterian Churchyard.
7. Will of Timothy Woodruff, abstracted in New Jersey Post-Revolutionary Documents, Calendar of
    Wills, 1796-1800, copy sent to me by Paula Sacco, Pittsburgh, PA.
8. Duncan, p. 55, in which this Isaac (with his family) is incorrectly identified as Isaac Bonnell,
    1-3-2-2-3, CB300164.
9. CB Database.

1-3-1-4-8   CB300197

SAMUEL[5] BONNELL (Isaac[4], Nathaniel[3], Nathaniel[2], William[1]) was born 1 October 1750[1] in New Jersey, probably in Elizabethtown, Essex (now Union) co. He is apparently the Samuel Bonnell, son of Isaac, who was baptized with his sister Mary in St. John's Episcopal Church, Elizabeth, Essex (now Union) co, NJ, on 19 August 1755[2,3]. He was married and had several children[4]. He is also apparently the Samuel Bonnel, householder, who was listed among the rateables of Elizabeth twp, Town Ward, Essex co, NJ, in January 1779 and February 1780[5]. In 1780 he is listed as owner of 1 acre of land[5]. His wife died 17 August 1788[4], and he died 18 November 1798 in Elizabeth[4]. On 11 January 1799, Robinson Thomas was appointed administrator, together with Moses Austin and Samuel Smith, to make an inventory of Samuel's estate. No record exists of the inventory or its disposition to heirs[3].

Children:
1. child, d. 18 Aug. 1777[4].
2. child, d. 18 May 1789[4].
   others?

REFERENCES:
1. Bible Records and Wills, Boudinot Chapter DAR, Elizabeth, NJ. Wade, Bonnell & Crane Bible.
    Records from Bible owned by Helen Bertha Crane, 220 South Broad St., Elizabeth, NJ.
    Copied by Evelyn Leary Ogden. Copied and sent to me by Homer Baldwin in 1959.
2. IGI-NJ, Christenings in St. John Episcopal Church, Elizabeth, NJ.
3. CB Database.
4. NEHGR, Vol. 44, p. 359, and Vol. 45, pp. 46, 50.
5. Gen Mag of NJ, Vol. 43, p. 30, New Jersey Rateables, 1778-1780, by Kenn Stryker-Rodda.

1-3-1-7-1   D66   CB300135

STEPHEN[5] BUNNELL (James[4], Nathaniel[3], Nathaniel[2], William[1]) was born 6 July[22] 1731[8,22] at Scotch Plains,[8] Essex (now Union) co, NJ. Stephen's wife was MARY _____, as attested by several deeds in[4] Ohio. I find no record of their marriage, which must have taken place in New Jersey. Several references[8,10] say that she was a widow, MARY (DANIELS) BLACKFORD, and

I don't know any reason to question it. The earliest record I have found which identifies her is the paper labeled "Notes on Family" inserted in the Bunnel-Swain Family Bible,[8] published in 1842. Nothing indicates when these "Notes" were compiled, but certainly it was long after the event, and probably long after most of the entries in the Bible record.

It is asserted that Mary was the daughter of Ebenezer and Mary Daniels,[10] of Piscataway, Middlesex co, NJ, and the widow of Nathaniel Blackford,[10] also of Piscataway, just across the county line from Westfield, Essex co, where Stephen was born and raised. Assuming this to be so, we are faced with a problem. (See my article in *The Bunnell/Bonnell Newsletter,* Vol. VII, No. 2, pp. 25, 26.[23]) Nathaniel Blackford and Mary Daniels were married 20 August 1759 in the Scotch Plains Baptist Church in Westfield[11]. She was his second wife[12]. His first wife, Frances Leforge,[13] was apparently the mother of his children[12]. Nathaniel died in March or April 1764,[12] and Mary could not have been married to Stephen Bunnell until after that date.

However, most of the Family Group Sheets I have received from various correspondents[14-19] give birthdates for the first four children of Stephen and Mary as abt 1755, abt 1759, abt 1761, and abt 1764. Based on these dates, a marriage date for Stephen and Mary is suggested as about 1754, manifestly impossible for the widow Blackford. There are three possibilities:

    1. The birth dates for James, Jonas and Brazilla and David may be incorrect. The various lists I have seen[14-19] seem to have come from a single source, and none is supported by any evidence of birthdate or age at any period of life, not even a census record. James was married, but I don't find a date. Brazilla never married. Jonas married around 1790, when he would have been 31. David married in 1796 when he would have been 32. These seem like late first-time marriages to me.
    2. Stephen may have had another wife before he married Mary. It seems unlikely that he remained single until age 33 in 1764, the earliest he could have married Mary (Daniels) Blackford. If there was a first wife, she could have been the mother of the first three or four children, assuming their birthdates are correct.
    3. The first marriage, if there was one, may have been childless, and Mary (Daniels) Blackford could have been the mother of all the children, IF the birthdates conform to the revised Family Group Sheet[20] sent to me by Nona Bassett, Merced, CA. The evidence for her set of dates is no better, but they seem to fit the situation more reasonably, and I have chosen to use them in the list below. Note that Stephen's will lists Stephen, Jr. (who was born in 1767) as the second son. It must be recognized, however, that other evidence may be found which will correct or confirm this conclusion.

During the Revolutionary War Stephen served for a time as a private in Capt. Samuel Jones's company, Lt. Col. Joseph Hasbrouck's Fourth Regiment of the militia of Orange co, NY[2,10].

His father's will, proved 16 October 1788,[1] provided that Stephen was to have part of the plantation "where I live" along land of John Shotwell of 80 acres. It was about this time that Stephen and his family, together with other families from East Jersey, removed to a new settlement in Mays Lick, in what was then Mason co, VA, but is now in Mason co, KY. This part of Virginia was admitted to the Union as the state of Kentucky on 1 June 1792. That year he appears on the tax records of Mason co, KY, for the first time, with 265 acres of land, 45 head of stock, and three black males, apparently slaves[9].

Prior to 1804 Stephen purchased land in Adams co, OH, but apparently never moved there. On 12 February 1805 Stephen and Mary Bunnell, of Mason co, KY, sold 21 acres of this land[4]. In October 1808 Stephen and Mary Bunnell, Sr., of Mason co, KY, sold 125 acres on the Ohio Brush Creek to their youngest son Nathaniel[4]. Then, on 2 March 1809 Stephen and Mary Bunnell of Mayslick, Mason co, KY, sold 104 acres in Meigs twp, Adams co, OH, at the mouth of Cedar Creek[4].

Stephen continued to be taxed every year in Mason co, KY, until 1809; in the latter year no land was mentioned. Around 1808 they removed from Kentucky to Warren co, OH, locating on section 10, Clear Creek twp[21]. He is included on the 1810 tax list of Franklin twp, Warren co[5].

Stephen died in Clear Creek twp, Warren co in late 1812 or early 1813[7]. He and his wife, who died before him, were both buried in the old Clearcreek Baptist Cemetery in Ridgeville, Warren co[8]. His will, dated 13 October 1812 and probated 16 February 1813, reads as follows:[7]

"At a Court of Common pleas held at Lebanon in the County of Warren within the State of Ohio on the sixteenth day of February A.D. 1813. Were Present:
The Hon. Francis Dunlavy Esqr. presiding Judge, Ignatius Brown, Jacob D. Lowe and George Harlan, Esquires, Associate Judges. The following will was proven in open court by two of the subscribing witnesses, to wit, Fergus McLean and John Blair, on the 16th February A.D. 1813, which will is in following words, to wit,

In the name of God Amen. I Stephen Bunnell Sen[r] of Warren County and State of Ohio being in a lingering state of health do make and declare this writing to be my last will and Testament as follows, viz, in the first place I do give devise and bequeth that my daughter Rhoda Bunnel shall have fifty dollars of the property as money that I leave at my death and to James Bunnel my Son one dollar and to Stephen Bunnel my Son one dollar and Jonas Bunnel my Son one dollar and to David Bunnel my Son one dollar and to Nathaniel Bunnel my Son one dollar and then that Mary Bunnel my daughter shall have all the Ballance of my estate whether personal or real money or effects whatsoever nature or kind they may be or whatsoever they may be found and I do hereby direct that the Executors of this my last will Testament as soon as conveniently after my death pay all and every such Legacies or bequests that is mentioned in this writing which is my last will and testament. And I do nominate and appoint Nathaniel Bunnel my son and Ephraim Blackford husband to Mary my Daughter to be executor of this my last will and Testament and do hereby revoke all former wills that I have heretofore made and make and declare this writing to be my last will and testament. In witness I Stephen Bunnel Sen[r] have set my hand and seal this thirteenth day of October in the Year of our Lord one thousand eight hundred and twelve.

Stephen Bunnel

Signed sealed and delivered by Stephen Bunnel when perfectly in his senses in presence of us whose names we have subscribed here as witnesses in the same---witnesses' names.
Luther Russel
Fergus McLean
John Blair"

His son Brazilla, who is not mentioned in the will, had died in 1796.

Children (birthdates are very tentative):
1. 310272. James, b. about 1765[20] (or about 1755[14-19]).
2. 310273. Stephen, b. 25 June 1767[8, 14-19, 20].
3. 310274. Jonas, b. about 1769[20] (or about 1759[14-19] or 29 Aug. 1759[22]).
4. 310275. Brazilla, b. about 1771[20] (or about 1761[14-19]).
5. 310276. David, b. about 1773[20] (or about 1764[14-19]).
6. 310278. Rhoda, b. about 1777[20] (or about 1780[14-19]); m. Amos Hart[8].
7. 310277. Nathaniel, b. 3 July 1778[14-19, 20].
8. 310279. Mary, b. about 1779[20] (or about 1782[14-19])(or 21 July 1773[22]); m. Ephraim Blackford[7]; d. 28 Mar. 1828[10].

REFERENCES:
1. NJ Wills - Vol. VII. Will of James Bonnell, 28 May 1788, proved 16 Oct. 1778.
2. Rev War - NY, pp. 161, 162.
3. Kentucky Ancestors, Vol. 3, No. 2, Oct. 1967, p. 52: Mason County Kentucky Court & Other Records, contrib. by Mrs. Lula Reed Boss, Maysville, KY. Deed Book H, p. 377. Sent to me by Marjorie C. Gibbs, Union Springs, NY.
4. Adams Co., OH Deeds, 1797-1806 and Adams Co., OH Deeds, 1806-1812, by T. L. C. Genealogy, Miami Beach, FL, 1990, Vol 4, p. 187, Vol. 5, p. 27, Vol. 6, pp. 348, 393. Sent to me by Christine D. Kraft, Lawrence, KS.
5. Early Ohio Tax Records, compiled by Esther Weygandt Powell, 1971, p. 449, published by the Ohio Historical Society. Sent to me by Christine D. Kraft.
6. Ohio, The Cross Road of Our Nation, Records & Pioneer Families, by Mrs. LeMaster, January-March, 1964, p. 2. Warren Co. 1810 Tax List. Sent to me by Doris Bunnell Thomas, Garden Grove, CA.
7. Warren co, OH, Will Book 1, pp. 41, 42, 43, photocopied and sent to me by Claude A. Bunnell.
8. Bunnel-Swain Bible Records. Bible published by H & E Phinney's, Cooperstown, NY, 1842. Original owner was Merritt Bunnel, grandson of Stephen. Owned by the Warren County Historical Society in 1957. Copy of records sent to me by Mrs. Lyle A. Snyder , Fellsmere, FL.
9. Mason co, KY, Tax Book, 1790-1810, on LDS Film # 008,400, extracted and sent to me by Mrs. William S. George, Phoenix, AZ.
10. Duncan, p. 52.
11. NJ Marriages, p. 647.
12. NJ Wills - IV, pp. 44, 45.
13, NJ Wills - II, p. 297 and NJ Wills - III, p. 195.
14, Ltr. 25 Feb. 1960 from Homer Baldwin - line of Mrs. Charles (Nettie) Glaser.
15. Ltr. 1961 from Mable Mae (Bunnell) McClamrock.
16. Ltr. 19 Sept. 1967 from Nina Osborn Roberts.
17. Ltr. 5 Apr. 1987 from John Paul Grady.
18. Ltr. 6 June 1984 from Judith L. Osborn to Ruthelle Finnerty. Ref: the records of Mable Mae (Bunnell) McClamroch.

19. Family Group Sheet compiled by Nona Bassett. Ref: Nina O. Roberts.
20. Revised Family Group Sheet compiled by Nona Bassett. No references.
21. *History of Warren co, OH*, W. H. Beers & Co., 1882, A Reproduction by Unigraphic, Inc., 1971, pp. 894, 895, sent to me by Mrs. Harry Atleson, Cuyahoga Falls, OH.
22. CB Database.
23, Bunnell/Bonnell Newsletter, Vol. VII, No. 2, pp. 25, 26.

1-3-1-7-3   D67   CB300134

ABRAHAM[5] BONNELL (James[4], Nathaniel[3], Nathaniel[2], William[1]) was born 3 September 1736[7] (or 27 August 1736[11]) at Scotch Plains, Westfield twp, Essex (now Union co), NJ. According to a reference in his father's will, Abraham sold some land to his father on 29 April 1760.[1] Soon after this he married JANE JENKINS, who was born about 1745[5]. He is probably the Abram Bunnell who enlisted 3 March 1776[8] as a private in the Essex co militia during the Revolution,[6] but his service was probably brief. He was exempt from military service in March 1779 and February 1780 when he was taxed in Westfield on 39 acres of improved land, 1 horse and 3 cattle.[2] In 1780 he had in addition 2 hogs.[2] Under the terms of his father's will in 1788, Abraham inherited the center portion of the homestead at Scotch Plains, between the portions of his brothers Stephen and Daniel.[1] He is found in the tax lists of Westfield, Essex co, NJ, in 1796, 1810, 1811, 1812, 1813 and 1815.[3] He seems also to have owned some land in Chatham, Morris co, since he appears on a tax list there in 1814.[3]

Abraham wrote his will on 27 September 1817:

> "In the Name of God, Amen. I Abraham Bonnel of the Township of Westfield, County of Essex and State of New Jersey do make and publish this my last will & Testament in manner & form following:
>
> 1st. I order all my just debts and funeral charges to be paid out of my moveable estate.
>
> 2d. I give and bequeath unto my wife Jane Bonnel two cows, one horse & riding chair, bed- bedstead & cord, bedding & curtains, & a sufficiency of household furniture to keep house with for her to use and dispose of as she thinks proper, also I give to my said wife Jane Bonnel the whole use of my house and plantation as long as she remains my widow.
>
> 3d. I give and bequeath to my son Stephen Bonnel a lot of land with the dwelling house and all the buildings thereon where I now live, Beginning at Jotham Meekers corner being a stone, thence S.E. (allowing the variation) one hundred feet, thence S.W. (allowing the variation) two hundred feet, thence N.W. (allowing the variation) four hundred & forty six feet, and from thence two hundred feet to the Street, and from thence to the place of Beginning which lot of land with all the buildings &c. thereon I give to him and to his heirs and assigns forever.
>
> 4th. I give and bequeath unto my four sons James Bonnel, Samuel Bonnel, William Bonnel and Stephen Bonnel all the remainder of my lands and tenements to be equally divided between them in quality to them and to their heirs & assigns forever, and I do hereby appoint Jotham Frazee Esqr., Rueben Woodruff and David Osborn as commissioners to make said division and that their judgement shall be final.
>
> 5th. I give and bequeath unto my son Abraham Bonnel twenty five dollars if he should return home in three years after my decease, if not it is my will that the said twenty five dollars be paid to his daughter Julian Bonnel.

6th. I give to my daughter Susanna Bishop fifty dollars out of my moveable estate to her, her heirs and assigns forever.

7th. I give unto my daughter Elizabeth Whitehead one dollar out of my moveable estate to her, her heirs and assigns forever.

8th. I give to my grand son Ezra Fatout, when he arrives at full age, Fifty dollars to be paid out of my moveable estate to him, his heirs & assigns forever.

9th. I give to my grand daughter Rebecca Blackford fifty dollars to be paid out of my moveable estate, to her and her heirs and assigns forever.

10th. I give to my grand daughter Julian Bonnel fifty dollars to be paid out of my moveable estate to her & to her heirs & assigns forever.

11th. The remainder of my moveable estate that shall remain after the aforesaid legacies is paid out it is my will that it should be equally divided among my four sons, namely, James Bonnel, Samuel Bonnel, William Bonnel & Stephen Bonnel.

12th. I hereby appoint & constitute David Osborn and Dennis Cole referees to decide all matters of difference should there any arise in the settlement of my estate among my legatees or between the legatees & Executors hereinafter named and their judgement shall be final & decisive.

13th. I hereby appoint Reuben Woodruff & my son Stephen Bonnel Executors of this my last will and Testament hereby revoking all former wills by me made.

In Witness whereof I have hereto set my hand and seal this twenty-seventh day of September in the year of our Lord One thousand eight hundred & Seventeen.
Signed, sealed published & declared by
the sd. Abrm. Bonnel to be his testament
& last will in presence of us.
Jacob Stanberry, Isaac Miller,   Abraham Bonnel (L.S.)"[4]
Jacob F. Stites.

Jane (Jenkins) Bonnell died before her husband. Her gravestone read "This stone erected to the memory of Jane wife of Abraham Bonnell who died July 5, 1819 in the 74th year of her age."[5]   Abraham died 5 February 1820[9] at 83 years 5 months and 8 days[11]. They were buried in the Scotch Plains Baptist Churchyard[11]. His will was probated in Essex co on 10 February 1820.[4]

The following list of children has some documentary support, primarily Abraham's will, but much of it depends on data provided by Abraham's great grandson George Boardman Bunnell and by the research of Homer E. Baldwin, a descendant of Susannah (Bonnell) Bishop.

Children:
    1. 310398. Rebecca[10] or Mary[12], m. _____ Blackford; d. before 1817[4].
          Children (surname Blackford):[4]
          1. Rebecca.
    2. 310395. Susannah[4], b. 15 Feb. 1765[9]; m. 31 Aug. 1783 James Bishop[9];
          d. 24 May 1836.[9]
          Children (surname Bishop):[9]
          1. Moses.   3. James.   5. Mary.
          2. Abraham.   4. Rachel.
    3. 310399. Nathaniel, b. 1766; d. 3 Nov. 1776, age 10 years[5].
    4. 310391. James[4], b. 1772[7].

5. 310400. Sarah, b. 1772; d. 3 Nov. 1776. age 4 years[5].

6. Abraham, d. in infancy[9].

7. 310594. Abraham[4].

8. 310396. Elizabeth[4], b. about 1780[9], m. _____ Whitehead[4]. (George Boardman Bunnell said she was married three times.[12])

9. 310392. Samuel[4], b. 1781[9].

10. 310393. William[4], b. 25 December 1782[13].

11. 310397. Esther[9], b. abt. 1786; m. Aaron Faitout[9]; d. 27 Dec. 1804[9].
    Children (surname Fatout):[4]
    1. Ezra.

12. 310390. Stephen[4], b. about 1789[9].
    Duncan[10] adds a 13th child, Daniel, but I find no other reference to him.

REFERENCES:

1. NJ Wills - Vol. VII, Will of James Bonnell.
2. Gen Mag of NJ, Vol. 43, No. 3, p. 132, New Jersey Rateables, 1778-1780, by Kenn Stryker-Rodda.
3. New Jersey Tax Lists.
4. Will of Abraham Bonnel, docket #3092, A True Copy from the Surrogate of Essex County, NJ, sent to me by Alice Weigand, Spokane, WA, 15 Feb. 1992.
5. Gravestones in the Scotch Plains Baptist Cemetery copied by Frederick Conkling and sent to me by Homer E. Baldwin.
6. Rev War - NJ - 1, p. 525.
7. IGI-NJ.
8. Union & Middlesex co, NJ, Hist.
9. The Bonnell-Bunnell Line of Homer E. Baldwin of Greensburg, PA, compiled and sent to me by Homer Baldwin, along with supportive correspondence 1959 to 1965.
10. Duncan, p. 53.
11. CB Database.
12. Ltrs. 6 Jan. 1908 and 3 July 1911 from George Boardman Bunnell to John A. Biles.
13. Ltr. 22 July 1987 from Connie Wilson, El Cerrito, CA, citing LDS Library Film 909298 on Wills, Marriages and Deaths, Crawford co, PA, 1852-1854.

1-3-1-7-8 D68 CB300136

DANIEL[5] BONNELL (James[4], Nathaniel[3], Nathaniel[2], William[1]) was born 30 March 1751[1,2] in Scotch Plains, Westfield, Elizabethtown, Essex (now Union) co, NJ. During the Revolution he served as a private at various times in the Continental Army, in the Essex co militia, and in Capt. Moses Munson's company, Eastern Battalion of the Morris co militia[7]. He appears as a single male on the tax list for Elizabeth twp, Westfield Ward in March 1779[3]. On 20 June 1779[2], in the Westfield Presbyterian Church, he married MARTHA HEWES or HUGHES[2]. She was born 14 June 1761[1] in New Jersey. In February 1780 Daniel was again listed among the taxables in Westfield Ward, this time as a householder, no longer a single male, with 1 cow and 1 pig[3]. He appears in the 1781 tax list in Westfield ward also[4]. In 1786 he was a member of the Scotch

Plains Baptist Church in Elizabeth twp[2]. His father's will, probated in 1788, left him one third of his father's "plantation."[5] In 1793 his name was listed on the roster of the militia of Essex co, NJ[6].

In a query published in the journal *Genealogy and History* in 1947, a great great granddaughter of Daniel cited a family tradition: "He eloped ca 1780 with Martha Hughes, b ca 1751 of a Tory family; & it is presumed they married in NJ; may have lived in Scotch Plains (now in Union co). With family ca 1794-5 left NJ & lived a year near Lexington, Fayette co, KY. Daniel in meantime secured land grant in Butler co, OH, cleared the land & built a cabin; returned to KY; thence journeyed to NJ to sell land owned there; on return trip was murdered. Widow Martha (& posthumous dau.) 1796-7 left KY for the new home in Ohio where Martha may have m again. Daniel & Martha had 4 dau's & 5 sons, including Matthew and Samuel. Samuel (next to the youngest child) was b 23 Oct. 1795. . . Matthew Bounell b 7 Aug. 1785 near Elizabeth, NJ. . . "[16]

However, it would appear that his land was in Columbia twp, Hamilton co, OH, rather than in Butler co. Also, it is doubtful that he was murdered. The *Freeman's Journal* of Saturday 27 October 1798 reported that "Thursday last a man by the name of Daniel Bunnel, who formerly lived at Columbia, was picked up in the Ohio, a small distance above that place, drowned: he lay in 3 or 4 inches of water, beside a skiff in which he was descending the river--an inquest was held on the body, their verdict accidental death. He had some whisky on board, of which, probably he drank too freely, and being alone fell a victim to his own indiscretion."[8]

Thus, his death occurred on or before 25 October 1798. On 7 November 1798 the widow Martha Bonnell and Ephraim Blackford were appointed administrators of his estate in Hamilton co, OH[9]. In 1799 his widow appeared as a petitioner in Hamilton co[9]. The inventory on Daniel's estate was presented to the Probate Court of Hamilton co by Ephraim Blackford on 10 April 1799[9]. On 15 February 1811, in court in Warren co, OH, guardians were provided for the four youngest children[14]. Noah and Daniel chose George Harrisbarger for their guardian, and Samuel, Daniel's twin, chose Adam Keever. The court appointed George Harrisbarger as guardian for Catherine. Martha (Hughes) Bonnell married (second) Samuel Foote, as his second wife[2]. She died 20 May 1838 in Warren co, OH[2]. She was buried in Springboro Cemetery in Warren co[15].

Children:
1. 310413. Mary, m. Sept. 1799 Shobal Vail[10]; d. 1851[10].
2. 310414. Matthew[11], b. 7 Aug. 1785[2,16].
3. 310416. Abigail, b. 9 Jan. 1792[1]; m. 24 Mar. 1808 George Keever[12]; d. 25 Oct. 1852[1].
    Children (surname Keever)[13]:
    1. Martin.   2. Moses H.
4. 310417. Noah, b. Apr. 1794[14].
5. 310415. Samuel[16], b. 25 Oct. 1796[14].
6. 310418. Daniel, b. 25 Oct. 1796[14].
7. 310419. Catherine, b. posthumously 25 Mar. 1799[14]; m. 19 Nov. 1815 John Milton Bunnell[12] (1-3-1-7-1-2-2); d. 3 Jan. 1859[15].
    perhaps others.

REFERENCES:
1. Virkus, Vol. VII, p. 412.
2. Duncan, p. 53.
3. Gen Mag of NJ, Vol. 43, No. 3, p. 131, New Jersey Rateables, 1778-1780, by Kenn Stryker-Rodda.
4. New Jersey Tax Lists.
5. NJ Wills - Vol. VII, copies sent to me by Homer E. Baldwin, Greensburg, PA, and Paula Sacco, Pittsburgh, PA.
6. NJ in 1793, p. 135.
7. Rev War - NJ - 1, pp. 158, 525.
8. Freeman's Journal, Vol. III, No. 19, Saturday, 27 Oct. 1798, photocopy sent to me by Claude A. Bunnell.
9. Abstract of Book 1 & Book A, Probate Record 1791-1826, Hamilton co, OH, pp. 51, 53, copied and sent to me by Mrs. Harry Atleson, Cuyahoga Falls, OH.
10. *History of Butler co, OH*, p. 654, copy sent to me by Claude A. Bunnell.
11. *The National Cyclopedia of American Biography*, Vol. XLI, p. 193.
12. *Warren co, OH, Marriage Records*, compiled by Willard Heiss, 1977, copied and sent to me by Mrs. Harry Atleson.
13. Beers' *History of Warren co, OH*, p. 912, copied and sent to me by Mrs. John Hegeman, Dayton, OH.
14. *Gateway to the West*, Vol. X, 1977, p. 55, Warren co, OH, Guardianships, 1804-1817., copied and sent to me by Ellen Dorn, Alhambra CA.
15. CB Database.
16. *Genealogy and History*, 15 Feb. 1947, Washington, DC, query submitted by a daughter of Thomas Aaron Bounell, M.D., great grandson of Daniel, copied and sent to me by Claude A. Mitchell, Muskegon, MI.

1-3-2-2-1   D69   CB300042

ABRAHAM[5] BONNELL (Abraham[4], Isaac[3], Nathaniel[2], William[1]) was born 4 August 1732[1] in Chesterfield, Burlington co, NJ. Perhaps as early as 1740 his parents moved to Kingwood, Hunterdon co, NJ. In the late 1750s he married ELIZABETH FOSTER[3], daughter of Abraham and Elizabeth (Moore) Foster[4]. She was born 17 May 1743[1] in Southampton, Suffolk co, Long Island, NY[4].

Abraham served as a lieutenant during the French and Indian War in 1758[17]. At the early age of twenty years he had begun the purchase of large tracts of land from the West Jersey Society[13]. By the time he was forty he had bought almost 2000 acres, most of which he sold, as favorable opportunity presented itself[13].

He established himself as a tavern keeper and had a license, perhaps in company with his father, to operate the Boars Head Tavern, the location of which is not known[13]. However, in 1767 he purchased the property ever since known as the Bonnell Tavern at Clinton in Hunterdon co[13]. (Other sources say that this property was part of the land bought by his father on 16 December 1752[9], and that his father gave it to him[11].) Abraham maintained his license at the tavern in

Clinton for the rest of his life[13]. His application for the license in 1768 has been preserved as follows:[13]

> "To the honourable the Judges of the Court of Quarter Sessions for the County of Hunterdon now convened at Trenton - - -
> "The Petition of the Subscriber Hunbly Sheweth - - -
> "That your Petitioner has for several Years past been favour'd with a Licence to keep a publick House in the Township of Bethlehem, and having hitherto preserved the good oppinion of his Customers, humbly hopes your Honours will indulge him with a Licence for the ensuing Year and Your Petitioner as in duty bound will ever pray.
> "May 2d, 1768 - - -   /s/ Abrm Bonnel
>
> "We the subscribers do recommend the above Abraham Bonnell as a person well qualified for keeping a Publick House, and hopes your honours will grant him a Licence for that purpose - - -"

The signatures of the following subscribers were listed: James Clifford, Arch. Stewart, Nath. Dunham, Adam Hope, Francis Quick, Danel Donham, David McKinney and Joseph Gordin.

The tavern was the voting place for the northern part of Hunterdon co, and in 1770 it was chosen by the township committeeman as the Bethlehem Township meeting place[13]. Abraham became an active leader in the growing discontent with British rule, and his tavern was a center of the resistance movement. It was here in 1775 that the men of the community met to organize the first regiment of Minute Men in New Jersey, after news of the battle of Lexington arrived[13].

During the American Revolution he was a member of the Provincial Congress at Trenton, NJ, in 1775[17]. He was a member of the Sons of Liberty, one of three chosen to represent lower Hunterdon co, NJ, at the meeting in Bethlehem twp 11 March 1776[13]. He "served as a Lieutenant Colonel, Colonel Joseph Beavers's Second Regiment, Hunterdon County New Jersey Militia, 1776; Lieutenant Colonel, Colonel Mark Thompson's Regiment, New Jersey Militia, 1776; (two thousand men were detached under ordinance of July 18, 1776, for service in the Flying Camp; regiment consisted of two companies from Somerset County, two companies from Sussex County, and four companies from Hunterdon County;) in service until October 7, 1776; Lieutenant Colonel, Colonel Beavers's Second Regiment, Hunterdon County New Jersey Militia, January 31 to March 3, 1777, and served at Millstone; stationed at Alexandria, Hunterdon County, May, 1777; (commission as Lieutenant Colonel dated May 6, 1777;) on rolls, October, 1777; stationed at Alexandria, Hunterdon County, April, 1778; in service, June, 1778; on rolls, November, 1780, - during the Revolutionary War."[6,8] He distinguished himself at the battle of Monmouth and was personally praised by General Washington for his bravery in battle[11].

After the war Abraham continued to play a prominent role in his community, serving as a member of the Hunterdon co Board of Freeholders and the Bethlehem township committee[13,14].

NEW JERSEY ARCHIVES, Vol. III, *Newspaper Extracts, 1779*, states: "On Tuesday, 29 June 1779, sold the house of Col. Abrah Bonnell in Bethlehem, a plantation situated in said township on Musconetcung

Mountain, containing 230 acres with a log tenement thereon, a small piece of meadow and an excellent orchard. Hunterdon County, New Jersey Gazette, Vol. II #77, Wednesday, 26 May 1779."[18]

Col Abram Bunnel appears among the rateables of Bethlehem twp, Hunterdon co, in June 1778, rated on 40 acres of land, 2 horses, 3 head of cattle and 1 pig[19]. The listing of rateables in Bethlehem twp in September 1780 identifies him simply as Abraham Bunnel, with 38 acres, 3 horses, 2 pigs and a tavern[19]. *Hunterdon County Taxpayers 1778-1797* lists him as Abraham Bonnel, Bethlehem in 1785; Abraham Bonal, Bethlehem in 1786; Abraham Bonol, Bethlehem in 1789 and 1790; and Abraham Bonnell, Kingwood in 1797[12].

He died 1 November 1797 and his widow died 27 June 1822. They were buried in the Bethlehem Presbyterian Church Cemetery, at Grandin, between Pittstown and Clinton, Hunterdon co, NJ. Their gravestones read: "Col. Abraham Bonnell d. November 1797 aged 65 yrs & 3 ms. Elizabeth Bonnell d. June 1822 aged 79 yrs & 1 mo."[12] He died intestate, but the abstract of his probate record in the *Calendar of wills--1796-1800* reads: "1797, Nov. 29. Bonell, Abraham, of Bethelem Twsp., Hunterdon Co. Int. Adm'rs--Clement Bonnell and Alexander Bonnell. Fellowbondsmen--Henry Bailie and Charles Stewart; all of said Co. Lib. 37, p. 208. 1797, Dec. 5. Inventory, £2,495.16.6; made by Ralph Guild and Nehemiah Dunham. 1799, May 10. Account by the Adm'rs; total £2637.0.5. File 1176J."[16]

A record in Book 1, *PETITIONS OF HUNTERDON COUNTY, NJ*, reads as follows: "Division of the Real Estate of Abraham Bonnell} Hunterdon County} Whereas application being made to us the subscribers, Judges of the court of Common Pleas for the County affores[d] by Alexander Bonnell, That David Frazer & John C. Rockhill Esq[r] & Capt. Ralph Guild may be appointed Commissions to Divide into nine equal parts all those seven tracts of Land Situate in the Townships of Bethlehem & Kingwood in the County aforesaid Late the property of Abraham Bonnell Dec[d]. And having met agreeable to Advertisement, & hearing the prayer of Petitioner & no objections being made we Do agreeable to the prayer of the Said Petitioner appoint the said David Frazer, John E. Rockhill & Ralph Guild, Commissioners pursuant to an act Intestate an act for the more Easy Partition of Lands held by Coparceners &c., Passed the Eleventh day of Nov. 1799[?]. Given under our hands & Seals the 27th day of Sept. 1799. /s/ Jos. Reading, Thos. Reading, Dan[l] Hunt."[7]

On 17 March 1800 the three commissioners appeared before Judge Daniel Hunt and took the required oath to perform the duties required of them according to the best of their skill, knowledge and judgement.

"This may certify that we, the subscribers commissioners appointed by Joseph Reading, Thomas Reading and Daniel Hunt Esquires, Judges of the Inferior Court of Common Pleas, of the County of Hunterdon, to divide the real Estate of Abraham Bonnell late of the Township of Bethlehem in the County of Hunterdon aforesaid dec[d]. having proceeded in the Division thereof, agreeable to our appointment, and having given notice by advertisement, printed in the Federalist and New Jersey State Gazette, of the time and place of making allotment, by ballot, for the shares of the said Estate, as divided, agreeably to law---we met the twenty seventh day of September in the year of our Lord one thousand eight hundred at the House of Clement Bonnell Innkeeper in the Township of Bethlehem aforesaid - being the time and place advertised as aforesaid for making the said allotment - and proceeding in the presence of Divers spectators, to the balloting for the Said Shares - when Henry Carricuff was appointed by us the said Commissioners to draw the tickets of the names and the numbers of the shares, which he did in the following order - the tickets of the name - and the tickets of the numbers being <u>mixed</u>? up close and put into separate places he drew -

      1st The Heirs of Newell Godley dec[d]   and opposite No. 8.

      2d Alexander Bonnell   and opposite No. 3.

3^d Clement Bonnell	and opposite No. 1.
4th Clement Bonnell	and opposite No. 9.
5th Charles Bonnell	and opposite No. 4.
6th Alexander Bonnell	and opposite No. 2.
7th John Bonnell	and opposite No. 5.
8th Charles Bonnell	and opposite No. 6.
9th John Bonnell	and opposite No. 7.

when all the tickets were finised drawing.

Therefore--the said John Bonnell is intitled to shares, number five and number seven, of the Division of the real Estate of the said Abraham Bonnell dec^d, Clement Bonnell to shares number one and number nine--Alexander Bonnell to shares number two and number three--Charles Bonnell to shares number four and number six and the Heirs of Newell Godley dec^d to share number eight---Now all the aforesaid shares are fully represented and described on the Maps and field Book of the aforesaid Division, hereto annexed, reference being had to the respective numbers thereon will at large appear --- In Witness whereof we have hereunto set our hands and seals the fourth day of October Anno Domini one thousand eight hundred. David Frazer

Jn° Rockhill

Ralph Guild"[7]

Children:

1. 310032. Mary V., b. 18 June 1760[1]; d. 1760[18].
2. 310033. John, b. 16 May 1762[1].
3. 310034. Jeremiah, b. 16 Dec. 1763[1]; d. 1763[18].
4. 310016. Clement duMont, b. 4 Jan. 1766[1].
5. 310035. Alexander, b. 31 Jan. 1768[1].
6. 310036. Newell, b. 25 Apr.[1](or Mar.[10]) 1770[1]; m. Joseph Godley[9]; d. 1793[9].
   Children (surname Godley)[9]:

1. Sarah.	2. Mary.	3. Mahlon.

7. 310198. Charles Foster, b. 13 Dec. 1781[1].
8. 310197. Abraham, b. 10 Dec. 1783[1]; d. before Sept. 1799[7].

REFERENCES:

1. "Bible Records copied from the Records in possession of late Arthur Franklin Bonnell of Whitehouse, N.J. Nov. 30- 1914 L.G.F." in the Pennsylvania Historical Society, Philadelphia. Copy sent to me by Clement M. Bonnell III. Printed in the Bunnell/Bonnell Newsletter, Vol. II, No. 2, p. 10.
2. Gravestones in Bethlehem Presbyterian Church Cemetery, Grandin, NJ, transcribed August 1971 by Thomas B. Wilson, Genealogist, for Mrs. Max Thelen, Jr. Copy sent to me by Clement M. Bonnell III.
3. Bonnell.
4. Ltr. 6 Apr. 1914 from Addie Watts Crawford, Canton, PA, to John A. Biles.
5. NJ Wills - Vol. IV, p. 49.
6. Deats, Ltr. 15 Feb. 1927 from The Adjutant General, State of New Jersey, to Hiram E. Deats.
7. Petitions of Hunterdon co, NJ, Book 1. Division of the Real Estate of Abraham Bonnell. Pages 1 and 2 of 9 pages, photocopied and sent to me by Paula Sacco, Pittsburgh, PA.
8. Rev War - NJ - 1, pp. 336, 342, 357.
9. Deats, Wm. M. Pettit's Bonnell Line.
10. The Bible of Charles Foster and Deborah (Leigh) Bonnell, which lists the births of all of Abraham's children. The month of Newell's birth is the only variance in date. This Bible is now owned by Clement M. Bonnell III.

11. Historic Guide Posts, by Samuel Harden Stille, No. 4. The Old Bonnell Tavern, in the Plainfield, NJ, Courier-News, Friday, 21 April 1933. Photocopy sent to me by Mrs. E. B. Brown, Liberty, NY, 22 Nov. 1959.
12. Hunterdon co, NJ.
13. Union Township, Rural Recollections, by Andrew C. Herdan, 1988, sent to me by Clement M. Bonnell III.
14. The First 275 Years of Hunterdon County 1714-1989, by Hunterdon County Cultural and Heritage Commission, sent to me by Robert E. Dils.
15. Bunnell/Bonnell Newsletter, Vol. VI, No. 3, p. 34, April 1992.
16. NJ Wills - Vol. IX, p. 37. .
17. Deats, citing New Jersey Archives, Vol. IX, p. 185.
18. Duncan, p. 54.
19. Gen Mag of NJ, Vol. 47, No. 3, p. 118, New Jersey Rateables, 1778-1780, by Kenn Stryker-Rodda.
20. CB Database.

1-3-2-2-2   D70   CB300162

JACOB[5] BONNELL (Abraham[4], Isaac[3], Nathaniel[2], William[1]) was born, perhaps in 1735[2] in New Jersey (probably in Chesterfield twp, Monmouth co, or perhaps in Kingston, Middlesex co). The only certain reference to this Jacob is the bequest of £5 he received by the terms of his father's will dated 28 January 1768[1]. I have found only one other Jacob Bonnell of about the same age in New Jersey: 1-3-1-2-2-1, son of Benjamin. There has been a great deal of confusion and blending of the records for these two men, with very few records to work on.

Several researchers have stated that this was the Jacob who married Mary Schooley on 27 November 1760[2,3,7]. No contemporary evidence is cited to make the connection. The letter from Grace Gridley Roscoe to Addie Watts Crawford on 19 January 1921[4] offers better evidence that it was Benjamin's son who married Mary Schooley. They were Quakers, as were many of their descendants.

Since Jacob, son of Benjamin, was a Quaker who would likely have been opposed to military activity, I believe it is logical to assign the several records of military service to this Jacob, son of Abraham. During the French and Indian War Jacob Bonnell served as an ensign in a New Jersey regiment in 1758/59 and as a commissioned officer in 1759/60[5]. During the Revolution he served as a private in the militia of Somerset co, NJ[6].

The Family Group Sheet for Abraham Bonnell, Sr., prepared by H. Russell Bonnell, gives Jacob's birth date as 1735 and says he died 14 October 1811[2]. Since it also says that Jacob married Mary Schooley, it is not clear which Jacob these dates apply to. Sources cited are *New Jersey Archives*, Vol. 1, pp. 33 and 49, and *The History of The Shinn Family in Europe and America*, by Josiah H. Shinn, 1903, neither of which I have seen.

My own best guess is that he died before May 1778, perhaps in service, and that the Catherine Bunnill who appears that month on the tax list for Kingwood twp, Hunterdon co, was his widow[8]. She appears again in February 1780, in Amwell twp, Hunterdon co, as a householder, owning 90 acres of improved land, and with a single man, James Shaw, living in her household[9].

By June 1780 it would seem they were married. The 90 acres are listed under his name, he is not called a single man, and she does not appear[9].

Jacob does not appear on any of the tax lists which I have seen, and no other references which might apply to him have come to my attention.

REFERENCES:

1. NJ Wills - Vol. IV, p. 49.
2. Family Group Sheet on Abraham Bonnell, Sr., compiled by H. Russell Bonnell, Logan, UT, 12 Mar. 1961, and sent to me on 4 Apr. 1961.
3. *Documents Related to the History of New Jersey*, Vol. 5, ed. by Scott , Records of Rahway and Plainfield Monthly Meeting of Friends From 1687 to 1825:

    "Jacob Bonnel and Mary Schooley, both of Mendham, were married at Mendham, 11th month, 21st, 1761."

    Sent to me by Paula Sacco, Pittsburgh, PA.
4. Ltr. 19 Jan. 1921 from Grace Gridley Roscoe to Addie Watts Crawford. See References, under 1-3-2-2 Abraham for substantial extract.
5. CB Database.
6. Rev War - NJ - 1, p. 513.
7. Duncan, p. 55.
8. Gen Mag of NJ, Vol. 48, No. 2, p. 76, New Jersey Rateables, 1778-1780, by Kenn Stryker-Rodda.
9. Gen Mag of NJ, Vol. 47, No. 2, p. 83.

1-3-2-2-3   D71   CB300164

ISAAC[5] BONNELL (Abraham[4], Isaac[3], Nathaniel[2], William[1]) was born between 1740 and 1745 probably in Hunterdon co, NJ. His father left him £5 in his will dated 28 January 1768, and he and his mother were named executors of the will[1]. Apparently he was among the men from the Morris co, NJ, companies sent to Maj. Duykinck at Amboy, NJ, on 6 July 1776[6], and the Isaac Bonnell of Kingwood, NJ, listed in 1778 in the *Revolutionary Census of New Jersey*, by Ken Stryker-Rodda[4]. He is listed in the *Official Roster of Revolutionary Soldiers Buried in Ohio*[10]. He married CATHERINE SEVERNS[9], daughter of Samuel and Mary Severns[13]. She was around twenty years younger than Isaac. He was over 35 when their first child was born and she must still have been in her teens. This could have been a second marriage for Isaac, although I have found no evidence for a prior one. Isaac Bonnill owned 50 acres of improved land in Kingwood twp, Hunterdon co, in May 1778 and a house and lot in Kingwood in January/February 1780[2]. He appears in *Hunterdon County Taxpayers 1778-1797* as Isaac Bonhill, Kingwood, in

1780 and 1785, Isaac Bonnell, Kingwood, in 1786, and Isaac Bonnill, Kingwood in 1789[5]. He was probably also the _____ Bonbill, Kingwood, in 1779[5]. He also owned taxable property in Alexandria twp, Hunterdon co, in July 1785 (the first extant tax list for that twp) and in July 1786[3]. Other than the fact that sons William and Jesse were said to have been born in New Jersey, this is the last reference to this Isaac Bonnell in New Jersey that I have found.

Isaac and Catherine seem to have lived for a time in Loudon co, VA, since the last three or four of their children were apparently born there. Isaac witnessed a deed there in 1797[12]. (It is just possible that he was the Isaac Bunnell who witnessed a deed on 16 August 1798, from Henry Owsley and wife Martha of Lincoln co, KY, to William Reed of Mason co, KY, for land in Mason co[8].)

They moved next to Crawford co, PA, where he bought 200 acres in tract 1294 from Francis Holmes and James Herreatte on 1 June 1808[14]. In 1810 he appears in the census in Wayne twp, Crawford co, PA: 10311-2111[15]. On 12 October 1812 Isaac Bunnell, miller, (Note that Catherine's father, Samuel Severns, was a mill owner in New Jersey[13].) and wife Catherine sold tract 1294 to Thomas Cochran for $4000[14]. In September 1814 he bought three parcels of land in Madison twp, Guernsey co, OH, from members of the Huffman family[16]. Here he laid out the town of Winchester[17]. Sales of lots in Winchester by Isaac and his heirs appear on the Guernsey co records for the next 20 years[16]. Isaac appears in the 1820 census in Madison twp, Guernsey co: 100111-01201[15]. The same year he was appointed on 18 July as Commissioner to pay bills for the road from Winchester to Fairview[16]. He is also listed in the 1825 tax list in Guernsey co[18]. He appears again in the 1830 census in Madison twp, Guernsey co: 00000000001-000010001[15].

Isaac died intestate in Guernsey co (15 June?) 1834 and his estate was probated there. Letters of Administration were granted 19 June 1834 to Jonathan Bonnel and John Dillon[20]. He was buried in Winterset, Madison twp[10]. In April 1836 some of his heirs petitioned the Court of Common Pleas of Guernsey co to partition and distribute the real estate owned by Isaac Bonnell at the time of his death[21]. The real estate consisted of the following pieces:

> The northwest quarter of Section 14, Township 3, Range 1, of the unappropriated lands in the military district, containing 160 acres more or less.
> The southwest quarter of Section 14, Township 3, Range 1, of the unappropriated lands in the military district, excepting 15 acres included in the town plat of New Winchester, containing 145 acres more or less.
> Lots #3, #4, #37 and #38 in the town of New Winchester[21].

These lands were sold at auction in October 1836 for a total of $3453.25. The widow Catherine received a third as her dower right, and the remainder, after deducting expenses, was divided among the children and/or their assigns[21]. On 12 April 1837 Catherine sold her dower interest in Section 14, Township 3, Range 1, to her son William for $600[16].

Catherine Bonnell died in 1839 in Madison twp. Her will, dated 5 May 1837 and probated 8 April 1839, is recorded in Guernsey co, but mentions only one child, her son Isaac, Jr. Her will reads as follows:

In the name of the benevolent father of all, I Catharine Bonnell of the County of Guernsey in the state of Ohio do make and publish this my last will and testament.

<u>First</u>. It is my will that all my just debts and funeral expenses be paid out of my estate.

<u>Second</u>. I give and devise all the residue of my estate to my grand children, the sons and daughters of my son Isaac Bonnell to them and their heirs and assigns forever. <u>Third</u>. I appoint Nathan Evans of the said County of Guernsey, executor of this my last will and Testament. I do hereby revoke and annul all former wills by me made. In testimony whereof I hereunto set my hand and seal this 5th day of May in the year of our Lord Eighteen hundred and thirty-seven.

her
Catharine X Bonnel. (Seal)
Mark

Signed, sealed, acknowledged, published, and declared by the said Catharine Bonnell as and for her last will and Testament in the presence of us who sign the same as witnesses in her presence and in the presence of each other at her request.

Nathan Barnes

Nathan Evans[22].

Children[21]:

1. 310064. Samuel, b. 22 Feb. 1780.
2. 310066. Jonathan, b. 13 Nov. 1781[15].
3. 310065. Daniel, b. about 1785·
4. 310067. Mary, b. 1787 NJ[23]; m. 181x Jacob Shipman[21]; d. 1861 OH[23].

   Children (surname Shipman)[23]:

1. John	3. Jane.	4. Francis R?
2. Lewis.	others?	

5. 310073. John, b. about 1788.
6. 310074. William, b. 18 Mar. 1791.
7. 310075. Jesse, b. about 1794.
8. 310078. Sarah, b. 1796; m. 27 Nov. 1817 John Dillon[21].
9. 310079. Isaac, b. 20 Feb. 1800.
10. 310089. Catherine, b. 11 Aug. 1802[11] VA; m. 27 Feb. 1823 John Wherry[11]; d. 18 Dec. 1885[11].

    Children (surname Wherry)[11]:

1. David.	4. Samuel Severns.	7. Andrew Dillon.
2. Isaac.	5. Harriet Ann.	8. Matthew Matlin.
3. Mary Evaline.	6. John Patterson.	9. Sarah Catherine.

11. 310092. Nancy Jane, b. 1 Aug. 1804[15] VA or 19 Aug. 1805[19]; m. 19 Apr. 1827[19] Andrew Finley Linn[21]; d. 17 Feb. 1867[19].

    Children (surname Linn)[19]:

1. Fernando E.	6. Margaret.	10. Andrew Finley.
2. Absolem M.	7. William Albert.	11. child, d. y.
3. Snoden Sargent.	8. John Alfred.	12. George.
4. Ann Catherine.	9. Rebecca Ann.	13. Nancy J.
5. Sarah Agnes.		

FIFTH GENERATION

REFERENCES:

1. NJ Wills - IV, p. 49.
2. Gen Mag of NJ, Vol. 48, p. 76, New Jersey Rateables, 1778-1780, by Ken Stryker-Rodda.
3. CB Database, citing Gen Mag of NJ, Vol. 54, p. 552.
4. *Revolutionary Census of New Jersey*, Ken Stryker-Rodda, 1972, p. II-21.
5. Hunterdon co, NJ.
6. CB Database, citing *Papers of Wm. Livingston*, Carl E. Prince, Editor, 1979.
7. Duncan, p. 55, where Isaac is listed correctly as the son of Abraham, but all other data shown apply instead to Isaac Bonnell, 1-3-1-4-5, CB300194.
8. *Kentucky Pioneers and Their Descendants*, by Ila Earle Fowler, 1978, p. 144 (Deed Book E, p. 324), sent to me by Marjorie Gibbs, Saratoga Springs, NY.
9. Query in *Boston Transcript*, 13 Aug. 1930, sent to me by Homer Baldwin and Gwen Quickel.
10. *Official Roster - Revolutionary Soldiers 1775-1783 Buried in Ohio*, sent to me by Althea Statum.
11. Ltr. 27 Oct. 1967 from Mrs. George H. Huls.
12. Ltr. 15 Sept. 1998 from Charlotte Blair Stewart.
13. *West Jersey Society Tract Dwellers, 1782-1788*, p. 128, and *Sussex County Deed Abstracts*, p. 95 (Deed Book B, p. 283), sent to me by Claude A. Bunnell.
14. Title search of property in Crawford co, PA, bought and sold by Isaac Bunnell, sent to me by J. Richard Bunnell.
15. CB Database - including census records.
16. CB Database - Guernsey co real estate transactions.
17. *Guernsey County, A Household Guide*, Wills twp, sent to me by Don Bonnell.
18. 1825 Tax List - Guernsey co, OH, sent to me by Althea Statum and John Paul Grady.
19. FGS - Andrew Finley and Nancy Jane (Bonnell) Linn, sent to me by D. Eileen Linn.
20. Probate Record, Isaac Bonnell's estate, sent to me by Claude A. Bunnell.
21. Petition for Partition of Isaac Bunnell's estate, Court of Common Pleas, Guernsey co, OH, 17 April 1836 et seq., sent to me by Charlotte Blair Stewart. See below for complete text.
22. Will of Catharine Bonnell, sent to me by Claude A. Bunnell and Ilene Grimes.
23. FGS - Jacob and Mary (Bonnell) Shipman, sent to me by Charles Marsteller.

Following is the complete text of the Petition for Partition (Reference #21):

Pleas. Before the Honorable Corrington W. Searle, President Judge, and James G. Brown, William Skinner and Stuart Spear, Esqurs., Associate Judges of the Court of Common pleas of the County of Guernsey in the State of Ohio, of the October term of said court in the year of our Lord one thousand eight hundred and thirty six.

Philo P. Bonnell, George W. Bonnell	Petition for Partition
Theodore M. Bonnell, Sarah Thomas,	17 April term 1836.
William Carlile & James Spence, Jr.	Be it Remembered that heretofore to wit on the
Vs.	Eight day of January in the year of our Lord
Catharine Bonnell, widow of Isaac	one thousand eight hundred and thirty six, Philo
Bonnell, dec[d] and Samuel Bonnell	P. Bonnell, Geo. W. Bonnell, Theodore M.
Jacob Shipman & Mary his wife	Bonnell, Sarah Thomas, Wm. Carlile and James
John Bonnell, William Bonnell	Spence, Jr., filed in the office of the Clerk of the
John Dillon and Sarah his wife,	Court of Common Pleas within and for the County
John Wherry and Catharine his wife	of Guernsey in the state of Ohio, their Certain
And Andrew F. Linn & Nancy his wife.	Petition for partition against Catharine Bonnell,
	Widow of Isaac Bonnell deceased, and Samuel

Bonnell, Jacob Shipman and Mary his wife, John Bonnell, William Bonnell, John Dillon and Sarah his Wife, John Wherry and Catharine his wife, and Andrew F. Linn and Nancy his wife, in these words, to wit-
To the Honorable the Court of Common pleas for the County of Guernsey in the state of Ohio at the Term of March 1836. The petition of Philo P. Bonnell, George W. Bonnell, Theodore M. Bonnell, Sarah Thomas, William Carlile

and James Spence, Jr., respectfully represents, that Isaac Bonnell, late of the said county of Guernsey, deceased, departed this life on or about the 15th day of June, 1834, seized and possesed in fee simple of the following described tracts of land and town lots, that is to say, the north west quarter of section fourteen in township three, and Range one of the unappropriated lands in the military destrict situate in the said County of Guernsey and containing one hundred and sixty acres more or less--also the south west quarter of section fourteen in township three and Range one of the unappropriated lands in the military destrict situate in said Guernsey County, excepting so much of the last named quarter section as is included in the town plat of the town of New Winchester, which was laid off on the said quarter section and which town plat is supposed to contain about fifteen acres. The part of the said quarter section of which the said Isaac Bonnell dec[d] died seized and possessed as aforesaid being estimated to contain one hundred and forty five acres be the same more or less, also four Lots numbered Three, Four, Thirty seven and Thirty eight, in the Town of New Winchester aforesaid:- Your petitioner further shows that the said Isaac Bonnell, dec[d], died intestate leaving to survive him: his widow Catharine Bonnell and his children and heirs at law as follows. To wit, Samuel Bonnell, Jonathan Bonnell, Daniel Bonnell, Mary Shipman who is intermarried with Jacob Shipman, John Bonnell, William Bonnell, Jesse Bonnell, Sarah Dillon, who is intermarried with John Dillon, Isaac Bonnell, Catharine Wherry, who is intermarried with John Wherry & Nancy Linn who is intermarried with Andrew F. Linn:- all of whom as well your petitioners as the said widow and children reside in the said County of Guernsey except the said Samuel Bonnell who resides in Venango County, Pennsylvania, and your petitioner Sarah Thomas who resides in Ohio County, Virginia:- Your petitioners further shew that since the death of the said Isaac Bonnell, dec[d], Your petitioners, the said Philo P. Bonnell, George W. Bonnell and Theodore M. Bonnell, have acquired by purchase the share and proportion of the said Jonathan Bonnell in and to the said tracts of land & Town lots, and that as tenants in Common with the other parties in interest, herein named, they are entitled to one undivided thirty third part thereof, in fee simple. That your petitioner, the said Sarah Thomas has acquired by purchase the share and proportion of the said Daniel Bonnell, in and to the same tracts of Land & Town lots and that she is entitled to one undivided eleventh part thereof in fee simple- That your petitioner the said William Carlile has acquired by purchase the share and proportion of the said Jesse Bonnell in and to the same tracts of land and Town lots and that he is entitled to one undivided eleventh part thereof, in fee simple- That your petitioner, the said James Spence, Jr., has acquired by purchase the share and proportion of the said Isaac Bonnell in and to the same tracts of lands and town lots and that he is entitled to one undivided eleventh part thereof, in fee simple- and that the said Samuel Bonnell, Mary Shipman, John Bonnell, William Bonnell, Sarah Dillon, Catharine Wherry and Nancy Linn, are each entitled to one undivided eleventh part of the same tracts of land and town lots, in fee simple - all subject to the dower of the said Catharine Bonnell, who is entitled to dower therein as the widow of the said Isaac Bonnell, dec[d]. Your petitioners therefore pray that the said Catharine Bonnell widow as aforesaid and the said Sam[l] Bonnell, Jacob Shipman and Mary his wife, John Bonnell, W[m] Bonnell, John Dillon and Sarah his wife, John Wherry & Catharine his wife and Andrew F. Linn and Nancy his wife be made defendants to this petition; and that, on the hearing thereof, this Honorable Court will order and direct that the dower of the said widow in and to the said tracts of Land and Town lots, be set off & assigned to her-- and that partition thereof, be had and made and the several parts and proportion of your petitioners therein be set off and divided to them, in severalty or that the parts & proportion of each of the said parties in interest therin be set off and divided to them in severalty as to your honors may seem most proper. And your petitioners as in duty bound will ever pray &c James M. Bell Atty for pet[s].

And afterwards, to wit at the next term of the Court of Common pleas began and held at and in the Court house of the County of Guernsey aforesaid on the fourth day of April in the year of our Lord one thousand eight hundred and thirty six Came the demandants and filed due proof of the publication of notice to the defendants as required by law, which proof is as follows to wit. Notice Petition for Partition. Philo P. Bonnell, George W. Bonnell, Theodore M. Bonnell, Sarah Thomas, William Carlisle and James Spence, Jr., demandants (vs) Catharine Bonnell, widow of Isaac Bonnell deceased, and Samuel Bonnell, Jacob Shipman and Mary his wife, John Bonnell, William Bonnell, John Dillon and Sarah his wife, John Wherry and Catharine his wife and Andrew F. Linn and Nancy his wife, defendants. Notice is hereby given to the above named defendants that the above named demandants have this day filed their petition in the office of the Clerk of the Court of Common pleas, for the County of Guernsey in the State of Ohio, praying that partition may be had and made of certain lands and town lots, situate in said Guernsey County, and particularly described in said petition, being the real estate of which the said Isaac Bonnell, deceased, died seized and possessed, in fee simple---and praying further, that the dower therein of the said widow be set off and assigned to her,

and that the several parts and proportions of the said demandants, therein, as stated and set forth in the said petition be set off and divided to them in severalty, as to the said court may seem most proper. Said petition may be acted on at the next term of said court. James M. Bell Attorney for demandants January 9, 1836. 3W[?]
The State of Ohio Guernsey County ss. Court of Common pleas March Term 1836. Personally appeared in open court James M. Bell, who being sworn, says, that an advertisement, of which the annexed is a copy was published in the "Guernsey Times" a newspaper printed & published in the Town of Cambridge in said Guernsey County and in general circulation in said county at least forty days prior to the 4th day of April 1836. Sworn to and subscribed in open court this 4th day of April 1836. Ja^s M. Bell. Before me Moses Sarchet Clk. Printers fees $2.50--

And afterwards at this same court here held to wit on the Eighth day of April in the year last aforesaid On motion to the court by Mr. Bell counsel for demandants, It is ordered that, by the oaths of Jacob G. Morton, Robert Campbell and Richard Scott, one full and equal third part of the lands & premises in the said petition described be assigned and set off to the said Catharine Bonnell as her dower estate, and that by the like oaths of the same Jacob G. Morton, Robert Campbell and Richard Scott, partition be made of said lands and premises subject to said dower estate for the following proportions to wit, to the said Philo P. Bonnell, George W. Bonnell & Theodore M. Bonnell, each one equal third (sic) third part, to Sarah Thomas, William Carlisle, James Spence, Jr., Samuel Bonnell, Mary Shipman, John Bonnell, William Bonnell, Sarah Dillon, Catharine Wherry and Nancy Linn, each one equal eleventh part thereof, and it is further ordered that a writ of partition issue to the Sheriff of Guernsey County Commanding him to cause said dower to be assigned and said partition to be made accordingly. And thereupon on motion of said petitioners this cause was continued until the next term of the Court of Common pleas aforesaid at and in the Court house of the County of Guernsey aforesaid to be held:-

And afterwards to wit on the Fourteenth day of April in the year of our Lord one thousand eight hundred and thirty six the Following writ of Partition was issued to the Sheriff to wit The State of Ohio, Guernsey County ss: To the sheriff of said County, Greeting: We command you that without delay by the oaths of Jacob G. Morton, Robert Campbell and Richard Scott, you cause Catharine Bonnell, widow of Isaac Bonnell deceased, to be endowed of one full third part of the following real estate situate lying and being in the county of Guernsey aforesaid, that is to say; the north west quarter of section fourteen, in Township three and Range one of the unappropriated lands in the military destrict, containing 160 acres more or less,- also the southwest quarter of section fourteen, intownship three and Range one of the unappropriated lands in the military destrict, excepting so much of said last mentioned quarter section as is included in the town plat of the town of New Winchester which was laid off in the said quarter section and which town plat was supposed to contain about fifteen acres. The said quarter exclusive of said town plat, being estimated to contain 145 acres, more or less.- Also in lots numbered three, four thirty seven and Thirty Eight, in the town of New Winchester aforesaid.- by metes and bounds according to law; - and also, that, in like manner and by the like oaths of the same Jacob G. Morton, Robert Campbell and Richard Scott, you cause partition to be made of the same lands and premises, subject to said dower estate, among the following persons and in the following proportions, to wit: To Philo P. Bonnell, George W. Bonnell, and Theodore M. Bonnell, each one equal thirty third part:::- To Sarah Thomas, William Carlisle, James Spencer, Jr., Samuel Bonnell, Mary Shipman (who is intermarried with Jacob Shipman), John Bonnell, William Bonnell, Sarah Dillon (who is intermarried with John Dillon), Catharine Wherry (who is intermarried with John Wherry) and Nancy Linn (who is intermarried with Andrew F. Linn), each one equal eleventh part thereof, and that your proceedings in the premises you distinctly certify under your hand to our court of Common pleas with and for the said County of Guernsey on the first day of their next term together with this writ. Witness Corrington W. Searle President Judge of our said Court of Common pleas this 14. Day of April A. D. 1836. Attest. Moses Sarchet Clk.

And afterwards, to wit: at the next term of the Court of Common pleas aforesaid Continued and held at and in the Court house of the County of Guernsey aforesaid on the Sixth day of July in the year of our Lord one thousand eight hundred and thirty six. On motion to the court by Mr. Bell, counsel for the petitioners and upon producing the proceedings of the Sheriff, and the report and proceedings of the Commissioners hereinbefore appointed, in the words and figures following, to wit: ""I have executed this writ by the oaths of the within named commissioners whose

FIFTH GENERATION

report is herewith returned June 9th 1836. My fees $1.95, viz,- For executing writ, $1.00. Travelling fees 95c. John Beymer Sheriff G. C. --- The State of Ohio, Guernsey County (seal)..I the subscriber, a Justice of the peace within and for said County of Guernsey, do hereby certify that, on this day, the above named Jacob G. Morton, Robert Campbell, & Richard Scott, were by me duly sworn to perform the duties required of them by the foregoing order, given under my hand and seal this 25th day of April A.D. 1836. William Carlisle, Justice of the peace.
We the Commissioners appointed in the cause named in the within writ to assign dower to Catharine Bonnell, widow of Isaac Bonnell, late of the County of Guernsey in the State of Ohio, deceased, in the real estate mentioned and described in the within writ of Partition and also to make partition of the same real estate subject to said dower estate between the parties named in the said writ, and having been duly sworn upon actual view of the premises, do assign to the said Catharine Bonnell, for her dower estate, so much of the said real estate as is contained within the following limits, viz: Beginning at a post, in the centre of the Steubenville road on the east boundary line of the south west quarter of section 14 in Township three and range one (military) thence North 68 poles, thence west 44 poles 16 links, thence South 5 ° East 80 poles, 15 links to the said Steubenville road, thence South 65° west 18 poles 9 links, to the east end of the town of New Winchester, thence South 23° East 14 poles, thence south 15° west 4 poles, 6 links, thencs south 15½° East 49 poles, thence South 57° East 12 poles, 7 Links, thence south 80 1/4° East 13 poles 3 ½ links, thence north 74 1/2° East 64 poles 18 links, and thence North 95 poles 20 Links to the place of Beginning, and estimated to Contain seventy acres & forty five hundredths of an acre, be the same more or less--and being part of both the said quarter section mentioned in the said writ. And upon a further view of the said premises we are of opinion that the same cannot be divided according to the demand of the said writ without a manifest injury of the Value thereof, and thereupon we do estimate the value thereof, subject to said dower estate, in each of the said quarter sections, and including the remainder after such dower estate shall have determined as follows, that is to say the said North west quarter of section fourteen in Township three and Range one at the sum of thirteen hundred and sixty dollars ($1360)- the said south west quarter of Section fourteen in Township three and Range one (excepting so much thereof as is included in the Town Plat of the Town of New Winchester) at the sum of Twenty one hundred and seventy five dollars ($2175)- The said lot numbered three in the said town of New Winchester, at the sum of twenty dollars, the said lot numbered Four in the said Town of New Winchester, at the sum of Twenty dollars, the said lot numbered thirty seven in the Town of New Winchester at the sum of Ten dollars, and the said Lot numbered thirty eight, in the said Town of New Winchester at the sum of Ten dollars. Given under our hand this Fifth day of July A.D. 1836- Robert Campbell, J. Morton, Richard Scott. Filed, viz: Commissioners J. G. Morton - 3 days $3.00; Robert Campbell - 2 days $2.00, Richard Scott - 2 days $2.00 - - Surveyor Otho Brashear 2 days $4.00. Chainman, Levi Carter 2 days 1.50, Saml Miller 2 days $1.50 - - Total $14.00, and the same being examined, It is ordered that the said proceedings and report be and the same are hereby approved and confirmed. And thereupon neither of the parties electing to take said estate at the valuation thereof, as returned by said Commissioners. On motion of the petitioners it is ordered that said estate be sold at public auction by the Sheriff of said county of Guernsey, according to the statute in such case made and provided, and therefore on motion this cause was continued until the next term of the Court of Common pleas at and in the Court house of the County of Guernsey aforesaid to be held:--

And afterwards to wit: on the 20th day of July in the year of our Lord one thousand eight hundred and thirty six the following order of sale was issued to the Sheriff, to wit: The State of Ohio, Guernsey County, ss. Court of Common pleas, July Term 1836. Partition; July 6th 1836. On motion to the Court by Mr. Bell, counsel for the petitioners and upon producing the proceedings of the Sheriff and the report and proceedings of the Commissioners thereinbefore appointed and the same being examined, it is ordered that said proceedings and report be and the same is hereby approved & confirmed, and thereupon neither of the parties electing to take said estate at the valuation thereof, as returned by said Commissioners, On motion of the petitioners it is ordered that said estate lying and being in the County of Guernsey aforesaid, that is to say: the North west quarter of Section Fourteen in Township three and Range one of the unappropriated lands in the military destrict, containing one hundred and sixty acres more or less, also the south west quarter of section Fourteen, in Township Three and Range one of the unappropriated lands in the military destrict, excepting so much of said last mentioned quarter section as is included in the Town plat of the Town of New Winchester, which was laid off on the said quarter section, and which town plat is supposed to contain about fifteen acres, the said quarter section exclusive of said Town plat being estimated to contain 145 acres more or less; also in lots number three, four, thirty seven and thirty eight in the Town of New Winchester, aforesaid, be sold at public auction by the sheriff of said County of Guernsey according to the statute in such case made and provided.-- I, Moses

Sarchet, Clerk of the Court of Common pleas for said County of Guernsey, do hereby certify, that the above is a true copy of the order of sale made in the above cause at the term aforesaid, of said court "seal". Given under my hand and the seal of said court this 20th day of July, A.D. 1836. Moses Sarchet, Clk.

And afterwards, to wit: at the next term of the Court of Common pleas aforesaid, Continued and held at and in the Court house of the County of Guernsey aforesaid on the Fifth day of October in the year of our Lord one thousand eight hundred and thirty six, on motion to the Court by Mr. Bell, counsel for the petitioners, and upon producing the proceedings of the sheriff and the sale by him made in pursuance of a former order of this court, which proceeding is as follows, to wit: "Sheriff Sale. By virtue of an order to me directed made by the Court of Common pleas for the County of Guernsey in the state of Ohio at their July term 1936. In a petition for Partition, wherein Philo P. Bonnell, George W. Bonnell, Theodore M. Bonnell, Sarah Thomas, William Carlisle and James Spence, Jr., were demandant, and Catharine Bonnell, widow of Isaac Bonnell, dec⁴, and Samuel Bonnell, Jacob Shipman and Mary his wife, John Bonnell, William Bonnell, John Dillon, Sarah his wife, John Wherry and Catharine his wife, and Andrew F. Linn and Nancy his wife, were defendants, I will sell at Public auction at the door of the Court house in the Town of Cambridge in said Guernsey County, on Saturday the 10th day of September 1836 between the Hours of 10 A.M. And 4 P.M. The following real estate situate in said County of Guernsey--that is to say:- the north west quarter of section Fourteen, in Township three and Range one, of the unappropriated lands in the military destrict, containing 160 acres more or less; also the south west quarter of section Fourteen, in Township three and Range one of the unappropriated lands in the military destrict, excepting so much of said last mentioned quarter section as is included in the town plat of the town of New Winchester, which was laid off on the said quarter section and which town plat is supposed to contain about fifteen acres, the said quarter section exclusive of said town plat being estimated to Contain 145 acres more or less, and also the Lots number 3, 4, 37 and 38, in the town of New Winchester aforesaid, subject to the dower of Catharine Bonnell, widow of Isaac Bonnell, deceased, as the same has been set off and assigned to her, and including the remainder after the determination of said dower estate: John Beymer, Sheriff. July 6, 1836. I Received this writ August 4th 1836, and in pursuance of the Command thereof and having caused public notice of the time and place of sale to be given for at least 30 days before the day of sale by advertisement in the "Guernsey Times" a newspaper printed in the town of Cambridge, Guernsey County, Ohio (a copy of which advertisement is hereto annexed), I did on the 10th day of September 1836 at the Court house in said Guernsey County, at public auction sell the tracts of Land and Town lots described in the within order and annexed advertisement, as follows, that is to say: the said North west quarter of section Fourteen in Township three and Range one of the unappropriated lands in the military district, Containing 160 acres more or less, to William Bonnell for the sum of Sixteenhundred and thirty five dollars ($1635). The said south west quarter of section Fourteen in Township three and Range one of the unappropriated lands in the military district, excepting so much of said last mentioned quarter section as is included in the two plat of the town of New Winchester, which was laid off on the said quarter section, and which town plat is supposed to contain about 15 acres (the said quarter exclusive of said Town plat being estimated to contain 145 acres more or less) to the said William Bonnell for the sum of Seventeen hundred & sixty five dollars (1765) which said two tracts of Land were so sold subject to the dower of Catharine Bonnell, widow of Isaac Bonnell, deceased, as the same has been set off & assigned to her, and including the remainder after the determination of said dower estate. The said tn lot number three in the said Town of New Winchester to thesaid William Bonnell, for the sum of Seventeen dollars ($17). The said tn lot number Four in the said Town of New Winchester, to the said William Bonnell for the sum of twenty-one dollars & fifty cents ($21.50). The said tn lot number thirty seven, in the said town of New Winchester to Daniel D. Fordyce, for the sum of Eight dollars ($8.) And the said tn lot number thirty eight in the said Town of New Winchester to John Fordyce for the sum of six dollars and seventy five cents, said sum being in each case more than two thirds the approved value and the highest and best bids made therefore. My fees $74.43. Viz, Advertisement $5.37. Poundage. $69.06 . October 3rd, 1836. John Beymer Sheriff of the County of Guernsey in the state of Ohio, and the same being examined, It is ordered that said proceedings and sale be and the same is hereby approved & confirmed, and thereupon it appearing that the consideration money of said estate has not been paid by said purchasers into the hands of the sheriff, It is ordered that the Sheriff on receiving payment of the consideration money or taking sufficient security therefore, to the satisfaction of the court, execute and deliver to each of the said purchasers a deed in fee simple, for the part of said estate so sold him, and it is further ordered that, out of the same consideration money, the said sheriff pay the costs and expences of this suit, amounting to one hundred & fourteen dollars & fourteen cents, and that he distribute the residue of said money or securities between the said parties, according to their Just rights and proportions.

1-3-2-2-4 D72 CB300163

JOHN[5] BONNELL (Abraham[4], Isaac[3], Nathaniel[2], William[1]) was born about 1745[2], probably at Kingwood, Hunterdon co, NJ. In his father's will, dated 28 January 1768[1], he was given £5 and a tract of 100 acres in Gloucester co, NJ, "bounded by a branch of Great Egg Harbor River known as Myery (Miry) Run." He died before 6 July 1811, when his heirs sold this tract of land to George West of Burlington, NJ[3]. The name of his wife has not been found. John does not appear on any of the New Jersey tax lists I have seen, although CB Database cites a reference to him on a customer account at the fulling mill in Grandin, Hunterdon co, on 20 November 1776[5].

His children, John and Rachel were both residents of Alexandria twp, Hunterdon co, in 1811[3].

Children[3]:
1. 310429. Mercy, m. before 20 Apr. 1799 Obed Coalman[3].
2. 310430. John C., b. 4 Apr. 1778[4].
3. 310431. Rachel, m. Andrew Fleming[3].

NOTE: Is this the John Bonnell of NJ who applied for a Revolutionary War pension (S6676)?[6] Probably not.

REFERENCES:
1. NJ Wills - Vol. IV, p. 49.
2. Family Group Sheet, Abraham Bonnell, Sr., compiled by H. Russell Bonnell, Logan, UT, and sent to me in 1961.
3. Hunterdon co, NJ, Deed Book P, p. 506, recorded 20 March 1812, photocopied and sent to me by Paula Sacco, Pittsburgh, PA. See The Bunnell/Bonnell Newsletter, Vol. I, No. 3, pp. 4, 5. Following is an abstract of all significant data:
   "This Indenture made this sixth day of July in the year of our Lord one thousand eight hundred and eleven. Between John Bonnel and Jemima, his wife and Andrew Fleming and Rachel his wife, formerly Rachel Bonnel, all of the township of Alexandria in the County of Hunterdon in the State of New Jersey of the first part, and George West, Esquire of the City of Burlington in the State aforesaid of the other part. Witnesseth that the said John Bonnel and Jemima his wife and Andrew Fleming and Rachel his wife for and in Consideration of the sum of [not legible] Dollars current lawful money of the United States . . . do grant, bargain and sell, . . . unto the said George West, all that certain tract of Land formerly surveyed to Abraham Bonnel on or about the year of our Lord one thousand seven hundred & thirty seven 1737, Situate, lying and being at or near Great Egg Harbour River in the County of Gloucester in the State of New Jersey aforesaid duly recorded in the Surveyor Generals office at Burlington in Lib. M, folio 333. bounded as followeth. Beginning at a maple tree by a branch of sd River called Myery run on the South side of the said

branch, thence extending North sixteen degrees West thirty one chains and a half to a stake and thence North seventy three degrees East thirty five chains to a white oak, thence South eleven degrees East thirty two chains to the aforesaid run thence bounding by the several courses of the same to the place of beginning. Containing one hundred acres of Land and allowance for Highways be the same contained in the reputed bounds more or less. Which tract of Land was left by will of said Abraham Bonnel dated the eighth day of January 1768 to his son John Bonnel who also died without disposing thereof, leaving Issue, Mercy, John and Rachel, and the said Mercy having since married Obed Coalman, together with her said Husband conveyed their share in said land to said John & Rachel by Indenture dated 20th April A.D. 1799, the whole being now the property of the parties of the first part."

4. Gravestone of John Bonnel, Jr., in Mt. Pleasant Cemetery, Alexandria twp, Hunterdon co, NJ, copied by Paula Sacco.
5. CB Database.
6. *Index of Revolutionary War Pension Applications.*
7. Duncan, p. 55.

1-3-3-1-1   D70   CB300039

JACOB[5] BONNELL (Benjamin[4], ?Samuel[3], Nathaniel[2], William[1]) was born probably in the 1730s, or even earlier, in Essex co, NJ[1]. On 27 November 1760, in Mendham, Morris co, NJ, he married MARY SCHOOLEY[2], daughter of William and Elizabeth (French) Schooley[5]. Jacob and his wife were Quakers and members of the Mendham Monthly Meeting[7]. On 9 July 1768 Jacob purchased 9.53 acres in Mendham twp from Thomas Milledge and Abraham Byden[7]. He appears in the tax lists in Mendham from 1779 to 1794[8]. Duncan says he served as a private in the Revolution from Morris, NJ[6]. His Quaker religion makes this questionable. There were other Jacobs. He died between 2 April 1795, when he purchased property in Roxbury twp, Morris co, NJ, from Mark Walton[4], and 1 April 1797, when his widow Mary and his children sold the property to Israel Canfield and Jacob Losey[4].

Children:
1. 320082. Mercy, b. 26 Apr. 1764[2]; m. (first) Jacob Simcock[3]; m. (second) Daniel Mills (or Miller)[3].
2. 320084. Henry, b. 28 Nov. 1767[2].

REFERENCES:
1. Letter 28 Nov. 1855 from Richard Brotherton, Dover, NJ, to Charles Bonnell CB331672, Waterloo, NY.
2. NYGBR, Records of Rahway and Plainfield [NJ] Monthly Meeting of Friends (formerly held at Amboy and Woodbridge). Communicated by Hugh D. Vail, Esq. Births, Vol. X. pp. 130, 140, 141. Marriages, Vol. ?, p.?
3. FGS - Jacob Bonnell and Mary Schooley, submitted by Viola Bunnell Kuhni, Midway, UT.
4. Morris co, NJ, Deed Book D, p. 190.
5. Handwritten chart of Schooley ancestry sent to me by Mrs. Russell S. Cooke, Springfield, IL.
6. Duncan, p. 55.

NOTE: Duncan listed this Jacob as the son of Abraham (1-3-2-2). In the 1920s Grace Gridley Roscoe and Carolyn Syron Valentine discovered the 1855 Richard Brotherton letter and misinterpreted it to mean that this Jacob was the son of Benjamin Bonnell (1-3-1-2-2). Relying on their interpretation, in my book, Volume I of *The Bunnell/Bonnell Family in America*, I published a "correction" of Ruth Duncan's statement. Now having found the actual letter as written by Richard Brotherton, I can correct my own misstatement. Note that Mary Schooley was Richard Brotherton's great aunt.

1-3-3-1-2 CB300054

BENJAMIN[5] BUNNELL or BONNELL (Benjamin[4], ?Samuel[3], Nathaniel[2], William[1]), was born about 1744[4], probably in Essex co, NJ. As a child he moved with his parents to Mendham, Morris co, NJ. Little is known of his early life. Like many of his relatives and neighbors, he was a member of the Society of Friends (Quaker)[7].

During the Revolution many of the Quakers found their sympathies to lie with the Loyalists who supported the British side of the conflict. So it was with Benjamin. However, unlike most Quakers, he became actively involved in the conflict. In March 1779 Benjamin Bunnel of Succassuny, Morris co, was indicted for knowingly passing counterfeit $30 bills[3]. This is almost certainly the Benjamin of this article. Whether he suffered any consequences does not appear. About this time Benjamin was married to Sarah, whose maiden name may have been Jones[1]. (The Mendham tax list for June 1780 includes two householders, James Jones and Daniel Jones[5].)

On 6 August 1781 Benjamin was in New York City, where he enlisted as a corporal in the loyalist American Legion, Capt. James Wogan's company, serving under Brigadier General Benedict Arnold[1]. On the 6th of September the American Legion took part in Arnold's attack on New London, CT, and its protecting forts, Fort Trumbull and Fort Griswold[1]. Benjamin's company, assigned to the west side of the Thames River[1], was involved in the capture of Fort Trumbull and the burning and plunder of New London[8]. Benjamin Bonnell was disowned by the Society of Friends "for conduct of a warlike nature."[7]

As the war came to a close in early 1783, the stream of Tories fleeing to other parts of the British empire became a flood. The third major wave of Loyalists destined for the River Saint John, Nova Scotia (now New Brunswick) took ship at the end of June, departing New York about 8 July 1783[1]. Paul Bunnell lists eleven ships comprising this fleet[1]. He quotes the evacuation records of New York: "Benjamin Bonnell, farmer, from New Jersey, assigned to unit No. 15, captain William Wright on the ship, *William*, with wife, and two children under ten years of age, dated July 1783."[1] About two weeks later they arrived in Parrtown, Nova Scotia (now Saint John, New Brunswick)[1].

It was more than a year later that Benjamin finally received a grant of 10 acres of land on the west side of the Saint John River along the seashore[1]. Paul Bunnell quotes the landgrant in toto[1]. It was dated 11 August 1784 to "give and grant unto Matthew Hains," and 111 others, including

FIFTH GENERATION

Benjamin Bonnell[1]. Each grantee received 10 acres out of a total tract of 120 acres[1]. This land proved inadequate as farm land for a family, and the following year he and 60 other Loyalists received another grant of the Long Reach property farther up the Saint John River[1]. It consisted of 1280 acres on the east side of the river, to be divided according to rank[1]. As a corporal, Benjamin's lot was lot No. 1, 200 acres stretching out on the bank of the river[1].

Here they cleared the land, built their house, raised their growing family and developed the farm which supported them for the next 23 years[1]. On 25 May 1809, however, they sold the farm on Long Reach to Tertullus Theal of Saint John for £121[1]. On 11 January 1810 Benjamin paid £20 to John and Elizabeth Crab for 200 acres on the opposite side of the river in Greenwich Parish[1]. Years later, by date of 13 November 1824, he sold 100 acres of this property to his son Isaac[1]. On 28 June 1827 Benjamin wrote his will, as follows[1]:

"In the name of God, Amen.
I, Benjamin Bunnell, of Long Reach, Parish of Westfield and County of Kings, Yeoman, being of sound mind and memory although weak and infirm of body But knowing that it is appointed once for all to die--I do make and ordain my last will and testament in manner and form as follows -- viz. principally and above all I give and recommend my soul unto the hands of the Allmighty God that gave it, and my body I recommend to the earth -- to be buried in a Christian-like manner. Nothing doubting but at the general resurrection I shall receive the same again -- THROUGH the mighty power of GOD. And as touching such wordly . . . as it hath pleased God to bless me in. I leave and bequeath it in manner and form as follows

FIRST
I allow all my just debts to be paid.

Secondly
I leave and bequeath unto my beloved wife Sarah -- all the profits arising from the farm at the Devil's Back known by lot no. twenty-nine, it being the South half of the same containing one hundred acres more or less together with the use of two milk cows and six sheep -- with all the moveables and household furniture therein during her natural period of life or while she lives --

Thirdly
I leave and bequeath to my son Benjamin twenty-five pounds currency. To my son Joseph twenty-five pounds current money and to my son Simeon fifty pounds current money. And to three of my daughters Sarah, Aphia and Eleanor, I bequeath ten pounds currency apiece or to each if it remains to be had after. The others get their shares -- or otherwise whatever remains after my sons' share or what is mentioned is to be divided between the three Daughters mentioned. Each share and share alike. All these shares mentioned to be raised or got from the sale or profit of what I leave in my beloved wife's hands at her decease.

Lastly
I do make constitute and ordain Thomas Fowler and Isaac Cawson both of the Long Reach and County of Kings to be my executors of this my last will and testament. Dated this 28th day of June in the year of our Lord One Thousand Eight Hundred and Twenty-Seven.
Signed sealed and delivered
in the presence of us   Benjamin Bunnell
Joseph Purdy
Sarah Purdy"

Benjamin died 17 February 1828[5]. His wife survived him[1].

FIFTH GENERATION

Children:
1. 006840. Sarah Elizabeth, b. about 1779[7]; m. about 1816[7] Joseph Purdy[1].
2. 004745. Aphia, b. about 1781[7].
3. 000301. Benjamin, b. 1789[7].
4. 006841. Joseph, b. 1790[7].
5. 006715. Eleanor Ann, b. 1797; m. 20 Aug. 1816[1] Joseph Fanjoy[1].
      Children (surname Fanjoy)[6]:

1. Isabella.	5. Simeon.	8. Charles Thomas.
2. Benjamin Bunnell.	6. William.	9. Rebecca.
3. Edward Albert.	7. Joseph.	10. Elizabeth.
4. Sarah Ann.		

6. 000031. Simeon, b. about 1798[7].
7. 006708. Isaac, b. about 1800[7].

NOTE:

There is no clear evidence that Benjamin Bonnell, the Loyalist, was the same person as Benjamin the son of Benjamin 1-3-3-1. Barring new evidence to the contrary, I believe the circumstantial evidence is convincing:

1. The evacuation record says specifically that he was a farmer from New Jersey.
2. He was originally a Quaker, as were most if not all the other known children of 1-3-3-1.
3. Although he was a Quaker, he engaged in anti-Revolutionary activity.
      a. Passing counterfeit money. This was largely supplied by the British to embarrass and cripple the patriot economy.
      b. Joining this to his actual enlistment and service in the British forces completes the picture.
4. Richard Brotherton, a devout Quaker, in his 1855 letter says he never knew Benjamin and apparently never knew what became of him. This would be consistent with the circumstances. Benjamin fled to New Brunswick before Richard was born. The family probably did not talk about the only member who actively chose the wrong side in the Revolution and who was disowned by the Society of Friends for his military activity.
5. Benjamin named a daughter Eleanor, apparently after his mother, and a son Simeon, apparently after his brother who died as a young man. Neither of these names was common in the American family at this time. Simeon seems to have been used exclusively by Benjamin 1-3-3-1 and his descendants for several generations.

NOTE 2:

Recent (2007) DNA test results suggest that current descendants of this Benjamin Bonnell are probably not descended from William Bunnell the immigrant. Further tests are necessary to clarify this matter and to determine at what point in the family tree the above record is incorrect. There are at least three weak links in this line.

REFERENCES:
1. *THUNDER OVER NEW ENGLAND, Benjamin Bonnell, Loyalist,* by Paul J. Bunnell, A.G., U.E.L., 1988.
2. Letter 28 Nov. 1855 from Richard Brotherton, Dover, NJ, to Charles Bonnell CB331672, Waterloo, NY.
3. Indictment of Benjamin Bunnel, Mar. 1779, copy sent to me by Paul J. Bunnell.
4. *Vital Statistics from New Brunswick Newspapers*, Vol. 1-2-3, 1784-1828, notice sent to me by Carole Bonnell.

5. Gen Mag of NJ, Vol. 45, No. 3, p. 125.
6. Children of Joseph and Eleanor (Bonnell) Fanjoy, sent to me by Claude B. Mitchell.
7. CB Database.
8. *The Battle of Groton Heights*, by Rev. H. E. Burnham, 1926.

1-3-3-1-3   CB300058

AARON[5] BONNELL (Benjamin[4], ?Samuel[3], Nathaniel[2], William[1]) was born 30 March 1749[1], probably in Mendham twp, Morris co, NJ[2]. On 13 April 1772[3,4], in Morris co, NJ, he was issued a license for his marriage to ANN BROTHERTON[1,3,4], daughter of Henry and Mercy (Schooley) Brotherton[5]. She was born 7 September 1753[1] in Morris co. The bondsmen for the marriage license were Aaron's father Benjamin Bonnel, Hezekiah Freeman, and John Clark[4].

Ann's father died at the end of 1773 or early in 1774. His will provided for his wife and the education of the children, with all assets to be sold and divided equally among the children when Mercy, the youngest reached the age of 18[10]. Aaron Bunnel, householder, 4 horses, 3 cattle, 1 pig, appears on the list of taxables for Mendham, Morris co, NJ, in June 1778[6], and again in June 1780[6] as Aaron Bonnill, 34 acres improved land, 4 horses, 3 cattle. On 1 September 1786 Aaron Bonnel of Mendham mortgaged lands "situate near Rockaway River, whereon the said Aaron Bonnel now dwells"[9].

On 24 September 1789, the children of the deceased Henry Brotherton, including Ann (Brotherton) Bonnell, with her husband Aaron, sold a 15-acre parcel of their father's estate in Mendham to their brother William Brotherton for £50[11]. The deed was witnessed by Nathaniel and David Bonnell, presumably Aaron's brothers. This suggests that Ann's sister Mercy was now eighteen and that the time had come to settle their father's estate and to divide the proceeds among them.

About 1788 Aaron and Ann, with the first 8 or 9 of their children, moved to western Pennsylvania. In the 1790 census he appears in Washington co as "Aron Bundle": 2-2-6-0-0[7]. In 1793 his name appears on the tax rolls of Pike Run twp, Washington co, PA[5]. On 16 August 1799 he purchased of Andrew and Sarah Smith a tract of 100 acres in West Bethlehem twp on the North Fork of Ten Mile creek[5]. He paid £100 for it[5]. He appears in the census in West Bethlehem twp, Washington co, in 1800: 00201-01001[8], and in 1810: 02001-00111[8]. There he died about 18 March 1814, intestate[5]. The following year, on 6 October 1815, the deeds of Morris co, NJ, show that Ann (Brotherton) Bonnell sold 106 acres in Randolph twp, Morris co, NJ, to her nephew, Richard Brotherton[8].

It would seem that the widow Ann and some of the children continued to live on the farm in West Bethlehem twp. Nothing was done about dividing the estate among the heirs until 1831, when son Benjamin petitioned the Washington co court for appraisement of the land and partition among the children[5]. The land was valued and appraised at $948.13 ½ on 27 March 1832, but the court decided that the land could not be beneficially divided[5]. Benjamin then purchased the farm from the other heirs[5]. Ann (Brotherton) Bonnell was still living in 1832[5].

Children:

1. 014402. Elizabeth, b. 21 Jan. 1773[1]; m. William Schooley[5]; d. 2 Dec. 1831.
2. 002142. Moses, b. 3 April 1774[1].
3. 002141. Henry, b. 29 July 1776[1].
4. 009764. Mary, b. 23 June 1778[1]; m. James Buckingham[5,13].
   Children (surname Buckingham)[13]:
   1. James D.   others.
5. 005764. Sarah, b. 31 Jan. 1780[1]; m. Thomas Hutton[5].
6. 001523. Anna, b. 22 Nov. 1781[1]; m. Edward Wallace[5]; d. before 1832[5]
   Children (surname Wallace):

1. Mary.	4. William.	6. Edward.
2. Ann.	5. Thomas.	7. John.
3. Richard.		

7. 005686. Mercy, b. 25 Feb. 1784[1], in NJ; m. about 1804 Thomas Iiams[5,12]; d. 21 May 1867[12].
   Children (surname Iiams)[12]:

1. William R.	5. John.	9. Ann.
2. Rebecca.	6. Elizabeth.	10. Nancy.
3. Sarah.	7. Thomas.	11. Charity.
4. Mary.	8. Elenora.	

8. 000295. Benjamin, b. 12 Apr. 1786[1].
9. James, b. 13 Sept. 1788[1]; apparently died in infancy.
10. 005685. John, b. 29 Apr. 1791[1].
11. 014403. Eleanor, b. 29 Apr. 1793[1]; m. Thomas Moore[5]; d. before 1832[5].
    Children (surname Moore):

1. Ann.	4. Esther.	6. Narcissa.
2. Eunice.	5. William.	7. Aaron.
3. Thomas.		

12. 014404. David, b. 17 June 1795[1].
13. 012467. William, b. 28 July 1797[1].

REFERENCES:

1. The Hatfield Family Bible, owned in 1965 by Mrs. Ruth Amer, 729 Beekman Ave., Medford, OR. She was the great great granddaughter of Aaron and Ann (Brotherton) Bonnell. The following extract copied by Mrs. Amer and sent to me by Mrs. Floyd Nielson on 7 September 1965.
   "Aaron, son of Benjamin & Eleanor Bonnell, was born 3 mo 30th 1749
   "Anne, wife of Aaron Bonnell & daughter of Henry & Mercy Brotherton, b. 9th mo 7th, 1753
   "Elizabeth daughter of Aaron & Anne Bonnell born 1st M. 21, 1773
   "Moses son of Aaron & Anne Bonnell, born 4th M. 3rd, 1774
   "Henry son of Aaron & Anne Bonnell born 7th M. 29th, 1776

FIFTH GENERATION

"Mary daughter of Aaron & Anne Bonnell born 6th M. 23rd, 1778

"Sarah daughter of Aaron & Anne Bonnell 1st M. 31, 1780

"Anne daughter of Aaron & Anne Bonnell 11th M. 22, 1781

"Mercy daughter of Aaron & Anne Bonnell born 2nd M. 25, 1784

"Benjamin son of Aaron & Anne Bonnell born 4th M. 12th, 1786

"James son of Aaron & Anne Bonnell born 9th M. 13th, 1788

"John son of Aaron & Anne Bonnell born 4th M. 29th 1791

"Eleanor daughter of Aaron & Anne Bonnell born 4th M. 29th 1793

"David son of Aaron & Anne Bonnell born 6th M. 17th 1795

"William son of Aaron & Anne Bonnell born 7th M. 28th 1797"

2. Letter 28 Nov. 1855 from Richard Brotherton, Dover, NJ, to Charles Bonnell CB331672, Waterloo, NY.
3. NJ Marriages, p. 28.
4. Marriage License of Aaron Bonnell and Ann Brotherton from the files of the New Jersey Secretary of State. Copy sent to me by Marilyn W. Lynch:

"Aaron Bonnell

Benj.n Bonnell	Bond
Hezekiah Freeman	for
& John Cook	license

To

His Excellency.

Know all men by these presents,

That we Aaron Bonnell, Benjamin Bonnell, Hezekiah Freeman & John Cook all of the County of Morris & Province of N.J. holden and do stand justly indebted unto His Excellency William Franklin Esq Captn General Governor and Commander in chief over the Province of N.J. the sum of Five Hundred Pounds of current lawful Money of N.J. to be paid to his said Excellency William Franklin Esqr his Successors or Assigns : For the which Payment well and truly to be made & done, we do bind ourselves our Heirs, Executors and Administrators, and every of them, Jointly & Severally firmly by these Presents.

Sealed with our Seals; Dated this thirteenth Day of April Annoque Domini One thousand Seven Hundred and Seventy-two.

The Condition of this Obligation is Such,

That whereas the above-bounden Benjamin Bonnel, Hezekiah Freeman & John Cook have obtained License of Marriage for the above Bounden Aaron Bonnel of the one Party, and for Ann Brotherton of the other Party: Now, if it shall not hereafter appear, that they the said Aaron Bonnel & Ann Brotherton have any lawful Let or Impediment, of Pre-contract, affinity or Consanguinity, to hinder their being joined in the Holy Bands of Matrimony, and afterwards their living together as Man and Wife; then this obligation to be void, or else to stand and remain in full Force and Virtue.

Sealed & Delivered in	
the Presence of	Aaron Bonnel
Malm McCourry	Beniam Bonnel
	Hezekiah Freeman
	John Cooke"

182

5. *Genealogy of Brotherton, Bonnell Families of Morris co, NJ and Hamilton, Clermont co, OH*, by Margaret Watson Cooke - 1966.
6. Gen. Mag. of NJ, Vol. 45, No. 3, p. 122.
7. *First Census of the United States - 1790, Heads of Families - Pennsylvania*, page 255.
8. CB Database.
9. Book C, Morris co mortgages, page 93, extract sent to me by Jerome Hatch, Chicago, IL.
10. NJ Wills - Vol. V, p. 67.
11. Morris co, NJ, Deeds, Book L, p. 343.
12. FGS, Thomas & Mercy (Bonnell) Iiams, prepared and sent to me by Roberta W. Iiams, Springboro, OH.
13. Letter 26 Dec. 1990 from Mary Burdick, Watertown, MA.

1-3-3-1-4 CB300059

NATHANIEL[5] BONNELL (Benjamin[4], ?Samuel[3], Nathaniel[2], William[1]) was born about 1758[1] in Mendham twp, Morris co, NJ (or in Newark, Essex co, NJ). His father settled in Mendham twp, where Nathaniel grew to manhood. He married (first) ELIZABETH LIKENS[1] in Morris co (Was she daughter of the William Likens[2] who appears in the 1778 and 1780 tax list in Mendham twp?) Nathaniel appears among the rateables for Mendham twp in June 1780 as Nath[l] Bonil as a householder owning 10 acres of improved land and 2 pigs[2]. He was also apparently the Nathaniel Bonnell who was listed in Mendham in the militia census in 1793[3]. (The only other Nathaniel in Mendham was over the age limit for inclusion in the census.) He, with his brother Simeon, was probably the Nathaniel Bonnell who enlisted in 1775 as a private in the First Regiment of the New York Line during the Revolution[9].

Like his half-brother Jacob, Nathaniel later removed to Junius, Seneca co, NY, where in 1806 he bought 80 acres of land in the northwest part of lot 66 from Thomas Bills[4]. His occupation was noted as shoemaker. He was a Quaker[7]. He appears in Junius in the census in 1810: 01001-00000[4]. It would appear that Elizabeth was no longer living and that son Nathaniel was the only child living with him. On 9 March 1811 he bought 29 more acres from Thomas Bills for $250[4]. One of the witnesses to the deed was Henry Bonnel[4], son of Nathaniel's half-brother Jacob.

Some time in this decade Nathaniel married again, this time to CATHERINE _____[5]. They appear in the 1820 census in Junius: 000001-00001[4]. On 6 February 1824 he sold a small piece of his property in Junius to Samuel Lunda[4]. Nathaniel made his will on 9 February 1833[5]. Heirs listed in the will included his wife Catherine, son Darius of Rochester, NY, daughter Pamelia, wife of Charles Tripp of Dansville, NY, son Nathaniel of Sheffield, OH, daughter Perthania, wife of Zina Tripp of Watson, NY, and after the death of his wife, Catherine Conner[5]. Nathaniel and his wife appear in the 1840 census in Waterloo, Seneca co, NY: 00100000001-0000001[4]. Nathaniel died at Waterloo on 29 June 1845[5], and his wife must have died somewhat before. His will was filed for probate on 17 July 1845 by Catherine Conner of Waterloo[5]. What her connection was to Nathaniel and his family is unknown. [Catherine M. Conor was born 11 June 1800, daughter of Charles and Agnes Connor[4]. She died 6 March 1858 in Waterloo and was buried in the Quaker Cemetery[4].] His will reads[5]:

"I Nathaniel Bonnel of the town of Waterloo, county of Seneca and State of New York, being in usual health and sound mind, do make and publish this my last Will and testament in manner and form following, viz. 1st, I give and bequeath unto my beloved wife Catharine Bonnell all my estate both real and personal during her natural life to be used and occupied by her during her said natural life for her own proper use benefit and behoof. Second, I give and bequeath to my son Darius Bonnel the sum of five dollars, and to my daughter Pamelia Tripp the sum of twenty dollars. Third, I give and bequeath to my son Nathaniel Bonnel the sum of fifty dollars, and to my daughter Perthania Tripp the sum of fifteen dollars. Fourth, The above legacies contained in the Second and Third items of this my said last will and testament, are to be paid as soon as may be after the decease of my said wife. Fifth, I give and bequeath unto Catharine Conner all my real estate after the death of my said wife, and to her heirs and assigns forever. Sixth, If their shall be any personal property remaining after the decease of said wife it is my will that the same shall be the property of the said Catharine Conner and her heirs and assigns. Seventh, If any of my heirs shall bring any demands against my estate, he she or they shall forfeit the legacies contained in the foregoing.
Eighth, I nominate constitute and appoint my friends William Bowdish and Isaac Mosher Executors of this my last will and testament hereby revoking all other and former wills by me at any time heretofore made. In witness whereof I have hereunto set my hand and seal this ninth day of February in the year of our Lord one thousand eight hundred and thirty three."

"Seneca county ss: Catharine Conner of Waterloo in the county of Seneca, being duly affirmed, says that Nathaniel Bonnell, late of the town of Waterloo, in the county of Seneca, deceased, died a natural death on the twenty ninth day of June last, in the said town of Waterloo, in the county of Seneca, where he resided previous to & at the time of his death; That the said deceased died having a last will & testament, now here in court produced, which relates to both real & personal estate, & in which William Bowdish & Isaac Mosher are named as executors; That the said deceased left no widow. That he left children his heirs at law & next of kin whose names & places of residence are as follows, to wit.- Darius Bonnell, residing in the city of Rochester, Pamelia Tripp, wife of Charles Tripp, residing in the town of Dansvill, Steuben county, N.Y., Nathaniel Bonnell, residing in the town of Sheffield, Ashtabula county, Ohio, & Perthania Tripp, wife Zina Tripp, residing in the town of Watson, Lewis county, N.Y. That the above are all & the only heirs at law & next of kin of the said deceased and are all of lawful age.
Subscribed & affirmed to this 17th}
Day of July 1845, before me   }   Catharine Conner
        John Morgan, Surrogate of Seneca county."

Children:
1. 003449. Simeon[1,6], b. 15 Nov. 1783[1].
2. 320211. Pamelia[1,5], b. 21 July 1785[1]; m. 1807[1] Charles Tripp[1,5].
        Children (surname Tripp)[1]:
        1. Daniel.   3. Uriah.   5. George.
        2. Simeon.   4. Elizabeth.
3. 032244. William[1,6], b. 26 Jan. 1786[1].
4. 320210. Darius[1,5,6], b. 13 Jan. 1788[1].
5. 320223. Perthania[5], b. 179x; m. Zina Tripp[5].
6. 320224. Nathaniel[1,5,6], b. 22 Aug. 1797[8].

REFERENCES:
1. Family data compiled by Nathaniel's great great granddaughter Lois Louise Tripp, Avon, NY, in 1943. Copied and sent to me by Homer E. Baldwin 5 Dec. 1959.

2. Gen Mag of NJ - Vol. 45, No. 3, pp. 122, 125.
3. NJ in 1793, p.251.
4. CB Database.
5. Will of Nathaniel Bonnell, Seneca co, NY, Will Book B, p. 388. Photocopy sent to me by Claude A. Bunnell.
6. Letter 28 Nov. 1855 from Richard Brotherton, Dover, NJ, to Charles Bonnell CB331672, Waterloo, NY.
7. List of 1810 Quakers in Waterloo twp, Seneca co, NY, sent to me by Claude A. Bonnell.
8. Bonnell history compiled by Clara (Witt) Bonnell-Dawson for her sons. Sent to me 8 Nov. 1992 by Max B. Davis, Garden Grove, CA.
9. *New York in the Revolution as Colony and State*, by James A. Roberts, 1898, p. 19.

1-3-3-1-5 CB300060

SIMEON[5] BONNELL (Benjamin[4], ?Samuel[3], Nathaniel[2], William[1]) was born probably in Mendham twp, Morris co, NJ. Richard Brotherton said that he died as a young man[1]. No other information about this man has yet come to my attention, although he is probably the Simeon Bonnell who enlisted in 1775 in the First Regiment of the New York Line during the Revolution[2]. It is interesting to note that his brother Benjamin had a son, a grandson, a great grandson, and a great great grandson who all bore the name Simeon. His brother Aaron had a grandson Simeon. His brother Nathaniel had a son, a grandson and a great grandson named Simeon. Otherwise Simeon is a rare name in the Bunnell/Bonnell family.

REFERENCES:

1. Letter 28 Nov. 1855 from Richard Brotherton, Dover NJ, to Charles Bonnell CB331672, Waterloo, NY.
2. *New York in the Revolution as Colony and State*, by James A. Roberts, 1898, p. 19.

1-3-3-1-6 CB300061

DAVID[5] BONNELL (Benjamin[4], ?Samuel[3], Nathaniel[2], William[1]) was born about 1762, probably in Mendham twp, Morris co, NJ. He married MARY ANN MASTERS in New Jersey[2]. References to this man during his early life in Mendham twp are meager at best. Some of the listings of David and/or David, Jr., in Sharon Holley's analysis of Mendham tax records may well apply to him[3]. Richard Brotherton wrote in 1855 that Benjamin's son "David removed with a view of going to Redstone" [PA, as his brother Aaron did] "but settled in the upper part of Virginia. When he left here he had two sons, Thomas and John."[1]

Although the western boundaries of Virginia, Maryland and Pennsylvania had already been settled before the late 1790s, when David took his family west, he actually settled in Bedford co, PA. At the time of the 1800 census they were living in Londonderry twp, Bedford co, PA. He is listed as David Bundle, with 1 male and 2 females under 10, a male and a female from 10 to 16, 1 male from 16 to 26, and 1 male and 1 female from 26 to 45[5,8]. In 1804 he appears as executor of the will of Henry Amerine, Sr., of Bedford co[5,8]. In the triennial assessment of 1808 in Bedford co

David paid a tax of 99 cents on 25 acres of warranted land, 175 acres of improved land and 2 cows[6]. On 1 February 1810 he was appointed by Pennsylvania Governor Simon Snyder to the position of Justice of the Peace in the district including Londonderry twp, Bedford co[7]. David Bonnell appears in the 1810 census in Londonderry twp with 1 male under 10, 1 between 10 to 16, 2 between 16 to 26, and 1 male over 45; also, 2 females under 10, 1 between 10 to 16, 2 between 16 to 26, 1 between 26 to 45, and 1 female over 45[8]. In 1813 David witnessed the will of John Hains in Bedford co[5,8]. David and Mary Ann appear in the 1820 census of Londonderry twp living alone, both over 45[8]. The 1830 census of Londonderry twp lists them as 1 male and 1 female between 60 and 70[5,8]. In 1834 he sold land in Bedford co to C. Wolford[5,8], and in 1835 he bought land from George Karchner, again in Bedford co[5,8].

David died before before 4 February 1836, when his sons Henry and John, were appointed administrators of his estate[9]. At the April 1838 session of the Bedford co Court, the administrators petitioned for the sale of his real estate[5]. Mary Spies copied the following notes in the Bedford co court house:

> Orphan's Court Docket No. 5, p. 374: To the Honorable Judges of the Orphans' Court of Bedford Co. at April Term 1838. The petition of Henry Bonnell & John Bonnell administrators of David Bonnell late of Londonderry Twp. show that personal estate of the intestate is insufficient to pay the debts.
> Inventory & conscionable appraisment filed in Registers Office -- 52.22
> Debts due by intestate -- 184.89
>
> Land adjoining George Miller heirs
>   Cornelius Devore
>   Christian Wolford[5]

The date of death of Mary Ann (Masters) Bonnell has not yet been found.

Children:
1. 032245. Thomas[1,2], b. about 1784.
2. 004488. John[1,2], b. 25 Apr. 1788[2].
3. 032346. Phebe[10], b. about 1790; m. _____ Wolford[10].
4. 004487. Henry[2], b. about 1795.
5. 027543. Mary[8,10]; b/ about 1812[8]; m. Solomon Albright[8].
   others.

REFERENCES:
1. Letter 28 Nov. 1855 from Richard Brotherton, Dover, NJ, to Charles Bonnell CB331672, Waterloo, NY.
2. *Descendants of David & Mary Ann Bonnell*, compiled by Jean Ansteth Kennedy 1976-1981.
3. *Tax Ratables 1778-1822, Mendham and Randolph Townships, NJ, Bonnell Family - Acres Taxed*, study prepared by Sharon Holley, Budd Lake, NJ, April 1988.
4. *New Jersey in 1793*, by James S. Norton, 1973, p. 251.
5. Individual Chronology - David Bonnell (Bunnell), compiled and sent to me in 1988 by Mary B. Spies, Spokane, WA.
6. Letter 2 July 1992 from Clement M. Bonnell, III, Milford, NJ.

7. Commission copied and sent to me in 1988 by Mary B. Spies:
   Bedford co, PA, Deed Book G, page 832
   "Pennsylvania   In the name and by authority of the commonwealth of Pennsylvania, Simon
   Snyder Governor of the said commonwealth, to David BONNELL of the County of Bedford
   sends greetings. Know you that reposing especial trust and confidence in your integrity, judgment
   and abilities, I the said Simon Snyder, have appointed and by these presents do appoint and
   commission you the said David BONNELL to be a Justice of the Peace in the district numbered
           including Londonderry Township in the Coounty of Bedford, hereby giving and
   granting unto you full right and title, to have and execute all and singular the powers jurisdictions
   and authorities, and to receive and enjoy all and singular the lawful emoluments of a Justice of
   the Peace aforesaid, agreeable to the constitution and laws of the commonwealth, to have and to
   hold this commission and the office hereby granted unto you the said David BONNELL so long
   as you shall behave yourself well. Given under my hand and the seal fo the state at Lancaster
   this first day of February in the year of our Lord one thousand eight hundred and ten and of the
   commonwealth the thirty fourth.
   By the Governor   N. B. Baeleau secy.
   Recorded the 23 day of February A.D. 1810   David Mann, Recorder"
8. CB Database
9. Photocopy of the Bond of Henry and John Bonnell as administrators of David's estate, sent to me by
   Joan Flavel, Gold Beach, OR.
10. Letter 4 March 2001 from Joan Flavel, Gold Beach, OR.

1-3-7-1-1 D28iii CB300172

JOHN[5] BONNELL (Joseph[4], Joseph[3], Nathaniel[2], William[1]) was born in Elizabethtown, Essex
(now Union) co, NJ, probably in the late 1730s or early 1740s. The will of his father Joseph,
dated 3 November 1761 and proved 5 December 1761, specified that his son John was to be
supported until his death, when the lands were to be sold and the money divided between the
remaining two sons, Sinecy Bonnel and Doctor Wats Bonnel[1]. I find no further record of him,
although it would appear that he was already dead when his brother Sinesy made his will on 19
August 1777.[3]

REFERENCES:
     1. NJ Wills, Vol. IV, p. 49.
     2. Amer Fam - Long Island, p. 61.
     3. NJ Wills, Vol. V, p. 52.

1-3-7-1-2 D28v CB300170

DOCTOR WATTS[5] BONNELL (Joseph[4], Joseph[3], Nathaniel[2], William[1]) was born in
Elizabethtown, Essex (now Union) co, NJ, in the late 1730s or early 1740s. He is called "Dr.
Wats" in his father's will dated 3 November 1761[1]. Every other reference to him that I have seen
also calls him Doctor Watts Bonnel(l), but I have been unable to determine whether he was a
medical doctor or whether "Doctor Watts" was his given name; I suspect the latter. He married
EUNICE BALL[2,3], daughter of Nathaniel Ball of Connecticut Farms[2,3], Essex co, NJ. He
appears in the tax lists of Springfield, Essex co, in 1779 and 1780[4], and in 1781, 1782, 1783 and

187

1789[5], and that of Orange twp, Essex co from 1810 to 1815, 1820 to 1822[5], and in that of Chatham, Morris co, NJ, in 1806 and 1807[5].

They lived in Springfield, Essex co, for a number of years, until 1 May 1804, when he and his wife sold their house and eight acres of land in Jefferson Village, Springfield twp, "on which Bonnel now lives" to Langhorn Burton Raynor of New York City for $1000[7]. They took a mortgage for $750, which was paid in full by 4 March 1805[6]. The Bonnells then moved across the Passaic River and bought 64 acres in Chatham, Morris co, at a place called the Long-Hill[8]. On 10 February 1808 they sold this property to Miller Walker and moved to Orange twp, Essex co, NJ, where they seem to have remained for the rest of their lives[6,7].

I have not found a record of the deaths of Doctor Watts or Eunice, nor any account of children, although various sources state that he had six children or none at all.

REFERENCES:
1. NJWills - Vol. IV, p. 49.
2. Littell, p. 32.
3. Extract from a Ball genealogy compiled and sent to me by Joseph Scukanec, Flint, MI, citing the Frank C. Ball collection, Ball State University, Muncie, IN.
4. Gen Mag of NJ, Vol. 43, No. 2, p. 80, New Jersey Rateables, 1778-1780, by Kenn Stryker-Rodda.
5. New Jersey Tax Lists.
6. Essex co, NJ, Mortgages, Book D, p. 249, Book G, p. 134, Book H, p. 763, Book I, p. 247, Book L, p. 578.
7. Essex co, NJ, Deeds, Book I, p. 488, Book P, pp. 307, 309, Book T, p. 366, Book X, p. 13.
8. Morris co, NJ, Mortgages, Book F, p. 179.
9. Morris co, NJ, Deeds, Book Q, p. 396.

1-3-7-1-3   D73   CB300168

JOSEPH[5] BONNELL (Joseph[4], Joseph[3], Nathaniel[2], William[1]) was born about 1734/35 in Elizabethtown, Essex (now Union) co, NJ. He married PHEBE _____ [1]. He died 7[2] (or 5[3]) March 1761[2,3] at the age of 26 years, and was buried in the Presbyterian Cemetery at Connecticut Farms, Essex co, NJ, near the grave of his only child[2,3]. His will, dated 23 January 1761, was proved 24 November 1761[1]. An abstract gives the following: Joseph Bonnel of Elizabeth, Yeoman, give to my wife, Phebe, my moveable estate and 35 pounds. Brother Synesey, my apparel; land to be sold and my father, Joseph Bonnel to have the rest of the cash from the sale of the land. My wife, my father, Joseph Bonnel and Moses Baldwin, Executors. Witnesses - Samuel Walter, Jacamiah Smith and Obadiah Smith[1]. [Did Phebe marry (second) Jacob Jennings?[4]]

Children:
1. 310291. Joseph, b. 24 Feb. 1760[5]; d. 14 Sept. 1760[2,3].

REFERENCES:
1. NJ Wills - Vol. IV, p.49.
2. CT Farms Church Records.

3. CT Farms Cem Inscriptions.
4. DAR Index of Spouses, Vol. III, p. 106: "Bonnell, Mrs. Phoebe = Jacob Jennings, Patriot
    Index, Vol. I, p. 368", copied and sent to me by Miss Marian E. Biles, Greene, NY.
5. Duncan, p. 55.

1-3-7-1-5   D74   CB300169

SYNESY[5] BONNELL (Joseph[4], Joseph[3], Nathaniel[2], William[1]) was born about 1746/47 in Elizabethtown, Essex (now Union) co, NJ. His brother, Joseph, Jr., left his apparel to Synesy in his will of 3 November 1761[2]. His wife was PUAH[1] BALL, daughter of Nathaniel[9] and Esther (Osborn)[4] Ball[4,9]. On 29 June 1775 he was one of the Elizabethtown volunteers in the Revolutionary Army company of Capt. Richard Townley under the command of Col. Elias Dayton.[10]

He was only 31 years old when he died at Connecticut Farms, Essex (now Union) co, NJ, on 22 February 1778[3]. He was buried in the Presbyterian cemetery there next to the grave of his brother Joseph, Jr[3]. His widow married (second) John Sallae, by whom she had three more children[4]. An abstract of Synesy's will is as follows: 19 Aug. 1777. Sinesey Bonnell of Elizabeth give to my wife, Puah, 35 pounds, grain livestock, fire wood and use of my part of the plantation until sold, then she is to use the money to bring up the children. All lands to be sold after the death of my mother, Sarah Bonnell. Daughters, Rachel, Lois and Phebe the money that remains, when they are 18. Executors - wife, Puah and friend, Elias Whitehead. Witnesses - Benjamin Hait, Solomon Line and Sarah Cambel. Proved 11 March 1778[1]. Puah Bonnell appears in the tax list in Springfield, Essex (now Union) co, NJ, in July and October 1781[8].

Children[1]:
1. 310301. Rachel.
2. 310302. Lois, b. 6 Apr. 1772[5,6]; m. 19 Nov. 1790 Gabriel Johnson, son of Uzal
            Johnson[5,7]; d. 26 Apr. 1827[5].
            Children (surname Johnson)[5]:

1. Sinesy.	4. Pamela.	7. Mariah.
2. Charles.	5. Aaron.	8. William.
3. Electa.	6. Uzel E.	9. child.

3. 310303. Phebe.

REFERENCES:
1. NJ Wills - Vol. V, p. 52.
2. NJ Wills - Vol. IV, p. 49.
3. CT Farms Church Records.
4. Duncan, p. 56.
5. Littell, pp. 193, 194.
6. Homer E. Baldwin, Greensburg, PA, informed me that the birth of Lois Bonnell on 6 April
    1772 is noted in the Johnson-Sayre Bible.

7. CB Database, citing Gen Mag of NJ, Vol. 19, p. 21.
8. New Jersey Tax Lists, pp. 300, 301.
9. Extract from a Ball genealogy compiled and sent to me by Joseph Scukanec, Flint, MI, citing the Frank C. Ball collection, Ball State University, Muncie, IN, and Dr. Joseph L. Druse, E. Lansing, MI.
10. New Jersey Genealogy, 8 volumes with index, *Jersey Genealogy*, Q. & A. Column in *Newark Evening News, 1901-1918*, Vol. L, p. 57, #642, sent to me by W. Jerome Hatch, Chicago, IL.

1-3-7-7-1   D75   CB300147

DAVID[5] BONNELL (David[4], Joseph[3], Nathaniel[2], William[1]) was born in 1739/40[1] (or 1748[14]) at Connecticut Farms, Essex (now Union) co, NJ. In current genealogical sources he is usually called David Elias Bonnell, but no reference to him in his lifetime or at his death gives him a middle name. "David Elias" seems to have been a family tradition among later generations of his descendants. On 21 November 1762[4], at Westfield, Essex (now Union) co, NJ, he married TEMPERANCE WADE[4], daughter of Daniel, Sr., and his first wife Elizabeth[15, 16] Wade[4]. In 1793 Daniel Wade, Sr., left £10 to his daughter, Temperance, wife of David Bonnell[13, 16]. She was born about 1741[3] at Elizabethtown, Essex (now Union) co, NJ.

David and Temperance lived apparently lived out their lives in Springfield, Essex (now Union) co, NJ, where David, Jr., appears on the tax list in 1779 and 1780 as a householder among the rateables of Springfield twp, Essex co, NJ[7]. Another reference to David Bonnell in the Springfield tax list in September 1789[8] may apply to this David, or it may refer to his father David.

Although this seems not to have been one of the David Bonnells who was resident in Mendham, Morris co, NJ, during this period, he may well have bought land there as a speculation. It should be noted that almost all of his purported children except the oldest, Ithamer, lived in Mendham at some time in their adult lives.

The date of David's death has not been ascertained, but when Temperance died in Springfield at age 82 on 4 April 1824, she was called widow of David Bonnell. His death may have occurred many years before. The place of their burial does not appear.

This account of David and Temperance is mostly circumstantial. It depends a great deal on the family research done by descendants of son Ithamer and sent to me by Iva Bunnell Adams in 1962. No contemporary evidence has been found to prove that David[4] 1-3-7-7 had a son David. Neither can I find evidence to prove conclusively that he did not. Until further evidence becomes available, I will stick with this placement of David[5] on the family tree.

However, after considerable study, I no longer believe that this is the David Bonnell who was resident in Mendham, Morris co, NJ, for 25 or 30 years before his death on 27 August 1800 and burial in Hilltop Cemetery, Mendham. In all likelihood that was David[5] 1-3-1-4-2 CB300191. Possibly most or all of the children listed here were the children of David[5] CB300191.

Children:
1. 310281. Ithamer, b. 15 Jan. 1767[4].
2. 310282. Elias, b. 1770[4].
3. 310283. Henry, b. 15 Oct. 1772[4].
4. 310284. Sarah, b. about 1773[4]; m. 29 Oct. 1795 Joseph Gardner[10].
5. 310285. Luther, b. 8 Sept. 1775[4].
6. 310286. Stephen C., b. 1777[4].
7. 310287. David, b. 25 Apr. 1779[4].
8. 310288. Elizabeth (Betsey), b. about 1783[4]; m. Ebenezer Sturges[4].
         Children (surname Sturges):
         1. Tempe.   perhaps others.
9. 310289. William, b. 3 Aug. 1788[4].

REFERENCES:
1. Inscriptions in Hilltop Cemetery, Presbyterian Church, Mendham, NJ, in Cemetery Description Books, by county, in the Newark, NJ, Historical Society, extracted by W. Jerome Hatch, Chicago, IL.
2. Madison Church Records, pp. 26, 299.
3. Death Notices in The Palladium of Liberty, in Marriage Notices Copied from Newspapers Published in Morristown, NJ, by Frederick Alexander Canfield, extracted by W. Jerome Hatch.
4. Family Group Sheet for David Elias Bonnell, compiled and sent to me in 1962 by Iva Bunnell Adams, Midway, UT.
5. Morris co, NJ, Mortgages, Book B, pp. 169, 194, and Book C, p. 273.
6. Proceedings of the New Jersey Historical Society, Vol. 66, p. 118, in research papers of Ruth C. Duncan.
7. Gen Mag of NJ, Vol. 43, No. 2, p. 80, New Jersey Rateables, 1778-1780, by Kenn Stryker-Rodda.
8. New Jersey Tax Lists, p. 300.
9. Tax Rateables, Mendham and Randolph Townships, NJ, Bonnell Family - Acres Taxes, prepared by Sharon Holley, Budd Lake, NJ, 1988, copy sent to me by W. Jerome Hatch.
10. Gen Mag of NJ, Vol. 4, No. 1, pp. 9, 30.
11. Morristown Church Records, Combined Registers, 1742-1885, p. 23.
12. Duncan, p. 56.
13. CB Database, citing Essex co Probate records 07776G-7781G, Vital Records of Union co, Vol. 1, p. 94, and Palladium of Liberty, 22 April 1824.
14. Amer Fam-Long Island, p. 61.
15. Wade Genealogy, by Stuart Charles Wade, 1900, p.245.
16. NJ Wills - Vol VIII, p. 385.

NOTE:
See 1-3-1-4-2, CB300191. It is entirely possible that this entire account from his marriage in 1762 to his death in 1800 belongs instead to David Bonnell 300191, and that this David 300147 was born about 1748 and probably died young. No contemporary evidence I have found makes either identification more likely than the other.

1-3-7-7-2   CB300154

NATHANIEL[5] BONNELL (David[4], Joseph[3], Nathaniel[2], William[1]) was born at Connecticut Farms, Essex (now Union) co, NJ, in 1746[10]. No contemporary evidence has been presented to prove that Nathaniel was the son of David and Hannah (Thompson) Bonnell. See the article in *The Bunnell/Bonnell Newsletter*[14] which weighs the pros and cons of this identification.

In 1774?[6] (or about 1767[15]) he married ANNA COZAD[6] of Mendham, Morris co, NJ, daughter of Samuel and Ann (Clark) Cozad[6] . She was born in 1754[6]. They lived in that part of Mendham twp, Morris co, NJ, which in 1806 was set off as Randolph twp. A mortgage dated 27 September 1774 refers to "premises in Mendham twp Beginning in the road above Nathaniel Bunnels where the line of Kirkbride's Lot on which Zophar Riggs lately lived crosses the Road, &c." Nathaniel's name appeared on tax lists in Mendham twp from 1778 to 1796[4,7] and on tax lists in Randolph twp from 1806 to 1814[3]. Nathaniel may have been the person listed in the Morris co militia in 1793 from Mendham, although he was over the upper age limit of 45 years[13]. His son Nathaniel, Jr., had not yet reached the minimum age of 18.

Anna Bonnell was admitted to the Presbyterian Church in Mendham in 1800[15]. The will of Samuel Cozad of Mendham, dated 15 February 1806 and probated 5 March 1811, mentions his "daughter Anne, wife of Nathaniel Bunnel."[15] Nathaniel and Anna were listed as "of Mendham" on 12 May 1804 when they sold 52 acres to Nathaniel Clark for $787.50, and as "of Randolph" on 28 October 1809 in a deed for 3.66 acres to Archibald Otis for $287.50 and on 8 May 1812 in a deed for 3.37 acres to Samuel T. Lawrance for $42.50[1]. On 5 March 1808 Nathaniel and Anna mortgaged a 30-acre tract of land in Randolph twp to Henry Pierson to secure payment of $256.81[2].

All sources available to me list seven children for Nathaniel and Anna, but not always the same seven. Numbers 4 through 8 appear on all lists. However, some omit Phebe and Hannah[6,12]. Others omit Elizabeth and Henry instead[11]. Until further clarification is available, I have chosen to retain all nine children on the list.

Nathaniel died at Randolph on 25 April 1814[10]. His widow, "Wid. Anna Bonnel," was received 9 June 1820 as a charter member of the Mount Freedom Presbyterian Church in Randolph, on transfer from the Mendham Presbyterian Church[5]. She died 17 September 1828[5].

Children (all born at Mendham, NJ):
1. 310376. Phebe, b. 8 July 1772[11]; m. 1 Apr. 1792 Henry Bonnell (1-3-7-7-1-3)[8]; d. 15 June 1845[11].
2. 310375. Elizabeth (Betsey), b. 1776[6]; m. 26 June 1795 Reuben Hulbert[7]; d. 1850[6].
   Children (surname Hulbert)[6]:
   1. Louis.   3. Elizabeth.   5. Berthania.
   2. Phebe.   4. Jane.
3. 301374. Henry, b. 1777[6].
4. 310377. Nathaniel, b. 26 Aug. 1782 [16] or 1779[6,12].

5. 310378. David Thompson, b. 17 Oct. 1783[11] (or 1782[6])(or 26 Oct. 1783[12]).
6. 310379. Aaron Pitney, b. Sept. 1784[6,11,12].
7. 310382. Anna, b. 24 Mar. 1786[9]; m. 4 Nov. 1804 Jacob Drake[6]; d. 3 Nov. 1865[6,9].
   Children (surname Drake)[6]:
   1. Rhoda Ann.   3. Margaret.   4. Catharine.
   2. Eliphalet.
8. 310380. William, b. 3 Aug. 1788[12].
9. 310381. Hannah, b. 1788[11]; m. Reuben Morris[11].

REFERENCES:
1. Morris co, NJ, Deeds , Book H, p. 535; Book S, p. 510; Book W, pp. 57, 421, 478.
2. Morris co, NJ, Mortgages, Book F, pp. 414, 474.
3. NJ Tax Lists, pp. 299, 310, 424.
4. Holley, tax records.
5. Mt. Freedom Church records.
6. Clark record.
7. Gen. Mag. of NJ, Vol. IV, No. 1, p. 31; Vol. 45, No. 3, p. 122.
8. Newark Gazette, 26 July 1792.
9. Morris Gen Soc, Vol. 4, No. 2, p. 14.
10. Adams, Family Group Sheet - David Bonnell.
11. Gray, Family Group Sheet - Nathaniel Bonnell.
12. Carroll, Notes - pp. 2, 3.
13. NJ in 1793.
14. Bunnell/Bonnell Newsletter - Vol. VIII, No. 3, pp. 35-39.
15. CB Database.
16. Madison Church Records, p. 26.

1-3-7-7-5 D29vii CB300153

OLIVER[5] BONNELL (David[4], Joseph[3], Nathaniel[2], William[1]) was born at Connecticut Farms, Essex co (now Union twp, Union co), NJ, about 1759[1]. He died in 1806[2] and was buried in the Presbyterian Cemetery at Connecticut Farms[2]. It seems odd that a man who lived for 47 years, apparently in the same place all his life, left no record except that of his burial.

REFERENCES:
1. Adams, Family Group Sheet - David Bonnell.
2. CT Farms Cem. Inscriptions.

1-3-7-7-6 D76 CB300150

JOSEPH[5] BONNELL (David[4], Joseph[3], Nathaniel[2], William[1]). "He was born on the 21 day of April AD 1761 in the township of Elizabeth," Essex (now Union) co, NJ, "and has the record of his age in his family Bible in his possession."[1] He lived as an apprentice to Andrew Ross "in the war time, and was an apprentice to him in May 1777 at which time he became 16 years of age, and continued an apprentice until he was 21 years old."[1]

"In the month of May 1777 while a resident of the township of Elizabeth, he was drafted in the Infantry of the New Jersey Militia into monthly duty, in the Regiment of Col. Samuel Potter, in the company commanded by Captain Stephen Chandler and was stationed 1 month in Elizabeth Town & quartered with one _____ Ogden. Kept guard along the shore between Elizabeth Town Point and the Blazen Star which was on the lines opposite Staten Island - the enemy were at Staten Island. From this time until the month of July 1781 he continued in the Infantry service on monthly duty (and never refused a tour of duty during the war) and performed his duty by keeping guard on the New Jersey lines, along the shore above mentioned, and was most of the time at Elizabeth Town Point, Halsteds Point, Tremblys Point or at the Blazing Star, between Elizabeth Town and Amboy, during which time some of the enemy were almost all of the time at Staten Island opposite the New Jersey shore.

"He was called a minute man, & always held himself in readiness for duty at a minutes warning, - was sometimes commanded by Captn: Stephen Chandler, at other times by Captn: Wood, at others by Captn: David Woodruff & at others by Captn Samuel Herriman - sometimes was in the regiment of Col: William Crane at others, in Col: Samuel Potter's, but cannot specify the particular months, nor the number of times he served on monthly tours under each - he performed actual service in monthly duty more than one third of the time, and when not on monthly duty was frequently out on alarm.

"In the month of July 1781, while a resident in Elizabeth Town, New Jersey, he enlisted in the 3 months service in the Infantry of the militia under Captain Henry Van Blarcom in the Regiment of Col: Seely, - he joined the Regiment at Morristown, N.J. and marched from thence through Hanover to the North River to Dobbs ferry at the Sloat, opposite White Plains a short distance above Fort Lee, and remained there under the command of General Elias Dayton for one month, - at the expiration of the month he returned through Hackensack, Paterson, Acqueckanonck & Newark to Connecticut farms, & there served the residue of the 3 months, and was discharged without receiving any certificate of service or discharge.

"In June 1780, he was in the Battle at Connecticut farms, and also at Springfield, went to both battles on alarm, in the engagement at the farms he placed himself under Lieut: Seeley of the Continental service,- saw Moses Ogden an officer of the Continental service, there, who was killed on that day. In the engagement at Springfield he was under the command of Captn: Herriman and assisted in taking the baggage of British Col: Fox with two pack horses, his servant & barber, together with a British soldier, prisoner.

"At the expiration of the 3 months service, he volunteered in the militia in Captain Elicum Littel's company of Artillery and continued in that service until the close of the war in 1783. He can safely say he has performed more than two years actual service & fully believes that he has performed as much as three years actual service."[1]

He married NANCY LYON[11]. She was born 27 January 1762[9]. Their first two children died in childhood. They were buried in the graveyard of the Presbyterian Church at Connecticut Farms, where a double headstone made of red sandstone marked their graves. It was signed by J. C. Mooney, a local stonecutter, and read as follows:

FIFTH GENERATION

"In Memory of Aaron & Phebe
Son & daughter of Joseph &
Nancy Bonnel. Aaron died
Aug. 25, 1793 aged 8 years
11 months & 10 days. Phebe died
Dec 10th 1789, aged 1 year 2 mo
& 10 days.
I take these little Lambs said He
And lay them in my breast
Protection they shall find in me
In me be ever blest."[10]

After the War Joseph was a member of the Essex co militia[4]. From September to December 1794 he served under Capt. Canfield during the insurrection in western Pennsylvania known as the Whiskey Rebellion[9].

Nancy (Lyon) Bonnell was admitted to membership in the Presbyterian Church at Connecticut Farms on 24 April 1802[9]. Joseph was admitted in 1817[9]. They remained members there for the rest of their lives[9].

Joseph's name appears in various probate and real estate records over the years. In 1802 he was executor, with Stephen Townley, of the estate of Charles Townley[7]. In 1805 he served as administrator of Robert Wade's estate[6]. On 16 January 1806 Joseph Bonnel & Nancy his wife sold a tract of land, a little over ¼ acre in Connecticut Farms to Peter William Teller and Samuel Teller for $144. It was bounded southeast by the road leading from Newark to Connecticut Farms meeting house, southwest by the Morris Turnpike road, northwest by land of said Joseph Bonnel and east by land of Eliazer Campbell[7]. In 1810 he was administrator of the estate of Miller Baker in Union twp[9]. The following year he was the executor of his father's estate[9]. On 30 August 1813 Timothy Miller mortgaged a 5-acre lot in Union twp to Joseph Bonnel to secure payment of $250[6]. On 25 April 1819 Jacob G. and Susan Broadwell mortgaged two tracts of land in Springfield twp, Essex co, to secure payment of $462.34 to Jonas Wade and $377 to Joseph Bonnel on or before 1 April 1820[6]. Tax records are extant listing Joseph Bonnel (or Bunnel) in 1812, 1813, 1814, 1815, 1821 and 1822[5].

He appears in the 1830 census (1 male 70-80 years, 1 female 20-30 years and 1 female 60-70 years)[9] and the 1840 census (1 male 70-80 years, 1 female 30-40 years and 1 female 70-80 years)[9], both in Union, Essex (now Union) co, NJ. Nancy died 20 January 1846[3] at the age of 83. He died 23 June 1849[3]. They were buried in the Presbyterian Cemetery at Connecticut Farms, Essex (now Union) co, NJ[3]. His estate was probated in 1849 in Essex co, file no. 13792G[9]. In the 1850 census in Union twp, Joseph Bonnel was listed in the mortality schedule as a widower and a tailor[9]. His daughter Nancy was listed as living in the household of her brother-in-law William Day in Union twp[11].

Children:
    1. 310295. Aaron, b. 12 Sept. 1784; d. 23 Aug. 1793, age 8 yrs. 11 mo. & 10 ds.[10]

2. 310294. Phebe, b. 1 Oct. 1788; d. 10 Dec. 1789, age 1 yr., 2 mo. & 10 days.[10]
3. 310296. Phebe, b. about 1791; m. William Day[8].
          Children (surname Day):[8]
          1. Charles.   3. Mary.   4. William.
          2. Samuel.
4. 310297. Joanna, b. 6 Dec. 1794; m. 17 Jan. 1826 James Wilson Wade[2].
5. 310298. Nancy, b. 7 Oct. 1803[3]; bapt. Conn. Farms Pres. Ch. 11 Dec. 1803[2];
          d. 7 Aug. 1874[3].

REFERENCES:
    1. Rev. War pension appl. (S2087).
    2. CT Farms Church records.
    3. CT Farms Cem. Inscriptions.
    4. NJ in 1793.
    5. NJ Tax Lists.
    6. Essex co, NJ, Mortgages, Bk G, p. 319; Bk K, p. 537; Bk N, p. 157.
    7. Essex co, NJ, Deeds, Bk F, pp. 269 & 358; Bk L, p. 892.
    8. Duncan, p. 57.
    9. CB Database.
  10. NJ Burial Grounds, p. 110.
  11. Adams, Family Group Sheet - David Bonnell.

     NOTE: Marilyn Ward Lynch compiled a genealogy of The Bonnel/Bunnill Family, completed in July 1990. She lists among the children of Joseph and Nancy a daughter Keziah and a son John. I have not found any reference to these children anywhere else, and Mrs. Lynch gives no source.

     A John Bonnell CB002474, son of Joseph Bonnell CB003083, was born in Essex co, NJ, in October 1804. There are numerous descendants, but we have been unable to determine the ancestry of this Joseph. It is possible that Joseph 003083 is the same person as Joseph 300150, but except for being in the right place at the right time, I have seen no evidence to support it.

1-3-7-7-8 D77 CB300152

WILLIAM[5] BONNELL (David[4], Joseph[3], Nathaniel[2], William[1])was born at Connecticut Farms, Essex co (now Union, Union co), NJ, in 1765[1]. About 1790 he married NANCY WOODRUFF, daughter of Josiah and Patience (Wade) Woodruff[1]. She was born 6 June 1772[1]. Nancy's father, Josiah, died the year of their marriage. In the probate of his estate she was listed as the wife of William Bonnele[6]. William was a member of the Essex co Militia[5]. William and Nancy were admitted to membership in the Presbyterian Church at Connecticut Farms, she on 14 January 1803 and he on 7 May 1803[6]. William received all of his father's real and personal estate at his father's death in 1811[1]. He was a farmer and ropemaker[1].

William's name is found in the tax records in Union twp, Essex co, in 1812, 1813, 1815, 1821 and 1822[7]. Among the real estate dealings recorded in Essex co we find that William Bonnell bought three acres at Connecticut Farms from John and Mary Smith for $124 in February 1802[1]. On 29

July 1811 Elias and Mary Crilley mortgaged a small plot of land to William Bonnell to secure payment of $100[8]. William and Nancy Bonnel sold two parcels of land to Stephen Hedley, Jr., Joseph Durin and Thomas Brown on 9 May 1812. One parcel of 1 ½ acres was adjacent to William's property in Union twp, and the other was nearby[9]. On 27 January 1818 William and Nancy sold a tract of land for $265 to Alexander Smith. She made her mark in signing[1].

William died 4 February 1828[1,2,3]. Nancy appears in the 1830 census in Springfield and in the 1850 census in Union, both in Essex (now Union) co, NJ[6]. She died 3 February 1859[1,2,3]. They, with their infant sons Oliver and David, were buried in Section III, Row G, in the Connecticut Farms Presbyterian Church Cemetery[2,3]. William's will, dated 6 February 1827, probated 9 February 1828, and recorded in Will Book D, page 616, reads as follows:

"In the Name of God Amen, I, William Bonnel of Township of Union, County of Essex and State of New Jersey do make and publish this my Last will and Testament in manner and form as follows viz: 1st I Give and bequeath to my wife Nancy Bonnel the use of all my real Estate as long as she remains my widow. I also Give and bequeath to my said wife Nancy all my Personal Property except what is hereinafter devised to my son William J. Bonnel, to do with and dispose of as she thinks proper. 2nd I Give and bequeath to my Daughter Sally Blake one Dollar. 3d. I Give and devise to my son Oliver Bonnel the one equal undivided half of my salt Meadow. 4th. I Give and devise to my son William J. Bonnel all my real Estate (excepting one equal undivided half of the salt Meadow above devised to my son Oliver) after the marriage or decease of my wife Nancy Bonnel and I also give and bequeath to my said son William the following Personal Property viz: All the Rope works and Tackling, one stove in the Barn, one open stove in the Dwelling House (Large), one Clock, one Corner Cupboard, one 1 Horse waggon and Harness, one sleigh and all my farming utensils and the said William is to satisfy and pay all the just demands against me. Lastly I appoint my two sons Oliver Bonnel and William J. Bonnel Executors of this my Testament and Last will. In Testimony whereof I have hereunto set my hand and seal this Sixth day of February in the year of our Lord one thousand Eight Hundred and Twenty seven.   William Bonnel."
"Signed sealed published
and declared by the said William
Bonnel to be his Testament and
Last will in the presence of us
Caleb S. Miller
Caleb M. Dulea
Jas. R. Camp"[10]

"Inventory of the Personal Property of William Bonnel Late of Union Essex County New Jersey Decd. made by us the Inscribers the 16th Day of feby A.D. 1828.

Wearing apparel	75.00
Household furniture	320.00
Corn Rye oats & flour & Meat	60.00
Sheep swine Cattle etc	75.00
Implements of Husbandry	65.00
Debts	64.50

	659.50

Appraised by us the day and year above written.

Jas. R. Camp

Benjamin Winans"[10]

The gravestone which stood in the burial ground at Connecticut Farms, now lost, read:

"W. B. In memory of William Bonnel, who departed this life, February 4, 1828. In the 63 year of his age.

"Many are the afflictions of the righteous.

But the Lord delivereth him out of them all."--Psalms xxiv 19[1].

Nancy's will dated 11 June 1856 is as follows:

"In the name of God Amen. I Nancy Bonnel of the Township of Union in the County of Essex and State of New Jersey being feeble in body but of sound mind, memory and understanding (for which blessing i thank my God) do make and publish this my last will and testament in manner folowing that is to say: First it is my will, and I do order that all my just debts and funeral Expenses be duly paid and satisfied as soon as conveniently can be after my decease. Item I give and bequeath to my Grand son Edward A. Blake twenty five Dollars in money & my Boston Rocking Chair. Item I give and bequeath to my Grand son William H. Bonnel Fifty Dollars in money alsoe my Clock. Item I give and bequeath to my Grand son Joseph R. Bonnel Twenty five Dollars in money. Item i give and bequeath unto Sharlot Isabel Bonnel Forty Dollars in money, half a Dozen Silver tea spoons, all my wearing apparel, my homespun Blanketts, alsoe all my linnen of whatsoever kind it may be. Item I give and bequeath unto my Grandson William H. Bonnel my large family Bible. Item I give and bequeath unto my daughter in law Margaret Bonnel widow of my son William J. Bonnel decd. all the remainder of my property whatsoever and wheresoever to her and her heirs forever. Lastly I hereby appoint Margaret Bonnel widow afforsaid Executrix and my grand son William H. Bonnel Executor of this my last will and testament: In witness whereof i have hereto set my hand and seal this Eleventh day of June AD 1856. Signed Sealed published and declared by the said Nancy Bonnel to be her last will and testament In the presence of us

James W. Wade

Samuel S. Doty

her

Nancy X Bonnel

mark"

Children:

1. 310383. Sarah, b. 26 Dec. 1792[1]; m. 12 May 1814 Stephen Blake.[2]
    Children (surname Blake):[11]
    1. Edward A.
2. 310384. Oliver, b. 3 Feb. 1793; d. 13 Sept. 1793[1,2,3].
3. 310385. Oliver, b. 28 Mar. 1795[1].
4. 310386. David, b. 22 May 1805[3] (or 1804[1,2]); bapt. 20 July 1805[2]; d. 11 Oct. 1806[3] (or 1805[1,2]).
5. 310387. William Jones, b. 17 Mar. 1808[1].

REFERENCES:

1.. Amer. Fam. - Long Island, pp. 61, 62, 63.
2. CT Farms Church records.
3. CT Farms Cem. Inscriptions, p. 171.
4. Duncan, p. 57.

5. NJ in 1793.
6. CB Database.
7. NJ Tax Lists, pp. 300, 424, 425.
8. Essex co, NJ, Mortgages, Book K, p. 22.
9. Essex co, NJ, Deeds, Book 7, p. 58.
10. Photocopy of Will of William Bonnel and Inventory.
11. Photocopy of Will of Nancy Bonnel.

SIXTH GENERATION

1-1-6-3-4-1 D30i CB310099

CHARLES[6] BUNNELL (Benjamin[5], Benjamin[4], Benjamin[3], Benjamin[2], William[1]) was born 19 January 1759 in Derby[1], New Haven co, CT, and was baptized there on 22 January 1759 in St. James Protestant Episcopal Church[1]. He married RHODA[1] ELTON[5]. He appears in the 1790 census of Derby CT: 1-2-1-0-0[2]. (Charles and Rhoda apparently had no children of their own. It is possible, even likely, that the two males under 16 years counted in the 1790 census were two of the sons of his deceased cousin Isaac. At least, they do not appear with their mother in the 1790 census[2].)

In October 1798 the northern part of Derby where they lived was included in the new town of Oxford, New Haven co, CT. Charles served there as a Selectman. He appears in the Oxford census records in 1800: 0021-0101, 1810: 10001-00001, 1820: 100001-00001-AGR-1, and 1830: 0000000001-0000000001[5]. "Esq. Charles Bunnell, an unselfish, public spirited, worthy and respected citizen; and held a prominent place in the confidence of the people. His residence was that of the late Harry Sutton[4]. He died 17 March 1838 in Oxford, New Haven co, CT, without issue[1]. His widow appears in the 1850 census in Oxford, living with Lucius and Rhoda Fuller[5]. She died 8 April 1851 in Oxford at the age of 91[1]. They were both buried in the Oxford Congregational Church Cemetery[3].

His will, probated in Oxford, reads as follows: "I, Charles Bunnell, of Oxford give to my wife Rhoda Bunnell one horse and one horse wagon; 2 good cows; $200 in money; all household furniture including clock & case; all the provisions in the house & cellar; a small strip of land in Oxford and the use and improvement of my land during her natural life.

"To my two brothers, Benjamin and Reuben Bunnell, all my real estate, after the decease of my wife to be divided equally.

"I appoint Elias Scott, Executor. Signed: Charles Bunnell, 9 Nov. 1835. Witnesses: Nathan B. Fairchild, Harry Osborn and Roswell Cable."[3]

Rhoda's will, probated in Oxford, reads as follows: "I, Rhoda Bunnell, give to Rhoda Fuller all my real estate. In the event of the death of Rhoda Fuller, it is to go to her children: Hannah, Charles B. and Rhoda B. Fuller.

"To my sister, Esther Bunde, all my wearing apparel and household furniture.

"To Julia Warner, my gold beads.

"To Harriet Fuller, daughter of Lucius T. & Rhoda Fuller, my best feather bed.

"To Charles B. Fuller, son of Lucius T. & Rhoda Fuller, one small feather bed.

"To Charles Blackman $50 in a note against Charles & Elijah Blackman of $150.00.

"To Nathan Elton, son of Nathan, dec. $50 from the above mentioned note.

"I appoint Elias Scott Executor. Signed: Rhoda Bunnell, 3 July 1846. Witnesses: Nathan Mansfield, Maria Mansfield and Eunice Scott."[3]

REFERENCES:
1. New Haven - Jacobus, p. 365.
2. Census 1790.
3. Duncan, p. 33.
4. Derby, pp. 235, 236.
5. CB Database.

1-1-6-3-4-2 D78 CB310100

BENJAMIN B[6][3]. BUNNELL (Benjamin[5], Benjamin[4], Benjamin[3], Benjamin[2], William[1]) was born 19 July 1763 at Derby, New Haven co, CT[1]. In Oxford Parish, town of Derby, he married (first) 22 November 1786[1] MARY TWITCHELL[1], daughter of Joseph and Elizabeth (Tomlinson) Twitchell[1]. She was born 10 February 1760 in Derby[1]. Their home was included in the new town of Oxford, New Haven co, CT, in 1798, and Benjamin appears there in the 1800 census: 2101-0011, the 1810 census: 11101-01002, the 1820 census: 000211-10011-AGR-4, and the 1830 census: 000000101-0000000011[4]. Mary (Twitchell) Bunnell died 6 August 1833 at Oxford[3]. Benjamin was married (second) 8 October 1835[3], by Rev. Charles Smith[4], to ANNA[1] GUNN[3], who was born in Naugatuck, New Haven co, CT, about 1767[1]. Benjamin appears in the 1840 census in Oxford: 0000000101-0000000011[4]. He died 20 September 1840 at Oxford, CT[1]. He was buried with his first wife, Mary, in St. Peter's Church Cemetery[3] in Oxford. His widow Anna appears in the 1850 census in Oxford[4]. She died 14 March 1849[1] at Naugatuck, where her death was recorded in St. Michael's Protestant Episcopal Church[1].

His will, probated in Oxford, reads: "I, Benjamin Bunnell, give to my wife, Anna Bunnell in addition to the $50 which I have heretofore given her as jointure or legacy in my estate, $50 more to be paid to her out of my estate.

"I also give to Anna Bunnell, one brass kettle, one swine, and the water of my farm sufficient to fat the same.

"I also give to Anna Bunnell, one fire screen and one calico bedspread.

"I give to my three sons, Chester, Reuben and Renus Bunnell, all my real and personal estate that shall remain after paying the above request, to be divided equally between them.

"I appoint Elias Scott, Executor. 2 June 1840. Signed: Benjamin Bunnell. Witnesses: Nathan Mansfield, John R. Bassett and George Scott."[3]

Children (by first wife)(born in Oxford):
1. 320001. Chester[1], b. 12 Apr. 1788[1]; m. 12 Feb. 1814 Roxy Dunning[1]; d. 8 Mar. 1843[3].
2. 320002. Richard[1], d. young[3].
3. 320003. Reuben[1], b. 30 Oct. 1795[1]; m. 19 Sept. 1822 Mary Ann Smith[3]; d. 3 Oct. 1851[3].
      Children (surname Bunnell):[3]
      1. Mary Ann.   2. Charles Smith.   3. Henry Hobart.
4. 320004. Renus[1], b. 14 May 1799[1]; m. 4 Sept. 1826 Temperance Baldwin[1]; d. 1 Sept. 1866[3].
      Children (surname Bunnell):[3]
      1. Catherine.   2. Lyman.   3. Benjamin Barton.
?5.   Mary[2], b. 14 May 1799[2].

REFERENCES:
1. New Haven - Jacobus, p. 365.
2. Biles Manuscript, p. 6.
3. Duncan, p. 58.
4. CB Database.

1-1-6-3-4-3 D79 CB310101

REUBEN[6] BUNNELL (Benjamin[5], Benjamin[4], Benjamin[3], Benjamin[2], William[1]) was born 24 December 1765 at Derby[1], New Haven co, CT. He married SARAH SACKETT[1], daughter of Jonathan Sackett[1]. She was born about 1767[1]. Reuben appears in the 1790 census in Derby: 1-0-2-0-0[2]. That part of Derby was incorporated in the new town of Oxford, New Haven co, CT, in 1798, and there he spent the rest of his life. He appears there in the census in 1800: 2001-2101, in 1810: 00201-02010, in 1820: 000001-00101-Mfg 1, in 1830: 000000001-000000001, in 1840: 0000000001-0000000001, and in 1850 as a farmer[4]. According to the *History of Christ Church, Quaker Farms, in Oxford, CT,* Reuben was made Chorister (to 'set the psalm') of St. Peter's Episcopal Church in Oxford in 1788, Clerk in 1812 and Treasurer in 1817[3]. He was Senior Warden of the church for 35 years.[3] His wife died 6 September 1851[1], and he died 2 February 1853[1], both at Oxford[1], New Haven co, CT. Both were buried in St. Peter's Episcopal Church Cemetery in Oxford[3].

Reuben's will, probated in Oxford, reads: "I, Reuben Bunnell, will that the barn standing on my homelot, belonging to John L. Fairchild, shall remain his.

"I will that all my household furniture be equally divided between my daughters, Ruth Ann Hodge and Clara Fairchild.

"I give to my four grandchildren, children of my son Horace, deceased, $20 each and $20 to my granddaughter, Lavinia Bunnell.

"I will that the remainder of my estate be equally divided between my four children, namely: Lavinia Hitchcock decd, Ruth Ann Hodge, Clara Fairchild and Charles Bunnell.

"Chauncey M. Hatch, Executor. 17 April 1852. Signed: Reuben Bunnell. Witnesses: Huldah C. Hatch, Grace D. Baldwin and Betsey E. McLean."[3]

Children:
1. 320011. Lavinia[1], b. about 1789 (or about 1802); m. _____ Hitchcock[1]; d. 1 May 1850[3], age 61[3].
2. 320010. Horace[1], b. about 1795[1]; m. (first) Mary A. _____[3]; m. (second) 16 Nov. 1840 Mrs. Fanny Sperry[3]; d. 18 Nov. 1848[1].
   Children (surname Bunnell)(by first wife):[3]
   1. John A.
3. 320012. Charles[1] A[4,5] or L[3], b. about 1796[3] or 1793[4]; m. (first) 28 Nov. 1819[4] Almyra Gunn[5]; m. (second) 29 Mar. 1827 Ticphena Bablet(??)[4].
   Children (surname Bunnell)(by first wife):[5]
   1. Ira H.   ? son?   ? daughter?
   Children (surname Bunnell)(by second wife):[4]
   2. Almira.   4. Reuben.   6. Ann M.
   3. John.   5. June E.   7. Horace D.
4. 320008. Ruth Ann[1], b. 8 Feb. 1798[1]; m. 22 Mar. 1815[1] Chauncey Hodge[1].
   Children (surname Hodge):[3]
   1. Charles K.   2. Albert L.
5. 320009. Clara[1], b. 1800[4]; m. 26 Jan. 1825[3] John L.[3] Fairchild[1].

SIXTH GENERATION

REFERENCES:
1. New Haven - Jacobus, p. 365.
2. Census 1790.
3. Duncan, p. 59.
4. CB Database.
5. E-mail 13 Apr. 2004 from Joanne B. Rexford, Vero Beach, FL.

1-1-6-3-6-1   D80   CB310001

LUKE[6] BUNNELL (Isaac[5], Benjamin[4], Benjamin[3], Benjamin[2], William[1]) was born 28 February 1758[1] at Derby,[1] New Haven co, CT. He married (first) 31 March 1785,[1] at Derby[1] BETTY BATES[1], daughter of Benjamin and Abigail (Hine) Bates[1]. She was born 10 October 1757[1] at Derby[1]. A few days before his marriage, on 26 March, Luke bought 1 acre 68 rods of land at Quaker's Farm Purchase lying next to the land of his father-in-law Bengamin Bates[4]. Quaker's Farm was part of Oxford Parish in the town of Derby[6]. Betty died at Derby 1 April 1786[1].

Luke married (second) 21 December 1786[1] in Derby SARAH BUCKINGHAM[1], daughter of Ebenezer and Abigail (Andrews) Buckingham[3]. She was born 1 March 1762[3] in Derby. The Oxford Parish Congregational Church record at Derby shows that Luke and Sarah Bunnell were admitted to membership on 25 September 1788[5]. Luke appears in the 1790 census in Derby: 1-0-2-0-0[2].

On 7 February 1795 Luke purchased an acre of land at Quaker's Farm from Elihu Bates and sold half of it back to him nine days later[4]. His wife Sarah bought three acres at Quaker's Farm from Roger Perkins on 4 August 1798[4]. It was in October 1798 that the Oxford Parish in the northern part of Derby was separated and set off as the Town of Oxford[6]. Luke appears in the census in Oxford in 1800: 3001-1101, in 1810: 02101-10010, in 1820: 000201-01001-MFG3, and in 1830: 0000000001-000010001[5]. On 9 May 1809, Luke, serving as administrator for his father's estate, sold land on the west side of Woodbury Road to Elijah Harger for $30.00[4]. He sold some of his own land at Quaker's Farm in 1815 to Levi Candee and in 1824 to Tom Bennett[4]. On 8 February 1826 he sold 1 acre and 10 rods to his son Leverett for $15.94[4].

Luke died in the decade before 1840, when his widow appears in the Oxford census: 001-0000010001-AG. When the 1850 census was taken, Sarah was living with her son Joel in Barkhamsted, Litchfield co, CT[5]. She died there on 23 March 1856[3].

Children (by second wife):
1. 320016. Betty[1], bapt. 21 Sept. 1788[1]; m. 4 Feb. 1815[3] Augar Curtiss[3]; d. 1867[3].
     Children (surname Curtiss)[3]:
     1. Esther E.   3. John R.   4. Jane M.
     2. Sarah H.
2. 320017. Leverett[1], b. 13 May 1792[1]; m. Philena _____ [3]; d. 9 Sept. 1826[3.]
     Children (surname Bunnell):[3]
     1. James A.

3. 320018. Alma[1], bapt. 5 July 1795[1]; d. 19 May 1805[3].
4. 320019. Joel[1], b. 14[1] (or 6[3]) Oct. 1796[1]; m. 23 Jan. 1823 Phoebe (Edith) Gaines[3]; d. 14 Aug. 1872[3].
    Children (surname Bunnell):[3]
    1. Henry.   2. Martha.
5. 320020. Hervey[1], b. 6 July 1799[1]; m. (first) 11 Jan. 1824 Eliza Hinman[3]; m. (second) Pamela _____[3].
    Children (surname Bunnell):[3]
    1. Harvey.   2. John C.
6. 320021. Mary[1], bapt. 23 Dec. 1804[1]; m. about 1828[4] Isaac Collins Bunnell[3] 1-1-6-3-6-9-1.

REFERENCES:
1. New Haven - Jacobus, p. 365.
2. Census 1790.
3. Duncan, pp. 59, 60.
4. Gillen.
5. CB Database.
6. Derby.

1-1-6-3-6-2 D81 CB310002

ISAAC[6] BUNNELL (Isaac[5], Benjamin[4], Benjamin[3], Benjamin[2], William[1]) was born 11 May 1759[1] at Derby[1], New Haven co, CT. On 22 October 1780[1], in the Oxford Parish Congregational Church[1] at Derby, he married HANNAH TYLER[1]. Isaac died before 1790. His widow Hannah appears in the 1790 census in Derby, CT: 0-1-2-0-0[2]. (She had four sons under the age of 16. Where were the other two? I suggest that they were living with Isaac's cousin Charles, whose 1790 census record shows two males under 16[2], although Charles and his wife had no children of their own.) Hannah Bunnell died in April 1802[1] at Oxford (formerly Derby), New Haven co, CT, at age 44. The real estate she owned, two acres and a house in Oxford, was inherited by her four children in equal undivided shares[4].

Children:
1. 320025. Clark[1], b. 4 June 1781[3]; m. 18 Feb. 1802 Elinor Rhodes[3]; div.7 Aug. 1814[3]; d. 25 Jan. 1822[3].
    Children (surname Bunnell):[3,5]
    1. Isaac A.   3. Burnett.   4. Caroline.
    2. Marcus.
2. 320404. Samuel S.[3], b. about 1782/3; m. (first) 10 Sept. 1805 Sarah Hill[3]; m. (second) _____ _____[5].
    Children (surname Bunnell)(by first wife):[3]
    1. Isaac Samuel.   ? others?
    Children (surname Bunnell)(by second wife):[5]
    2. daughter.   3. daughter.

3. 320403. Isaac[3], b. about 1784/5; d, 24 Dec, 1814[3].
4. 320026. Charity[3], b. about 1787; d. 4 Nov. 1817[3].
            Children (surname Bunnell)[3]:
            1. Hannah.

REFERENCES:
    1. New Haven - Jacobus, p. 365.
    2. Census 1790.
    3. Duncan, pp. 60, 61, 62, 115.
    4. Bunnell/Bonnell Newsletter, Vol. 12, No. 1, pp. 10, 11.
    5. Biles Manuscript, p. 264.

1-1-6-3-6-3   D82   CB310003

WILLIAM[6] BUNNELL (Isaac[5], Benjamin[4], Benjamin[3], Benjamin[2], William[1]) was born 16 December 1761[1] at Derby[1], New Haven co, CT. He served as a private for seven months in the Connecticut troops in the Revolution[4]. He married 26 March 1783[1], in the Oxford Parish Congregational Church at Derby, SARAH DORMAN[1], daughter of Samuel and Sarah (Wooding) Dorman[1], who was born 1 November 1760[1] in New Haven[1], New Haven co, CT.

William appears in the 1790 census of Derby, CT: 1-2-3-0-0[2], in the 1810 census of Derby: 00111-02003[5], and in the 1810 census: 21001-11001[5], the 1820 census: 010101-01001[5], and the 1830 census: 000000001-001010001[5] in Oxford, New Haven co, CT. On 3 August 1832 he applied for a pension for his service in the Revolution: "On this 3ᵈ day of August 1832 personally appeared in open Court, before the Probate Court of said District at Derby now sitting, William Bunnell resident of the Town of Oxford in the County of New Haven, and State of Connecticut, aged 71 years, who, being first duly sworn according to law, doth, on his oath, make the following Declaration, in order to obtain the benefit of the Act of Congress passed June 7, 1832:--That he entered the service of the united States under the following named officers, and served as herein stated:-that is to say

"First states, as he believes, 1777 he was drafted & detached from the Company of Militia of said Oxford then forming [by act?] Of the Town of Derby to perform a tour of 2 months service and was ordered to Newfield as it was then called, where he joined a company under the command of Capt. Daniel Holbrook & served with sᵈ company at sᵈ Newfield, Stratford, Milford & New Haven where he was discharged at the expiration of sᵈ two months, which he thinks was in the Spring of the year.

"In the same year afterwards, as he believes, in September 1777 he was drafted & ordered to Oyster River, a place between Milford and New Haven for a tour of duty of one month which he performed under the command of Lieutenant Ranford Whitney. He does not remember any other officer, if there was any other in sᵈ service & no other of the Company but Samˡ Hawkins now living.

"In the same year he was required by acting commissary Thomas Horsey to transport one load of Provisions continental stores to Newtown in Fairfield County which took up four days in going & returning & two loads to Woodbury Now Southbury which employed him 2 days each making in the whole eight days. He cannot state the months in which this service was done.

"In August & September 1778 He performed a tour of duty for two months at Milford having been again drafted for that purpose. His Captain was now _____ Peck of Milford (he does not recollect his first name) and Thaddeus Baldwin of Derby was Ensign. Having finished this tour & returned home he was immediately ordered back & detained another month, before other troops came on & relieved this company. We were stationed along the shore as guards.

"In the fall of the next year 1779 he served two months at New Haven being drafted & ordered there. David Daggett was Captain of the Company in which he served. Nathan Parsons[?] of Derby was Lieutenant & one Pinto (whose first name he does not recollect nor that of the Ensign) was orderly Sergeant. They were stationed in the City of New Haven & served as guards during said term.

"This applicant was several times ordered out on sudden alarms during the war. But he cannot particularly specify. Sometimes he was detained no longer than to get part of the way to Milford & sometimes a few days.

"He was born in Derby in that part which is since the town of Oxford on the 16th day of December 1760 & has always lived in sd towns. This record is on my father's family bible.

"He states that he is acquainted with Deacon John Carrington & Captain Alva Bunnell of sd Derby & Revd Ashbel Baldwin of Oxford & Capt. Job C[   ] of the same town who will testify to his character for credibility and their [   ] of his service as a soldier of the revolution."[4]

A Certificate of Pension (#S17317) was issued on 24 September 1833 at the rate of $23.33 per annum retroactive to 4 March 1831, to be paid semi-annually[4].

William died by September 1836 in Oxford[3]. His probate record in Oxford contains the following: "Oxford, Sept. 28, 1836. To Charles A. Ingrot, Judge of the Court of Probate, New Haven District. Sir: It is our request that Horace Candee of the Town of Oxford be appointed on the Estate of William Bunnell, late of Oxford, to settle and adjust the claims according to law. Signed: Sarah Bunnel, Chester Bunnell, Cynthia Hendrix, William Bunnel, Erastus Bunnell, Isaiah Bunnell, Abel Bunnel and Sheldon Bunnel."[3]

Also, the following document was submitted to the Probate Court: "We the subscribers Heirs at Law of William Bunnell, late of Oxford deceased, being all legally able to act, do hereby agree and have each a distribution of all the Estate of said deceased both Real and personal to our satisfaction as witness our hands. Dated, Oxford May 14th, 1837. Signed: Abel Bunnel, Sheldon Bunnel, Chester Bunnell, Alson Hendryx, Cynthia Hendryx, Erastus Bunnell and Isaiah Bunnell."[3]

Oxford Deeds, Vol. 13, p. 526, has the following deed of sale: "June 3, 1835, Abel & Sheldon Bunnell of Colebrook, William Bunnell of Farmington; Chester & Erastus Bunnell & Alson & Cynthia Hendrix of Oxford and Isaiah Bunnell of Bridgeport sold 10 acres of land to Truman Tomlinson."[3]

Children:
1. 320595. Chester, b. about 1783[5]; bapt. 27 Apr. 1783[5]; d. young[5].
2. 320596. Abel, b. 2 Mar. 1784[5]; bapt. 5 Sept. 1784[5]; m. (first) Angelina _____[3]; m. (second) Roxey Simons[3]; d. 21 Mar. 1861[3].
   Children (surname Bunnell)(by second wife):[3]
   1. son, d. young.   3. Alanson D.   4. Angeline R.
   2. William S.
3. 320597. Sheldon, b. 3 Mar. 1786[5]; bapt. 1788[5]; m. 3 Sept. 1807[6] Anna Morehouse[3,6]; d. 20 Mar. 1861[3].
   Children (surname Bunnell):[3,6]
   1. Nancy Ann.   3. Maryette.   5. Ira S.
   2. John Maxson.   4. Lyman Phelps.   6. Henry Rood.
4. 320598. Cynthia, b. about 1787[5]; bapt. 15 Feb. 1789[5]; m. Alson Hendrix[3].
5. 320599. Sarah, b. about 1789[5]; bapt. 20 Aug. 1789[5]; probably the child who d. 16 Mar. 1804[5].
6. 320600. Chester, b. about 1791[5]; bapt. Feb. 1791[5].

SIXTH GENERATION

7. 320601. Erastus, b. about 1793[5]; bapt. 20 Jan. 1793[5]; m. (first) Nov. 1821
Charlotte Norton[3]; m. (second) Clarinda _____[3]; d. 29 June 1873[3].
Children (surname Bunnell)(by first wife):[3]
1. Charles Burr.   4. Amos Orville N.   7. Cynthia.
2. Laura.   5. Emeline M.   8. Mary E.
3. Jeanette Hannah.   6. Susan Martha.   9. Lucy A.
Children (surname Bunnell)(by second wife):[3]
10. Harriet L.   11. George W.
8.   William. (on evidence of documents cited above.)
9. 320603. Isaiah, b. about 1803[6]; bapt. 21 Dec. 1803[6]; m. Maria B. Tuttle[3];
d. 1 May 1838[3].
Children (surname Bunnell):[3]
1. Smith Wheeler.   2. Merrit F.   3. Thomas B.

REFERENCES:
1. New Haven - Jacobus, p. 365.
2. 1790 census.
3. Duncan, p. 62.
4. Rev. War Pension appl.
5. CB Database.
6. Biles Manuscript, pp. 265, 266, 267.

1-1-6-3-6-5   D83   CB310005

PHILEMON B.[6] BUNNELL Isaac,[5] Benjamin[4], Benjamin[3], Benjamin[2], William[1]) was born 26
September 1767[1] at Derby[1], New Haven co, CT. His wife was RUTH BOTSFORD,[2] daughter
of Samuel and Elizabeth (Watkins) Botsford[2]. She was born 22 July 1766.[3] Philemon appears
in the 1800 census: 30010-10010, the 1810 census: 01010-22010, the 1820 census:
000001-00201, and the 1830 census: 000000001-001000001, all in the town of Derby.[3] He
died in 1833 at Derby. His son Alva was administrator for the probate of his estate[3].

Children:
1. 320098. David[2], b. about 1795[2]; m. (first) Ann _____[2]; m. (second) Julia (Coger)
Bowen[2].
Children (surname Bunnell)(by first wife):[2]
1. Ann Amanda.   2. David L.   3. Sarah A. J.
2. 320099. Alva[2], b. Dec. 1797[3]; m. (first) 2 May 1823 Hannah Wheeler[2]; m.
(second) 28 Feb. 1836 Lucy (Perkins) Barns[2]; d. 22 Apr. 1883[2].
Children (surname Bunnell)(by first wife):[2]
1. Mary.   3. Roxanna.   4. George W.
2. Hannah A.
Children (surname Bunnell)(by second wife):[2]
5. Sarah Jane.   6. Mary Elizabeth.
3. 320101. Elizabeth[2], b. about 1800[3]; m. 2 Jan. 1823[2] Willard Barnes[2].

208

4. 320102. Ann[2], b. about 1805[3]; m. 13 Mar. 1826[2] David Webster[2]; d. 5 May 1873[2].

    probably others from the evidence of the census records.

REFERENCES:
1. New Haven - Jacobus, p. 365.
2. Duncan, pp. 62, 63.
3. CB Database.

1-1-6-3-6-6   D84   CB310006

TRUMAN[6] BUNNELL (Isaac[5], Benjamin[4], Benjamin[3], Benjamin[2], William[1]) was born about 1770[1] in Connecticut. About 1794[4] he married ANNA _____ [1]. He appears in the 1800 census: 10010-20010[3,4], the 1820 census: 01001-21002[3] or 000001-21002[4], the 1830 census: 00000001-00010001[3,4], and the 1840 census: 000000001-1000010001[4], all in Oxford, New Haven co, CT. He was a member of the Christ Church in the Quaker Farms section of Oxford[2]. Anna died 21 June 1832[2] at the age of 66[2]. Truman died 1 May 1848[1] at Oxford[1].

Children (born in Oxford):
1. 320549. Polly[1], b. 28 June[4] or 28 July[2] 1796[2,4].
2. 320548. John Lewis[2], b. 16 June 1798[2]; m. 29 Nov. 1821 Clarinda Hosmer[2].
        Children (surname Bunnell):[2]
        1. Clarinda.   2. Solomon J.
3. 320550. daughter[2], b. 13 Aug. 1800[2].
    The census records suggest they may have had one or two other daughters.

REFERENCES:
1. New Haven - Jacobus, p. 365.
2. Duncan, p. 63.
3. Duncan census files.
4. CB Database.

1-1-6-3-6-7   D85   CB310007

DAVID[6] BUNNELL (Isaac[5], Benjamin[4], Benjamin[3], Benjamin[2], William[1]) was born about 1775, probably in that part of Derby, New Haven co, CT, later set off as the town of Oxford. About 1796 he married MARY[3] (POLLY)[1,2] LOCKWOOD[2]. She was born 28 May 1777[2], the daughter of Ezra and Hannah (Clauson) Lockwood[2]. They apparently lived in Oxford, since the births, baptisms and deaths of their children were recorded in the vital records of the town and of the Congregational Church in Oxford. When their first child died in 1798 he was buried, however, in the Old Cemetery in Watertown, Litchfield co, CT[2]. This may have been the home of Mary's parents.

David and Polly joined the Oxford Congregational Church on 26 May 1799[3]. In 1808 they were dismissed from the Oxford church and recommended to the Congregational Church in Watertown[3]. Whether they actually moved to Watertown and joined the church there is not clear. Very soon after, they removed to Stamford, Fairfield co, CT, where David appears with his family in the 1810 census: 01210-10010[3]. He died, and his estate was probated in Stamford in 1813[3]. His widow Polly appears in the 1830 census: 0-00001101[3], and in the 1840 census (as Mary): 0-010001101[3], both in Stamford, where she had been admitted to the First Congregational Church on 23 June 1839[3]. She died 2 January 1842[2,3], although the CB Database cites Spencer Mead's abstracts of the Stamford probate records, Vol. 2, p. 305, stating that her estate was probated in Stamford in 1841[3].

Children:
1. 320531. Orin[2], b. 7 May 1797[2]; d. 10 Feb. 1798[2].
2. 320532. Lockwood[2], b. 25 Nov. 1798[2]; m. 1819 Ann Waterbury[2]; d. 1825[2].
3. 320529. Elizabeth Ann[2], bapt. 14 Dec. 1799[2].
4. 320533. son[3], b. 2 Sept. 1800[2]; d. 8 May 1801[2].
5. 320530. Augustus[2], bapt. 25 Apr. 1802[2].
6.   daughter[2], d. 21 Dec. 1806, age 3[2].
7. 320578. Nancy Eloiza[3], bapt. July 1808[3].

REFERENCES:
1. New Haven - Jacobus, p. 366.
2. Duncan, p. 63.
3. CB Database.

1-1-6-3-6-9 D86 CB310052

NATHAN[6] BUNNELL (Isaac[5], Benjamin[4], Benjamin[3], Benjamin[2], William[1]) was born about 1782[1,2,3], probably in that part of Derby, New Haven co, CT, later set off as the town of Oxford. He married CURRANCE _____ [1]. Nathan appears in the 1810 census: 2001-0001[4] in Watertown, Litchfield co, CT. In 1815 he was apparently the administrator of the estate of his nephew Isaac Bunnell CB320403 in Watertown[2]. Jo Gillen researched the land records of Watertown, CT, and found that Nathan and Currance sold their ¼ interest in 21 acres on Jack's Hill, so called, and that Nathan was listed as grantee in six deeds between September 1807 and February 1816[1].

Sometime after this, they moved to Onondaga co, NY[1], where he appears in the 1820 census: 011110-00010-AG3[4], and in the 1830 census: 0000001-0000001001[4], both in the town of Manlius. In 1840 they appear in the town of Dewitt, Onondaga co: 00000001-00000001001[4]. Currance seems to have died sometime in the following decade, since in the 1850 census Nathan, age 68, was recorded as living in DeWitt with his son Isaac C. Bunnell[4]

Children:
1. 320030. Edmund H., b. about 1804[1,4]; m. Ann _____[4]; d. after 1850[4].
    Children (surname Bunnell):[4]
    1. Esther A.   4. Elizabeth.   7. Nathan T.
    2. Francis A.   5. Harriet M.   8. Mary.
    3. John A.   6. Jane P.   9. Charlotte.
2. 320875. Isaac Collins, b. about 1807[4], or Dec. 1802[1]; m. (first) about 1828 Mary
    Bunnell[2] 320021; m. (second) Jane A. _____[2]; d. 28 June 1896[2].
    Children (surname Bunnell)(by first wife):[2]
    1. Caroline.   3. Almon.   4. Rachel A.
    2. Jabe Collins.

REFERENCES:
1. Gillen, pp. 32, 33, 34.
2. Duncan, pp. 61, 62, 63, 64.
3. Bunnell/Bonnell Newsletter, Vol. 12, No. 1, p. 11.
4. CB Database.

1-1-6-4-1-1   D32i   CB310250

JAMES[6] BUNNELL (Isaac[5], Solomon[4], Benjamin[3], Benjamin[2], William[1]) was born 16 February 1767[2,3], probably in Lower (now Middle) Smithfield twp, Northampton (now Monroe) co, PA. According to Biles[2], he never married, but remained with his father on the farm "in the Hollow in Middle Smithfield twp. If I am not mistaken, James ventured away from home at least once. I believe him to be the James Bunnell who appears in the 1790 census in Bucks co, PA, as a free white male of 16 years and upwards[1]. He was 23 years old at the time. Perhaps he had traveled down the Delaware River with farm produce or lumber to sell. In any case he was taxed as the owner of 63 acres in Middle Smithfield in 1798[4]. He also appears on Middle Smithfield tax lists from 1815 to 1833[4]. He died 6 February 1844 and was buried in the Coolbaugh cemetery, Monroe co[2].

It is interesting to note that he was a resident of four Pennsylvania counties during his lifetime without ever moving off the farm in Lower (later Middle) Smithfield twp. He was born in Northampton co in 1767. He was taxed in Wayne co in 1798 and in Pike co from 1815 to 1833. He died and was buried in Monroe co.

REFERENCES:
1. Census 1790- PA, p. 56.
2. Biles Manuscript, p. 13.
3. CBR NE PA, p.407.
4. CB Database.

1-1-6-4-1-3   D87   CB310252

GERSHOM[6] BUNNELL (Isaac[5], Solomon[4], Benjamin[3], Benjamin[2], William[1]) was born 12 July[1] or (30 June[2]) 1770[1,2] in Lower (now Middle) Smithfield twp[1], Northampton (now Monroe) co, PA. On 8 October 1794[1] he married (first) LANAH (ELEANOR) TOCK[1]. She was born 10 July 1770[1]. Gershom appears on the 1796 tax list in Middle Smithfield twp[2], assessed on 60 acres[5], and again in 1797[2]. In 1798 he was assessed on 131 acres including 1 hut house, 20 x 30, of hewed logs[2]. He appears in the 1800 census: 01121-31020[2] and in the 1810 census: 1013-2201[2], both in Middle Smithfield twp, Wayne co, PA. After the death of his father in 1812, Gershom occupied the homestead in "The Hollow"[3].

His wife Lanah died 15 October 1813[1]. He married (second) 27 June 1814[1] Mrs. LEONORA (SMITH) BRINK[1], who was born 24 September 1774[1] in Delaware (now Lehman) twp[1], Northampton (now Pike) co, PA. In 1814 he was elected elder of the Reformed Dutch Church in Smithfield[2] In 1816 Rev. John Boyd, appointed by the Presbytery of New Brunswick, reorganized the church, and ordained John Turn and Gershom Bunnell ruling elders[5]. (In 1816 he bought a clock case for $16 from cabinetmaker John Turn of Middle Smithfield twp[6].) Gershom appears on Middle Smithfield tax lists from 1814 to 1821[2]. He is listed in the 1820 census in Middle Smithfield twp, Pike co: 210012-0021-AG[2]. He died 2 December 1828[1] at the old homestead in Middle Smithfield twp[1] and was buried in the Coolbaugh cemetery there[1]. His widow married Jacob Morey as her third husband[1]. She died 7 June 1835[1] at Mount Bethlehem[1] (probably Mount Bethel, Northampton co, PA).

Children (all born in Middle Smithfield)(by first wife):
1. 320182. Eleanor[1], b. 27 Feb. 1795[1]; m. William Pennell[1]; d. 4 Mar. 1854[1].
    Children (surname Pennell)[1]:
    1. Gershom Bunnell.
2. 320181. Martha[1], b. 23 Oct. 1797[1]; m. 1 July 1820[2] Daniel Bensley[7]; d. 6 Mar. 1863[1] without issue[7].
3. 320180. Mary[1], b. 25 Sept. 1799[1]; m. 25 June 1816[1] Elijah Quigley[1]; d. 23 Aug. 1869[1].
    Children (surname Quigley}[1]:

1. Eleanor.	4. Jane.	7. Amy.
2. Sarah.	5. Mary.	8. Benjamin.
3. Elizabeth.	6. Catherine.	

4. 320183. Hannah[1], b. 29 Sept. 1803[1]; m. Isaac Quigley[1]; d. 1839[1].
5.   Henry[1], d. young[1].
6. 320178. Benjamin[1], b. 18 Feb. 1808[1]; m. 17 Oct. 1831 Hannah Gross[1]; d. 5 Nov. 1855[1].
    Children (surname Bunnell):[1]

1. Martha.	4. Ellen.	6. Benjamin.
2. Gershom L.	5. Daniel.	7. Mary.

7. 320179. John[1], b. 24 Dec. 1811[1]; d. 26 Jan. 1826[1].

Children (by second wife):

8. 320184. James[1], b. 25 Feb. 1818[1]; m. 14 Aug. 1842 Julian Ann Walter[1]; d. 21 Apr. 1871[1].

Children (surname Bunnell):[1]

1. Theodore W.	5. Susanna W.	8. James Madison.
2. Mary Jane.	6. Sarah Ellen.	9. Michael W.
3. Henry W.	7. Gershom Walter.	10. Lydia.
4. Elizabeth D.		

9. 320185. Gershom[1], b. 6 Jan. 1821[1]; d. 17 June 1903[1].

10. 320186. Henry[1], b. 18 July 1823[1]; m. 4 Mar. 1854 Lydia Smith[1]; d. 9 May 1895[1].

Children (surname Bunnell):[1]

1. Gersham H.	2. James.

REFERENCES:

1. Biles Manuscript, pp. 20, 21, 23, 28, 29. "Record taken from old Gershom Bunnell Bible, Bushkill, Pa."
2. CB Database.
3. CBR NE PA, p. 407.
4. Tioga NY History, p.121.
5. Wayne PA History, pp. 1094, 1096.
6. *Arts of the Pennsylvania Dutch*, by Earl F. Robacker, A. S. Barnes and Co., Inc., New York, 1965, p. 29. Sent to me by Beverly Sorensen, Northbrook, IL.
7. NEHGR, Vol. 93, p. 205.

1-1-6-4-1-4   D88   CB310253

JOHN[6] BUNNELL (Isaac[5], Solomon[4], Benjamin[3], Benjamin[2], William[1]) was born 11 August 1772[6] in Lower (now Middle) Smithfield twp,[6] Northampton (now Monroe) co, PA. About 1795 he married (first) HANNAH JAYNE[6], daughter of John and Cornelia (Decker) Jayne[6]. She was born 3 July[4] 1776[4,6] in Lower Smithfield twp[6]. On 9 January 1797 he purchased 100 acres of land on the west branch of the Owego Creek[9], a part of the Park Settlement[8], about 3 miles above the point were the Owego Creek enters the Susquehanna River at Owego. Park Settlement lay on the west side of the Creek in what was then the town of Owego, Tioga co, NY. The land now lies in the present town of Candor, Tioga co, NY. He was a shoemaker and farmer[8], but he is said to have paid for his farm chiefly with bounties obtained from trapping wolves[6]. John Bunnell appears there in the 1800 census: 20010-00100[4,5]. He and his wife were charter members of the Baptist Church on Owego Creek 1 May 1802[7], and John was chosen its first deacon[8].

In March 1809 they sold their farm (which since 1806 had been in the town of Spencer, Tioga co) to Lyman Truman[9] and moved to a farm of approximately 100 acres which he purchased along the Owego Creek[9] in the town of Berkshire, Broome co, NY. John appears there in the 1810 census: 22010-10010[4], and in the 1820 census: 101201-00010[4]. In 1822 the town of Berkshire was transferred to Tioga co, NY, and in 1824 the town of Newark, where their farm was situated, was set off from Berkshire. The 1825 New York state census in the town of

Newark records that their family consisted of 4 males (2 voters and 1 subject to military duty) and 1 female[4,5]. They appear again in the town of Newark in the 1830 Federal census: 01010001-0000001[4]. Hannah died there on 7 November 1837[3] and was buried in the West Newark Church Cemetery[3] in the town of Newark (since 1862 the town of Newark Valley). In February 1838 John sold the farm in Newark to his son Isaac. A year later he purchased 39 acres of land in the town of Richford, Tioga co, NY. He married (second) in 1838 or 1839 BETSEY _____[1]. He died 15 January 1840[1] at Richford[1], Tioga co, NY. He was buried in the West Newark Church Cemetery with his first wife Hannah[3].

John Bunnell made his will on 25 May 1839 (Surrogate's Office, Tioga Co, NY, Book D, p. 418.) It provided forst for the payment of his debts. Then he left $100 to his son William B. Bunnell and $300 to his eldest son Isaac Bunnell. Any remaining sums of money were to be divided equally among his five younger sons - John J., David, Henry, William B. and Benajah. His two youngest sons William B. and Benajah were to receive "two featherbeds with sufficient clothing for the same to be divided equally between them." All of his wearing apparel was to be divided equally by sons John J. and David.
All the rest of his personal property and real estate was left to his beloved wife Betsey Bunnell so long as she remained his widow. After her death or remarriage, the real estate was to be divided equally among his six surviving sons. His son Henry Bunnell and John R. Hubbard were appointed executors.
The will was submitted for probate 12 March 1840, an inventory of the estate was filed on 8 June 1840, and the final settlement was filed 2 September 1844[1].

Children (by first wife):
  1. 320212. Isaac[1], b. 27 May 1797[6] or 13 June 1795[10]; m. (first) about 1815 Rachel Brink[9]; m. (second) 1844 Fanny Lodemia Jackson[9]; d. 4 Sept. 1869[10].
      Children (surname Bunnell)(by first wife):[9]

1. Annie.	4. Orville Mortimer.	7. Elizabeth.
2. John.	5. Hannah Jayne.	8. Temperance.
3. Margaret.	6. Mary.	

      Children (surname Bunnell)(by second wife):[9]

9. William Luther.	11. James Torry.	12 Currance Meranda.
10. Isaac Melanchon.		

  2. 320213. John J.[1] (James[9] or Jayne[6]), b. 1799[6]; m. Sarah J. Sawyer[9]; d. 1885[9].
      Children (surname Bunnell):[9]

1. Calaickey.	5. Isaac S.	9. Elizabeth.
2. William Chelson.	6. Mary A.	10. John James.
3. child.	7. Sarah P.	11. Emeline B.
4. Nathaniel Pomeroy.	8. Aaron Miles.	12. Abram S.

  3. 320214. David[1], b. 18 June 1802[9] (or 1801[6]); m. about 1823 Mary Mae Everett[9]; d. 29 or 30 Aug. 1865[9].

Children (surname Bunnell):[4,9]

1. Benjamin J.	5. Mary Jane.	8. Sarah Melissa.
2. Samuel Ford.	6. Nancy E.	9. Chelson Dallas.
3. George Alfred.	7. Henry D.	10. Marcus Fayette.
4. James Smitchell.		

4. 320215. Henry Jayne[1], b. 23 Dec. 1803[6]; 1828 Eliza Livermore[6]; d. 5 Feb. 1890[6].
Children (surname Bunnell):[4,6]

1. John Gardner.	3. William Henry.	5. Mary Emeline.
2. Charles Arnold.	4. James Harlo.	6. Sarah Eliza.

5. 320222. Ann Eliza[2], b. 1 June 1806[2]; d. 11 Aug. 1817[2].

6. 320218. James[2], b. 14 Sept. 1808[2]; d. 22 May 1809[2].

7. 320219. Gershom[2], b. 9 May 1810[2]; d. young[2].

8. 320220. Jesse[2], b. 17 Feb. 1811[2]; d. 17 Apr. 1811[2].

9. 320221. Cornelia[2], b. 22 Mar. 1817[2]; d. 1 July 1817[2].

10. 320216. William B.[1], b. 29 July 1818[9] (or 29 June 1814[4,6]); m. Zippora Elizabeth Livermore[4]; d. 22 Apr. 1868[4]
Children (surname Bunnell):[4]

1. Charlotte Elizabeth.	2. Cora R.

11. 320217. Benajah[1] J.[9] (Jayne[6]), b. about 1821[6]; m. (first) Anna Elizabeth Doyle[6]; m. (second) Clarissa Myers[4]; d. 8 Mar. 1871 aged 50 years[11].
Children (surname Bunnell)(by second wife):[4]
1. Mina E.

12.   child[8].

13.   child[8].

14.   child[8].

NOTE: For a greatly expanded account of John Bunnell and his family, see *The Bunnell Families - Tioga County, NY*, by Charles Everett Bunnell, P. O. Box 1507, Fairfield Glade, TN, 38558. Phone: (931) 707-1444, E-mail: bunnellfamily.com. A copy is on file at the Tioga County, NY, Historical Society, Owego, NY, and perhaps others. My own copy will eventually be placed in the Wyoming co, PA, Historical Society, Tunkhannock, PA.

REFERENCES:
1. Will of John Bunnell - Will Book D, p. 418, Tioga co, NY.
2. Gravestone inscriptions, Jenksville Cemetery, Tioga co, NY.
3. Ltr 14 Aug. 1975 from Mrs. Paul Bunnell, Holton, MI, with cemetery records of the West Newark Cemetery, Town of Newark, Tioga co, NY.
4. CB Database - census, 1800, 1810, 1820, 1825, 1830.
5. Ltr. 21 Feb. 1978 from Christopher Bock, Kansas City, MO.
6. Biles Manuscript, p. 31.
7. *History of Tioga, Chemung, Tompkins and Schuyler Counties, New York*, Everts & Ensign, 1879, page 136.
8. Tioga Gazetteer, pp. 200, 241, 248.
9. *The Bunnell Families - Tioga County, NY*, by Charles Everett Bunnell.
10. *Bunnell and Allied Families*, by Joan England Murray, Palatine, IL, 1990.
11. Gravestone inscriptions, East Rush Cemetery, Susquehanna co, PA.

1-1-6-4-1-5   D89   CB310255

HENRY BUNNELL[6] (Isaac[5], Solomon[4], Benjamin[3], Benjamin[2], William[1]) was born 3 July 1778[1] in Lower Smithfield twp[2], Northampton (now Monroe) co, PA. He married MARY NIHART[1] of Pocono[3], Northampton (now Monroe) co, PA. She was born about 1779[2] in Bethlehem[4], Northampton co, PA. Henry appears in the 1800 census in Lower Smithfield twp, Northampton (now Monroe) co, PA: 102-001[4]. The first five of their children were born in Middle Smithfield[1], but in the spring of
1809 he removed to Walpack, Sussex co, NJ[1], and bought a farm on Flat Brook[2], where all the rest of the children were born[1]. (The move may have been a bit later than 1809, since the CB Database finds Henry in the 1810 census in Middle Smithfield, Wayne co, PA: 1011-201[4]. These numbers, however, do not seem to correspond to Henry's family as we know it.)

In Walpack he was a farmer and a blacksmith[1]. He died in Walpack 4 August 1826[1] and was buried in the Old Walpack Churchyard[1]. His sons Henry and Gershom were appointed administrators of his estate[4]. His widow Mary remained on the farm in Walpack twp, where she appears in the 1830 census: 01-0110001[4] and the 1840 census: 100-0011001[4]. In the 1850 census Mary, age 72, was still living on the farm, now owned by her son David[1,4]. She died 27 April 1856[4] and was buried beside her husband in the Old Walpack Churchyard[1].

Children:
1. 320226. George, b. 26 Jan. 1800[2], d. young[2].
2. 320227. Julia, b. 15 Mar. 1802[2]; m. Jesse Diamond[2] (or Dimon[3]); d. 1835[2].
      Children (surname Diamond or Dimon)[2]:
      1. John.   2. Isaac.   3. Oliver.
3. 320228. Gershom R., b. 29 Jan. 1804[2]; m. 21 Jan. 1826 Anna C. Bergstreser[2];
      d. 27 Dec. 1869[2].
      Children (surname Bunnell):[2]
      1. Annie C.   3. Mary.   4. Hannah.
      2. Henry Jackson.
4. 320229. David, b. 1 Mar. 1806[1,2]; m. 16 Sept. 1828 Catharine Smith[1,2]; d. 26 Feb.
      1894[2].
      Children (surname Bunnell):[2]
      1. James. M.   5. Mary M.   9. Purcilla.
      2. John I. Blair.   6. Henry.   10. Martha J.
      3. Thomas Grattan.   7. Catherine.   11. Franklin Pierce.
      4. Sarah Ann.   8. Joseph Wesley.
5. 320230. Robert, b. 24 (or 14[3]) Mar. 1808[2]; m. Eunice Barry[2]; d. 29 Nov. 1839[2].
      Children (surname Bunnell):[2]
      1. Henry J.   3. James.   5. Alizena.
      2. Robert Gabriel.   4. Albert F.
6. 320321. Isaac B., b. 20 July 1810[2]; m. (first) Margaret LaBar[2]; m. (second) Oct.
      1871 Marcy Mingle[2]; d. 20 Mar. 1895[2].

Children (surname Bunnell)(by first wife):[2]

1. Charles LaBar.	3. Sarah E.	4. J. Leslie.
2. John Fletcher.		

7. 320232. James, b. 25 Jan. 1812[2]; m. Mary Ann Hull[2]; d. 28 Sept. 1879[2].

Children (surname Bunnell):[2,5,6]

1. William Hull.	7. Hannah Jane.	12. Clarence.
2. Lucinda Margaret.	8. Julia Ella.	13. Florence Estella.
3. Emma Harriet.	9. Lavinia.	14. David Hume.
4. Gershom.	10. Jacob Walter.	15. John Hull.
5. Sarah Elizabeth.	11. Benjamin Franklin.	16. Eva.
6. Anna.		

8. 320233. Barnett, b. 20 May 1815[2]; d. young[2].

9. 320234. John, b. 26 Mar. 1817[2]; m. 19 Oct. 1839 Marsa Lanterman[2]; d. 1 June 1900[2].

Children (surname Bunnell):[2]

1. Peter DeWitt.	5. Annie M.	8. Isaiah C.
2. Mary Phoebe.	6. Martha.	9. Nehemiah.
3. Sarah Caroline.	7. Marcus.	10. Isabell.
4. Jennie.		

10. 320247. Mary, b. 16 Feb. 1819[2]; m. John Hull[2]; d. 25 Oct. 1888[2].

Children (surname Hull):[2]

1. Melissa J.	3. Emma C.	4. Anna Mary.
2. Jessie Fremont.		

11. 320248. Henry, b. 17 June 1821[2]; m. (first) Elizabeth Garess[2]; m. (second) Hannah Floyd[2]; m. (third) Mary L. Lanterman[2]; m. (fourth) Elizabeth France[2]; d. 20 Dec. 1894[2].

Children (surname Bunnell)(by first wife):[2]

1. Samuel Corey.

Children (surname Bunnell)(by second wife):[2]

2. Mary Elizabeth.   3. Hannah Jane.

Children (surname Bunnell)(by third wife):[2]

12. 320249. Eleanor, b. 29 Dec. 1823[2]; d. 1864 unmarried[2].

REFERENCES:
1. Snell, p. 226.
2. Biles Manuscript, pp. 37, 44.
3. Bonnell, pp. XIV-26, 30.
4. CB Database.
5. "Ma's brothers and sisters", listed in a diary kept by one of the sons of Hannah Jane (Bunnell) Smith, on a page copied and sent to me by William Tidball, Summerland, BC, on 29 Oct. 1994.
6. 1860 census, Wayne twp, Lafayette co, WI, extracted on page 22 in *Through the Century, A History of South Wayne, Wisconsin (1899-1989)*, sent by William Tidball.

SIXTH GENERATION

1-1-6-4-1-6   D32vi   CB310256

WILLIAM[6] BUNNELL {Isaac[5], Solomon[4], Benjamin[3], Benjamin[2], William[1]) was born 2 October 1780[1], in Lower (now Middle) Smithfield twp[1], Northampton (now Monroe) co, PA. He remained at home unmarried[2]. His mind became weak and he was sometimes called "Crazy Billy"[2].

REFERENCES:
1. CBR NE PA, p. 407.
2. Biles Manuscript, p. 13.

1-1-6-4-1-7   D90   CB310257

DAVID[6] BUNNELL (Isaac[5], Solomon[4], Benjamin[3], Benjamin[2], William[1]) was born 23 April 1783[1] in Lower (now Middle) Smithfield twp[1], Northampton (now Monroe) co, PA. In his early manhood he lived for several years in Wallpack, Sussex co, NJ[1]. In 1804 he settled at Bethany in Dyberry twp, Wayne co, PA[3]. On 5 March 1805[1] he married PARTHENIA KELLAM[1], daughter of John and Sally Killam[5]. She was born 5 March 1786[2] in Palmyra twp, Northampton (now Pike) co[2], PA. He cleared much of the timber from his farm and erected a house and a blacksmith shop where he carried on his trade of blacksmithing[3]. Bethany was the first county seat of Wayne co, and David used to accommodate boarders at his house when court was in session[3]. For many years he served as justice of the peace[3]. The organization meeting for the establishment of the Baptist Church at Bethany was held at his house in 1809[3], and he and his wife were members[3].

David appears in the 1810 census in Dyberry twp, Wayne co: 1011-201[4] and in Bethany, Wayne co in the 1820 census: 41001-1201[4] and in the 1830 census: 1121011-1120101[4]. In 1839 he sold his property in Bethany[3]. The next year he appers in the census in Berlin twp, Wayne co, PA: 00011001-00111001[4]. With his sons, Henry, Z. K. Pike, and John K., he bought some 750 acres, mostly a wild tract of land in Dyberry and Texas twps, Wayne co[3]. He soon built a new home by the Bunnell Pond in Texas twp[3]. He and his sons erected a sawmill at the outlet of the Pond and began lumbering and clearing the land[3]. The 1850 census of Texas twp, Wayne co, lists David, age 67, and wife Pathenia, age 64[4].

David Bunnell died at his home in Texas twp in September 1854[2] (or 1855[3]). His widow moved back to Bethany. She appears there in the 1860[4] and 1870[4] census living with her daughter Eunice, Mrs. Brooks Lavo. She died at Bethany in 1875[2]. They were buried in Glen Dyberry cemetery, Honesdale[3,4] (or in Bethany[1]), Wayne co, PA.

Children:
1. 320235. Rockwell·, b. 2 Apr. 1806[2]; m. Flavilla Brooks[2]; d. 12 Jan. 1892[2].
   Children (surname Bunnell):[5]
   1. Stewart Wallace.   3. Delia.   5. Minerva.
   2. Marvice.   4. Parthena.   6. Julia.

or[2]

1. Julia.	3. Wallace.	5. Morris.
2. Parthenia.	4. Sarah Jane.	6. Hortense.

or[4]

1. Parthena.	4. Stewart Wallace.	6. Morris W.
2. Minerva T.	5. Lydia E.	7. Brice Blare.
3. Julia F.		

2. 320236. Eleanor, b. 22 Nov. 1807[2]; m. Isaac Parsons[4] Olmstead[2]; d. 1843[3].
   Children (surname Olmstead)[5]:

1. Oscar.	3. Caroline.	5. Hattie.
2. David.	4. Evelyn.	6. Eleanor.

3. 320237. Eunice B., b. 6 Jan. 1810[2], m. Brooks Lavo[2]; d. 15 Nov. 1876[2].
   Children (surname Lavo)[2]:

1. Parthenia L.	4. Mary.	7. Henrietta.
2. Malvina.	5. Henry.	8. Amanda.
3. Mortimer.	6. Sarah.	9. Eugene.

4. 320238. Henry, b. 17 Oct. 1811[2]; m. (first) 1 Sept. 1836 Amanda Page[2]; m. (second) 4 Mar. 1855 Lydia Ann (Schofield) Bunnell[2]; m. (third) 26 Sept. 1861 Mary Bunnell[2]; d. 19 Dec. 1872[2].
   Children (surname Bunnell)(by first wife):[2]

1. David Montgomery.	4. Mary E.	6. Calvin Page.
2. Louisa Priscilla.	5. William Henry.	7. Amanda C.
3. George F.		

   Children (surname Bunnell)(by second wife):[2]

8. Judson Willard.	9. Irving W.

   Children (surname Bunnell)(by third wife):[2]

10. Edward Elmer.	12. Ida Belle.	14. Ellery Pike.
11. William Fletcher.	13. Harry Horatio.	

5. 320239. Zebulon Montgomery Pike, b. 6 July 1813[2]; m. 27 June 1839 Clarinda Bonham[2]; d. 5 June 1857[2].
   Children (surname Bunnell):[2]

1. Oliver Hamlin.	4. Martha J.	7. Isabel Alice.
2. Ellery J.	5. Helen M.	8. Eugene P.
3. Amelia S.	6. Oscar E.	

6. 320240. Charles Forsythe, b. 6? July? 1815[2]; m. (first) 1844 Ada A. Norton[2]; m. (second) Harriet A. Norton[2]; m. (third) Sallie Mariah Newton[2]; d. 3 Oct. 1875[2].
   Children (surname Bunnell)(by first wife):[2]

1. Clark.	2. Hattie.

   Children (surname Bunnell)(by second wife):[2]

3. Jane Adelaide.

   Children (surname Bunnell)(by third wife):[2]

4. Caroline Rosella.	5. Mary Augusta.

7. 320241. John Kellam, b. 14 Jan. 1817[2]; m. 10 Nov. 1841 Ann S. Brownscombe[2];
d. 2 Apr. 1902[2].
Children (surname Bunnell):[2]
1. Caroline Amelia.   4. Hattie E.   6. Sarah Emma.
2. George W. or G.   5. Frank Clark.   7. John Kellam.
3. William B.

8. 320242. Sarah E., b. 11 Dec. 1820[2]; m. Rev. Gilbert Bailey[2]; moved to Los
Angeles, CA[2].
Children (surname Bailey)[5]:
1. Gilbert.   3. Howard.   5. William.
2. Charles.   4. Wayland.   6. daughter.

9. 320243. David S., b. 19 Nov. 1821[2]; m. Henrietta Tomlin[2].
Children (surname Bunnell):[4]
1. Edward B.   4. William S.   7. Clifton Marssy.
2. Gertrude F.   5. Alfreda.   8. Rubena.
3. Orlando S.   6. Arabella S.   9. Albion B.

10. 320244. Harriett A., b. 21 May 1824[2]; d. as a young woman, unmarried[3].

11. 320245. Abigail Jane, b. 9 Oct. 1826[2]; m. William Stockdale[2]; d. in Illinois[2].
Children (surname Stockdale)[5]:
1. Minnie Jenneu.   2. Bunty Barrie.

REFERENCES:
1. CBR NE PA, pp. 143, 407.
2. Biles Manuscript, pp. 47', 48.
3. *History of Wayne, Pike and Monroe Counties, Penn.*, by Alfred Matthews, 1886, pp. 505, 825.
4. CB Database.
5. Pages 28, 32 and 33 of a typed document, identified as "taken from records of John Killam, Jr., Northbrook, Ill.", sent to me by Beverly Sorensen, Northbrook, IL, 18 Mar. 1978.

1-1-6-4-1-8   D32viii   CB310259

BARNETT[6] BUNNELL (Isaac[5], Solomon[4], Benjamin[3], Benjamin[2], William[1]) was born 16 (or 26[2]) February 1789[1], in Middle Smithfield twp[1], Northampton (now Monroe) co, PA. He was baptized 19 April 1789 at the Dutch Reformed Church at Smithfield, Northampton co, PA[2]. He served as a private in Capt. John Dornblazer's detachment from Northampton, Lehigh and Pike counties, PA, in 1812[3]. He married CHARITY DICKERSON[1], who was born 19 September 1789[2] in New York[2], the daughter of Simeon and Mary Dickerson[2]. He owned a farm in Middle Smithfield on what was afterwards known as "Barney Hill"[1]. He appears in tax lists in Middle Smithfield, Pike co, from 1814 to 1833, and in the Pike co census in 1830: 1000001-21002. Thirty years later he appears in the 1860 census in Pahaquarry twp, Warren co, NJ, living with his son Isaac[2]. He died 19 June 1864[1] at Millbrook[1], Pahaquarry twp, Warren co, NJ, at his son Isaac's home[1].

Children:
1. 320950. Eleanor, b. 12 Apr. 1822[1]; m. Milton Armstrong[1].

2. 320951. Mary, b. 21 Aug. 1824[1]; m. F. L. Smith[1]; 9 children[1]; d. 1872.
3. 320952. Julia, b. 12 May 1827[1]; m. George Fenicle[1].
          Children (surname Fenicle)[1]:
          1. Horace.   2. Emma.
4. 320953. Isaac, b. 7 Jan. 1830[1]; m. 10 Feb. 1859 Eliza R. VanCampen[1].
          Children (surname Bunnell):[1,2]
          1. Anna Augusta.   3. Lavinia.   4. Oliver.
          2. William Preston.
5. 320954. Martha H., b. 30 Apr. 1832[1]; d. 24 Aug. 1849[1].
6. 320955. Rachel, b. 2 July 1834[1]; d. 13 July 1835[1].
7. 320956. Elizabeth, b. 28 Jan. 1837[1]; m. John Sitgreaves[1].
8. 320957. David, b. 29 Oct. 1839[1]; d. May 1864[1].
9. 320958. John, b. 4 July 1842[1]; m. (first) Phoebe Gameford[1]; m.(second) Martha _____ [2].
          Children (surname Bunnell)(by first wife?):[1]
          1. John.   2. George.
          Children (surname Bunnell)(by second wife):[2]
          3. Isaac.

REFERENCES:
1. Biles Manuscript, pp. 60, 61.
2. CB Database.
3. PA Archives, 2nd Series, Vol. XII, p. 129.

1-1-6-4-3-6 D91 CB310242

BENJAMIN[6] BUNNELL (Benjamin[5], Solomon[4], Benjamin[3], Benjamin[2], William[1]) was born 29 October 1788[1] in Lower (now Middle) Smithfield twp[1], Northampton (now Monroe) co, PA. On 23 December 1806[4] (or 1809[5]) he married MARY EVA OZIER[1], who was born 30 December 1787[1] (or 11 October 1787[3]). The 1810 census of Lower Smithfield twp, Northampton co[3] shows Benjamin and Mary with 1 boy under 10 (son John) and 1 girl under 10 (daughter Amanda? or a daughter who died young?).

During the late 1820s they moved to Luzerne (now Wyoming) co, PA, locating on "The Neck"[1] in Washington twp. He was a shoemaker[1]. In the 1830 census of Tunkhannock twp, Luzerne co, PA[3], Benjamin and Mary are listed with 1 male between 10 and 15 (son Isaac), 3 males between 15 and 20 (sons Daniel, Benjamin and Charles), and 1 female under 5 years (daughter Mary). Son John died 21 May 1830[1] and was not counted in the census.

They were still living on "The Neck" when the 1840 census of Washington twp, Luzerne co, PA[3], was taken. Benjamin and Mary are shown as between 50 and 60 years of age. Their household also included 1 male between 5 and 10, 1 male between 20 and 30, 1 female between 10 and 15, 1 female between 15 and 20, and 1 female between 20 and 30. Probably the male and female between 20 and 30 represent one of their sons and his wife, but most of the other young people do not seem to fit into their immediate family. They could have been relatives, or orphan children Ben and Mary took in to raise, or to help with the farm and house work.

Sometime between 1840 and 1850 Benjamin and Mary moved from "The Neck" to Bunnell Hill[1], in what was then Braintrim twp, but is now Meshoppen twp, Wyoming co, PA. The census of 1850[3] shows that Benjamin Bunnel, 61 years old, was a farmer owning real estate valued at $1000. His wife Mary was 62. They were living alone.

Ten years later, the census of Meshoppen twp, Wyoming co, PA[3], shows that Benjamin, age 72, a farmer, now owned real estate valued at $1500 and had personal property worth $500. He and Mary now had living with them their grandson, John Luce, age 28, his wife Ann, age 22, and son Riley, age 1 year. John Luce was the son of their adopted daughter Amanda, who married Abram Luce.

By 1870[3], Benjamin, at age 82, had retired from farming, though he still owned the farm, now valued at $2500, on which they lived with their son and daughter-in-law, Isaac W. and Amelia Bunnell and their four sons.

Benjamin's great-niece, Mrs. Sarah Dunlap, in 1914 wrote: "I lived with grandfather James Bunnell, one of the six brothers of Wyoming county, from the time I was 9 until I was 22. His brother,'Uncle John', we always called him, was a dear old man whom I remember well. Whe he came to visit grandfather, he always read a chapter in the Bible, and they prayed together. I also remember Uncle Solomon, and Uncle Benny, who was such a devout man; and the four brothers, all over 70, sat in a row at a camp meeting on Rattlesnake Hill, in 1871, and partook of the Lord's supper together, just a year or two before the first one went home."[6]

Mary Eva (Ozier) Bunnell died 21 August 1874[1] at the age of 86 years, 7 months and 20 days. Benjamin died 27 February 1880[1,2] at his home on Bunnell Hill[1], aged 91 years, 3 months and 29 days[2]. They were buried in the cemetery at Vosburg on "The Neck" in Washington twp, Wyoming co, PA, although only his gravestone can be found today[2]. If there was ever a stone for Mary, it has not survived the years.

Children:
     1. 320172. John[1], b. 26 Oct. 1809[1]; d. 21 May 1830[2].
     2. 320169. (adopted[1]) Amanda[1], b. 1810[5]; m. 1825[5] Abram Luce[1,5].
          Children (surname Luce):
            1. Elizabeth.   3. Euphemia.   5. Letitia.
            2. Mary Ann.   4. Benjamin.   6. John.
     3. 320075. Daniel[1], b. 8 Oct. 1811[1]; m. 9 May 1832 Mary Ozier[1]; d. 26 Aug. 1898[1].
          Children (surname Bunnell):[1]
            1. Charles G.   4. Charlotte.   7. William.
            2. David.   5. A. Oziah.
            3. Eliza Ann.   6. George W.
     4. 320170. Benjamin[1], b. 31 Mar. 1813[1]; m. 30 Sept. 1834 Margaret Sterling[1]; d. 2 Mar. 1894[1].

Children (surname Bunnell):[1]

1. Amanda Malina.	5. Laura Hester.	9. Calvin Sterling.
2. Judson Webster.	6. Margaret E.	10. Walker Sterling.
3. Solomon.	7. Sarah Elizabeth.	
4. Doyle Adelbert.	8. Ematury (Emma T.).	

5. 320168. Charles[1], b. 8 July 1815[1]; m. 3 Nov. 1838 Nancy McAdams Little[1].

Children (surname Bunnell):[1]

1. Benjamin Little.	4. Theodore Armstrong.	7. Charles R.
2. Allen Alonzo.	5. Emogene.	
3. Mary Elizabeth.	6, Caroline J.	

6. 320171. Isaac W.[1], b. 27 Feb. 1817[1]; m. Amelia A. (Millicent?) Bond[3].

1. Gershom A.	5. Mary.	9. Perrin S.
2. Alonzo L.	6. David.	10. Calvin A.
3. George G.	7. Edgar B.	
4. Rebecca.	8. Morris B.	

7. 320173. Mary[3], b. 3 Dec. 1827[3].

REFERENCES:
1. Biles Record, p. 103.
2. Gravestone inscriptions in Bunnell Cemetery on "The Neck" at Vosburg, Washington twp, Wyoming co, PA.
3. CB Database - census records 1810-1870 and records of Smithfield Church, Shawnee, PA.
4. Family data of Stanley A. Smith, Pullman, WA, citing family historian Mary (Overfield) Rice as the source.
5. DAR Vol. 92, p. 105; Vol. 132, p. 216; Vol. 147, p. 221.
6. Localized History of the Bunnell Family, 1913-1914, compiled by family historian Mary (Overfield) Rice for the 1914 Bunnell Family reunion, and published in the weekly newspaper, *Meshoppen Enterprise*.

1-1-6-4-3-7   D92   CB310241

JOHN[6] BUNNELL (Benjamin[5], Solomon[4], Benjamin[3], Benjamin[2], William[1]) was born 13 August 1790[1,3] in Lower (now Middle) Smithfield twp, Northampton (now Monroe) co, PA[1]. On 10 July 1810[1,2] he married MARY PLACE[1], daughter of James and Phoebe (Winans) Place. She was born 7 November 1793[1] (or 7 September 1795[3]), christened 9 November 1795 at Middle Smithfield. He lived on the home farm till his father's death in 1814, when he purchased from his brother-in-law William Jayne, the farm in Braintrim (now Meshoppen) twp, Luzerne (now Wyoming) co, PA[1]. He remained there one year and then exchanged it for the land on "The Neck" in what is now Washington twp, Wyoming co[1]. In the fall of that year, 1815, he was converted to Methodism by the preaching of Rev. Mr. Lane at a camp meeting held on "The Neck"[5]. He became a class leader in 1816 and maintained his interest in and service to the church for the rest of his life[5]. In 1836 he built another home on "The Neck" near Vosburg Station in Washington twp, where he and Mary and their family made their home until 1847[1]. He then sold the second homestead on "The Neck" to his son John, Jr., and bought a large property in Tunkhannock twp, Wyoming co, PA, just outside the present Tunkhannock Borough.

Here he built another home. His wife Mary died 3 November 1851[1,3] and was buried in the family cemetery near their home on "The Neck," where two of their children were already interred[1,3]. On 4 October 1854, in Greene, Chenango co, NY, he was married (second), by Rev. H. Gee, to ARMENIA FELLOWS, widow of Rev. George Evans[2]. She was born 3 October 1803 at Sullivan, Tioga co, PA[2]. John appears in the 1820 census in Tunkhannock twp, Luzerne co, PA: 0201-14011, in 1830 in Tunkhannock twp, Luzerne co: 200201-123001, in 1840 in Washington twp, Luzerne co: 11200001-0101101, 1850 in Tunkhannock twp, Wyoming co, with wife Mary, in 1860 in Tunkhannock twp, Wyoming co, with wife Armenia and three of her Evans children, Elizabeth, Sarah and Armenia, and in 1870 In Forkston twp, Wyoming co with wife Armenia, her daughter Armenia Ross age 25 and granddaughter Dora Ross age 5[4]. John died 11 August 1872[1,3] and was buried with his first wife Mary in the family cemetery on "The Neck"[1,3]. His widow Armenia died 26 September 1880[2].

Children (by first wife):

1. 320027. Benjamin[1], b. 24 Oct. 1811[1]; m. 17 Jan. 1833 Sarah Ann Little[1];
    d. 12 Aug. 1896[1].
    Children (surname Bunnell):[1]

1. James Armstrong.	3. Melvina Inez.	5. Robert Elwell.
2. John Hamilton.	4. Mary.	6. Amanda Elizabeth.

2. 320163. James[1], b. 10 Apr. 1814[1]; m. 15 Oct. 1837 Mary Harding[1];
    d. 10 Jan. 1899[1].
    Children (surname Bunnell):[1]

1. Savanna Evaline.	3. Nelson George.	4. Mary.
2. Frank Charles.		

3. 320166. Lydia[1], b. 22 Mar. 1816[1]; m. 2 Mar. 1835[1] George Sumner[1];
    d. 8 Apr. 1897[1]
    Children (surname Sumner)[1]:

1. Archibald Bannatyne.	6. Corington James.	10. Maria Ann.
2. John Bunnell.	7. Mary Lucy.	11. Armenia Irene.
3. Benjamin Edward.	8. Martha Amanda.	12. Ida Sarah.
4. Savana A.	9. Elnora Inez.	13. George Gilbert.
5. Corington A.		

4. 320167. Anna[1], b. 18 Nov. 1817[1]; m. 25 Feb. 1836[1] William Overfield[1];
    d. 11 Mar. 1854[1].
    Children (surname Overfield)[1]:

1. Mary Harriet.	4. Paul James.	7. Ettaline Amanda.
2. Lydia Elizabeth.	5. John Bunnell.	8. Charles Nesbitt.
3. Sarah Helen.	6. Martha Lydia.	

5. 320252. Elizabeth[1], b. 2 Jan. 1819[1]; m. 18 Nov. 1834[2] Archibald Bannatyne[2];
    d. 27 Mar. 1854[1].
    Children (surname Bannatyne)[1]:

1. Robert W.	4. Ann.	6. John W.
2. Savannah.	5. Lydia.	7. James.
3. Mary.		

6. 320253. Savannah[1], b. 2 June 1820[1]; d. 5 Apr. 1841[1,3], unmarried.
7. 320254. Mary[1], b. 24 Feb. 1822[1]; m. 15 Aug. 1839[1] Jacob Place Biles[1]; d. 22 Aug. 1889[1].
    Children (surname Biles)[1]:

1. Helen Marr.	5. Sarah.	9. Jacob Monroe.
2. James Monroe.	6. Emily Amanda.	10. Martin Luther.
3. Aaron.	7. Anna Eliza.	11. Elmore Llewellyn.
4. Mary.	8. John Addison.	12. Albert Sidney.

8. 320255. Sarah[1], b. 12 Mar. 1824[1,3]; m. 18 Oct. 1842[1] Isaac Osterhout Smith[1]; d. 6 Apr. 1881[1,3].
    Children (surname Smith)[1]:

1. John Draper.	3. Mary Melissa.	5. Hernando Cortez.
2. Leander Bannatyne.	4. Amanda Larissa.	

9. 320256. John[1], b. 19 Apr. 1826[1]; m. 24 Sept. 1846 Rebecca Place[1]; d. 10 Sept. 1872[1,3].
    Children (surname Bunnell):[1]

1. Amanda.	4. Mary.	7. Anna.
2. Sarah.	5. Martha L.	8. Ella.
3. William.	6. Hannah.	

10. 320164. Aaron[1], b. 13 Jan. 1828[1]; m. 22 Apr. 1849 Clementine Lane[1]; d. 7 Jan. 1894[1].
    Children (surname Bunnell):[1]

1. Clara Rosaletta.	4. Mary Frances.	7. Minnie Josephine.
2. Bessie Amanda.	5. Alma E.	8. Eleanor Roena.
3. John Gilbert.	6. James Lane.	9. John Walter.

11. 320257. Charles[1], b. 21 Mar. 1830[1,3]; d. 5 Apr. 1830[1,3].
12. 320258. Amanda Merritt[1], b. 3 Mar. 1831[1]; m. 29 Sept. 1853[1] Gilbert Merritt Chamberlain[1]; d. 6 Feb. 1917[1].
    Children (surname Chamberlain)[1]:

1. Sarah Theressa.	2. Mary Alice.

13. 320259. Charles[1], b. 4 July 1833[1]; m. 28 Jan. 1854 Amanda Viola Blakeslee[1]; d. 19 Mar. 1901 s.p.[1].
14. 320260. George Nesbit[1], b. 2 Mar. 1838[1]; m. 2 May 1858 Frances Elizabeth Bardwell[1]; d. 13 Jan. 1904[1].
    Children (surname Bunnell):[1]

1. Charles Marsh.	2. Lenna Marsh.	4. Katharine Maria.
2. George Harmon.		

NOTE: John Addison Biles, in his manuscript on the Bunnell Family, wrote about these children, his mother, aunts and uncles:

    "This is a most remarkable family for size in weight and strength. John weighed over three hundred pounds. Benjamin nearly as much. James, Aaron, Charles, and George at times weighed nearly two hundred and fifty. All, both men and women, with exception of two or three, weighed over two hundred pounds. John was called the giant of Wyoming County, and on one occasion at least in a contest on a lifting machine, drew the machine to its limit at twelve hundred pounds. Several of his brothers were nearly as strong."[1]

SIXTH GENERATION

REFERENCES:
1. Biles Manuscript, p. 112, 113, 118, 120, 126, 129, 135, 138, 143, 146, 147.
2. Memoir of John Bunnell et al., by his granddaughter Mary H. (Overfield) Rice. (See below.)
3. Gravestones in the Bunnell Cemetery on "The Neck", Washington twp, Wyoming co, PA, copied by William R. Austin.
4. CB Database - census records.
5. Luzerne, Lackawanna and Wyoming co, PA.

Following is the text of the Memoir of John Bunnell, by Mary H. (Overfield) Rice, handwritten by her in November 1905. Notations and corrections by John Addison Biles appear in italics.

"Memoir of Grandfather - John Bunnell, Senior

John was the second son of Benjamin and Catherine Barry Bunnell, who in their early days lived in Delaware *Kingwood, NJ,* or more likely, in some valley along the Delaware river. He was born August 13, 1790, and presumably, was named after John Barry - Commodore in command of the ship Lexington in the war of 1812. His parents moved from their pioneer home to the vicinity of Stroudsburg, now Monroe county, Penna., intending to settle in the far-famed Valley of Wyoming in Luzerne county; but the new of the terrible Indian Massacres, July 3, 1778, *French & Indian War 1754 to 63,* deterred them.

When but twelve years old, while raking and binding wheat alone in the field, John became so deeply impressed by the sensible presence of his Creator, that, kneeling on his sheaf, he dedicated his future services to Him whom he resolved to serve.

The eldest son - Benjamin Jr. being apprenticed to learn the shoemaker's trade, it early fell to the lot of John, whose Father died young, to assume his place and assist his Mother in providing for the large family left to her maternal care.

He had the supreme privilege of standing on the deck of the first steamer - Clermont, in 1807, which was built by Robert Fulton, when New York city was a small place, and her suburbs were not. He married Mary Place - July 10, 1810; and when their eldest child - Benjamin was one year old, 1812, they came by the way of the old Easton turnpike, through Moscow and Slocum Hollow, now Scranton, to Braintrim, Luzerne county since Wyoming county, and located on the farm known as the Solomon Bunnell property, situated on the hill near a mile above Black Walnut.

They brought their stock with them, and were four or five days making the journey from Stroudsburg, Monroe country(sic). Their one horse being too wild for his wife to ride and carry their child; so John rode carrying the little one while his faithful wife walked and driving the cows - plodded on. The following morning after their arrival, five of her toe nails came off; and eventually, they all came off through the agony of suffering incurred by walking from Stroudsburg to Black Walnut, over the wilderness paths so rough and unbroken.

Soon afterward, this farm was exchanged with his brother-in-law William Jayne whose wife was Elizabeth Bunnell, for that one on the "Neck" in Washington township, now owned by Nelson Bunnell. Here was developed the first real Homestead, where the other thirteen children were born and reared, or died.

John Bunnell's Record of their Children.

Benjamin	born	October 24, 1811.	Died	August 12, 1896.
James	"	April 10, 1814.	"	Jan. 10, 1899.
Lydia	"	March 22, 1816.	"	April 8, 1897
Anna	"	November 18, 1817	"	March 11, 1854.
Elizabeth	"	January 2, 1819.	"	March 27, 1854.
Savannah	"	June 2, 1820	"	April 5, 1841.
Mary	"	February 24, 1822	"	August 22, 1889.
Sarah	"	March 12, 1824.	"	April 6, 1881.
John	"	April 19, 1826	"	September 11, 1872.
Aaron	"	January 30, 1829	"	January 7, 1894.
Charles	"	March 21, 1830	"	April 5, 1830.
Amanda Merritt	"	March 3, 1831	"	Feb. 6, 1917.
Charles	"	July 4, 1833	"	March 19, 1901.
George Nezbert	"	March 2, 1838	"	July 13, 1904.

Their Marriages:

Benjamin to Sarah Ann Little	January 17, 1833	(5) No. of Children.
James to Mary Hardin	October 15, 1837.	Four.

SIXTH GENERATION

Lydia to George Sumner	March 22, 1835	Eleven.
Anna to William Overfield	February 22, 1836	Eleven.
Elizabeth to Archibald B. Bannatyne	November 18, 1834	Seven.
Mary to Jacob P. Biles	August 15, 1839.	Nine.
Sarah to Isaac O. Smith	October 18, 1842	Five.
John to Rebecca Place	September 1, 1846	Six.
Aaron to Clementine Lane	April 22, 1849	Nine.
Amanda M. to Gilbert M. Chamberlain	September 29, 1853	Two.
Charles to Amanda Viola Blakslee	January 28, 1854	None.
George N. to Frances E. Bardwell	May 2, 1858	Four.

I heard grandfather John Bunnell tell my mother Mary Biles that his tally of his grandchildren was eightyfour. He took a paper from his pocket with his record on it. John A. Biles.

All of John's family came to Wyoming county in due time from Monroe county, with the exception of his sister - Martha, (Patty) who married John Place - (brother to Mary Place Bunnell) who remained on the Place *Bunnell* Homestead *in MiddleSmithfield.*

Great-grandmother - Catherine Barry Bunnell lived very near to Grandfather's in those early days, accompanied by her youngest daughter - Catherine, Katy or Kate. After her marriage to Doctor Benjamin Carney, Great-grandmother lived alone until Catharien's return, after her husband journeyed West, and never returned. After several intervening years, Catherine became the second wife of Benjamin Crawford, and moved to Auburn township, Susquehanna County, Penna.

We find in the "Wyoming County, Penna. History" of 1786 to 1880, the following: "Methodism was one of the pioneer institutions of Washington township. In the spring of 1815, John Bunnell located on the "Neck", and was converted under the preaching of Rev. George Lane in the fall of 1815, at a great Camp meeting in the same locality. Preaching services were held several years previous to 1815, on the "Neck"; and at Carney flats along the Susquehanna river, the schoolhouse was built about 1800.

"John Bunnell was made Class leader in 1816, with the following names as some of the members: Mary, wife of John Bunnell, David Jayne and wife-Mary Barry, Abram Vosburgh and wife, William Alden and wife, Jonathan Kellogg and wife, and George Evans who afterwards was educated by the Oneida Conference of the Methodist Episcopal Church, and became a power for God's cause."

In the pioneer days of the Susquehanna Valley, goods were "hauled" from Philadelphia and New York on the old-fashioned Conestoga wagons, each drawn by four, five or six horses. Also from Easton, the centre mart of the Delaware Valley, the merchandise was purchased by our pioneer ancestors and transported to Wilkes-Barre and Sunbury, yea, on up the Susquehanna river by Conestoga wagons which were well adapted to the rough, rooty highways. They have immense wheels; and high over the great hind wheels arched the wagon's ledge in a grand sweep, descending with a boat-like curve to the smaller front wheels, whence it rose again, ending high over the wheeler's haunches, like the prow of some old ship over the sea. A massive thing of solid timber with panneled sides it is, having red wheels and running gear and blue body, somewhat toned by the weather. For emigration, these great, cumbersome vehicles answer both purposes of transporting goods and lodging. Cotemporaneous with the Conestoga wagon in the early years, was the "Durham boats" on the Susquehanna and Delaware rivers, also a means of transportation of goods from Sunbury up the stream, when ten or twelve miles would be considered a fair day's work. They floated down stream like arks. Until the completion of the Easton and Wilkes-Barre turnpike in 1807, the Conestoga wagons and "Durham boats" were the only means of transportation known.

A Durham boat is so named because it was built at Durham, Bucks county, Penna., along the Delaware river. These boats had lenght - sixty feet, breadth of eight feet and depth of two feet; and with fifteen tons of lading they drew about twenty inches of water. They had decks at each end and running boards for "poling" at the sides. Masts with sails were erected on them when a favorable wind blew, and a steersman and two polers on each side constituted the crew. The boats built on the Susquehanna were similar, but larger and carried larger crews. Trips extended up the Susquehanna river to Towanda, Bradford county.

These public burden-bearers, were often drafted into Grandfather - John Bunnell's service, in transmitting the commodities of large farming operations in exchange for goods to be utilized by his numerous and rapidly increasing family, and others.

His ancestry dating back to Colonial days, conferred in his Teutonic and Germanic origin a clear title to all the characteristics of a good settler: hence his noble example of sobriety, thrift and perseverance in clearing, cultivating and bringing up his farm to its highest possibilities.

He practiced early, the laudable principle of returning to his a just compensation for its goodly harvests. In his fertilizing operation, our Mother remembered the childhood panoramic beauty of the ploughing under of a field of buckwheat while in blossom, to enrich the soil preparatory to a new seeding.

SIXTH GENERATION

Every child had their allotted work. When our Mother, Elizabeth and Savannah were in their early teens, they had the hoeing of a field of potatoes three times over during their growth, which yeilded two hundred bushels when gathered in the autumn.

A plot of flax was reared each season; afterward came the <u>pulling</u>, probably by the children, then the <u>rotting</u>, after which it went through the process of <u>braking</u> by Moses Bertran, who was Grandfather's rollicking brother-in-law. Then followed the <u>swingling</u> which resolved the transfored product into <u>tow</u> and <u>flax</u>. Now, twirling the distaff and with measured jogging of the little wheels, came the rhythmic hum of spinning the wondrous yarn by Grandmother and her girls- hired or otherwise. After this, the skeins were boiled in ashes and water (weak lye) and washed thoroughly for the weaving. Lydia, the eldest daughter was the weaver. Some of the choicest fibre ofthe flax was spun as carefully as possible, doubled and twisted, and oftentimes bleached for the making of sewing thread, or it was colored blue in the indigo dye tub, or black with barks and soft soap for the making of the family wardrobe.

Through the fruit of the loom, came yard upon yard of the intricate web of linen for the manufacturing of sheets, pillow cases, straw ticks, shirts, trousers, dresses, aprons, yea- even bed curtains to be affixed to the tester frame, so as to fashion a canopy high over the great goosefeather bed. Blue and copperas colored threads were striped or checked in the linen cloth for the womens' wear, so as to vary the style and variety of the home made apparel.

During the summer of 1825, Grandfather Bunnell's little daughter Anna would stay all night with his Mother when alone. The monrning of November 18th, she told her Grandmother that it was her birthday, and this was the reply: "When I was a child in Ireland, little girls were set to spinning tow on the little wheel, on the morning when <u>eight</u> years old!" Poor martyred children! Grandfather kept a flock of sheep, which furnished munificent fleeces for more carding, washing, spinning, coloring, designing and weaving for bedding and clothing when the Frost King ruled over the land. How everyone worked! However, there was bounteous provision always enough and to spare for home and the stranger at the gate. Poor men found work and honest pay always at Grandfather's. Aunt Amanda remembers when the fun-seeking boys had painted the face of an odd, drunken character black, and otherwise bullied and worried him. *(Larry - from Ireland.)* Dear, compassionate Grandfather caused the poor wretch to be brought in and laid before the open fire, while with warm water and cloth, he kneeled beside the soiled, abused victim and attempted to wash and cleanse, as <u>he</u> supposed, the <u>bruised</u> face and alleviate the poor man's condition!

* * * * * *

Our Mother often told us that when a young woman when she was doing the house work, she became weary of placing a large plate of beef bones on the table for finishing. She said one day to her Father: "Daddy, I do get <u>so</u> <u>tired</u> of putting this great plate of beef bones on the table!" He smilingly replied: "Ah Anna, if you get a husband who will provide plenty of beef bones for you, I shall be very thankful!" She often thought of her rich home with ample supplies, after becoming a pioneer's wife!

* * * * * *

In the early days before canals and railroads were known, Grandfather- John Bunnell, with an ark, *(as I learned it, he had his Ark made up river where he began to load them.)* ascended the Susquehanna river every year as far as Cayuga Lake, N.Y., for an ark load of plaster, which was the chief and favorite fertilizer of the farmers then. Probably a number of barrels of salt were also added.

Floating down the broad stream to his own harbor at the "Neck" with his cargo, he would leave what was needed for his own use; and then re-load with grain, lumber, potatoes and the residue of plaster, and move off again to the southern farmers from Sunbury on to Harrisburg or farther below until all was disposed of.

Or with his Conestoga wagon laden with the rich yieldings of a productive farm, to Easton which was the first market for the pioneer's grain by the way of the Easton and Wilkes-Barre turnpike - the very earliest, and was built in 1807. The turnpike from Berwick to Mauch Chunk called the "Lehigh and Susquehanna" was chartered March 19, 1804, and was constructed and finished in 1810.

During his absence, the farm was carried on by his two eldest sons - Benjamin and James; and Grandmother with her phalanx of helpful girls manned the balance with precision, sternness and great success. One trip he made to Easton in 1834, while he probably was laying in building materials for the second Homestead now owned by Elias Treible which was built that year, he purchased for his <u>three</u> eldest daughters - Lydia, Anna and Elizabeth - each a pretty set ot table ware good enough for a Queen, also each a wedding dress of <u>blue</u> <u>silk</u>.

The old Homestead was owned by the second son - James for many years, while the second Homestead built in 1834 *(From my Mother, I learned that they moved into the new (Treible) house in 1836.)* became a sacred Mecca, to which the many married children returned whenever possible. Archibald B. Bannatyne, a Scotchman from Rothsay, Scotland, was the builder of the palatial new home; and won Grandfather's third daughter Elizabeth as his bride - November 18, 1834.

* * * * * *

Grandfather was a thoroughbred stalwart physically, financially, loyally, spiritually. He was a six-footer, muscular and of a goodly appearance. Financially, he had no honorable superior. He gave as good as a <u>three</u> thousand dollar farm to each of his twelve married children. Loyal to his Country, during the Civil War, he promised each grand-son who enlisted the sum of two hundred dollars. To his namesakes he increased the premium to three hundred; and the folllowing named "brave boys" responded to their Country's call: John Hamilton Bunnell, Charles Franklin Bunnell, Benjamin E. Sumner, Paul James Overfield, John Bunnell Overfield, Robert W. Bannatyne, John Draper Smith. Also, his fourth son - Aaron Bunnell enlisted as Lieut. Spiritually, after selling the second Homestead at Vosburg to his third son - John Bunnell Jr., he purchased a large tract of land just out of the town of Tunkhannock; built the third Homestead in 1847; and became intimately identifies with the Tunkhannock Methodist Episcopal church interests all along the remaining years of his sojourning here. In the building of the new Church in 1868, Grandfather became one of the chief contributors towards its erection.

His faithful wife died Nov. 3, 1851, leaving one daughter- Amanda M., the youngest, to preserve the sacredness of the home inviolate to his peacefulness and comfort. Several years afterward, he married Armenia, widow of Rev. George Evans, of Greene, N.Y., to whom he faithfully fulfilled a husband's obligations of protecting love and care, as also to the four children: Elizabeth, Sarah, Frank and Armenia, whom she brought with her.

#See Obituary on page 44, written it is supposed, by his eldest step-daughter - Mrs. Almeda McDonald of Greene, N.., who was a talented writer; and in her published Book of Poems, dedicated one of the finest - "John Ironsides", as a beautiful tribute to Grandfather's nobleness of character and indomitable will in the Right.

Obituary of John Bunnell Senior, of Tunkhannock,
Wyoming County, Penna., as Written by his Step-daughter-
Mrs. Almeda McDonald, Greene, N.Y.

Born - August 13, 1790.　　　　　　　　Died - August 11, 1872.

"And he was not, for God took him."

When men at the close of a long life of duty are called from labor to reward, from toil to rest, those who watch the bark of life receding from Time's shore, feel like congratulating the soul that goes on its voyage to the Great Beyond. Mr. Bunnell was one of the few living to see the wonderful changes of the last 75 years. He stood ont he deck of the first steamer- the Clermont - 1807, built by Robert Fulton 62 years ago, when New York was a small place, and Brooklyn and all the suburbs were not.

His *grand*parents, moved from *the* Delaware *at Kingwood, N.J.,* to Stroudsburg *Middlesmithfield*, Penna., intending to settle in the far-famed Valley of wyoming, in Luzerne county; but the news of the terrible Indian massacre deterred them. *(Massacre 16 Oct. 1755 at Penns Creek)*.

Subsequently, Mr. Bunnell located in Washington township, Wyoming county, near Vosburg, where he built up two Homesteads with the aid of his faithful wife - Mary Place, reared 13 children above the age of 21, *& 1 died at 2 weeks old*, and walked hand in hand with God's work all along the years.

He then sold the second Homestead on the "Neck" to his third son - John Bunnell Junior, purchasing a large property at Tunkhannock and building the third Homestead in 1847. He became largely identified with the interests of the Methodist Episcopal Church there, being considered as one of the chief contributors towards the building of the new Church in 1868. His wife died November 3, 1851.

Several years afterward, he married Armenia, widow of Rev. George Evans, Greene, N.Y., to whom he faithfully gave a husband's care and protection, also four children which she brought with her.

"A man of iron will, of splendid power of physical endurance, where he went, he carried civilization, making the 'Desert to rejoice and blossom like the rose.'"

He said as other men felt called to follow some profession, he felt called to be a farmer. Perhaps some vision of his Lord who once walked on earth amid the ripening ears of corn, may have influenced his imagination from boyhood; for he once said that being but a boy of twelve, alone in the wheat field, and seeing how all things grew and were upheld by some Power unseen, but intelligent, he fell to weeping, and then and there made a covenant with God that when he should be a man and have a house of his own, he would serve Him. He was faithful to this covenant as long as he lived. His influence in the Church of God can not be computed. He stood a long lifetime as firmly in his place of duty as the pillar which holds the structure stands in its place. Of such childlike faith as to take God at His word, he was vexed by no subtle questions of doctrine, but was able through life to commit his ways to "Him who careth for us."

It is better than any patent of nobility to be descended from such a man as this: true to his God, his country, and the obligations of family and society. "He rests from his labors and his works do follow him."

"I am so tired I must go home" were among his last words. He was buried on his eighty-second birthday. *Aug. 13, 1872.*

Thus one by one the men of the olden time are passing away, but if the young men who crowd into their places are as loyal, true and good, America long will continue to be --

"The land of the free and the home of the brave."

Copied by Mary H. Rice,
　126 Mulberry St., Scranton.
　Nov. 3, 1905.

229

SIXTH GENERATION

Grandmother - Mary Place
was married to John Bunnel, July 10, 1810
She was born September 7, 1793; Died November 3, 1851.

Her father - James Place was a Scotchman *or French* who resided in Monroe county, died there and was buried in the Coolbaugh Cemetery, near Stroudsburg *5 miles north*. Her mother - Phoebe Winings *Winans* was an English*Dutch*woman, and after her Husband's death, came north to be with her children in Wyoming and Bradford counties. While with her daughter - Rosannah who married Alexander *P.* Biles of Porterville, Bradford county, Penna., she passed on to the Promised Land, and was buried in the Biles Grave-yard, in Porterville. *(J. P. Biles farm.)*

After Grandmother - Mary Place's marriage to John Bunnell, they located in Monroe Co where the eldest child - Benjamin was born. When a year old, they came to the farm now known as the Solomon Bunnell property, above Black Walnut, she walking from Stroudsburg. In the spring of 1815, they moved to Washington township, int he beautiful locality beside the Susquehanna river known as the "Neck," where a home was developed from the forest vast, and thirteen children grew to manhood and womanhood. At a notable camp meeting in the fall of 1815, in the vicinity of the "Neck," Grandmother thus described her unique conversion. She said: "A deep solemnity was resting on the great congregation; numbers were <u>falling helplessly</u> here and there under the <u>power of conviction</u>. There stood Daddy (her husband - John Bunnell) and Granny (her mother-in-law - Catherine Barry Bunnell) not far from me; and I thought to myself - "What would they say to me if I should fall too?" (Great-grandmother was a rigorous Baptist). The next thing I knew, I was sitting on the ground where I had fallen, with all of them around me shouting and rejoicing, and I <u>was happy as a fool</u>?"

* * * * * *

King Lemuel's lesson of chastity and praise of a virtuous woman in the thirty-first chapter of Proverbs, is a faithful symposium of our grandmother - Mary Place Bunnell's home life as wife and mother. In the varied duties of dairying, scrubbing, scouring, washing, ironing, knitting, mending, spinning wool and flax, weaving, cooking, embroidering dainty caps and sewing, so completely crowding the long days of a pioneer's wife, grandmother was a perfect housekeeper - a model manager and disciplinarian.

The ways of her household were always before her; she never ate the bread of idleness. Her children blessed her; her husband honored her. Early in March, 1830, as customary each spring, Grandfather journeyed up the Susquehanna river to Cayuga Lake, N.Y. for an ark load of plaster. During his absence, March 21, 1830, her eleventh child - Charles was born. On Grandfather's return, everything seeming favorable, he resumed his journey down the river to complete the traffic among the farmers, so profitably and opportunely opened. But Death came April 5, 1830, and took the young infant away; and Grandmother bore her suffering and bereavement, surrounded by her faithful children and ministering friends. During this sad experience, Grandfather passed on down the river to Sunbury and Harrisburg, continuing the sale of his plaster to resident farmers along the route farther south towards the Chesapeake Bay until his stock was exhausted, making an absence of several weeks before his return. Only God's amazing and sure foundation of Christian grace and wisdom could sustain in those hours of loneliness and trial. His grace sufficed!

April 5, 1841, her fourth daughter, Savannah born June 2, 1820, who was an amiable, handsome, spiritual woman, through the mal-practice of a professed physician, gave up her bright young womanhood to suffering and death; and Grandmother again quaffed the cup of grief to its dregs.

But a decade of years passed on; the third Homestead at Tunkhannock had been built, and life was full of fruition and promise, when disease prostrated the aging form; and November 3, 1851, her spirit died to earth to awaken in Heaven leaving an example worthy of all emulation. Although reared without educational advantages, she was second to none in matured judgement, social amentity, steadfast integrity and religious character, which insured a good name always which is rather to be chosen than earth's greatest riches, or tomes of worldly knowledge.

Let her greatest eulogy be: She was a true help meet to her noble, Christian husband - John Bunnell!

Mary H. Rice wrote the above June 6, 1903, }
for M. Minnie Emory, Los Angeles, California.}

Obituary of Mary Place Bunnell.

Mrs. Mary Place Bunnell, wife of John Bunnell died of dysentery, at Tunkhannock, Wyoming county, Penna., November 3, 1851, in her fifty-ninth year. Experiencing the pardoning love of God thirty-five years since, she united with the Methodist Episcopal Church and remained a worthy and faithful member until admitted to the Church triumphant in Heaven.

For some four weeks, she endured with great patience and resignation the most intense suffering.

Possessed naturally of a very vigorous constitution, death did not find so easy a victim. Being called to her bed-side, at which we had frequently knelt during her illness, a few hours previous to her departure, we found her as usual firmly tursting in Him who "is a stronghold in the day of trouble."

She passed peacefully and triumphantly away - enjoying the bliss-inspiring assurance, that whether living or dying, she was the Lord's!" In her death, the Methodist Episcopal Church has lost an excellent member; a husband has been deprived of a devoted companion; and a large circle of children are bereaved of an affectionate mother.

Husband and children! Your loss is irreparibly great! To whom can you betake yourselves for consolation and support in this dark hour of affliction but to Him who doth not afflict willingly?

May this providence be so sanctified to the good of this deeply afflicted family, that all the children, very soon, may be enriched with that holiness without which no man shall see the Lord! Remember one of the dying expressions of that sainted mother: - "I hope they will seek the Lord!"

(Rev..) Dewitt C. Olmstead.

Tunkhannock, Nov. 13, 1851.

Memoir of Mrs. Armenia Bunnell,
Second Wife of Grandfather - John Bunnell.
Born: October 3, 1803. Died: September 26, 1880.

Mrs. Armenia Bunnell was born October 3, 1803, at Sullivan, Tioga county, Penna. Her grandfather - Nathan Fellows went from Vermont in 1801 to Pennsylvania, with a colony of thirty young men, all unmarried except Mr. Fellows. She was the first white child born in her township, and it was named after her. Her grandfather gave her two thousand acres of land, so that she seemed to have a good start in life. The land on which Elmira, N.Y. is built, could then have been bought for $1.25 per acre; but on account of coal, the colony preferred to settle near Blossburg.

The freshness and beauty of this early life always remained in her memory. Often in her later life, she expressed a wish to be again in the unbroken wilderness by the stream of running water or the cool, clear spring.

She was the child of a Presbyterian mother, and the minister of Vermont used to come down to the settlement, to hear the children say the catechism, and to advise and encourage the young flock growing up so far from New England; and these seasons of pastoral visitation were a delight to all, both young and old.

The Methodists began to preach in the colony when she was seventeen years old; and in their meetings she was converted and felt that with these people, her home must be. She was united in marriage to Rev. George Evans (his third wife), a Methodist minister, December 11, 1825, at Sullivan, Tioga county, Penna., by Rev. John McKeene; and her earnest life work now commenced.

She was privileged to see the marvellous growth and prosperity of the Methodist Episcopal Church; and was one who received every number of the Christian Advocate. It was her wish that a copy of her beloved paper should be buried with her, and that of September 23, 1880 was chosen. She was a woman of intense patriotism and loyalty.

Her grandfather - Nathan Fellows was a Captain in the Revolution, and present with General Washington's army during the memorable winter at Valley Forge. Her family were English both on the father's and mother's side, having come over in the ship next after the Mayflower. Her religious life was one of the most perfect repose. She lived a life of faith, having confidence in the promises of the Lord to his people. Sunday evening, September 26, 1880, she entered the rest of the eternal Sabbath.

In the death of this venerable and lovely woman, her friends feel that being "absent from the body she is pressent with the Lord," and that she has passed with that great congregation which is - "faultless before the throne of God."

She was united in marriage the second time to John Bunnell, Tunkhannock, Penna., a man devoted to the interests of the Methodist Episcopal Church through a long life. She survived him eight years.

Almeda McDonald, Daughter,
Greene, N.Y.

1-1-6-4-3-8   D93   CB310249

SOLOMON[6] BUNNELL (Benjamin[5], Solomon[4], Benjamin[3], Benjamin[2], William[1]) was born 21 July 1792[1,2] in Lower (now Middle) Smithfield, Northampton (now Monroe) co, PA[1]. On 19 August 1812[1] he married ELEANOR PLACE[1], daughter of James and Phoebe (Winans) Place[1]. She was sister to Mary Place, his brother John's wife, and John Place, his sister Martha's husband[1]. She was born 22[1] (or 23[2]) December 1794[1,2] in Middle Smithfield twp[1], Northampton (now Monroe) co, PA. In 1812 they moved to Luzerne (now Wyoming) co, PA[5]. He bought a large tract of land and first settled near the Susquehanna River, but in 1814 or 1815 he located on a farm on Bunnell Hill in Braintrim (now Meshoppen) twp, where he remained for the rest of his life[5]. In a letter written in 1979, Solomon's great-great-granddaughter, Genevieve (Love) Newton, said that Solomon "lived in the old red house, which was between the house and cow-barn on the farm where I was born."[8]

231

Solomon and Eleanor were early members of the Methodist Episcopal Church[5]. They were listed in the Methodist class held in the Skinners Eddy church from 1858 to 1861[7]. Eleanor's death on 4 February 1859 was reported in the class records[7]. Solomon transferred for a few years to the class held at the Scranton Corners church on Bunnell Hill, but is found again in the Skinners Eddy class records from 1865 until his death[7].

An interesting deed, dated 18 March 1839, grants over 200 acres on the Susquehanna River to Solomon Bunnell for $69.55 paid to the Commonwealth of Pennsylvania[9]. It appears that this was to clear his title to property he had previously purchased from owners who held it under the original Connecticut title. The money he paid would be used to compensate people who had purchased the land from the Penn proprietors but had never settled on the land. The bitter controversy known as the Pennamite War between the settlers from Connecticut, who called the area Westmoreland co, CT, and the Pennsylvania authorities who established the same area as Luzerne co, PA, began before 1770 and was not resolved legally until 1782, when the territory was formally judged part of Pennsylvania. For the settlers on the ground closure did not come for many years, as this deed indicates.

Solomon appears in the 1820 census: 20111-2001[3], in 1830: 002001-020011[3], and in 1840: 0000101-0002001[3], all in Braintrim twp, Luzerne co, PA. In the 1850 census in Braintrim twp, Wyoming co, PA, Solomon and Eleanor appear with their daughter Aurelia and two grandchildren, Emily and Solomon Gay[3]. Eleanor died 4 February 1859 aged 64 years, 1 month and 13 days[1,2]. In the 1860 census in Meshoppen twp, Wyoming co, PA, Solomon's family is not with him, but he has a couple of ladies keeping house for him[3]. In 1870 he appears living with his son John Solomon Bunnell and family on the old homestead in Meshoppen twp, Wyoming co, PA[3]. Although he lived as a farmer for 60 years on the same farm, political boundary changes over the years made it appear that he had moved from time to time.

Solomon died at his home 22 May 1874 without leaving a will[1,2,10]. In August of that year son John petitioned the Orphan's Court in Wyoming co to partition the real estate, which was sold and divided according to law among the surviving children and grandchildren[10]. Solomon and Eleanor were buried in the family cemetery on the homestead on Bunnell Hill with a number of their children and grandchildren[2].

Children:
1. 320273. Elizabeth, b. 30 Nov. 1812[1]; m. 1829[1] Ansel Gay[1,4,10]; d. 1865[1].
   Children (surname Gay):[1,4,10]
   1. Amanda.   7. James P.   13. Armina A.
   2. Emily.   8. Calvin S.   14. Almeda.
   3. Savannah.   9. Eleanor B.   15. Mary.
   4. Solomon Bunnell. 10. Treadway.   16. Lorenzo D.
   5. Charles.   11. John B.   17. Harriet.
   6. George.   12. Eleanor.
2. 320274. Anna, b. Dec. 1815[2] (or 17 Aug. 1814[1]); d. 2 Jan.[1,2] 1818[2] (or 1817[1]).

3. 320272. John Solomon, b. 20 May 1816[1]; m. 19 May 1836 Laura Maria Whitcomb[1]
d. 23 Jan. 1887[1].
Children (surname Bunnell):[1]
1. Irene. 4. Henry Clay. 7. Emma Delphine.
2. Ahira Lehman. 5. Albert.
3. Wesley. 6. George Marbel.
4. 320275. James, b. 14 Feb. 1818[1]; m. 3 Feb. 1842 Mary Ann Luce[1]; d. 28 May
1884[1].
Children (surname Bunnell):[1]
1. Warren. 4. Wellington R. 7. Eleanor Gertrude.
2. Harrison M. 5. Mary Elizabeth. 8. Carrie.
3. Irene C. 6. Frederick Lester.
5. 320276. Mary Ann, b. Feb.[2] (or 10 July[1]) 1819[1,2]; d. 10 Aug. 1820[1,2].
6. 320277. Eleanor, b. 15 Apr. 1822[1]; m. William Cooley[1,10], d. 5 Oct. 1855[1].
Children (surname Cooley):[1,4,10]
1. Olive. 3. Aurelia. 4. Mary.
2. Warren Lester.
7. 320278. Aurelia, b. 14 June 1823[1]; m. 25 Nov. 1851[1] Isaac Carter[1,4,10];
d. 27 Oct. 1876[1].
Children (surname Carter):[1,4,10]
1. Ziba. 3. Scott. 4. Frank.
2. Mary Emogene.
8. 320051. Phoebe, b. Mar. 1824[2] (or 11 Mar. 1825[1]); d. 11 Feb. 1825[2] (or 1826[1]).
9. 320081. daughter, b. and d. 15 Jan. 1830[1,2].
10. 320085. daughter, b. 7 May 1832[1,2]; d. 8 May 1832[1,2].

REFERENCES:
1. Biles Manuscript, pp. 149, 150, 155, 156.
2. Gravestones in Bunnell Cemetery on Bunnell Hill, Meshoppen twp, Wyoming co, PA, copied by William R. Austin about 1962.
3. Census microfilms, Luzerne co, PA, 1820, 1830, 1840; Wyoming co, PA, 1850, 180, 1870.
4. CBR NE PA, pp. 313, 1574.
5. Luzerne, Lackawanna and Wyoming cos., PA, p. 518.
6. *Montrose Democrat*, newspaper, 10 June 1874.
7. Records of the Skinners Eddy, PA, Methodist Church.
8. Ltr. 15 January 1979 from Genevieve Love (Mrs. Paul M. Newton) to E. J. Mowry.
9. Deed, photostat sent to me by Doris (Bunnell) Thomas:
"The Commonwealth of PENNSYLVANIA. TO ALL TO WHOM THESE PRESENTS SHALL COME, Greeting:
"Know Ye, That in consideration of the sum of sixty nine Dollars and fifty five cents in full now by Solomon Bunnell, there is granted by the said Commonwealth unto the said Solomon Bunnell a certain tract of land being part of Lot No. 14 Situate in Braintrim one of the seventeen townships, Luzerne County Beginning at a corner, thence up Susquehanna River, north forty one degrees west one hundred and three perches to a corner, thence by a part of Lot No. 14 north sixteen degrees and thirty minutes east one hundred and sixty perches to a spanish oak, and north seventy four degrees west twenty perches to a corner, thence by Lot No. 13 north sixteen degrees and thirty

minutes east one hundred and sixty nine perches to a corner, thence by Lot No. 18 south sixty nine degrees east one hundred and ten perches to a corner, and thence by the residue of Lot No. 14 south sixteen degrees and thirty minutes west three hundred and ninety nine perches to the Beginning, Containing two hundred and nineteen acres and ninety two perches and allowance etc.

"Which said tract of land was resurveyed by virtue and in pursuance of an Act of Assembly entitled An Act for Offering Compensation to the Pennsylvania claimants of certain lands within the seventeen townships in the County of Luzerne and for other purposes therein mentioned passed the 4th of April 1799 and the supplements thereto passed the 15th of March 1800 and the 6th of April 1802 and certified to John Frink whose right in and to said part of Lot or tract by virtue of sundry conveyances and other assurances in law became vested in the said Solomon Bunnel with the appurtenances.

"To Have and to Hold the said Tract or Parcel of Land, with the appurtenances unto the said Solomon Bunnel and his heirs to the use of him the said Solomon Bunnel his heirs and assigns forever.
Free and Clear of all restrictions and reservations as to Mines, Royalties, Quit=rents, or otherwise, excepting and reserving only the fifth part of all gold and silver Ore, for the use of the Commonwealth, to be delivered at the Pit's Mouth, clear of all charges.

"In Witness Whereof, John Gebhart, Secretary of the Land Office of the said Commonwealth hath hereto set his hand, and the Seal of the Land Office of Pennsylvania hath been hereunto affixed, the eighteenth day of March in the year of our Lord, one thousand eight hundred and thirty nine and of the Commonwealth the sixty third.

Attest, Jos. Henderson   Deputy Secretary Land Office
                                                Enrolled in Patent Book H, Vol. 40 Page 524"

10. PARTITION. (transcribed and typed copy sent to me by Doris (Bunnell) Thomas.)
     "In the Matter of the real estate of Solomon Bunnell, late of the township of Meshoppen, deceased.
     WYOMING COUNTY SS;
          "The Commonwealth of Pennsylvania to the Sheriff of said county, Greeting:
     LS   Whereas, at the Orphan's Court held at Tunkhannock in and for the county of
               Wyoming on the 17th day of August A.D. 1874 before the Honorable William
               Elwell President and his Associate Justices of the said court, by petition of
     John Bunnell was presented, setting forth that the petitioner was a son of Solomon Bunnell, late of township Meshoppen, said county deceased. That the said Solomon Bunnell died about the 22 day of May A D 1874, intestate; seized in his demesne as of fee of and in a certain messuage and tract of land situated in the township of Meshoppen, county of Wyoming and state of Pennsylvania, bounded on the North by the lands of John Bunnell, on the East by the lands of Robert Dunlap, on the South by the Susquehanna river, and on the West by lands formerly of Nicholas Overfield, containing one hundred and sixteen acres, more or less with appurtenances. That the said Solomon Bunnell had five children; Elizabeth intermarried with Ansel Gay, John Bunnell, James Bunnell, Eleanor intermarried with William Cooley, Aurelia intermarried with Isaac Carter. That the said Elizabeth Gay died before the said Solomon Bunnell, having had twelve children: Amanda intermarried with Wm Dunmore, Emily intermarried with J. Wesley McMicken, Savanna intermarried with Morris La Barre, Solomon B. Gay, Charles Gay, James Gay, Calvin Gay, John B. Gay, Eleanor intermarried with Morris Vanscoten*, Armenia intermarried with John Anderson, Lorenzo Gay and Harriet Gay. That Amanda Dunmore died before her mother, leaving, to survive her, George Dunmore, Elizabeth intermarried with Albert M. Douglas, Solomon Dunmore, Seth Eddy Tibbitts, Morris Dunmore and Ella A. Tibbitts. That

SIXTH GENERATION

Eleanor Cooley died before the said Solomon Bunnell, leaving to survive her, Olive intermarried with Gideon Lobdell and Lester Cooley. That Aurelia Carter died before the said Solomon Bunnell, leaving to survive her Imogene intermarried with Alonzo Parker and Ziba Carter. That under and by virtue of the intestate laws of this commonwealth it belongs to the said John Bunnell and James Bunnell, each to have one-fifth part of said real estate in fee, and to the said Emily McMicken, Savanna La Barre, Solomon B. Gay, Charles Gay, James P. Gay, Calvin Gay, John B. Gay, Eleanor Vanscoten, Armenia Anderson, Lorenzo Gay, Harriet Gay, each to have one sixtieth part of said real estate in fee, and to said George Dunmore, Elizabeth Douglass, Solomon Dunmore, Seth Eddy Tibbitts, Morris Dunmore and Ella A. Tibbitts, each to have one three hundred and sixtieth part of said real estate in fee; and to the said Olive Lobdell and Lester Cooley each to have on-tenth part of said real estate in fee; and to the said Imogene Parker and Ziba Carter, each to have on-tenth part of said real estate in fee. That no partition of said real estate having been made, the petitioner prays the Court to award an inquest to make partition of said real estate to and among the aforesaid parties according to their respective rights.

"And now, Aug. 17th 1874, on the presentation of the above petition and on due proof and consideration of the premises an inquest is awarded for the purposes therein mentioned, and the Sheriff is directed to give notice of the time and place of the meeting of the inquisition by publication in one weekly newspaper published in Wyoming County for four weeks before the meeting at the inquest, and that a paper be sent to all parties intereasted, whose residence is known, and not personally served.

BY THE COURT.

"We therefore command you that taking with you twelve good and lawful men of your bailiwick, you go to and upon the premises aforesaid and there in the presence of the parties aforesaid, by you to be warned, if being warned they will be present, and having respect to the true valuation thereof and upon Oaths and affirmations of the said twelve good and lawful men you make partition to and among the heirs and legal representatives of the said intestate in such proportions as by the laws of this commonwealth is directed, if the same can be done without prejudice to or spoiling the whole. But if the said partition can not be made thereof without prejudice to or spoiling the whole, then you cause the said inquest to inquire and ascertain whether the same will conveniently accomodate more than one of the said representatives of the said intestate without prejudice to or spoiling the whole and if so how many it will as aforesaid accomodate, describing each part by metes and bounds, and returning a just valuation of the same.

"But if the said inquest, by you to be summoned as aforesaid to make the partition or valuation, shall be of opinion that the premises aforesaid with appurtenances, cannot be so parted and divided as to accomodate more that one of said representatives of the said intestate, that you cause the inquest to value the whole of said real estate, with the appurtenances, having respect to the true valuation thereof according to law.

"And that the partition or valuation so made, you distinctly and openly have before our said Justices at Tunkhannock, at an Orphan's Court to be there held on the third Monday of November next, after such an inquest shall be made, under your hand and seal, and under the hands and seals of those whose oaths and affirmations you shall make such partition or valuation.

"Have you then and there this writ.

"Witness the Honorable William Elwell, President Judge of our said court the 17th day of August, A.D. 1874.   A. B. FITCH, Clerk O C

"Notice is hereby given by virtue of the above writ of partition to me directed an inquest will be held and taken on the premises therein described, on the third day of November A.D. 1874, at ten o'clock A.M., for the purpose of making partition of said real estate as by the said writ I am commanded, at which time and place all parties interested in said real estate are hereby notified to attend if they think proper.

EDWIN STEPHENS, Sheriff"

*Eleanor Gay married Marshall Vanscoten, not Morris - wra.

1-1-6-4-3-9   D94   CB310244

ISAAC[6] BUNNELL (Benjamin[5], Solomon[4], Benjamin[3], Benjamin[2], William[1]) was born in Middle Smithfield twp, Northampton (now Monroe) co, PA 18 February 1795[1]. His father died in 1814, and soon Isaac, his mother, and all but one of his siblings had moved from the Delaware River valley to the valley of the Susquehanna River in what is now Wyoming co, PA. There he married, in 1815[1] ANNA DEPEW OVERFIELD[1], daughter of Paul and Hannah (DePew) Overfield[1]. She was born 13 March 1796[1] in Braintrim twp, Luzerne co (now Meshoppen twp, Wyoming co), PA.

They began married life on a farm in Braintrim twp, just a few miles from that of her parents. All their children were born there. He must have continued to own some property in Middle Smithfield, since he appears in the tax records there in 1815 and 1816[6]. One of the few references to Isaac which have been found is his appearance in the account book of Paul Overfield, 3d, blacksmith, his wife's cousin. On 28 April 1819 Isaac was charged 90 cents for sharpening a plow share and 13 drag teeth and for laying a colter[5].

Isaac appears in the 1820 census: 100100-20101 and in the 1830 census: 211001-012001, both in Braintrim twp, Luzerne co (now Meshoppen twp, Wyoming co)[2]. His farm was in that part of Meshoppen twp known as Bunnell Hill. There he died on 26 June 1832[3] and was buried in lot 39, Overfield Cemetery, now in Meshoppen twp[3]. He was only 37, the first of the twelve children of Benjamin and Catherine Bunnell to die. He left his wife with eight children ranging in age from 16 years down to 2.

His widow Anna appears in the 1840 census in Braintrim twp, Luzerne co: 0111-0101001[2]. She died 10 October 1842[3] and was buried with Isaac in Overfield Cemetery. Their daughter Marguerite, who had drowned in 1836[1], was interred in the same lot[3].

Children:
    1. 320053. Hannah, b. 20 Mar. 1816[1]; m. 5 July 1835[1] Samuel Bloomfield Howard[1].
            Children (surname Howard):[1]

1. Harris M.	6. Charles.	11. Hattie.
2. Margaret.	7. Mary.	12. Ella.
3. Isaac.	8. Henry D.	13. infant.
4. Edmund Bunnell.	9. Lucy.	14. infant.
5. Sarah.	10. Frederick.	

2. 320055. John W., b. 23 Mar. 1818[1]; m. 22 Feb. 1840 Lucy Sumner[1]; d. 21 Mar. 1892[3].

Children (surname Bunnell):[1]

1. George Lewellyn.   4. Sarah M.   7. Ida Theressa.
2. Nicholas S.   5. Porter.   8. Elmer Sumner.
3. Lydia Ann.   6. John Judson.   9. Jennie.

3. 320054. Marguerite, b. 27 Mar. 1820[1]; d. 9 Aug. 1836[1].

4. 320056. Rebecca Keeler, b. 23 May 1822[1]; m. 3 June 1848[1,5] Rudolphus Schoonover Davis[1,5]; d. 22 July 1902[1].

Children (surname Davis):[1]

1. Anna Harriet.   3. Theodore Cuyler.   5. Isaac Bunnell.
2. Orra Frances.   4. Bertha Lena.   6. Henry Winter.

5. 320060. Charles, b. 7 June 1824[1]; m. Emma Major[1]; d. 16 June 1854[1].

Children (surname Bunnell):[1]

1. Isabell.   2. Frank.

6. 320057. Edmund, b. 29 Aug. 1826[1] m. 6 Feb. 1851 Eliza Rebecca Overfield[1]; d. 21 Sept. 1906[3].

Children (surname Bunnell):[1]

1. Pauline S.   4. Llewellyn L.   7. Seth Keeney.
2. Minnie Alzara.   5. Anna Augusta.
3. Sarah L. Ozier.   6. Nettie Arnold.

7. 320058. Isaac Overfield, b. 12 Aug. 1828[1]; m. 1 Jan. 1855 Marilla S. Place[1]; d. 8 Jan. 1900[1].

Children (surname Bunnell):[1]

1. Eva Diantha.   2. Anda (or India).   3. Harvey Place.

8. 320059. Anna, b. 28 Mar. 1831[1]; m. 2 July 1852[1] Dr. Sydney Campbell.

Children:[1]

1. Alice.   4. G. Draper.   7. Terry.
2. Addison J.   5. Nettie.   8. Perry.
3. William H.   6. Hattie.

REFERENCES:

1. Biles Manuscript, pp. 158, 159, 164, 165, 167, 168.
2. Census Microfilms - 1820, 1830, 1840, Braintrim twp, Luzerne co, PA.
3. Records of Overfield Cemetery, Meshoppen twp, Wyoming co, PA.
4. Wyoming co marriages taken from the *"Wyoming Patrol & Republican Standard"* newspaper, as extracted in *Lest-We-Forget*, journal of the Wyoming County Historical Society, Vol. 7, No. 1, p. 20.
5. *Meshoppen Enterprise* newspaper, 29 Aug. 1917 - "A Leaf from the Account Book of Paul Overfield 3d," printed in the account of the 1917 Bunnell-Overfield family reunion, by Mary H. Rice, Historian.
6. CB Database.

1-1-6-4-3-11   D95   CB310261

JAMES[6] BUNNELL (Benjamin[5], Solomon[4], Benjamin[3], Benjamin[2], William[1]) was born 29 May 1799[1] in Middle Smithfield twp[1], Wayne (now Monroe) co, PA. While still in his early teens he moved with his mother and most of his siblings to Luzerne (now Wyoming) co, PA.

In 1818[1], he married LOUISA[3] (LOVICA[1])(ALVISIA[8]) RUSSELL[1,6,7], daughter of Alban and Hannah (Hartwell[7])(or Alcott[6]) Russell[6,7,8], early settlers in what is now Russell Hill in Washington twp, Wyoming co, PA. She was born 25 May[1])(or April[8]) 1798[1,8] in Killingly[8], Windham co, CT. They settled on a farm in Braintrim twp, Luzerne co (now Meshoppen twp, Wyoming co), PA, where they raised their nine children and several grandchildren besides.

James appears in the 1820 census: 20001-2001[2], in the 1830 census: 120001-111001[2], and in the 1840 census: 0012001-1211101[2], all in Braintrim twp, Luzerne co, PA. He and Louisa appear in the 1850 census[2] in Braintrim twp, Wyoming co, PA, with their six youngest children. James's nephew Charles Bunnell, son of Isaac, was living with them working on the farm.

By 1860 all the political boundary changes had been completed. In the census that year[2] James and Louisa appear in Meshoppen twp, Wyoming co, PA. Of their children, only daughter Eleanor was still at home with them. But they also provided a home for three grandchildren: Sarah and Landis Safford, ages 15 and 11, children of their daughter Hester, who died in 1850, and Frances Baldwin, age 2, daughter of their daughter Roxanna, who died in May 1860. The 1870 census[2] lists James, age 71 and "Luvina", age 72 Bunnell, on a farm valued at $4000. Their personal property was valued at $1000. Two of their grandchildren, Landis Safford, age 21, and Frances E. Baldwin, 12, were wtill living with them.

Louisa died 29 December 1872[3]. James survived her until 4 May 1879[3]. They were buried in Lot 29, Overfield Cemetery[3] in Meshoppen twp, where their daughter Roxanna Baldwin had been buried some years before[3].

Children:
    1. 320262. Hester A., b. 11 Oct. 1819[1,4]; m. 16 Oct. 1842[9] Laban L. Safford[4],
            d. 18 June 1850[1,4].
            Children (surname Safford):[1,2]
            1. Sarah E.   2. Landis Barton.
    2. 320263. Sally[1] (Sarah A.[9]), b. 7 Feb. 1821[1]; m. 27 Apr. 184x[9] Daniel Cooley[1];
            d. Feb. 1913[1].
            Children (surname Cooley):[1]
            1. James.   3. Anderson.   5. Isaac B.
            2. Eva.   4. Emma.
    3. 320264. George, b. 16 Nov. 1822[1]; m. (first) 10 June 1850 Eleanor Russell[1];
            m. (second) 23 Oct. 1870 Mary Jane Wakeley[1]; d. 12 Dec. 1899[1].
            Children (by first wife)(surname Bunnell):[1]
            1. Byron James.   2. Samantha.   3. Bentley R.

Children (by second wife)(surname Bunnell):[1]

4. Etta Eliza.	6. Clifford A.	8. Eva Louisa.
5. Lewis Monroe.	7. Lucy E.	9. Adeline E.

4. 320265. Isaac B., b. 16 Jan. 1825[1]; m. 13 June 1856 Adaline E. Russell[5]; d. 5 Mar. 1861[1].

Children (surname Bunnell):[1]

1. Catherine Tracy.	3. Daniel Cooley.	4. Hester Ann.
2. Eva Ellen.		

5. 320266. Lucinda, b. 17 Oct. 1826[1]; m. 12 Dec. 1855[1] James Humphrey Bird[1], d. 19 Feb. 1914[1].

Children (surname Bird):[1]

1. James Bunnell.	3. Oscar M.	7. Omeigh.
2. Ella E.	5. Ida L.	8. Edward.
3. Orin J.	6. William.	

6. 320268. Barton Russell, b. 12 May 1829[1]; m. 20 July 1861 Sarah Bird[1]; d. 12 Feb. 1925[3].

Children (surname Bunnell):[1]

1. Isaac Cooley.	5. Henry Dunlap.	9. Katherine.
2. John L.	6. Rose May.	10. James Elliot.
3. Louisa Abigail.	7. Arthur Harder.	
4. Anna Rebecca.	8. Nancy Belle.	

probably another daughter Emma R., d. 6 May 1873, age 6.

7. 320267. Catherine, b. 4 June 1831[9]; m. 7 Dec. 1854[1] Jacob Jackson Manning[1]; d. 6 Oct. 1920, age 98[1].

Children (surname Manning):[1]

1. James L.	4. Stella.	7. Blennie.
2. Charles A.	5. Angie.	8. Ella.
3. Emma.	6. Sarah.	9. George B.

8. 320270. Roxanna J., b. 4 Apr. 1837[1]; m. 4 July 1856[1] Charles B. Baldwin[1]; d. 16 May 1860[1].

Children (surname Baldwin):[1]

1. Frances Eveline.	2. Arthur Cameron.

9. 320269. Eleanor, m. 30 June 1861 George[1] (or A.[5] Maines[1,5].

Children (surname Maines):[1]

1. Cameron.	3. Mary.	5. Arthur.
2. Sally.	4. Dolly.	

REFERENCES:

1. Biles Manuscript, pp. 175, 176, 177, 178, 180, 181, 182, 183.
2. Census Microfilms: 1820, 1830, 1840, Braintrim twp, Luzerne co, PA.
   1850, Braintrim twp, Wyoming co, PA.
   1860, 1870, Meshoppen twp, Wyoming co, PA.
3. Records of Overfield Cemetery, Meshoppen twp, Wyoming co, PA.
4. Gravestone in Bunnell Cemetery, Auburn Four Corners, Susquehanna co, PA, copied by WRA.

5. Marriages printed in the *Wyoming Intelligencer*, 10 July 1861, as extracted in *Lest-We-Forget*, journal of the Wyoming County Historical Society, Vol. 11, No. 1, 15 Sept. 1991, and Vol. 13, No. 2, 15 Feb. 1994.
6. CBR NE P, p. 1146.
7. *Jayne History*, by Lillian Jayne Dull and Ruth Jayne Hardy, 1960, p. 32.
8. NEHGR, Vol. 118, p. 135, *David Russell (c. 1673-1752) of Killingly, Conn.*
9. Duncan, pp. 68, 69.

1-1-6-4-3-12   D96   CB310262

GERSHOM[6] BUNNELL (Benjamin[5], Solomon[4], Benjamin[3], Benjamin[2], William[1]) was born 15 December 1803[1,2] in Middle Smithfield twp[1], Wayne (now Monroe) co, PA. While still in his teens he moved with his mother and siblings to the new home on the Susquehanna River in what is now Washington twp, Wyoming co, PA. At age 16, he was probably one of the two males of 10 to 16 years who appeared in the 1820 census living with his widowed mother Catharine Bunnell on "The Neck" in Tunkhannock twp, Luzerne co (now Washington twp, Wyoming co), PA[3].

On 1 January 1823[1,8], in Tunkhannock twp, Luzerne co[8], he married SARAH KELLOGG[1,2,8], daughter of Jonathan and Elizabeth (Smith) Kellogg[8]. She was born 4 September 1805[1,2,8] in Newport twp, Luzerne co, PA[8]. They began housekeeping on the Charles Place farm on "The Neck" in Tunkhannock twp[1]. Soon they moved across the Susquehanna River to a farm on Grist Flats in Windham twp, Luzerne co (now Mehoopany twp, Wyoming co), where their first child was born[1]. They moved back to the old home on "The Neck" before their daughter was born in September 1828[1]. Gershom appears in the 1830 census there in Tunkhannock twp: 01001-123001[3]. About 1830 he joined the Methodist Episcopal Church, a religious connection which he always maintained.

In 1833 Gershom paid $3.00 per acre for a farm in Auburn twp, Susquehanna co, PA, previously owned by Jabez Sumner[1]. This was his home for the rest of his life. His descendants live there yet. He appears there in the 1840 census: 000111000100-001101000010[4], and in 1850, when his father-in-law, at age 83, lived with them[5].

Gershom died at his home 8 June 1855[1,2] and was buried in the Bunnell Cemetery[2] at Auburn Four Corners, which had been established on a part of his farm[9]. His son Jonathan continued to operate the farm, and the widow Sarah lived with him. She appears in the 1860[6], 1870[6] and 1880 census[7] with Jonathan and his family. Her death occurred 19 December 1881[2] in Elk Lake[8], Dimock twp, Susquehanna co, apparently at the home of her daughter. She was buried with Gershom in the Bunnell Cemetery[2].

Children:
>   1. 320401. Jonathan, b. 19 Apr. 1825[1]; m. 8 Oct. 1851 Charlotte E. Fargo[1];
>   d. 8 Mar. 1914[2].
>   Children (surname Bunnell);[1]
>   1. Alice.   2. Gersham W.   3. Frederick Seward.
>   2. 320402. Nancy, b. 7 Sept. 1828[1]; m. 4 Sept. 1850[1] Frederick Fargo[1]; d. 20 Apr.
>   1884[8].
>   Children (surname Fargo):[1]
>   1. Sarah H.   2. A. Wilson.   3. Charlotte Francesca.

REFERENCES:
>   1. Biles Manuscript, pp. 185, 186.
>   2. Gravestones, Bunnell Cemetery, Auburn Four Corners.
>   3. Census Microfilms - 1820, 1830, Tunkhannock twp, Luzerne co, PA.
>   4. 1840 census - transcribed in *Susquehanna County Historical Society Newsletter*, Vol. 8, No. 1,
>   May 1997, p. 31. Also transcribed in the files of Ruth Cost Duncan.
>   5. 1850 census - Files of Ruth Cost Duncan and CB Database.
>   6. 1860, 1870 census - CB Database.
>   7. *1880 United States Census and National Index*, Family History Resource File.
>   8. Data extracted from *The Kelloggs in the Old World and the New*, by Timothy Hopkins, 1903,
>   Vol. 1, pp. 314, 687, and sent to me by Helen K. McCracken, Towanda, PA, in 1969.
>   9. Stocker, pp. 82, 85.

1-1-6-5-4?1   D34ii   CB010506

GERSHOM[6] BONNELL, (son? of Gershom[5], Solomon[4], Benjamin[3], Benjamin[2], William[1]) was
born about 1757[2] in Connecticut[1]. During the Revolution he took the Loyalist part and served
as a private under Captain Elyath Miller in the Oliver Delancey Regiment in 1779[1]. After the
war he removed to Sheffield, Sunbury co, New Brunswick, Canada, where in 1782[2] he was
married to LAVINIA COY[1,2]. She was born about 1761[2] in New Brunswick[2], daughter of
Edward and Amy (Titus) Coy[1] of Gagetown, Queens co, NB[1]. In 1801 Gershom received a
land grant in Burton Parish, Sunbury co, NB, for his Revolutionary War service[1,2]. In 1819 he
made an additional petition for land in Sussex? co*, NB (MF #F4183, CNNB Archives)[2]. In
1845, at age 87, he resided in Fredericton, Sunbury co, NB[2]. He was receiving a Revolutionary
War pension[2]. His wife Lavinia died 5 February 1846[2], and he died the same month in
Fredericton[2].

Children:
>   1. 027345. Rebecca, b. about 1783[2].

NOTE: Ruth Duncan believes that the Joseph Bunnell who married Esther Gilbert had a brother
Gershom and that they were both the sons of Gershom, Jr. If this is the Loyalist Gershom, I

would have to agree that the only one of Gershom, Sr.'s sons who could have been the father was Gershom, Jr., baptized in 1732. But **it is important to remember that no evidence has been found to support this conclusion.**

*At least at the present time there is no Sussex co in New Brunswick or in any of the Maritime Provinces of Canada.

REFERENCES:
1. *Bunnell/Bonnell Newsletter*, Vol. VIII, No. 1, p. 12, including notes compiled by Paul J. Bunnell.
2. CB Database.

1-1-6-5-4?2   D97   CB013196

JOSEPH[6] BUNNELL (son? of Gershom[5], Gershom[4], Benjamin[3], Benjamin[2], William[1]) was born about 1763[1] in Connecticut. In March or April 1782 he enlisted for a year in the regiment commanded by Col. Samuel B. Webb and part of the time by Lt. Col. Ebenezer Huntington in the Connecticut line[1]. He was honorably discharged in March 1783[1]. He does not appear in the 1790 census in Connecticut when he was a single man. On 7 April 1793[2], in Weston, Fairfield co, CT, he married ESTHER GILBERT[2] who was born in 1766. They appear in the 1800 census in Norwalk, Fairfield co, CT: 30010-10010[4] and in the 1810 census in Weston, Fairfield co, CT: 00001-10110[4]. (Where were all the sons in 1810?). On 31 March 1818 Joseph Bunnell applied for a pension based on his service in the Revolution:[1]

> "I Joseph Bunnell of Weston in the County of Fairfield and State of Connecticut being duly sworn depose and say that I served as a Soldier in the army of the United States in the Revolutionary war for the term of one year commencing in the month of April to the best of my recollection 1782 in the third Connecticut Regiment commanded by Col. Samuel B. Webb in the first company in sd Regiment commanded by Capt. Bulkley and received an honorable discharge from said service which I have lost considering it of no value at this late period of time. I am poor and very infirm of body and stand in need of help from the Public for my support - and further say not -"[1]

He was granted a pension of $8.00 per month commencing on 31 March 1818[1]. The pension was reviewed in 1820 when Joseph signed the following statement in court:

> "BE IT REMEMBERED, that in the County Court, held in and for the County of Fairfield in the District and State aforesaid, on this 14th day of June 1820 the same being a Court of Record, and halving a Seal, under the Authority of said State, personally came and appeared in open Court, Joseph Bunnell, aged 56 years, resident in the Town of Weston in the County of Fairfield in said State, and being affirmed according to Law, doth on his Oath declare that he served in the Revolutionary War, as follows: that is to say in the year 1782 in the month of March he enlisted into the Regiment commanded by Col. Webb, (and Lieut.-Col. Eben[r] Huntington a part of the time) in the Connecticut line, on the continental establishment, for the term of one year, and faithfully served out said term, and was honorably discharged in March 1783 which discharge he has lost - that the original Declaration made by him, for the purpose of obtaining a Pension, under the Act of Congress of the 18th of March, 1818, was dated the 31 day of March 1818, that in pursuance thereof he was entered in the List of Pensioners, and received a Pension Certificate No. 1673.

And I do further solemnly swear that I was a resident citizen of the United States, on the 18th day of March, 1818, and that I have not since that time, by gift, sale, or in any manner, disposed of my property, or any part thereof, with intent thereby so to diminish it as to bring myself within the provisions of an Act of Congress, entitled "An Act to provide for certain persons engaged in the land and naval service of the United States in the Revolutionary War," passed on the 18th day of March, 1818; and that I have not, nor has any person in trust for me any property or securities, contracts or debts due to me; nor have I any income other than what is contained in the Schedule herein annexed, and by me subscribed. And I do further declare that my occupation is that of a Collier, but I have not been able to earn my support during several years past on account of being very badly ruptured, and am now failing fast in consequence of said rupture; and that I have a family residing with me, viz. a wife named Esther aged about 54 years who has become very infirm, & is troubled with a complaint which it is apprehended with terminate in the consumption and a daughter named Susannah aged about 18, who has been at times very ill & is subject to the spitting of blood - and that I have no means of supporting my said family, except the property hereafter stated and my labour & my pension - and that the schedule of my debts hereto annexed is correct & true, all which is subscribed by me the day and year aforesaid.

/s/ Joseph Bunnell"[1]

The following document was appended to the foregoing as evidence of Joseph Bunnell's need:

"At a County Court, held in and for the County of Fairfield in the District and State of Connecticut, on the 14th day of June 1820, the same being a court of Record, and having a seal, by virtue of the laws of said State.

Personally appeared, in open Court, Joseph Bunnell a resident in the town of Weston in the County of Fairfield in said State, and exhibited and subscribed the following Schedule, and made affirmation that the same is a true and perfect Schedule of all his income and property (necessary clothing and bedding excepted) viz.

One small house & 4 acres of land adjoining -
one cow - 6 chairs - 1 broken porridge pot -
1 old tea kettle cracked - 2 stone jugs - 3 old knives & forks
3 earthen plates - 1 axe - 1 rake - 2 old chests - 3 old barrels
1 small table - one old bible -

Joseph Bunnell[1]

"Account of debts the subscriber now owes --viz.

To Martha Osborn by note	$ 17.50
To Eliphalet Coley by note	16.25
To George Cannon by note	10.47
To Isaac M. Sturges by book	11.00
To Giles Bunnell by note	40.00
To Silliman Godfrey by note	3.25
To Eben' Godfrey by book	4.63
To Samuel Gilbert by book	17.20
To John Sturges by note	50.00
To Thomas Squire by book	20.00
found due by Court	$190.30

/s/ Joseph Bunnell"[1]

The census of 1820 in Weston lists him as 000001-01001-MFG1[4]. (Daughter Susannah appears in the 10 to 16 year column.) In 1835 it was reported that he was still on the pension roll at age 72[1]. Nothing has yet been learned about when or where he and Esther died.

Children:
1. 320049. Zar[3], b. about 1796[4]; m. (first) Eliza A. _____[5]; m. (second) 12 Mar. 1843 Mrs. Julia Ann Cook[5].
   Children (by first wife)(surname Bunnell):[5]
   1. Joseph Allen.   2. Julia Elizabeth.   3. Almira.
   Census records suggest two or three older daughters.
2. 320048. Beale[3], b. 28 Dec. 1797[5]; m. Anna Davis[6]; d. 5 Apr. 1863[5].
   Children (surname Bunnell):[6]
   1. Samuel Gilbert.   5. Elizabeth B.   9. George Burr.
   2. Anna Davis.   6. Beale David.   10. Joseph Frederick.
   3. Harriet B.   7. John Wesley.
   4. Sarah H.   8. William Henry.
3.   Caroline[3], b. 179x[4].
4. 320050. Giles[3], b. 15 Oct. 1801[3]; m. 10 Oct. 1825 Abigail Ogden[3]; d. 11 Oct. 1852.[3]
   Children (surname Bunnell):[3]
   1. Ebenezer Bradley. 4. Theodore.   7. Frances Christine.
   2. David King.   5. Mary Esther.   8. Lewis Giles.
   3. Alva.   6. Sarah Ann.
5. 320052. Susannah[1], b. about 1803[1].

REFERENCES:
1. Revolutionary War pension file S36,448, obtained from the National Archives and sent to me by Claude A. Bunnell.
2. *Families of Old Fairfield*, by Donald Lines Jacobus, Vol. II, p. 180.
3. Biles Manuscript, p. 236.
4. CB Database, 1800, 1810, 1820 census.
5. Duncan, p. 69.
6. Cutter - CT, Vol. II, p. 783.

Note: As in the case of Joseph's assumed brother Gershom above, I must emphasize **that no evidence has been found which links this Joseph with Gershom, Jr.**

1-1-6-5-5-1 D98 CB310009

JAMES[6] BUNNELL (Joseph[5], Gershom[4], Benjamin[3], Benjamin[2], William[1]) was born 12[1] or 21[3] December[1,3] 1768[1,3] in Litchfield co, CT[7]. In 1797[4] he married AZUBA CARTER[1], who was born 16 April 1768[1] in Connecticut[1]. James appears in the 1800 census: 20010-10010[3], and in the 1810 census: 10010-31010[3], both in Litchfield, Litchfield co, CT. He was a blacksmith[1]. Azuba died 23 June 1816[1], a week after the birth of her youngest son[1].

James's mother, the widowed Abiah (Kirby) Bunnell, came to keep house for him and to help raise the younger children[1]. They lived in Washington twp, Litchfield co, where he appears in the 1820 census: 110001-11001[3].

In 1830 James was probably the 60 - 70 year old man in the household of his son Elijah in New Preston, Washington twp, Litchfield co[3]. Elijah and his family moved in May 1833 to Bridgewater twp, Susquehanna co, PA[7]. James either went with him[1] or followed soon after. Apparently, he appears there in the 1840 census as a man of 70 - 80 years in Elijah's household. He died 5 August 1841[1] at his son's home and was buried on the farm[1]. The stone that marks his grave can still be seen there[6].

Children:
1. 320152. Ephraim Kirby[1], b. 6 Aug. 1798[1]; m. (first) 31 Dec. 1823 Roena Griswold[2]; m. (second) 6 Mar. 1828 Cornelia Stone[2]; d. 3 June 1881[1].
   Children (surname Bunnell)(by second wife):[2]
   1. Emily.   4. William Henry.   7. Kirby C.
   2. Cornelia Jane.   5. Harry Dwight.
   3. Martha Matilda.   6. Avis Amelia.
2. 320153. Avis[1], b. 1[1] of 21[5] June 1800[1]; m. 27 May 1821[5] Daniel Landon[1,5]; d. 1882[1].
   Children (surname Landon):[1]
   1. William.   2. Louisa.   3. Avis.
3. 320151. Elijah[1], b. 6 Jan. 1803[1]; m. (first) 28 May 1826 Lucy Stone[2]; m. (second) 21 Feb. 1865 Elmira Juliet (Wright) Stone[2]; d. 20 Sept. 1873[1] or 30 Sept 1872[2].
   Children (surname Bunnell)(by first wife):[2]
   1. Ephraim Kirby.   3. Dotha Ann.   5. Lucy Jane.
   2. William.   4. Truman S.   6. Harry.
4. 320154. Lucy[1], b. 27 Feb. 1805[1]; m. Charles A. Farnham[1]; d. 19 July 1878[1].
   Children (surname Farnham):[1]
   1. Sarah Jane.   3. James.   5. Lucy.
   2. Charles.   4. John.
5. 320155. Matilda[1] May[4], b. 24[1] or 14[4] July 1807[1]; m. (first) 8 Aug. 1833[1] (or 13 Feb. 1842[5]) Harry Stone[1]; m. (second) 1853[1] _____ Way[1]; d. 5[1] or 8[4] Aug. 1853[1].
   Children (surname Stone):[1]
   1. Merritt H.
6. 320156. Dotha Ann[1], b. 10[1] or 19[4] June 1810[1]; m. 27 Nov. 1834[5] Joseph H. Tooley[1,5].
   Children (surname Tooley):[1]
   1. Jane E.   3. Martha Dallas.   5. Clara Beaumont.
   2. Emma Josephine.   4. Nettie.   6. Joseph.
7. 320150. James Andrew[2], b. 18[1] or 13[4] July 1813[1]; m. 27 May 1839 Mary Ann Hall[2]; d. 20 May 1886[8].

Children (surname Bunnell):[1]
1. Frederick Hall.   3. Lyman Walton.   4. Welcome Lemon.
2. Robert Oscar.

8. 320149. Samuel Carter[1], b. 16 June 1816[1]; m. 12 Oct. 1840 Amy Amanda Hall[2]; d. 26 Feb. 1884[2].
   Children (surname Bunnell):[2]
   1. Franklin Milton.   3. Homer Franklin.   5. Mary Jane.
   2. Edward Samuel.   4. Annie (or Amy) E.

REFERENCES:

1. Biles Manuscript, pp. 192, 193, 194, 195, 197, 198, 200, 203, 204, 211.
2. Duncan, pp. 69, 70, 133, 134.
3. Duncan Files -1800 and 1810 census, Litchfield twp, Litchfield co, CT.
   1820 and 1830 census, Washington twp, Litchfield co, CT.
   Special "Bunnell" file at the Connecticut State Library.
4. "Bunnell Geneology", comprising the Bunnell ancestry and the descendants of James and Azuba (Carter) Bunnell, handwritten around 1900 on blank pages an a printed account book headed "Account of Grain Sold". Although it is not signed, the writer was a descendant, who referred to Samuel Carter Bunnell as "Uncle Samuel.".
5. Early Bunnell marriages extracted from Vital Records Town of Litchfield, CT, by Mrs. Clarence Bunnell, Winsted, CT, and sent to me 4 April 1961.
6. Photo of the gravestone of James Bunnell taken and sent to me by Mrs. Paul Carlson, Montrose, PA, 22 May 1997.
7. Stocker, pp. 351, 387.
8. Gravestones in Dimock Cemetery, Susquehanna co, PA, copied by William R. Austin.

1-1-6-5-5-2 D99 CB310010

JOEL[6] BUNNELL (Joseph[5], Gershom[4], Benjamin[3], Benjamin[2], William[1]) was born in 1770[1]. He married (first) MOLLY[5,6] _____, who was born about 1771[6]. Joel appears in the 1800 census[2,8]: 00010-20011 in Cornwall, Litchfield co, CT. Joel and Joseph Bunnell of Cornwall sold two pieces of land in Warren twp and one in Cornwall twp to Burritt and Ruth (Crofut) Jennings on 13 July 1801[3]. In 1806 Joel purchased 121 acres from John Welch, half in the town of Cornwall and half in Goshen[3]. His residence was apparently on the Cornwall side near the village of East Cornwall[2,3]. The Cornwall and Goshen land records include a number of transactions to and from Joel Bunnell in the next couple of decades[3].

Joseph and Joel, their two youngest sons, are called twins in several of the accounts[1,5,7], but that does not seem to be supported by the census records[2,8]. Molly, wife of Joel Bunnell, died 15 April 1818 at the age of 47, according to her gravestone in the cemetery in Cornwall[6]. Joel appears in the 1820 census in Cornwall[2,8]: 020101-00201. Two of the males (Joel and his oldest son Hiram) were engaged in farming.

Joel married (second) CONTENT _____, widow of Joseph Sanford, Jr.[3,7]. She brought with her several pieces of land as her dower right from her first marriage[3]. Some of these they later deeded to his sons Hiram and Joseph[3]. Duncan and the CB Database cite the Goshen Congregational Church records to state that Content Bunnell died 16 April 1833 at the age of 55[7,8]. However, I find in Ruth Duncan's abstracts of the Goshen land records a brief abstract of an agreement dated 14 April <u>1836</u> between Joel Bunnell and wife Content of Cornwall and Joseph Bunnell of Goshen regarding two pieces of land in Goshen[3].

Joel is listed in the 1840 census in Cornwall[2], but the only person shown is a woman of 60 to 70 years. It is possible that this represents Joel himself, recorded in error on the wrong side of the list. It would match his record in the 1830 and 1850 censuses. He last appears in the census of 1850[2,8] living in Goshen next to his son Joel, Jr.[4]. His age is given as 80 years.

Joel died 21 November 1854[1,5,7] in Bristol, Hartford co, CT[1,5,7], and was buried in the Cornwall cemetery[7].

Children:
1. 320765. Irene[8], b. about 1798[8]; m. 30 June 1822[8] Elisha Clark[5,8].
   Children (surname Clark):[4]
   1. George Osborn.　2. Hiram.　3. others?
2. 320766. Hiram[8], b. 1800[5]; m. 10 Sept. 1826[1] Lucy Barker[1]; d. 1865[1].
   Children (surname Bunnell):[8]

1. Myron.	4. Harriet.	7. Calvin.
2. Austin.	5. Joel.	8. Elijah.
3. Sarah.	6. Hiram Ives.	9. Ann Eliza.

3. 320767. Joseph[8], b. about 1801[8]; m. (first) Caroline Sanford[7]; m. (second) 29 Mar. 1830[7] Maria Price[7]; d. 13 Apr. 1845[8].
   Children (suname Bunnell)(bt second wife):[7]

1. Edgar G.	3. Maria L.	5. Joseph B.
2. Wolcott.	4. Elizabeth M.	

4. 320768. Joel[8], b. 1810[6]; m. 2 Mar. 1834[7] Fanny Abigail Palmer[7]; d. 1877[7].
   Children (surname Bunnell):[7,8]

1. Amanda C.	4. Austin H.	7. Dwight Henry.
2. Mary Ann.	5. Oscar Palmer.	8. Walter Joel.
3. George M.	6. Charles Monroe.	

NOTE: Is he the Joel Bunnel who served as a private in Daniel Deming's Co. in the War of 1812? Duncan, p. 47, says it was Joel[5] D57 CB300097, but this seems unlikely.

REFERENCES:
1. Biles Manuscript, pp. 213, 218.
2. Duncan census files, Cornwall, CT - 1800, 1820, 1830, 1840; Goshen, CT - 1850.
3. Duncan land records files - Cornwall and Goshen, CT.
4. Duncan files - Page 19 from a history of Goshen, CT.

5. *History of Cornwall*, by Edward Starr - extract sent to me by Mrs. Clarence H. Bunnell, Winsted, CT.

6. Gravestones in cemetery at Cornwall, CT, copied and sent to me by Mrs. Clarence H. Bunnell.

7. Duncan, pp. 70, 135, 136.

8. CB Database - census records - Cornwall, CT - 1800, 1820, 1830, Goshen CT - 1850.

1-1-6-5-5-3   CB310013

JOSEPH[6] BUNNELL (Joseph[5], Gershom[4], Benjamin[3], Benjamin[2], William[1]) was born in 1770[1], probably in Connecticut. Little is known about his early life - he does not appear in the census records in 1790, 1800 or 1810. By 1797 he was married (first) to _____ _____. The Biles manuscript says she died in 1804 leaving three children. Fanny is omitted from the Biles list, but all the other children are called children of the second (also name unknown) wife. When Joseph died he left a widow Lucy, who has been presumed to be the mother of the last nine children. A careful perusal of the census records, the known birth dates and Joseph's will, leads me to believe that Lucy was the mother of only the last six children. Perhaps she was the third wife instead of the second. In any case Joseph's first wife (or wives) died after presenting him with seven children, and he married, by 1810, LUCY _____.

In 1811 they moved (from Litchfield co, CT?) to the town of Sterling, Cayuga co, NY, where they were among the first settlers[3]. Their home was about 1 ½ miles northeast of Sterling center[3]. There they lived for the rest of their lives. The Baptist Church of Sterling, which later became the Baptist Church of Hannibal, was organized at their home[3]. Joseph appears in the 1820 census in Sterling: 210001-21010-AG[7].

In 1841 Joseph wrote his will[2]:

> "The Last Will and testament of Joseph Bunnell of the Town of Sterling, County of Cayuga and State of New York. I, Joseph Bunnell, considering the uncertainty of this mortal life and being of sound mind and memory (blessed be God for the same) Do make and publish this my Last will and testament in manner and form following, that is to say.
>
> FIRST. I give and bequeath Abia Bunnell, formerly my daughter, now Abia Brouk, one cow, and to my daughter, Damarris Bunnell formerly, now Damarris Denney, I give and bequeath seventy five cents, also to my daughter Lucy Bunnell I bequeath one cow, also a home at my home until she shall be otherwise provided for. Also to my son Leman Bunnell I give and bequeath one dollar. Also to my son Miles Bunnell I give and bequeath one dollar. Also to my son, Joel Bunnell I give and bequeath one dollar. and also to my daughter Fanny Bunnell, now Fanny Cooper, I give and bequeath one dollar. Also to my daughter, Calista Bunnell formerly, now Calista Lake, I bequeath one dollar. and to my son Anthony Bunnell I give and bequeath one dollar. And also to my son, Alva Bunnell, I give and bequeath one dollar; to my beloved son Amasa Bunnell, I give and bequeath my farm together with all my farming utensils, and what stock may be on the farm left, excepting that in before mentioned , that may Son Amasa is to have all the above mentioned property bequeathed to him after my deceas and the deceas of Lucy my wife.

LASTLY. I do hereby appoint Amasa Bunnell, my son, Executor to this my Last will and testament, hereby revoking all former wills by me made.

In Witness whereof, I have hereunto set my hand and seal this Sixth day of November in the year of our Lord one thousand eight hundred and forty one.

Joseph Bunnell   (L.S.)

Signed, Sealed, Published and declared by the above named Joseph Bunnell to be his last will and testament in the presence of us who have hereunto subscribed our names as witnesses in the presence of the testator, the day and year above written.

Mary L. Clark
Polly Clark
Benjamin Clark"   Recorded in Book H of Wills, at page 377.

Joseph died in the Town of Sterling on 16 May 1845[2], survived by his widow Lucy and 11 of his 13 children. (His heirs at the time of probate also included the following grandchildren: Miles, Ephraim, Lemuel and William Colton, Louisa and Emeline Lake.[2]) The will was probated 4 January 1848. (The widow Lucy had died 25 September 1847[2,4], daughter Calista Lake on 1 March 1845[1], and daughter Lucy on 23 September 1847[1]. Daughter Abigail Colton, not mentioned in the will, had died 28 April 1835[1].) It would be interesting to know why Joseph had only one "beloved son" and why he made such a one-sided disposition of his estate.

Children (by first wife):
1. 320032. Leman, b. about 1797[7]; m. Sarah _____[7].
    Children (surname Bunnell):[7]
    1. Laura.   2. Amanda.   3. Judson.
2. 320770. Miles, b. 2 Mar. 1798[1]; m. 27 Dec. 1823[1] Beula Baxter[1]; d. 18 Sept. 1869[1].
    Children (surname Bunnell):[1]
    1. Eliza A.   3. Emilinda.   5. Juliaette.
    2. Almira B.   4. Sarah Jane.   6. Joseph.
3. 320036. Abigail, m. 1819[7] Julius Colton[7]; d. 28 Apr. 1835[1].
    Children (surname Colton):[2]
    1. Miles.   3. Lemuel.   4. William.
    2. Ephraim.
4. 320034. Fanny, b. 1802[4]; m. 1820[4] John Cooper II[4]; d. 14 July 1879[4].
    Children (surname Cooper):[4]
    1. Alva.   3. Jane D.   5. Peter William.
    2. Joseph.   4. Caroline.
5. 320080. Anthony S., b. about 1803[7]; m. 9 Apr. 1840[5] Julia Harvey[5]; d. 20 Sept. 1853[1].
    Children (surname Bunnell):[6]
    1. Mary J.   4. Lucy.   7. John C.
    2. Joseph.   5. Nettie.   8. Harriet.
    3. Ellen.   6. Henrietta.

6. 320771. Joel, b. about 1804[7]; m. Britania Mead[1]; d. 7 Dec. 1867[1].
        Children (surname Bunnell):[7]
        1. Frederick.   4. Mary.   7. Samuel W.
        2. Douglas.   5. Anna.
        3. Hannah.   6. Alexander.
7. 320061. Calista E.; m. _____ Lake[2]; d. 1 Mar. 1845[1].
        Children (surname Lake):[2]
        1. Louisa.   2. Emeline.

Children (by last wife):
    8. 320064. Abia, b. 30 June 1811[1]; m. Nicholas Brouk[2]; d. 17 Aug. 1853[1].
    9. 320066. Amasa, b. 10 Feb. 1814[1]; m. 10 May 1842[7] Catharine Gilchrist[7];
        d. 13 Sept. 1888[1].
        Children (surname Bunnell):[7]
        1. William.   2. Marion.   3. Myron.
10. 320067. Demarris, b. 26 June 1816[1]; m. George Denny[2]; d. 6 Aug. 1848[1].
11. 320070. Alvah Curtis, b. 20 Dec. 1818[1]; d. 1892[1].
        Children (surname Bunnell):[1]
        1. Belle.
12. 320033. Joseph, b. 9 June 1821[1]; d. 28 Apr. 1834[1].
13. 320035. Lucy, b. 28 Mar. 1828[1]; d. 23 Sept. 1847[1].

REFERENCES:
    1. Biles Manuscript, p. 192, 220, 222, 223.
    2. Will and probate notes sent to me by Daisy Ruth (Cooper) Johnson in 1969.
    3. *History of Cayuga County, New York, 1789-1879*, by Elliot G. Storke.
    4. Descendants of John Cooper II and Fanny (Bunnell) Cooper, sent to me by their great granddaughter Daisy Ruth (Cooper) Johnson.
    5. Weddings in Marshall co, IN, 1836-1850, Book 1, p. 98, extract sent to me by Mary Katherine DeLong in 1990.
    6. Descendants of Anthony S. and Julia (Harvey) Bunnell sent to me in 1997 by their great grandson Donald S. Patterson, M.D.
    7. CB Database.

1-1-6-5-5-4   D100   CB310011

ELIJAH[6] BUNNELL (Joseph[5], Gershom[4], Benjamin[3], Benjamin[2], William[1]) was born in Connecticut, probably Litchfield co, 12 July 1770, calculated from his age given on his gravestone[1,2]. The 1850 census record tends to confirm this date[7]. However, if it is accurate, the year 1770 cited as the birth year of Elijah's twin brothers Joel and Joseph must be incorrect.

"Elijah Bunnell of Litchfield" and MARY PRATT were married 21 February 1795 in the Congregational Church at New Preston, in Washington Town, Litchfield co, CT[4]. They lived in the towns of Litchfield and Warren, where Elijah had interests in a saw mill and an iron forge along the Shepaug River[3]. Elijah appears in the 1800 census in the town of Warren, Litchfield co, CT: 00010-10010[7]. He and his wife were both between 26 and 45 years of age, with a girl (daughter?) under ten.

Sometime before December 1811 they left Connecticut and moved across the border to New York state, where they settled in Philipstown, then in Dutchess co, but after 1812 in Putnam co. They lived at Canopus Hollow[5], in that part of Philipstown which in 1839 was set off as the Town of Putnam Valley[7]. He owned and operated a forge and triphammer on Canopus Creek. Having no sons of his own[5], he raised his nephew Joel, son of Joseph Bunnell[5]. Another nephew, Ephraim Kirby, son of James Bunnell, also lived with him as a boy[5]. A tradition in Ephraim K.'s family says that he assisted his uncle Elijah to forge a chain to stop English vessels from ascending the Hudson River during the War of 1812[5].

Elijah appears in the 1810 census in Philipstown, Dutchess co, NY: 11010-00001[7]. Elijah, himself, is listed as age 26-45, but his wife is over 45. The daughter? no longer appears and had probably died. she would have been at most 15 years old in 1810. The two young males were probably Elijah's nephews: Ephraim, b. 1798, and Joel, b. 1804.

Elijah appears in the Philipstown census in Putnam co, NY, in 1820: 001111-01001-AG[7]. Both Elijah and his wife were over 45 years of age. In 1830, again in Philipstown, Putnam co: 01000001-211001[7], the picture changes. His wife's age falls in the 30-40 group. I believe this indicates a change in wives. Mary is a common enough name so that it would not be surprising that he married one Mary in 1795 but that a different Mary survived him in 1855. Presumably, his first wife died and he remarried soon. The 1840 census, taken in Putnam Valley, Putnam co: 000000001-0011001[7], gives his wife's age again as 30-40. She seems to have aged less than 10 years in this decade, but made it up by 1850 when the census of Putnam Valley included Elijah Bunnell age 80, born in Connecticut, farmer, with real estate worth $6000, and his wife Mary age 55, born in Connecticut[7].

Elijah died 14 January 1855 in Putnam Valley at the age of 84 years, 6 months and 2 days[1,2]. He was buried in the Methodist Cemetery at Adams Corners in the town of Putnam Valley[1,2]. His widow Mary died 23 April 1866, aged 72 years 10 months and 17 days[1,2]. Born in 1793, she was 23 years younger than her husband. She was buried at Adams Corners with Elijah and their daughter Lucy[1,2].

Children:
1. 320775. Lucy, b. 2 Jan. 1824; d. 30 Oct. 1845[1,2].
?2.   Avis, b. 2 Apr. 1826; d. 25 Jan. 1830[2]. (g.s. calls her daughter of Elijah and Lucy, probably an error for Elijah and Mary - wra)

REFERENCES:
1. NYGBR, Vol. 49, p. 179. Gravestones in Putnam co, NY.
2. *Old Gravestones of Putnam County, NY*, by Barbara Smith Buys.
3. Duncan files - Land records, Danbury, Warren and Litchfield, CT.
4. *Early Connecticut Marriages*, Vol. V, p. 76.
5. Biles Manuscript, pp. 222, 223.
6. Duncan, p. 70.
7. CB Database.

SIXTH GENERATION

1-1-6-5-5-5   CB310040

EMMONDS[6] BUNNELL (Joseph[5], Gershom[4], Benjamin[3], Benjamin[2], William[1]) The only references to the existence of this man are found in the Biles Manuscript. On page 192 the fifth and last child of Joseph and Abiah (Kirby) Bunnell is listed as   "(Heman or (Emmonds(?)".

On page 220, in the article on Miles Bunnell, son of Joseph and grandson of Joseph and Abiah (Kirby) Bunnell, we find, "Miles, son of Joseph . . . After the death of his mother in 1804 he went to Litchfield, Conn. and lived with his Uncle Emmonds. He married Dec. 27, 1823 Beula Baxter . . ."

On page 221: "Joseph, son of Miles and Buela (Baxter) Bunnell was born Apr. 15, 1835 at Cold Springs, Putnam Co., N.Y." . . . "He well remembers his father's uncle Elijah Bunnell of Canopus Hollow, Putnam Co., N.Y., who owned and operated a forge there, and used to visit them while his father lived Cold Springs, N.Y. He also remembers his father's uncle Emmons Bunnell of Litchfield, Conn."

That is all. No reference to an Emmonds Bunnell has been discovered in census records, deeds, wills or vital statistics, to support the statements in the Biles Manuscript.

1-1-6-5-9-2   D36ii   CB310042

NOAH[6] BUNNELL Noah[5], Gershom[4], Benjamin[3], Benjamin[2], William[1]) was born 9 October 17676[1] in Connecticut. He married REBECCA _____ [2]. Noah Bunnel, cooper, appears in the Rhinebeck Precinct, Dutchess co, NY, account book, showing a debit in March 1788 and a credit in 1789[3]. He appears in the 1790 census in Clinton, Dutchess co, NY[6]. Besides his wife, some of his younger siblings may have been living with him. Noah's father, Noah, Sr., died 11 December 1790, while at Noah, Jr.'s home in Hyde Park, Clinton twp[3]. As eldest son, Noah, Jr., was allotted 2 shares of his father's estate, including 2 equal thirds of Noah, Sr.'s cooper shop[4]. His brothers divided the rest of the cooper's tools among them.

Noah Bunnell, Jr., died 14 October 1794 at the age of 27 years and 5 days[6]. On 10 December 1794 his widow Rebecca was appointed administratrix of his estate, with Thaddeus Lawrence, cordwainer, and Isaac Russell, farmer, as sureties. Thaddeus Lawrence attested to the death of Noah by declaring under oath that he was present at Noah's funeral on 16 October 1794[2].

Children:
    1. 320078. Levi, b. between 1790 and 1794; m. 13 Nov. 1813 Lois Mosher.
            Children (surname Bunnell):[5]

1. George.	4. Jane.	6. Henry.
2. Mary.	5. Richard M.	7. William Jackson.
3. Egbert.		

REFERENCES:

1. Biles Manuscript, p. 224.
2. Letters of Administration, estate of Noah Bunnell; photocopy sent to me by Jacqueline Bunnell-Ogden.
3. Letter 23 July 2000 from KINSHIP to Brenda Bunnell Griffin.
4. Record of probate of the estate of Noah Bunnell (Sr.) in the Town and for the district of New Milford, CT. Photocopy sent to me by Brenda Bunnell Griffin.
5. Letter 25 May 2000, from Jacqueline Bunnell-Ogden citing the probate record of Noah's son George.

1-1-6-5-9-3 D101 CB310043

SALMON BEARDSLEY[6] BUNNELL (Noah[5], Gershom[4], Benjamin[3], Benjamin[2], William[1]) was born 9 May 1769[1] in Connecticut. On 6 July 1791, in Mew Milford, Litchfield co, CT, Salmon and his widowed mother Mary were appointed administrators of his father's estate[2]. After the reserve for the widow's third, the remainder was divided into equal shares, of which the eldest son, Noah, Jr., received two shares and each of the other children one share. The court record of the disposition lists Salmon's share as follows:[2]

> 1 Choristers Companion, 1 Bedstead & cord.
> 2 Setts Truss hoops, 1 Grindstone
> part of sett of Coopers tools to Divide
> 1 Bottle, 1 Musical magazine
> about ½ an acre Land, Lot No. 1
> 1 part in the House [after the death of their mother].

On 25 May 1804, in Dutchess co, NY, he married LOIS LEETE, daughter of John and Lydia (Leete) Leete of Amenia, Dutchess co, NY[3,4]. She was born 11 April 1778 in Guilford, New Haven co, CT[3]. This is certainly the "Solomon Bunnell" who appears in the 1810 census in the town of Stanford, Dutchess co, NY: 20110-11010[10]. The following year[10] they moved to a farm on the Susquehanna River in the town of Windsor, Broome co, NY, where Salmon had purchased land on 6 July 1808[5] and 3 February 1812[5]. The last three children were born in Windsor[6], the youngest, posthumously, only ten days after Salmon died on 30 November 1815[7]. He was buried in a cemetery on the main road between the villages of Windsor and Ouaquaga in the town of Windsor[7]. Infant son John Frederick was probably buried in the same cemetery.

In a letter dated 15 January 1816, Eber Leete, brother of Lois, wrote to another brother, "We have lately had letters from the westward announcing the Death of Brother Salmon B. Bunnel on the first day of December. He took cold & had a fever set in which terminated in death in three weeks. We have not heard from them since - Brother Hearvey has gone out."[14] In July 1816[14] Lois took her five little children back to her parents home in the town of Stanford, Dutchess co, NY[6]. Here her brother John Leete, Jr., was appointed guardian of the children[8]. On 5 May 1817, John Leete, Jr., as guardian, and Lois Bunnell sold 42 acres of the Windsor land to Amasa Bird of Windsor with the following deed[8]. It is not clear whether this was all the land they owned in Windsor. If not, there must have been other tracts sold since none of the family returned to Broome co.

This Indenture, Made the fifth day of May in the year of our **Lord** one thousand eight hundred and seventeen Between John Leete Jr. of the town Stanford county of Dutchess and State of New York Guardian of Myron L., Theron B., Ruth L., Alexander H. and Salmon B. Bunnell, infant children of Salmon Beardslee Bunnell late of the town of Winsor County of Broome and State aforesaid deceased by order ot the chancellor of the state aforesaid, and Lois Bunnell late wife of the said Salmon Beardslee Bunnell, now of said town of Stanford of the first part, and Amasa T. Bird of said town of Windsor of the second part, Witnesseth, that the said parties of the first part, for and in consideration of the sume of <u>fife</u> hundred and sixty six dollars, money of account of the United States, to them in hand paid, by the said party of the second part, the receipt whereof is hereby confessed and acknowledged, have granted, bargained, sold, remised, released, aliened and confirmed, and by these presents, do grant, bargain, sell, remise, release, alien and confirm unto the said party of the second part, and to his heirs and assigns forever, all that certain piece or parcel of land being part of Lots number one hundred and five and one hundred & eight in Abijah Hammond's Patent lying and being in said town of Windsor bounded and described as follows, (viz) beginning at the southeast corner of lot number one hundred and eight at two birches proceeding from one root on the west bank on the Susquehannah River, thence running north eighty seven degrees west (as the needle pointed in 1788) seventy four chains and eighty three links to a stake and stones, thence north three degrees east six chains and one link to a stake and stones, thence south eighty seven degrees east sixty six chains and thirty one links to a stake and stones standing on the west bank of the Susquehannah River, thence down said river as it winds and turns to the place of beginning, containing forty two acres, one rood and thirty two rods of Land. Reserving the privilege of passing and repassing on the south side of said Lot with a team or carriage as the case may be or with cattle, by supporting one half of the lane fence when the privilege is used, to the rear of Lot number one hundred and eight so as to get only land belonging to the parties of the first part. Together with all and singular the hereditaments and appurtenances thereunto belonging, or in any wise appertaining, and the reversion and reversions, remainder and remainders, rents, issues and profits thereof; and all the estate, right title, interest, claim and demand whatsoever of the said parties of the first part, either in low or equity, if, in and to the above bargained premises, with the said hereditaments and appurtenances. To have and to hold . . .
(The rest of the deed is the usual legal boilerplate.)

Lois Bunnell appears in the 1820 census: 200000-10010[10] and in the 1830 census: 0001-00001001[10], both in the town of Stanford, Dutchess co, NY. In 1832 she moved to Decatur[14], Otsego co, NY[6], where she remained for two years, then to Fayetteville, Onondaga co, NY[6]. In July 1839 Lois and her daughter Ruth went to Lafayette twp, Walworth co, WI, where her son Alexander had located about two years previously[14]. They immediately took up a claim of 320 acres on Section 20. Half was purchased for Lois and 80 acres each for the sons[6]. After his marriage, son Alexander sold his land in Lafayette twp and bought property in neighboring Spring Prairie twp[6], where Lois appears living with him in the 1840 census[10]. After only three years in Spring Prairie Alexander returned to Lafayette and purchased his mother's 160-acre farm[6]. Lois died 6 September 1850 "at Elkhorn", Walworth co, WI[9], probably at home on the farm with Alexander, whose post office address was Elkhorn[[6].

Children:
    1. 320104. Myron Leete, b. 4 Apr. 1805[11]; m. 29 Aug. 1827 Ann Maria Fish[11].
    2. 320105. Theron Beardsley, b. 11[11] or 12[12] Nov. 1808[11, 12]; m. 15 Mar. 1850
            Catherine Brown[11]' d. bef. 1860[10].
            Children (surname Bunnell):[11]
            1. Frank Albert.

SIXTH GENERATION

3. 320106. Ruth Leete, b. 11 Feb. 1810[11]; m. 5 Jan. 1841 James Fuller[11];
d. 23 Jan. 1843[11].
Children (surname Fuller):[11]
1. Charles.
4. 320107. John Frederick, b. 11[11] or 12[6] Jan. 1813[6,11]; d. in infancy[11].
5. 320108. Alexander Harvey[12] (or Henry[11]), b. 11[11] or 12[6] Jan. 1813[6,11]; m. (first)
24[11] or 29[12] Nov. 1839[11,12] Mary Dyer; m. (second) 27 Apr. 1848
Harriet H. (Newell) Dyer[11].
Children (surname Bunnell)(by first wife):[11]
1. Myron Clark.   2. Charles Dyer.   3. Mary Lucretia.
Children (surname Bunnell)(by second wife):[11]
4. Lois Narcissa.   5. Julia Arvilla.
6. 320109. Salmon Beardsley, b. 10 Dec. 1815[11]; d. 3 Aug. 1837[13].

REFERENCES:

1. Biles Manuscript, p. 224.
2. Probate Record, Noah Bunnell, Sr. Court of Probate, District of New Milford, CT, pp. 57-61.
Photocopy sent to me by Brenda Bunnell Griffen, May 2001.
3. *Families of Early Guilford, CT*, compiled by Alvan Talcott, 1984.
4. *The Ancestors and Descendants of Havilah and Dorcas Gale Bunnell*, by Adele Andrews, 1935.
5. Grantee Index of Deeds, Broome co, NY, Courthouse.
6. *History of Walworth County, Wisconsin*, p. 929.
7. Gravestone, Ouaquaga Cemetery, Broome co, NY, in DAR vol. 72, p. 65.
8. Grantor Deed, Dutchess co, NY, Book 14, pp. 360, 361.
9. Death Notice, *Poughkeepsie Teller*, Dutchess co, NY - Mrs. Lois Bunnell.
10. CB Database - census records, 1810, 1820, 1830, 1840.
11. Duncan, pp. 70, 71.
12. Family Records, compiled by Merrill I. Bunnell.
13. *Burying Grounds of Sharon, Conn., Amenia and North East, NY*, 1903, p. 189.
14. *Leete and Gayle Genealogy*, Dec. 1863, in Ruth Duncan's files, by James Dudley of Poughkeepsie,
NY. from Mr. L. C. Bennett, Ithaca, to the Connecticut Historical Society, where this copy
of manuscript pages 21 - 25 was made.

1-1-6-5-9-4   D102   CB310044

HAVILAH[6] BUNNELL (Noah[5], Gershom[4], Benjamin[3], Benjamin[2], William[1]) was born 18 April 1772[1,3], probably in Litchfield co, CT. He is mentioned in the account of the administration of his father's estate on 1 November 1791 in New Milford, Litchfield co, CT[4]. His share of the estate was a gun, part of a share of cooper's tools, about one half acre of land, and an interest in the house after his mother's death[4]. Havilah and his brother Salmon, on 7 July 1794, deeded property in New Milford in the vicinity of the Quaker settlement[2].

As a young man he settled in Amenia, Dutchess co, NY, where on 7 April 1800 he married DORCAS GALE[2], who was born 9 November 1777[3], in Dutchess co. Adele Andrews concluded on circumstantial evidence that she was probably the daughter of Noah and Phebe (Mead) Gale of Amenia[2]. Havilah appears in the 1800 census in Stanford twp, Dutchess co,

255

NY: 10220-00200[5]. He evidently did not own property there as his name does not appear in the land records of the county[2]. In any case they evidently remained in Dutchess co only a few years before removing to the town of Bainbridge, Chenango co, NY[2]. Their son Salmon was born there in June 1806[2]. An old family record, dated 17 February 1849 gives the following: "Havilah and Dorcas Bunnell were brought to see the great necessity of attending to the concerns of a future state in 1811 and went forward and gave themselves in covenant May 12, 1811, and gave their children baptism 1812." The record does not state where[2].

Havilah Bunnell's name first appears in the land records of Chenango co, NY, 28 June 1814 when he purchased and mortgaged property in Bainbridge[2]. Later records suggest that he operated a sawmill on this property[2] and the Biles Manuscript states that he did so[1]. Biles also explained that the property was in South Bainbridge, which after 1857 became the town of Afton[1]. In 1820 the property was sold at foreclosure sale[2].

The account book of Reuben Kirby of Bainbridge records four transactions with Havilah Bunnell: 26 July 1821, 8 March 1821, 13 April 1822, and 18 March 1823 when Kirby settled with Havilah Bunnell and balanced all accounts "to this date". Both men signed[2]. On 1 May 1823 Havilah bought a part of lot No. 78 in Bainbridge[2]. (In 1839 this property was deeded to Hiram Bunnell by the other heirs[2].)

Havilah Bunnell died 18 September 1823[2], most likely in Bainbridge where he seems to have spent most of his adult life[2]. Although there are some family traditions that he lived for a time in Franklin, Delaware co, and in Windsor, Broome co, NY[2], these are probably confused recollections of his brothers Salmon Beardsley and Sebah. Every record found from 1806 to 1823 calls him "of Bainbridge"[2]. His grave has not been found[2], nor have the graves of his young sons Heman and Noah. I suspect they lie unmarked in an old cemetery in the present town of Afton.

On 1 May 1824 Dorcas Bunnell repurchased the South Bainbridge property which had been lost in 1820[2]. Shortly before 1831 Melancthon B. Jarvis came to Unadilla, Delaware co, NY, from Norwalk, CT. His second wife, Clarissa Jennings, died that year, and some time before 1839 he married the widow Dorcas Bunnell[2]. In 1839 both Melancthon and Dorcas signed a deed with other heirs of Havilah Bunnell, at which time they were of Bainbridge[2].

Dorcas lived the later years of her life with her daughter Betsey Vail in Unadilla[2]. In the New York state census of 1865 she is listed as a member of this family, and Dutchess co, NY, is given as her birthplace[2]. She was buried in the Jarvis lot in the churchyard of St. Matthew's Church in Unadilla. Her gravestone bears the following inscription: "Dorcas/wife of/M. B. Jarvis/ Died Oct. 13, 1865/Ae. 87 yrs./11 mo./4 d.[2]

Children:[2,3]
        1. 320112. Hiram, b. 5 Dec. 1800; m. about 1830 Fidelia Melendy; d. 5 Feb. 1884.
                Children (surname Bunnell):
                1. Salina.   2. George H.   3. Emily.

2. 320113. Malinda, b. 13 May 1802; m. 23 Feb. 1826 Milo Smith; d. 29 Sept. 1878.
   Children (surname Smith):
   1. Emily.   2. Edgar O.
3. 320114. Salina, b. 18 June 1804; m. Hiram Gillette; d. 3 or 8 May 1882.
   Children (surname Gillette):
   1. Edward Augustus. 3. Ellen.   5. Charles H.
   2. Oscar S.   4. Henriette G.
4. 320115. Salmon, b. 30 June 1806; m. 10 Dec. 1829 Flavia Day; d. 11 Dec. 1882.
   Children (surname Bunnell):
   1. Ellen Augusta.   3. Edward Salmon. 5. Ervetus Franklin.
   2. Martha Jane.   4. Augustus Loretto. 6. Rheu Emma.
5. 320116. Heman, b. 22 Mar. 1809; drowned 28 Aug. 1814.
6. 320117. Noah, b. 30 Mar. 1812; drowned 1 June 1818.
7. 320118. Phebe Emmeline, b. 24 Feb. 1814; m. 10 Sept. 1833 Solon P. Hubbell;
   d. 20 Oct. 1865.
   Children (surname Hubbell):
   1. Arthur O.   2. Josephine E.   3. Emma J.
8. 320119. Betsey Caroline, b. 2 Dec. 1815; m. prob. 16 Oct. 1839 Moses B. Vail;
   d. 11 May 1881.
   Children (surname Vail):
   1. Merton W.   3. Orissa T.   4. Elizabeth H.
   2. Eleanor G.
9. 320120. Heman Gale, b. 23 Apr. 1821; m. 20 Sept. 1848 Elizabeth Ann Wetmore;
   d. 26 Oct. 1859.
   Children (surname Bunnell):
   1. Kossuth Eugene.   2. Arthur Howard.

REFERENCES:
1. Biles Manuscript, p. 227.
2. *The Ancestors and Descendants of Havilah and Dorcas Gale Bunnell*, by Adele Adams, 1935.
   Most of this account is based on Miss Adams' excellent work, from which many statements
   have been taken verbatim.
3. *The Connecticut Nutmegger*, Vol. 11, No. 4, March 1979, pp. 592, 593. Family Bible of Salmon
   Bunnell, owned by Miss Adele Adams.
4. Probate Record, Noah Bunnell, Sr., Court of Probate, District of New Milford, CT, pp. 57-61.
   Photocopy sent to me by Brenda Bunnell Griffin, May 2001.

1-1-6-5-9-5 D103 CB310045

SEBAH[6] BUNNELL (Noah[5], Gershom[4], Benjamin[3], Benjamin[2], William[1]) was born 25
February 1774[1] in Fairfield co, CT[1], and was baptized 29 May 1774 in the Congregational
Church in Derby, New Haven co, CT[2]. He inherited one share in his father's estate in 1791,
consisting of "part sett of Coopers tools, 1 half Barrel Cask; 2 old Casks, 1 new Dial, 1 Singing Book/Laws; 4
Cyder Barrels, 2 -3 Barrel Casks, 1 hoe; 1 old Bed tick;
½ an acre of Land Lott No. 6, a part in the house."[3] On 19 September 1799 he married (first)

ELIZABETH WAY of Litchfield co, CT, daughter of Thomas and Zillah (Ford) Way[2]. She was born 6 August 1766 in Waterbury, New Haven co, CT[2]. Sebah was counted in the 1800 census in the town of Chenango, Tioga co, NY: 00000-10010(sic)[4]. Their residence was apparently in that part of the town which later became the town of Windsor, Broome co, NY[1].

About 1890 Sebah's son Nehemiah wrote *A SKETCH of the HISTORY of the RACE of BUNNELLS*, principally a short account of his father's life followed by a longer one on his own career. In 1946 his manuscript was typed and printed, bound together with accounts of the Robinson and Baldwin ancestors of Edwin Franklin Baldwin. The booklet is titled *JOHN ROBINSON AND HIS DESCENDANTS*. Extracts from the Sketch give us the best picture of the life of Sebah and his family:

" . . . Sebah, Noah's fifth child, was born in Fairfield, Connecticut, February 25, 1771[sic, probably a typo]. He became acquainted with Elizabeth Way, who came from Litchfield County about the same time. They were married September 19, 1799, commenced housekeeping in a little settlement near Windsor village. Orpha Ofelia was born August 10, 1800 in Windsor. Lucy M. was born in a little settlement below Windsor called Sugar Creek. Nehemiah was born July 25, 1807, two miles above Windsor Village in the town of Windsor. Levi C. was born in Walton, N.Y., January 29, 1910[sic]. When my father and mother came to Windsor, it was all new. . . . I think that Sanford and Colesville all belonged to Windsor, and that there were but few inhabitants scattered through that country. . . . Jony-cake and venison were their principal diet. The people used to take their rye and corn and row it up the river in a canoe near to Harpursville to get their grinding. . . .

" . . . My father suffered all these privations and disadvantages until after all his children were born in the wilderness as it was. There werre a great many pine trees growing along the river at Windsor at that time. . . . A short time before his youngest daughter was born father got a notion that he could do better down the river, a few miles below Windsor at a little settlement called Sugar Creek. There wasn't much road in those days. Father took his axe and went down to the river and selected a large pine tree. He cut it down, he cut hewed and cut out a canoe eighteen or twenty feet long. He took his goods, his wife and two little girls on board and set sail. He soon landed at Sugar Creek, safe and sound, a little settlement between Windsor and Towanda on the Susquehanna River. I never knew what my father did for a livelihood while there, but he lived there and his third youngest daughter was born May 9, 1805. A short time before his oldest son was born, he left Sugar Creek. He took his goods, his wife, his three little girls, went up the river two miles above Windsor village and there his oldest son was born, July 25, 1807. There my father learned the art of making whiskey out of rye. A short time before his youngest son was born, he took his goods, his wife, his three little girls, and twelve pound baby boy and left Windsor entirely, and went to Walton, Delaware County, N. Y., and there his second and last son was born., January 29, 1810. There my father learned the art of sawing lumber out of pine logs for building purposes. After a turn of time my father took his goods, his wife, his three little girls and two little boys and moved to Franklin, Delaware County, N.Y. There my father learned the art of laying stones into arches for setting boilers into stills for the purpose of making whiskey out of rye. After he had lived in Franklin long enough, he took his goods and his little family and moved to Kortwrite[sic], Delaware County, N. Y., seven miles above Delhi village on the Delaware River to a little place called Bloomville. There he practised what he had learned in Windsor about making whiskey out of rye for six years.

"Father was an industrious man. He was always doing something. He was rather a genius, he could turn his hand to almost any business. After he left the still, he was elected constable. That took his time mostly for one year. . . . Most of the people lived in log houses, had no money nor way to make money. A man worth $2000. was considered rich. A man could get but fifty cents a day, or a bushel of rye for a days work,-- a woman, seventyfive cents a week, a young man, $8 a month by the year. There was no money in the country. Some responsible men issued their three-cent, six-cent, and ten-cent bills. They called them shin-plasters. They passed for money in the vicinity where that man was known. Father had passed through all these pressing times. He had not accumulated anything ahead. His children could not earn much, yet his boys were getting large enough to earn a little, if he was with them. He left Bloomville with his family and stopped at a place called Elk Creek, about five miles northwest from Bloomville. There he taught their winter school. After that he decided to try his hand on a contract for fifty acres of new land. He thought his boys were coming on so they would be able to help him. He bought a possession on a contract for fifty acres of new land, a little log house and two or three acres of land, part of it cleared. The place was one mile and one half north of Meredith Square. My oldest sister was at work in Franklin. She had worked away from home more or less for three or four years. My second sister had worked out some.

"In the spring, father planted some potatoes and corn and half an acre of beans. He had a noble corp of beans, and his corn and potatoes were good. He worked out by the day a good deal of his time. We lived on that place for four years. The next winter he was taken sick with pleurisy. The doctor came and bled him, He lay helpless five or six weeks, and it was a long time before he could do any work. Early in the spring my second sister married a poor man. That did not make it any better for us. During the four years we lived on that place, we raised some of our living on the place, and made some sugar. Father found a quarry of stone on the place that were very nice and smooth. He tried one for a grind stone. We had to go a mile to grind our axes. He selected a stone that was about the right thickness and made a grindstone. He put a shaft through the middle of it and put a crank on each end. He put my brother on one end and me on the other and we ground up a new axe in an hour. That advertised his grindstone business. There were but few grindstones in that region. Grindstones were scarce. Father made a good many grindstones and that helped him a good deal. The landlord was an old tyrant. He though[sic] there was money in the grindstone business, and he ejected father off and he had to leave. Father's constitution was considerably impared[sic] by hard labor and hard fare and his strength began to give way. Now I will leave my father in that little log house with his family, north of Meredith Square, and go back to Franklin, a mile or two south of Franklin village.

"I will mention a few incidents that I recollect while there or a few years afterwards. . . . . I recollect my father and mother leading me over the hill on Sunday morning to the Presbyterian meeting house in Franklin vallage to church. . . . . I recollect when we got to Bloomville we stopped in a little house a little off the road. Father went to work in a whisky still for the storekeeper.. . .

"You might ask where father was all this time. Father was in a whiskey still from daylight until nine o'clock at night. Father and all his brothers and sisters were brought up under the old Presbyterian blue laws, and I don't think any of them departed from them so far as the law was concerned. My father came in at nine o'clock Saturday night. Sunday morning the family were all up on time. Any child that was not wanted to help about breakfast took his bible and sat down to read. And every child had to sit down with his bible and look over after him. Through the day they had to have a good book of some kind and stay in the house, if they did not go to church. There was no church there, except the Methodist. Father did not encouraqge them much to go there. He did not like them much. Every neighbor or neighbor's child new better than to step into his door for a Sunday call.

" . . . I was ten years old that July. Father taught singing school. He gave his pupils both at the singing school and the district school that they need not think that they had come there to play. They must understand that they had come there to learn.

"During all this time, father had not been with his children much in the daytime, so mother had the care of the children mostly. The children were afraid of father. When he said anything to a child, or whipped them, he did it to have it stayed done. Mother could not control her children quite as well, as they would take advantage of her sometimes. She was brought up to hard work. Her father commenced on a new lot, cleared it up, and lived and died on it. Mother worked hard, spinning, weaving, knitting, and she did all she could to help along, and had the children work all they could. My mother was brought up strictly an Episcopalian. Her father belonged to the church of England. She experience religion among the Methodists in Boonville when quite young.

" . . . . Father's constitution was considerably impared by hard labor, and his strength began to give way, but his boys were getting able to do a great deal of hard work. He took up a new lot in the southwest part of the town, or just over the line in the town of Delhi. He built a log house on it and moved in. Father went to work with his boys to chop and clear the land, so as to raise our living, hoping eventually to pay for it and have a home. We cleared some of the land and burned the maple and birch timber into coal, what we could for the Delhi market. We got five dollars for one hundered bushels of coal. We managed to get a horse team and wagon. We worked out some by the day, drew and laid stone wall by the rod. We raised some flax. Mother and my youngest sister used to spin and weave and knit for other people. They made woven flax into pants, frocks, skirts, and sheets. They did anything to make a living. During the time we lived there, we raised crops away from home, . . . cut hay away from home, drew and laid stone wall away from home and worked by the day. I worked by the month nine months one year. During the time we lived there, my oldest sister was sick one whole year. She was not confined to her bed nor to the house all the time. She doctored with a doctor fifteen miles off in Franklin one whole year. She got no help. Then she went to Tom Soman's doctors house. She stayed there a few weeks, came home cured, and had worked enough to pay her doctor's bill whill living there.

"Mother fell down stairs and hurt herself terribly while living there.

". . . . In the fall we left that place and moved on the hill one mile and one half toward West Meredith, and there I was married November 4, 1829. There mother died December 29, 1829. Soon after mother died, my father and sister moved to Masonville. In June, 1829, my oldest sister was married to Wakeman Hull, a widower. He was in comfortable circumstances. My father and sister kept house a while in Masonville. After that we spent some time in Towanda, Pennsylvania". [On 18 December 1838 Sebah Bunnel of the Borough of Towanda, Bradford co, PA, appeared in the Bradford co Court of Common Pleas to sign a deposition to assist his sister Lucy in obtaining a pension based on the Revolutionary War service of her deceased husband Ebenezer Keeler. Sebah gave his age as now 64 years[6].]

"When father first came to Windsor, on going through the woods from one neighborhood to another, a mile or so, he got lost and lay in the woods all night. He froze his feet so badly that his toes had to be taken off both feet, all but two or three. The old doctor . . . that attended him . . . took of his toes. Then father studied medicine with that doctor. After my sister was cured by the Tom Soman doctor, my father turned his attention to that system of practice. He did not practice medicine, but after mother died, he practiced medicine in Masonville, also in Towanda, Pennsylvania, after the Tom Soman system. In 1841, he came back to Brainbridge[sic], Chenango County and married a widow, Collar, in June, 1843. He died in the seventieth year of his life, in the neighborhood of Melody[sic] Hill, and was buried there.

"Now with regards to myself, I shall have to turn back to that little log house north of Meredith Square . . .I was about thirteen years old at that time. I passed through several revivals and after that I left the place north of Meredith Square and went to the neighborhood of Peak's Brook. They had quite a revival there. My youngest sister experienced religion and my mother and sister were baptised and united with the Baptist Church. There my father changed his views and became a believer in the Baptist principles."[1]

Sebah Bunnell appears in the 1810 census in Franklin: 20010-21010[4] and the 1820 census in Meredith: 020010-0101-AG2[4], both in Delaware co, NY. Nehemiah says that his father died in the seventieth year of his life, therefore between his marriage in June 1843 and his 70th birthday on 25 February 1844. His place of burial has not been found. There is an old graveyard on Melendy Hill in what was then South Bainbridge, now the town of Afton, but few of the graves are marked with surviving stones. He may have been buried in the same location as his brother Havilah.

Children:
    1. 320862. Orpha Ofelia, b. 10 Aug. 1800[1]; m. June[1] (or 15 Dec.[5]) 1829[1,5]
                        Wakeman Hull[1,5].

Children (surname Hull):[5]

 1. Julia M.   2. Aaron S.   3. George J.
 2. 320863. Betsey, b. 5 Aug. 1802[1]; m. 25 Mar. 1821 Nathaniel Valentine[1].
         Children (surname Valentine):
         1. Milo[1].   2. Marca.
 3. 320864. Lucy M., b. 9 May 1805[1]; m. Richard Jarvis[1]; d. 1881[1].
         Children (surname Jarvis):[1]
         1. Elizabeth.   2. Lucy Jane.
 4. 320865. Nehemiah Beardsley, b. 25 July 1807[1]; m. 4 Nov. 1829 Luna Baldwin[1];
         d. 10 May 1892[1].
         Children (surname Bunnell):[1]
         1. Sarah Jane.   3. Harriet.   4. Elizabeth M.
         2. Elmer.
 5. 320866. Levi Cramer, b. 29 Jan. 1810[1].

REFERENCES:
   1. Bunnell Sketch, including descendants of Sebah Bunnell compiled by Edwin Franklin Baldwin.
   2. Duncan, p. 72, 73.
   3. Probate Record, Noah Bunnell, Sr., Court of Probate, District of New Milford, CT, pp. 57-61.
         Photocopy sent to me by Brenda Bunnell Griffin, May 2001.
   4. CB Database - census 1800, 1810, 1820.
   5. *Descendants of George Hull*, pp. 68, 69, sent to me by Joan Murray.
   6. From the National Archives, the pension applications of Ebenezer Keeler and his widow Lucy
         (Bunnell) Keeler, including a deposition by her brother Sebah Bunnell, sent to me by Alice D.
         Gedge, Riverton, UT. Sebah's deposition follows in part:

"Personally appeared in open Court in the Court of Common Pleas of Bradford County, the same being a Court of Record Sebah Bunnel of the Borough of Towanda, Bradford Co. aforesaid, who being duly sworn doth depose and say That he is the Brother of Lucy Keeler Wife of the late Ebenezer Keeler, a Revolutionary Soldier who as such drew his Pension for many years previous to his death. That this deponent is now Sixty four years of age and his Sister the said Lucy Keeler was seventy two years of age last March, as this deponent verily believes from the statements made to him by his Father and Mother and from the Records of the ages kept in the Family Bible. That the said Lucy Keeler was married to the said Ebenezer Keeler in New Milford in Connecticut in the year of our Lord one thousand seven hundred and Eighty six as appeared by the Records of their family kept in the Family Bible. . . ."

1-1-6-5-9-6   D36vi   CB310046

ZETHAN[6] BUNNELL (Noah[5], Gershom[4], Benjamin[3], Benjamin[2], William[1]) was born 19 April 1776[1] in Connecticut. He inherited one share in his father's estate in 1791. His share consisted of part of a sett of cooper's tools, two singing books, 3 cider barrels, a rag coverlet, 2 table spoons, etc., plus ½ acre of land, Lot No. 9, and one share in the house after the death of his mother.[2] He married (first) CYNTHIA HUNTINGTON[3], daughter of Daniel and Sybilla Huntington of Woodbury, Litchfield co, CT. She was born 1 April 1774 in Woodbury[4] and died there 24 February 1804, "wife of Zalmon Bunnell, aged 30"[4].

Zethan married (second) 17 February 1805[5], in the Second Church of Christ in Hartford, Hartford co, CT, JERUSHA HUTCHINSON[5,6], daughter of Rev. Elisha and Jerusha (Cadwell) Hutchinson[6]. She was born 24 June 1786 in Pomfret, Windsor co, VT[6]. Their marriage did not last very long. In the Litchfield co, CT, Superior Court records we find: "Jerusha Bunnell of Hartford married Zelhun Bunnell of Hartford in 1803(sic). He abused her and then deserted her. She was granted a divorce in Nov. 1808."[7] She married (second) 6 November 1814 Hon. Titus Brown[6]. She died 25 May 1863 in Francestown, Hillsborough co, NH[6].

I have not found any further record of Zethan Bunnell. Ruth Duncan initially said in her book that Zethan and Jerusha removed to Oakland co, MI. Search there might find trace of him, but I suspect that this statement may represent confusion with the fact that their son Edwin moved to Oakland, Alameda co, CA, in later years and died there.

Children (by second wife):
1. 320400. Edwin Fairbanks, b. 25 Sept. 1807[6]; m. 3 May 1833 Adeline Woodbury[6]; d. 11 Dec. 1891.
    Children (surname Bunnell):
    1. Mary W.   2. child, d. young.   3. George Woodbury.

REFERENCES:
1. Biles Manuscript, p. 224.
2. Probate Record, Noah Bunnell, Sr., Court of Probate, District of New Milford, CT, pp. 57-61. Photocopy sent to me by Brenda Bunnell Griffin, May 2001.
3. *Ancestors and Descendants of Havilah and Dorcas Gale Bunnell*, by Adele Andrews, 1935, p. 61.
4. *History of Ancient Woodbury, CT*, by William Cothren, 1879, reprint 1992 by Heritage Books, Inc., pp. 68, 250.
5. *Families of Early Hartford, CT*, by Lucius Barnes Barbour, pp. 108, 333.
6. Ahnentafel Chart for Edwin Fairbanks Bunnell-Hodgkin.PAF, 15 Jan 1998, sent to me by Christine D. Kraft, 14 Jan. 1998. Citations include, among others, *History of Francestown, NH*, by Cochrane & Wood; *Town Records of Pomfret, VT*, by M. Sawyer; *Pomfret, VT*, by H. H. Vail.
7. Ltr, 1989, from Ruth Duncan with additions and corrections to her book.
8. Duncan, p. 36.
9. CB Database

1-1-6-5-10-1   D37i   CB310053

NATHANIEL[6] BUNNELL (Nathaniel[5], Gershom[4], Benjamin[3], Benjamin[2], William[1]) was born 7 December 1769 at Newtown, Fairfield co, CT[1]. I have found no other reference to this person, unless . . . Is he perhaps the same person as the Nathaniel Bunnell CB004130 who appears in the 1800 census: 00110-00101-00 and in the 1810 census: 01311-10011, both in Albany, Albany co, NY[2]?

REFERENCES:
1. Jacobus, Vol. I, p. 360.
2. CB Database.

1-1-6-5-11-1   D104   CB310201

DANIEL[6] BUNNELL (Isaac[5], Gershom[4], Benjamin[3], Benjamin[2], William[1]) was born in 1772[1,5] in Newtown, Fairfield co, CT[1,5]. He moved with his parents from Connecticut to New Brunswick, Canada, in 1783 after the Revolution. After his father's death in 1791 he had the responsibility for the care and charge of the rest of the family[1]. About 1795 he married (first) _____McLEOD[1], daughter of William McLeod, Sr.[1], and went to live with her on the McLeod grant at Lower Millstream[1]. *Echoes of the Past*, about the Millstream area, says that the first log house at Lower Millstream was built by an Englishman Daniel Bonnell, in 1785 (probably an error for 1795), and was later owned by his great-great grandson, H. C. Coy[6]. It is recorded that the Millstream was much deeper and swifter than now, and it broadened out into a small lake[6]. Mr. Bonnell built his cabin on the shore of the lake and nearby constructed a boat house for the Durham boats that were the first means of transportation in those days[6]. His wife died in childbirth in 1799[1], and their infant son soon followed her[1]. That year, with his mother, he signed the deed selling his father's initial grant in Clifton, NB, to William Frost[6]. Years later, on 27 July 1814, another deed referring to the same property has the signatures of all his brothers and sisters and recites in part, "wheras our said brother Daniel at the time he conveyed the said lot to William Frost had the care and charge of our father's family upon him and did what was in his power toward the support and maintenance of the same and did convert the purchase money for the said lot to our use and benefit."[1,6]

Very soon, before 12 June 1800[1], he married (second) EMMA SPRAGUE[1], daughter of William and Elizabeth Sprague of Sussex, Kings co, NB[1]. She was born about 1776[1,5] at Cherryfield, Washington co, ME[1,5]. Together, on 12 June 1800, they signed the conveyance of the east half of Lots 4 and 5 at Lower Millstream which had come to Daniel with his first marriage[1]. They moved to Penobsquis, in the Parish of SussexVale, Kings co, NB, where he was listed on the assessment of the Parish in 1800[7]. Daniel was a carpenter and millwright[1]. In 1817 he submitted a petition for land in Westmoreland co, NB[7]. In 1823 he was one of the 16 founding members of the United Baptist Church in Penobsquis[4]. He died 16 January 1841[1,2] at the age of 68[1] in Penobsquis. His wife died the same year[1,2] and they were buried in Pioneer Cemetery in Penobsquis, NB[1,2].

Children (by first wife):
    1. 320392. Samuel, b. and d. in 1799[1].

Children (by second wife):
    2. 320062. Crandall, b. about 1803[2]; m. 10 May 1831[6] or 29 Oct. 1829[5] Catherine
              Fitzgerald[1,2]; d. 11 Sept. 1847[1,2].
              Children (surname Bunnell):[6,7]
              1. William Calvin.   4. James C.   7. Daniel.
              2. Mary Ann.   5. Lydia.   8. Crandall J.
              3. Emma (or Amy).   6. John Calvin.
    3. 320110. Daniel, b. about 1806[5,6]; m. (first) 21 Aug. 1832 Emma Graves[3];
              m. (second) 28 Nov. 1858 Anna (Vail) Steward[5].
              Children (surname Bunnell)(by first wife):[5]
              1. Alfred Murray.

4. 320063. Emma, b. 1808[5,6]; m. 26 May 1831 Daniel Goddard[3,5].
   Children (surname Goddard):[6]

1. John Calvin.	5. Mary Ann.	8. Titus.
2. Elizabeth.	6. Daniel Wager.	9. Willard.
3. Catherine.	7. LeBaron.	10. Wealthy.
4. Crandal.		

5. 320111. Elizabeth, b. July 1809[5]; m. 28 July 1831 LeBaron Graves[3,5]; d. 12 Nov. 1859[1,3].
   Children (surname Graves):[6]

1. Elizabeth.	3. Amanda.	5. Helen.
2. John.	4. Mary.	6. William.

6. 320088. Jane, b. about 1815[5]; m. 23 Dec. 1839 Robert Long[1,5].
7. 320121. Lucy, b. about 1811[5]; m. 20 Nov. 1834 John Walters[1,5].
8. 320090. Sarah, b. 1820[5].
9. 320097. Love, b. about 1823[5]; m. 1843[1] John Hall[1,5].

REFERENCES:
1. *Bunnell/Bonnell Newsletter*, Vol. 11, #3, pp. 3,4, 5, 6., article compiled by Betty Andrews Storey.
2. Gravestones of Daniel, Sr., and Crandall Bunnell - photos sent to me by Betty Andrews Storey.
3. King co, NB, vital statistics, collected and sent to me by Carole Bonnell, Spanaway, WA.
4. *The History of the United Baptist Church at Penobsquis*, by Grace McLeod & Phyllis Hall - 1981.
5. Family Group Record - Daniel and Emma (Sprague) Bunnell, compiled by Carole Bonnell, 1 Sept. 1993.
6. Family Group Sheet, David (sic) Daniel Bonnell, compiled by Harold A. Bonnell, 15 June 1991.
7. CB Database.

1-1-6-5-11-5   D106   CB310205

JOHN[6] BONNELL (Isaac[5], Gershom[4], Benjamin[3], Benjamin[2], William[1]) was born in 1779[1] in Newtown, Fairfield co, CT[1]. He removed to New Brunswick, Canada, with his parents in 1783. In 1809 he was granted lot #35 of 400 acres at Millstream, Kings co, NB[1]. He married MARY McLEAN[1] of Sussex, Kings co, NB[1], before 1813. She was born about 1782[1]. some time after the birth of all their children, they removed to Mabou, Inverness co, Cape Breton Island, NS[1]. John died at Mabou in 1831[1] and was buried in the Presbyterian Graveyard at Mabou[1]. After his death, Mary with her six children walked from Mabou, NS, to Sussex, NB, a distance of some 400 miles, to return to the scenes of her earlier years[1]. She appears in the 1851 census as a widow, age 69, living with her son Daniel in Studholm Parish, Sussex, Kings co, NB[3]. She died 23 July 1857, age 75[2], and was buried in Roachville Cemetery, Studholm Parish[2].

Children:
   1. 320188. Ruth, b. 17 Mar. 1813[1]; m. 12 Apr. 1853 Charles Dodd[1]; d. 13 Aug. 1870[1].
      Children (surname Bonnell):
      1. Clarissa, b. 1837[1]; d. 1876[1].

2. 320189. Mary, b. 1815[1]; d. 5 Feb. 1892[1] unmarried[1].

3. 320197. Rachael, b. about 1817[1]; m. 1837 Thomas Tinling[1].
   Children (surname Tinling):[1]
   1. Edward.   4. William.   6. Thomas.
   2. Mary Elizabeth. 5. Amanda.   7. Isaac.
   3. John.

4. 320076. Isaac, b. 1818[1]; m. Martha McLean[1]; d. 8 Jan. 1888[1].
   Children (surname Bonnell):[1]
   1. Mary.   3. John.   5. Albert E.
   2. Olive.   4. Annie.

5. 320208. Sarah, b. 1821[1]; m. 9 May 1840 William Ode Dunfield[1]; d. 1883[1].
   Children (surname Dunfield):
   1. Naomi Lulu.

6. 320077. Daniel, b. 17 Apr. 1822[1]; m. (first) Margaret Eliza McLean[1]; m. (second)
   11 Apr. 1871 Janet T. Tait[1], d. 10 Nov. 1904[1].
   Children (surname Bonnell)(by first wife):[1]
   1. William.   3. Margaret E.   5. Mary M. (Jennie M.)
   2. Frances "Annie". 4. Daniel.
   Children (surname Bonnell)(by second wife):[1]
   6. William.   7. Frederick John.   8. Joseph.

REFERENCES:
1. FGS and bio - John Bonnell, prepared by Harold A. Bonnell, Woodstock, NB, 15 June 1991 and 15 Apr. 1992.
2. Vital Records - census, gravestone and marriage records gathered by Carole Bonnell, Spanaway, WA.
3. CB Database.

1-1-6-5-11-6 D105 CB310204

ISAAC[6] BONNELL (Isaac[5], Gershom[4], Benjamin[3], Benjamin[2], William[1]) was born about 1780[1] in Newtown, Fairfield co, CT[1]. He moved with his parents soon after to New Brunswick, Canada. He was married (first) 11 January 1802[1], in New Brunswick, by Rev. Scovil to SARAH FOWLER[1]. She was born 24 March 1787[1] at Hammond River, Kings co[1], NB, daughter of Weeden and Elizabeth (Sherwood) Fowler[1]. On 11 December 1809 he was granted Lot 10 at Sudholm Millstream, NB, consisting of 190 acres[1]. Four years later he sold the lot to John Slipp[3]. In April 1815 he was granted lot 5 of 305 acres near Collina, NB, and sold it to Leonard Slip the following October[3]. Sarah (Fowler) Bonnell died between 1815 and 1818 at Collina, Kings co, NB[1].

For his second wife Isaac married 24 June 1819 ELIZABETH BLEAKNEY[1,2], who was born in 1801 in Petitcodiac, Albert co, NB[1]. Isaac appears as administrator of the estate of his step-father James Dugan in February 1822[2]. Isaac was baptized by Elder Innis and united with the Baptist Church in Norton, Kings co, NB[1]. He and his wife "Betsy" were two of the eight original organizers of the First Studholm Baptist Church in Collina on 12 June 1840, and Isaac was the first Clerk[1]. They appear in the 1851 census at Moss Glen Studholm, NB[2,3]. He was a millwright[3]. He died 8 June 1860[1], and Elizabeth died 20 March 1875[1], both in Brunswick, Queens co, NB[1].

Children (by first wife):

    1. 320140. Jerusha, b. about 1803[3]; m. 28 Jan. 1822 Jacob Mires[1,2]; d. about 1889[1].

    2. 320065. Elizabeth, b. about 1805[1]; m. 4 June 1822 Joseph Sherwood[1].

    3. 320141. Rebecca, b. about 1808[1]; m. 8 May 1828 John Coy[1]; d. 1890[1].

        Children (surname Coy):[1]

1. Isaac.	5. Eliza J.	9. Asa.
2. Deborah.	6. Joseph Bonnell.	10. Benjamin Jesse.
3. John Bonnell.	7. Alfred.	11. Rebecca.
4. Frances.	8. Amy.	

    4. 320161. *Mary, b. 27 Aug. 1810[1]; m. John McGregor[1]; d. 23 June 1869[1].

        Children (surname McGregor):[1]

1. Sarah Ann.	4. Mary.	7. Lois Parker.
2. Eleanor Jane.	5. Daniel Smith.	8. Eliza Miles.
3. Esther.	6. Isaac Bonnell.	9. Blanche Louise.

    5. 320162. *Margaret, b. 27 Aug. 1810; m. Daniel Bacon.

        Children (surname Bacon):

1. Sarah.	3. John L.	4. William B.
2. Mary L.		

    6. 320165. Sarah Ann "Sally", b. 6 Nov. 1812[1]; m. 20 Feb.[1] or 14 Mar.[2] 1830[1,2] Gabriel Fowler[1,2]; d. 3 Mar. 1884[1].

        Children (surname Fowler):[1]

1. William.	5. Emily A.	9. Isaac W.
2. Samuel O.	6. Wilford D.	10. Newton G.
3. Sarah E.	7. Ammon.	11. John W.
4. Hiram G.	8. Levina V.	12. George F. M.

    7. 320174. Rachel, b. 6 Nov. 1814[1]; m. (first) 1832 Charles Clark[1]; m. (second) Isaac Coy[1]

        Children (surname Clark:[1]

1. Margaret.	5. Sarah.	9. Isaac.
2. Lydia.	6. Maria.	10. Wellington Jackson.
3. Leah.	7. David.	
4. Levi.	8. Harriet.	

Children (by second wife):

    8. 320175. John Sherwood, b. 1824[3] (or 1826[1]); m. 9 May 1846 Mary Ann Brown.

        Children (surname Bonnell):[1]

1. Ruth.	3. Rachael.	5. Hannah.
2. Mary Jane.	4. Charles H.	6. John B.

9. 320068. Isaac Bleakney, b. 1825[1]; m. 9 July 1847 Jemima Fowlie[1]; d. 4 Mar. 1885[1]

      Children (surname Bonnell):[1]

1. Sarah A.	4. Elizabeth.	6. Mary A.
2. Isaac W.	5. George W.	7. Araminta.
3. Eloise.		

10. 320269. Justus (or Justice) Johnston[1], b. 1827[1]; m. 2 June 1848 Mary Jane Chapman[1]; d. 1 Dec. 1854[1].

      Children (surname Bonnell):[1]

1. Henry Allen.	2. Margaret E.	3. Lydia I.

11. 320177. Jemima, b. 1829[1]; bapt. 1848[1]; m. 1 Aug. 1852 James H. Wanamaker[1].

12. 320071. George W., b. 16 June 1833[3]; m. 5 Dec. 1853 Bethia Fowlie[1]; d. 28 Apr. 1902[1].

      Children (surname Bonnell):[1]

1. John Sherwood.

13. 320176. Robiah "Roby", b. about 1834[1]; m. 26 July 1854 Howard D. Gray[1].

      Children (surname Gray):[1]

1. Johnston.	4. Angela Evaline.	6. Jemima.
2. Sarah Elizabeth.	5. Wilford.	7. Minda.
3. Esther Jane.		

14. 320187. David Daniel, b. 1844[1]; m. Mary A. _____ [1].

      Children (surname Bonnell):[1]

1. Newton.	3. Isaac.	5. Mary A.
2. Daniel.	4. Elizabeth.	

NOTE: CB Database includes one more child for the first marriage, Jane 320303, b. 1816, citing IGI records.

NOTE: *Data on these two daughters comes from an early version of the family records compiled by Harold A. Bonnell. In the 1992 version cited in the References, he combines the two as Mary Margaret, showing the marriage to John McGregor and the McGregor children. There is no mention of Daniel Bacon or the Bacon children. CB Database lists one daughter, Mary Margaret, but gives her both marriages, first John McGregor and second Daniel Bacon. However, her gravestone, as quoted by Harold Bonnell makes it clear that she died as the wife of John McGregor.

Harold's decision to combine these two as one may have been influenced by the father Isaac Bonnell's obituary which stated that he had six children by each wife. For this reason Harold suggested that Jemima, by the second wife, may not belong to this family. Whatever the correct situation regarding Mary and Margaret, I believe we should ignore the statement in the obituary.

REFERENCES:

1. FGS and bio - Isaac Bonnell, prepared by Harold A. Bonnell, Woodstock, NB, 15 Apr. 1992.
2. Vital Records - census, gravestone and marriage records gathered by Carole Bonnell, Spanaway, WA.
3. CB Database.

1-1-6-5-11-7   D107   CB310206

JUSTUS[6] BONNELL (Isaac[5], Gershom[4], Benjamin[3], Benjamin[2], William[1]) was born about 1790[1] in Collina, Studholm Parish, Kings co, NB[1]. He was bondsman in February 1822 for the estate of James Dugan[1]. Justus was a farmer. He petitioned for land in Kings co in 1824 and in Queens co in 1832[3]. On 22 July 1838[1] he married MARGARET BAXTER[1,2], daughter of Capt. Simeon Barton Baxter. It has been asserted that she was born in Ireland, about 1795, and immigrated to New Brunswick in 1832[1]. They appear in the 1851 census in Studholm Parish, Kings co, NB[2]. Justus died 7 April 1869 in Collina, NB[1,2]. His widow died there 18 February 1871[1,2]. They were buried in the Kierstead Mountain Cemetery in Collina[2].

Children:
- 1. 320079.   Justus Sherwood, b. 27 July 1839[1]; m. 6 Feb. 1866 Jemima Filinda Kierstead[3]; d. 15 Nov. 1892[1,2].

  Children (surname Bonnell):[1]
  1. Hannah Elizabeth.   3. Adam.   5. Hetty Jemima.
  2. Wilda Ann.   4. Weldon Thomas.   6. Mabel Armintha.

REFERENCES:
1. FGS and bio - Justus Bonnell, prepared by Harold A. Bonnell, Woodstock, NB, 15 Apr. 1992.
2. Vital Records - census, gravestone and marriage records gathered by Carole Bonnell, Spanaway, WA.
3. CB Database.

1-1-6-5-13-3   D39iii   CB310060

STEPHEN[6] BUNNELL (Job[5], Gershom[4], Benjamin[3], Benjamin[2], William[1] was born 22 November 1778 at Newtown, Fairfield co, CT[1]. Sometime after 1790 Stephen accompanied his father in the move to what is now the town of Colesville, Broome co, NY. Until 1806 the county was Tioga, and until 1807 the town was Chenango[6]. In 1807 the town of Windsor was taken from Chenango, and it was not until 1821 that the town of Colesville was set off from Windsor[6]. His son Stephen, Jr., in 1852, said he was born 30 June 1806 in Windsor, NY[4]. Stephen's wife was probably ABIGAIL _____[2], and they must have been married while the area was still known as Tioga co, NY.

Deeds recorded in the Boome co Court House show that he bought land in the town of Chenango in 1813 and sold it in 1832[3]. He appears in the 1820 census in the town of Windsor (Colesville?): 000010-21010-AG[5], and in the 1830 census in the town of Chenango: 01000001-00100001[5]. What is now the city of Binghamton was included in Chenango until 1855[6]. It is likely that Stephen and his family lived in or near Binghamton (then called Chenango Point), since they were members of the First Presbyterian Church there[2]. Sons Byron and Stephen were both married in that church, and the family was dismissed from that church to the Congregational Church in 1834[2]. Stephen, Sr., apparently died before 1840, when his widow appears in the census of the town of Chenango, Broome co, NY: 0001-000020001[5].

Probable Children:[2]
    1. 320793. Byron, b. 1800[5]; m. 2 June 1828 Lucy Lounsbury[2].
        Children (surname Bunnell):[5]
        1. Joseph.   2. Sarah L.
    2. 320794. Stephen, b. 30 June 1806[4]; m. 6 Mar. 1833 Mercia Markham[2].
        Children (surname Bunnell):[5]
        1. Benjamin Moscow.
    3.   Amanda.
    4.   Sophia.

REFERENCES:
    1. New Haven - Jacobus, p. 360.
    2. Records of the First Presbyterian Church, Binghamton, NY.
    3. Broome co, NY, Deed Book 4, p. 64; Mortgage Book 5, p. 270.
    4. *Ohio Records & Pioneer Families*, Quarterly Publication of the Ohio Historical Society, Vol. 21, p. 156.
    5. CB Database.
    6. *Historical and Statistical Gazetteer of New York State*, by J. H. French, Seventh Edition, 1860

1-1-6-5-13-5   D108   CB310061

BRADLEY[6] BUNNELL (Job[5], Gershom[4], Benjamin[3], Benjamin[2], William[1]) was born 26 January 1784 at Newtown, Fairfield co, CT[1]. He married CHARLOTTE HOUGHTON[3], daughter of James Houghton, Jr.[2] She was born in 1785 in Windsor, Windsor co, VT[3]. They removed to New York state, first settling in Homer, Cortland co, NY, where their son Willard was born in 1814[3]. Bradley was farming in Barre, Genesee (now Orleans) co, NY, when he appears there in the 1820 census: 300110-11010[5]. It was here that he obtained a diploma from the Medical Society of Orleans co, NY[5].

Before 24 March 1824 they moved to Rochester, Monroe co, NY, where son Lafayette and daughter Frances were born[5]. Bradley appears there in the 1830 census: WD1-1211001-1001101[5]. In 1832 Dr. Bunnell moved his family to Detroit, Wayne co, MI, then a small French village mostly dependent on fur trading and lumbering[3]. On 5 October 1835 Bradley bought land in Buena Vista twp, Saginaw co, MI[5]. (Did he ever live there?)

In 1850 Bradley appears in the census of Buffalo, Erie co, NY, as a doctor[5]. Four years later his wife Charlotte died in LaCrosse, LaCrosse co, WI[3]. Bradley moved across the Mississippi River to live with his son Willard, at whose home in Homer, Winona co, MN, he died in 1856[3]. He was buried in the Homer Cemetery[3]. Bradley and Charlotte were said to be the parents of twelve children, six of whom lived to maturity[3,4].

Children:
    1. 320660. Charlottte[2,5], b. 1810[5]; m. (first) Dec. 1833 James Smith[5]; m. (second) James Lester Montford[2,5].

2. 320658. Anna Maria[2,5], b. 1812 VT[5]; m. 18 Jan. 1831 Stephen H. Van Rennsselaer[6]
3. 320351. Willard Bradley[2,3,5], b. 1814[3]; m. 20 July 1837 Matilda Desnoyer[2,3,5];
  d. 1861[5].
  Children (surname Bunnell):[2]
  1. David Porter.   4. Frances Matilda.   7. Irene.
  2. John Bradley.   5. Minneowah.   8. Willard Bradley.
  3. Louise Ann.   6. Minnie.
4. 320661. James Lester[5], b. 1817[5].
5. 320352. Lafayette Houghton[2,3,5,7], b. 13 Mar. 1824[7]; m. 24 Aug. 1859 Sarah A.
  Smith[7]; d. 22 July 1903[7]. He was the author of *Discovery of Yosemite*.
6. 320659. Frances Augusta[2,5], b. 1830[5]; m. Peter L. Bowen[5].

Note: The CB Database gives Bradley a middle initial B., but I have not found any
    reference to support it.

REFERENCES:
  1. New Haven - Jacobus, p. 360.
  2. Family Chart - Bradley Bunnell, compiled and sent to me by Claude B. Mitchell, Muskegon, MI..
  3. Bunnell Family data compiled by Ray Bunnell LeMay and sent to me by Willard Walls Bunnell,
      Madison, CT.
  4. *Lafayette Bunnell and the Discovery of Yosemite*, Chapter I, p. 10, page sent to me by Patricia A.
      Bunnell, Canton, MI.
  5. CB Database.
  6. Marriages Copied from Newspapers of New York State, by Nancie Davis, West Columbia, SC.
  7. *The Bunnell/Bonnell Newsletter*, Vol. VII, No. 2, pp. 16-20.

1-1-6-5-13-7   D39viii   CB310037

BILLY[6] BUNNELL (Job[5], Gershom[4], Benjamin[3], Benjamin[2], William[1]) was born 17 June
1789[1,2], probably in Brookfield, Fairfield co, CT[1]. He died 14 February 1810 at Colesville,
Broome co, NY, and was buried there[1].

REFERENCES:
  1. Biles Manuscript, p. 238.
  2. Ltr. 18 October 1961 from James R. Bird, Medford , NJ.

1-1-7-1-2-2   D109   CB310105

HEZEKIAH[6] BUNNELL (Daniel[5], Hezekiah[4], Hezekiah[3], Benjamin[2], William[1]) was born 21
March 1758 at Harwinton,Litchfield co, CT[1]. During the Revolution he enlisted as a private in
the First Company, Second Battalion, Gen. James Wadsworth's State Brigade in 1776[2]. His
uncle Titus Bunnell was ensign in the same company[2]. Hezekiah Bunnel enlisted again for 3

months in Capt. Asa Bray's company, Col. Roger Enos' Regiment in 1778[2]. He married MABEL _____ [3] (Was her maiden name Bunnell?[4] Probably not.)

Hezekiah appears in the 1790 census in Watertown, Litchfield co, CT: 1-0-2-0-0[5]. In 1795 he settled in Plymouth, Litchfield co, CT. He died there 24 November 1797 and was buried in the Old Cemetery at Plymouth Center[3] (Northbury Cemetery at Plymouth). His probate record in Plymouth contains the following: "Dec. 5, 1797, Plymouth. Hezekiah Bunel who lived on a farm of mine was a few days ago accidentally killed, he has left a widow and one child. He possessed no real estate, but left some personal property, and there are some debts to pay. I have thought it would be necessary that Administration should be had on his Estate. The widow is feeble and declines Administer - she wishes the bearer Mr. Daniel Adkins, a friend to the deceased might be appointed Administrator. From my knowledge of Mr. Adkins I believe he will do well. I am your humble servant, David Smith. To the Hon. Joseph W. Hopkins, Esq."[6]

Mabel Bunnell appears in the 1800 census: 00-0101[7] and in the 1810 census: 00-00101[7], both in Plymouth, Litchfield co. I have found no record of her death.

Children:
1. 320031. Orrel, b. 7 July 1787[3]; m. 25 Nov. 1818 Chester Painter[3]; d. 20 Aug. 1819[3].
   Children (surname Bunnell):[3]
   1. Charlotte.
   Children (surname Painter):[6]
   2. Orrel.

REFERENCES:
1. New Haven - Jacobus, p. 366.
2. *The Record of Connecticut Men of the Military and Naval Service During the War of the Revolution 1775-1783*, edited by Henry P. Johnston, pp. 396, 620.
3. Vital Records, Church and Cemetery Records, and Probate Records compiled by Ruth C. Duncan in the Connecticut State Library.
4. *Revolutionary Soldiers Buried in Litchfield County*.
5. *Heads of Families at the first Census of the United States Taken in the 1790 - Connecticut*, p. 76.
6. Duncan, p. 75.
7. CB Database.

1-1-7-1-2-4 D110 CB310107

DANIEL[6] BUNNELL (Daniel[5], Hezekiah[4], Hezekiah[3], Benjamin[2], William[1]) was born 11 April 1763[1] (or 1761[2]) at Harwinton, Litchfield co, CT[1]. On 10 August 1832 he submitted a claim for a pension based on service in the Revolution as follows:

That he entered the service of the United States under the following named officers, and served as herein stated - viz:

1st. In the month of June or July 1776, he enlisted for the term of four months into a copy of state troops commanded by Capt. (name not recollected) of the regiment of Col. ... Mead, went with his party from Farmington to Horseneck and there joined the company, which was there stationed. He served with the company through the term of 4 months and was then verbally discharged. During this tour, he was frequently engaged in skirmishing parties, knew no regular officers at the post.

2nd. In the year 1777, soon after Danbury was burnt, he was drafted for a tour of 3 months into a company of detached militia (officers not recollected) went from Farmington through Danbury to Westpoint, joined a company there, and served 6 or 8 weeks and was there discharged.

3rd. In the month of July 1779 he engaged as a substitute for   Wilson, on a tour of 1 month, went to Horseneck, joined a company commanded by Cap. Amos Barnes of the regiment commanded by Col. Andrew Adams which was stationed there, served one month, and was there discharged.

4th. In the month of March 1782, he enlisted into a company of State troops for the term of 8 or 9 months, commanded by Lieut.   Hubbard of Col. Thomas Grosvenor's regiment - went to Litchfield, Con. and there joined the company, marched thence through New Milford to Westpoint and joined the regiment, was stationed there till the end of the term and was discharged at New Windsor, the latter part of December 1782. On this tour he served about the post most of the time, and was normally employed in boating provisions and stores on the river.   He recollects that there was a large force stationed at and near Westpoint while he was there, that he saw Gen. Washington and many other officers.

In answer to the interrogatories propounded, he says to the
1st. He was born in Harwinton, Litchfield County on the 11th day of April 1761.
2nd. His birth was recorded in the town records of Harwinton.
3d. When called in service he was living in that part of Farmington, now Burlington, lived in New
        Haven about 6 years immediately after the war, and has ever since lived in Burlington.[2]

Daniel married ELIZABETH GILLETT[4]. He appears in the 1790 census: 1-1-2-0-0[3], the 1800 census: 11011-01010[5], both in Bristol, Hartford co, CT, and in the 1810 census: 01101-00101[5], the 1820 census: 000101-00011[5], and the 1830 census: 000001001-000000101[5], all in Burlington, Hartford co, CT. In 1832, living in Burlington, he applied for his Revolutionary War pension, signing his name as "Daniel Bunnel".[2] His application was not approved, because of insufficient information, and additional documents were submitted from time to time. Lemuel Whitman, Judge of Probate, Farmington District, added several personal notes to the documents. On 9 January 1833 he wrote:

> "I have had no previous acquaintance with this applicant, but from inquiry I understand he sustains a fair character for truth and honesty and is quite poor. He appears to be a man of naturally weak intellect and defective memory, and his deafness, infirmities, and other misfortunes seem to have almost destroyed all he ever had. I can have no doubt but that he has been engaged in most of the service he states, perhaps in the whole, and perhaps in more that he has no recollection of. It is very difficult, if not impossible, from any information to be had from him, to ascertain the precise amount of the revolutionary service he has performed, and it must therefore be left to the discretion of the department on the case furnished."[2]

On 1 November 1833 Judge Whitman wrote:

> "I believe it is impracticable to obtain any further or better evidence in support of the service of Daniel Bunnel that has before been transmitted . He will relinquish his claim for a pension for such part of his service as the Department shall think ought not to be allowed. With respect to his service in 1776, though he was then under "the military age" I have no doubt but he performed it. The account he gives of his skirmishes with the tories (who were numerous about Horseneck) and of his boyish adventures with them, though I did not think them of sufficient importance to detail in his declaration, leaves no doubt on my mind, but that he was in the service he stated in his first particular. I hope his claim will receive all the favor it is possibly entitled to."[2]

On 24 September 1834 a letter from the War Department to Judge Whitman brought a final close to the case:

"Sir:

Daniel Bunnel having claimed to have served in Col. Grosvenor's Regt., of State troops, recourse was not in the first instance had to the Continental rolls. There being a field officer of that name, Lt. Col. Grosvenor of Col. Durkee's Regiment of the Continental Army, it was thought possible on the receipt of your letter, that the claimant might have confounded the Continental with the State service. On examination of the rolls of that Regiment, it appears that Daniel Bunnel enlisted into Capt. Warner's Co., to which Lt. Hubbard belonged, on the 20th April, 1782, and deserted on the 7th August following. Having by this offense forfeited all emoluments which might have arisen from his previous service, the rejection of his claim has been confirmed. The papers remain on file."[2]

No record of the deaths of either Daniel or his wife Elizabeth has been found. Daniel was still living on 7 July 1835, when the last reference is made to him in the documents in his pension file.

Children:

1. 320526. Chester, b. about 1791; m. (first) Electa Stone; m. (second) 20 Jan. 1828 Sylvia E. Griswold; d. 2 June 1871, age 80.
Children (surname Bunnell)(by first wife):[4]

| 1. Charles. | 3. Eliza Ann. | 5. Albert. |
| 2. William Perkins. | 4. Charlotte. | 6. Angeline. |

Children (surname Bunnell)(by second wife):[4]

7. Giles Griswold.	10. Mary L.	12. Lucia A.
8. Henrietta Sylvia.	11. Almeron A.	13. Fidelia E.
9. Wales Theodore.		

2. 320528. Daniel, b. about 1799; m. 19 April 1841 Polly Hill; d. 14 Feb. 1860 age 61.

REFERENCES:

1. New Haven - Jacobus, p. 366.
2. Revolutionary War pension application No. 3367, R1432.
3. *Heads of Families at the First Census of the United States Taken in the Year 1790 - Connecticut*, p. 35.
4. Duncan, p. 75.
5. CB Database.

1-1-7-1-2-5   D111   CB310108

LEMUEL L.[6] BUNNELL (Daniel[5], Hezekiah[4], Hezekiah[3], Benjamin[2], William[1]) was born about 1767[1] in Harwinton, Litchfield co, CT. His wife was MARIEL BENHAM[1], who was born 10 January 1765 in Farmington, Hartford co, CT[1]. She was the daughter of Joel and Esther (Andrews) Benham[1]. Lemuel appears in the 1800 census in Bristol, Hartford co, CT: 21010-10100[2]. He died at Burlington, Hartford co, CT, 1 February 1809[1,3] and was buried in the Center Cemetery there[1,3].

Lemuel's probate record in Burlington contains the following: "Probate Office, 16 Feb. 1809.
"Whereas Ebenezer Benham of Burlington in sd. district hath applied to this Court for letters of

Administration on the estate of Lemuel Bunnel late of sd. Burlington decd. & whereas the right of appointment appertains to Maria Bunnel widow of sd. decd. or to Daniel Bunnel of sd. Burlington brother of sd. decd.

"These are therefore to notify the sd. Maria & Daniel to appear before sd. Court of Probate at the office of the Judge of sd. Court in Farmington in sd. district on the 20th day of Feb. instant at two of the clock in the afternoon, if they see cause then & there to show reasons, if any they have, why the sd. appointment should not be made. To any indifferent person to serve & return. Signed: John Treadwell, Judge of sd. Court."

"At a Court of Probate holden at Farmington, on the 12the day of December A.D. 1809 Bliss Hart Esqr. & Ebenezer Benham Adm. on the estate of Lemuel Bunnel late of Burlington decd. having obtained an act to sell real estate of sd. decd. for the payment of the debts charges and allowances to the amount of $666.55 no move that the residue of sd real estate may be distributed according to law.

Whereupon this Court do appoint Col. Abr Pattibone & Misses Chauncy Brooks & Chancey Gagles, all of sd Burlington distributors, they or any two of them to make distribution of sd real estate to the widow & heirs of sd decd as follows: (viz): To Marial Bunnell sd Widow of sd decd the use and improvement of one third part of the whole real estate of sd decd during her natural life, and Joel, Polly, Hezekiah, Thedy, Sibble, children of sd decd to each of them respectively and to their heirs for ever, one equal part or portion of all the real estate of sd decd remaining unsold & make return of their doing to this Court."[1]

Mariel Bunnell survived her husband for many years. She appears in the 1810 census in Burlington, CT: 01100-21001[2], and again in the 1850 census in Burlington living with her son Hezekiah[2]. She died 7 April 1852[1,3] and was buried beside her husband[1,3].

Children:

1. 320694. Joel, b. 5 Feb. 1793[3]; m. 26 Feb. 1818 Fanny Gridley[1,2]; d. 4 July 1876[3].
   Children (surname Bunnell):[1,2]
   1. Warren Gridley. 3. Norris W.   5. Adeline Alice.
   2. Lemuel W.   4. Sheldon L.
2. 320697. Polly.
3. 320695. Hezekiah, b. about 1799[3]; m. 8 Sept. 1829 Amanda Shepard[1,2]; d. 29 Jan. 1881[3].
   Children (surname Bunnell):[1,2]
   1. Marcus.   4. Theda.   7. Charles.
   2. Lyman Benham.   5. Ai.   8. Clarilla.
   3. Seymour.   6. Jennette.
4. 320698. Theda.
5. 320699. Sybil, m. Challings S. Wheeler[4].
   Children (surname Wheeler):[4]
   1. Hiram M.   three others.

REFERENCES:
1. Duncan, pp. 75, 76.
2. CB Database.
3. Burlington Cemetery Inscriptions, copied 29 March 1975.
4. *History of White County, Indiana*, p. 394.

1-1-7-1-2-7   CB310039

MILES[6] BUNNELL (Daniel[5], Hezekiah[4], Hezekiah[3], Benjamin[2], William[1]) was born about 1775 in Connecticut (probably in Bristol, Hartford co). He appears three times in the land records of Bristol[1]. On 3 December 1792 he purchased a share in 25 acres of land from his brother Lemuel, and on 23 October 1793 he sold that share to Solomon Whitman, Jr. On 2 April 1793 he leased land to his brother Daniel. He married AMELIA[4] (MILLY[5]) DOUD, daughter of Amos and Sarah (Norton) Doud[5]. In 1800, when their first child was born, they lived in Danbury[2], (or Waterbury[3]), CT. Soon after, they removed to Luzerne co, PA, and settled near his brothers-in-law Nehemiah Maine and David Doud along the Wyalusing Creek in what is now Jessup twp, Susquehanna co, PA[6,7]. This item from the *Wilkes-Barre Gazette,* Luzerne co, PA, reprinted in *History of Bradford County, PA,* gives some insight into the dangers of pioneer living:

> "Aug. 6, 1802.--At Wyalusing, Mr. Nehemiah Main, accompanied by Mr. Miles Bunnel, went into the wheatfield of the latter, where he espied a huge bear. With his trusty rifle he drew upon the monster and shot him through the thigh, and then advanced to close combat. As soon as within reach the bear raised himself up, and grasping our hero in his paws, threw him upon the ground, bit him through the thigh in three places, and wounded him severely in the arm. After a considerable struggle, with the assistance of Mr. Bunnel, he extricated himself from his adversary, when they returned to the attack with more success, and succeeded in dispatching the bear. Mr. Main, with the assistance of Mr. Bunnel, returned home. He was confined ten days with his wounds."[8]

The 1810 census shows them living in Bridgewater twp, Luzerne (now Susquehanna) co, PA. The census lists one male and one female at age 45 or upwards and two males and two females under ten years of age[9]. Life was hard for Miles and his family. The tax records of Bridgewater twp show that their school taxes were waived from 1813 to 1818 for their first five children because Miles was too poor to pay them[10]. In 1816 50 acres of his land in Bridgewater twp, Susquehanna co, was sold at Sheriff's sale[11]. Before 1820 Miles and his family moved down the Wyalusing Creek to Rush twp, Susquehanna co, PA, where he appears in the 1820 census: two males under 10, one 16 to 18, one 16 to 26, and one over 45; one female under ten, two 10 to 16 and one 26 to 45[9]. The tax records of Rush twp show that Miles was too poor to pay the school taxes for his three youngest children in 1830[10]. That is the last record I have found which refers specifically to Miles Bunnell. The 1830 census of Rush twp lists his son Amos as head of household, but includes a man and a woman between 50 and 60 years old[9]. These might have been Miles and Amelia, but if so it doesn't account for their young children.

On 5 April 1853 Amos' son James Monroe Bunnell wrote a letter to his uncle David M. Bunnell which included: "your mother and father is wal you could expect they ar geting old you now your mother sends hur respects to you and your woman"[12] This would seem to indicate that Miles and Amelia were still living in Rush, if that is the appropriate interpretation. Miles does not appear in the 1840 or 1850 census records. No date or place of death has been found. However, an intriguing notice was published in *The Susquehanna Register, and Northern Farmer*, Montrose, Susquehanna co, Pa, on Thursday, 28 June 1838:

"Poor old Bunnell.--From the following statement given by Noah Wadhams Esq. in the last Wyoming Republican, it would seem that this unfortunate old man has ended his earthly career by being drowned. The description given of the body found, answers so well that there can be no doubt of his identity. Bunnell was an early settler in this vicinity; but for several years past, his family has been broken up and scattered, and he has been a wretched outcast, wandering about in a state of mental derangement, generally carrying a huge pack containing a curious assortment of all the miscellaneous trash he could pick up in the streets or door-yards.

The following is the statement alluded to :--

The subscriber was called on by some of the citizens of Plymouth township, on the 21st day of May last, and informed that a dead body had been found in a gully, on the lower end of Plymouth flats. As it was reported that the Coroner was from home, I proceeded to summon a jury, who, being affirmed, after examining the body, returned a verdict that the deceased came to his death by drowning. He was supposed to have been a man who had been wandering about the country in a deranged state, and who had told the people his name was BUNNELL. He was buried as decently as circumstances would admit, as to appearance he had been dead some time before discovered--probably 12 or 14 days.

June 15, 1838   NOAH WADHAMS, J. P."[13]

I know of no other Bunnell to whom this could apply. If it were not for the line in the letter to David M. Bunnell I would probably assert that Miles Bunnell drowned in the Susquehanna River about the end of May 1838.

Children:

1. 320015. Martin, b. 11 Dec. 1800[3]; m. 22 Apr. 1827 Irena Anna Keator[3]; d. 30 June 1879[2].
            Children (surname Bunnell)[2,3]
            1. infant son, d. y.   5. Charles H.   9. Elvira Lydia.
            2. Sarah A.   6. Abigail Amelia.   10. Elmore D.
            3. Cornelius Keator.   7. George H.   11. Anna A.
            4. Lewis Martin.   8. Andrew Putnam.
2. 320022. Amos, b. 11 Dec. 1803[14]; m. 1827 Amelia Ann Williams[14]; d. 16 Feb. 1899[14].
            Children (surname Bunnell):[14]
            1. James Monroe.   5. David Lorenzo.   8. Sarah A.
            2. child, d. y.   6. Mary Evaline.   9. Silena E.
            3. Laura E.   7. Adaline Celestia. 10. Clarissa Marcelia.
            4. Francis Hamilton.
3.   Abigail, b. about 1806[10]; m. Albert Leonard; d. 9 Apr. 1892 in her 87th year; buried in Rush Center cemetery[15].
4. 320023. Sarah N., b. about 1808[10]; d. 16 May 1846; buried at Lawton, PA[4].
5. 320024. David M., b. about 1815[16]; m. (first) _____ _____[16]; m. (second) Mary Ann Butler[16]; d. 20 Nov. 1895[16].
            Children (surname Bunnell)(by first wife):[16]
            1. Sarah C.

Children (surname Bunnell)(by second wife):[16]

2. Delia.	5. George.	8. Almyra.
3. James.	6. Harriet C.	9. Franklin.
4. John.	7. Elizabeth (Betsy).	

6.   Hezekiah, b. about 1819[10]; m. Margaret L. _____ [17].

Children (surname Bunnell):[17]

1. Charles A.	4. Abigail J.	6. Susanna.
2. Peter S.	5. Martin Luther.	7. Viola.
3. Sarah Maria.		

7.   Hannah, b. about 1820[10].

8.   Rhoda, b. about 1824[10].

REFERENCES:

1. Bristol, CT, land records, sent to me by Ruth C. Duncan, West Simsbury, CT. 16 May 1990.
2. Gravestones in Lyons Street Cemetery, Herrick twp, Susquehanna co, PA.
3. Martin Bunnell Family Bible record.
4. Gravestone of Sarah N. Bunnel, Snyder Cemetery, Lawton, Susquehanna co, PA.
5. *The Descendants of Henry Doude,* by Rev. W. W. Dowd 1885, p. 15.
6. *History of Susquehanna County, Pennsylvania,* by Emily C. Blackman 1873, p. 286.
7. *Centennial History of Susquehanna County, Pennslyvania,* by Rhamanthus M. Stocker 1887, p. 357.
8. *History of Bradford County, Pennsylvania,* published by L. H. Everts & Co. 1878, p. 449.
9. 1810, 1820, 1830 census Susquehanna co, PA.
10. *Journal of Genealogy and Local History* of the Susquehanna County Historical Society. Vol. 10, No. 2, p. 59; Vol. 11, No. 1, pp. 17, 18, Vol. 12, No. 2, p. 28.
11. Sheriff's Deed to Ephraim Fairchild, Jr., Susquehanna County Quarter Session, Vol. 2, p. 97.
12. Letters 5 April 1853 and 2 February 1857 from James Monroe Bunnel to his uncle David M. Bunnell.
13. "Poor old Bunnell" - From *The Susquehanna Register and Northern Farmer,* Montrose, PA, Thursday, 28 June 1838.
14. Amos Bunnell Family Bible record.
15. Gravestone in Rush Center Cemetery, Rush twp, Susquehanna co, PA.
16. Letter 8 Sept. 1987 from Ival E. Paulsen.
17. CB Database.

1-1-7-1-3-1   D112   CB310111

ABEL[6] BUNNELL (Jesse[5], Hezekiah[4], Hezekiah[3], Benjamin[2], William[1]) was born 29 April 1758 at Farmington, Hartford co, CT[1]. He was baptized 9 July 1758 in the Episcopal Church in Bristol, Hartford co, CT[1].

Duncan states that he had a first wife, name unknown, and that they were the parents of one son[2]. He married (second?) 2 October 1784, SILENCE SCOTT in the Congregational Church in Wolcott, New Haven co, CT[3]. They settled before 1790 in Claremont, Cheshire (now Sullivan) co, NY, where he appears in the first Federal census: 1-2-2-0-0[3]. He appears in the census in Claremont, Cheshire co, successively in 1800: 42010-11010[3], 1810: 10301-02101[3], and 1820: 000111-00111-AGR3[3].

Silence (Scott) Bunnell died 15 March 1823 in Claremont at the age of 63[1,4]. She was buried in Old Village Cemetery, Claremont[4], where there daughters Ruth and Sally had been buried earlier[4]. *The History of Claremont, NH*, indicated that they were the parents of 18 children, although there seems to be no reason to accept that as fact.

Before the end of 1823, Abel married (third?) CLARISSA (YORK) DODGE, widow of Ebenezer Dodge[5]. She was mother of 9 or 10 children by her first husband[5]. Her daughter Clarissa became the wife of Abel's son Caleb[5]. Abel appears again in the 1830 census in Claremont, now part of Sullivan co, NH: 0001000001-01000101[3].

Abel died in Claremont 27 September 1847[1,4] and was buried beside his wife Silence in the Old Village Cemetery[4]. Following the record of his gravestone in *Claremont Grave Stone Records*, the compiler, Charles B. Spofford, wrote, "He was known as "Bear" Bunnell, and tradition gives this reason: In the early days of the town he chanced to meet an enormous bear. He had no weapon, but neither had he any notion of retreating; so he threw mud in the animal's eyes until it was blinded, and then killed it with a fence rail."[4]

Before listing Abel's children, I should note that I have found definite evidence for only three of them. Son Philip's son Lyman B. Bunnell wrote to John Biles in 1907 that his father's parents were Abel and Silence (Scott) Bunnell[6]. Two daughters, Ruth and Sally, buried in the Old Village Cemetery, are called specifically daughters of Abel and Silence Bunnell on their grave stones.[4]

Claude Bunnell's Database lists only 5 children: Caleb, Jesse, Clara, Philip and Levi[3].

Duncan, pp. 76 and 77, lists a male child, name unknown, by the first wife, and two children, Jesse and Clara, by Silence Scott[2].

Nona Bassett lists ten children: Abel, Philip, Jesse, Seth, Amasa, Ruth, Sally, (and, she says, "I added") Clara, Caleb and Amanda[7].

The Family Record sent to John Biles by Harriet E. Bunnell, granddaughter of Abel's brother Bela, states that Abel buried two daughters Ruth and Sallie and that his son Abel went to live in Troy, NY, and died there[8].

Lyman B. Bunnell in his letter to John Biles said, "My father had a brother Abel who went to Troy, NY, lived and I suppose died there had two daughters. I know nothing of them. I have a letter at home written to my father from Troy, NY. He had other brothers and sisters I don't know how many. My father often spoke the names of Seth, Amesa, Ruth, Salley. I supposed them to be brothers and sisters. My father' mother's name was Silence Scott. Abel was younger than the others. All this I learned from father not records."[6]

Careful review of the census records does not support inclusion of all these names. My own best estimate of a correct list is as follows:

Children (by first wife):
1. 000001. ?James, b. 7 June 1784; m. Susan _____; d. 23 Mar. 1855.

Children (by second wife):
2.   ?son, b. about 1786-88; d. between 1790 and 1800?
3.   Ruth, b. about 1790[4]; d. 20 Aug. 1822, age 32[4].
4. 320718. Caleb, b. 1792[3]; m. Clarissa Dodge[5].
        Children (surname Bunnell):[3]
        1. Calvert.   4. Charles Alonzo.   7. Evelina.
        2. Luther Wellington. 5. Edward Richmond. 8. William D.
        3. Elovin.   6. Clarissa Jane.   9. Abel.
5. 320717. Jesse, b. 21 Mar. 1794[3]; m. Betsey Hyatt[3]; d. 3 Feb. 1869[3].
        Children (surname Bunnell):[3]
        1. son, d. young. 3. Mary.   5. Judy A.
        2. dau. d. young. 4. Eliza.   6. Fitch H.
6. 320716. ?Clara, b. 1795(1800?)[2,3]; m. _____ McDuffy[2,3].
7. 320719. Philip, b. 23 Oct. 1796[6]; m. (first) 22 Mar. 1828 Mary Ann Leighton[6]; m. (second) 2 May 1832 Mary Worthley[6]; d. 23 July 1893[6].
        Children (surname Bunnell)(by first wife):[6]
        1. Sarah A.   2. Albion Smith.
        Children (surname Bunnell)(by second wife):[6]
        3. Thomas W. or R. 5. Edwin H.   7. Freeman W.
        4. Lyman B.   6. Philip Doodridge.
8.   Sally, b. about 1798[4]; d. 4 Apr. 1818, age 20[4].
9.   Abel, b. about 1802-3[6,8].

REFERENCES:
1. New Haven - Jacobus, p. 366.
2. Duncan, pp. 76, 77.
3. CB Database.
4. *Grave Stone Records from the Ancient Cemeteries in the Town of Claremont, New Hampshire*, by Charles B. Spofford, 1896.
5. *Genealogy of the Dodge Family*, by Joseph T. Dodge, 1898, pp. 527, 528.
6. Ltr., 14 Dec. 1907 from Lyman B. Bunnell, Phillips, ME, to John A. Biles.
7. Ltr., 28 Nov. 1988 from Nona Bassett, Merced, CA.
8. Ltr. 14 Oct. 1907 from Harriet E. Bunnell, Claremont, NH, to John A. Biles.

1-1-7-1-3-3 D113 CB310118

JESSE[6] BUNNELL (Jesse[5], Hezekiah[4], Hezekiah[3], Benjamin[2], William[1]) was born 19 June 1763 at Farmington, Hartford co, CT[1], and was baptized 7 August 1763 in the Bristol, CT, Episcopal Church[1]. He married RHODA _____[2] at least by 1792. Their son Chester was born in CT and baptized 9 June 1793 in St. Matthew's Episcopal Church in East Plymouth, Litchfield co, CT[3]. They moved soon after this to Claremont, Cheshire (now Sullivan) co, NH, where second son Charles was born in 1796[4].

Jesse appears in the 1800 census in Claremont: 21010-20010[2]. This is probably the Jesse Bunnell of Newport (next door to Claremont), Cheshire co, NH, who bought land in Vermont from Benjamin Hinman on 28 June 1802.

Jesse died 24 January 1810 at Claremont at the age of 47[1]. His widow Rhoda appears in the 1810 census in Cheshire: 00000-30010[2]. I find no further record of Rhoda, but I suspect she married again and may well have moved to Otsego co, NY, where her two sons were married.

Children:
- 1. 320878. Chester, bapt. 9 June 1793[1]; m. 22 Feb. 1822 Polly Hyatt[2]; d. 22 Apr. 1864[2].
  Children (surname Bunnell):[2]
  1. Samuel H.
- 2. 320879. Charles Gilbert, b. 12 May 1796[4]; m. 24 Feb. 1816 Mary Brooks[4]; d. 8 May 1876[5].
  Children (surname Bunnell):[4]

1.Charles Gilbert.	6. Amelia.	11. Martha.
2. Jason.	7. Sarah.	12. Sylvia G.
3. Ira.	8. Mary.	13. Elisha Sherman.
4. Jesse.	9. Frances Melvina.	14. William Taylor.
5. Mary.	10. Valentine Brooks.	

- 3. 320880. Sylvia G.[3]
- 4. Mary Amanda, b. 18 Mar. 1807[6]; m. 21 Apr. 1825 Ralph Henry Delong[6]; d. Dec. 1845[6].
  Children (surname DeLong):[6]

1. Edwin Lutheran.	4. Mary Amanda.	7. Anna.
2. Edgar Pitt.	5. William Gilbert.	
3. Henry Peter.	6. Albert.	

REFERENCES:
1. New Haven - Jacobus, p. 366.
2. CB Database.
3. Duncan, p. 77.
4. Family Bible - Charles Gilbert Bunnell, photocopy sent to me by Carolyn Rankin, Madison, WI.
5. Probate Book 5, page 222, Genesee co, NY, extract sent to me by Carolyn Rankin.
6. Family Group Sheet - Ralph Henry DeLong, sent to me by Mary Katherine DeLong.

1-1-7-1-3-4   D114   CB310114

BELA[6] BUNNELL (Jesse[5], Hezekiah[4], Hezekiah[3], Benjamin[2], William[1]) was born 27 August 1765[1] at Farmington, Hartford co, CT[1] and was baptized 20 October 1765 in the Episcopal Church at Bristol, Hartford co, CT[1]. About 1787, at Bristol, CT, he married (first) EUNICE GILBERT[2,3]. She was born about 1767[4]. Bela appears in the 1790 census in Bristol, CT: 2-0-2-0-0[5]. Their first four children were born in Connecticut, but about 1796 they moved to

Claremont, Cheshire (now Sullivan) co, NH, where Bela bought a farm on Green Mountain[2]. The previous owner had begun to clear the land and had built a log house[2]. Bela and his family lived in the log house for a few years before building the frame house which was still standing 100 years later[2], and may be yet.

Bela appears in the 1800 census in Claremont, Cheshire co, NH: 2001-3101[6]. On 10 April 1804 his wife Eunice died in Claremont at the age of 36 years[4], leaving five children, ages 7 to 14. She was buried in the Old Village Cemetery at Claremont[4]. Very soon, Bela married (second) LOIS MATHEWS, daughter of John and Olive (Rice) Mathews[1,7]. She was born 7 September 1783 at Bristol, CT[7]. She and Bela were first cousins, since their mothers were sisters.

Bela was counted in the 1810 census in Claremont, Cheshire co: 1001-1211[6]. He died later that year on 17 November 1810 at Claremont[4] and was buried in the Old Village Cemetery there[4]. His children by his first wife were old enough to be on their own or to help their step-mother. However, his widow was left with 3 small children of her own, with another one on the way. Then Lois herself became sick and died on 11 November 1814 at Claremont[2,7]. Around 1900 Olive Elvina (Bunnell) McDuffee wrote: "My father died Nov. 17, 1810. My mother died Nov. 11, 1814. . . . . . Mother gave me to Uncle John Mathews. I went there to live at the age of six years."[7] Probably similar arrangements were made for the other three young children.

Children (by first wife):
  1. 320885. Beda, b. 16 Oct. 1789[7]; m. Susan Peck[8].
      Children (surname Bunnell):[8]
      1. Lavinus.   3. Climenda.   4. Susan Peck.
      2. Cephas.
  2. 320886. Sheldon, b. 13 Aug. 1791[2,7,9]; m. 22 Nov. 1815[2] Elizabeth Robinson[9];
      d. 12 Dec. 1861[2,9].
      Children (surname Bunnell):[9]
      1. Laura.   4. Levi.   7. George Willis.
      2. Robert Robinson.   5. Warren.   8. Harriet Elizabeth.
      3. Hannah Rich.   6. Charles.
  3. 320888. Milla, b. 19[7] or 12[10] Mar. 1793[7,10]; d. 8 June 1890[7].
  4. 320889. Clara, b. 6 Feb. 1795[7]; m. (first) 31 Jan. 1816 Leman Cowles[7];
      d. 24 Jan. 1884[3].
      Children (surname Cowles):[2]
      1. Albert.   3. Edwin.   5. Tracy.
      2. Sarah.   4. Eunice.
  5. 320887. Polly, b. 3 Feb. 1797[7]; m. Palmer Johnson[2].
      Children (surname Johnson):[2]
      1. Clarissa.   5. Esther.   8. Martha.
      2. Gilbert.   6. Job.   9. Sarah.
      3. Mary.   7. Emma.   10. Eunice.
      4. Amos.

6. 320890. Willis, b. 22 Apr. 1799[4]; d. 6 Sept. 1802[4].

Children (by second wife):
    7. 320891. Eunice, b. 11 Mar. 1805[7]; m. John Mitchell[8]
        Children (surname Mitchell):[7]
        1. Walter.
    8. 320892. George Willis, b. 20 Dec. 1807[7] or 1806[6]; m. Mahala Perkins;
        d. 13[6] or 17[10] Nov. 1870[6,10].
        Children (surname Bunnell):[10]
        1. Nathaniel Perkins. 3. Mary W.   4. Alice Marie.
        2. Orlando Ephraim.
    9. 320893. Olive Elvina, b. 19 May 1809[7]; m. 10 Feb. 1834 Nathaniel McDuffee[7];
        d. 17 July 1902[7].
        Children (surname McDuffee):[7]
        1. Henry Lynn.   4. George.   6. Ellen.
        2. Sarah.   5. Jane (Jennie). 7. Anna.
        3. Charles.
   10. 320029. Bela Vinson, b. 19 June 1811[7]; m. 31[7] or 1[6] Dec. 1837[6,7] Ruth
        McDuffee[6,7]; d. 1 Nov. 1888[7] or 1 Nov. 1882[6].
        Children (surname Bunnell):[6]
        1. Elvira Jane.   2. Gilbert.   3. Zerah.

REFERENCES:
    1. New Haven - Jacobus, pp. 366, 1559.
    2. Ltr. 14 Oct. 1907 Harriet E. Bunnell, Claremont, NH, to John A. Biles.
    3. VT Death Records, Film 324, 1870-1908 - Clara (Bunnell) Cowles, copied by Becky West Rutledge.
    4. *Grave Stone Records from the Ancient Cemeteries in the Town of Claremont, New Hampshire*, by Charles B. Spofford, 1896.
    5. *Heads of Families at the First Census of the United States Taken in the Year 1790 - Connecticut*, page 35.
    6. CB Database.
    7. Ltr. 6 July 1987 from Doris M. Denton, Pleasant, CA.
    8. Biles Manuscript, p. 246.
    9. Ltr. 26 Oct. 1978 from Mrs. James L. Magner, Omaha, NE.
  10. Duncan, pp. 77, 147, 148.

1-1-7-1-3-6 D41vi CB310116

SETH A. (ALVAH?)[6] BUNNELL (Jesse[5], Hezekiah[4], Hezekiah[3], Benjamin[2], William[1]) was baptized 9 December 1770 in the Episcopal Church at Bristol, Hartford co, CT[1]. Seth was mentioned in his father's will dated 7 June 1782 and probated[2] in 1786. On 4 April 1793 he sold land, inherited from his father in Bristol, CT, to his brother Jesse[3]. Like most of his father's family, he removed to Claremont, Sullivan co, NH, where he was a blacksmith[4]. Numerous references to Seth Bunnell in New Hampshire and Vermont have been found, but it is

282

not clear that they all refer to this Seth. However, after extensive study, I believe the following account is reasonable and, barring new data to the contrary, probably accurate[19] .

Seth married (first) 2 April 1799, in Claremont, NH, REBECKAH RICE[5]. A few days earlier, on 27 March 1799, he took the oath as a freeman of the State of Vermont[6]. He seems to have spent most of his life in Derby, Orleans co, VT, on the Canadian border, but may have actually lived in Canada some of the time[4,9]. Deeds show that he purchased land in Vermont on 25 May 1801, 30 November 1801, 29 December 1801, 26 November 1804, 27 July 1805, 9 July 1806, 13 July 1808, and 14 May 1811[7]. He appears in the 1810 census in Derby: 3011-02001[8], apparently still with his first wife. (Was he also the Job Bunnel who appears in the 1800 census there? 10100- 00200-00[8]. I do not find any Job or any other Bunnell that would fit this record.) Rebeckah died, and he married (second) OLIVE ASHLEY, who was born in 1788, daughter of Col. Samuel and Lydia (Doolittle) Ashley[9]. Seth appears in the 1830: 10000001-1210001[8] and 1840 census in Derby: 001000001-00110001[8], with his second wife. He died in Derby 2 March 1841 and was buried in the Derby Center Cemetery[10].

Children (by which wife?):
    1. 320959. Levi D[2].
        Children (probably)(surname Bunnell):
        1. Jennie Sarah.
    2. 320961. Horatio Nelson, b. 1803[15]; m. Sally Ann Chamberlain[15]; d. 1868[15].
        Children (surname Bunnell):[13]

1. Rosalia F.(or B.).	4. Alva.	7. Hannah Rebecca.
2. Orrin Nelson.	5. Laura A.	8. Willie Lucius.
3. Walter Seth.	6. Levi Dexter.	9. Edgar Edward.

    3.   Alvah, b. about 1804[12]; m. 30 Aug. 1846 Catherine McCormick[12]; d. 16 Apr. 1851[12].
    4. 012578. Eli, b. 1811 (or 12 June 1819[12,14]); m. 15 Jan. 1853 Mary Ann Phoebe Caulder[20]; d. 12 Sept. 1883[20].
        Children (surname Bunnell):[14,20]
        1. Alvah Alonzo.   2. Emma Pease.   3. Theodora Augusta.
    5. 320964. Laura[8]; b. about 1813; m. 22 Oct. 1832 Walter Child[8].
    6. 320965. Harriet E., b. 1815-1819 (or about 1808[10]); m. 26 June 1837 Rev. Jesse W. Spencer[120]; d. 24 Oct. 1842[10].
        Children (surname Spencer):[10]
        1. Mary R.
probably others.

Children (by second wife):
    7.   Lucinda, b. 7 Feb. 1825; m. 17 Sept. 1846 Prindle Partridge.
    8. 320960. Lucius Doolittle, b. Dec. 1826[16,17]; m. (first) 4 Dec. 1848 Melinda (or Matilda) Emeline Watts[18]; m. (second) 26 Nov. 1881 Mrs. Alvira Wells[16]; d. 2 June 1910[17].

Children (surname Bunnell)(by first wife):[11,15]

1. Seth Alva.   3. George Henry.   5. Lillie E.
2. Lucius Augustus.   4. Hattie Emma.

perhaps others.

REFERENCES:
1. New Haven - Jacobus, p. 366.
2. Duncan, p. 38, 39.
3. Bristol, CT, Land Records, Vol. 4, p. 18, researched by Ruth C. Duncan.
4. Family records sent to John A. Biles.
5. Marriage record copied in Concord, NH, by Becky Rutledge.
6. *History of Derby, VT*, pp. 34, 35, sent to me by Clifton C. Cilley, Sr.
7. Derby, VT, Land Records researched by Becky Rutledge.
8. CB Database.
9. *Doolittle Family Genealogy,* pp. 271, 172, sent to me by Roxana A. Smith.
10. Copies of photographs of gravestones in the Derby Center Cemetery, from Becky Rutledge.
11. Data sent to me 12 Oct. 1987 by Ruth C. Duncan, citing Roxana A. Smith.
12. Vital Records, Montpelier, VT, researched by Becky Rutledge.
13. Ltrs. 18 May 1992, 15 May 1992, 9 June 1992, Becky Rutledge to Clifton C. Cilley, Sr. - research in Vital Records of Vermont and New Hampshire.
14. Ltr. Nov. 1959 from Mary A. Vann, daughter of Alvah Alonzo Bunnell.
15. Ltr. 25 Feb. 1992 from Clifton C. Cilley, Sr.
16. Certified copy of marriage record of Lucius D. Bunnell, sent to me by Roxana A. Smith.
17. Ltr. 30 June 1931 from Veterans Administration, Bureau of Pensions, to Miss Josephine H. Bunnell, Henniker, NH.
18. Pedigree Chart for Lucius Doolittle Bunnell prepared by Roxana A. Smith, 16 Feb. 1993.
19. Bunnell/Bonnell Newsletter, Vol. VII, No. 4, pp. 46- 50.
20. Record of Bunnell Family From 1819, obtained from Elmer Hall, son-in-law of Alvah Alonzo Bunnell, and sent to me by William B. Bunnell, Concord, NH.

1-1-7-1-3-9   D41viii   CB310118

LEVI[6] BUNNELL (Jesse[5], Hezekiah[4], Hezekiah[3], Benjamin[2], William[1]) was baptized 21 December 1777 at Bristol, Hartford co, CT[1]. He was mentioned as a beneficiary in his father's will dated 7 June 1782[2].

REFERENCES:
1. New Haven - Jacobus, p. 366.
2. Duncan, pp. 38, 39.

1-1-7-1-4-2   D115   CB310121

NATHANIEL[6] BUNNELL (Nathaniel[5], Hezekiah[4], Hezekiah[3], Benjamin[2], William[1]) was born 9 May 1758 at Farmington, Hartford co, CT[1]. He served a few months in the Revolution under his uncle Titus Bunnell. "At the age of 20 he enlisted at New London, CT, in the Continental army and was present 6 September 1781 when Arnold burned the town"[2,5]. He married (first) (Dinah Tubbs?[5], _____ Hart?[5]). He appears in the 1790 census living at Bristol, Hartford co, CT: 1-1-2-0-0[9]. On 17 February 1795 he married (second) RHODA BATES[5,6], whose first husband was _____ Hotchkiss[5,6]. (She had at least one child, a son James, by her first husband[5].) She was born 6 October 1761[5,6]. Nathaniel appears in the 1800 census in Bristol: 11010-31010[10], in the 1810 census in Burlington, Hartford co, CT; 20101-12101[10], and in the 1820 census in Burlington: 010001-21201[10]. According to the land records of the towns of Bristol and Burlington, Nathaniel sold land in Bristol in 1787 and purchased property in Burlington in 1807, 1813 and 1815[4]. He was a farmer[3]. He died 22 August 1828 in Burlington[3]. His widow Rhoda appears in the 1830 census in Burlington living with her son Thomas[10]. By 1840 she was living with her son Allen in Bristol[1], and was still with Allen when the 1850 census was taken in Burlington[10]. She died 29 July 1852[5,6].

Children (by first wife):
    1. 320684. Anna Hart[5,6]; m. Lemuel Wiard[5,6].
        Children (surname Wiard)[11]

1. Albert H.	4. son.	7. child.
2. Alonzo H.	5. Beulah.	8. Laura.
3. Almeron.	6. Lucyann.	

    2. 320013. Russell[5,6,8], b. about 1788[10]; m. Lucinda _____ [10]; d. after 1850[10].
        Children (surname Bunnell):[8,10]

1. daughter.	5. daughter.	9. Reuben.
2. daughter.	6. Thomas James.	10. William.
3. daughter.	7. daughter.	11. Larkin A.
4. daughter.	8. Nancy.	

    3. 320014. Enos, b. 25 May 1792[7]; m. (first) 22 Oct. 1817 Theodotia Upson[7]; m. (second) 24 May 1837 Matilda Moses[3]; d. 12 June 1864[3,7].
        Children (surname Bunnell)(by first wife):[3,7]

1. Fidelia.	4. Almeron A.	7. Allison.
2. Upson.	5. Virgil.	8. Albert Virgil.
3. Julius.	6. Addison.	9. Laura Ann.

        Children (surname Bunnell)(by second wife):[3]
        10. Albert Martin.

Children (by second wife):
    4. 320689. Dinah, b. 12 Dec. 1795[5]; m. (first Charles (or George) Warner[5]; m. (second) Royal Grover[5]; d. 23 Apr. 1875[5].
        Children (surname Grover):[3]
    5. 320690. Laura, b. 24 Mar. 1798[5]; d. 27 Aug. 1828, unmarried[5].
    6. 320691. Phileta, b. 10 Feb. 1800[5]; d. 15 Nov. 1815, unmarried[5].
    7. 320687. Allen, b. 7 Feb. 1802[5,6]; m. 8 Feb. 1826 Rhoda Atwater[6]; d. 20 May 1873[5].
        Children (surname Bunnell):[6,10]

1. Caroline.	4. Susannah.	6. Thomas.
2. Emilie.	5. Rhoda.	7. Sterling.
3. Charles Rollin.		

8. 320692. Susannah, b. 27 Oct. 1804[3]; m. 31 Oct. 1833[3] David B. Clark[3,5];
            d. 16 May 1834[5].

9. 320688. Thomas, b. 9 Nov. 1806[5]; m. (first) 15 May 1829[3] Permelia Bunnell[3,5]
            320216; m. (second) 1 June 1865 Louise Nancy Clements[5]; d. 11 Feb.
            1895[5].
            Children (surname Bunnell)(by first wife):[5]

1. Olive.	4. Allen Thomas.	7. Albert.
2. Rachel Sophronia.	5. Angeline.	8. Susan Jane.
3. Susannah.	6. Romanta A.	

            Children (surname Bunnell)(by second wife):[5]

9. Arthur Clemence.	11. Carrie Mae.	13. Leon Thomas.
10. daughter, stillborn	12. Lura Genevieve.	14. Charles Rupert.

REFERENCES:

1. New Haven - Jacobus, p. 366; and Farmington Vital Records, Barbour Collection, copied and sent to me by Mrs. Clarence Bunnell.
2. Biles Manuscript, p. 251.
3. Duncan, pp. 78, 141, 142, 143.
4. Bristol and Burlington, CT, Land Records, extracted by Ruth C. Duncan.
5. Ltrs. from Mae Bunnell Cook, Terryville, CT, daughter of Thomas 320688, to John A. Biles, 18 Nov. 1909, 24 Nov. 1909, 21 Jan. 1910, 21 Oct. 1910, 29 June 1911.
6. Ltrs. from Charles Rollin Bunnell, Bristol, CT, grandson of Allen 320687, to John A. Biles 11 Nov. 1907, 18 Nov. 1907.
7. Ltrs. from Addison Bunnell, son of Enos 320014, to John A. Biles, 25 Nov. 1907, 9 Dec. 1907.
8. Ltr. from Russel Bunnell 320013 to Allen Bunnell 320687 6 Oct. 1833.
9. Census 1790, Connecticut, p. 35.
10. CB Database.
11. Descendants of Anna Hart Bunnell, compiled and sent to me by Korlean Beardsley, Rockwell, TX, 14 Nov. 2006.

1-1-7-1-5-1   D43vi   CB310130

AMBROSE[6] BUNNELL (Titus[5], Hezekiah[4], Hezekiah[3], Benjamin[2], William[1]) was born 22 March 1765 in Burlington, Hartford co, CT[2]. He married 4 July 1793 ROSANNA WOODRUFF[3]. daughter of Elisha and Ann (Griswold) Woodruff[3]. She was born 19 April 1773 in Farmington, Hartford co, CT[3]. They appear in the 1800 census in Plymouth, Litchfield co, CT: 20010-40010[4]. They removed first to Onondaga co, NY[2], where he appears in the 1810 census in the town of Onondaga: 311110-32210[4]. He was elected overseer of the poor in the town of Onondaga in 1812 and 1813[4]. Later they moved to Mobile, Mobile co, AL[3], or, south, perhaps to North Carolina or Tennessee[2]. Ambrose died in 1817[2], and Rosanna died in 1865[3].

Children:
     1. 320122. Anson[2], b. 1794[4].
     2. 320321. Adna[2], b. 1795[4].

3. 320346. George[2] William[5], b. 1800[4]; d. 26 Dec. 1842[5]; author, newspaper editor and volunteer in the War for Texas independence[5].
4. 320347. Ambrose[2], b. 1803[4]
5. 320348. Asa[2], b. 10 Oct. 1807[4]; m. Lovina Amelia _____ [4]; d. 6 Apr. 1866[4].
   Children (surname Bunnell):[4]

   1. Sarah Jane.   3. Celia Ann.   5. Ruth.
   2. Albert Porter.   4. Alfred Sydney.
6. 320349. Gad W.[2], b. 1812[4]; m. Neoma _____ [4].
   Children (surname Bunnell):[4]

   1. Oscar.   2. Emeline.   3. Elwood
7. 320350. Hartley[2], b. 1818[4].

The census records suggest that there were also several daughters in this family.

REFERENCES:

1. New Haven - Jacobus, p. 366.
2. Biles Manuscript, p. 258.
3. Duncan, p. 40.
4. CB Database.
5. *The Bunnell/Bonnell Newsletter*, Vol. III, No. 3; Vol. VI, No. 1, and Vol. X, No. 2.

1-1-7-1-5-2   D117   CB310128

SOLOMON[6] BUNNELL (Titus[5], Hezekiah[4], Hezekiah[3], Benjamin[2], William[1]) was born 29 December[3] 1766[1,3] at Burlington, Hartford co, CT[3]. In January 1797, at Plymouth, Litchfield co, CT, he married RACHEL HILL[4]. They lived all their lives in Plymouth, where he appears in the 1800 census: 1002- 101[6], the 1810 census: 21010-21010[5], the 1820 census: 220104-32311[6], the 1830 census: 001010001-00001001[6], and the 1840 census: 0000100001-000001001[6]. Solomon died 14 August 1845 at the age of 79[3,4]. His probate record in Plymouth contains the following: "Estate worth $2651.05 part of which was 80 acres of land in Plymouth."[4]. Rachel appears in the 1850 census in Plymouth living with her bachelor son Ambrose. She died 29 March 1852, at the age of 78[3,4]. They were buried together in the Old Cemetery in Plymouth[4].

Children:

1. 320123. Amanda[2], b. 4 Nov. 1797[4]; m. 1 Jan. 1824[4] Nathaniel Bailey[2,4].
   Children (surname Bailey):[2]

   1. son.   2. son.   3. Rose.
2. 320124. Merrit[2], b. 17 Oct. 1799[4]; m. (first) 15 June 1825 Mehitable Clark[4]; m. (second) 1 Jan. 1843 Louise Osborn[4]; d. 7 May 1869[4].
   Children (surname Bunnell)(by first wife):[4]

   1. Lucian Augustus.   2. Mariah Margaret.   3. Henry Martin.
3. 320125. Charrie[2], b. 15 Jan. 1802[4]; d. 24 May 1884[4], unmarried.
4. 320126. Parmelia[2], b. 23 Aug. 1804[3,4]; m. 15 May 1829[4] Thomas Bunnell[2,4] 1-1-7-1-4-2-9, q.v.; d. July 1864[4].

5. 320127. Mansfield[2], b. 18 Nov. 1806[4]; m. 24 Apr. 1833 Sophronia A. Miller[4]; d. after 1880[4,6].
   Children (surname Bunnell):[4]
   1. Florilla S.
6. 320128. Edwin[2], b. 23 Mar. 1810[4]; m. (first) 21 Feb. 1826 Jeanette Lowrey[4]; m. (second) Dec. 1840 Mrs. Caroline (Lowrey)[6] Vose[4]; d. 10 Apr. 1893[4].
   Children (surname Bunnell)(by first wife):[2,4]
   1. Martha Janet.   2. William Edwin.
7. 320129. Solomon[2], b. 14 July 1812[4]; m. 19 Sept. 1836 Helen Wilmot[4]; d. 24 June 1859[4].
   Children (surname Bunnell):[4]
   1. Hubert W.   2. Helen Geraldine.   3. Edwin C.
8. 320130. Margaret[4], b. 9 Jan. 1815[4]. Probably died young. Her nephew did not remember her[2].
9. 320131. Ambrose[2], b. about 1817[4]; d. unmarried[2] 16 Apr. 1868[4].

REFERENCES:
1. New Haven - Jacobus, pp. 366, 511.
2. Ltr. 30 Apr. 1907 from William E. Bunnell, son of Edwin 320128, to John A. Biles.
3. Biles Manuscript, pp. 259, 260.
4. Duncan, pp. 78, 79, 150, 151.
5. Census records copied by Ruth C. Duncan.
6. CB Database.

1-1-7-1-5-4   D116   CB310126

TITUS JEFFERSON[6] BUNNELL (Titus[5], Hezekiah[4], Hezekiah[3], Benjamin[2], William[1]) was born 19 July 1769 at Farmington, Hartford co, CT[1,2]. He married POLLY (or MARY) COOK, daughter of Arba and Mary Cook[3]. She was born 13 May 1782[4] in Connecticut. Their first two children, at least, were born in Plymouth, Litchfield co, CT, and baptized in the Plymouth Congregational Church[5]. He appeared in the 1810 census of Plymouth, CT, as Titus Bunnell, Jr.: 20011-1110[4]. About 1815 they removed to North Carolina. The *Montgomery County, North Carolina, Equity Records* contain the following:

> :Docket of Superior Court 1807-1824. Titus Bunnell was in the clock business with two others, "Bunnell, Tyrell and Langdon" from Oct. 1819 until sometime the first part of March 1821. Titus and the others were into an apparent squabble over the finances of the business. It seems that they had let out more clocks on a credit basis than on a cash basis and when they did take in any money it was not divided equally. Titus bought the two other partnership rights in March 1821 to become the sole owner."[5]

In 1823 they sold land in Plymouth, CT, that Polly (Cook) Bunnell had inherited from her parents. Titus appeared in the 1830 census in Montgomery co, NC: 001100001-1011001[4,7] and in the 1840 census in Montgomery co on the west side of the Yadin and PeeDee rivers[6]: 0001100001-00100001[4,6,7]. They lived in what is now Stanley co, formed in 1841 from

Montgomery co. Deeds of 25 Nov. 1836 and 6 December 1844 for land on "Waters of Mountain Creek" mention Titus Bunnell's corner. Their land was apparently in what is now North Albemarle twp, Stanley co, NC. After undergoing numerous problems related to unpaid bills, he sold the clock business[8].

Titus and his family moved from North Carolina to Hancock co, IL, in 1845[8]. They appear there in the 1850 census living with their daughter and son-in-law Polly and Randal Howell[7]. Polly died 19 February 1851[4] and Titus died 19 August 1856[4]. They were buried at Round Prairie Cemetery in Schuyler co, IL[9].

Children:
    1. 320701. James Canfield, bapt. 14 Dec. 1805[5].
    2.   Mary (Polly), bapt. 26 June 1808[5]; m. Randal Howell[7]
             Children (surname Howell):[7]

1. Juliet.	3. Charlotte.	4. Martha.
2. James C.		

    3.   Madison (?)[10].
    4. 320074. Louis Hart, b.12 June 1822[9]; m. 21 Dec. 1847 Minerva Ellen Bayles[9]; d. 10 Jan. 1898[9].
             Children (surname Bunnell):[9]

1. Horace Taylor.	5. Mary A.	8. Emma E.
2. Sylvester Jefferson.	6. Arby M.	9. Laura S.
3. Jerome B.	7. Elmer Ellsworth.	10. Severn.
4. Louis Whitney.		

    others?

REFERENCES:
    1. New Haven - Jacobus, p. 366.
    2. Vital Records of Farmington, CT, in the Barbour Collection, State Library, Hartford, CT, copied by Mrs. Clarence Bunnell.
    3. Land Records of Plymouth, CT, researched by Ruth E. Duncan.
    4. CB Database.
    5. Duncan, p. 78.
    6. Genealogical notes researched by Marian E. Biles
        1840 census, Montgomery co, NC.
        Deed Book 2, p. 342, Stanley co, NC.
    7. Genealogical notes researched by Bess R. Hubbard.
        1830 and 1840 census, Montgomery co, NC.
        1850 census, Hancock co, IL.
        Deed Book 2, p. 347, Stanley co, NC.
    8. Family record compiled by Mrs. Katharyn Sluder.
    9. Ltrs and Family Group Sheets compiled by Dorothy Hammerlund.
    10. Biles Manuscript, p. 261.

1-1-7-1-5-6 D118   310129

ALLEN[6] BUNNELL (Titus[5], Hezekiah[4], Hezekiah[3], Benjamin[2], William[1]) was born 11 December 1772[1] (or about 1774[census records]) in Farmington, Hartford co, CT[2]. He married (first) in 1800, in Plymouth, Litchfield co, CT, CLARISSA ALVORD[2], daughter of Thomas and Anna (Bow)(Lucas) Alvord[2]. She was born about 1781 in Middletown, Middlesex co, CT[2]. They appear in the 1800 census: 00100- 00100[4,5] and the 1810 census: 00010-30010[5], in Plymouth, Litchfield co. Allen was a captain in the 26th Regiment in the War of 1812[2]. Clarissa died 21 December 1819 in Plymouth at the age of 38[3]. Allen appears as a widower with his children in the Plymouth census in 1820: 100001-11200[4,5]. On 3 October 1822, in Bristol, Hartford co, CT[2], he married (second) SALLY PECK, daughter of Lamant and Sarah Peck[2]. She was born about 1784[2]. They appear in the census record of Plymouth in 1830: 00100001-00001101[4], in 1840: 00000000- 00002001[4], in 1850: Allen at age 76 and Sally at age 66[5], and in 1860 census: Allen at age 86 and Sally at age 87[4,5]. He was a farmer. The land records of Plymouth contain many deeds of transactions by Allen Bunnell between 1815 and 1848[6]. In 1823 he was administrator of the estate of Anna Alvord. He died 20 July 1860 in Plymouth at the age of 87[2]. His widow appears in the 1870 census in Bristol, CT, at age 86 living with James and Sarah Peck[4,5]. She died there 20 March 1874 at the age of 90[2]. Allen and his wives were buried in the Old Cemetery in Plymouth[2].

Allen's will, probated in Plymouth, reads as follows: "I, Allen Bunnell give to my wife, Sally Bunnell, all the property of every kind and nature that she brought with her, at the time of our marriage, and that she has, or may have inherited, or that it may have accumulated since, in any, to be hers.

"I give to my daughter, Harriet Smith, $1000.00.

"I give $200 to my granddaughter, Candace Tuttle; $200 to each of my grandsons: James E. Smith, William W. Bunnell and Watson A. Bunnell. $200 to my daughter-in-law, Harriet Holcomb and $100 to my grandson, Edmund Plumb.

"I give all the rest and residue of my property unto my Executor in trust, to pay over the same, at the decease of my wife (if she survives me, if not, at the end of two years after my decease) to the Treasurer of the American Home Missions Society to be applied to the charitable uses and purposes of said Society and under its direction.

"All my shop tools, farming tools, household furniture, bed and bedding to be appraised and sold to pay my debts, funeral charges, etc.

"Oliver Smith, son-in-law, Executor. Signed: Allan Bunnell. 18 March 1859. Witnesses: Charles L. Grannis, Sheldon H. Tracey and Mary J. Tracey."[2]

Sally declined to accept the legacy and devise of her husband on 18 October 1860[2].

Children (by first wife):
1. 320607. Harriet, b. 31 Jan. 1801[2]; m. Oliver Smith[2]; d. 28 Jan. 1892[2].
    Children (surname Smith):[2]
    1. James E.
2. 320708. Caroline, b. 3 May 1803[2]; m. 14 Aug. 1821 Ebenezer Plumb[2]; d. 1869[2].
    Children (surname Plumb):[2]
    1. Edmund.
3. 320609. Laura (Louise), b. 22 Feb. 1808[2]; d. 11 Mar. 1841[2].
4. 320610. Eliza, b. 28 Dec. 1812[2]; m. 9 Mar. 1851 Albert Carpenter[2].
5. 320611. Allen T., b. 1814[2]; m. Harriet N. Johnson[5]; d. 8 Dec. 1850, age 36[2] "on his passage home from California[7].

Children (surname Bunnell):[2]
1. George E.   3. Lyman J.   4. Watson Allen.
2. William W.

REFERENCES:
1. Biles Manuscript, p. 261.
2. Duncan, pp. 79, 80, 151.
3. New Haven - Jacobus, pp. 366, 511.
4. CT census records, researched by Ruth C. Duncan.
5. CB Database.
6. Plymouth, CT, land records, researched by Ruth C. Duncan.
7. Ltr. 29 June 1911, Mae (Bunnell) Cook, Terryville, CT, to John A. Biles.

1-1-7-1-5-7 D119 CB310131

ASA[6] BUNNELL (Titus[5], Hezekiah[4], Hezekiah[3], Benjamin[2], William[1]) was born 24 May 1776 in Farmington, Hartford co, CT[1]. The land records of Bristol, Hartford co, CT, show that Samuel Gaylord sold land in the 5th Tier of Bristol to Asa Bunnell "of Plymouth," Litchfield co, CT, on 28 December 1804[2]. From the same source we learn that on 2 December 1809 Titus Bunnell, Jr., Asa's brother, recovered judgement against Asa, "late of Plymouth," in the amount of $2928.99[2]. It would be interesting to view the original documents to see what this was about. In any case it suggests that Asa continued to live in Plymouth until he left the area to move south. The 1810 census finds him alone in Laurens co, SC: 00010-00000[3], apparently engaged in farming.

After only a few years he removed to Montgomery co, NC, where he purchased land on the east side of the Pee Dee River. About 1818 or 1819, probably in Montgomery co, he married MARTHA ANN[4] (SMITH?[5]), who was born about 1801 in North Carolina[6]. Asa appears in the 1830 census in Montgomery co, east of the Pee Dee and Yadkin Rivers: 0110101-31001-1[6]. (Montgomery co west of the Pee Dee and Yadkin Rivers, where his brother Titus located, was later set off as Stanly co.) Among the early deeds extant in Montgomery co is one by which Asa Bunnel sold two tracts of land to Samuel Hurley for $100 on 23 October 1837, 1st tract 100 acres on the waters of Uwharrie joining Henry Coltharp and 2nd 40 acres on Spencers Creek joining Hezekiah Tolbert[7]. He appears on the 1840 census in Montgomery co (east side of river): 02010001-003101-0[6]. In the 1850 census of Montgomery co Asa is listed as a farmer on 250 acres with his wife Martha and two sons, Washington, age 17, and Durham, age 14[6].

Asa died in Montgomery co on 4 March 1859[4]. Letters of Administration on his estate were granted to Alexander A. McCaskill, his son-in-law[4]. At the April 1859 term of the Montgomery co Court of Pleas and Quarter Sessions, his widow Martha Ann petitioned the Court to appoint a committee to view the estate and to allot to her sufficient to maintain her and her family for one year[4]. This was done, and at the October 1859 term the committee reported that they had allotted to her one bed and furniture, one wheel and pair of cards and the sum of $35 to be paid to her by the administrator[4]. The date of her death has not been found.

Children:

1. 320741. Thomas, b. June 1820[3]; m. 19 Feb. 1845 Sarah Smith[8,9]; d. Jan. 1902[8].
   Children (surname Bunnell):[8]

1. John M.	4. James Thomas.	7. Sarah C.
2. William M.	5. Terry Catherine.	8. Minerva L.(Lucinda[3])
3. David R.(Daniel Robert[3]).		
	6. Elethia Ellen.	

2. 320742. Stephen P., b. about 1822[3]; m. Sarah P. _____ [3]; d. 1867[3].
   Children (surname Bunnell):[3,5]

1. Rosetta A.	4. Martha.	7. William.
2. Sarah Elizabeth.	5. Laura Jane.	8. Thomas.
3. Mary.	6. John P.	9. Adam.

3. 320743. Martisha, b. 1824[3].
4. 320744. Martha, b. 1826[3]
5. 320746. Rejoicy, b. about 1829; m. 23 Aug. 1844 Alexander A. McCaskill[5,8,9].
   Children (surname McCaskill):[8]

1. Frances M.	4. Malinda.	6. Martin.
2. Archibald.	5. Daniel.	7. John.
3. Laura A.		

6. 320745. Mary Ann, b. 4 Sept. 1830[6]; m. about 1846 John Nixon Talbot[6]; d. 28 Aug. 1909[6].
   Children (surname Talbot):[3,6]

1. Mary Elizabeth.	5. Peter N.	8. Ralph S.
2. John.	6. George Frank.	9. John H.
3. Margaret A.	7. Fannie.	10. Harris G.
4. Stephen Bragg.		

7. 320747. George Washington, b. about 1832[3]; m. 4 Sept. 1851 Winnie Jane Smith[5,9].
   Children (surname Bunnell):[3,10]

1. Martha.	5. Daniel Milton.	9. John A.
2. Sarah E.	6. Lucinda.	10. George Lee.
3. Allen Bragg.	7. Christian.	11. Archibald B.
4. Nancy.	8. Frances F.	

8. 320748. Durham P., b. about 1836[3]; m. Mary A. _____ [3].
   Children (surname Bunnell):[3]

1. Martha C.	2. John W.	3. James Lomas.

REFERENCES:

1. Vital Records of the Town of Farmington, CT - photocopy of birth record sent to me by Bess R. Hubbard, Fuquay-Varina, NC.
2. Bristol, CT, land records, Vol. 9, pp. 89 & 463 - index compiled by Ruth C. Duncan.
3. CB Database.
4. Petition of Martha Ann Bunnell to the Court of Pleas & Quarter Sessions, Montgomery co, NC. Photocopy sent to me by Bess R. Hubbard.
5. Bunnell family records, compiled by Katharyn Sluder, Westminster, MD.
6. 1830, 1840, 1850 census data copied by Bess R. Hubbard.

7. Montgomery co, NC, deeds, extracted by Bess R. Hubbard.
8. Asa & some descendants, compiled by Cylvia Whiteside, copy sent to me by Ruth C. Duncan.
9. IGI-North Carolina, 1988 version.
10. The family of George Washington Bunnell, compiled by his granddaughter Ella (Bunnell) Edge.

1-1-7-2-2-1   D44i   CB310133

JOSEPH[6] BUNNELL (Jacob[5], Deliverance[4], Hezekiah[3], Benjamin[2], William[1]) was born 23 July 1757 at Branford (later North Branford), New Haven co, CT[1]. He served several enlistments as a soldier in the Revolutionary War[2]. He married (first) 8 June 1778 HANNAH BUTLER[3]. She died 6 March 1802 at the age of 43 and was buried in the North Branford Cemetery[4]. In August 1803, at North Branford, he married (second) ABIGAIL PALMER, daughter of John and Elizabeth (Harrison) Palmer, and widow of Hanan Hale[6]. She was born at Branford, 21 October 1762[6]. Joseph appears in the census in Branford in 1810: 00101-10111[5], 1820: 100011-00001-AG[5], and 1830: 0000000001-000000001[5]. Except for the male under 10 years in 1820, the young people included in the 1810 and 1820 census are apparently Abigail's three children by her first husband, Sally, Nabby, and William Hanan Hale. Joseph seems not to have had any children of his own.

Joseph applied for a pension on 7 August 1832. On 26 December 1832 he appeared in court to add to and explain his application. The pension was approved and issued on 21 March 1833 at the rate of $71.66 per annum to commence on 4 March 1831[2]. He died at North Branford 14 January 1837[6] of 1836[4,5]. His widow died there on 7 January 1844[6].

REFERENCES:
1. New Haven - Jacobus, p. 366.
2. Pension application S10403, photocopied and sent to me by Claude A. Bunnell. A major extract follows:

   "On this seventh day of August AD 1832 personally appeared in open court before the Court of Probate for the District of New Haven in Connecticut being a court of record now sitting Joseph Bunnel a resident of North Branford in the county of New Haven and State of Connecticut aged 75 years who being first duly sworn according to law doth on his oath make the following declaration in order to obtain the benefit of the act of Congress passed June 7, 1832 - That he entered the service of the United States under the following named officers and served as herein stated - That in the winter of 1776 he enlisted in the company of Captain Reuben Rose in the Connecticut State Troops as he thinks they were called for three months of which Jared Robinson was Lieutenant, & one Truesdale ensign - that he thinks there was another lieutenant by the name of Potter - that he was marched to New York & on to Long Island - that he with his company were employed in cutting Alders in a swamp for fascines & in building breastworks - that he was Sergeant of the company - that he was reviewed while with the company once by General Thompson & once by Lord Sterling - that he served at that time three months & was discharged before the enemy came to New York.
   That in May 1777 he enlisted for eight months in the company commanded by Captain James Peck in Colonel Roger Eno's regiment in the Connecticut Militia as he thinks - that he thinks Aaron? Bradley was lieutenant & John Francis was Ensign, but he is not confident as to the names of these last mentioned officers - that he was marched in this company through Derby, Newtown & Danbury in the State of Connecticut to Fishkill in the State of New York - that there

Colonel Meigs & Wyllys Regiment joined them - that he was marched up the river to attend the motions of the enemy who were sailing up the river to join Burgoyne - that afterward he was marched down the river again - that he served at this time eight months & was discharged on the first day of January 1778 - that he was Sergeant of this company - that he thinks he recollects that Augustus Barker was Adjutant & Eli Leavenworth Major of Col. Meigs regiment, but will not state positively.

That some time afterward in the winter, but in what year he cannot now recollect, except that it was before the enemy came to New Haven, he was drafted for two months, to serve as a guard on the Shore of Long Island sound, West of New Haven.

that afterward he served as a guard of the row galley New Defence at Branford & New London for one month, which galley was built at Branford & after was taken by the enemy.

that afterwards a short time before Cornwallis was taken, the precise year & month he cannot now recollect, he served for two months as a guard at Stoney creek - that he was Sergeant of the guard there kept.

that he was born in North Branford, then part of the town of Branford, but now made into a separate town - that he was born on the 23^d day of July AD 1757 - that there is no record of his age in existence to his knowledge, that he has always lived in the town in which he was born, both at the times when he entered the service & ever since - that he never received any written discharge from the service - that he has no documentary evidence of any kind - that he is known to the Rev. Matthew Noyes of North Branford, who can testify as to his character for veracity & to his belief of the declarants services as a soldier of the revolution.

. . . .

/s/ Joseph Bunnell"

Rev. Matthew Noyes and Jonathan Munson, both of North Branford, testified to Joseph Bunnell's "undoubted veracity" and reputation as a soldier of the revolution.

Elihu Root and John Potter, both of North Branford, testified that they enlisted at the same time as Joseph Bunnell and confirmed his account of their service.

"On this 26th day of December AD 1832 personally appeared in open court before the Court of Probate . . . Joseph Bunnel a resident of North Branford . . . aged seventy five years. . . . doth on his oath make the following declaration in addition to and explanation of a declaration heretofore made and sworn to by him . . . on the seventh day of August AD 1832 . . .

That in the winter of 1776, he enlisted for three months in the company of Connectictu State troops commanded by Reuben Rose, that Jared Robinson was Lieutenant & one Truesdale ensign of s^d company - that the declarant served as a Non-commissioned officer, viz as a Sergeant, for the full term of three months in this s^d company in the service of the United States; that by reason of old age & the consequent loss of memory, he cannot now recollect the precise time, i.e. either the precise day or month in which he was discharged from service, in s^d company, than those mentioned in s^d declaration, to which this is an addition & explanation, nor the Christian names of s^d Ensign Truesdale & Lieutenant Potter mentioned in s^d former declaration, nor the names of any officers of any other company, or the name of any general officers with whom he served, other than those mentioned in his s^d former declaration, but that he is certain that he served for the full term of three months in s^d Rose's company as a Sergeant, as above stated."

He made the same declaration for his other periods of service and signed again "Joseph Bunnell."

Another former soldier testified to his service, as follows:

"I Abel Hoadley of Branford in the county of New Haven and State of Connecticut being duly sworn depose & say - that I am sixty-eight years of age, that I am well acquainted with Joseph Bunnel who has subscribed & sworn to the foregoing declaration - that near the close of the war of the revolution I was drafted to serve in the Connecticut militia as a guard at Stoney Creek in s^d Branford - that I served in s^d guard to the best of my recollection two months in the fall of the year at s[d] Stoney creek - that s[d] Bunnell was Sergeant of s[d] guard & had the command of it during the two months in which I served - that I recollect no other officer besides s[d] Bunnel there - that I know that s[d] Bunnel served as a Sergeant of s[d] guard - that I saw him daily during s[d] two months acting as Sergeant aforesaid - that I remember sleeping on the floor nights with s[d] Bunnel- that the enemy were in the habit of coming to Thimble Island a few miles opposite Stoney creek in Long Island - that s[d] guard were stationed there to watch s[d] enemy, & were in actual service during the whole of s[d] two months - that s[d] Bunnel & myself were in actual service during the whole of s[d] two months - that by reason of my age & the decay of my memory I cannot swear positively as to the precise year, or month or day in which s[d] service of s[d] Bunnel & myself commenced & ended, but I knew that it was but a short time before the close of s[d] revolutionary war & according to the best of my recollection not less than two months. . . ." signed "Abel Hoadley"

3. CT Marriages - Bailey, Vol. 1, p. 14.
4. Duncan, p. 40.
5. CB Database.
6. Hale, House, p. 147.
7. Census 1790, p. 92.

1-1-7-2-2-3 D120 CB310135

JACOB[6] BUNNELL (Jacob[5], Deliverance[4], Hezekiah[3], Benjamin[2], William[1]) was born 12 December 1761 at Branford, New Haven co, CT[1].

Duncan, p. 80, says that Jacob, b. 12 Dec. 1761, "served as a 2nd. Lt. in the company of 57 volunteers raised for Minute Men Jan. 13, 1777"[2]. On page 40, however, she stated that his father Jacob, b. 6 April 1734, "served as a 2nd Lt. in the company of 57 men who volunteered to be Minute Men in Capt. Samuel Ellis' company of 13 Jan. 1777"[2]. In view of the fact that Jacob, Jr., was barely 15 years old, I conclude that Jacob, Sr., is the person meant. The source of the statement is found on page 613 of Rev. War - CT, listing Minute Men and Volunteers - 1776: "Samuel Eels is accepted captain; Samuel Baldwin 1st Lieut.; and Jacob Bunnell 2[d] Lieut. of a company of 57 Volunteers raised in the town of Branford, Jan. 13, '77"[14].

On the other hand, in the Bunnell cemetery records Ruth Duncan gathered is the burial in Old Northford Cemetery, North Branford, CT, of: "Jacob 2nd Lt. Capt. Ell's Co. Rev. War d 11 Aug. 1802" and "Hannah wife Jacob d. 13 July 1888, age 27 yrs."[7]. If this was actually an inscription on Jacob's gravestone, placed at the time he died, it would have to be given credence, since Jacob, Sr., was still living in the area. I suspect that the statement was added in some way by a descendant years later.

On 28 September 1786, at Northford, New Haven co, CT[1], Jacob was married by Rev. Williams[4] of the Northford Congregational Church, to HANNAH HOTCHKISS[1], daughter of Samuel and Mary (Goodsell) Hotchkiss[1]. She was baptized 1 November 1761 in the Northford

Congregational Church[1]. She died 13 July 1788 at the age of 27[1,7]. Jacob married (second) ROSANNA[5] KIMBERLY[6]. He appears in the 1790 census: 1-1-2-0-0[3] and in the 1800 census: 12011-31011[4] for Brandford, CT.

Between 1788 and 1802 Jacob's name occurs from time to time in the land records of the town of Branford[5]. In 1788 Jacob, Sr., deeded land to him that Jacob, Sr., had inherited from his father Deliverance Bunnell[5]. In 1798 Jacob, Sr., deeded 1/5 part of his lands in North Branford and Northford to each of his sons. They in turn agreed that their parents should live on the land for their natural lives[5]. In 1802 Jacob, Jr., bought 3 acres of land on the Great Hill in Northford from his brother Samuel.

Jacob died at Northford 11 August 1802[1,7], only 40 years old. He was buried in the Old Northford Cemetery with his first wife[7]. Solomon Linsley was appointed administrator of his estate[5]. The probate record notes that the estate was insolvent[8], although there were several parcels of land to be sold. On 23 October 1804 Rosanna Bunnell sold two parcels of her dower of her husband Jacob Jr to his brother Joseph[5]. I have found no further record of Rosanna. She probably remarried, as she had a family of young children to raise.

Children (by first wife):
    1. 320539. Jacob, b. 10 Feb. 1787[9]; m. 13 May 1818 Mary (Polly) Rogers[6]; d. 27 Feb. 1838[9].

        Children (surname Bunnell)[6]:

1. Nancy Woodruff.	3. Emeline.	5. Adaline Augusta.
2. Luzerne.	4. Selina.	6. Cornelia.

Children (by second wife):
    2. 320540. Hannah H., b. about 1789; m. (first) 13 Dec. 1807 Enoch Sears[4]; m. (second) 1813 Lemuel Cook; d. 19 Mar. 1825.
    3.   Sinai[6], m. 10 July 1825 Lemuel Cook[10,11], as his second wife.
    4.   Bill[6].
    5.   Potter[6] (accidentally shot by his own hand[6]).
    6.   Olive[6] Maria[12], admitted to Northford Congregation Church 19 Nov. 1820[12] and dismissed to 1st Church in New Haven in 182-[12]. Was she the Olive Bunnell of Southington, b. 23 June 1805, who married George Fenn of Watertown on 27 Nov. 1828 and who died 21 Oct. 1888 in Meridan at age 84 yrs & 4 mo?[13] Children: John T. & Louisa Fenn[13].

NOTE: It is possible that the last four children were Rosanna's children by a prior marriage, but they (Sinai and Olive at least) seem to have used the surname Bunnell, and the Charles Foote genealogy lists them as children of Jacob and Rosanna.

REFERENCES:
    1. New Haven - Jacobus, pp. 366, 448.
    2. Duncan, pp. 40, 80.

3. Census 1790, p. 92.
4. CB Database.
5. Branford, CT, Land Records, extracted by Ruth C. Duncan.
6. Genealogical Record of Deacon Charles Foote of Northford, CT, (unpublished), extracts sent to Ruth C. Duncan by Wesley F. Patience, Millville, NJ.
7. Connecticut Cemetery Records gathered by Ruth C. Duncan.
8. Connecticut Probate Records at the CT State Library, extracted by Ruth C. Duncan.
9. Hale's Collection of cemetery Records, CT State Library, extracted by Ruth C. Duncan.
10. Newspaper Marriages filed at the CT State Library, extracted by Ruth C. Duncan.
11. Vital Records in the card file at the CT State Library, extracted by Ruth C. Duncan.
12. Church Records at CT State Library, extracted by Ruth C. Duncan.
13. Family and Bible Records at the CT State Library, extracted by Ruth C. Duncan.
14. Rev. War - CT, p. 613.

1-1-7-2-2-5 D121 CB310137

SHERMAN[6] BUNNELL (Jacob[5], Deliverance[4], Hezekiah[3], Benjamin[2], William[1]) was born 3 April 1766 at Branford, New Haven co, CT[1]. Duncan, p. 81, states that his wife's name is unknown[3]. The Biles Manuscript states that his first wife is unknown, but that he married (second) POLLY NORTON[4]. However, the Branford land records make it clear that Sherman's wife was SARAH (SALLY) and that she was probably a sister to Anne Smith who married Sherman's brother Samuel[2]. The indications are thus that she was SARAH SMITH, daughter of Dow and Anne Smith. Vol. 16 of the Branford land records, on page 406, records an 1810 deed whereby Dow Smith gave land to Sherman and Sally Bunnell, Samuel and Anne Bunnell, Rebecca Smith, Daniel P. and Hannah Augur, 24 acres being the land of his first wife Anne Smith[2]. Several deeds of a similar nature to the Smith siblings were recorded in 1804[2]. I have not found any confirmation that there was a second marriage. It seems to be confused with the first marriage of Sherman's nephew Samuel Augustus Bunnell.

Sherman first appears in the Branford land records in 1797 when he bought a ¾ acre lot in the Second Society from Isaac and Thankful Smith[2]. It must have been about this time that he married Sarah. The following year he received a 1/5 share of his father's lands, agreeing to a stipulation that his parents would live on the land for their natural lives[2]. Sherman appears in the 1810 census: 2001-1001[6]; in 1810: 11010-22010[6]; in 1820: 100101-00101-AG2[6]; and in 1830: 000000001-000000001[6], all in Branford, New Haven co, CT, and in 1840 in North Branford (recently set off from Branford): 0000000001-000000001[6].

Sherman and Sally Bunnell, together with Samuel and Anna Bunnell, sold 26 acres in Branford to Isaac Tainter in 1810[2]. In 1813 Sherman sold his 1/5 share of his father's land to his brother Samuel[2]. From time to time other land transactions appear on the Branford records, including a deed of 1825 from Sherman to his son Hezekiah for land in the west part of the Second Society, including the "house where Sherman now lives."[2] "Capt." Sherman died 30 January 1847 in North Branford[5]. The Hale cemetery records include the burial of a Sally Bunnell in the North Branford Cemetery[5]. No date is given, but this may well be the burial of Sherman's wife.

Children:
   1. 320614. John S., b. about 1798[3]; m. (first) 13 Sept. 1820 Mary (Lucy) Pierpont[3];
          m. (second) 2 Aug. 1855 Eunice Keller[3]; d. 25 Feb. 1864[3].
          Children (surname Bunnell)(by first wife):[3]
          1. Mary Ann.   4. William E.   6. George S.
          2. dau., d.y.   5. child, d.y.   7. Lucas Pierpont.
          3. son, d.y.
   2. 320615. Hezekiah, b. about 1802[3]; m. 29 July 1829 Mary Abigail Harrison[3]; d.
          1 Feb. 1849[3].
          Children (surname Bunnell):
          1. Jane.[3]   3. Lemira.[4]   4. Mary Louisa.[3,4]
          2. Grace.[3,4]
   3. 320613. Daniel, b. about 1805[3]; d. 23 Aug. 1808[3].
   4. 320616. Joseph[4], b. about 1812[6]; m. Sylvia L. Markham[4,6].
          Children (surname Bunnell):[6]
          1. Sylvia Elizabeth.   3. Joseph Gilbert.   5. Samuel M.
          2. Mary Sophia.   4. Sherman A.
   5.   Mary[4].
   6.   Jerusha[4].

REFERENCES:
   1. New Haven - Jacobus, p. 366.
   2. Branford, CT, Land Records, extracted by Ruth C. Duncan.
   3. Duncan, pp. 81, 153.
   4. Biles Manuscript, p. 241.
   5. Hale's Collection of Cemetery Records, CT State Library, extracted by Ruth C. Duncan.
   6. CB Database.

1-1-7-2-2-6   D122   CB310138

SAMUEL[6] BUNNELL (Jacob[5], Deliverance[4], Hezekiah[3], Benjamin[2], William[1]) was born at
Branford, New Haven co, CT[1], about 1768[2].
Probably before 1795 he married ANNA SMITH, daughter of Dow and Anna (Linsley) Smith[1].
She was born about 1774 in Branford. Samuel's name is found in the Branford land records in
Volumes 13 to 17, buying or selling property in almost every year from 1797 to 1814[3]. In 1798
his father divided his property among his five sons, each agreeing that his parents would live on
the land during their natural lives[3]. In 1804 and again in 1810 Samuel and Anna shared in the
distribution of land by Dow Smith to his daughters[3].

Samuel appears in the 1800 census: 00010-40010[4], in 1810: 20010-22110[4], and in 1830:
10010001-01011101[4], all in Branford, New Haven co, CT. Anna (Smith) Bunnell died 14
December 1837 at the age of 63[2] (22 December per Northford Church records[2]). By 1840
Samuel had removed to Waterbury, New Haven co, where he appears in the census:
00000000101-0001001-AG[4]. In 1860 he was 91 years old, living with his son Samuel Augustus
in Branford[4]. He lived to be about 94 years old[5], dying in Branford on 8 January 1861[2].

Children:
1. 320585. Susanna[7], b. before 1800[4].
2. 320589. Eunice[7], b. before 1800[4]; m. 25 Dec. 1822 Worcester Cooper[2]; d. age 98[5].
   Children (surname Cooper):[5]
   1. Edward.　　　　2. Eliza Ann.　　　3. Charles H.
3. 320593. Abigail[7], b. before 1800[4]; d. unmarried[7].
4. 320590. Polly[7], b. before 1800[4]; m. 27 May 1826 Lyman Palmer[2].
5. 320594. Alvira[7], m. 25 Aug. 1822 James Benton[6].
6. 320586. Samuel Augustus[7], b. 15 Aug. 1805[2]; m. (first) 6 Nov. 1823 Mary
   Horton[6]; m. (second) Catherine (_____) Kelsey[5]; d. 3 Oct. 1887[5].
   Children (surname Bunnell)(by first wife):[5]
   1. Caroline Elizabeth. 4. Jane Elizabeth.　　7. Sidney Cleveland.
   2. Sarah Ellen.　　　　5. John Dwight.　　　8. Elliott Augustus.
   3. Esther Amelia.　　　6. George Willis.
7. 320588. Frederick[7], b. about 1807; d. 13 July 1856, age 49[2].
8. 320587. Willis S.[7], b. about 1808[2]; m. Sept. 1828 Mary Montgomery[2]; d. 5 April
   1884, aged 76 yrs., 1 mo., and 19 days.
   Children (surname Bunnell):[5]
   1. Jane Louise.　　　　3. Anne Elizabeth.　　5. Edward Russell.
   2. Willis Montgomery 4. Mary Josephine.
9. 320591. Mary[7] Minerva[2], b. 30 Oct. 1810[5]; m. 7 Oct. 1838[2] Seth Bradley[5].
   Children (surname Bradley):[5]
   1. Mary Josephine.　　2. Seth Thomas.
10. 320592. Russell Reynolds[7], b. 19 Aug. 1818[7]; m. 6 June 1841 Alexia Worell
    King[2]; d. about 1900[2].
    Children (surname Bunnell):[7]
    1. child, d.y.　　　　3. Charles Worell.　　5. Alice Elizabeth[2]
    2. William Russell.　4. Josephine Alice.　　6. Frank Smith.

REFERENCES:
1. New Haven - Jacobus, p. 366.
2. Duncan, pp. 81, 154, 155, 156.
3. Branford, CT, Land Records, extracted by Ruth C. Duncan.
4. CB Database.
5. *Genealogical and Family History of the State of Connecticut,* W. R. Cutter et al., editors, 1911,
   Vol. 3, pp. 1576, 1577, 1578.
6. Marriages from Connecticut Newspapers - Town of Waterbury, CT - extracted by Ruth C. Duncan.
7. Genealogical Record of Deacon Charles Foote of Northford, CT, (unpublished), extracts sent to Ruth C.
   Duncan by Wesley F. Patience, Millville, NJ.

1-1-7-2-2-7　D123　CB310139

STEPHEN[6] BUNNELL (Jacob[5], Deliverance[4], Hezekiah[3], Benjamin[2], William[1]) was born about
1776 at Branford, New Haven co, CT[1]. On 2 May 1796, in North Haven, New Haven co, CT[1],
he married (first) PATTY BLAKESLEE[1], daughter of Oliver and Elizabeth (Humiston)

Blakeslee[1]. She was born 26 April 1776 at North Haven, CT[1]. In 1798 Stephen and his brothers each received a 1/5 share of the land owned by their father Jacob in North Branford and Northford, all the sons agreeing that their parents would live on the land for their natural lives[11].

Stephen appears in the 1800 census in Branford: 10100-00100[8]. Before the middle of the decade he seems to have left Branford, since in 1805 Stephen "of Plymouth," Litchfield co, sold his share of his father's lands to his brother Samuel[11]. "Stephen of Plymouth" sold another plot of land in Branford to James Potter in 1807[11]. He didn't remain in Plymouth long - the following year his son Stephen was baptized in Dragon Bridge and died the next day. He was buried in what is now the Fair Haven Cemetery. Stephen appears in the 1810 census in New Haven, New Haven co, CT: 21010-02010[8]. From that time until his death he lived in the section of New Haven first called Dragon Bridge and later Fair Haven. The New Haven land records contain numerous references to his real estate transactions there and to those of his children[12]. He appears in the New Haven census in 1820: 120010-22010-AG1[8], in 1830: 00101001-00100001[8], and in 1840: 000010001-000000001-MFG1-NC1[8].

Patty (Blakeslee) Bunnell died at Fair Haven 9 April 1842[6] and was buried in the Fair Haven Cemetery[6]. On 5 December 1842 Stephen was married (second) by Rev. J. B. Beach of Fair Haven to Mrs. CHLOE EVARTS[8,10]. On 3 December 1843 Chloe was dismissed from the Northford Congregational Church and recommended to the Methodist Episcopal Church in Fair Haven[8].

Stephen died 22 April 1850[6] at Fair Haven and was buried in the cemetery there with his first wife and infant son[6]. His grandson George Bunnell was executor of his estate[8]. Chloe was married again on 13 April 1851 at New Haven, by Rev. J. E. Searles, to Amherst J. Finch of North Haven, New Haven co[8]. She died 9 April 1862 in New Haven at the age of 66[2].

Children (by first wife):
1. 320037. son, b. and d. 24 Mar. 1797[1,8].
2. 320038. Oliver Blakeslee, b. 22 Dec. 1797[1]; m. Elizabeth Grannis[1,13]; d. 29 Oct. 1834[1].
   Children (surname Bunnell):[8]

1. Maria M.	4. Lucius.	6. Mary E.
2. George.	5. Charlotte.	7. Olive.
3. Elizabeth A.		

3. 320039. Olivia Eliza, b. Mar. 1800[2]; d. 8 May 1871 unmarried[2].
4. 320040. daughter, b. and d. April 1801[2].
5. 320041. Lois, b. 29 May 1802[2]; m. 19 Oct. 1821 Anson Grannis[13]; d. 18 July 1887[13].
   Children (surname Grannis):[13]

1. Margaret Louise.	3. Anson Smith.	5. Esther Maria.
2. George S.	4. Smith.	

6. 320042. David L., b. 25 July 1804[2]; m. 16 Mar. 1830 Wealthy Ann Potter[2].
   Children (surname Bunnell):[2]
   1. Selleck J.

7. 320043. Patty, m. 19 Apr. 1826 Ebenezer Alling[2].

8. 320044. Stephen, b. 8 Apr. 1808[2]; bapt. 23 July 1808[7]; d. 24 July 1808[7].

9. 320045. Bela, b. 13 Sept. 1809[2]; bapt. 6 Nov. 1811[2]; m. 7 Dec. 1830 Emily C.
   Jacob[2]; d. 18 Feb. 1848[2].
   Children (surname Bunnell):[2]
   1. Marshall B.   2. Marshall S.

10. 320047. Nancy Elizabeth, b. 1816[8]; bapt. 28 Nov. 1821[8].

11. 320046. Willis, b. about 1819[2]; m. 28 Jan. 1849 Mary L. (Wedmore) Somers[2];
    d. 18 Jan. 1895[2].
    Children (surname Bunnell):[8]
    1. Esther Maria.   2. Willis S.   3. Julia E.

REFERENCES:
1. New Haven - Jacobus, pp. 229, 230, 367.
2. Duncan, pp. 81, 82, 157, 158.
3. New Haven Vital Records, extracted by Ruth C. Duncan.
4. Vital Records in the card file at the CT State Library, extracted by Ruth C. Duncan.
5. Hale's Collection of Cemetery Records extracted by Ruth C. Duncan.
6. CT Cemetery records gathered by Ruth C. Duncan.
7. CT Church Records in the CT State Library, extracted by Ruth C. Duncan.
8. CB Database.
9. Family and Bible records in the CT State Library, extracted by Ruth C. Duncan.
10. CT Newspaper Marriages, extracted by Ruth C. Duncan.
11. Branford, CT, Land Records, extracted by Ruth C. Duncan.
12. New Haven, CT, Land Records, extracted by Ruth C. Duncan.
13. *Descendants of Edward Grannis*, by Frederick A. Strong, 1927, pp. 70, 71, 111, 112.

1-1-9-2-4-2   D124   CB310020

NATHANIEL[6] BUNNELL (Israel[5], Ebenezer[4], Nathaniel[3], Benjamin[2], William[1]) was born 21 January 1775 in the town of Wallingford[1], New Haven co, CT, and was baptized 29 January (or June[3]) 1775[1,4] by Parson John Foote of the Cheshire Congregational Church. On 27[1,4] (or 18[2,3]) 1796[1] in Cheshire he married THANKFUL BRISTOL[1], daughter of Amos and Thankful (Tuttle) Bristol[1]. She was born 11 March 1777 in Wallingford[1] and was baptized 4 May 1777 in the Cheshire church[1].

Nathaniel lived all his life in the town of Cheshire (it was the northwestern part of the town of Wallingford at the time of his birth), where he appears in the census of 1800: 10100-00101[3], of 1810: 11210-00010[3], of 1820: 000201-00010-AG3[3], of 1830: 00000001-00000001[3], of 1840: 110000001-000001[3], and of 1850 when Nathaniel, age 75, and his wife "Mary" (sic) were living by themselves[3]. I presume that an error by a census taker or copyist is responsible for the "Mary", although in his Database Claude Bunnell lists Nathaniel's wife as "Thankful Mary Bristol"[3].

During his long life in Cheshire, Nathaniel was active in the buying and selling of real estate[9,10]. Thankful inherited land from the estate of her father, and they sold 16 acres of it to her brother-in-law Samuel Preston in 1799[10]. Nathaniel received several parcels of land by gift from his father, and more when his father's estate was probated in 1813[9,10]. The Cheshire land records include dozens of deeds reflecting Nathaniel's real estate activity[9,10]. The most unusual is the deed of 1 May 1830 to his newborn grandchild Lambert, son of Amos[10]. This apparently covered Nathaniel's home, since he retained in the deed the use of one-half of the house for the natural lives of himself and his wife[10]. Since the infant was now a property owner, his father Amos was appointed his legal guardian to look after his property.

The 1830 census indicates that Nathaniel and his two sons were farmers. Bishop Lines notebook states that "Mr. Munson says that Nathaniel Bunnell went to Spain to learn the art of Morrocco leather"[9]. John Biles reported that Nathaniel "owned a small farm in Cheshire, and also engaged in manufcaturing shoes in St. Croix, West Indies"[6].

Thankful died 18 June 1856 at Cheshire[8]. Nathaniel died 9 December 1857 at Cheshire[8], and was buried in the Old Hillside cemetery there.

Children:
1. 320557. William, b. 4 Nov. 1798[8]; d. 3 Aug. 1801[4].
2. 320558. William, b. 12 Nov. 1800[8]; m. (first) 18 Oct. 1826 Sally Seeley[5]; m. (second) 5 June 1836 Loiza Lines[5].
   Children (surname Bunnell)(by first wife):
   1. William, d. y.[7]   others?
3. 320559. Amos, b. 30 June 1802[4]; m. 17 Feb. 1828 Laura Russell[4]; d. June 1845[2].
   Children (surname Bunnell):[2]
   1. Lambert.   2. Alfred.   3. Eliza.
4.   child, d. 18 Feb. 1804[4].

REFERENCES:
1. New Haven - Jacobus, pp. 320, 367.
2. Duncan, pp. 82, 158.
3. CB Database.
4. *History of Cheshire, Connecticut, From 1694 to 1840*, by Joseph Perkins Beach, 1912, pp. 343, 435, 448, 471.
5. Waterbury Marriages in *The Connecticut Nutmegger*, Vol. 27, No. 2, p. 264.
6. Biles Manuscript, p. 277.
7. Vital Records in the card file at the CT State Library, extracted by Ruth C. Duncan.
8. Cheshire, CT, Vital Records, extracted by Ruth C. Duncan.
9. Notebook of the Right Reverend Edwin S. Lines, D.D., Protestant Episcopal Bishop of the Diocese of Newark, NJ, copied & sent to me by Judith Bruce, Monument, CO.
10. Cheshire, CT, Land Records, extracted by Ruth C. Duncan.
11. *The Bristol Genealogy*, by Warren Edwin Bristol, 1967, p. 42.

1-1-9-2-4-3   D125   CB310014

RUFUS[6] BUNNELL (Israel[5], Ebenezer[4], Nathaniel[3], Benjamin[2], William[1]) was born 19 March 1777 in the town of Wallingford, New Haven co, CT[1,3], and was baptized 4 May of that year in the Congregational Church at Cheshire, New Haven co, CT[1,4]. At 20 years old, in 1797, Rufus graduated from Yale College in New Haven[6]. He began the study of medicine[5], but did not complete it. Instead, about 1799, he moved to Meredith, Delaware co, NY, to set up a mercantile partnership with Samuel A. Law[5,6]. He appears in the 1800 census in Meredith: 002-0[10]. In 1802 he joined a new militia company in Meredith as ensign, and served as lieutenant in 1804 in Erastus Root's regiment[6]. On 4 March 1804, in the United Congregational Church in Bridgeport, Fairfield co, CT[10], he married DIANTHA FITCH[3], daughter of Abner and Elizabeth (Root) Fitch[3]. She was born 18 February 1778[3] at Coventry, Tolland co, CT[6].

In 1806 Rufus resigned from his militia regiment[6]. He and his partner Samuel Law moved to Delhi and Kortright, Delaware co, NY, where they added the manufacture of potash and pearlash, along with lumbering for the Philadelphia market to their previous business[5,6,10]. Rufus appears in the 1810 census in Kortright: 3001-0001[10]. Later that year the partners removed to Philadelphia, PA, and opened a lumber yard at 9th and Cherry Streets[5,6,10]. They did well until the war broke out and a nation-wide depression ruined many businesses. Their business still appears in the Philadelphia directory in 1814[10], but that year they found it necessary to dissolve their partnership[5]. Rufus seems to have returned to Delaware co, since the land records of Cheshire co, CT, show that Rufus "of Deleware" sold land he inherited from his father to his brothers Nathaniel and Ebenezer in 1815[11].

About the year 1816 Rufus moved his family to New York City and entered into partnership with Joseph D. Beers in the money-exchange and brokerage business[5]. The business was expanded into the south, and in 1823 Rufus took charge of the branch office in Charleston, SC. He remained in that position until the spring of 1825, although he was experiencing deteriorating health. Hoping to improve his condition he and his wife sailed for England, but he rapidly became worse and his wife brought him home immediately. He died in a hospital in Cambridge, MA, on 11 June 1826[3,5]. He was buried in Mountain Grove Cemetery in Bridgeport, CT[2]. He left an estate estimated at $200,000 to $300,000[10].

His widow Diantha appears in the 1830 census in New York City: 00003-0000201[10]. In New York she was a member of the Brick Church[10]. She removed to Bridgeport, Fairfield co, CT, where in 1835 she was admitted to the United Congregational Church[10]. A Diantha F. Bunnell was married on 24 October 1842 to Edward Foster at the New Haven Trinity Protestant Episcopal Church. The CB Database believes this to be the widow of Rufus[10], but it appears that she was the daughter of Rufus's brother Jairus, q.v. I note, however, that the widow Diantha Bunnell appears in the 1850 census living with her son William Rufus Bunnell in Bridgeport[10]. She died 16 June 1858 at the age of 80 in Bridgeport and was buried with Rufus in the Mountain Grove Cemetery there[2]. Her will, probated in Bridgeport, reads as follows:

"I, Diantha Bunnell, widow of Rufus Bunnell, decd give to Cornelia S. Bunnell, wife of my son William R., as a token of my regard and esteem, and as some compensation for the many attentions and services rendered by her to me in health and sickness, all the silver plate I die possessed of and being the family plate of my deceased husband and myself.

"I give to Sarah Matilda Bunnell, wife of my son Thomas F., my two parlor pier glasses now in her possession in Trenton, N. J.

"I give to Sarah Matilda and Cornelia S. Bunnell, all my wearing apparel and to said Cornelia S. Bunnell such household furniture, beds that are now in her possession.

"I give to my son William R. Bunnell those two certain two-story houses and lots on which the same stand, known as 291 and 293 situated in South Sixth St. In Jersey City, N.J., in trust for the following uses and purposes, viz: to pay out of the rents, income and profit thereof, the interest on the mortgage of said property and to pay the balance of such rents, income and profits annually to my son James F. Bunnell during his natural life for his sole and separate use. And I do further direct that if my sons William R. & T. F. and J. F. Shall unanimously agree in writing to any division of property, then the above trust shall cease and determine? and the several portions so agreed on shall several belong to the said William R., T. F. and J. F. Bunnell. And if no such division is made, then on the death of James F. Bunnell, I give said property to William R. and T. F. Bunnell.

"I give all the rest and residue of my estate, real or personal, of any kind and nature and whereever situated to my said children William R., T. F. and J. F. Bunnell, in equal one third portions. I appoint William R. Bunnell, Administrator on the estate of Rufus Bunnell dec.

"I appoint William R. Bunnell and Sherwood Sterling, Executors. Signed: Diantha Bunnell. 26 May 1858. Witnesses: E. W. Fairchild, E. W. Chapin and Wm. K. Lesley."[5]

Children:

1. 320157. George, b. 1805[3]; d. 1806[10].
2. 320158. William Rufus, b. 6 Mar. 1806[3]; m. (first) 6 June 1837 Sarah Haight[3]; m. (second) 28 Jan. 1836 Cornelia Sterling[3]; d. 6 Nov. 1872[2].
   Children (by first wife)(surname Bunnell):[3]
   1. Diantha Fitch.   2. Rufus William.
   Children (by second wife)(surname Bunnell):[5,10]
   3. David Sterling.   6. Julia Haight.   9. Henry.
   4. Sarah.   7. Katharine Sterling. 10. John Sterling.
   5. James Sterling.   8. Anna Strong.   11. Cordelia Waterman.
3. 320159. James Fitch, b. 27 Mar. 1807[3].
4. 320160. Thomas Fitch, b. 29 Nov. 1808[3]; m. Sarah Matilda McCoy[9]; d. 10 Aug. 1888[9].
   Children (surname Bunnell):[5,9]
   1. Cora McCoy.   2. Isaac McCoy.   3. Frances McCoy.

REFERENCES:

1. New Haven - Jacobus, p. 367.
2. Mountain Grove Cemetery, Bridgeport, CT, records gathered by Ruth C. Duncan.
3. Ltr. 11 Mar. 1871 from William Rufus Bunnell to Henry Jackson Bunnell.
4. *History of Cheshire, Connecticut, From 1694 to 1840*, by Joseph Perkins Beach, 1912, p. 349.
5. Duncan, pp. 82, 83, 84, 158, 159, 160, including the following extract from *Yale College Biographical Sketches* on pp. 82 and 83:
"After graduation, Rufus began the study of medicine; but soon after the year 1800 was persuaded by his former fellow townsman, Samuel A. Law to settle in Meredith, N.Y. where he engaged in business. In 1806 they removed to Delhi, N. Y.and there, and in the town next above it, Kortright, in addition to his previous business, engaged in

the manufacture of pot and pearl ashes, and in lumbering on the Delaware River for the market of Philadelphia, in partnership with his wife's second brother, Dr. Thomas Fitch.

"In 1810 the partners removed to Philadelphia, and opened a lumber yard, which they managed with profit until the spring of 1812. Business being then seriously impaired by the state of the country, the partnership was dissolved. At the close of the war, in 1815, Mr. Bunnell removed to New York City and entered into partnership with Joseph D. Beers, in the money-exchange and brokerage business. This business they extended to the principal places in the south, connecting with it the factorage of cotton, and also dealing in that article on their own account. In 1823 he took personal charge of the branch office in Charleston, South Carolina and continued there until the spring of 1825, when he sailed for England, in the hope of benefiting his health which was generally delicate and was then more impaired than usual. Before sailing he had risked a large amount on the probable advance of the price of cotton, and on finding in England that prices had fallen greatly, the impending loss so affected him in his feeble state of health that he became insane. His wife brought him home immediately, but he did not rally and he died suddenly, from an attack of cholera morbus, in a hospital in Cambridge, Massachusetts on 11 June 1826 in his 50th year."

6. Biles Manuscript, p. 277'.
7. Notebook of the Right Reverend Edwin S. Lines, D.D., Protestant Episcopal Bishop of the Diocese of Newark, NJ, copied & sent to me by Judith Bruce, Monument, CO.
8. *Root Genealogical Records, 1600-1870*, by James P. Root, 1870, pp. 187, 188.
9. *Genealogy of the Norris Family*, p. 196.
10. CB Database.
11. Cheshire, CT, Land Records, extracted by Ruth C. Duncan.
12. Bridgeport, CT, Land Records, extracted by Ruth C. Duncan.

1-1-9-2-4-6   D126   CB310023

VIRGIL[6] BUNNELL (Israel[5], Ebenezer[4], Nathaniel[3], Benjamin[2], William[1]) was born 21 September 1784[1], in Cheshire, New Haven co, CT, and was baptized 7 November 1784[2,3] by Parson John Foot[3] of the Cheshire Congregational Church. As a young man he removed from Cheshire to Delaware co, NY, where he resided for the remainder of his life. On 18 May 1811 he married FRANCES (FANNY) BLISH[1], daughter of Capt. Aaron and Roxie (Webster) Blish[1,4] of Harpersfield, Delaware co, NY. She was born 21 November 1793 in Connecticut[1].

In Delaware co Virgil settled first in Delhi for several years. In 1812 he served as lieutenant in the 87th militia in Delaware co[1], and in 1815 was promoted to captain[1]. That year, while still in Delhi, he sold several pieces of his property in Cheshire, CT[5]. In 1816[1] he moved to Stamford in the same county. The Cheshire land records in 1817 show other transactions by "Virgil Bunnell of Stamford, NY," selling his property there[5]. He appears in the census of Stamford in 1820: 100110-11010-AG[6] and in 1830: 0110101-110101[6.] They were still living in Stamford in 1837 when he sold (probably the last of) his property in Cheshire to his sister Jerusha (Bunnell) Brandin.

Before 1850 they moved again to the town of Kortright, in Delaware co, where, like his brother Rufus, he conducted a mercantile business. The local history refers to him among other early prominent citizens of the village of Bloomville in Kortright twp as "Virgil Bunnell and son George, the latter being a man of particularly fine presence and a successful merchant, doing business in the store now occupied by M. F. Allison"[7]. Virgil appears in the 1850 census in Kortright[6] at age 65, a merchant, with wife Frances, age 48(sic), children Roxy age 35, George age 32 merchant, and Frances age 22[8]. 20-year-old James Smith was also a member of his household[8].

Virgil died 19 October 1859 in Delhi[1], and was buried there[9]. Letters of administration on his estate were granted to his sons-in-law John G. Webster and James A. Rich - recorded 7 January 1860[10]. His widow Frances, age 67, appears in the 1860 census living with her daughter Roxcy Rich in Stamford, Delaware co[6].

Children:
- 1. 320652. Jane Ann, b. 12 Dec. 1812[1]; m. 9 June 1835 Matthew Bryce[1].
  Children (surname Bryce):[1]
  - 1. Frances Jeanette.
  - 2. George Oscar.
  - 3. Willis Bunnell.
  - 4. Washington.
  - 5. Roxce Ann.
  - 6. Flora Marianda.
- 2. 320654. George, b. 19 July 1817[1]; d. 14 Jan. 1854[1].
- 3. 320653. Roxce Blish, b. 10 Nov. 1821[1]; m. James A. Rich[1].
  Children (surname Rich):[1]
  - 1. Mary.
  - 2. Fanny.
  - 3. Virgil Bunnell.
  - 4. Thomas.
  - 5. George Bunnell.
  - 6. James.
  - 7. Ella Jane.
- 4. 320656. Frances A.[1] (or C.[11]), b. 5 Feb.[1] (or 19 Dec.[11]) 1830[1,11]; m. 24 Aug. 1857[10] John Griffin Webster[1,10]; d. 1869[1] (or 28 Feb. 1870[11]).
  perhaps others.

REFERENCES:
1. Biles Manuscript, pp. 280, 281.
2. New Haven - Jacobus, p. 367.
3. *History of Cheshire, Connecticut, From 1694 to 1840*, by Joseph Perkins Beach, 1912, p. 349.
4. *Biographical Review - The Leading Citizens of Delaware County, NY*, 1895, p. 696.
5. Cheshire, CT, Land Records, extracted by Ruth C. Duncan.
6. CB Database.
7. *Centennial History of Delaware County, NY, 1797-1897*, David Murray, etc., 1898, p. 471.
8. Census records extracted by Ruth C. Duncan.
9. Duncan, p. 84.
10. Bunnell/Bonnell notes extracted by Zoe Magden, Tacoma, WA.
11. *History and Genealogy of the Gov. John Webster Family of Connecticut*, by Wm. H. Webster and Melville R. Webster, 1915, page 865.

1-1-9-2-4-7   D45vii   CB310024

ISRAEL[6] BUNNELL (Israel[5], Ebenezer[4], Nathaniel[3], Benjamin[2], William[1]) was born 25 April 1787[1] in Cheshire, New Haven co, CT, and was baptized 17 June 1787[2] by Parson John Foot[3] of the Cheshire Congregational Church. On 23 November 1808 his father gave him 13+ acres of land, part of his own farm in Cheshire[4,5]. He married 28 December 1809[1], in Cheshire, BEULAH HITCHCOCK[1,2], who was born 5 May 1792[1]. They moved almost immediately to the town of Smithville, Chenango co, NY, where Israel appears in the 1810 census: 00100-00100[6].

Israel acquired more land in Cheshire when his father died in 1813, and sold 10 acres to his brother Nathaniel in 1815 for $275[4,5]. In 1818 he sold almost 23 acres in Cheshire to Charles Shelton of Cheshire[4,5]. He appears in the 1830 census in Smithville: 2220101-101001[6]. In 1837 Israel and Beulah Bunnell, "of Smithville" deeded property in Cheshire to his sister Jerusha Brandin[4]. Apparently they moved soon after to the town of Greene, Chenango co, NY, just south of Smithville, since they appear in Greene in the 1840 census: 00132001-011001[6], and again in the 1850 census[6], when he was called a farmer with real estate valued at $4000. Israel was said to be age 63 and Beulah 58. They died before the next census, Israel on 9 September 1852, age 65[7], and Beulah on 30 April 1853 at age 61[7]. Their gravestone in the Old Cemetery, Smithville Flats, lists Beulah as "Laura Bunnel, wife of Israel"[7], and John Biles concluded that Israel survived his first wife and married a second time. I would sooner believe that "Laura" on the gravestone was an error, but a check of the probate records in Chenango co would clear the matter up.

Children:
1. 320651. Edward[1], b. 10 Sept. 1810[8]; m. (first) about 1844 Rosanah Kelley[9]; m. (second) 1865 Deborah King[9]; d. 1871[9].
    Children (surname Bunnell)(by first wife):[9]
    1. Oliver.   3. Rufus Parker.   4. Nettie S.
    2. James Israel.
2. 320631. Mary O.[1], b. 14 July 1818[8]; m. William Bates[1].
3. 320632. Augustus L.[1], b. 28 Mar. 1820[8]; d. 1 May 1854[8].
4. 320633. Rufus[1], b. 12 Nov. 1821[8]; d. 1870[8], possibly murdered[9].
5. 320639. Frederick D.[1], b. 31 May 1824[8]; m. 23 Dec. 1845 Lovisa Tem Broeck[1]; d. 26 Jan. 1874[8].
    Children (surname Bunnell):[1,8]
    1. James Madison.   5. Derrick Tem Broeck. 8. Thomas Lee H.
    2. Frederick D.   6. Jane Ann.   9. Andrew Jackson.
    3. John Miller.   7. Margaret.   10. George Washington
    4. Mary Ophelia.
6. 320640. Elizabeth[1] Jerusha[6], b. 3 Dec. 1825[8]; m. (first) Canfield Tyler[1,9]; m. (second) 1881 John Parsons[8]
    Children (surname Tyler):[6,8]
    1. Elmer.   2. Adelaide.   3. Leroy.
7. 320634. James M.[1], b. 3 Dec. 1827[8]; 30 Apr. 1850[8] Uretta Tem Broeck[8,9]; d. 10 Aug. 1864[8].
8. 320636. Andrew Jackson[1], b. 32 May 1829[8]; d. 2 May 1855[8].
9. 320637. Antoinette E.[1], b. 22 Aug. 1831[8]; m. Charles Rorapaugh[1,9]; d. 5 Nov. 1904
    Children (surname Rorapaugh):[9]
    1. Fred.   2. Bert J.
10. 320638. Israel[1], b. 10 Oct. 1833[8]; d. 1834[8].

REFERENCES:

1. Ltr. 11 Dec. 1907 Andrew Jackson Bunnell (grandson of Israel) to John A. Biles.
2. New Haven - Jacobus, p. 367.
3. *History of Cheshire, Connecticut, from 1694 to 1840*, by Joseph Perkins Beach, 1912, pp. 349, 385.
4. Cheshire, CT, Land Records, extracted by Ruth C. Duncan.
5. Notebook of the Right Reverend Edwin S. Lines, D.D., Protestant Episcopal Bishop of the Diocese of Newark, NJ, copied & sent to me by Judith Bruce, Monument, CO.
6. CB Database.
7. Reference Notes copied in the DAR Library, Washington, DC, by Claude A. Bunnell 2 Oct. 1994.
8. Biles Manuscript, pp. 282, 283, 284, 285.
9. Ltr. 14 Jan. 1907 Rufus Parker Bunnell (grandson of Israel) to John A. Biles.

1-1-9-2-4-8   D127   CB310142

JAIRUS[6] BUNNELL (Israel[5], Ebenezer[4], Nathaniel[3], Benjamin[2], William[1]) was born 21 July 1789[1] and was baptized 6 September 1789[2] by Parson John Foot[3] of the Congregational Church in Cheshire, New Haven co, CT. On 26 September 1810[1] he married MARTHA LINCOLN[1], who was born in June 1790 in Vermont[4]. In 1813 he inherited some of his father's land, and on 25 October 1814 he sold a strip of 100 rods to his brother Nathaniel[6]. That year he was made a freeman of the town of Cheshire[3].

During the next couple of decades Jairus' name is found frequently in the real estate records of Cheshire[6,13]. He appears in the 1820 census in Cheshire: 300010-10010-AG[5]. John Biles wrote, "He was engaged for many years in the shoe business on the island of St. Thomas, West Indies."[1] His sixth child, Martha Elizabeth, 2nd, died in 1849 at age 20, and her death notice in the New Haven Vital Records adds that she was born in the West Indies[7]. (Her birth was recorded however in the New Haven Protestant Episcopal Church[8].) This probably explains why Jairus does not appear in the 1830 census.

In 1830 James Punderford won a judgement in Cheshire against Jairus Bunnell and Elias Mouthrop(?), dealers, under the firm name of Jairus Bunnell & Co.[6] Before 1840 he removed to New Haven, New Haven co, CT, where he appears in the census that year: 000020011-01200001-MFG4[5]. Jairus appears in the directories of the city of New Haven in 1840, 1841-2 as a shoemaker at 21 Fleet St., corner of Prout, and in 1843-4. In the 1850 census, in Orange, New Haven co, Jairus 61 is called a shoemaker, with wife Martha 60 and daughter Mary 15[5,14]. Jairus died 10 March 1860[10] in Orange[14]. His widow Martha died 23 November 1872[10]. They were buried in Evergreen Cemetery, New Haven, with most of their children[10].

Children:
1. 320572. Jairus Edwin, b. 13 May 1812[1]; m. 30 Nov. 1843 Zillah M. Morgan[7]; d. 2 Oct. 1845[10].
2. 320573. Cyrus Brooks, b. 29 Nov. 1813[1]; m. 30 Nov. 1848 Sarah A. Hart[]; d. 15 Apr. 1856[10].
3. 320571. Dennis Dowd, b. 29 Oct. 1815[1]; m. 29 Oct. 1839 Eliza Ward[7,8,11,12] (Was her name Sybil Eliza?[4,5] or did he have a second wife Sybil _____?); d. 3 Nov. 1852[10].

Children (surname Bunnell):[4]

    1. James E.   2. Ellen R.   3. Homer Augustus.

4. 320574. Martha Elizabeth, b. 13 Nov. 1818[1]; d. 12 Sept. 1824[10].

5. 320575. Diantha Fitch, b. 28 July 1826[1]; m. 24 Oct. 1842 Edward Foster[7,12] (or Fritt[1]).

    Children (surname Fritt):[1]

    1. Leslie.   3. Edward Cyrus.   4. Henry Lincoln.

    2. Elizabeth Ann.

6. 320576. Martha Elizabeth, b. 12 Sept. 1829[8]; d. 3 Sept. 1849[10].

7. 320577. Mary Jerusha, b. 20 Sept. 1834[8]; m. 2 Jan. 1855 Thomas B. (or R.) Post[11]; d. 17 Sept. 1901.

REFERENCES:

1. Biles Manuscript, p. 286.
2. New Haven - Jacobus, p. 367.
3. *History of Cheshire, Connecticut, from 1694 to 1840*, by Joseph Perkins Beach, 1912, p. 349.
4. Duncan, pp. 84, 160.
5. CB Database.
6. Cheshire, CT, Land Records, extracted by Ruth C. Duncan.
7. New Haven Vital Records, extracted by Ruth C. Duncan.
8. Church Records on file in the CT State Library, extracted by Ruth C. Duncan.
9. New Haven City Directories, extracted by Ruth C. Duncan.
10. Cemetery Records gathered by Ruth C. Duncan.
11. Newspaper Accounts of Marriages in the CT State Library, extracted by Ruth C. Duncan.
12. Vital Records in the card file at the CT State Library, extracted by Ruth C. Duncan.
13. Notebook of the Right Reverend Edwin S. Lines, D.D., Protestant Episcopal Bishop of the Diocese of Newark, NJ, copied & sent to me by Judith Bruce, Monument, CO.
14. Census Records extracted by Ruth C. Duncan.

1-1-9-2-4-9 D128 CB310143

EBENEZER[6] BUNNELL (Israel[5], Ebenezer[4], Nathaniel[3], Benjamin[2], William[1]) was born 29 January 1792 at Cheshire[1], New Haven co, CT, and was baptized 18 March 1792[2,3] by Parson John Foot[2] of the Congregational Church in Cheshire. He lost his hearing as a result of an accident in childhood[1].

From 1814 to 1816 Ebenezer's name appears frequently in the land records of Cheshire, CT, probably related, for the most part, to real estate inherited from his father's estate in 1813. A number of deeds in 1818 and 1819, however, refer to him as Ebenezer Bunnell of Canandaigua, Ontario co, NY. On 7 January 1819 he married ABIGAIL HOTCHKISS[1], probably back in Cheshire.

Ebenezer appears in the 1820 census in Canandaigua twp, Ontario co, NY: 00001-10101-MFG[5] and in the 1830 census, also in Canandaigua twp: 210001-211001[6,7]. Ebenezer of Canandaigua appears one final time in the land records of Cheshire, CT, in 1829 when he signed a release of

309

property from his father's estate[4]. They were apparently still living in Canandaigua twp in 1838 when their son Rufus J. was buried in Pinebank Cemetery In Cheshire, Canandaigua twp.

Very shortly, however, they removed to Grass Lake, Jackson co, MI, where Ebenezer appears in the 1840 census: 1001001-1011001-AG1[5]. The 1850 census in Grass Lake, MI, lists Ebenezer Bunnell age 58, born in Connecticut, a farmer, his wife Abigail age 53, born in Connecticut, and children Maria age 25, born in New York, Diantha age 20, born in New York, Dan V, age 15 New York, Jenett 13 New York, and Lambert 9 Michigan[5]. Abigail died 15 April 1859[9] and Ebenezer died 13 October 1861[1], both at Grass Lake, MI.

Children:
1. 320730. Jerusha Dowd, b. 25 Oct. 1819[1]; m. 10 May 1838 Cyrus G. Grinell[1]; d. 1 Nov. 1881[1].
2. 320729. Henry Martin, b. 28 May 1821[1]; m. 14 Nov. 1849 Catherine Longyear[1]; d. between 1900 and 1910[5].
   Children (surname Bunnell):[5]
   1. George.   2. Addie.   3. Mary.
   four others.
3. 320737. Matilda Ann, b. 22 May 1823[1]; m. (first) 18 Apr. 1841 James M. Watkins[1]; m. (second) 28 Aug. 1860 James W. Elliott[1]; d. 25 Feb. 1886[1].
4. 320731. Mary Amelia, b. 25 Aug. 1825[1]; m. 27 Feb. 1851[1] Zerah[5] Patterson[1,5].
5. 320732. Harriet Diantha, b. 10 July 1829[1]; m. 1864[1] or 1862[5] Thomas Cowley[1,5].
6. 320738. Rufus J., b. 28 Feb. 1832[1]; d. 1 Feb. 1838[1,8].
7. 320733. Daniel Virgil, b. 30 Nov. 1834[1]; m. 8 Dec. 1858 Mary A. Graham[1]; d. 5 Mar. 1885[1].
   Children (surname Bunnell):[5]
   1. Mary K.   3. Charles H.   4. Nellie.
   2. Maggie.
8. 320734. Jeanette N., b. July 1837[1]; m. 6 Oct. 1879 Peter Clement[1].
9. 320735. Lambert Fritt, b. 2 May 1841[1]; m. 1872 Lucy Cook[1].

REFERENCES:
1. Biles Manuscript, p. 287.
2. *History of Cheshire, Connecticut, from 1694 to 1840*, by Joseph Perkins Beach, 1912, p. 349.
3. New Haven - Jacobus, p. 367.
4. Cheshire, CT, Land Records, extracted by Ruth C. Duncan.
5. CB Database.
6. Duncan, p. 85.
7. 1820 and 1830 census records sent to me by Nona Bassett, Merced, CA.
8. Ltr. 20 Aug. 1970 from Clyde Maffin, Ontario co Historian to Zoe Magden.
9. Death Notices in Connecticut Newspapers, extracted by Ruth C. Duncan.

1-1-9-2-4-10 D129 CB310144

DENNIS DOWD[6] BUNNELL (Israel[5], Ebenezer[4], Nathaniel[3], Benjamin[2], William[1]) was born 6 August 1794 in Cheshire[1], New Haven co, CT, and was baptized 28 September 1794[2,3] by Parson John Foot[2] of the Congregational Church in Cheshire. He inherited land in Cheshire from his father's estate in 1813. In August and September 1815, preparing to leave Cheshire, he sold several parcels totalling over 20 acres[4,5]. He removed to Canandaigua[1], Ontario co, NY, where, on 10 February 1818, he married ELIZA DURAND[6,7]. She was born in Cheshire, CT, and was baptized there by Parson Foot on 13 October 1798[2,8]. She was the daughter of Munson and Ada (Hotchkiss) Durand[9]. Dennis appears in the 1820 census in Canandaigua, Ontario co, NY: 10001-001-AG1[10].

By 1823 Dennis was ready for another move. He sold the last of his property in Cheshire to his brother Jairus[4]. He moved to Niagara co, in the extreme northwest corner of New York State. He settled in Porter twp, Niagara co, where he purchased land from the Holland Land Compan - lot 50 in Section 00 township 15 range 08 - on 17 December 1823[11]. He appears in the 1830 census in Porter twp, Niagara co: 100001-010001[10]. (Where were the other three sons?). The obituaries of his sons William and Dennis, Jr., list their birthplace as Lewiston, the next town to the south. Perhaps Lewiston was the nearest post office to their home in Porter twp. In 1832 their son Elias died at the age of 11 years[7], and on 13 August 1833[7,12] daughter Martha died at 8 months[7] (or 3 months[12]).

Sometime between 1830 and 1835 they removed to Rochester, Monroe co, NY[7], where they lived until 1837. In that year their next moved took place, to Calhoun co, MI, where they settled in the town of Marshall[7]. While living there he became a minister of the Methodist Episcopal Church[1]. He appears in the 1840 census of Calhoun co, MI: 1011101-000001[14].

Dennis died 3 March 1850 in Battle Creek, Calhoun co, MI[13], and was buried in the Oak Hill cemetery in Battle Creek. His widow Eliza was living in the village of Battle Creek when the 1850 census was taken on 29 July[14]. With her were son Augustus, his wife Catherine and their infant daughter Annis, and her sons William R., Dennis D., and Charles[14]. Very soon Eliza left Michigan and returned to Canandaigua, Ontario co, NY, to be among old friends[7]. She died there on 20 October 1850[7]. Her sons erected a stone over her grave inscribed to "Our Mother and Sister, Eliza Bunnell died Oct. 20, 1850 aged 50 years. Martha J. Bunnell died Aug. 13, 1833 aged 3 mo."[12] A stone for their brother Elias who had died in 1832 is next to it.

Children:
1. 320749. Augustus, b. 13 Aug. 1819[1]; m. Catherine Emeline White[1]; d. 6 Apr. 1896[15].
   Children (surname Bunnell):[1]
   1. Annis E.   3. William E.   5. Charles Clifton.
   2. Dennis A.   4. Zoe May.
2. 320755. Elias, b. 1821[7]; d. 1832[7].

311

3. 320751. William Rufus, b. 5 Sept. 1823[1]; m. Lucy Jones[1]; div.[15]; d. Feb. 1873[15].
            Children (surname Bunnell):[10]
            1. Charles Albert.   2. William.   3. Clara.

4. 320752. Dennis Dowd, b. 13 Aug. 1826[1]; m. (first) 7 Nov. 1859 Mrs. Ann Eliza
            (Crosby) Fizette[15]; m. (second) 14 Sept. 1871 Mrs. Martha (_____)
            Scott[15]; d. 1 Sept. 1888[13].
            Children (surname Bunnell)(by first wife):
            1. Ida[15].   3. Lily Ann[15].   5. child[1].
            2. Oscar[15].   4. child[1].
            Children (surname Bunnell)(by second wife):
            6. Walter.

5. 320756. Martha Jane, b. 12 Dec. 1832[1]; d. 13 Aug. 1833[12].

6. 320753. Charles Clay, b. 5 Oct. 1835[1]; m. 22 Sept. 1872 Mrs. Flora A. (Groves)
            Springer[7]; d. 17 April 1908[7].
            They had no children, but he adopted Annie and Marie Springer,
            daughters of his wife's first marriage[15].

REFERENCES:
1. Biles Manuscript, p. 287.
2. *History of Cheshire, Connecticut, from 1694 to 1840*, by Joseph Perkins Beach, 1912, p. 349.
3. New Haven - Jacobus, p. 367.
4. Cheshire, CT, Land Records, extracted by Ruth C. Duncan.
5. Notebook of the Right Reverend Edwin S. Lines, D.D., Protestant Episcopal Bishop of the Diocese of Newark, NJ, copied & sent to me by Judith Bruce, Monument, CO.
6. Marriages in New York State, gathered by Nancie Davis, West Columbia, SC.
7. Zoe Magden's notes, as compiled in the files of Ruth C. Duncan.
8. Baptism record of Eliza Durand, sent to me by Zoe Magden.
9. *The Hotchkiss Family*, 1985 - extract sent to me by Charlotte Blair Stewart, Windber, PA.
10. CB Database.
11. *Western New York Land Transactions, 1804-1824, Extracted from the Archives of the Holland Land Company*, by Karen E. Livsey, published by Genealogical Publishing Co., Inc. - extracts sent to me by Charlotte Dunn, San Diego, CA.
12. Gravestone copied by Mrs. Albert Bunnell, Canandaigua, NY.
13. Obituary of Dennis D. Bunnell *in New Haven Palladium*, 26 March 1850, sent by Zoe C. Magden.
14. 1840 and 1850 census of Calhoun co, MI, sent by Zoe C. Magden.
15. Duncan, pp. 85, 160, 161.

1-1-9-5-3-1 D130 CB310403

JAIRUS B.[6] BUNNELL (Jairus[5], Jairus[4], Nathaniel[3], Benjamin[2], William[1]) was born about 1771[1] at Branford, New Haven co, CT. He was married about 1796 to HULDAH _____[1], who was born about 1777[1]. Jairus appears in the 1800 census: 10010-20010[2], 1810 census: 11010-21010[2], 1820 census: 01001-01110-AG[2], and 1830 census: 10001001-00003001[2], all in Branford, New Haven co, CT. His father deeded 22 acres in Branford to him in 1816[3]. He was a farmer[2]. Huldah died 6 December 1830, age 53 years.

In the 1850 census, after the northern part of the town was set off as North Branford, Jairus appears there at age 79, living with his daughter Delia[2]. He died 26 June 1852, age 81 years[1]. He and Huldah and their daughter Hannah were buried in the Congregational Church Cemetery in North Branford[1].

Children:

    1. 320869. Lewis, b. about 1797[1]; m. 9 Nov. 1823 Mehitable Ball[4]; d. 3 Feb. 1881 age 84.
          Children (surname Bunnell):[6]
          1. Delia Ann.
    2. 320870. Hannah (B.?), b. about 1798[1]; d. 2 Apr. 1820 age 21[1].
    3. 320871. Anna, b. about 1800[2]; m. Dec. 1839 Zina Ball[5].
          Children (surname Ball):[6]
          1. Edwin L.
    4. 320872. George, b. 25 July 1804[2]; m. 16 Sept. 1829 Frances A. Rose[2]; d. after 1881[2].
          Children (surname Bunnell):[6]
          1. Albert B.   3. George Wallace.   4. Samuel Rose.
          2. Hannah Elizabeth.
    5. 320873. Delia, b. about 1808[1]; d. unmarried 4 Feb. 1897 age 89[1].

REFERENCES:
    1. Connecticut Cemetery Records gathered by Ruth C. Duncan.
    2. CB Database
    3. Branford, CT, Land Records extracted by Ruth C. Duncan.
    4. Biles Manuscript, p. 290.
    5. Vital Records in the card file of the Connecticut State Library, extracted by Ruth C. Duncan.
    6. Duncan, pp. 85, 86, 161, 162.

1-1-9-5-4-1   D48i   CB310063

NATHANIEL[6] BUNNELL (Nathaniel[5], Jairus[4], Nathaniel[3], Benjamin[2], William[1]) was born 26 June 1776 at Farmington[1], Hartford co, CT, and was baptized the same day according to the records of the West Avon Congregational Church[2,3]. His father died when he was four months old, and his mother Abigail was appointed his guardian[3]. He died 4 January 1811 by drowning near Portland, Cumberland co, ME[3]. (Jacobus says he drowned near Portland, Mass.[2], but there is no Portland in Massachusetts, now or in the past. CB Database cites the records of the West Avon Congregational Church for the place of death.[3]) His probate record suggests that he was probably a blacksmith[3].

REFERENCES:
    1. Farmington, CT, Vital Records, extracted by Mrs. Clarence H. Bunnell, Winsted, CT.
    2. New Haven - Jacobus, p. 362.
    3. CB Database.
    4. Duncan, p. 42.

SIXTH GENERATION

1-1-9-5-5-2 D49ii CB310154

JOHN[6] BUNNELL (John[5], Jairus[4], Nathaniel[3], Benjamin[2], William[1]) was born 29 December 1779 in Branford[1], New Haven co, CT, and was baptized 25 June 1780 by Rev. Williams of the Northford Congregational Church in Branford. He was lost at sea in 1802[3] and died without issue[1].

REFERENCES:
1. New Haven - Jacobus, p. 367.
2. CB Database.
3. Church Records collected in the Connecticut State Library, extracted by Ruth C. Duncan.
4. Duncan, p. 43.

1-1-9-5-5-3 D49iii CB310155

LUTHER[6] BUNNELL (John[5], Jairus[4], Nathaniel[3], William[1]) was born 20 March 1782 in Branford[1], New Haven co, CT, and was baptized 9 June 1782 by Rev. Williams of the Northford Congregational Church in Branford[2]. He served in the War of 1812 as a private in the 27th Regiment, Amos Fowler, Commander[3]. He appears in the tax list in the town of Branford in November 1817: List $1.97, tax $.08[4]. He appears occasionally in the land records of the town of Branford in the 1820s and later, principally regarding land which had been in his parents' estates[5].

Luther appears in the 1830 census in Branford: 0010011-00000000101[2], and in the 1840 census in North Branford: 000000011-00000000101-AG1[2]. His mother Puah (or Pure) was living with him. He died 31 December 1849[6] without issue[1]. Apparently he never married. His estate was distributed among his brothers and sisters on 6 December 1852[3].

REFERENCES:
1. New Haven - Jacobus, p. 367.
2. CB Database/
3. Duncan, p. 43.
4. Tax List, Town of Branford, Connecticut, November, 1817, printed in *The Connecticut Nutmegger*, Dec. 1993, pp. 384, 385.
5. Land Records of the towns of Branford and North Haven, CT, extracted by Ruth C. Duncan.
6. Records of the Old Northford Cemetery in North Branford, CT, gathered by Ruth C. Duncan.

1-1-9-5-5-4 D131 CB310156

JESSE[6] BUNNELL (John[5], Jairus[4], Nathaniel[3], Benjamin[2], William[1]) was born 12 June 1784 at Branford[1], New Haven co, CT, and was baptized 15 August 1784[2] by Rev. Williams of the Northford Congregational Church in Branford[3]. His wife was AMELIA FOOTE[1], daughter of Daniel and Hannah (Potter) Foote[1]. She was born about 1787[2]. Jesse appears in the tax list in the town of Branford in November 1817: List $5.10, tax $.10[4]. At various occasions in the

1820s Jesse bought or sold property in Branford[5]. He also appears in the 1820 census: 100010-00100[3] and the 1830 census: 0010001-1000001[3], both in Branford, New Haven co. After the division of town of Branford, Jesse appears in the 1840 census in North Branford: 000010001-00010001-MFG1-AG3[3]. The 1850 census in North Branford shows Jesse 62, his wife "Emeline" 62, son Daniel 30, and daughter "Altezeera" 22[3]. In 1860 Jesse was listed as a day laborer, age 74 with his wife "Emily" 74[3]. He died 3 September 1866 in North Branford. His widow Amelia , 83, appears in the 1870 census in North Branford living with her daughter and son-in-law[3].

Children:
1. 320619. Daniel Foote, b. about 1820[1]; sailor[3]; moved to Geauga co, OH[3].
2. 320620. Alteziera (Altezeera, Alzina), b. about 1828[1]; m. 23 Dec. 1855 Alonzo H. Blakeslee[3].

REFERENCES:
1. New Haven - Jacobus, p. 367.
2. Duncan, p. 86.
3. CB Database.
4. Tax List, Town of Branford, Connecticut, November, 1817, printed in *The Connecticut Nutmegger*, Dec. 1993, . 384.
5. Branford, CT, Land Records, extracted by Ruth C. Duncan.

1-1-9-5-5-5   D132   CB310157

NATHANIEL[6] BUNNELL (John[5], Jairus[4], Nathaniel[3], Benjamin[2], William[1]) was born 6 February 1787 at Branford[1], New Haven co, CT. On 3 March 1814 he married SALLY TODD[1], who was born about 1795[2]. Nathaniel appears in the tax list in the town of Branford in November 1817: List $6.11, tax $.14[3]. He is listed in the 1820 census: 000010-10100-MFG[4] and the 1830 census: 1000002-000101[4], both in the town of Branford, and in the 1840 census: 000100001-00000001-AG1[4], in the town of North Branford. In the 1850 census of North Branford Nathaniel age 60 appears with his wife Sally 55 and son John 21[4]. The Branford and North Haven, CT, land records contain deeds and other references to Nathaniel from time to time throughout this period[5].

Nathaniel died 11 January 1854 at North Branford[1,6]. His widow appears in the 1860 census in North Branford living with her son John[7]. She was probably the Sally, widow of Nathaniel Bunnell, who died in New Haven, CT, 13 January 1880, at the age of 84 years[8]. They were buried in the Old Northford Cemetery in North Branford[6].

Children:
1. 320439. Ann Augusta, b. 8 Apr. 1815[9]; m. 27 Sept. 1835 Frederick Tyler Elliott[9]; d. 13 Feb. 1901[10].
     Children (surname Elliott):[10]
     1. Harriet Augusta.   3. Sarah Clark.   4. Evelina Ann.
     2. Mary Jane.

2. 320440. John Nathaniel, b. 1828[2]; d. 1893 unmarried[2].

REFERENCES:
1. New Haven - Jacobus, p. 367.
2. Duncan, p. 86.
3. Tax List, Town of Branford, Connecticut - November, 1817, printed in *The Connecticut Nutmegger*, Vol. 26, No. 3, Dec. 1993, p. 384.
4. CB Database.
5. Land Records of Branford and North Haven, CT, extracted by Ruth C. Duncan.
6. Connecticut Cemetery Records, gathered by Ruth C. Duncan.
7. 1860 census, Branford, New Haven co, CT, extracted by Ruth Duncan.
8. Bunnell death notices in *Beckwith's Almanac - 1881*, sent to me by Dorothy Cotton, Dixon, CA.
9. *Family History and Genealogy of the Descendants of Robert Augur*, by Edwin P. Augur, 1904, p. 51, in the files of Ruth C. Duncan.
10. *Genealogy of the Descendants of John Eliot*, by Willimena H. Eliot Emerson, pp. 164, 165, in the files of Ruth C. Duncan.

1-1-9-5-5-8   D133   CB310160

AUGUSTUS (BARNES[8])[6] BUNNELL (John[5], Jairus[4], Nathaniel[3], Benjamin[2], William[1]) was born 16 May 1795 at Branford[1], New Haven co, CT. He was baptized 9 August 1795 by Rev. Matthew Noyes[3] of the Congregational Church at Northford in the town of Branford. His wife was SALLY THORPE[1], daughter of Abner Thorpe[2,5]. She was born in 1800[3].

Augustus appears in the 1820 census: 100100-00010-AGR1[3], the 1830 census: 020001-10001[3], and the 1840 census: 1100001-0010001-AG1[3], all in North Haven, New Haven co, CT. He was a farmer. The land records of North Haven include a number of transactions by Augustus and Sally Bunnell, mostly involving land in Branford and North Haven inherited from their respective parents[5]. He died 26 February 1847[1] at North Haven. His widow Sally married (second) Jared Leete[4]. She died 5 October 1853[4].

Children:
    1. 320802. Henry, b. 23 Jan. 1820[6]; m. 30 May 1857 Abigail Williams Munson[2]; d. 23 Mar. 1893[6].
        Children (surname Bunnell):[2]
        1. Ellen F.   3. Henry Ellsworth.   5. Oliver B.
        2. Jennie L.   4. George Louis.
    2. 320803. Willis, b. 1823[6]; m. 27 May 1853 Catherine Palmer[2]; d. 1888[6] (or 17 Nov. 1889[2]).
        Children (surname Bunnell):[2]
        1. Frank Elizur.   3. Carrie Marilla.   5. Mary J.
        2. Henderson Floyd. 4. William A.
    3. 320804. George Hoadley, b. 1824[6]; m. 11 Oct. 1847 Harriet E. Fitch[2]; d. 1890[6].
        Children (surname Bunnell):[2]
        1. Nellie F.   2. Henrietta F.   3. Hattie A.
    4. 320805. John, b. Oct. 1826[2]; d. 30 Nov. 1826, age 1 month[7].

5. 320806. Sarah, b. 1826[3].
6. 320807. John Luther[8], b. 1829[3]; m. Maria C. Bradley[8].
    Children (surname Bunnell):[3,8]
        1. Medora Ann.   2. Ida A.   3. Etta.
7. 320808. James Lewis, b. about 1839[3]; m. Maria Glynn[3]; d. 1897[3]
    Children (surname Bunnell):[3]
        1. Clara A.   2. William Austin.   3. James.

REFERENCES:
1. New Haven - Jacobus, p. 368.
2. Duncan, p. 87.
3. CB Database.
4. *Families of Early Guilford*, p. 786.
5. Land Records of North Haven, New Haven co, CT, extracted by Ruth C. Duncan.
6. Connecticut Cemetery Records gathered by Ruth C. Duncan.
7. Church records in the Collection of the Connecticut State Library, extracted by Ruth C. Duncan.
8. Ltr. 6 July 1987 from Capt. Harry A. Stowell, Ret., St. Augustine, FL.

1-1-9-5-5-9 D49ix CB310161

ELIZUR[6] BUNNELL (John[5], Jairus[4], Nathaniel[3], Benjamin[2], William[1]) was born 4 May 1798 at Branford[1], New Haven co, CT. His father deeded land to him in 1823 in Northford parish in the town of Branford[5]. He died 7 May 1833[2] in North Branford, New Haven co, without issue[1]. He was buried in the Old Northford Cemetery in North Branford[3]. Distribution of his estate was made to his siblings: Anna, Luther, Jesse, Nathaniel, Lucy Tyler, Betsy Rose and Augustus[4].

REFERENCES:
1. New Haven - Jacobus, p. 368.
2. Church Records in the Collection of the Connecticut State Library, extracted by Ruth C. Duncan.
3. Connecticut Cemetery Records gathered by Ruth C. Duncan.
4. Connecticut Probate Records extracted by Ruth C. Duncan.
5. Branford, CT, Land Records, extracted by Ruth C. Duncan.

1-1-9-5-6-5 D134 CB310072

JAMES MUNSON[6] BUNNELL (Abraham[5], Jairus[4], Nathaniel[3], Benjamin[2], William[1]) was born 1 August 1802[1] in Rensselaerville, Albany co, NY[3] He married _____ _____ on 15 April 1822[1]. He lived in Herkimer co, NY[2], where he died in 1829[1].

Children:
1. 320204. Arminta, b. 26 June 1823[2].
2. 320205. Oscar, b. 14 Apr. 1824[2]; m. 4 Nov. 1844 Alida Levesee[3]; d. 29 July 1865[3].
    Children (surname Bunnell):[3]
        1. Elizabeth.   3. Alderette.   4. Sarah S.
        2. Edson.

3. 320206. Sophia, b. 14 June 1827[2].
4. 320207. Munson, b. 7 Mar. 1829[2]; m. Elizabeth _____ [3].
      Children (surname Bunnell):[3]

1. Ella P.	3. Jefferson M.	5. Harriet A.
2. Henry B.	4. Charles T.	

REFERENCES:
1. New Haven - Jacobus, pp. 362, 363.
2. Duncan, p. 87.
3. CB Database.

1-1-9-6-2-2   D135   CB310165

EBENEZER[6] BUNNELL (David[5], Abner[4], Nathaniel[3], Benjamin[2], William[1]) was born 25 July 1769 at Wallingford[1] (now Cheshire), New Haven co, CT, and was baptized 30 July 1769 by Parson Foot[2] of the Cheshire Congregational Church. On 2 July 1788 he was married by Parson Foot to LOLY CURTIS[1,2,3], daughter of David and Eunice (Perkins) Curtis[4]. Ebenezer appears in the 1790 census in Cheshire: 1-1-2-0-0[5], suggesting that they had a son who died young and a daughter born before the 1790 census was taken. Another daughter and son David were born by May 1793.

The rest of Ebenezer's life is shrouded in mystery. According to son David's account, written in 1831, his father "was a sea-faring man, and died at sea when I was two years old."[6]. This is the only reference to Ebenezer's death I have discovered, except for the probate record of Ebenezer's father David[7] in 1810, which indicated that Ebenezer was deceased by that time. However, an Ebenezer Bunnell, son of David, married ELIZABETH MEYER, daughter of Jacob, on 28 December 1795 at St. Peter's Lutheran Church (the Stone Church) in Rhinebeck, Dutchess co, NY[8]. I know of no other Bunnell man to whom this could apply. It seems possible that he left his family to go to sea and never returned to Cheshire, where he was presumed dead after the passage of time. I have found no further record that could apply to him.

In any case, his wife Loly married a second time about 1799[6], but her new husband died after a short time[6]. She and her three children moved to "the head of the Delaware River,"[6] (this should mean somewhere in Delaware co, NY. After a few years they moved to New York City, where her son David was apprenticed to a stone-cutter[6]. Soon after, she moved back to the Delaware with her daughters[6]. They removed again to the town of York, Livingston co, NY, where Loly was still living in 1831[6].

From all the circumstantial evidence, it seems clear that the older daughter was the Octavia Bunnell, b. 16 December 1788[9], who married Joseph Lurvey 25 April 1805[9]. She died in 1813[9] and was buried in Newton's Cemetery in York, Livingston co, NY[10]. By extension, the Lola Bunnell who married Joseph Lurvey's brother Jacob was certainly the second daughter of Ebenezer and Loly Bunnell[11].

Children:

1.   ?son, d. young?[5].
2.   Octavia, b. 16 Dec. 1788[9]; m. 25 Apr. 1805 Joseph Lurvey[9]; d. 16 May 1813[9,10].

        Children (surname Lurvey):[9]

1. Jacob.	3. Lolyann.	5. Benoni.
2. James.	4. Mary.	6. Loretta.

3.   Lola, b. 21 Dec. 1790[11]; m. Jacob Lurvey[11]; d. 25 Mar. 1864[11].

        Children (surname Lurvey):[11]

1. Sarah Maria.	3. Susan.	4. Edwin.
2. John.		

    4. 320534. David C., b. 20 May 1793.

REFERENCES:

1. New Haven - Jacobus, p. 368.
2. *History of Cheshire, Connecticut, from 1694 to 1840*, by Joseph Perkins Beach, 1912.
3. *Early Connecticut Marriages*, by Frederic W. Bailey, Vol. 3, p. 58, reprinted 1968 by Genealogical Publishing Co.
4. Duncan, p. 87.
5. Census 1790 - Connecticut, p. 93.
6. *The Travels and Adventures of David C. Bunnell*, written by himself, 1831.
7. CB Database.
8. Ltr. 23 July 2000, Arthur C. Kelly to Brenda Bunnell Griffin, Scottsdale, AZ.
9. Family Bible of Joseph Lurvey, copy sent to me by Leota M. Cannon, Stamford, TX
10. Lurvey graves in Newton's Cemetery, York, Livingston co, NY, sent to me by Charlotte Dunn, Los Angeles, CA.
11. *The Peter² Lurvey Family of Essex County, Massachusetts, Maine, and Vermont*, by John Bradley Arthaud and Ernest Hyde Helliwell, III, Part Three, in The New England Historical and Genealogical Register, Volume 155, April 2001, pp. 170-173.

1-1-9-6-3-1 D136 CB310025

MOSES ATWATER⁶ BUNNELL (Abner⁵, Abner⁴, Nathaniel³, Benjamin², William¹) was born 18 November 1774 at Wallingford[1] (now Cheshire), New Haven co, CT, and was baptized 20 August 1775[1,2] by Parson Foot[2] of the Congregational Church of Cheshire[1] in the town of Wallingford.

Abner, his father, deeded 18 acres in Cheshire to Moses in 1803[4]. On 5 February 1804, at Cheshire[1], Moses married LOWLY HITCHCOCK[1], daughter of Eliakim and Lowly (Hull) Hitchcock[1]. She was born 11 February 1776 in New Haven[3], New Haven co, CT, and was baptized 26 May 1776 in the First Congregational Church of New Haven[1]. They removed almost at once to Blanford, Hampshire (now Hampden) co, MA, where they spent the first years of their married life. Here Moses seems to have been associated with Russell Atwater, a relative of his mother's family. On 12 January 1808 Moses A. Bunnell of Blanford, MA, sold five acres of land in Cheshire, CT, to his brother Abner, Jr.[4]. This was land which was left to him by his grandfather Moses Atwater[4], who died in Cheshire on 2 October 1805[1].

About the year 1809 they left Blanford and moved to the town of Russell, St. Lawrence co, NY[3]. His cousin Russell Atwater was one of the principal settlers of the town, which was named after him[7]. Moses appears in the 1810 census in Russell: 20320-20010[5]. In Russell he was the keeper of a tavern[8] or hotel[3]. The War of 1812 (Mr. Madison's War to the people of northern New York) was a period of fear and excitement, with raids on both sides of the border with Canada and the British capture of Ogdensburg, St. Lawrence co. It has been asserted that Moses served as a captain of militia during the war, but I have not found the evidence for the statement. In 1813 Moses was listed on a committee to improve the cemetery and to get a deed, and he served as a vestryman at its incorporation on 10 April 1819[8].

In 1819, however, they moved again, this time to the town of Canandaigua, Ontario co, NY, where he bought land from his brother Abner[8]. Moses appears in the 1820 census in Canandaigua: 120101-31110-AG[5]. His last child was born here, but Canandaigua didn't satisfy him long. In 1826 he sold the land back to brother Abner and took up a farm in the town of Henderson, Jefferson co, NY[8]. Here they spent the rest of their lives. Moses appears in Henderson in the 1830 census: 01010001-00110001[5], in the 1840 census: 000210001-000030001[5], and in the 1850 census when he was listed as age 75, with wife Sally (sic) age 74, daughter Frances age 34 and son George 27. He was a farmer with real estate worth $5000[5].

Moses died at Henderson on 14 February 1852[3]. His will was probated 1 July 1852 at the Surrogate Court in Watertown, Jefferson co, NY[9]. The probate record states, "That the heirs and next of Kin of said deceased are as follows and none other or others, viz: Moses A. Bunnel of Henderson aforesaid. Reuben A. Bunnel of the city of Rochester. Alfred Bunnel of Henderson aforesaid and George Bunnel of Henderson. Nancy Herendeen of Salem, county of Washtenaw and state of Michigan. Cornelia B. Hawkins of the city of Oswego. Frances J. Harmon of the town of Adams, Jefferson county and Sarah Crittenden of Texas in the county of Oswego, all children of said deceased and of full age and that Lowly Bunnel of Henderson aforesaid of full age is the widow of said deceased. . . ."[9] The only child no longer living was daughter Jane. The will itself follows:

"I, Moses A. Bunnel, of the town of Henderson in the county of Jefferson and state of New York of the age of seventy four years, considering the uncertainty of this mortal life and being of sound mind and memory do make publish and declare this my last will and testament in manner following, that is to say, First I give and bequeath to my son George Bunnel, all that forty acres of land in the said town of Henderson aforesaid deeded to me by Daniel McNeil & Sally his wife including all on the south side of the road deeded to me at the same time by the said McNeil excepting the west half of the upright part of the house where I now reside and the door yard in front of the same, reserving the privilege of going and returning to and from the spring of water ont he said forty acres and using the same for the purpose of watering cattle. I also give and devise to my son George Bunnel one undivided third part of seven and a half acres of cedar land which on sixth town point, so called. Second, I give and bequeath to my son Reuben A. Bunnel all the remaining part of my farm on which I now reside in the said town of Henderson containing one hundred and forty seven acres and the privilege of going to the spring of water on the above mentioned forty acres for watering cattle, subject to all the incumbrances which may be left by me on all the above described premises at the time of my decease. I also give and devise to my son Reuben A. Bunnell two undivided third parts of the seven and a half acres of cedar land on the point, so called. And I further give and bequeath to my son Reuben A. Bunnel all my horses, cattle, sheep, hogs, farming tools and implements and personal property which I may have or own at my decease. Third, I give and bequeath to my daughter Frances J. Bunnel the sum of one hundred dollars to be paid to her by my son Reuben A. Bunnel at my decease in consideration of the bequest herein made to him by me. And lastly I do hereby nominate and appoint my sons Reuben A. Bunnel and George Bunnel to be the executors of this my last will and testament, hereby revoking all other wills by me made. In Witness whereof I have hereunto set my hand and seal this 23[d] day of April in the year of our Lord one thousand eight hundred and forty nine. Moses A. Bunnel Seal.

"The above instrument consisting of one sheet was at the date thereof signed sealed published and declared by the said Moses A. Bunnel as and for his last will and testament in presence of us who at his request and in his presence and in the presence of each other have subscribed our names as witnesses thereto. Samuel Boyden residing in the town of Hounsfield, county of Jefferson. E. S. Robbins residing in the town of Hounsfield, County of Jefferson."[9]

Lowly lived with her son George on the home farm until she died on 12 October 1867[3]. She appears in the 1860 census as Lola A.Bunnel 84, with her son George in Henderson[5]. Moses and Lowly were buried at Sacketts Harbor, Jefferson co, NY. On 11 October 1911 the old Bunnel home at Henderson was burned to the ground. It was owned at the time by George's son Reuben A. Bunnel and had been owned by Bunnels for eighty years[10].

Children:
1. 320641. Moses Atwater, b. Oct. 1804[5]; m. 11 May 1831 Deborah Harrington[5]; d. after 1880.
   Children (surname Bunnell):[5]
   1. Moses Atwater.   3. Mercy.   5. Reuben A.
   2. Cornelia.   4. Marcus.   6. Sarah Crittenton.
2. 320642. Jane, b. about 1805[5]; d. probably before 1830[5].
3. 320643. Reuben Ashman, b. about 1806[5]; 10 Apr. 1850 Eliza S. Rogers[5]; d. between 1870 and 1880[5].
   Children (adopted)[10] (surname Bunnell):[5]
   1. Lorinda Rogers.
4. 320644. Nancy, b. about 1807[5]; m. Kellup Harrendeen[5,9].
5. 320646. Cornelia, b. about 1811[5]; m. Rufus Hawkins[5,9].
   Children (adopted)(surname Hawkins):[10]
   1. Cornelia.   2. Rufus.
6. 320647. Alfred, b. 13 June 1813[10]; m. 1843 Nancy Judson Harmon[5,9,10]; d. 16 Feb. 1895[11].
   Children (surname Bunnell):[5]
   1. Robert Franklin.   2. George Reuben.
7. 320648. Frances Jane[11], b. about 1816[5]; m. 1852 Samuel Harmon[5,9,10] as his fifth wife[11].
8. 320649. Sarah, b. 1 June 1817[12]; m. Almon Crittenton[9,12]; d. 26 Dec. 1894[12].
9. 320650. George, b. 10 May 1823[12]; m. 14 Oct. 1857 Laurentine Gilman[3]; d. 6 Dec. 1893[12].
   Children (surname Bunnell):[10]
   1. Reuben Ashman.

REFERENCES:
1. New Haven - Jacobus, pp. 66, 368.
2. *History of Cheshire, Connecticut, from 1694 to 1840*, by Joseph Perkins Beach, 1912.
3. *History of Jefferson County, New York*, L. H. Everts & Co., 1878, p. 390.
4. Cheshire, CT, Land Records, extracted by Ruth C. Duncan.
5. CB Database.
6. *Ulster Scots and Blandford Scouts*, by Sumner Gilbert Wood, 1928, reprint 1997 by Heritage Books, Inc., p. 222.

7. *History of the North County* (New York State), by Harry F. Landon, Vol. a, p. 228. Published by Historical Publishing Co., 1932.
8. Research of Nona Bassett, Merced, CA.
9. Will and probate record of Moses A. Bunnel deceased.
10. Ltr. 8 Dec. 1911 from Mrs. Reuben A. Bunnel (son of George), Henderson, NY, to John A. Biles.
11. Additions and corrections to my Moses Atwater Bunnell account submitted by LuAnne Bunnel, Green Valley, AZ.
12. Gravestone inscriptions in Evergreen Cemetery, Roberts Corners, Henderson, Jefferson co, NY, sent to my be Riley H. Kirby, Upper Marlboro, MD.

1-1-9-6-3-3   D137   CB310026

CHESTER[6] BUNNELL (Abner[5], Abner[4], Nathaniel[3], Benjamin[2], William[1]) was born 16 March 1778 at Wallingford[1] (now Cheshire), New Haven co, CT, and was baptized 3 May 1778[1,2] by Parson John Foot[2] of the Congregational Church of Cheshire in the town of Wallingford. As a young man he moved to the town of Canandaigua, Ontario co, NY. Before 1800 he married ANNA ATWOOD. Although her maiden name does not seem to appear in any contemporary document that has come to light, it is attested by the Ontario County Historian in 1972, saying, "Last week I visited the cemetery and found her stone which definitely says Annie Atwood, wife of Chester Bunnell."[4]

On 26 February 1800 Chester agreed to purchase 75 acres on land in township 9 in the third range in Ontario co, the south half of lot #56, for $309 to be paid over four years[6]. He appears in the 1800 census: 00100-10100[3] and in the 1810 census: 20110-21010[3], both in the town of Canandaigua, Ontario co, NY. Chester died 13 April 1811[7]. He was probably buried in the Pinebank Cemetery in Cheshire, Canandaigua twp, where his widow was interred many years later. However, no gravestone marks his grave. What caused his death is unknown. He was only 33 years of age. His brother Abner and a friend John Brocklebank were appointed administrators of his estate[5]. Since most of the little we know about Chester's life is found in legal documents filed in Ontario co, I have transcribed several of them as follows:

22 April 1811, Assignment of Letters of Administration:[5]

"The people of the State of New York, by the grace of God free and Independent
L.S. To Abner Bunnel brother and John Brocklebank friend of Chester Bunnel late of the town of Canandaigua in the county of Ontario deceased. Whereas the said deceased as is alledged died intestate, having whilst living and at the time of his death Goods, Chattels or credits within this state by means whereof the granting administration and also the auditing allowing and final discharging the account thereof doth appertain unto us - and we being desirous the goods Chattels and Credits of the said deceased may be well and faithfully administered, applied and disposed of Do grant unto the said Abner Bunnel and John Brocklebank full power by these presents to administer and faithfully dispose of all and singular the said goods Chattels and Credits - To ask demand recover and receive the debts which unto the said deceased whilst living at the time of his death did belong, and to pay the debts which the said deceased did owe, so far as such Goods Chattels and credits will thereto extend and the law require, hereby requiring you to make or cause to be made a true and perfect Inventory of all and singular the goods Chattels and credits of the said deceased which have or shall come to your hands possession or knowledge, and the same so made to exhibit or cause to be exhibited into the office of the Surrogate of the County of Ontario at or before the expiration of six Calendar months from the date hereof: and also to render a just and true account of administration

when thereunto required. And we do by these presents depute institute and appoint you the said Abner Bunnel and John Brocklebank Administrators of all and singular the Goods Chattels and credits which were of the said Chester Bunnel deceased. In Testimony Whereof we have caused the seal of office of our said Surrogate to be hereunto affixed -- Witness Reuben Hart Esquire, Surrogate of our said County at Canandaigua the twenty second day of April in the Year of our Lord one thousand eight hundred and Eleven - 1811.. and of our Independence the thirty-fifth. Reuben Hart."[5]

6 June 1811, Inventory of the estate[5] (Some of the list is hard to decipher and I don't guarantee a perfect transcription.)

"Ontario County. L.S. Whereas Administration of the Goods, Chattels and credits of Chester Bunnel of the town of Canandaigua in the County of Ontario deceased was granted on the twenty-second day of April AD1811 unto Abner Bunnel and John Brocklebank and whereas the said Abner Bunnel and John Brocklebank for divers good causes have refused further to act have returned into the office of the Surrogate of the County of Ontario the letters of administration heretofore granted and the same is hereby revoked. Reuben Hart Surrogate
June 6 A. 1811.
The following Inventory of the Estate of Chester Bunnel was on the sixth day of June exhibited by the administrators into the office of the Surrogate of the said County of Ontario/Vir/

3 chests	$3.00	amount brot up	11.69	brot up	$18.18
3 tables	2.00	Iron pot	1.50	11 knives & forks	4.50
3 old chairs	0.14	tin teakittle	0.75	1 pewter teapot	[??]
3 bedsteds	1.50	[??] tin pail & [??]	0.375	3 old tin cups	0.25
1 do	0.50	3 tin basins	0.375	1 tin strainer	0.125
1 [??]	0.50	1 tin pail	0.375	3 tin pint measures	0.375
3 old barrels	0.375	4 Iron flats	1.25	1 [??] bottle	0.125
1 wash tub	0.375	1 grid Iron	0.25	1 earthen pot	0.125
1 small keg	0.10	1 frying pan	0.375	3 earthen platters	0.125
1 bread tray	0.375	1 Currycomb	0.50	6 plates	0.25
1 old chest	0.25	1 small [??]	0.12	6 plates	0.50
1 old Gun	2.00	one wood pail	0.31	1 pitcher	1.25
1 [??] bucket	0.25	tin & copper pot	0.19	1 wood salt celler	0.06
1 old Lantern	0.25	1 candlestick	0.19	1 pint bowl	0.10
	11.09		18.18		22.34

amount brot over	$22.34	amount brot up	$26.02
1 pint tumbler	01.12	1 puter bason	1.00
1 creamer & sugar bowl	0.25	1 tin bason	0.10
sett tea cups & saucers	0.50	1 large Iron kettle	4.00
one earthen bowl	0.06	one [??]/feather bed & beding	15.00
set knives & forks	1.50	2 bed [??]	0.50
2 butcher knives	0.75	1 straw bed & beding	3.00
1 old tea canister	0.125	fire shovel & tongs	0.87
1 tin [??]	0.125	Cloathing	16.00
2 wood boxes	0.25		
	26.02		66.58

The aforegoing Inventory being exhibited by Abner Bunnel and John Brocklebank Administrators of Chester Bunnel deceased with their letter of Administration the following Letter of Administration granted to John Brocklebank and Josiah Robinson."[5]

The "following Letter of Administration" is identical in text to the original above and I omit it[5].

Almost 11 years after Chester's death his widow and children finally got title to the property he had contracted for in 1800 from Oliver Phelps. This deed, filed in Book 38, pages 167-169 in Ontario County Deeds in 1821, describes how it happened:[6]

"Whereas, Oliver Phelps, now deceased, by Augustus Porter his Attorney or agent, did on the twenty-sixth day of February in the year eighteen hundred covenant and agree with Chester Bunnel, then of the Town of Canandaigua, county of Ontario & State of New York, but now deceased, to convey to the said Chester Bunnel his heirs or assigns in fee simple on or before the first day of January in the year eighteen hundred and four seventy five acres of land in Township number nine in the third range in said county of Ontario, it being the south half of lot number fifty six, in consideration of the said Chester Bunnel's fulfilling on his part his covenant of that date first aforesaid, which was of the effect here stated, that is to say, that the said Chester should pay to said Phelps the sum of three hundred and nine dollars together with the lawful annual interest thereon annually by the first of January in the year eighteen hundred & four, the same being divided in four equal payments the last falling due the time last aforesaid, also that the said Chester should pay all taxes which had or should be levied on said land & also that said Chester should or would erect a house & make a settlement on said premises within six months from the date of said covenant, all of which covenants on the part of said Chester were to be strictly performed or the said Phelps, as was especially agreed in and by said covenant to be acquitted & discharged from the fulfilment of the covenant on his part. And Whereas by the said covenant it does not appear nor does it appear by the bond executed at the time of said covenant that the said Chester ever paid the said Phelps, his heirs executors administrators or assigns any part of said sum mentioned in said covenant to be paid said Phelps, but that on the contrary the said covenant of the said Chester was wholly broken & unfulfilled, though it is understood that the said Chester while in life did claim of the said Oliver while in life & of his administrator since the decease of the said Oliver - & that the administrator of the said Chester still continues to claim of the administrator of the said Oliver for work and labor by him the said Chester done & by others employed by and on account of the said Chester for the said Oliver a sum which the administrator of the said Chester contends is equivalent to the amount of the covenant & bond of the said Chester with the interest which has accrued thereon which was executed by the said Chester to the said Oliver as aforesaid, but which the administrator of the said Chester cannnot legally offset against the said bond as the same has been assigned by the said Oliver to the State of Connecticut & by said State of Connecticut by its proper officers assigned to Gideon Granger who now holds the same, and as the administrator of the said Chester can in no way satisfy by any assets coming into the hands of the administrator of the said Oliver, the claim which he urges against the said Oliver's estate as the same are to be applied to Judgment creditors which will in all probability absorb the whole of all assets coming to the administrator of the said Oliver to be administered.
    And Whereas the parties of this instrument conceiving it no more that justice and equity that the widow and heirs of the said Chester, deceased, ought in some way to have relief are willing to release all their right & title to the aforesaid land for the benefit of the widow & heirs of the said Chester Bunnel deceased, which release is to be considered as full ample & complete satisfaction of any claim the said Chester's estate may have against the said Oliver's estate by the parties to this instrument.
    Now therefore know all men by these present that We Gideon Granger and Zachariah Seymour individually and Zachariah Seymour & James Smedley as Trustees & Devises of the last Will & Testament of Oliver L. Phelps deceased. all of the Town of Canandaigua, County of Ontario & State of New York, in consideration of the premises and to close all differences and demands between the estates of said Chester & said Oliver & for and in consideration of one dollar to us in hand paid by Anna Bunnel widow & relict of said Chester deceased & of Polly Bunnel, Vina Bunnel, Chester Bunnel, Charles Bunnel, Susan Bunnel & Henry Bunnel, heirs of the said Chester Bunnel deceased, the receipt whereof at and before the unsealing and delivery of these presents is acknowledged, have given granted released and forever Quit Claimed and by these presents do give grant release & forever Quit Claim unto the said Anna widow & relict of the said Chester deceased and unto the said Polly, Vina, Chester, Charles, Susan & Henry, heirs of said Chester deceased in the manner herein hereafter particularly mentioned, all our right title interest claim or demand of in & to the following described piece of land situate in Township Number nine in the third range in the county of Ontario & State aforesaid, being seventy five acres of land, off the south side

of lot number fifty six & bounded east, west and south by the lines of the lot & north by a line parallel with the south line & distant from it far enough to contain said quantity of land, it being the same land contracted by said Phelps to said Bunnel as aforesaid. To have and to hold the one third part of said described premises with the tenements hereditaments and appurtenances thereto appertaining to the said Anna widow & relict of the said Chester Bunnel deceased during her natural life and unto the said Polly Vina Chester Charles Susan and Henry, heirs of the said Chester deceased, their heirs & assigns, after the decease of the said Anna widw & relict of the said Chester deceased forever, and the remaining two third parts of the aforesaid described premises with the tenements hereditaments and appurtenances thereto appertaining to the said Polly Vina Chester Charles Susan & Henry, heirs of the said Chester deceased, their heirs & assigns, forever, to the use benefit & behoof of the said Anna widow and relict of the said Chester deceased of the one third part of said described premises as of the tenements hereditaments and appurtinences thereunto appertaining during her natural life and to the use benefit and behoof of the said Polly Vina Chester Charles Susan & Henry, heirs of the said Chester dceceased their heirs and assigns after the decease of the said Anna widow & relict of the said Chester deceased forever and to the use benefit and behoof of the said Polly Vina Chester Charles Susan and Henry heirs of the said Chester deceased of the other two third parts of said described premises as of the tenements hereditaments appurtenances thereto appertaining their heirs and assigns forever."[6]

Chester's brother Abner comes back into the picture in this deed dated 23 February 1822[8]. It would be interesting to learn how Abner became such a large creditor against Chester's estate, and how and why he was appointed trustee under the act of 10 June 1812.

"This Indenture made the twenty third day of February in the year one thousand eight hundred and twenty two between Abner Bunnel of the town of Canandaigua of the first part and Polly Knowles wife of Isaac Knowles, formerly Polly Bunnel, Lovina Ward wife of Moses Ward, formerly Lovina Bunnel, Chester Bunnel, Charles Bunnel, Susan Bunnel and Henry Bunnel of the same place of the other part witnesses. Whereas in and by the act entitled 'An act for the relief of the heirs of Chester Bunnel deceased' passed June 10th 1812 the said Abner Bunnel is appointed a Trustee to receive from Augustus Porter and Peter B. Porter a deed of the north half of lot number fifty six in town ship number nine in the third range of townships in the county of Ontario in trust for the benefit of the creditors and heirs of Chester Bunnel deceased and is authorized to sell and convey the said premises and to pay over the avails thereof or so much thereof as may be necessary together with the personal property of the deceased to discharge the debts of the said deceased to the administrators of the said deceased; which avails it is declared in and by the said act shall be considered as assets in the hands of the said administrators for the payment of the debts of the said deceased and the remainder if any to be paid to the heirs of the said deceased or their guardian or guardians to be distributed equally among the said heirs. And whereas the said Abner Bunnel is himself a creditor of the said Chester Bunnel deceased having a Judgment against John Brockelbank and Josiah Robinson administrators of the estate of the said Chester in the Court of Common pleas of the county of Ontario docketed on the twenty seventh day of June one thousand eight hundred and twelve for the sum of sixteen hundred and twenty nine dollars and seventy one cents, which judgment is the oldest against the said Chester and has priority to any other claim or demand against his estate. And whereas John Brockelbank and Josiah Robinson were appointed administrators of the estate of the said Chester Bunnel and have removed out of the state of New York and there are no administrators of the said estate. And whereas the said Abner Bunnel hath pursuant to the said act received from the said Augustus Porter and Peter B. Porter a conveyance of the north half of the said lot number fifty six and hath executed a bond pursuant to the directions of the said act to the heirs of the said Chester Bunnel. And whereas the said Abner Bunnel is disposed to appropriate the said premises to the benefit of the heirs of the said Chester Bunnel and to allow the full value thereof upon his said judgment and for that purpose has sold the said premises to the said parties of the second part who are the heirs of the said Chester Bunnel deceased for the sum of nine hundred dollars. Now therefore this Indenture witnesses that the said Abner Bunnel for and in consideration of the premises and of the sum of Nine hundred dollars which he hereby acknowledges to have received of the said parties of the second part and which he hereby covenants to apply and allow on the said juegment so obtained by him, hath granted bargained sold conveyed and confirmed and by these presents doth grant bargain sell convey and confirm unto the said parties of the second part their heirs and assigns forever the said north half of lot number fifty six in township number nine in the third range of townships in the county of Ontario containing seventy five acres together with the hereditaments and appurtenances thereunto belonging and all the right title and interest of the said Abner Bunnel to the same and to every parth thereof To have and to hold the said premises with the [??????] the said parties of the second part their heirs and assigns to their only proper use benefit and behoof forever. In witness whereof the said Abner Bunnel hath hereunto set his hand and seal the day and year first above written."[8]

Was the act of 10 June 1812 for the relief of the heirs an act of Ontario co, or was it enacted by the legislature of the state of New York? Chester's descendants might find that there is more to be learned about this matter in legislative records.

It appears that the heirs had had to sell the original property comprising the south half of lot 56, since there is a deed on file in Ontario co Deed Book 43, p. 602, in which Charles Bunnell repurchases that property from James Parshall for $50[9].

The widow Ann Bunnel appears in the 1830 census in Canandaigua: 0001-01000001[3], and probably in the 1840 census in the town of South Bristol, Ontario co, NY[3], living with Mary (Phelps) Bunnel, widow of Ann's son Chester, Jr. Widow Anna appears in the 1850 census in Canandaigua at the age of 79, with real estate valued at $1800[3]. She died 4 September 1861 and was buried in Pine Bank Cemetery in Cheshire, town of Canadaigua[10].

Children:
      1. 320353. Polly[6], b. about 1800[3]; m. before 1822 Isaac Knowles[8].
                  Children (surname Knowles)(living with uncle Henry Bunnell in 1850):[11]
                  1. Maria.   2. William.
      2. 320354. Lovina[6], b. about 1802[3]; m. before 1822 Moses Ward[8].
                  Children (surname Ward):[11]
                  1. Chester B.   3. William.   5. Sarah.
                  2. Andrew.   4. Moses.
      3. 320355. Chester[6], b. about 1804[3]; m. about 1826 Mary Phelps[11].
                  Children (surname Bunnell):[11]
                  1. Ambrose.   2. Aaron H.
      4. 320356. Charles[6], b. 4 July 1805[11]; m. (first) 5 Sept. 1829 Margaret Maria
                Barlow[11]; m. (second) after 1877 Mrs. Mary Ann Harvey[11]; d. 13 Aug.
                1894[11].
                  Children (surname Bunnell):[11]
                  1. Jonathan.   5. William Tecumcia. 9. Mary Jane.
                  2. Charles Barlow.   6. Byron Lord.   10. Margaret Josephine.
                  3. Alby Monroe.   7. George.   11. Sarah Ann.
                  4. Joseph Almie.   8. Susannah Maria. 12. Harriet Elviry.
      5. 320357. Susan[6], b. about 1808[3]; m. about 1827 Russell D. Salisbury[3].
      6. 320358. Henry[6], b. about 1811[3]; m. Mrs. Elizabeth E. (Penoyer) Brown[12];
                d. 1888[11].
                Children (surname Bunnell):[12]
                1. Francis H.   3. Charles M.   4. Elizabeth.
                2. George Madison.

REFERENCES:

1. New Haven - Jacobus, p. 368.
2. *History of Cheshire, Connecticut, from 1694 to 1840*, by Joseph Perkins Beach, 1912.
3. CB Database.
4. Ltr. 25 May 1972 from Clyde Maffin, Ontario County Historian to Nona Bassett.
5. Inventory of estate of Chester Bunnel, Ontario co Surrogate's office, Book 4, pp. 181, 21, 202, photocopy sent to me by Nona Bassett, Merced, CA.
6. Ontario co Deed Book 38, pp. 167-169, photocopy sent to me by Mary (Bunnell) Swift, Shaker Heights, OH.
7. Duncan, p. 88.
8. Ontario co Deed Book 44, pp. 366-368, photocopy sent to me by Mary (Bunnell) Swift.
9. Ontario co Deed Book 43, p. 602, photocopy sent to me by Mary (Bunnell) Swift.
10. Ltr. 20 Aug. 1970 from Clyde Maffin, Ontario co Historian to Zoe C. Magden.
11. Research by Nona Bassett.
12. Ltr. 26 Mar. 1961 from Mrs. Albert Bunnell, Canandaigua, NY.

1-1-9-6-3-4 D138 CB310176

ABNER[6] BUNNELL (Abner[5], Abner[4], Nathaniel[3], Benjamin[2], William[1]) was born 24 September 1780 at Cheshire[1], New Haven co, CT, and was baptized 12 November 1780[1,2] by Parson Foot[2] of the Congregational Church at Cheshire. On 3 October 1802, at Cheshire[1,2] he was married (first) by Parson Foot[2] to AZUBA HULL[1,2], daughter of Abijah and Rachel (Thompson) Hull[1]. She was born 5 July 1780[1] and was baptized 15 July 1781[1] at Cheshire. In October 1803 they moved to the town of Canandaigua[3], Ontario co, NY, where his brother Chester had settled a year or two before. They lived there the rest of their lives.

Abner was a carpenter, joiner and builder[3]. A letter written in 1911 by his grandson Walter King to Walter's cousin Anna Bunnell includes the following: "An incident or two of early history may be of interest, Grandfather Bunnell was a Col. in the war with Great Britain under General Wadsworth of Genneseo, he was ordered with his regiment to go to Buffalo to prevent an attack of the British, he had between 2 and 300 Indians with him. He reached Buffalo just as the British were leaving after setting fire to the place. Some time after the close of the war there was a sham battle in which Grandfather had a prominent part. When it was over Gen. Wadsworth who was commander made an address to the troops in the course of which he said soldiers you have all acquitted yourselves nobly. I wish I could say as much of your officers, it stirred grandfathers blood. He resigned his commission, took off his military apparel and then gave the General a piece of his mind in good earnest. Grandfather built the academy in Canandaigua and the family lived in part of it while it was being built."[4] The deaths of three of Abner's children were reported in *The Ontario Repository*, an early weekly newspaper. Abner Horton Bunnell in 1809 was "son of Abner, when Eliza died in 1813 she was "daughter of Capt. Abner," and when A. Hull died in 1815 he was "son of Major A. Bunnell." Abner's title of Col. came later, probably from continued service in the local militia.

Abner appears in the census in Canandaigua in 1810: 1011-2001[5]; in 1820: 200230-21110-AG[5]; in 1830: 1010102-010002[5]; and in 1840: 00002001-0010011[5]. Azuba (Hull) Bunnell died 10 December 1822[6,7] at Canandaigua[7]. Abner married (second)(before 1830?[5]) GERTRUDE V. AVERILL[6], sister of his son-in-law Elisha Averill[6]. She was born about 1797 in Vermont. The census records suggest that Abner's household usually included an extended family. In 1850 in Canandaigua the census[10] lists Abner age 69, carpenter, realestate $14,000, Gertrude 53, Abner's son Frederick 42 carpenter $1000 and his wife Juliette 38 and their children Anna S. 3 and William F. 1, Abner's granddaughter and Gertrude's niece Frances B. Averill 21, and Catherine Hollin age 12, born in Canada.

By 1860 Abner 79 was listed as a retired carpenter with real estate of $19,000 and wife Gertrude 64. Gertrude died 14 March 1865[8] and was buried in the West Avenue Cemetery in Canandaigua[8]. Abner's last appearance in the census in Canandaigua was in the 1865 census conducted by New York State. Abner 84, house-joiner, was living with his widowed daughter-in-law Juliette Maria (Bunnell) Bunnell and her children.

During his long life in Canandaigua Abner Bunnell was a prominent citizen of the village and the county. Besides his activities as a carpenter and builder, he dealt extensively in real estate, and many of his deeds are recorded in the Ontario co courthouse[13]. He sold some land to his brother Moses in 1819 and bought it back in 1826 when Moses decided to move to Jefferson co. He was appointed administrator of his brother Chester's estate and was involved in carrying out the provisions of the legislative act for the relief of Chester's widow and children.

Abner died 10 September 1867[6,8] and was buried with Gertrude in the West Avenue Cemetery in Canandaigua[8]. His gravestone calls him Col. Abner Bunnell[8]. His will, proved 14 November 1867, reads:[12]

I, Abner Bunnell of the Village of Canandaigua in the County of Ontario, and State of New York do make, ordain, publish, and declare, this to be my last Will and Testament, int he manner following, that is to say.--
First I direct that all my just debts, and funeral expenses shall be paid by my Executors hereinafter named, and that a suitable monument be erected at my grave, by them.
Secondly I give and devise unto my Wife Gertrude Bunnell during the term of her natural life, the use of the House and Lot, situate on the East side of Main Street, in the village of Canandaigua wherein I now reside. I also give and bequeath to my said wife Gertrude, the use, during her natural life, of all him household furniture (excepting my Secretary and Bookcase) and, also my family library, the same to be used by her with care and kept in as good order and condition as reasonable and proper use thereof will allow. I also give and bequeath to my said Wife, Gertrude, during her natural life, the interest on the sum of Two thousand dollars, which said sum I direct to be safely invested, and the interest thereon, to be paid to her, semi-annually by my Executors hereinafter named, which said bequest and devises shall be accepted by her in lieu of dower.
Thirdly After the decease of my said wife, said sum of two thousand dollars shall be given to my grandchildren, Anna Bunnell and William F. Bunnell, children of my son Frederick Bunnell, deceased, share and share alike, if both be living, but in case of the death of either of my Grandchildren, said sum of Two thousand dollars shall go to the survivor of them. The personal property hereinbefore bequeathed to my wife, for life, I direct shall after her decease be disposed of as follows. My son Orpheus Bunnell shall have my Secretary, Bookcase and family library. The Household furniture my daughter Mary King shall have.
Fourthly All my real estate after the decease of my said wife, I authorize, empower and direct my Executors hereinafter named, or the survivor of them, or their successors to sell, as soon as my be, at private sale, at such prices and on such terms as to them shall seem just and proper and most of the benefit of all parties concerned and the proceeds thereof to divide equally between my son Orpheus Bunnell and my daughter Mary King. And in case of the decease of either of them before the death of my wife, the sum which would be payable to such deceased shall go to his or her heirs.
Fifthly I give and bequeath unto my daughter Mary King the sum of Two thousand five hundred dollars, to be paid one year after my decease. I also give and bequeath to my grandsons Talma Averill and Selden Averill the sum of

three hundred dollars each, to be paid to them one year after my decease. I also give and bequeath to Fanny Babcock, widow of Pliny F. Babcock, deceased, the sum of three hundred dollars, to be paid to her one year after my decease.

Sixthly I give and bequeath to my son Orpheus Bunnell all my tools and lumber in my joiner shop. I also give and bequeath to my said son, Orpheus Bunnell, the interest on the sum of Four Thousand dollars, which sum I direct my Executors, hereinafter named, to invest, and the interest thereof to pay to him, semi-annually during the term of his natural life, said interest to be computed from the date of my decease.

Seventhly After the decease of my said son Orpheus Bunnell, I direct and bequeath the said sum of Four Thousand Dollars to be paid to the child or children of my said son Orpheus, if he has any child or children, then living and him surviving. In case he leaves no child or children then, the interest on the sum of one thousand dollars thereof, shall be paid to his widow (if he shall leave a widow) during her natural life. In case he leaves no child or children or widow him surviving, at his decease thesaid sum of Four Thousand dollars, and in case he leaves a widow, the sum of Three Thousand dollars shall be paid to the children then living of my daughter Mary King, my daughter Harriet Averill, and Anna Bunnell and William F. Bunnell, my Grandchildren and children of my deceased son Frederick Bunnell, share and share alike. I also direct that after the decease of the widow of my said son Orpheus, should he leave a widow him surviving, the one Thousand dollars of which she receives the interest during her natural life shall be paid to my said Grandchildren last above mentioned who may then be living, share and share alike.

Eighthly All the rest residue and remainder of my property not hereinbefore disposed of I give, bequeath and devise to my said son Orpheus bunnell and my daughter Mary King, share and share alike.

Ninthly In case there should not be sufficient assets for the payment of the legacies hereinabove mentioned and bequeathed I direct that all bequests to my wife shall be fully paid and carried into effect, and that all other bequests hereinbefore made be paid pro rata.

Lastly I do hereby make nominate and appoint Elijah S. Gregory and Hiram Metcalf of Canandaigua aforesaid, to be the Executors of this my last Will and Testament, hereby giving and granting to them full power and authority to do and perform every act and thing proper and necessary to carry this my last Will and Testament into full effect, here by revoking all former wills by me made.

In testimony whereof I have hereunto subscribed my name and affixed my seal this Fifth day of January in the year of our Lord One thousand Eight hundred and Sixty.

Abner Bunnell   {Seal}

The above Instrument, written on two sheets of paper, was subscribed by the said Abner Bunnell, the Testator therein named, in our presence and acknowledged by him to each of us, and he at the same time declared the above instrument so subscribed to be his last Will and Testament, and we at his request have signed our names as witnesses hereto and opposite our names our respective places of residence.

Henry M. Field of Canandaigua New York

J. Wells Taylor of Canandaigua Ontario Co. New York"

Whereas, I, Abner Bunnell, of the village of Canandaigua, in the County of Ontario & State of New York, have made my last Will & Testament in writing, bearing date the fifth day of January in the year of our Lord one thousand eight hundred and sixty, in & by which I have made nominated and appointed Elijah S. Gregory & Hiram Metcalf of Canandaigua aforesaid, to be the executors of my said Will & Testament;

And whereas, the said Elijah S. Gregory is now deceased & said Hiram Metcalf has become a person of unsound mind:

Now Therefore, I do, by this my writing, which I hereby declare to be a Codicil to my said last Will & Testament & to be taken as a part thereof, order & declare that my will is that Alexander H. Howell, of Canandaigua aforesaid be & he hereby is substituted, nominated & appointed as sole executor of my said last Will and Testament instead of said Elijah S. Gregory & Hiram Metcalf, hereby giving & granting unto said Alexander H. Howell, as such Executor, the same powers and authority granted to said Gregory and Metcalf in and by said last Will & Testament & full power to do and perform every act and thing proper and necessary to carry said last Will and Testament into effect.

And lastly, it is my desire that this Codicil be annexed to & made a part of my last Will & Testament as aforesaid to all intents and purposes.

In Witness whereof I have hereunto set my hand and seal this twenty eighth day of February, in the year of our Lord one thousand eight hundred and sixty five.

329   Abner Bunnell {Seal}"[12]

Children:
 1. 320675. Mary Hull, b. 20 Feb. 1804[6]; m. 29 Sept. 1825[11] Earl Douglas King[4]; d. Dec. 1887[6]
    Children (surname King):[3]
    1. Algernon Sidney. 2. Walter Deming. 3. Malcolm Graeme.
    (Was there another son Fred?)
 2. 320673. Abner Horton, b. 18 Sept. 1805[6]; d. 18 May 1809[6].
 3. 320674. Frederick K., b. 7 July 1807[6]; m. 22 Oct. 1840[6] Juliette Maria Bunnell[6] 1-1-9-7-5-2-3; d. 13 July 1856[6]
    Children (surname Bunnell):[3,6]
    1. Anna Stillman. 2. William Frederick.
 4. 320676. Harriet, b. 2 Dec. 1809[6]; m. Elisha P. Averill[6]; d. 18 Oct. 1859[6].
    Children (surname Averill):
    1. Fitch[4].   3. Selden[3,12].   4. Frances[3].
    2. Talma[3,12].
 5. 320677. Eliza Ann, b. 19 Dec. 1811[3]; d. 29 Apr. 1813[3].
 6. 320678. A. Hull, b. 10 Jan. 1814[3]; d. 6 Aug. 1815[3].
 7. 320679. Orpheus, b. 9 Sept. 1816[6]; m. Mary Taylor[3,4]; d. 1 Feb. 1879 s.p.[3]

REFERENCES:
 1. New Haven - Jacobus, pp. 368, 886.
 2. *History of Cheshire, Connecticut, from 1694 to 1840*, by Joseph Perkins Beach, 1912, pp. 349, 385, 448.
 3. Biles Manuscript, p. 297.
 4. Ltr. 14 Sept. 1911 from Walter Deming King, South Haven, MI, to Anna Stillman Bunnell, Canandaigua, NY.
 5. CB Database.
 6. Ltr. 4 Aug. 1907 from Anna Stillman Bunnell (Abner's granddaughter) to John A. Biles.
 7. Ltr. 20 Aug. 1970 from Clyde Maffin, Ontario County Historian to Zoe Magden, Tacoma, WA.
 8. Ltr. 4 Dec. 1970 from Clyde Maffin, Ontario County Historia to Nona Bassett, Merced, CA.
 9. 1865 New York State census, Canandaigua, Ontario co, NY, extracted & sent to me by Nona Bassett.
 10. 1850 Federal census, Ontario co, NY, extracted & sent to me by Nona Bassett.
 11. Bunnell/Bonnell marriages in New York State, gathered and sent to me by Nancie Davis, West Columbia, SC.
 12. Will of Abner Bunnell, photocopy sent to me by Nona Bassett.
 13. List of Abner Bunnell's grantor deeds compiled by Nona Bassett.

1-1-9-6-3-7 D139 CB310029

REUBEN[6] BUNNELL (Abner[5], Abner[4], Nathaniel[3], Benjamin[2], William[1]) was born 17 July 1786 at Cheshire[1,2], New Haven co, CT, and was baptized 23 July 1786[1,2] by Parson Foot[2] of the Congregational Church at Cheshire. On 28 September 1806 he was married at Cheshire by Parson Foot to PHILOME HULL[1,2], daughter of Thelus and Mary (Newton) Hull[1]. She was born about 1793 and was baptized 11 May 1804 in the Cheshire Congregational Church[1]. Reuben appears in the 1810 census in Cheshire, CT: 101-001[3].

SIXTH GENERATION

On 19 December 1814 Reuben and his mother Sarah were appointed administrators of his father's estate[4,5]. Soon after this Reuben removed to Canandaigua, Ontario co, NY, where his brothers Chester and Abner were already settled. He bought a piece of land from brother Abner[6]. On 18 July 1816, when the administrators Sarah and Reuben sold several pieces of land in Cheshire, CT, to settle the estate, Reuben was identified as "of Canandaigua, NY."[4,5] He appears in the census record in Canandaigua in 1820: 21001-10001[6] and in 1830: 0102101-001000011[3]. On 9 August 1827 Reuben bought 75 acres in the northern part of the town from Joseph Phelps for $1400 on west side of property owned by his brother Abner[7]. Then on 5 December 1831 he added an adjacent 1/2 acre lot, purchasing it from the widow Ellathea Brown for $47.50[8].

Reuben died 24 February 1839 in Canandaigua and was buried in the Pioneer Cemetery there[9]. His will was probated 30 March 1839[10,11,12,13]. I have not seen a copy of the will, but I have copies of several deeds which refer to it. In May 1844 Reuben, Jr., and his brother Abner 2d paid $500 to their brother Jesse and his wife for their share of the 75 acres Reuben, Sr., had purchased from Joseph Phelps[10]. Then on 1 January 1848 Abner 2d sold his share to Reuben, Jr., for $600[11]. On 16 September 1848 John and Mary Vermilya received $500 from Reuben for their share of the farm and the estate[12]. Finally, on 30 October 1850 Reuben paid $400 to Charles S. Bunnell for a quitclaim to the 75 acres and to release all claim which Charles may have had against the estate[13]. All of these deeds, in addition to the sale of the land, contained references to provisions in the will of Reuben, Sr., providing for the support and maintenance of Temperance Phelps and the support of Philome Bunnell and the payment of a legacy to Mary Vermilya[10,11,12,13].

By 1850 the title to the property was consolidated in the hands of Reuben, Jr., together with the dower right of his mother Philome. And on 18 November 1850 Philome and Reuben sold the entire property to Asbury Christian for $4,295.31[14]. The 1850 census in Canandaigua lists Philome 61 living with her son Reuben 37, his wife Jane 28 and their daughter Jane E. 3[3,6]. Reuben's brother Charles 28[3,6] and Temperance Phelps 72[3,6] also lived with them. I have been unable to discover what relationship, if any, existed with Temperance Phelps. The date and place of Philome's death has not been found.

Children:
  1. 320669. Jesse H., b. 1809[15]; m. 14 Oct. 1835 Ruth Ann Parker[15]; d. 12 Nov. 1869[15]
  2. 320667. Reuben, b. about 1814[9]. m. Jane _____ [9]; d. 3 May 1851[1].
       Children (surname Bunnell):[6]
       1. Jane E.
  3. 320670. Abner, b. about 1819[9]; d. 9 Mar. 1863[9].
  4. 320672. Mary, b. about 1820[16]; m. about 1837 John Vermilya[12,16]; d. 9 Jan. 1873[16].
       Children (surname Vermilya):[16]
       1. Marietta.   3. Dwight.   4. William J.
       2. Jane.

331

5.   Charles S.[13]   [The CB Database considers this Charles to be the same
                            person as Charles Henry Bunnell and lists him thus:
5. 320668. Charles Henry, b. about 1822[3]; m. Sarah Quick[3]; d. 8 January 1896[3].
            Children (surname Bunnell):[3]
                1. Henry Charles.   2. Orren V.   3. Amanda.

                            I (WRA) don't think there is sufficient evidence for this
                            identification.]

REFERENCES:
1. New Haven - Jacobus, pp. 368, 890.
2. Cheshire, pp. 349, 385, 448.
3. CB Database.
4. Cheshire, CT, deeds abstracted by Nona Bassett.
5. Cheshire, CT, land records abstracted by Ruth C. Duncan.
6. Research by Nona Bassett, Merced, CA.
7. Deed, 9 Aug. 1827, Joseph Phelps to Reuben Bunnell, Ontario co Deed Book 46, pp. 217, 218,
    photocopy sent to me by Mary (Bunnell) Swift, Shaker Heights, OH.
8. Deed, 15 Dec. 1831 Ellathea Brown to Reuben Bunnell, Ontario co Deed Book 52, p. 87,
    photocopy sent to me by Mary (Bunnell) Swift.
9. Ltr. 4 Dec. 1970 from Clyde Maffin, Ontario County Historian to Nona Bassett.
10. Deed 27 May 1844 Jesse H. and Ruth Ann Bunnell to Reuben Bunnell and Abner Bunnell 2d,
    Ontario co Deed Book 84, pp. 333-335, photocopy sent to me by Mary (Bunnell) Swift.
11. Deed 1 Jan. 1848 Abner Bunnell 2d to Reuben Bunnell, Ontario co Deed Book 84, pp. 335, 336,
    photocopy sent to me by Mary (Bunnell) Swift.
12. Deed 16 Sept. 1848 John and Mary Vermilya to Reuben Bunnell, Ontario co Deed Book 93,
    pp. 255-257, photocopy sent to me by Mary (Bunnell) Swift.
13. Deed 30 Oct. 1850 Charles S. Bunnel to Reuben Bunnell, Ontario co Deed Book ? , pp. 214, 215,
    photocopy sent to me by Mary (Bunnell) Swift.
14. Deed Philome Bunnell and Reuben and Jane M. Bunnell to Asbury Christian, Ontario co Deed Book
    93, pp. 320, 321, photocopy sent to me by Mary (Bunnell) Swift.
15. Duncan, p. 89.
16. Ltr. 7 Nov. 1988 from May (Bunnell) Swift.

1-1-9-6-3-10   D52x   CB310174

ELIAS[6] BUNNELL (Abner[5], Abner[4], Nathaniel[3], Benjamin[2], William[1]) was born 4 October 1795
at Cheshire[1,2], New Haven co, CT, and was baptized 17 January 1796[1,2] by Parson Foot[2] of the
Congregational Church at Cheshire. Like his brothers he removed to Canandaigua, Ontario co,
NY. He is listed in both the 1820 census: 010100-00101[3] and the 1830 census:
000001-010001[3] in Canandaigua twp. He was apparently married before 1820, and probably
had a daughter born between 1820 and 1825[3]. Was the Ann Eliza Bunnell of Canandaigua who
married Samuel Fennow of Tyrone 18 April 1841 in Canandaigua his daughter?[4]

REFERENCES:
1. New Haven - Jacobus, p. 368.
2. Cheshire, pp. 349, 448.
3. CB Database.
4. Marriages in New York State, gathered by Nancie Davis, West Columbia, SC.

1-1-9-6-5-1   D140   CB310179

ENOS[6] BUNNELL (Enos[5], Abner[4], Nathaniel[3], Benjamin[2], William[1]) was born 25 April 1777 at Cheshire[1], New Haven co, CT. As a young man, about 1802, he moved to the Grand River valley at Brant's Ford[2] in what is now Brant co, Ontario, CAN. In 1806 he built the second cabin in the settlement then known as Mississauga Hill, more recently the site of the Brantford Armories[2]. About 1809 Enos married SARAH WEIR[2,5]. He acquired a farm of 184 acres on Fairchild's Creek which had originally been leased by Capt. Joseph Brant for 999 years to John B. Rosseau[3]. All his children were born on the farm.

On 11 June 1810 Enos sold his right to the estate of his father in Cheshire, CT, to his brother Wareham for $75[4]. In 1830 Enos moved to the then Village of Brantford and soon established himself in the commercial life of the community[2]. When Enos died has not been found, but his wife Sarah died 6 December 1880[5].

Children:
1. 320897. Maria Jane, b. 29 Mar. 1809[5]; 5 Feb. 1835 Jacob Choate[5].
    Children (surname Choate):[5]
    1. Alexander Bunnell.   3. Jane.   5. Clara.
    2. Sarah Augusta.   4. Lawrence.
2. 320896. Sarah[5], m. Rev. John Kennedy[5]; d. 1 June 1890 s.p.[5]
3. 320895. Alexander[5]; m. Caroline Clench[5]; d. 3 July 1871[5].
    Children (surname Bunnell):[5]
    1. Henry, d. young.
4. 320028. Enos, b. 1818[3]; m. Cornelia Kennedy[5]; d. 12 Sept. 1875[2,5]
    Children (surname Bunnell):[5]
    1. Arthur Kennedy.   3. Sarah Cornelia.   5. Grace Augusta.
    2. Charles Samuel.   4. John Alexander.   6. Effie Maria.
5. 320898. Augusta[5]; m. 23 May 1866[5] David Canfield[5]; no children[5].

REFERENCES:
1. New Haven - Jacobus, p. 368.
2. "Bunnell Family One of Oldest," article by John Merriam published 21 June 1978 in the *Brant News*, Brantford, Ontario, CAN, copy sent to me by Cynthia Bunnell, Brantford, Ontario, and reprinted in the *Bunnell/Bonnell Newsletter*, Vol. 3, No. 4, p. 7.
3. *History of the County of Brant, Ontario*, by F. Douglas Reville, 1920, p. 337, photocopy sent to me by Ellen Dorn, Manhattan Beach, CA.
4. Lines, p. 21.
5. Chart - Ancestors and Descendants of Enos Bunnell, who came to Brantford, Ontario in 1802, compiled by Cynthia Bunnell - 1988.

1-1-9-6-5-2   D141   CB310180

WARHAM or WAREHAM[6] BUNNELL (Enos[5], Abner[4], Nathaniel[3], Benjamin[2], William[1]) was born 25 April 1781 in Cheshire[1], New Haven co, CT, and was baptised 24 June 1781[1,2] by Parson Foot[2] of the Congregational Church at Cheshire. On 23 September 1805, at New Haven,

New Haven co, CT, he married ANNA PIERSON STILLMAN[1]. She was born 5 March 1787 at New Haven[3], the daughter of Ashbel and Mary (Storer) Stillman[3]. Warham was a sea captain at the time of his marriage[4].

On 11 June 1810 Wareham bought his brother Enos' right in the estate of their father for $75[5]. Wareham was for many years a sea captain on a packet ship from New Haven to the West Indies[6] During the War of 1812 he was once captured by the English, the cargo destroyed, and the men left on an island from which they escaped after several weeks[6].

Warham appears in the census records in New Haven, New Haven co every decade from 1810 to 1860: In 1810 as W. Bunnel: 10010-10200[4]; in 1820 as Wareham Bunnel: 010010-11010[4]; in 1830 as Wareham Bunnell: 0000001-1001101[4]; in 1840 as Warham Bunnett: 0000001-000101101-MFG[4]; in 1850 as Warham Bunnell 69, Ann P. 63, Frances A. 43, Sarah J. 23, and Leman 3[4]; and in 1860 as Wareham Bunnell 79, retired sea master, wife Anna T. 73, Frances A. 52 teacher, and Susan L. (sic) 32[4].

Anna (Stillman) Bunnell died 25 November 1862[1] and Warham died 3 January 1864[1] in New Haven. They were buried in the Grove Street Cemetery in New Haven[3].

Was his name Warham or Wareham? The confusion seems to have been as great during his lifetime as it is now. His granddaughter Anna Stillman Bunnell consistently called him Wareham in her letters to John Biles, and she copied it that way from the family Bible[8]. The birth records of Cheshire, CT, published in the History of Cheshire list him as Wareham[2], but in the same history Parson Foot's record of baptisms calls him Warham[2]. Bishop Lines in his notebook refers to him several times as Wareham Bunnell[5], and both John Biles[6] and Ruth Duncan[3] list him that way. The census records, as indicated above, were inconclusive. To complete the confusion, I have a photocopy of a letter written 23 November 1837 to Hon. J. S. Edwards, Commissioner of Pensions in Washington, DC, which is clearly and beautifully signed "Warham Bunnell"[7].

Children:
1. 320563. Frances Ann, b. 25 Sept. 1806[8]; d. 4 May 1890[8].
2. 320564. William Henry, b. 1 Jan. 1809[8]; m. 22 Mar. 1842 Elizabeth Fuller
   Leeman[3]; d. 14 Dec. 1867[8].
   Children (surname Bunnell):[8]
   1. Leeman.
3. 320565. Juliette Maria, b. 4 Aug. 1811[8]; m. 22 Oct. 1840 Frederick Bunnell[3,9]
   1-1-9-6-3-4-3; d. 29 Mar. 1895[8]
   Children (surname Bunnell):[9]
   1. Anna Stillman.   2. William Frederick.
4.   Mary Pierson, b. 12 July 1813[8]; d. 27 Sept. 1814[8].
5. 320562. Alfred Augustus, b. 5 Sept. 1818[8]; d. 11 Sept. 1819[8].
6. 320566. Mary Atwater, b. 31 Mar. 1823[8]; d. 17 Mar. 1824[8]
7. 320567. Sarah St. John, b. 1 July 1827[8]; d. 1 Mar. 1893 unmarried[8].

REFERENCES:
1. New Haven - Jacobus, p. 368.
2. Cheshire, pp. 349, 448.
3. Duncan, pp. 89, 90.
4. CB Database.
5. Lines, p. 21.
6. Biles Manuscript, p. 303.
7. Ltr. 23 Nov. 1837 Warham Bunnell to J. S. Edwards.
8. Ltr. 8 Dec. 1907 Anna S. Bunnell to John A. Biles in which is copied the Wareham Bunnell family Bible record.
9. Ltr. 4 Aug. 1907 Anna S. Bunnell, Geneva, NY, to John A. Biles.

1-1-9-6-5-8   D142   CB310186

WILLIAM[6] BUNNELL (Enos[5], Abner[4], Nathaniel[3], Benjamin[2], William[1]) was born 20 September 1794 at Cheshire[1,2], New Haven co, CT, and was baptized 7 June 1795[1,2] by Parson Foot[2] of the Congregational Church at Cheshire. On 24 August 1815 he married CLARISSA STEVENS[3], daughter of Elisha and Agnes (Kimberley) Stevens[3]. She was born about 1792[3].

The next month Clarissa deeded over to William land in Waterbury, New Haven co, CT, she had inherited from her father[6]. William and Clarissa seem to have lived there from the time of their marriage[6]. The Waterbury land records contain half a dozen references to deeds by which William sold pieces of this land between 1815 and 1837[6]. The property was in that part of Waterbury known as Salem Society, or Salem Bridge Society[6]. This southern part of Waterbury was later set off as the town of Naugatuck.

The Naugatuck Congregational Church records contain a number of references to this family: A child of Mr. Bunnell died 24 September 1825 of dysentery at age 6 months[4]; another child, age 3, did of canker 20 October 1826[4]; his wife Clarissa was admitted to the church on 6 July 1828[4]; the three living children, Harriet, Elizabeth and Frederick were baptized on 19 July 1829[4]; and the youngest daughter Minerva was baptized 2 May 1833[4]. Clarissa (Stevens) Bunnell died 2 November 1835 at age 43 and was buried in Hillside Cemetery in Naugatuck.

Some time before 1860 William went out to Hudson, Summit co, OH, to live with his son Frederick, who had settled there in 1841. They appear there together in the 1860 census[8]. William died in Hudson 3 November 1875[3]. His body was returned to Connecticut and he was buried with his wife in Hillside Cemetery, Naugatuck.

Children:
1. 320132. Harriet H.[3], b. 11 Dec. 1816[7]; m. 2 June 1835 Henry Willis Lines[7]; d. 24 Feb. 1898[3].
   Children (surname Lines):[3,7]
   1. Henry Wales.   2. Edwin Steven.   3. Mary E.
2. 320133. Elizabeth, b. about 1818[4]; d. 22 Mar. 1875 age 57[4].
3. 320134. Frederick William[4], b. 6 July 1820[3]; m. 12 Jan. 1845 Maria Mansur[3]; d. 24 Apr. 1875[3].

4. 320135. Minerva, b. Mar. 1823[3]; d. 20 Oct. 1826[4].
5. 320136. Julie Ann[3], b. Mar. 1825[4]; d. 24 Sept. 1825[4].
6. 320137. Minerva Stevens, b. 11 Dec. 1830[4]; d. 30 Mar. 1880 age 49[4].

REFERENCES:
1. New Haven - Jacobus, p. 369.
2. Cheshire, pp. 349, 448.
3. Duncan, p. 90.
4. *Naugatuck, Connecticut, Congregational Church Records 1781-1901*, by Helen S. Ullman, p. 20. photocopy sent to me by Ruth C. Duncan.
5. *Ancient Burying Grounds of the Town of Waterbury, Conn.*, Mattatuck Historical Society Publications, Vol. 2 - 1917, p. 135, abstracted by Dorothy Cotton, Dixon, CA.
6. Waterbury, CT, land records abstracted by Ruth C. Duncan.
7. Lines, p. 8.
8. CB Database.

1-1-9-6-6-4   D54iv   CB310193

ELIAB[6] BUNNELL (Reuben[5], Abner[4], Nathaniel[3], Benjamin[2], William[1]) was born 6 April 1783 in Cheshire[1], New Haven co, CT. Although his older siblings are named in the list of baptisms by Parson Foot of the Congregational Church at Cheshire[2], Eliab and his younger sister are not. Perhaps their parents had changed their religious affiliation.

Eliab is mentioned in the probate record at Wallingford, New Haven co, CT, in 1794 when he inherited part of his father's land in Cheshire[3]. A deed dated 30 April 1798 by Eliab's sister Nabby Hotchkiss and her husband conveys "a certain piece of land in the estate of her father Reuben Bunnell . . . and lies on the East Side of land set out to Eliab from said estate. . ."[4]. In 1804 Eliab, his mother and his sisters sold 10 acres of land in Cheshire to Joel Parker, who apparently gave a mortgage to Eliab and his mother[5]. About this time Eliab seems to have moved to Winchester, Litchfield co, CT, the Annals of which record in 1805 that "This year Eliab Bunnell in company with Reuben Baldwin set up a work shop in which they made patent washing machines until about 1810 when Mr. Bunnell removed to Vernon, New York."[6] A number of families from Winchester and Torrington, CT, had settled in Vernon, Oneida co, NY, about ten years earlier[7].

That is as far as the paper trail has taken us for Eliab of Cheshire, CT. The remainder of this account depends on circumstantial evidence. I personally believe it to be factual, but have not yet found the necessary proof. Eliab's name is very unusual. Some researchers have misread old handwritten records as "Elias," while others, reading "Eliab," have assumed it was a mistake and corrected it to the more familiar "Elias". However, the rarity of the name allows us to suggest this continuation of this man's life. I am indebted to Nancy Bunnell, Flint, MI, for her persistence in searching out the documents to present this case.

Eliab Bunnell apparently moved very soon from Vernon, NY, to Washington, DC, where he married JANE M. ROBERTSON[8]. Their marriage license was dated 9 November 1812[8]. In

336

the War of 1812 Muster Rolls Eliab Bunnell is listed as a matross in the First Regiment District of Columbia Militia[9].

Eliab formed a partnership with William B. Robertson, probably his brother-in-law. In October 1815 they leased Lot 112 in Georgetown from Dr. Ninian Magruder[10]. On 12 July 1816 they purchased the lot from Dr. Magruder for $900[10]. They sold lot 112 to Clement Smith three days later for $2000[10]. Bunnell and Robertson were active in the real estate and mercantile business for at least the next ten years as evidenced by deeds and tax records[10]. In 1818 Eliab was assessed on $600 real property and $100 personal property[11]. The following year the firm of Bunnell and Robertson was assessed on four lots totaling $7300[11].

Eliab appears in the 1820 census in Washington DC: 200210-20020-MFG3[12]. I suggest that the 2 males under 10 were sons Henry and Reuben, that the 2 males 18-26 were hired employees, and that the 2 females under 10 were daughters Alba? and another not yet identified. Eliab himself was the male of 26-45 and wife Jane was one of the females 26-45. Eliab and the two 'employees' were the three men engaged in manufacturing. Eliab Bunnell a manufacturer in Winchester, CT, and Eliab Bunnell a manufacturer in Washington DC adds weight to my conclusion that they were the same person.

Eliab appears again in the 1830 census in Washington: 0111001-0110001[12]. The 2 children aged 5-10 have not been identified, even tentatively, but the male of 10-15 is probably son Reuben, the male of 15-20 is probably son Henry, and the female of 10-15 is probably the Alba Bunnell who married Joseph W. Amery in Washington on 11 October 1842.

The 1830 census is the last record we have found relating to Eliab and Jane Bunnell. Where and when they died is still unknown.

Children (constructed from the census records):
1. 027779. Henry, b. about 1813[13] (under 10 in 1820; 15-20 in 1830)[12]; m. 20 Dec. 1832 Permelia C. Amery, Charles co, MD[13]; d. before 1860[13].
   Children (surname Bunnell):[12,13]
   1. Mary Jane.
   2. Susanna Aurelia.
   3. Joseph?
   4. Richard.
   5. Eleazer?
   6. Sophia Virginia.
   7. Caroline Elizabeth.
   8. **Abner Eliab**.
   9. Roland (or Robert) C.
2. daughter, b. about 1815 (under 10 in 1820; 10-15 in 1830)[12].
3. 005484. Reuben W., b. 1817[13] (under 10 in 1820; 10-15 in 1830)[12]; m. 25 Apr. 1840 Mary J. Mullikin[13]; d. 22 Dec. 1860[13].
   Children (surname Bunnell):[12,13]
   1. George H.
   2. William.
   3. **Eliab Mullican**
   4. Catherine E.
   5. Elizabeth.
4. daughter, b. about 1819 (under 10 in 1820)[12].
5. son, b. 1820-1825 (5-10 in 1830)[12].
6. daughter, b. 1820-1825 (5-10 in 1830)[12]; probably Alba, m. 11 Oct. 1842 Joseph W. Amery.

NOTE: Two items of proof are needed for this account. First, proof that Eliab of Cheshire, CT, and Eliab of Washington, DC, are the same person. Second, proof that Henry and Reuben were sons of Eliab, though the fact that Henry named a son Abner Eliab and Reuben named a son Eliab Mullican leaves little doubt in my mind.

REFERENCES:
1. New Haven - Jacobus, p. 369.
2. Cheshire, pp. 60, 61.
3. Connecticut Probate Records abstracted by Ruth C. Duncan - Wallingford Dist. 285 8 Doc. 1794.
4. Lines, pp. 19, 20.
5. Cheshire, CT, Land REcords abstracted by Ruth C. Duncan - Deed Book 7, pp. 479, 481.
6. *Annals of Winchester, Conn.*, by John Boyd, 1873, excerpted and sent to me by Mrs. Clarence Bunnell, Winsted, CT, in 1960.
7. *Our County and Its People - Oneida County, NY*, by Daniel E. Wager, 1896, p. 567.
8. Certificate of Issuance of Marriage License, and *Marriage Licenses of Washington, DC, 1811-1830*, by Family Line Publishers 1988, p. 21.
9. Ltr. 22 June 2000 from Nancy Bunnell, Flint, MI.
10. List of deeds and other transactions of Eliab Bunnell in Washington DC, compiled by WRA from photocopies of documents obtained and sent to me by Nancy Bunnell.
11. 1818-20 Tax Records for District of Columbia. Photocopies of 2 pages sent to me by Nancy Bunnell.
12. CB Database.
13. Research by Nancy Bunnell, Flint, MI.

1-1-9-6-7-2   D55ii   CB310077

SAMUEL PRESTON[6] BUNNELL (Samuel[5], Abner[4], Nathaniel[3], Benjamin[2], William[1]) was born 12 July 1796 at Cheshire[1], New Haven co, CT, and was baptized 9 October 1796[1,2] by Parson Foot[2] of the Congregational Church at Cheshire. Very little has been learned about his life. His father died in 1808[1], leaving his mother with the care of the two children. In 1810 his grandfather Abner Bunnell died[1], and Samuel P. inherited land from Abner's estate[3]. He then needed a guardian to look after his property, and his mother Mary (Hitchcock) Bunnell was appointed for that purpose in 1811[3]. On 6 September 1812 she sold some of his land to Burrage Beach[4].

A Samuel P. Bunnel contracted to buy 100 acres of land in what is now Concord twp, Erie co, NY, on 5 June 1815 from the Holland Land Company[5]. The price of the land was $3.50 per acre[5]. It is not clear that he ever paid for the land or occupied it[5]. I know of no other Samuel P. Bunnell this could be, but it should be noted that he was not quite 19 years old at the time.

Also, could this be the Samuel Bunnell who married Mrs. Lydia Bradley 28 March 1839 at Waterbury, New Haven co, CT?[6]

REFERENCES:
1. New Haven - Jacobus, p. 363.
2. Cheshire, p. 349.
3. Connecticut probate records abstracted by Ruth C. Duncan.

4. Cheshire, CT, land records abstracted by Ruth C. Duncan.
5. *Western New York Land Transactions 1804-1824*, by Karen E. Livsey, Genealogical Publishing Co., Inc., 1990, p. 124, extracts sent to me by Charlotte Dunn, San Diego, CA.
6. *The Town & City of Waterbury, Connecticut from the Aboriginal Period to the Year 1895*, Vol. I, Joseph Anderson, ed., 1896. Appendix: FAMILY RECORDS by Miss Katharine Pritchard, p. 31, abstracted by Dorothy Cotton, Dixon, CA.

1-1-9-6-9-3   CB310219

MILES[6] BUNNELL (Jehiel[5], Abner[4], Nathaniel[3], Benjamin[2], William[1]) was born 17 November 1789[1] at Cheshire, New Haven co, CT. He married DEBORAH _____, who was born 23 August 1792[2]. They removed to Canandaigua, Ontario co, NY, where several of his brothers also located. There, a child of Miles, probably his oldest, died on 6 January 1813[3]. He volunteered at Buffalo, NY, on 9 September 1814 for service in the War of 1812 as a private in a company commanded by Capt. J. Pullin's in the regiment of New York Militia under the command of Lt. Col. Hopkins[4]. His service was for the relief of the American garrison at Fort Erie in Upper Canada[4]. He received an honorable discharge on 8 November 1814 at Batavia, Genesee co, NY[4].

Before the end of the decade Miles removed his family to a farm in Charlestown, Clark co, IN, where he appears in the 1820 census: 000010-20010[3]. Another moved took him to Westport, Oldham co, (Jefferson co before 1824), KY, where he appears in the 1830 census: 1100101-1011001[3]. In 1831 Miles Bonnell "of Jefferson co, KY" bought 80 acres of land in Bartholomew co, IN[7]. In 1833 Miles and Deborah Bunnel "of Bartholomew co" sold the 80 acres to Susanna Farbush[7]. The following year he bought lot 150 in Columbus, Bartholomew co, from James and Peggy McAchram[7]. Here he established a leather manufacturing business[2,3].

Miles Bonnell was a witness to the will of Anthony Head in Bartholomew co on 14 June 1836[2]. On 14 February 1838 Samuel Crittenden filed a lawsuit against him[2]. He appears in the 1840 census in Columbus: 00111011-0011001-MFG[3]. The two extra men in his household were probably employees. His wife Deborah died in Columbus 26 October 1849 and was buried in the City cemetery there[2,3]. Miles appears in the 1850 census in Columbus as a harness maker living with his daughter and son-in-law Mary and Joseph Mitchell[3]. On 18 November 1850 Miles acted as security for his son-in-law William Adams, administrator of the estate of John Adams[2].

On 28 September 1850 Congress passed an "act granting bounty land to certain officers and soldiers who have been engaged in the military service of the United States"[4]. On 24 December 1850 Miles applied for the bounty land citing his service as described above[4]. He signed the application "Miles Bunnell"[4]. His request was approved and he received Land Warrant No. 17793 for forty acres[5].

On 3 March 1855 Congress passed an act granting additional bounty land. Miles applied for this benefit on 21 March 1855[5]. His application this time stated that he was drafted in Canandaigua in August 1814 in a company commanded by Lieut. Bebee in Col. Hopkins' regiment of the New York Militia[5]. His discharge information was the same as in the first one[5]. He signed this application "Miles Bunnel"[5].

Miles died in Columbus on 16 February 1856[2] and was buried with his wife in the Columbus City cemetery[2]. Many years later a friend of his son Charles recalled that, "Old Miles Bunnell was also a tanner. His place was near the bluff north of Tipton Knoll. He was a very quiet old gentleman, a member of the Methodist Church and is dead long since. His eldest son, William, was lame from some disease in childhood. Charlie his second son was a playmate of mine, and a good fellow. . . . There was a daughter-Mary."[2]

Children:
1. 320209. child, d. 6 Jan. 1813[3].
2. 320359. Cinderella, b. 9 Sept. 1814[6]; m. 17 Mar. 1831 William Clifford Adams[6]; d. 21 Mar. 1846[6].
    Children (surname Adams):[6]
    1. infant, d.y.   3. Mary Ann.   5. Martha Ann.
    2. Ellen.   4. John M.   6. Cinderella.
3. 320086. Sally Ann, m. 13 May 1836 Andrew Jackson Devore[7].
4.   July Ann, m. 11 Nov. 1840 Stephen Dickerson[6,7].
5.   William, b. 1820-25[2].
6. 320089. Mary A., b. 1827[6]; m. 18 Nov. 1845 Joseph E. Mitchell[2]; d. 22 Nov. 1893[6]
    Children (surname Mitchell)"[3]
    1. Mary H.
7. 320091. Charles H., b. 1829[6]; m. (first) 24 July 1850 Nancy G. Young[7]; m. (second) 7 Apr. 1864 Catherine McCrea[7]; d. 18 Sept. 1893[6].
    Children (surname Bunnell)(by first wife):[7]
    1. Frankie W.   2. Mary J.   3. Joseph W.
    Children (surname Bunnell)(by second wife):[3]
    4. Rachel A.

NOTE: The gravestone of two children, Nellie and Jessie, is located in the same cemetery lot as that of Deborah Bunnell[7]. There are no dates on the stone. They were probably additional children of Miles and Deborah who died young and appear in no other record.

REFERENCES:
1. Jehiel Bunnell Family Bible.
2. Ltr. 9 Feb. 1987 from Greg Mobley, Bartholomew co Historical Society, to Evelyn Ingham, Escalon, CA.
3. CB Database.
4. Application for bounty land dated 24 Dec. 1850.
5. Application for bounty land dated 21 Mar. 1855.
6. Ltr. 8 Jan. 1996 from Carol J. (Guinn) Jenkins, Elizabethtown, IN, descendant of Arthur and Ellen (Adams) Guinn.
7. Research in records of Bartholomew co, IN, by Marjorie Gibbs, Saratoga Springs, NY.

SIXTH GENERATION

1-1-9-6-9-4   D143-Belosha   CB310220-Beloster

BELLOSTEE[6] BUNNELL Jehiel[5], Abner[4], Nathaniel[3], Benjamin[2], William[1]) was born 29 December 1791[1] at Cheshire[2], New Haven co, CT. [This name is very unusual, perhaps even unique. I have a photocopy of the Bible record in which Jehiel listed the births of his children[1], an original signature[6] and a photocopy of another signature[8], both by Bellostee himself, and a photocopy of a letter by A. O. Bunnell, Bellostee's nephew, listing the names of Jehiel's children[2]. Taken all together there can be no doubt that the name was BELLOSTEE.]

Bellostee moved with his parents before 1800 to Whitehall, Washington co, NY, where he grew up. He enlisted 25 May 1812 in Whitehall, NY, in Capt. Abel Foster's company in the 2nd Artillery Battalion[5], and served from 2 October 1812 in Capt. E. Badger's company, New York State Militia[3] (for service in the War of 1812)[3] until his discharge on 30 November 1812[3,5].

He married 15 December 1814 at Gorham, Ontario co, NY[3], ELIZABETH WILBER[3,4], who was born 21 October 1796 in Connecticut[4]. They lived for a while in Canandaigua, Ontario co, NY. While living there, on 8 November 1815, he wrote a poignant letter to his parents to inform them of the sickness and imminent death of his brother Rodney[6]. The 1820 census found them in Covington, Genessee (now Wyoming) co, NY: 010111-20101[5], where he was a farmer. Apparently, his parents and one or two of his brothers were present in his household. The census numbers are difficult to match up with what we know of his family.

In any case, most of the family moved shortly to Lima, Livingston co, NY, where the 1830 census finds the parents Jehiel and Statira living alone, and Bellostee's family is recorded as: 001001-121001[5]. Bellostee appears again in the 1840 census in Lima: 0000101-0212001[5]. On 10 December 1844, in Lima, Bellostee filed an affidavit in an effort to secure a pension for his mother, following his father's death[8]. Before 1850 they made one final move to Lockport, in Niagara co, NY.

The 1850 census shows Bellostee living in Lockport at age 58, employed as a painter. His wife Elizabeth was said to be 53[5]. That year, on 21 December, he filed application #64836 for bounty land based on his service in the War of 1812[5]. He received warrant #33705 for 40 acres[5]. On 29 March 1855, after Congress had provided for additional bounty land, he submitted his application #76944 and received warrant #28335 for an additional 120 acres[5]. Bellostee appears as a house painter in both the 1860 and 1870 census records in Lockport[5].

On 9 March 1871, in Lockport, he applied for a government pension (application #1774)[5]. It was approved, and he received certificate #777 for $8.00 per monnth[5]. Bellostee died 3 December 1875 in Lockport[7]. I have not found a reference to Elizabeth's death, but it would appear that she survived him.

Children:
    1. 320810. Julia Ann, b. 21 Apr. 1816[4]; m. 29 Nov. 1835 Hiram Parsell[4]; d. 14 Dec. 1905[4].

Children (surname Parsell):[4]
1. Walter C.   3. Pascal.   5. Julia Adelia.
2. James.   4. Hiram.

2. 320811. Jehiel, b. 26 Apr. 1818[4]; m. Elizabeth _____ [5].
Children (surname Bunnell):[5]
1. Wesley.   2. Samuel.

3. 320812. Jane Eliza, b. 21 Aug. 1820[4]; m. _____ Mitchell[5].
4. 320813. Harriet Louisa, b. 11 Apr. 1824[4].
5. 320814. Adelia Clarissa, b. 28 Sept. 1827[4].
6. 320815. Maria Annette, b. 2 Aug. 1831[4]; m. _____ Teall[5].
7. 320816. Elizabeth May, b. 3 Apr. 1833[4].

REFERENCES:

1. Jehiel Bunnell Family Bible.
2. Ltr. 10 Aug. 1907 from A. O. Bunnell to John A. Biles.
3. War of 1812 Pension Files, National Archives, abstracted by Charlotte Blair Stewart, Windber, PA.
4. Duncan, pp. 90, 91.
5. CB Database.
6. Ltr. 8 Nov. 1815 from Bellostee Bunnell to Jehiel Bunnell.
7. Biles Manuscript, p. 306.
8. Affidavit, 10 Dec. 1844, filed by Bellostee Bunnell in his mother's behalf.

1-1-9-6-9-5   CB310221

RODNEY[6] BUNNELL (Jehiel[5], Abner[4], Nathaniel[3], Benjamin[2], William[1]) was born 30 December 1793[1] at Cheshire[2], New Haven co, CT. Before 1800 he moved with his parents to Whitehall, Washington co, NY, where he grew up. By 1815 he and several of his brothers were living in Canandaigua, Ontario co, NY. In November his brother Bellostee wrote this letter to their parents:

"Mr. Jehiel Bunnel, Poultney, County of Rutland State of V.T.
Canandaigua   Nov. the 8th 1815.
O my Dear parents. O the unhappy news I have to inform you is such that I can heardly form letters. O with a bleading heart and a trembling hand and with wiping eyes. O I Cannot write but I must inform you that Rodney is very Sick and we Don't Expect that he will remain with us but a few hours longer altho he may this two or three Days but you my Dear friends and parents must not be surprised if you have a letter from me to morrow that he is no more. O my Dear? parent I Cannot write. I will write you immediately. O my Dear mother Strive to Bearit it with fortude. I will writ the perticulars.   Bellostee Bunnell"[3]

Rodney Bunnell died 18 November 1815 in Canandaigua[4].

REFERENCES:

1. Jehiel Bunnell Family Bible.
2. Ltr. 10 Aug. 1907 from A. O. Bunnell to John A. Biles.
3. Ltr. 8 Nov. 1815 from Bellostee Bunnell, Canandaigua, NY, to Jehiel Bunnel, Poultney, VT.
4. Biles Manuscript, p. 306.

SIXTH GENERATION

1-1-9-6-9-6   CB310222

ASAHEL[6] BUNNELL (Jehiel, Abner[4], Nathaniel[3], Benjamin[2], William[1]) was born 29 August 1796[1] at Cheshire[2], New Haven co, CT. Before 1800 he moved with his parents to Whitehall, Washington co, NY, where he grew up. With his brothers and his parents he moved to western New York, where he died 1 January 1831 in Lima, Livingston co, NY[1,3].

REFERENCES:
1. Jehiel Bunnell Family Bible.
2. Ltr. 10 Aug. 1907 from A. O. Bunnell to John A. Biles.
3. Biles Manuscript, p. 306.

1-1-9-6-9-7   CB310227

ZURIEL[6] BUNNELL (Jehiel[5], Abmer[4], Nathaniel[3], Benjamin[2], William[1]) was born 24 September 1801[1] at Cheshire[2], New Haven co, CT, (or more likely at Whitehall, Washington co, NY, where his parents appear in the 1800 census.) In 1820, at Albany, Albany co, NY, he married KEZIAH KETURAH VAN BENTHUYSEN[4], who was born 15 May 1796 in Albany, NY[4]. Zuriel died 21 May 1825 at Lima, Livingston co, NY[1,3]. His widow died 29 January 1877 at Horse Shoe Bend, co?, UT[4].

REFERENCES:
1. Jehiel Bunnell Family Bible.
2. Ltr. 10 Aug. 1907 from A. O. Bunnell to John A. Biles.
3. Biles Manuscript, p. 306.
4. CB Database.

1-1-9-6-9-8   D144   CB310224

DENNIS[6] BUNNELL (Jehiel[5], Abner[4], Nathaniel[3], Benjamin[2], William[1]) was born 15 September 1806[1] at Whitehall, Washington co, NY[2]. His wife was MARY BAKER[3], daughter of James and Mary (Parker) Baker[3]. She was born about 1812 in New York State[4]. They appear in the 1840 census in Lima, Livingston co, NY: 2001310001-0200010001[4], and in the 1860 and 1870 census in Dansville, Livingston co, NY, where Dennis was employed as a painter and paper hanger[4]. Mary died in 1881[3] and Dennis died 2[4] July[5] 1885[3] in Dansville.

Children:
1. 320093. Damaris Blake[4], b. Mar. 1833[6]; d. after Aug. 1914[7].
2. 320096. Sarah C.[5].
3. 320092. Asael Othello[4], b. 10 Mar. 1836[6]; m. 9 Apr. 1863 Anna M. Carpenter[3];
   d. after Aug. 1914[7].
   Children (surname Bunnell):[3,6]
   1. Anna Mae.   2. son.   3. Mark H.

4. 320094. Mark John[4], b. 25 Dec. 1837[6]; m. 1863 Josephine Bottume[6]; d. after 1914[7]
Children (surname Bunnell):[6]
1. Alice E.   2. George M.   3. Belle I.
5. 320095. Mary F., b. 12 Mar. 1853[6]; m. 28 Dec. 1882 Frank A. Willard[6]; d. after
Aug. 1914[7].
Children (surname Willard):[6]
1. Charles.

REFERENCES:
1. Jehiel Family Bible.
2. Ltr. 10 Aug. 1907 from A. O. Bunnell to John A. Biles.
3. *Dansville 1789-1902*, edited by A. O. Bunnell, compiled by F. N. Quick, pp. 9, 10, 11.
4. CB Database.
5. Biles Manucript, p. 307.
6. Duncan, pp. 91, 166.
7. Ltr. 6 Aug. 1914 Mary (Bunnell) Willard to John A. Biles.

1-1-9-7-5-1 D57i CB310080

JOEL[6] BUNNELL (Joel[5], Joseph[4], Nathaniel[3], Benjamin[w], William[1]) was baptized 13 March 1785 in the Congregational Church at Cromwell, Middlesex co, CT[1]. He served as a private from Middletown, Middlesex co, CT, in Samuel B. Northrop's Company, 37th Infantry, regular army, during the War of 1812[1]. He died 4 August 1814 at Fort Hale, ?, during the war[1]. His brother Raphael was the administrator of his estate[2].

REFERENCES:
1. Duncan, p. 47.
2. CB Database.

1-1-9-7-5-3 D145 CB310082

RAPHAEL[6] BUNNELL (Joel[5], Joseph[4], Nathaniel[3], Benjamin[2], William[1]) was born 20 February 1789[1] at Middletown, Middlesex co, CT[5]. He was baptized 17 October 1790 at the First Congregational Church in Cromwell, Middlesex co[7]. In 1791 his parents moved to Berlin, Hartford co, CT[5]. On 5 August 1810, according to the records of the Berlin-Kensington Congregational Church, he married SALLY STANLEY, "both of Berlin"[7]. Raphel appears in the 1820 census in Berlin: 1000010-30010- MFG[5], and nine of their twelve children were born there.

About 1827 they removed to New York State - to Candor, Tioga co, according to the Biles Manuscript[3]. In the 1830 census they appear in the town of Lansing, Tompkins co, NY: 3101001-0111001[5]. (Cynthia Anne (Vose) Bunnell said that her husband Charles was born 31 December 1832 in Scipio, Cayuga co, NY[1].) Raphael died 8 July 1839[1] (in Spencer, Tioga co,

NY[3]). His widow Sarah appears in the 1840 census in Ithaca, Tompkins co, NY: 1011-010000[5]. The 1870 census shows that widow Sally was living with her son Charles in Newfield, Tompkins co, NY[5]. She died 3 July 1873[1] (at Spencer, Tioga co, NY[3]). They were both buried in Ithaca, NY[1].

Children:

1.   child, d. Feb. 1811[4].
2. 320818. Harriet, b. about 1812[5]; m. Owen Shaw[3].
3. 320821. Sally Ann[1,2], b. about 1813[5]; m. George Monk[3].
     Children (surname Monk):[5]
     1. George William.
4. 320819. Stillman S., b. 5 Feb. 1814[5,6]; m. Catherine DuBois[6]; d. 9 Jan. 1889[5,6].
     Children (surname Bunnell):[5,6]
     1. Emilie Amelia.   3. Elizabeth.   5. Adelaide.
     2. Mariette Molly.   4. Leroy Sibley.   6. Byron H.
5. 320820. Samantha, b. about 1816[5]; m. Isaac DeBois[3].
6. 320822. William, b. about 1821[5]; m. Deborah Ann Grieves[3]; d. 10 Mar. 1876[5] or 1881[3].
     Children (surname Bunnell):[3,5]
     1. Julia Parthena.   3. Ida.   4. Minnie.
     2. Eva.
7. 320823. Melissa, b. about1823[5].
8. 320824. John Russell, b. about 1824[5]; Esther _____ [5].
     Children (surname Bunnell):[5]
     1. Oscar H.   3. Mary.   5. Gertrude.
     2. William W.   4. son.
9. 320825. Cornelius, b. 18 Oct. 1826[8]; m. Sarah Kyser[8]; d. 26 Mar. 1892[8].
     Children (surname Bunnell):[8]
     1. Charles.   2. William.   3. Harvey.
10. 320826. Truman, b. about 1829[5].
11. 320827. Charles, b. 31 Dec. 1832[1]; m. 11 Jan. 1866 Cynthia Anne Vose[1]; d. 10 Apr. 1900[1].
12. 320828. Alonzo, b. 22 Mar. 1839[5]; m. 12 Apr. 1865 Louise Valentine[2]; d. 4 Feb. 1910[5].
     Children (surname Bunnell):[2,5]
     1. Frank W.   3. Cora M.   5. Arrieanna G.
     2. Louise M.   4. Jennie.   6. Nora.

REFERENCES:
1. Ltr. 7 Dec. 1907 from Mrs. Charles Bunnell to John A. Biles.
2. Ltr. 13 Dec. 1907(?) from Alonzo Bunnell to John A. Biles.
3. Biles Manuscript, pp. 310, 311, 312.
4. Duncan, pp. 91, 92.
5. CB Database.

6. Family Group Sheet - Stillman S. Bunnell, prepared by Mrs. Richard W. Bunnell, Fullerton, CA.
7. Ltr. 2 Oct. 1963 from Frances Davenport, Head, History & Genealogy Section, Connecticut State
    Library, to Mrs. Richard W. Bunnell.
8. Records gathered by Beverly Sorensen, Northbrook, IL, including obituary and gravestone of
    Cornelius Bunnell.

1-1-9-7-5-5   D57v   CB310091

ZENAS[6] BUNNELL Joel[5], Joseph[4], Nathaniel[3], Benjamin[2], William[1]) was born in Berlin,
Hartford co, CT, and was baptized 6 November 1791 in the Congregational Church at
Kensington, Hartford co, CT[1]. He removed to Delhi, Delaware co, NY, in 1809[2]. He married
and had children, since he appears in the 1820 census in Aurelius, Cayuta co, NY: 10001-301
MFG[3] and in the 1830 census in Seneca Falls, Seneca co, NY: 120001-010101[3]. However, no
further records regarding Zenas and his family have so far come to light.

REFERENCES:
1. Duncan, p. 47.
2. Biles Manuscript, p. 310.
3. CB Database.

1-1-9-7-5-6   D146   CB310084

JOHN[6] BUNNELL (Joel[5], Joseph[4], Nathaniel[3], Benjamin[2], William[1]) was born about 1795 in
Berlin, Hartford co, CT[1]. He was baptized in February 1797 in the Congregational Church in
Kensington, Hartford co, CT[2]. On 2 July 1816 in Southington, Hartford co, CT, he married
ELIZA BARNES[2], who was born about 1798[2].

John appears in the 1820 census in Southington: 0001-010-MFG[1]. John and his wife were
admitted to the First Congregational Church of Southington on 5 August 1821[2]. John appears
in the 1830 census in Berlin, Hartford co: 000002-020001[1], and in the 1840 census in
Southington: 1000001-0000001[1]. He died 4 November 1845 at Southington[2].

The 1850 census of Berlin, Hartford co, found Eliza and her son John living with Royal and
Elizabeth Robbins[1]. Eliza was dismissed from the Southington church and admitted to the
Kensington Congregational Church on 22 June 1851[2]. Widow Eliza, age 60, appears in the
1860 census in Winchester, Litchfield co, CT, living with her daughter Mary and son-in-law
William Yale[1].

Children:
1. 320706. Maria Barnes, b. about 1818[1]; bapt. 23 June 1822[2]; m. 26 Nov. 1836
    Aaron Sage[3].
2. 320707. Rhoda Bateman, b. about 1822[1]; bapt. 23 June 1822[2]; m. 25 Oct. 1842
    Levi Merriam[3].

Children (surname Merriam):[2]
    1. Walter Henry.   2. Charles Andrew.
  3. 320708. Mary S., b. 1824[1]; bapt. 1 Jan. 1825[1]; m. 25 Nov. 1841 William H. Yale[1].
  4. 320709. John Edmund, b. about 1839[1,2]; m. (first) 17 July 1859 Martha A. Cramer[2];
        m. (second) 11 July 1864 Isabelle M. Allen[2]; d. 19 Feb. 1883[1].
        Children (surname Bunnell)(by second wife):[2]
        1. Alice.   3. child, d. y.   5. James Albert, d. y.
        2. Harry.   4. child, d. y.   6. child, d. y.
  5. 320710. Sarah Jane, b. 1841[1]; bapt. 30 July 1841[1].

NOTE: The Farmington Town Clerk's records also include the marriage of Martha A. Bunnell of Southington to Silas B. Talmadge, of Meriden, on 6 Aug. 1845 by Elisha C. Jones[3]. I suspect that she was another daughter of John and Eliza (Barnes) Bunnell. In the CB Database Martha is #003876.

REFERENCES:
  1. CB Database.
  2. Duncan, pp. 92, 167.
  3. Marriages in the records of the Farmington, CT, Town Clerk's office, sent to me by Stephen E. Baylor, Arlington, WA.

1-1-9-7-5-9 D57ix CB310086

EDMUND[6] (EDWARD) BUNNELL (Joel[5], Joseph[4], Nathaniel[3], Benjamin[2], William[1]) was born in 1797 in Berlin, Hartford co, CT[1]. He was baptized 12 October 1808 with three of his siblings in the Congregational Church in Kensington, Hartford co[2]. He married (first) in 1818[1] MARY SMITH[3], daughter of Elkanus Smith[3]. She was born about 1798[1]. Edmund appears in the 1840 census in Southington, Hartford co, CT: 0000001-1020001-AG[1]. Mary died 8 September 1846[5] at the age of 48[2] and was buried in Oak Hill Cemetery, Southington[5].

Edmund was married (second) 6 January 1850 by Elisha C. Jones in Southington to AMY (MATTHEWS[4]) WEBSTER[2], widow of Ira Webster[2]. She was born about 1789. Edmund and wife Amy appear in the 1850 census in Southington[6]. His occupation was listed as joiner. Amy died 22 August 1859, age 70[2]. In the 1860 census we find Edward (sic) Bunnell, age 55, joiner and carpenter, living with his daughter and son-in-law "Anna" (Amy E.) and Silas H. Smith in Southington[6].

Edmund died 14 October 1866[2] at Southington[1]. He was buried in Oak Hill Cemetery, Southington, beside his first wife[5]. His gravestone is apparently engraved "Edward Bunnell," with no other data[5].

Children:
  1. 320725. Charles E., b. 11 June 1820[6]; m. Sarah Morse[6]; d. 19 Oct. 1899[1].
        Children (surname Bunnell):[1]
        1. Sarah L.   2. Charles Henry.   3. Edmund Riley.

2.   Amy E., b. about 1823[6]; m. 2 Apr. 1843 Silas H. Smith[4]; d. 19 Nov. 1860[5]
            Children (surname Smith):
            1. Charles[5].   2. George[6].   3. Sylvia[6].
3. 320456. David W.[1], b. Apr. 1829[1]; d. after 1900[1].
4.   Emily Jane, b. 19 Apr. 1830[8] m. 1 June 1847 Anson T. Clarke[8];
            d. 27 July 1883[8].
            Children (surname Clarke):[8]
            1. Lenora H.   2. Mary E.   3. Leolian Frank.
5.   Sarah, b. about 1837[6,7].

REFERENCES:
   1. CB Database.
   2. Duncan, p. 47.
   3. Biles Manuscript, p. 310.
   4. Marriages in the records of the Farmington, CT, Town Clerk's office, sent to me be Stephen E. Baylor, Arlington, WA.
   5. Ltr. 2 Feb. 1992 from Mrs. Edmond Dube, Oak Hill Cemetery Association, Southington, CT, to Stephen E. Baylor.
   6. Ltr. 12 Nov. 1992 from Stephen E. Baylor.
   7. Ltr. 10 June 1993 from Stephen E. Baylor. Mr. Baylor and I corresponded at some length to resolve the confusion created by several late references to Edmund as Edward.
   8. *Cone Family in America*, by William Whitney Cone, p. 468.

1-1-9-7-5-10   D57x   CB310088

RUSSELL[6] BUNNELL (Joel[5], Joseph[4], Nathaniel[3], Benjamin[2], William[1]) was born in Berlin, Hartford co, CT. He was baptized 12 October 1808 in the Congregational Church in Kensington, Hartford co[1]. On 15 July 1847, at Plymouth, Litchfield co, CT, he was married by Rev. Ephraim Lyman to SARAH PICKWICK[2]. She was born in Wiltshire, England[2].

Children:
   1. 320279. Emeline A., b. 17 Nov. 1849[2]; m. 7 Jan. 1875 John Ervil Wells[2];
            d. 16 Jan. 1916[2]. Several children (surname Wells)[2].
   2. 320280. Sarah Amelia, b. 12 Aug. 1853[2]; d. unmarried 26 Mar. 1922[2].

REFERENCES:
   1. Duncan, p. 47.
   2. CB Database.

1-1-9-7-5-11   D57xi   CB310090

CYRUS ROBINSON[6] BUNNELL (Joel[5], Joseph[4], Nathaniel[3], Benjamin[2], William[1]) was born in Berlin, Hartford co, CT[2]. He was baptized in September 1814 in the Congregational Church at Kensington, Hartford co.[1]. He married (first) _____ _____[2]. Cyrus, age 35, appears in the

1850 census in Windsor, Hartford co, CT, as a marketman, living with Lumen Atwater[3]. His residence was still in Windsor in 1853, when on 24 February he married (second) MARY LOUISE MATTHEWS at Springfield, Hampden co, MA[2]. They appear with their two children in the 1860 census in Granby, Hartford co, CT[3]. He was listed as a shoemaker[3].

On 16 August 1862 he was enrolled at Granby in Company E, 10th Connecticut Regiment of Volunteers as a private[3]. He died in service on 30 December 1862[2,3] in Company B, 10th Regiment[2], at New Bern, Craven co, NC[3]. His widow applied for a pension on 23 October 1863[3]. She died 4 June 1890 at Worcester, Worcester co, MA, at age 68[3]. (Her birthplace was given as Bath, Sagadahoc co, ME[3].)

Children (by second wife):
    1. 320582. Cornelia Jane, b. 28 July 1853[2,3].
    2. 320581. Henry B.[2] of P.[3], b. 21 Feb. 1856[3]; m. 29 Nov. 1884 Rosalie Cardinal[3].

REFERENCES:
    1. Duncan, p. 47.
    2. Corrections and updates to Duncan, p. 47, sent to me by Ruth C. Duncan after publication of her book.
    3. CB Database.

1-1-9-7-6-1 D58i CB310226

SAMUEL[6] BUNNELL (Amos[5], Joseph[4], Nathaniel[3], Benjamin[2], William[1]) was born 29 November 1780 in Southington, Hartford co, CT[1]. He married PATIENCE _____ [2], who was born about 1780[2]. Samuel appears in the 1810 census in Farmington, Hartford co: 20010-11010[2]. He died 12 October 1813 while serving in the War of 1812[3]. His widow died 19 January 1831 at Farmington at the age of 51[2]. All five children were named in the probate of her estate[2].

Children (order?):
    1. 320552. Lucretia, b. 15 Dec. 1801[1]; m. 5 Jan. 1823 Samuel Warren[1].
    2. 320553. Sextus, b. about 1805[2]; m. 3 Oct. 1830 Lola Maritte How[1].
         Children (surname Bunnell):[2]
            1. child, d.y.   2. child, d.y.   3. child, d.y.
    3. 320556. Samuel, b. about 1812[2].
    4. 320554. Catherine, m. 15 May 1831 Luther Graham[2].
    5. 320555. Luanna, m. 26 June 1832 Benjamin Upson[4].

REFERENCES:
    1. Births and Marriages in the records of the Farmington, CT, Town Clerk's office, sent to me by
        Stephen E. Baylor, Arlington, WA.
    2. CB Database.
    3. Duncan, p. 47.
    4. Waterbury, CT, Marriages, from the Barbour Collection, printed in *The Connecticut Nutmegger*,
        Vol. 27, No. 2, page 264.

1-1-9-7-6-2   D147   CB310227

AMOS[6] BUNNELL Amos[5], Joseph[4], Nathaniel[3], Benjamin[2], William[1]) was born about 1790 in Southington, Hartford co, CT[1]. On 18 October 1809, at Southington, he was married by Rev. William Robinson of the First Congregational Church to LYDIA GRAHAM[3]. Amos appears in the 1810 census in Southington: 001-101[4].

According to records Ruth Duncan found in *Connecticut Men in the War of 1812*, Amos enlisted at Farmington, CT, on 2 August 1813, together with his brother Samuel, in Christopher Riley's company, 37th Regiment of Infantry in the Regular United States Army. However his discharge certificate[1] states that he was enlisted the 29th day of March 1814 as a private in captain C. Ripley's company, 37th regiment of Infantry and that he was discharged on 10 May 1815 at New London, CT. He received Warrant No. 3536 for 160 acres of bounty land for his service[2]. His discharge certificate describes him thus: "Said Amos Bunnel was born in the Town of Southington in the State of Connecticut is about twenty three years of age, five feet eight inches high, light complexion, blue eyes, brown hair, and by occupation, when enlisted, a Farmer."[1]

After his discharge he settled in Groton, New London co, CT, where he appears in the 1820 census: 200010-20110-AG[4]. Amos "died 4 April 1827 in Groton, Connecticut at the age of 40. (Hartford Courant, issue of 9 April 1827)"[5]. His widow married (second) 15 August 1830, in New London, New London co, CT, Harry Nichols[5].

Children:
> 1. 320612. child, b. 25 June 1810; d. 29 June 1810[3].
> probably others (1820 census).

REFERENCES:
> 1. Discharge certificate - War of 1812.
> 2. Warrant No. 3536.
> 3. *Ecclesiastical and Other Sketches of Southington, Connecticut*, by Heman R. Timlow
>   - Vital records abstracted by Ruth C. Duncan.
> 4. CB Database.
> 5. Duncan, p. 92.

1-1-9-7-6-3?   D151   CB004688

WILLIAM[6] BUNNELL (son of Amos[5]?[3,4], Joseph[4], Nathaniel[3], Benjamin[2], William[1]) was born 7 November 1792[4], possibly in Southington, Hartford co, CT. He married POLLY PRINGLE[3] who was born about 1796 in Connecticut[5]. This **may have been** the William Bunnell who appears in the census records of Waterbury, New Haven co, CT, in 1820: 10100-20010[6] and in 1830[6]. They settled in Unadilla, Otsego co, NY, where he appears on tax assessment rolls from 1831 to 1851[9]. He also appears there in the census records in 1840, 1850, NY1855, and 1860[10]. In 1840: 0010101-0012001[10]; in 1850 William, a cooper, wife Polly, and Maria Fancher, age 2[10]; in NY1855 William, a cooper, wife Polly and son Lyman[10]; and in 1860 William, cooper, and wife Polly[10].

Children:
1. 011558. Chauncey[1] Lewis[10], b. 1818[10]; m. (first) 27 Jan. 1839 Mary Maria
     Warner[10]; m. (second) 27 ____1843 Rebecca S. Longley[10]; m. (third)
     Juliett _____[10]; d. 13 Apr. 1893[10].
     Children (by third wife)[10](surname Bunnell): [1,10]
     1. Maria G.   2. Helen.
2. 002090. Catherine[1], m. Israel Mott[2].
3. 008168. Mary[1], m. _____ Gibits[2].
4. 008167. Betsey[1], m. Daniel Fuller[2].
5. 004689. William Lyman[1], b. 26 Sept. 1826[7]; m. Almira Aylesworth[1,10]
     d. 18 Jan. 1872[7].
     Children (surname Bunnell):[1,10]
     1. Mary Ellen.   2. Charles H.
6. 011530. Harriet[1] R.[10], b. 1828[10]; m. Rosal Wright[2].

NOTE: The parentage of this William Bunnell is very uncertain. Claude Bunnell's Database lists his parents as unknown[10]. Ruth C. Duncan, in *William Bunnell and His Descendants*, suggests that he was the son of William Bunnell 1-1-10-1-7 D62 CB300117[5], and I included him that way in the first edition of this book. On reviewing the data more carefully, however, I can find nothing to connect him to William 1-1-10-1-7.

John A. Biles, relying on letters from family members, decided he was the son of Amos Bunnell 1-1-9-7-6[4]. Esther Kennedy's DAR application combined Amos 1-1-9-7-6-2 with this William into Amos William, giving him the wife and children of William. We know that the son Amos instead married Lydia Graham and remained in Connecticut until his death in Groton, CT. He was not Amos William. But I am suggesting that William was a third son of Amos 1-1-9-7-6, although the 1800 and 1810 census records of Southington, CT, do not offer support for the theory. However, the William of this sketch and Amos' daughter Julia Katherine (grandmother of Esther Kennedy) both removed from Connecticut to Unadilla, NY. Their grandchildren considered themselves cousins of each other[2]. William's birth in late 1792 fits well between that of Amos about 1790 and Julia Katherine in 1796. **This is a very tentative identification which requires further research to prove or disprove.**

REFERENCES:
1. Ltr. 28 Jan. 1907 from grandson Charles H. Bunnell to John A. Biles.
2. Ltr. 13 Sept. 1912 from granddaughter Mary E. Morenus to John A. Biles.
3. DAR application of Esther Elvenia (Grannis) Kennedy sent to John A. Biles.
4. Biles Manuscript, p. 310A.
5. Duncan, p. 94.
6. 1820 and 1830 census records of Waterbury, CT, abstracted by Ruth C. Duncan.
7. *The Ancestors and Descendants of Havilah and Dorcas Gale Bunnell*, compiled by Adele Andrews, 1935, p. 86.
8. Reference Notes compiled by Claude A. Bunnell, No. 11 - V572-P6-NY State Census 1855 Town of Unadilla, Otsego co.
9. *The Bunnell/Bonnell Newsletter*, Vol. 12, No. 4, Nov. 1998, p. 67, compiled by Carole Bonnell.
10. CB Database.

SIXTH GENERATION

1-1-9-7-8-2

GEORGE[6] BUNNELL (Hull[5], Joseph[4], Nathaniel[3], Benjamin[2], William[1]).

REFERENCES:
> The only reference I have found to this person is in the list of children of Hull Bunnell provided in the manuscript written by John A. Biles.

1-1-9-7-8-3

JESSE[6] BUNNELL (Hull[5], Joseph[4], Nathaniel[3], Benjamin[2], William[1]).

REFERENCES:
> The only reference I have found to this person is in the list of children of Hull Bunnell provided in the manuscript written by John A. Biles.

1-1-9-7-8-6

LEVA[6] BUNNELL (Hull[5], Joseph[4], Nathaniel[3], Benjamin[2], William[1]).

REFERENCES:
> The only reference I have found to this person is in the list of children of Hull Bunnell provided in the manuscript written by John A. Biles.

1-1-9-7-8-8   D148   CB310423

HENRY[6] BUNNELL (Hull[5], Joseph[4], Nathaniel[3], Benjamin[2], William[1]) was born about 1802 in Southington, Hartford co, CT[1]. He married PHEBE GOODALE[1], who was born about 1795 in Southington[1]. Henry appears in the 1840 census in East Haddam, Middlesex co, CT: 011001-1000001[2] and in the 1850 census of Groton, New London co, CT, at age 48 with wife Phebe age 63 (probably a transcriber's error for 53), son Amos 15 and daughter Eliza 13[2]. Anna Goodale, age 80, was living with them[2]. In the 1860 census in Groton, Henry, age 58, farm laborer, was listed with wife Phebe, age 64[2]. In the same house son Amos, age 24, fisherman, lived with his wife Rosetta, daughter Amanda, and Polly Goodale, age 84[2].

Henry died 17 April 1866 in Groton[1]. His widow was baptized 3 March 1867 in the Poqunoc Bridge Baptist Church in Groton[1]. She died in Groton 3 May 1875[1].

Children:
> 1. Amos, b. 6 Sept. 1835[3]; m. Rosetta Bogue[1,3]; d. 13 Mar. 1916[3].

Children (surname Bunnell):[3]

1. Amanda E.	5. William Henry.	9. Lena.
2. Jane E.	6. Fanny Almira.	10. Herbert Elery.
3. Elfrida.	7. Mary Etta.	11. Tina May.
4. Abigail Ella.	8. Everett.	12. Lillian.

   2. Eliza, b. about 1838[1]; m. 29 Nov. 1855 Russell Bogue[1,3]; d. 7 Apr. 1898[3].

REFERENCES:
   1. Duncan, p. 93.
   2. Connecticut census records abstracted by Ruth C. Duncan.
   3. CB Database.

1-1-9-7-8-10   D149   CB310428

MARCUS[6] BUNNELL (Hull[5], Joseph[4], Nathaniel[3], Benjamin[2], William[1]) was born about 1810 in Farmington, Hartford co, CT[1]. He was married 1 May 1831, in Farmington, by Rev. Noah Porter, to ELIZA SMITH[2] who was born about1806[1]. On 2 February 1834 they were baptized as adults and admitted to the First Congregational Church of Southington, Hartford co, CT[1,4]. Marcus appears in the 1840 census in Farmington: 100001-110101[3]. He was a farmer and blacksmith[1]. He died 25 November 1849 in New Britain, Hartford co, CT, of lung fever at the age of 39[1]. Eliza Bunnell and her son George appear in the 1850 census in New Britain in the household of Edward and Jane Tubbs[4].
Daughter Mary appears in the 1850 census in New Britain living with Horace H. and Harriet Brown[4]. Widow Eliza Bunnell's membership in the First Congregational Church of Southington was withdrawn on 5 July 1867[4].

Children:
   1.   child, d. 22 Dec. 1833, age 6 weeks[1].
   2. 320902. Jane Ellen, bapt. 10 Aug. 1834[1]; m. 9 Mar. 1851 James Elliot Merriam[1];
             div. before 1866[1].
   3. 320903. Mahala Ann, bapt. 10 Aug. 1834[1].
   4.   child, d.10 Mar. 1836, age 10 weeks[1].
   5. 320904. Mary, b. about 1839[1].
   6. 320905. George, b. Feb. 1847[4]; m. 5 July 1869 Jennie D. Smith[4]; d. 24 Jan. 1907[4].
             Children (surname Bunnell):[4]
              1. Jennie L.   2. George Ayres.

REFERENCES:
   1. Duncan, p. 93.
   2. Barbour Collection of Vital Records in Connecticut State Library, abstracted by Mrs. Clarence H.
       Bunnell, Winsted, CT.
   3. 1840 Census, Farmington, Hartford co, CT, abstracted by Ruth C. Duncan.
   4. CB Database.

1-1-10-1-6-3   D150   CB310094

WILLIAM[6] BUNNELL (Joseph J.[5], Israel[4], Israel[3], Benjamin[2], William[1]) was born 28 October 1795 at West Avon, Hartford co, CT[1]. He was baptized 22 July 1796 in the Congregational Church at Avon, Hartford co[2]. He married (first) about 1819 BETSY HART, daughter of Levi and Elizabeth Hart[3]. He appears in the 1820 census in Colebrook, Litchfield co, CT: 0001-1010[1]. (If the census is correct it suggests that their oldest child was a daughter, placing their marriage date a year or two earlier than 1819.)

On 3 September 1821 William was admitted to membership in the Congregational Church in Colebrook, Litchfield co, CT[1,3]. His wife Betsy was admitted to the Barkhamsted First Congregational Church on 4 November 1827[1,3]. They may have lived in Winsted, Litchfield co, for a time[1], but they removed to Farmington, Hartford co, CT, where they were admitted to the Congregational Church on 9 September 1834[1,3].

William appears in the 1840 census in Farmington: 1001001-3001101 as a farmer[1,4]. (This does not correspond with the list of children below. Is this the wrong William, did the census taker get it wrong, or is our list of children incorrect?) They were dismissed from the Congregational Church in Farmington in 1842 to the Congregational Church at Plainville, Hartford co, CT[1]. Betsy (Hart) Bunnell died at Plainville 27 August 1845 at the age of 47[3] and was buried in West Cemetery, Plainville[5].

For his second wife William married 27 October 1845, in Farmington, CT, MARY (CLARK) ANDREWS, widow, of Winsted, Litchfield co, CT[3]. She was born in 1805[3]. She joined the church in Plainville in 1849[3]. William and Mary appear in the 1850 census in Farmington, CT, with his daughters Dolly W., age 15, and Ellen A., age 7[1,4]. They appear again, by themselves, in the 1860 census in Farmington[1]. In 1850 and 1860 William's occupation was listed as "Cooper." His wife Mary died in 1869, according to the records of the Plainville Congregational Church[3].

Children:
1. 320907. William Levi, b. 13 May 1820[3]; m. 12 Dec. 1842 Phebe Durand[3]; d. 24 July 1903[3].
   Children (surname Bunnell):[3]
   1. Lucas C.   3. William.   4. Harriet Rebecca.
   2. Alice E.
2. 320908. John Nelson[3], b. 5 Sept. 1827[1]; m. (first) 29 May 1854 Mary Jane Beecher[3]; m. (second) 3 Oct. 1891 Ann Eliza (Vanderveck) Marsh[1]; d. 11 Jan. 1911[1].
   Children (surname Bunnell)(by first wife):[3]
   1. son, prob. d. y.   2. Charles Beecher.
3. 320909. Jennette, b. about 1827[3].
4. 320910. Laurie A., b. about 1833[3].

5. 320911. Dolly W., b. about 1835[3].
6. 320605. Darwin Hart, b. 1836; bapt. 18 Sept. 1836[1]; m. (first) 9 Sept. 1857 Harriet
E. Chamberlain[1]; m. (second) 1892 Harriet Vivian Bragg[1]; d. 6 Oct.
1906[1].
Children (surname Bunnell)(by first wife):[1]
1. William Darwin.   3. L. S.   5. Madeline C.
2. Minnie H.   4. Linnie Sareno.
7. 320912. Ellen A., b. about 1843[3]; m. _____ Andrus[3].

REFERENCES:
1. CB Database.
2. Jacobus, p. 365.
3. Duncan, pp. 93, 94, 168.
4. 1840 and 1850 census records of Farmington, Hartford co, CT, abstracted by Ruth C. Duncan.
5. Ltr. 29 Apr. 1891 from Ruth C. Duncan.

1-3-1-2-2-3   D152   CB310239

BENJAMIN[6] BONNELL (Benjamin[5], Nathaniel[4], Nathaniel[3], Nathaniel[2], William[1]) was born 4
March 1751[3] in Springfield Ward, Elizabethtown, Essex (now Union) co, NJ. About 1770 he
married HANNAH WARD[1], who was born about 1754[10], daughter of David and Hannah
(Farrand) Ward[1]. He served as a private in the Revolution, in Captain Mead's company, First
Regiment of the New Jersey Continental Line[5]. He also served as a private in the
Commander-in-Chief's Guard, Continental Army[5]. These are the only references to any
Benjamin Bonnell in Stryker's register[5]. Marilyn Lynch, in her unpublished compilation *The
Bonnell/Bunnill Family*, includes this outline of his military service, most of which she
abstracted from *History of Chatham, NJ,* by Ambrose Ely Vanderpoel, published in 1959 by the
Chatham Historical Society:

"The commander-in-chief's guard was a famous organization. . . . The only resident of Chatham who was a member
of this distinguished corps was Private Benjamin Bonnel; but as he did not join until the spring of 1782, long after
Washington had left this region, he was not one of the 'fifty or sixty mounted guards' . . . who accompanied the
general on his trips to Short Hills.'

"Benjamin apparently had some problems about serving. He enlisted 9 Aug. 1777, as a private in the 3rd company,
under Capt. Conway, later Capt. Mead of the 1st New Jersey regiment, Col. Matthias Ogden, attached to Gen.
Maxwell's brigade. Benjamin deserted at Brandywine, Del.(sic) on 11 Sept. 1777. Benjamin apparently rejoined on
his own on 1 Apr. 1778. He fought in the Battle of Monmouth, 28 June 1778.

"Benjamin was promoted to the rank of corporal on 21 Jan. 1780. He fought at Connecticut Farms and at
Springfield, 23 June 1780. He deserted again on 13 Dec. 1780.

"A three hundred dollar reward was offered in advertisements for Benjamin Bonnel, John Burnett and John Yherts.
To collect the reward the men had to be 'apprehended and secured.' Which apparently happened.

"Benjamin and his friends were captured and 'was confined to the gaol of this county (Sussex) the 31st of December
last.' This notice was published in the Newtown newspaper, 7 Jan. 1781, by James Morrow, gaoler.

"Benjamin rejoined in Jan. of 1781 and was reduced in rank. He was detached to Morristown, 26 Feb. 1781 to Capt. Jonathan Foreman's 1st Co. of the 3rd Battalion of Lt. Col. Barter's 1st brigade in Gen. Muhlenberg's 1st division of light infantry, commanded by Gen. Lafayette.

"Benjamin was involved in the battle at Green Springs, VA, 6 July 1781 and at Yorktown, 19 Oct. 1781. He was transferred at Newburgh, NY, 30 Apr. 1782 to the commander-in-chief's guard, under Lt. Col. William Colfax.

"Benjamin was furloughed at Newburgh 6 June 1783, until ratification of the treaty of peace. He was discharged 3 Nov. 1783."[12]

For his service Benjamin earned the right to a warrant for bounty land, which he apparently sold to Obadiah Valentine. The warrant, #8161, was issued on 22 October 1789 to the heirs of Obadiah Valentine, late assignee, deceased.[10]

Throughout the period of his service in the war Benjamin appears on extant tax lists as a householder in Springfield, Essex co[2,7]. By the time of his discharge all of their children had been born except for the last two daughters, Phebe and Prussia.

Shortly after the war (beginning in July 1785) Benjamin appears also in the tax lists of Hanover twp (later Chatham twp), Morris co, NJ[7]. He seems to have joined the family business, operating grist and saw mills on the Passaic River between Springfield on the east side and Chatham on the west side. His father and uncles Nathaniel and John individually and in partnership had kept the mills going during the war[11]. Now Benjamin and several of his brothers and cousins became part owners. Littell says tersely that Benjamin's occupation was that of "bellows-maker,"[1] but I find no other reference to that activity. When the military census was taken in New Jersey in 1793 Benjn Bonnell Junr (age 42) and his son Enos Bunnell (age 17) appear in the "List of All the Militia enrolled in the County of Essex."[6]

His father died suddenly in November 1798, and Benjamin and his brother John were appointed administrators of the estate[4]. On 13 December 1805 Benjamin Bonnel of Essex co sold to each of his sons Enos and Matthias an equal one-third interest in "two sawmills . . . in the neighborhood of Chatham together with all the dams sluices ponds pondages races with all the appurtenances thereunto belonging." Each of the sons paid him $1000 for his share[8]

Benjamin died 9 October 1808, probably unexpectedly, since he died without making a will[4]. The Morristown newspaper *Palladium of Liberty,* said he died at Chatham (in Morris co) at age 52[10]. The paper got his age wrong, and I suspect it was wrong about the place also, unless he died suddenly while at work at the mill. I have seen no reason to believe that he ever lived any place except Springfield, Essex (now Union) co, although he owned the mill properties in Chatham for some years. The *New Jersey Calendar of Wills* listed him as Benjamin Bonnel of Springfield Township, Essex co, when the inventory of his estate was filed and sworn to by his son Enos Bonnel as administrator[4].

He was buried in Hillside Cemetery, Madison, Morris co, NJ[3], where his daughters Prussia and Jane had previously been buried[3]. The Vital Records of the Madison Presbyterian Church list him as Benjamin Bunnel, Jr., d. Oct. 9, 1808, age 57 yr, 7 mo, 5 da[3]. His widow Hannah was married (second) by Rev. Elias Riggs on 18 August 1810 at New Providence, Essex (now Union) co, to Elder Moses Miller of Warren, Somerset co, NJ[9,10]. She died at Springfield, Essex (now Union) co in 1823[10].

On 11 September 1810, by order of Orphans Court at the June 1809 term, Enos Bonnell, as administrator, advertised for sale 1 equal undivided 1/3 part of all mills and property situate on Passaic River owned by his father, consisting of 1 grist mill, 2 saw mills and 1 1/2 acres of land adjoining[10]. He sold the property on 12 November 1810 to Israel Day for $1230[10].

Children:
1. 320333. Prussia, bapt. 10 Apr. 1774 [10]; d. 26 Aug. 1781 in 10th yr.[3]
2. 320334. Enos, b. 26 Feb. 1776[3]; bapt. 14 Apr. 1776[10]; m. 1797[10] Rachel Ball[1]; d. 23 Jan. 1859[3]

   Children (surname Bonnell):[1,10]

1. Charlotte.	5. Benjamin B.	9. John Ball.
2. Almira.	6. Alfred Mahlon.	10. Mary.
3. Jane.	7. Matilda.	11. Eliza.
4. Elam Williams.	8. Harriet.	

3. 320335. Sally, b. 1778[10]; m. 31 Mar. 1811[9] Enos Baldwin Townley[1,9].

   Children (surname Townley):[1]

1. Joanna.	3. Hannah Mariah.	5. Elizabeth.
2. David E.	4. Effingham.	6. Enos.

4. 320336. Jane, bapt. 1 Feb. 1783[10]; d. 15 Sept. 1783, age 11 mo.[3]
5. 320337. Matthias L., bapt. 7 Nov. 1784[10]; m. 23 Aug. 1807 Sally Ward[3]; d. 27 June 1833[3].

   Children (surname Bonnell):[10]

1. Mehitable Louisa.	3. Moses Ward.	5. Jane Day.
2. Enos Johnson.	4. Joanna Day.	

6. 320338. Phebe, bapt. 20 May 1787[10]; Dr. Amos King[14].

   Children (surname King):[14]

1. Prussia.	2. Almira.

7. 320339. Prussia, bapt. 2 May 1790[10]; m. 4 Nov. 1807 Bonnel R. Brant[3]; d. 11 Jan. 1823 age 33[3].

   Children (surname Brant):[14]

1. Laura Adeline.	4. Lavenda Josephine.	7. Sarah.
2. Sofronia.	5. Elliet Constantine.	
3. Benjamin.	6. Margaretta.	

REFERENCES:
1. Littell, pp. 46, 47, 48, 120, 285, 440, 441, 462.
2. Gen Mag of NJ, Vol. 43, p. 79.
3. Madison Church Records, pp. 23, 24, 25, 26, 29.
4. NJ Wills, Vol. IX, p. 37; Vol. XI, p. 38.
5. Rev. War - NJ -1, pp. 61, 152, 158.

6. NJ in 1793, p. 133.
7. *New Jersey Tax Lists 1772- 1822*, Vol. 1.
8. Deed Record, Essex co, NJ, Books O, Q, and T.
9. *Records of New Providence Presbyterian Church*, compiled by Beacon Fire Chapter DAR, Summit, NJ, for the Newark, NJ, Historical Society, abstracted and sent to me by Philip S. Lacy.
10. CB Database.
11. *Chatham at War*, pp. 65, 184, 239.
12. Lynch, pp. 21, 22, 23.
13. Notes compiled by Gwen Quickel, Lake Jackson, TX, in November 1988.
14. Fern Bonnell, pp. 60, 61.

1-3-1-2-2-4   D153   CB310308

NATHANIEL[6] BONNELL (Benjamin[5], Nathaniel[4], Nathaniel[3], Nathaniel[2], William[1]) was born 20 March 1753 in Springfield, Essex (now Union) co, NJ[1]. On 19 February 1772 he married Sibah Hoel (Howell)[2]. Between 1772 and 1809 three adult Nathaniel Bonnells lived in this immediate area, and it is frequently extremely difficult to differentiate among them.

This Nathaniel is clearly the person listed in the New Jersey Rateables in February 1779 in Springfield Ward, Elizabeth twp, Essex co as Nathaniel Bunnell, householder[3]. No property or livestock were listed. In Springfield Ward in February 1780 he appears as Nathaniel Bonnel, Ju., again householder with no taxable property[3]. Apparently he was called Junior this time to distinguish him from his uncle Capt. Nathaniel Bonnel, who did not appear on the 1779 assessment. Uncle Nathaniel was assessed in 1780 on 3 acres and a sawmill, but was not listed as a householder[3].

This Nathaniel is probably also the person who was listed in tax assessments in Springfield as Nathaniel Bonnell, Jr., from 1781 to 1796[4], and as Nathaniel Bonnel from 1810 to 1813 in New Providence twp[4], which had been set off from Springfield in 1793.

Only two other contemporary records have been found which seem to apply to this Nathaniel: The baptism on 10 April 1774 of Calvin and Luther, sons of Nathaniel Bonnel, Jr.[5], and the death of a child of Nathaniel Bonnel Jr. on 30 January 1783[5], both from the Records of the New Providence Presbyterian Church. The graveyard of the church includes the gravestone of Mary Bonnell, daughter of Nathaniel and Tibbah, died 30 January 1783 at 7 years[5].

It is probably safe to say that Nathaniel was born and lived in the New Providence section of Springfield along the Passaic River. He does not seem to have taken part in the mill business as did his father, several uncles and several brothers. If he lived out his life in New Jersey or followed some of his brothers to Ohio is not known, and no record of the date or place of his death has been discovered.

Children:
1. 320438. Calvin[2], bapt. 10 Apr. 1774[5].
2. 320443. Luther[2], bapt. 10 Apr. 1774[5].

3. 320429. Mary, b. about 1776; d. 30 Jan. 1783[5].
4. 320497. Elijah[2].
5. 320498. Lockey[2].

REFERENCES:
1. CB Database.
2. Littell, p. 46.
3. Gen Mag of NJ, Vol. 43, pp. 79, 80.
4. NJ Tax Lists.
5. New Providence, NJ, Presbyterian Church.

1-3-1-2-2-5   D154   CB310238

SAMUEL[6] BONNELL (Benjamin[5] Nathaniel[4], Nathaniel[3], Nathaniel[2], William[1]) was born 10 February 1755[1] in Springfield, Elizabethtown, Essex (now Union) co, NJ. Samuel served as a private in the New Jersey Line of the Continental Army, enlisting in the First Battalion in the Second Establishment in late 1776 or early 1777[2]. When the Third New Jersey Regiment was formed in 1780 he was assigned to the company of Captain Richard Cox[2] and was later transferred to the First Regiment, still as a private[2]. Some DAR records assert that he served for seven years[3], but I have not found the records to support it. However, when he was awarded Bounty Land Warrant 8112 on 23 April 1790 for 100 acres of land his military grade was listed as Quarter Master Serjeant in the New Jersey Line[4]. A more intensive study of military records in the National Archives might reward his descendants with a clearer picture of his service.

He married ELIZABETH CRANE[5], who was born about 1760 in New Jersey (probably Essex co). The wedding took place about 1780[3] or a little later, perhaps after the war ended in 1783. Their first two children were baptized in the New Providence Presbyterian Church in the summer of 1786 or 1787[6]. (The community of New Providence on the Passaic River opposite Chatham, originally known as Turkey, was part of the Springfield Ward, Elizabethtown, Essex co, NJ. Springfield became a township on its own in 1793 and New Providence was set off from Springfield as a separate township in 1809. In 1857, Essex co was divided in two, with the southern half, including New Providence, established as Union co. Elizabeth is its county seat.)

Samuel and his family removed to Hamilton co, OH, about 1790, perhaps to take advantage of the warrant for bounty land. Claude Bunnell's Database cites the Cincinnati Historical Society for the statement that Samuel Bonnell was a member of Capt. James Flinn's company of militia volunteers on 25 January 1792[3]. On 10 July 1796 Samuel and Elizabeth sold a piece of land in Hamilton co to Gabriel Foster for $70[7]. On the division of the estate of his father, Capt. Benjamin Bonnell, Esq., Samuel inherited a fourth part of "the Old Grist Mill" in Chatham, Morris co, NJ. On 24 February 1801 Samuel Bonnell, "late of the township of Springfield, Essex co, NJ," sold his quarter share in the mill to his brother John Bonnell, "Junr." for $250[8].

Their home was in Mill Creek twp, Hamilton co, OH, (now part of the city of Cincinnati). A letter directed to him at that address was left for him at the Cincinnati post office 1 January

1806[3]. He appears on the tax rolls of Hamilton co in 1806, 1808 and 1809[3], and on the tax roll of Mill Creek twp, Hamilton co, in 1810[3]. Samuel died in July 1816 in Mill Creek twp and was buried in Pleasant Ridge Cemetery, now in Cincinnati[3]. His will was proved 22 July 1816 by James Lyon, Charles Paddock and William Paddock. Son Lewis Bonnell was named executor[7]. Final accounting was submitted to court by Lewis Bonnel on 16 February 1820[7].

His widow Elizabeth appears in the 1820 census: 000200-00101[9] and the 1830 census: 0-0000000001[9] in Mill Creek twp, Hamilton co. She died in 1935 and was buried with Samuel in Pleasant Ridge Cemetery[3].

Children:
1. 320285. Lewis Joseph, b. before summer 1787, bapt. summer 1786 or 1797[6]; m. 7 May 1812 Abigail Robinson[2]; d. 3 Sept. 1831[3].
Children (surname Bonnell):[3]

   1. Stephen R.   4. Jane.   7. Joanna.
   2. Samuel   5. Jonathan R.   8. Benjamin C.
   3. Elizabeth.   6. John K.

2. 320290. Jayne, b. before summer 1787; bapt. summer 1786 or 1787[6].
3. 320389. Lydia, b. 20 July 1791[11]; m. Samuel Maxwell Frazee[11].
Children (surname Frazee):[11]

   1. Sarah.   others?

4. 320288. Phebe[3], b. about 1795, m. 8 Apr. 1813 Moses Marsh[3].
5. 320286. Benjamin C., b. about 1798[3]; m. 21 Oct. 1821 Margaret Robeson[3]; d. 4 Apr. 1846[3].
Children (surname Bonnell):[3]

   1. Elizabeth.

6. 320287. Abigail, b. about 1800[3]; m. 19 Oct. 1820 Recompense S. Fraizer[10].

REFERENCES:
1. *Soldiers of the American Revolution Buried in Ohio*, Vols. 1929, 1938, 1959, published by the Daughters of the American Revolution.
2. Rev War - NJ -1, pp. 152, 158.
3. CB Database.
4. Index of Rev. War Pension Applications in the National Archives, Bicentennial Edition, by the National Genealogical Society, 1976, and copy of Samuel's Bounty Land Warrant Record Card, sent to me by Claude A. Bunnell.
5. Littell, p. 46.
6. Records of the New Providence Presbyterian Church, New Providence, NJ, abstracts of which were sent to me by Philip S. Lacy and W. Jerome Hatch.
7. Hamilton County Court and Other Records, Vol. II, p. 124, by Cummins, data sent to me by Mrs. Harry Atleson, Cuyahoga Falls, OH,
8. Morris co, NJ, Deed Book D, p. 478, abstract of which was sent to me by Claude A. Bunnell.
9. Census Records, Mill Creek twp, Hamilton oc, OH, 1820 and 1830, abstracted and sent to me by Mrs. Harry Atleson.
10. *Ohio Marriages Recorded in County Courts Through 1820--and Index*, by Jean Nathan ---Ohio Genealogical Society, 1996, abstracted and sent to me by Marjorie Gibbs.
11, *Ohio Records and Pioneer Families*, Vol. XIV, p. 36, sent to me by Mary Burdick, Watertown, MA.

1-3-1-2-2-6   D155   CB310240

JOHN[6] BONNELL (Benjamin[5], Nathaniel[4], Nathaniel[3], Nathaniel[2], William[1]) was born 18[2] March 1757[1] in Springfield, Essex[1] (now New Providence, Union) co, NJ. In most records he was called John, Jr., to distinguish him from his uncle John. He served as a private in the Revolutionary War[1]. In 1833 his pension application details his service as he remembered it:

"Declaration in order to obtain the benefit of the Act of Congress
Passed June 7th 1832
State of Pennsylvania, Wayne County

"On this 29th day of August AD Eighteen hundred and thirty three personally appeared in open Court before the Judges of the Court of Common Pleas now sitting **John Bonnell** a resident of Dyberry Township Wayne County and State of Pennsylvania aged Seventy Six years, who being first duly sworn according to law doth on his oath make the following declaration in order to obtain the benefit of the act of congress passed June 7th 1832.   That he entered the service of the United States under the following named officers and served as herein stated -

"That he enlisted a private in the early part of the Spring of seventeen hundred and seventy five (and he believes in April - for the term of one year) in Essex County, New Jersey, under Captain David Lyon. [word?] Matthias Clark and _____ Bateman were the lieutenants. The Regiment to which he was attached was commanded by Lieut. Col. Richmon and was marched to St. Johns passing through Elizabeth Town, New York, Albany, Tyconderoga and Crown Point. he remained with the regiment at St. Johns some time and whilst there was in a skirmish or engagement with the Brittish & Indians after which he returned to the Isle of Knox. The hardships that he had undergone in his march and whilst at St. Johns injured his health and he with many other soldiers were taken sick.   that he remained at the Isle of Knox for some weeks the time he cannot now recollect when he with other invalid soldiers at that place were ordered to Tyconderoga where he remained until he was dismissed with others, as he understood at the time by the order of General Schuyler, and he with Nathaniel Bonnell and Nehemiah Ward, soldiers in the same company, returned home together to Chatham New Jersey. He believes he was dismissed in October 1775 being in actual service six months at least and he believes more than that time. he also believes he received a written discharge by a Richard Varick but has since lost or mislaid the same -

"Some time after he returned home to Morris County New Jersey he was drafted and called out in the militia as a private for one month and served out the time, he does not distinctly recollect the name of his captain but well recollects that he was stationed with the Company at Elizabeth Town Point New Jersey remained there some time, was marched to Newark staid there about one week and returned again to Elizabeth Townpoint and staid untill the end of his enlistment for one month, was discharged and returned home. Soon after his return home he was again drafted for one month and called into service of the militia as a private and was stationed at Bergin in the State of New Jersey, he was ?lazing?? at Bergin Point at the time of the Battle on Long Island which he believes was in August 1776 and in the two last named tours he thinks that his Captain's name was Chandler from Elizabeth Town. he served his tour of one month and was discharged and returned home.

"That he was home but a short time before he was again drafted in the militia for one month, his captain's name was Wood and Seth Raymond was his Lieutenant - this was in the latter part of the Summer or early in the Fall of 1776. He was stationed at Woodbridge in New Jersey and was marched from there to Springfield and was in that battle, he believes that Col. Seely then had the command at any rate he saw him there, and also Col. Angel of the Continental Army, he served his term of one month and was discharged.   he was called out and served at other times but cannot recollect the precise time of service he was at the Battle of Monmouth in New Jersey.

"He was born in the month of March 1757 in Essex County New Jersey and resided in that state untill AD 1816 when he removed to Pennsylvania where he now resides - that at this time he has no documentary evidence of his service and that he knows of no person whose testimony he can procure who can testify to his service except David Leonard and Stephen Bedford whose depositions are hereto annexed. And that he hereby relinquishes any Claim whatever to a pension or annuity except the present and declares that his name is not on the pension roll of the agency of any state.

Sworn to and subscribed the day   John Bonnel
and year aforesaid
     G B Wescott

"We Joel Campbell, a clergyman residing in Honesdale Wayne County and Stephen Day residing in the same County hereby certify that we are well acquainted with John Bonnell who has subscribed and sworn to the above declaration, that we believe him to be seventy six years of age, that he is reputed and believed in the neighbourhood where he now resides to have been a soldier of the revolution, and that we concur in that opinion."[1]

Recognizing that the above account was John's recollection of events which occurred 58 years earlier, some reference to official records is useful. First, his enlistment date seems a little early, since the first shots of the Revolution did not occur until mid-April 1775, and the act providing for the enlistment of militia in each county was not passed by the Provincial Congress of New Jersey until 3 June 1775[3]. In his account of service in 1775 it is clear that he was serving in a regiment of the New York State Line rather that that of New Jersey. None of the officers he mentioned can be found in the *Official Register of the Officers and Men of New Jersey in the Revolutionary War*[3]. That is not conclusive in itself, but we find that Capt. David Lyon, Lt. Matthias Clark, Lt. John Bateman and Capt. Richard Varick were all officers in the New York regiments which served in the attack on St. John's, Montreal and Quebec[4]. Lt. Col. Richmon does not appear, but this was probably intended for Lt. Col. Pierre (or Peter) Regnier, who did command one of the five New York regiments[4]. The "Isle of Knox" was actually Isle aux Noix on the Richelieu River south of St. John's.

Although John himself does not appear in the list of enlisted men in the New York regiments, two New Jersey Bonnells do: Nathaniel and Simeon Bonnell were members of the First Regiment of the New York Line[4]. Nathaniel could have been John's brother or his cousin Nathaniel, Jr., but I prefer to believe that Nathaniel and Simeon were brothers, sons of Benjamin Bonnell 1-3-3-1 CB290008 of Mendham, NJ.

John Bonnell was a member of General Montgomery's army which left Fort Ticonderoga on 28 August 1775 and traveled up Lake Champlain and the Richelieu River to undertake the siege of Fort St. John on 8 September[5]. The fort finally surrendered on 2 November permitting the army to continue on to the capture of Montreal[5]. However, John's illness apparently kept him from participating in these early victories or the disaster at Quebec which followed.

John's service in the various call-ups of the New Jersey militia are easier to clarify. His captain in his first two tours was obviously Capt. Stephen Chandler of the First Regiment of Essex co[3]. The Battle of Long Island occurred on 27 August 1776[6]. On his next tour his Captain Wood was probably Daniel S. Wood, captain in the First Essex Regiment[3]. I could not identify Lt. Seth Raymond, however.

SIXTH GENERATION

The Battle of Springfield took place on 23 June 1780[7]. Col. Sylvanus Seeley was apparently the Col. Seely he remembered[3]. Col. Angel of the Continental Army was warmly cited for his part in the action in Major General Greene's report to General Washington the next day[7]. The Battle of Monmouth took place two years earlier on 28 June 1778[7]. Although the depositions of David Leonard and Stephen Bedford were not included in the copy of John's petition which I received, both men were included in the list of New Jersey militia[3].

John, Jr., appears in the 1780 tax list as a single man in Springfield Ward, Elizabeth Township, Essex co, NJ[8]. After the war he married NANCY DAY, daughter of Stephen and Damaris (Foster) Day[9]. At least two of their children were baptized in the New Providence Presbyterian Church[14]. Littell calls John "a tailor"[9]. John, Jr., appears in the tax records of Springfield from 1781 to 1796[11]. In 1793 his name was included on the list of all the militia enrolled in the County of Essex[10]. He was a contributor to the Madison Presbyterian Church in Morris co in 1793 and 1794[2]. In 1793 John and his brother Benjamin were administrators in the probate of their father's estate[12].

John, Jr., and his wife Nancy appear as residents of Essex co in the records of land transactions until 1806[2]. The tax records of 1806 to 1814 suggest that they had removed across the Passaic River to live in Chatham twp, Morris co, NJ[11], In any case, in the year 1816, together with Nancy's brother and John's sister, Stephen and Polly (Bonnell) Day[13], they left New Jersey to settle in Dyberry twp, Wayne co, PA[1,13]. On 29 August 1833 John applied for a pension based on his service in the Revolution[1]. It was approved at the rate of $30 per year retroactive to 4 March 1831[1].

On 3 November 1826 the eastern part of Dyberry twp had been set off as Berlin twp, Wayne co. John appears on the 1840 census of Berlin twp: 00000000001-000001[2] as well as on the census of pensioners that year[2]. He was 83 years old[2]. His pension was paid through 4 March 1841[1]. The pension agent was informed of his death on 4 March 1842, although the actual date of death was not given[1]. The date of his wife's death has not been found. A search of the cemeteries in Berlin twp would probably reveal the dates.

Children:
1. 320340. Stephen Day, bapt. 30 Sept. 1787[14]; m. 23 June 1811 Harriet Ball[14]; d. after 1840[13].
2. 320341. Polly Foster, bapt. 20 Sept. 1789[14]; m. _____ Wood[13].
3. 320344. Julia, b. 16 Sept. 1790[14]; m. 9 Aug. 1816 Rev. John M. Babbit[14]; d. 24 Dec. 1856[14].
   Children (surname Babbit):[14]
   1. Nancy Day.   2. Julia.
4.   Elijah, never married[13].
5. 320343. Barney, b. 18 Nov. 1799[2]; m. 1829[2] Lucy Brooks[13]; d. 1 Mar. 1868[2].
   Children (surname Bonnell):[14]
   1. Joanna Minerva.   3. Mary Frances.   4. Elijah Day.
   2. Jane Bruen.
6. 320342. Joanna, b. 1800-1810[2]; m. after 1845 Capt. Homer Brooks[13].

SIXTH GENERATION

REFERENCES:

1. Revolutionary War Pension Application File #S6676 of John Bonnell, photocopy obtained from the National Archives and sent to me by Claude A. Bunnell.
2. CB Database.
3. Rev War - NJ-1, pp. 30, 355, 384, 419, 504, 513, 665.
4. Rev War - NY, pp. 17, 19, 29, 47, 60.
5. *The American Heritage Book of the Revolution*, Richard M. Ketchum, Editor, 1958, American Heritage Publishing Company, Inc., p. 131.
6. *Rag Tag and Bobtail*, by Lynn Montross, 1952, Harper & Brothers Publishers, pp. 62-65.
7. *Historical Collections of the State of New Jersey*, by John W. Barber and Henry Howe, 1845, reprint 1990 by Heritage Books, Inc., pp. 192-194, 270, 340.
8. Gen Mag of NJ, Vol. 43, No. 2, May 1968, pp. 79, 80.
9. Littell, pp. 46, 48, 120, 121.
10. NJ in 1793, p. 133.
11. NJ Tax Lists, pp. 298, 301.
12. NJ Wills - Vol. IX, p. 37.
13. *Wayne, Pike and Monroe Counties, Pennsylvania*, by Alfred Mathews, 1886, pp. 511, 598, 599, 607-609.
14. Duncan, pp. 95, 170.

1-3-1-2-2-7 D156 CB310236

AARON[6] BONNELL (Benjamin[5], Nathaniel[4], Nathaniel[3], Nathaniel[2], William[1]) was born 4 March 1759[1,2] in Springfield, Essex (now New Providence, Union) co, NJ, where his parents lived all their lives (or in Chatham, Morris co, on the other side of the Passaic River, as he stated in his pension application).

He was 17 years old in 1776 whe he enlisted as a private in Capt. Sylvanus Seeley's company, Col. Ephraim Martin's Battalion, Brigadier General Nathaniel Heard's Brigade of New Jersey militia[1,3,4]. In this tour of duty he was marched to New York City, then transferred across the East River to Brooklyn[1]. On 26 and 27 August 1776 he took part in the Battle of Brooklyn, Long Island, which resulted in a major defeat for the outnumbered American forces[4]. During the night of 29 August, General Washington successfully evacuated his entire army, including young Aaron, across to Manhattan[4]. A week or so later Aaron was assigned to Fort Washington on the west coast of Manhattan[1]. He fell sick and was granted a furlough to recover at home[1]. The term of his enlistment expired before he was able to return to duty, and he was discharged[1].

The American army took up winter quarters in Morristown, Morris co, NJ, in January 1777[5], and Aaron enlisted for service in Col. Jeduthan Baldwin's Regiment of Artificers[1,3]. At Morristown he was employed in erecting a large frame shop for the use of the gunnery troops[1]. He continued in this service as an artificer, working at Morristown and Chatham, for the three months of his term of enlistment[1]. Following his two voluntary enlistments he was drafted into the "flying camp" or "Minutemen" of the New Jersey militia for service as needed during the remainder of the war[1]. He remembered specifically taking part in the Skirmish of Elizabethtown 25 February 1779[1,5] and the Battle of Springfield 23 June 1780[1,5].

On 29 May 1785 Aaron was married by Rev. Jonathan Elmore of the Presbyterian Church at New Providence to RACHEL CLARK[1,6], daughter of Henry Clark[7]. She was born 21 September 1762[1] in New Jersey[8]. Their first child, Pamela, was baptized in the New Providence Presbyterian Church[6]. Aaron appears in the tax records of Springfield twp, Essex (now Union) co, which included the village of New Providence, in 1789, 1795 and 1796[10]. In 1793 he was a contributor to the Presbyterian Church at Madison, Morris co, NJ[8]. That year he was listed as a member of the Essex co militia[9].

When Aaron submitted his application for a pension in 1832, he was asked the question, "Where were you living when called into service, where have you lived since the Revolutionary war, and where do you now live-" He responded, "At Chatham New Jersey and removed in 1803 to New York where I remained two years and removed to this County [Crosby co, OH] where I have since resided"[1]. Although Aaron spoke of Chatham, Morris co, NJ, on the west side of the Passaic river, as his home in New Jersey, all other references I have found relating to his place of residence indicate that he actually lived in New Providence, Essex co, on the east side of the river.

In 1803 Aaron moved his family to New York State[1]. CB Database states "to Saratoga co, NY," although I do not find the source of the statement. From there they removed to Hamilton co, OH, in the year 1805[1,2]. In 1807 he bought a tract of land in the northwest corner of Hamilton county, identified as range 1, tier 2, section 18[8]. It lay due north of the village of Harrison in what was then Crosby twp (now Harrison twp)[2]. He improved the land and farmed it until his death[2]. Aaron appears in the 1820 census of Crosby twp: 000101-00001-AG2[8] and also in the 1830 census of Crosby twp: 00002000001-000001001[8].

On 25 September 1832 he applied for a pension based on his military service[1]. The pension was approved on 10 May 1833 in the amount of $88.00 per year, retroactive to 4 March 1831[1].

Aaron died 4 October 1837[1] in Crosby (now Harrison) twp, Hamilton co, OH. On 28 November 1838 his widow Rachel applied for a widow's pension under the law passed 7 July 1838[1]. She died 8 July 1839[1] without ever receiving a pension[1]. Aaron and Rachel were buried in Park Cemetery, Harrison, Hamilton co, OH. On 22 January 1852 Clark Bonnell, as administrator of his mother's estate, filed an application for the pension which would have been due to her during the last year of her life[1]. The pension file does not indicate that it was paid[1].

Children:
1. 320146. Pamela Clark, b. 24 May 1786[1]; bapt. 2 July 1786[6]; m. (first) 1806 Henry Clark Miller Looker[10]; m. (second) Isaac Hull Butler[13]; d. 1836[13]. Children (surname Looker):[10]
   1. Emily Hewitt.
2. 320142. Rachel V., b. 12 Aug. 1788[1]; m. 16 June 1811 Robert Anderson[13]; d. before 16 Sept. 1816[13].
3. 320145. Clark, b. 18 Nov. 1790[1]; m. 7 Sept. 1811 Rachel[8] Elsey Wykoff[2]; d. 6 Dec.[11] 1864[2,11].

Children (surname Bonnell):[2,7,11]

1. Jane.	4. Oscar Samuel.	7. Robert Burns.
2. Susan.	5. Leonidas.	8. Lockey.
3. Marcus Seneca.	6. Delia Emily.	9. Samuel C.

4. 320143. Samuel, b. 15 Mar. 1793[1]; m. 7 Oct. 1824 Nancy Gilliland[13]; d. before 1839[1].

5. 320147. Benjamin, b. 6 Aug. 1796[1]; m. Mary Allen[13]; d. after 1860[8].

6. 320144. Allison Clark, b. 16 Mar. 1801[1]; m. 1 Nov. 1835 Catherine Hough Looker[12]; d. 16 Aug 1875[12].

Children (surname Bonnell):[8]

1. Edwin.	3. Alice.	5. Keator (Kate).
2. Henry.	4. Rufus.	6. Lucy.

REFERENCES:

1. Rev War pension appl. - Aaron Bonnell Pension File 13086.

"The State of Ohio, Hamilton County

On this 25th day of September 1832 personally appeared before me the undersigned a Judge of the Court of C.P. within and for said County Aaron Bonnell a resident of Crosby township in the County aforesaid, aged seventy three years, who being first duly sworn according to law doth on his oath make the following declaration in order to obtain the benefit of the act of congress passed June 7, 1832 -- That he entered the service of the United States under the following named officers and served as herein stated. Captain Sylvenus Seeley, the name of his Ensign was   Roberts his field officers were Col. Martin the name of his General was Heard the name of the Adjutant of his regiment was Jos. King. at Chatham New Jersey and marched from there to the City of New York and after remaining there a short time crossed over to Long Island and remained there till the American Army evacuated the Island and crossed over again to New York where he remained about one week and marched to Fort Washington where he was taken sick and obtained a furlow to return home to Chatam for a short time - and before his recovery the term for which he enlisted expired and was honorably discharged having served five months, this was in the year 1776 -- and he again entered the service as an artificer in the winter following - at Morristown N.J.& was engaged in erecting a large frame shop for the use of the gunnery and continued in the said service working at Morristown & Chatam three months the term for which he engaged -- and was discharged, and again entered the service in what was called the flying camp or minutemen and served under different officers whose names he can not now recollect, until the close of the war. during the period of the last named service he was in the battle of Springfield and at the Skirmish at Elizabethtown. that he is unable from bodily infirmity to appear in open Court to make oath to this his declaration. That he has no documentary evidence and that he knows of no person except the one whose deposition is herewith submitted whose Testimony he can procure who can testify to his service. He hereby relinquishes every claim whatever to a pension or annuity except the present and declares that his name is not on the pension roll of the agency of any state.

Sworn to and subscribed the day and year aforesaid   Aaron Bonnel

"Interrogatories propounded by the Justice to the applicant

1. Where and in what year were you born

Ans. In the year 1759 at Chatam New Jersey.

2. Have you any record of your age and if so where is it

Ans. None othere than the register of my birth in the old family bible now in my possession.

3. Where were you living when called into service; where have you lived since the Revolutionary war and where do you now live -

    Ans. At Chatam New Jersey and removed in 1803 to New York where I I remained two years and removed to this County where I have since resided.

4. How were you called in to service, were you drafted did you volunteer or were you a substitute & if a substitute for whom.

    Ans. The 5 months & 3 months tours I was a volunteer - & in the flying camp services I was drafted.

5. State the names of some of the regular officers who were with the troops when you served such continental and militia regiments as you can recollect and the general circumstances of yr service.

    Ans. Genl. Washington Genl. Lord Sterling Col Dayton Genl. Wayne - the general circumstances of my service as is contained in my declaration.

6. Did you ever receive a Discharge from the service & if so by whom was it given and what has become of it.

    Ans. None other than a verbal one fr my officers.

7. State the names of persons to whom you are known in your present neighborhood and who can testify to yr character for varacity & their belief of your services as a soldier of the revolution.

    Ans. Judge Othniel Looker Col Wakefield John D. Moore Danl Mason Dr. Crookshank.

Sworn & subscribed the day & year aforesaid   Aaron Bonnel

And I do hereby declare my opinion after the investigation of the matter & after putting the interrogatories prescribed by the war department that the above named applicant was a revolutionary soldier & served as he stated. Henry Lincoln,, J.P."

"On this twentyeighth day of November Eighteen hundred and thirty eight, personally appeared in open Court before the Honorable Judges of the Court of Common Pleas in and for the County of Hamilton aforesaid now sitting Rachel Bonnel aged seventy six years on the twenty first of September last past who being duly sworn according to law doth on her oath make the following declaration in order to obtain the benefit of the provisions of the act of Congress passed July 7th 1838 entitled an act granting half pay and pensions to certain widows - That she is the widow of Aaron Bonnel dec^d who was a private in Col. Ephraim Morgans regiment and afterwards a private in Col. Lindley and Ogdens Regiment in the New Jersey line during the war of the Revolution and also an artificer, all of which service will more fully and at large appear by reference to the declaration and proof of the said Aaron Bonnell dec^d now on file in the war office upon which a pension was granted to him under the provisions of the act of Congress passed 7th June 1832 which said pension certificate bears date May 10th 1833 and signed by Lewis Cass, then secretary of war. She further declares that she was married to the said Aaron Bonnel on the twenty ninth day of May in the year seventeen hundred and eighty five, that her husband the aforesaid Aaron Bonnell died on the fourth day of October Eighteen hundred and thirty seven, that she was not married to him prior to his leaving the service, but the marriage took place previous to the first of January seventeen hundred and ninety four, viz. at the time above stated - that she has no record evidence of her marriage   Rachel Bonnell

SIXTH GENERATION

"At the same time personally appeared before the Honorable Judges of said Court Abigail Johnson aged sixty nine years who being legally sworn deposes and says that she well knows the above applicant Rachel Bonnell widow of Aaron Bonnell deceased, that deponant was present at the marriage between the said Aaron Bonnell deceased and the said Rachel Bonnell which took place at New Providence Essex county in the state of New Jersey, that the marriage ceremony was performed by Jonathan Elmore a Presbyterian clergyman on the twenty ninth day of May seventeen hundred and eighty five and that they lived together as man and wife until the death of the said Aaron Bonnell which occured on the fourth day of October Eighteen hundred and thirty seven, that the said Rachel Bonnell has never since been married but still remains the widow of the said Aaron Bonnell deceased.   Abigail Johnson

"Copy of the Family Record of Aaron Bonnell deceased
"Aaron Bonnel born March 4th 1759 (fourth seventeen hundred & fifty nine) and Rachel his wife born September 21 1762 (September twenty first seventeen hundred and sixty two.)
"Pamela C. Bonnell born May 24 1786 (May twenty fourth seventeen hundred and eighty six)
"Rachel V. Bonnell born August 12th 1788 (August twelfth seventeen hundred and eighty eight.)
"Clark Bonnell born November 18th 1790 (November eighteenth seventeen hundred & ninety)
"Samuel Bonnell born March 15th 1793 (March fifteenth seventeen hundred & ninety three)
"Benjamin Bonnell born 6th August 1796 (August sixth seventeen hundred and ninety six)
"Alison C. Bonnell born March 16th 1801 (March sixteenth eighteen hundred and one.)"

"I Rachel Bonnell widow of Aaron Bonnell deceased depose and say that the above and foregoing is a true extract from the family Record of said Aaron Bonnell deceased - as entered in the family bible in the hand writing of said Aaron Bonnell deceased - with the exception of the dates here inserted in letters & figures in the original in figures only.
                                                Rachel Bonnell
Sworn to and subscribed before me
this 13th day of May 1839   Luther Hopkins, Justice of the Peace"

"State of Ohio, County of Hamilton
    Be it known that before the Court of Common Pleas in the County & State aforesaid holden at Cincinnati in said County on this 22nd day of January 1852 Personally appeared Clark Bonnell (administrator of the Estate of Rachel Bonnell deceased) and made oath in due form of Law that he is the duly appointed administrator of the Estate of Rachel Bonnell deceased, that he is a Son of Aaron Bonnell late of said County of Hamilton & deceased, And that his said father in his life time was a pensioner of the United States under the act of the 7th June 1832 at the rate of Eighty Eight Dollars per annum - that his father the said Aaron Bonnell died in the county of Hamilton & State aforesaid on the 4th day of October 1837 leaving Rachael Bonnell (deponent's Mother a widow the said Aaron surviving) & that his said Mother also died in the County of Hamilton aforesaid on the 8th day of July 1839 - leaving this deponent and two Brothers

(viz. Benjamin Bonnell & Allison C. Bonnell) his said father & mother
surviving - all of whom now resided in Hamilton County aforesaid & that this
deponent (as administrator of the Estate and as one of the above mentioned Children
of the said Aaron & Rachael deceased - hereby make application for the amount
of Pension due his said mother at her decease as the Widow of his father the said
Aaron Bonnell deceased. That in & in application he refers to the proof hereto
annexed & herewith presented - as well as the proof on file at the proper office of
Government in support of this his application - & further that his said Mother did
not in her life time receive a pension as the widow of her said late Husband the
said Aaron Bonnell deceased - to his knowledge and belief.

Clark Bonnel"

2. *History of Hamilton co, OH, 1789-1881*, by Henry A. & Kate B. Ford, p. 318B, and notes sent by Mrs. John W. Hegeman.
3. Rev War - NJ -1, pp. 59, 64, 70, 349, 355.
4. *The Battle of Brooklyn 1776*, by John J. Gallagher, 1995.
5. NJ Collections, pp. 165, 166, 385.
6. Records of the New Providence Presbyterian Church at Turkey, Essex (now New Providence, Union) co, NJ, abstracted and sent to me by W. Jerome Hatch and Philip S. Lacy.
7. Duncan, pp. 95, 96.
8. CB Database.
9. NJ in 1793, p. 133.
10. *The Compendium of American Genealogy*, Vo. VII, p. 359.
11. The Bonnell descent of Gladys Marcella (Fenton) Steebe, sent to me by Homer E. Baldwin.
12. *American Ancestry*, Vol. X, 1894, Joel Munsell's Sons, Publishers, p. 108.
13. William Bonnell Descendants thru Samuel & Aaron, MS compiled by Mrs. Russell S. Cooke, 1961.

1-3-1-2-2-9 D157 CB310311

PAUL[6] BONNELL (Benjamin[5], Nathaniel[4], Nathaniel[3], Nathaniel[2], William[1]) was born 7 November 1762[1] in Springfield twp, Essex (now New Providence, Union) co, NJ. He is said to have taken part, with his father and brothers, in the battle of Springfield in June 1780, although there is no indication he had joined the military service as yet. He enlisted in the spring of 1782 at Philadelphia as a private in Captain Christie's company, Colonel Richard Butler's Pennsylvania regiment[1]. He was marched from Philadelphia to Carlisle barracks where he remained until fall 1782[1]. He then marched to Lancaster, PA, where he guarded British prisoners for the remainder of his service[1]. He was discharged in July 1783[1]. On 11 June 1789 he received bounty land warrant #8998 and assigned it to Matthias Denman[3].

On 28 December 1783 in New Providence, Essex (now Union) co, he married MARY PARSONS[2] (or PIERSON[3]), daughter of William Parsons, Jr.[2] She was born in 1763 in New Jersey[3]. Paul appears on a tax list in Springfield twp, Essex co, in September 1789[4]. all of their children were apparently born at New Providence in Springfield twp[3]. The baptisms of the first three children are found in the records of the Presbyterian Church of New Providence[3].

Paul seems to have had an enduring interest in military life. He was apparently the Paul Bonnell who enlisted 14 April 1791 in Capt. Jonathan Rue Castle's company, Major Athomas Paterson's battalion, 2nd Regiment Infantry, U. S. Army for service in an expedition against the Indians. He was discharged 19 November 1791[3].

In 1804 or 1805 he moved his family to Ohio, settling in Hamilton co with several of his siblings. At first he began farming on a tract near Carthage in Hamilton co[5], but soon moved across the county line to Fairfield twp, Butler co, where he remained for the rest of his life[3,6].

In November 1812, Paul enlisted as a private in Capt. A. Edwards' company of the 19th Ohio Infantry Regiment[1]. He was with the forces of General William Henry Harrison when he built the fort at the rapids of the Maumee River which he named Fort Meigs[7]. The fort was besieged in March 1813 by a force of a thousand Canadians and 1200 Indians[7]. Unable to breach the fort, the enemy withdrew[7], but in this action Paul was wounded in the frontal bone of his head[1]. He was discharged 26 April 1814[1]. He enlisted again in the 17th Ohio Infantry Regiment on 1 February 1815 and was discharged 18 April 1815 at Chillicothe, OH[1]. He was described on his discharge certificate as "about Forty four years of age, Six feet high, Light complexion, Blue eyes, Sandy hair, and by occupation, when enlisted, a Sawyer."

In 1816 Paul applied for the bounty land to which he was entitled by his military service. Warramt #1-58 for 320 acres was finally issued to his heirs on 20 April 1833.[1] He also applied for an invalid pension under the law passed 30 April 1816, based on the wound he received at Fort Meigs. This was approved on 15 September 1818 and paid, retroactive to 29 January 1816 at the rate of $4.00 per month[1].

Congress passed another law on 18 March 1818 providing for pensions for Revolutionary War veterans. Paul applied on 19 March 1819 citing his service in 1782 and agreeing to release his right to the invalid pension in exchange for the War pension[1]. It was approved, and Certificate #15814 was issued for a pension of $8.00 per month beginning 12 March 1819[1].

Paul did not enjoy his pension very long. He died 26 August 1820 in Fairfield twp, Butler co, OH[1]. On 28 August his heirs filed for probate of his estate[3]. Apparently there was no will[3]. Whether his wife survived him or not is not clear. She was dead before September 1829 when the surviving children and grandchildren renewed Paul's application for bounty land and received approval in April 1833[1].

Children:
    1. 320444. Elizabeth[1], bapt. 1787[3]; m. Jerry[3] Caldwell[1,3].
    2. 320445. Abigail[1], bapt. 20 Apr. 1788[3]; m. 5 Nov. 1806 James T. Morton[8];
            d. before Mar. 1830[1].
            Children (surname Morton):[1]
            1. Anna Maria.   2. William.
    3. 320446. Johannah[1], bapt. 7 June 1789[3]; m. 11 Aug. 1804 Jonathan Line[8].
    4. 320447. Rachel[1], b. 29 May 1794[3]; m. 18 Feb. 1815 Aaron Jewel[8]; d. 1867[3].

SIXTH GENERATION

5. 320007. Jane[1], m. 26 May 1816 Hugh B. Hawthorne[8].
6. 320005. Mary[1], m. 5 Apr. 1819 Richard Easton[8].
7. 320006. Eli Phillips[1], b. 5 Nov. 1801[9]; m. 19 Oct. 1826 Eliza Wright[9];
   d. 7 Nov. 1851[9] (or 1857[3]).
   Children (surname Bonnell):[9]
   1. William W.   3. David W.   5. Clarissa Angeline.
   2. Mary H.   4. Sarah Jane.   6. Emily I.

REFERENCES:

1. Rev War pension appl - Paul Bonnel Pension File S42625, including documents relating to his service in the War of 1812. Some extensive excerpts follow:

"State of Ohio, Butler County
   "Before the subscriber Daniel Milliken an associate judge of the court of Common pleas for the county of Butler in the seventh circuit in the State of Ohio Personally appeared Paul Bonnel on the   day of March in the year of our Lord eighteen hundred and nineteen who being duly sworn according to law doth on his oath make the following declaration for the purpose of obtaining a pension under an act of Congfres entitled an act to provide for certain person engaged in the land and naval service of the United States in the revolutionary war - that he was fifty six years of age on the seventh day of November last, that some time during the Spring of the year seventeen hundred and eighty two (the day or month he does not recollect) at Philadelphia he enlisted to serve as a private soldier during the existence of the war between the United States and great Brittain in a company of light horse. He does not recollect the name of the Captain, he does not recollect whether a colonel was appointed to command the regiment he enlisted in the Pennsylvania line. during the Spring in which he was enlisted he was marched under the command of Lieutenant Jones from Philadelphia to Carlisle where they remained at the barracks . while he remained at Carlisle he was under the command of Colonel Butler, afterwards General Butler who was killed in St. Claire defeat.

The said Bonnel remained at Carlisle from the time that he arrived there as aforesaid untill the ensuing fall when he marched under the command of Colonel Butler to Lancaster of Pennsylvania - near where he was employed in guarding the Brittish Prisoners untill the termination of the revolutionary war. He believes that Colonel Butler commanded the whole of the troops employed as a guard at Lancaster during the time that he was employed as a soldier in the aforesaid guard. the said Bonnel further declares under oath that some time in July, as this declarant believes, of the year seventeen hundered and eighty three at Lancaster he was honourably discharged at which time he received five months pay. the said Bonnel delivered his written discharge and other documents relative to his services to his father. his father is now dead and knows not what has become of the aforesaid papers. the said Bonnel further declares that he believes he was discharged by Colonel Butler but is not certain. that the aforesaid services were performed during the revolutionary war against the common enemy & on the continental extablishment. that from old age & infirmities & from his reduced circumstances in life he absolutely stands in need of the assistance of his country for support that he has no further evidence within his power of having [?] to his aforesaid services.
Subscribe before me this 12th day of April 1819   Paul Bonnel
      Daniel Milliken"

"I Paul Bonnel do hereby release all my right & interest to a pension which was granted to me by J. C. Calhoun, Secretary of War on the 15th day of Septmeber A.D. 1818, said pension was granted in conformity with the law of the United States of the 30th April A.D. 1816 for a wound incurred by me while a private in the company of Captain A. Edwards of the 19th regiment. the said Paul is inscribed on the pension list roll of the Ohio agency & which commenced on the 29th day of January one thousand eight hundred and sixteen. I do hereby release the aforesaid pension provided a pension shall be granted on the above declaration & certificate, & otherwise the pension I have received to continue.   Paul Bonnel"

2. Littell, p. 46.
3. CB Database.
4. NJ Tax Lists, p. 301.
5. *History of Hamilton co, OH, 1789-1881,* by Hery A. & Kate B. Ford, p. 318B.
6. Duncan, p. 96.
7. *The Shaping of America, Vol. III of A People's History of the Young Republic*, by Page Smith, 1980, p. 606.
8. *Ohio Marriages Recorded in County Courts Through 1820 - An Index*, by Jean Nathan, Ohio Genealogical Society, 1996, abstracted and sent to me by Marjorie Gibbs.
9. Ltr. 23 Mar. 1960 from Leonard S. Bonnell, Mountainside, NJ, great grandson of Eli P. Bonnell.

1-3-1-2-5-2   D158   CB310358

NATHANIEL[6] BONNELL (Nathaniel[5], Nathaniel[4], Nathaniel[3], Nathaniel[2], William[1]) was born 15 June 1756[1], probably in Chatham, Morris co, NJ. During the revolutionary War he served in Capt. Abraham Lyons' company, 4th Battalion, 2nd Establishment of the Continental Line[9]. He also served in the militia of Essex co, NJ[9]. He appears as a single man in the tax records of Morris twp, Morris co, NJ, in January 1780[10].

On 15 June 1781 Nathaniel married MARTHA CRANE[1], daughter of Isaac and Mary (Miller) Crane[2]. She was born 3 October 1764[1]. Their home was in Chatham village in Morris twp, Morris co, NJ. Nathaniel was involved in the milling and lumber businesses with his father and other family ,members. In 1793 he was listed as a member of the militia of Morris co[3]. From 1800 to 1813 the Morris co deed and mortgage records include a number of transactions reflecting his active business interests[4]. He appears on the tax records of Chatham twp from 1806 (the year Chatham twp was created from Morris and Hanover twps) to 1813[6]. In1809 when his father's will was probated he received a bequest of $20, his father explaining that he had given Nathaniel "heretofore what I think proper"[5]. The following year Martha acquired 48 acres of land in New Providence from the estate of her father Isaac Crane[4].

Nathaniel died 15 April 1814[1] and was buried in the cemetery of the New Providence Presbyterian Church[4] across the river from Chatham. He died intestate, and his son Jonathan Crane Bonnell administered his estate[4]. After his death Martha's name continues to appear in the tax lists of Chatham twp[6]. She survived her husband until 30[1,2] (or 20[4,7]) June 1846[1,2,4,7]

Children:

1. 320432. Philemon, b. 29 Mar. 1782[1](or 1785[4]); bapt. 29 July 1787[8]; m. 26 Jan. 1806[4] Rachel Noe[1,4]; d. 22 Mar. 1863[1].
   Children (surname Bonnell):[2]
1. Huldah.	4. Nathaniel.	7. Maline.
2. Mary Noe.	5. Martha Crane.	8. Sally Doty.
3. Ellis.	6. John Noe.	

2. 320433. Huldah, b. 1 Sept. 1787[1]; bapt. 11 Nov. 1787[8]; m. (first) 22 Nov. 1806[4] Timothy D. Pettit[1,4]; m. (second) 10 Apr. 1810[4] David Noe[1,4]; d. 6 Mar. 1863[1].
   Children (surname Pettit):[2,7]
1. Benjamin.	2. Timothy Day.

   Children (surname Noe):[2]
3. Joseph Crane.	6. Ellis Frazee.	8. Jane Bonnel.
4. Mary.	7. David.	9. Huldah.
5. Martha Bonnel.		

3. 320430. Jonathan Crane, b. 29 Sept. 1790[1]; bapt. 13 Feb. 1791[8]; m. 2 Nov. 1814 Phebe Ward[1]; d. 14 Dec. 1865[1].
   Children (surname Bonnell):[1,2]
1. Mehetabel.	5. Charity Frost.	8. Phebe W.
2. Julia.	6. Emmaline.	9. Jonathan.
3. Emma.	7. Jane M.	10. David Ward.
4. Harriett.		

4. 320434. Mary, b. 29 Feb. 1792[1]; bapt. 16 June 1793[8]; m. 9 Jan. 1813[4]; Charles M. Day[1,4]; d. Sept. 1866[1].
   Children (surname Day):[7]
1. Elizabeth.	2. Matthias.

5. 320435. Jane, b. 3 July 1795[1]; m. 1817[4] John M. Stites[1,4]; d. 14 Aug. 1880[1].
   Children (surname Stites):[2]
1. William Crane.	2. Huldah.

6. 320436. Elizabeth, b. 11 Feb. 1797[1]; m. 18 Feb. 1829[4] Matthias Osborn[1,4]; d. 1 Jan. 1858[1].
   Children (surname Osborn):[2]
Mary Elizabeth.	2. Martha Jane.	3. Sarah Anne.

7. 320437. Sarah, b. 17 Feb. 1799[1]; m. James T. Lennington[1]; d. 1875[1].

8. 320431. Maline Miller, b. 22 July 1802[1]; m. 25 Nov. 1824 Elizabeth D. Walker[1]; d. 18 July 1849[1].
   Children (surname Bonnell):[2,4]
1. Mary Jane.	4. Priscilla A.	7. Edward N.
2. Mary Elizabeth.	5. Helen R.	
3. Adeline Salome.	6. Martha C.	

REFERENCES:

1. Bible of Jonathan C. Bonnel, records copied by Harold A. Sonn and published in *The New Jersey Genesis*, Vol. 8, No. 3, April 1961, pp. 322, 323.
2. Littell, pp. 48, 49, 50, 102, 120, 302, 310, 320, 409.
3. NJ in 1793, p. 247.
4. CB Database.
5. NJ Wills, Vol. XI, p. 38.
6. NJ Tax Lists, p. 299.
7. Duncan, pp. 96, 97.
8. Presbyterian Church records, New Providence, NJ, abstracted and sent to me by W. Jerome Hatch and Philip S. Lacy.
9. Rev War - NJ - 1, pp. 152, 513.
10. Gen Mag of NJ, Vol. 46, No. 1, Jan. 1971, p. 39.

1-3-1-2-5-3   D159   CB310359

CALEB GILBERT[6] BONNELL (Nathaniel[5], Nathaniel[4], Nathaniel[3], Nathaniel[2], William[1]) was born 4 November 1758[1], probably in Chatham, Morris twp, Morris co, NJ. He was given the name Caleb Gilbert by his parents at birth, but for much of his early life, including the period of his military service he signed his name Gilbert Bonnel. When later in life he reverted to using his original name it occasionally caused confusion with earlier records[1].

In the spring of 1778, probably in May, Gilbert enlisted, in Morris co, for nine months as a private in Captain Yellis (or Giles) Meade's company, Colonel Matthias Ogden's Regiment of the New Jersey Line, Continental Army[1,2]. He joined his regiment at Mount Holley and was marched to join the main army[1] moving to prevent the British force of General Clinton from returning safely to Staten Island and the Hudson River[3]. On 28 June the two armies met at the battle of Monmouth Courthouse at Freehold, NJ. The American troops were victorious on the field but were unable to prevent the British from escaping to Sandy Hook where they were picked up by the British navy[3]. Gilbert Bonnell took part in several lesser skirmishes as well, before he was discharged at the completion of his term of enlistment[1]. Although he did not mention it in his pension application, records show that he also served tours of duty in the New Jersey militia[2].

On 4 May 1787 Gilbert was married by the Reverend Jacob Van Arsdale, pastor of the Presbyterian Church at Springfield, Essex (now Union) co, NJ, to his cousin JOANNA WOODRUFF[1], daughter of Elijah and Mary (Bonnell) Woodruff[4]. She was born 10 May 1759[1]. They may have lived for sometime with Joanna's parents in Springfield, since Gilbert appears on a tax list in that town in 1793[5]. He also appears in the 1793 census of New Jersey militia as Caleb Bonnell in Essex co and Gilbert Bunnel in Morris co. Perhaps their sojourn in Springfield was only temporary.

In any case, on 15 March 1803 they sold their home in Morris twp, Morris co, to Margaret Conkling, widow, for $215[7]. They moved across the river to New Providence, Essex (now Union) co. The tax lists of New Providence twp include Gilbert Bonnel from 1810 to 1815,

Caleb in 1815 and G. Caleb in 1820[5]. On 19 July 1803 Margaret Conkling returned the property to "Gilbert Bonnel, late of Morris County" for the price she had paid for it[7]. "Gilbert Bonnel and Joannah his wife of Essex county," sold the property the same day to Gabriel Johnson of Morris co for $162.50[7].

When his father died in 1809 Caleb G. received his share of the estate[8]. On 18 April 1810 he and his wife sold his 1/8 interest in his father's 44-acre homestead and in the Chatham Old Mill[4,7]. He appears on the tax list of Chatham in 1810 and 1811[5]. About the 15th of March in 1810 Caleb purchased a house and 3-acre lot in New Providence twp from Isaac Meeker for $500, paying $250 down and giving Meeker a mortgage for the rest[1]. Caleb and Joanna never managed to achieve prosperity, although he was a weaver by trade[1]. His pension application describes the series of loans and mortgages he used in a frustrating attempt to pay for their home[1]. Finally, on 7 January 1819, they deeded the property to Caleb Meeker's widow Charity, the ultimate mortgage holder, in exchange for cancelling the burdensome debt[1].

On 9 April 1818 "Gilbert Bonnel" submitted his first application for a veteran's pension, stressing his financial need for help from his country[1]. It was rejected for lack of evidence[1]. Nine years later he tried again. On 27 April 1827 his revised application explained the long delay, provided corrected service data, and described his poverty and need in great detail[1]. This time it was approved in the amount of $8.00 per month.

Caleb died 2 May 1834[1] at New Providence[4] and was buried in the cemetery of the New Providence Presbyterian Church[4]. Joanna applied for a widow's pension on 25 October 1838, for which she received $30 per year. She died 17 (or 16) 1846 and was buried with her husband[4].

Children:
1. 320410. Charlotte, b. 21 June 1787[1]; d. 21 Sept. 1787[1].
2. 320406. Caleb Woodruff, b. 3 June 1788[1]; m. 13 Dec. 1823[1] Clarissa Canfield[4]; two children[1].
3. 320407. Elijah W., b. 3 Oct. 1789[1]; m. 26 Aug. 1815 _____ _____ [1]; d. 18 Dec. 1821[1].
4. 320408. Lewis, b. 15 Jan. 1792[1]; d. 22 Apr. 1792[1].
5. 320409. Mary W., b. 10 July 1793[1]; m. 24 Sept. 1814[1] Samuel G. Sisco[1]; a family of children[1].

REFERENCES:
1. Pension applications of Gilbert Bonnel and his widow, including a page from his Family Bible, photocopies obtained from the National Archives and sent to me by Claude A. Bunnell. Some extracts from the documents follow:

"On this eighteenth day of April 1827 personally appeared in open court being a court of record for the said county, Gilbert Bunnel, aged sixty eight years, resident in New Providence in said county, who being first duly sworn according to law doth on his oath declare that he served in the Revolutionary War as follows: that he enlisted for the period of nine months some time in the spring of the year (probably in May) 1778 in Captain Mead's company, Col. Matthias Ogden's Regiment, of the Jersey line and joined his regiment at Mount Holley that Spring, from whence he was marched & joined the main army before the battle of Monmouth, in which battle he was personally engaged, besides several skirmishes of less importance . . . "

"This deponent has two children Viz. Mary, married to Samuel Sisco, and removed with her husband to Ohio seven or eight years since, is poor and has a family of children. His son (only son) Caleb, aged about 38 years, is married, has two children, is a Shoemaker, is poor & has no residence except as a tenant; his health is infirm and is incapable of doing anything for the support of his father. This deponent occupies a room in the same dwelling with his son & sometimes keeps a separate table; he is by trade, a weaver, but has not followed his trade within the last year or two, in consequence of lameness and defect of eyesight; he occasionally works a little in a garden, & sometimes follows the plough for an hour or two. he is Sixty eight years old on the 4th November last & feels himself unable longer to maintain himself by his own exertions & hopes to obtain the bounty of his country in shape of a pension during the remainder of his life."

"This deponent has no land, no house, no horse, no cow, no sheep, no hog or pig, no waggon or cart, no plow nor sled, no notes, no bonds, no debts owe to him in any form or shape. He owes to several individuals in his neighborhood sundry small debts contracted for family necesaries, provisions &c. amounting probably to ten or twelve dollars which he expects & hopes to pay in some way. he has a wife, with whom he has lived about 50 years or nearly, her name is Joanna, aged about 68 years, is very infirm & scarcely competent to take charge of the little affairs of her house, and altogether unable to perform any hard labor."

"This deponent further states on oath, that he learned from his parents, that in his infancy he was baptized by the names of Caleb Gilbert, & that during his early life being always called Gilbert, he was in the habit of writing his name Gilbert Bonnel, & verily believes he was enlisted in 1778 under the name Gilbert Bonnel. It is about thirty years since he commenced writing his baptismal name Caleb Gilbert Bonnel since which period the greater part & perhaps the whole of his papers in which his name is used the whole name Caleb Gilbert is inserted. . ."

2. Rev War - NJ - 1, pp. 152, 513.
3. NJ Collections, p. 337 et seq.
4. CB Database.
5. NJ Tax Lists, pp. 296, 297, 300, 424.
6. NJ in 1793, pp. 142, 247.
7. Morris co NJ Deeds, Book H, pp. 246, 278, 280, Book T, p. 178.
8. NJ Wills - Vol. XI, p. 38.

1-3-1-2-5-6   D64vi   CB310363

JONATHAN[6] (Nathaniel[5], Nathaniel[4], Nathaniel[3], Nathaniel[2], William[1]) was born in March 1765[1], probably in Chatham, Morris twp, Morris co, NJ, and was baptized 23 June 1765 in the Presbyterian Church of New Providence, Essex (now Union) co, NJ[2,7]. He was "of Chatham, New Jersey" when he married ELIZABETH BRYANT[3,4], daughter of Cornelius and Hannah (Carteret?) Bryant[3,4]. She was born at Springfield, Essex (now Union) co, NJ, in 1768[3]. Jonathan died before 1799[3], and Elizabeth married (second) John Ballentine[3], and (third) Samuel Williams[3]. She had one daughter, Eliza H. Bannatine, b. 14 July 1799, by her second husband[3]. She outlived all three husbands and died 26 (or 21[7]) June 1845 at Elizabethtown, Essex (now Union) co, NJ[3]. She was buried in Mount Pleasant Cemetery[3].

Jonathan had apparently been estranged from his father for a number of years. Nathaniel's will, written 10 October 1809, more than ten years after Jonathan's death, included Jonathan among his heirs, with the proviso that, "If son, Jonathan, should not be living and had no lawful heirs, the $20 given to my daughter, Elizabeth, should be paid her out of estate which would have fallen to him."[5].

Children:
    1. 320072. Jonathan[3,4], b. 28 Feb. 1791[6]; m. Sabina Ferris[3]; d. 17 Sept. 1743[6].
        Children (surname Bonnell):[3]

1. George.	5. Jane.	9. Susan.
2. Eliza.	6. Gouverneur.	10. William.
3. Charlotte.	7. Pierre.	11. Lemuel.
4. John.	8. Sabina.	

    2. 320073. Charlotte[3,4], m. George Pattent[3]; no children[3]

REFERENCES:
1. Little, p. 48.
2. Records of New Providence Presbyterian Church, abstracted and sent to me by Philip S. Lacy.
3. *Carteret and Bryant Genealogy*, by C. R. Baetjer, 1887, pp. 23, 24, 28.
4. *Morris Area Genealogy Society Newsletter*, Vol. 6, #2, June 1993, p. 3, and #4, Dec. 1993, p. 3.
5. NJ Wills - Vol. XI, p. 38.
6. *Greenwich,Fairfield County, Conn. Cemeteries*, copied in Nov. 1907 by Mr. William A. Eardeley, Bonnell Cemetery at Steep Hollow on cross road to North Cos Cob, pp. 8, 9.
7. CB Database.

1-3-1-2-5-7   D64vii   CB310365

JACOB[6] BONNELL (Nathaniel[5], Nathaniel[4], Nathaniel[3], Nathaniel[2], William[1]) was born in May 1767[1], probably in Chatham, Morris twp, Morris co, NJ. He was baptized 14 June 1767 in the Presbyterian Church at New Providence, Essex (now Union) co, NJ[2,3]. In his later years he used to say that in his boyhood he had seen General Washington pacing back and forth in Mr. Morrell's door yard[4]. On 9 July 1789 he married MARGARET CRANE[3], daughter of Stephen and Jenny Crane[5].

Jacob and Margaret were members of the "Bottle Hill Meeting House" (now the Presbyterian Church of Madison), Morris co, for many years[6]. He was confirmed in the church in 1792[6]. From 1790 to 1819 he held a number of offices in the church, including moderator, clerk, elder and trustee[6]. In 1824 they transferred their membership to the new Presbyterian Church in the village of Chatham[6].

In 1793 "Jacob Bunnel" was listed as a member of the militia of Hanover twp, Morris co, which then included what became part of Chatham twp in 1806[7]. From 1792 until 1805 Jacob appears in the tax lists of Hanover twp[8]. After the establishment of Chatham twp he appears on its tax lists to 1822, the last year of the published lists[8].

Margaret's father died at year-end 1795. In his will he left each of his six daughters, including "Margaret (wife of Jacob Bonnel)" the sum of £50[5]. When Jacob's father Nathaniel died in 1809, his will left 58 acres of land in Great Swamp to his sons Gilbert, Jacob, William and Enoch, the land to be divided equally by Jacob Potter and Enos Bonnel[5]. The residue of the estate, after various bequests, was to be divided equally among all the children except Nathaniel, who had already received his share[5]. On 17 April 1810 Jacob bought for $245 from his brother Enoch the 11.29-acre tract in Great Swamp which had been Enoch's portion[9]. The same day he sold to Enoch, for $225 the 1/8 share he had inherited of his father's 44-acre homestead and the Chatham Old Mill on the Passaic River[9].

Jacob was a jeweler and clock maker[1,4,10]. The publication *NEW JERSEY, History of Ingenuity and Industry*, by James P. Johnson, on page 74 has a picture of an elaborate grandfather's clock made and signed on its face by Jacob Bonnell[10].

Margaret Bonnell died 14 September 1824 at the age of 55[3]. Jacob appears in the census of Chatham, Morris co, in 1830: 000000001-000001[3] and in 1840: 0000000001-00000011[3]. He died 23 February 1841 in Chatham[3,11] and was buried in Fairmount Cemetery in Chatham[11]. The inventory of his personal property for the probate of his estate listed six unfinished clocks, one "musick clock," and clockmaking tools[10].

Children:
1. 320411. Charles, b. 19 Dec. 1789[3]; m. 8 Aug. 1808 Abigail Woodruff[3].
2. 320412. Eunice, b. 21 Jan. 1792[3]; 20 July 1793[3].
3. 320413. Ann C., b. 10 Dec. 1793[3]; d. 21 June 1878[3].
4. 320414. Vashti, b. 10 Dec. 1795[3]; d. 15 Jan. 1836[11].
5. 320415. Maria, b. 14 Feb. 1799[3]; d. 1 Oct. 1799[3].
6. 320416. Amos, b. 9 Feb. 1801[3]; bapt. Mar. 1802[6]; d. 30 Sept. 1802[3]
7. 320417. Ezra, b. 24 Aug. 1802[3]; m. 26 Dec. 1825 Amy Underhill[3].
8. 320418. Job, b. 7 Dec. 1806[3]; d. 18 Dec. 1806[3].
9. 320419. Margaret, b. 23 Jan. 1801[3]; m. 1 May 1828 Caleb Underhill[3].
10. 320420. Angus (son, b. 1 Oct. 1812, bapt. 1812[6]); m. George Cheshire[3] (should this be Agnus or Agnes?)

REFERENCES:
1. Littell, p. 48.
2. Records of the New Providence Presbyterian Church abstracted and sent to me by Philip S. Lacy.
3. CB Database.
4. *History of Chatham, New Jersey*, by Ambrose Ely Vanderpoel, 1959, abstracted and sent to me by Gwen Quickel.
5. NJ Wills - Vol IX, pp. 90, 91; Vol XI, p. 38.

6. Madison Church Records, p. 24.
7. NJ in 1793, p. 297.
8. NJ Tax Lists, pp. 297, 301.
9. Morris co, NJ, Deeds, Book T, pp. 179, 342.
10. *NEW JERSEY History of Ingenuity and Industry*, by James P. Johnson, 1987, pp. 74,75.
11. Burials in Fairmount Cemetery, Chatham, NJ, abstracted and sent to me by W. Jerome Hatch in the New Jersey Historical Society, Newark, NJ.

1-3-1-2-5-12   D160   CB310372

WILLIAM[6] BONNELL (Nathaniel[5], Nathaniel[4], Nathaniel[3], Nathaniel[2], William[1]) was born in January 1783[1], probably in Chatham, Morris twp, Morris co, NJ. He was baptized 9 March 1783 in the Presbyterian Church of New Providence, Essex (now Union) co, NJ[2]. On 25 December 1806 he was married by Rev. Riggs[3] to SARAH DOTY[1,2,3], daughter of James and Nancy (Locey) Doty[1]. She was born 29 July 1789 in New Providence[4].

William appears on the tax lists of Chatham twp from 1806 through 1822[5]. On 25 June 1808 he bought 4.43 acres in Chatham twp from his father[6]. His father's will, dated 10 October 1808 and proved 27 July 1809, left him an equal share with three of his brothers in a 58-acre parcel in Great Swamp[7], as well as an equal share with all his siblings of the residue of the estate[7]. On 7 April 1810 he sold his 11.75-acre share in the Great Swamp tract to Benjamin Bruen[6]. A few days later, on 18 April, William bought the 1/8 share of his brother Caleb G. to their father's homestead lot and the Chatham Old Mill[6]. On 1 August he bought the 1/16 share of his sister Chloe and her husband Abraham Sampson[6].

William and his brother Enoch, who lived with him[1], together acquired a full half-share in the mill and homestead property[6]. Their cousin and brother-in-law Sylvanus Bonnell owned the other half through his purchases from other heirs. In 1823 William and Enoch borrowed $900 from Sylvanus and gave him a mortgage on their half-share of the mill (then known as the Franklin mill)[8].

William appears in the 1840 census in Chatham twp, Morris co: 00100002-01011101[3]. His wife Sally (Sarah) died 5 January 1843[2] and was buried in the cemetery of the Presbyterian Church in New Providence[2]. For his second wife he married MARY _____[3]. They appear in the 1850 census of Chatham[3,9], when William was listed as age 66, a miller, Mary age 42, and the two youngest children William F., age 22, and Sarah B., age 16. Mary died in October 1857[3]. William appears in the 1860 census in Chatham as age 78, miller and farmer[3]. With him, keeping house, was Anna Bonnell age 60[3], probably his niece, daughter of Jacob Bonnell.

William died 2 March 1861[3] at "Franklin, Morris co"[3], (probably at the Franklin Mill in Chatham). He was buried with his first wife in New Providence[3].

Children (by first wife):
1. 320100. Mary, b. 1807[11]; d. 1857[11].
2. 320452. Daniel Losey, b. 19 Sept. 1810[3,11]; m. 5 Jan. 1837 Sarah C. Potter[3,11]; d. 12 Oct. 1900[3,11].
   Children (surname Bonnell):[11]
   1. Eliza Day.   2. Harriet Newel.
3. 320449. Nancy Doty, b. 1 Dec. 1813[10]; m. 22 Feb. 1834 William Sayre[1]; d. 2 Sept. 1905[3].
   Children (surname Sayre):[10]
   1. Elizabeth Bonnell. 4. Emily Brown.   6. David Brown.
   2. John Francis.   5. Sarah Doty.   7. Mary Caroline.
   3. George.
4. 320448. Jane Caroline, b. Mar. 1816[11]; m. 4 Aug. 1844[3] David Sanders[11]; d. Aug. 1856[11].
   Children (surname Sanders):[11]
   1. William.   3. Cyrus.   4. Rodman.
   2. Frank.
5. 320450. Elizabeth, b. 22 Aug. 1818[3]; d. 28 Dec. 1840[2].
6. 320453. William Francis, b. Nov. 1827[4]; m. May 1854 Sarah Ann Morrell[11]; d. 9 Jan. 1890[11].
   Children (surname Bonnell):[3,11]
   1. Jonathan Elmer. 2. Willie, d. y.
7. 320451. Sarah B., b. 1833[11]; d. July 1863[11].

REFERENCES:
1. Littell, pp. 48, 141, 371.
2. Vital Records of the Presbyterian Church of New Providence, NJ, abstracted by Philip S. Lacy.
3. CB Database.
4. Duncan, pp. 97, 98.
5. NJ Tax Lists, pp. 300, 301.
6. Morris co, NJ, Deeds, Book R, p. 341; Book T, pp. 97, 178; Book W, p. 171.
7. NJ Wills - Vol XI, p. 38.
8. Morris co, NJ, Morgages, Book L, p. 1.
9. 1850 census, Chatham, Morris co, NJ, abstracted by Homer E. Baldwin.
10. Ltr. 21 Dec. 1907 from Mary Caroline (Sayre) Morgan to John A. Biles.
11. Ltr. undated from Harriet Newel Bonnell to John A. Biles.

1-3-1-2-5-13 D64xiii CB310373

ENOCH[6] BONNELL (Nathaniel[5], Nathaniel[4], Nathaniel[3], Nathaniel[2], William[1]) was born 5 October 1784[1,2] at Chatham, Morris co, NJ. On 28 November 1784 he was baptised in the Presbyterian Church at New Providence, Essex (now Union) co, NJ[2]. He never married, living most of his life with his brother William in Chatham. He was an heir of his father's estate in 1809[3]. In 1810 he bought brother Jacob's share of the Chatham Old Mill and their father's homestead[4] and sold to Jacob his share of the tract in the Great Swamp[4]. His name appears in the tax lists of Chatham from 1808 to 1816, 1818, 1820 to 1822[5]. In 1823, together with his brother William, he borrowed $900 from Sylvanus Bonnell, his cousin and brother-in-law, in return for a mortgage on their half-interest in the Old Mill, known by that time as the Franklin Mill[6]. When the census was taken in 1840 in Chatham he was counted in his brother's household[7]. Littell, writing in 1851, said that he was living with William[1]. He died accidentally on 5 October 1858 in Chatham and was buried in the Presbyterian Cemetery in New Providence[7].

REFERENCES:
1. Littell, p. 48.
2. Vital Records of the Presbyterian Church of New Providence, NJ, abstracted by Philip S. Lacy.
3. NJ Wills - Vol XI, p. 38.
4. Morris co, NJ, Deeds, Book T, pp. 179, 342.
5. NJ Tax Lists, pp. 296, 297, 300.
6. Morris co, NJ, Mortgages, Book L, p. 1.
7. CB Database.

1-3-1-2-7-1   D161   CB310316

JAMES[6] BONNELL (John[5], Nathaniel[4], Nathaniel[3], Nathaniel[2], William[1]) was born 10 October 1758[1] in Chatham, Springfield twp, Essex (now Union) co, NJ. He may have been the James Bonnel who served in the Revolution as Adjutant in the Continental Army regiment led by Colonel Oliver Spencer[2,3]. However, Stryker seems to imply that this service was by James Bonnell CB002976 of Sussex co, NJ[3], and I tend to agree. CB Database credits this service to both men[2].

In the early 1780s James married ROSA[1] or RHODA[4] BURNET[1,4], who was born about 1760, daughter of David and Abigail Burnet[10]. She and Mary Burnet, wife of his brother Jonathan, were sisters[1]. James appears in tax lists in Springfield twp, Essex (now Union) co, NJ, in 1781 and 1782[6]. In 1793 he was listed in the militia of Essex co, NJ[5]. Some time before 1806 they moved across the river to the Morris co side. They lived "by the Franklin Mill"[1] (previously known as the Chatham Old Mill) in Chatham. The tax lists of Chatham, Morris co, include James from 1806 until his death[6]. The taxes were then charged to the Heirs of James Bonnel at least until 1818[6]. The records of the Presbyterian Church of Madison, Morris co, show that he was a contributor to the church in 1794[4].

"Rhoda Bunnel" died 28 October 1805 in her 45th year[4]. James followed her in death less than two years later, on 22 September 1807[4]. They were buried in the Hillside Cemetery, Madison[4]. His son Elias was administrator of his estate when it was probated 29 September 1808[2]. The inventory was made by William Bonnell[2].

Children: (Note - The will of John Bonnell dated 7 September 1811 twice listed the surviving children of his son James, and I have assumed it to be the correct order of their births.)

1. 320395. Electa, b. about 1782[2]; m. 9 Nov. 1806[4] Abraham Walker[1,4]; d. 21 Nov. 1808[4].
   Children (surname Walker):[1]
   1. Rhoda.

2. 320393. Stephen Carter, b. 22 Jan. 1785[7]; m. 19 Aug 1806 Sarah (Sally) Simpson[1]; d. 4 Apr. 1852[7].
   Children (surname Bonnell):[1]
1. Catherine S.	4. Nancy.	6. Stephen Carter.
2. James M.	5. Electa.	7. Hannah Parcel.
3. Elias.		

3. 320394. Elias, b. about 1787[2]; m. 1808[2] Catherine Simpson[1,2]; d. 16 Feb. 1822[2].
   Children (surname Bonnell):[1]
   | 1. Edwin. | 3. Rhoda. | 4. Elias Freeman. |
   | 2. Caroline. | | |

4. 320396. Hannah, b. 23 Dec. 1790[2]; m. 4 Feb. 1810 Stephen Parcel[4].
   Children (surname Parcel):[1]
   1. John.

5. 320397. Nancy[1], b. about 1795.

6. 320398. David, b. 27 Nov. 1797[9]; m. Sarah Day Sayre[1]; d. 1 Dec. 1822[7].
   Children (surname Bonnell):[2]
   1. Harriet N.

7. 320399. Mahlon C., b. 27 Nov. 1797[9]; m. 1820 Sarah Primrose Oliver[8]; d. 4 Nov. 1865[9].
   Children (surname Bonnell):[1,2]
1. Joanna Price.	4. Henry W.	7. Mahlon.
2. David H.	5. Sarah A.	8. Cornelia P.
3. John P.	6. Salina.	

REFERENCES:
1. Littell, pp. 50, 51.
2. CB Database.
3. Rev War - NJ - 1, pp. 56, 57, 152, 383, 525.
4. Madison Church Records, pp. 23, 24.
5. NJ in 1793, p. 133.
6. NJ Tax Lists, pp. 297, 298, 301.
7. Gravestone inscriptions abstracted by W. Jerome Hatch from cemetery description books at the New Jersey Historical Society, Newark, NJ.
8. DAR Lineage Books, Vol. 88, p. 280; Vol. 97, p. 79.
9. Gray - Family Group Sheet.
10. Amer Fam - Long Island, pp. 72, 73.

1-3-1-2-7-3   D162   CB310318

JONATHAN[6] BONNELL (John[5], Nathaniel[4], Nathaniel[3], Nathaniel[2], William[1]) was born 12 May 1763[1] at Chatham, Springfield twp, Essex (now Union) co, NJ. On 10 August 1783, at New Providence, Springfield twp, Essex (now Union) co, Jonathan married MARY BURNET[2], who was born 9 January 1765, daughter of David and Abigail Burnet[3]. She and the wife of his brother James were sisters. Jonathan is found in the tax lists of Springfield twp, Essex co, for 1795 and 1796[4].

American Families - Long Island states that he lived all his life in Chatham, married there and all his children were born there[3]. It is apparent that most of that time their home was in that part of the village of Chatham on the east side of the Passaic River in Springfield twp, Essex co. Today the site is in Summit twp, Union co. On 17 March 1800 Jonathan and Mary "of the township of Springfield county of Essex and state of New Jersey" sold to Israel Day the 5-acre lot "in Chatham in town County and State aforesaid" bounded by the road from Chatham to Springfield, lands of Israel Day and Elias Dayton and the road from Chatham to Canoe Brook[5]. This was probably their home lot, and they must have moved across the river to Chatham in Morris co. The township of Chatham, Morris co was established in 1806. Previously, the village on the west side of the river was partly in Hanover twp and partly in Morris twp.

Jonathan died before 1806, when his widow Mary appears in the tax list of Chatham twp, Morris co[4]. She was listed there also in 1810, 1811 and 1813[4]. She died 13 March 1845[3] and was buried in the old burial ground at Madison (formerly Bottle Hill), Morris co[3]

Children:
1. 320484. Matilda[1], b. 11 Feb. 1784[6]; m. 20 Sept. 1803 Alexander Bruen[6]; d. 26 Nov. 1860[6].
   Children (surname Bruen):[6]
1. Juliette.	4. Harriet Emeline.	7. Charles Alexander.
2. Cyrenus.	5. Alfred Franklin.	8. James Harvey.
3. Jonathan B.	6. John Carter.	9. Charlotte Ward.
2. 320483. Ichabod, b. 1787[3]; m. 19 May 1810 Sarah Esther Parcel[3,7]; d. 10 Feb. 1816[3].
   Children (surname Bonnell):[1]
   1. Mary.
3. 320485. Joel, b. 27 Apr. 1791[3]; m. 1816[7] Arabella Halsey[1]; d. 19 Feb. 1880[7].
   Children (surname Bonnell):[1,7]
1. Albert A.	3. Joel.	5. Francis (or Frances).
2. Mary Anne.	4. Henrietta Frances.	6. Edward C.
4. 320486. Alva, b. 28 Aug. 1792[3]; m. 23 Jan. 1814 Nancy Ann Halsey[3]; d. 14 June 1832[3].
   Children (surname Bonnell):[1,3]
1. Alfred Halsey.	3. Elizabeth.	5. Sylvanus Sylvester.
2. Marcus Eggbert.	4. Joel Murton.	6. John.
5. 320487. John, "drowned at sea"[3].

REFERENCES:

1. Littell, pp. 50, 52.
2. Vital records of the Presbyterian Church of New Providence, NJ, abstracted and sent to me by Philip S. Lacy.
3. Amer Fam - Long Island, pp. 72, 73, 74.
4. NJ Tax Lists, p. 301.
5. Essex co, NJ, Deeds, Book E, p. 514.
6. Family Group Sheet compiled 5 July 1982 by Sharon Leon, Spokane, WA.
7. CB Database.

1-3-1-2-7-4   D163   CB310319

ISRAEL[6] BONNELL (John[5], Nathaniel[4], Nathaniel[3], Nathaniel[2], William[1]) was born 24 May 1765[1] in Chatham, Springfield twp, Essex (now Union) co, NJ. He married FANNY HAND[1] who was born about 1759[2]. Israel was listed in the militia of Morris twp, Morris co, NJ, in 1793[3]. He appears on the tax lists in Hanover twp, Morris co, in 1794 and 1795[4] and in Chatham twp, Morris co, in 1806, when Chatham twp was established, until 1822[4], the latest year published in this source. In 1795 he was a contributor to the Presbyterian Church at Madison, Morris co[5].

On 3 November 1808 his father, John Bonnell, "for and in consideration of the natural love and affection which he hath and beareth unto the said Israel Bonnel and for the better maintenance and livelihood of him the said Israel Bonnel" gave him a messuage of land containing 9.56 acres in Chatham twp on the south side of the Turnpike Road from Elizabethtown to Morristown[6]. When his father died in 1817 his will provided a bequest "To son Israel all the land I bought of Dr. Peter Smith lying between lands of Jacob Morrell and Wm. Spencer and also a small piece of land opposite my dwelling house across the river adjoining land of Jacob Morrell at the West end, the River on the south side, the mill pond on the east, and Land of Israel Bonnel on the north. Likewise I give and bequeath to my son Israel all my right in and on to the store of goods at his house and all the debts due for goods sold out of the same."[7]. Israel was appointed one of the executors of the estate[7].

Israel appears in the 1830 census: 00000001-000000001 and in the 1840 census: 0000000001-0000001001 in Chatham twp, Morris co, NJ[8]. His wife Fanny died 18 July 1848 in her 89th year[2], and Israel died 28 February 1849 in his 84th year[2]. They were buried in Fairmount Cemetery, Chatham[2].

Children:
1. 320501. Harriet[1], m. Lewis Freeman[1].
   Children (surname Freeman):[1]
   1. Lewis.   3. Sarah.   5. daughter.
   2. Francis.   4. son.
2. 320502. Sarah A.[1,2]; b. about 1795; d. 29 Aug. 1854 age 59[2].

3. 320503. Lewis[1] Hand[8], b. about 1800[8]; m. (first) 1830 Lucinda (_____) Ross[8]; m. (second) 14 Dec. 1834 Eliza C. Fink[8].
    Children (surname Bonnell)(by Sallie Butt)[8]
    1. Lewis Hand, b. 1842.

REFERENCES:
1. Littell, pp. 50, 52.
2. Gravestone inscriptions abstracted by W. Jerome Hatch from cemetery description books at the New Jersey Historical Society, Newark, NJ.
3. NJ in 1793, p. 247.
4. NJ Tax Lists, pp. 297, 300, 301, 424.
5. Madison Church Records, p. 24.
6. Morris co, NJ, Deeds - Book R, p. 359.
7. Amer Fam - Long Island, p. 72.
8. CB Database.

1-3-1-2-7-7 D164 CB310322

SYLVANUS[6] BONNELL (John[5], Nathaniel[4], Nathaniel[3], Nathaniel[2], William[1]) was born 28 February 1773[1,2,3] (or 28 January 1773[4] or 28 September 1773[5]) in Chatham, Springfield twp, Essex (now Union) co, NJ. In 1793 he was listed as a member of the Essex co militia[6]. In 1795 and 1796 he appears in the tax records of Springfield twp, Essex co[7].

On 9 May 1801 Sylvanus began to acquire his own interest in the milling business by purchasing for £500 a half-interest in the grist mill of Joseph and Mary Meeker on the Elizabethtown River in Elizabeth (now Union) twp, Essex (now Union) co, NJ[9]. He bought another mill in Elizabeth township the same day from John and Ruth Lum[9]. Over the next decade he bought a number of other properties in Elizabeth twp, either alone or in partnership with the Meekers[9]. At the same time he was acquiring property in Chatham, Morris co, where he appears in the tax records from 1810 to 1821[7].

On 28 February 1808[8, 11, 12] he was married by Rev. M. LaRue Perine of the Bottle Hill (now Madison) Presbyterian Church to his cousin NANCY BONNELL[1], daughter of Nathaniel and Mary (Simpson) Bonnell of Chatham, Morris co[1]. She was born in July 1778[1]. Their home was in the newly established Union twp on one of the properties where he owned a saw mill[9]. On 18 April they sold a half-interest in the sawmill property to Foster Day[9] and moved the family across the Passaic River to Chatham in Morris co[9]. Sylvanus seems to have stayed in partnership with Foster Day until he died[9].

He bought property in Chatham twp, where they remained for the next ten years[5,10]. They attended the Bottle Hill Meeting House (now the Presbyterian Church of Madison), the nearest church to their home[11]. Two of their children died in this decade and were buried in Hillside Cemetery beside the church[11]. When his father died in 1817 he served as one of the executors of the estate[5]. Under the terms of the will he received lands in Chatham village[5] as well as a share in lands in Wayne and Luzerne counties, PA.

About 1820 they moved back to Springfield, Essex (now Union) co, where he built a house at 504 Morris Avenue[5]. He named it "The Hemlocks"[5]. He appears on the Springfield tax records in 1820 and 1821[7]. Sylvanus was a member of the Chatham Committee of the Bottle Hill church, which was formed in 1824 by some of the church members to protest the building of a new church building at the old site[11]. They preferred that the new church be built closer to Chatham[11]. When they could not prevail many of the members withdrew and formed a new church of their own in Chatham village[11].

Still active in business, Sylvanus died suddenly of a fever on 9 December 1825[11,12,13]. He was buried in Hillside Cemetery with his infant children[11]. His wife Nancy and his partner Foster Day served as administrators of his estate[5]. Nancy and her children stayed on in their home in Springfield where she appears in the 1830 census: 011201-00221101[5] and 1840: 0001301-000030001[5]. Eventually she moved back to Chatham where she died 4 July 1851[11]. She was buried with Sylvanus in Hillside Cemetery[11].

Children:
1. 320423. Eliza, b.24 Dec. 1807[11,12] and adopted by Sylvanus and Nancy after their marriage[12]; m. 1 Dec. 1830 George Townly Sayre[5,11]; d. 22 Nov. 1890[11].
    Children (surname Sayre):[1,3,11]
    1. Sylvanus Bonnel. 3. Eliza.   5.Theodore.
    2. Edward.   4. Theodore Lyman.
2. 320424. Calvin, b. 29 Jan. 1809[12]; d. soon[12].
3. 320425. Calvin Day, b. 9 Apr. 1810[12]; m. 13 Dec. 1834 Julia Ann Croll[5]; d. 5 Aug. 1851[12].
    Children (surname Bonnell):[4,5]
    1. Mary Lantz.   4. Paul Insale.   5. Emma H.
    2. William Harvey. 5. John Calvin.   6. George Washington.
    3. Job Clark.
4. 320422. James Harvey, b. 30 June 1811[12]; m. 5 Mar. 1845 Rachel Ann Buffington[4]; d. 27 Oct. 1895[4].
    Children (surname Bonnell):[4]
    1. Sylvanus.   4. Nancy.   7. Harvey S.
    2. Edwin R.   5. Frank S.   8. Albert.
    3. Lewis.   6. Clark O.
5. 320426. John Wichliff, b. 14 July 1812[12]; m. (first) 1857 Rosanna Hoover[4]; m. (second) Apr. 1865 Eliza M. Pittman[4,5].
    Children (surname Bonnell)(by first wife):[4]
    1. Arthur F.
    Children (surname Bonnell)(by second wife):[4]
    2. Ida.   4. Bertrand.   5. Clel.
    3. Liffie.
6. 320427. Mary, b. 2 Sept. 1813[12]; d. 9 Oct. 1814[11].

7. 320428. Charlotte, b. 27 Aug. 1814[12]; m. 27 Mar. 1844 Abner Stites[1,13].
            Children (surname Stites):[1]
             1. Edward Morris.   2. Charlotte Morrell.
8. 320489. Margaretta, b. 27 Oct. 1815[12]; d. 6 Nov. 1815[11].
9. 320490. Julia Ann, b. 23 Sept. 1816[12]; d. 26 Aug. 1842[11].
10. 320491. Nancy, b. 11 Apr. 1818[12]; m. William Thompson[4].
11. 320492. Sylvanus, b. 31 Mar. 1819[12]; d. 12 Aug. 1859[11].
12, 320493. William, b. 31 Dec. 1820[12]; d. 31 Oct. 1908[3].

REFERENCES:
1. Littell, pp. 50, 52, 409, 438.
2. Amer Fam - Long Island, p. 73.
3. Duncan, pp. 99, 100.
4. Fern Bonnell, pp. 65, 68, 69, 71.
5. CB Database.
6. NJ in 1793, p. 133.
7. NJ Tax Lists, pp. 299, 301, 424.
8. Gen Mag of NJ, Vol. V, No. 4, pp. 119, 120.
9. Essex co, NJ, Deeds, Bk E, pp. 669, 671; Bk G, p. 560; Bk K, p. 536; Bk N, pp. 65, 627; Bk O, p. 147; Bk R, pp. 4, 630; Bk T, p. 577.
10. Morris co, NJ, Deeds, Bk U, p. 172.
11. Madison Church Records, p. 26.
12. "CHILDREN OF SYLVANUS & NANCY BONNEL, From the Family Records - a true copy", furnished by Nancy, the tenth child of Sylvanus Bonnel. Photocopy sent to me by Grover C. Smith, Benton, AR.
13. *Records of the Springfield Presbyterian Church: 1818-1943*, abstracted and sent to me by James P. Bonnell, Merced, CA.

1-3-1-2-7-9 D65ix CB310324

DAVID[6] BONNELL (John[5], Nathaniel[4], Nathaniel[3], Nathaniel[2], William[1]) was born 5 September 1778[1] in Chatham, Springfield twp, Essex (now Union) co, NJ. He was killed 27 December 1797[2] by the fall of a tree in the Great Swamp[1], Morris co, NJ. He was buried in Hillside Cemetery at Madison, Morris co.

REFERENCES:
1. Littell, p. 50.
2. Madison Church Records, p. 25.

1-3-1-4-5-1 D71i CB310341

DAVID[6] BONNELL (Isaac[5], Isaac[4], Nathaniel[3], Nathaniel[2], William[1]) was born about 1769[3] in Elizabethtown, Essex (now Union) co, NJ. By the will of his grandfather Timothy Woodruff, dated 6 February 1786, proved February 1799, he inherited 40 shillings to be paid when he became 21[1]. He appears in the militia census in Essex co, NJ, in 1793[2]. Little information has been discovered about his life. He may have been married to SARAH _____[4]. On 5 October

1802 he borrowed $160 from John Hanyon giving a mortgage secured by two half-acre lots that he owned in Elizabeth[3]. He was drowned at Elizabeth Old Point 20 July 1816 at the age of 47[3]. No record of children has been found. A reference was made to "Sarah wid. David Bonnel: under date of 3 September 1848 in the *Manuel of the First Presbyterian Church of Elizabeth - 1858*[4]. Was this David her husband?

REFERENCES:
1. NJ Wills - Vol. IX, p. 423.
2. NJ in 1793, p. 127.
3. CB Database.
4. *Gleanings From the West Fields*, Vol. XII, No. 6, p. 44, abstract sent to me by James P. Bonnell, Merced, CA.

1-3-1-4-5-2   D7ii   CB310343

NOAH[6] BONNELL (Isaac[5], Isaac[4], Nathaniel[3], Nathaniel[2], William[1]) was born about October 1770[1] in Elizabethtown, Essex (now Union) co, NJ. He was bequeathed £5 when he came of age in the will of his grandfather Timothy Woodruff, dated 6 February 1786 and proved 4 February 1799[2]. He never married.

He appears in the Essex co militia census in 1793[3]. Records show that in 1820 he loaned $140 to Mclancthon Freeman and $100 to William Milven, secured by mortgages on lots in Elizabeth[4]. He appears in the 1840 census of Elizabeth, Essex co, NJ: 000000001-0[4].

He died at Elizabeth 3 April 1856 at the age of 85 years, 6 months[1,4]. He was a boatman[4]. He was buried in the cemetery of the First Presbyterian Church of Elizabeth beside his father[1]. His brother Seth was appointed administrator of his estate in April 1856[4]. Seth died before final settlement of the estate, and Seth's wife Elizabeth was appointed administrator in his place on 6 April 1859[4]. The principal asset of the estate was a block of 50 shares of National State Bank worth $1500[4]. The final accounting on 13 July 1968 showed a total of $584.45 after expenses[4]. It was equally divided among Seth's three children, David W. Bonnel, Laura E. Horton and Abigail Price[4].

REFERENCES:
1. Elizabeth, NJ, Cemeteries, grave #1734.
2. NJ Wills - Vol. IX, p. 423.
3. NJ in 1793, p. 130.
4. CB Database.

1-3-1-4-5-3   D180   CB310342

SETH[6] BONNELL (Isaac[5], Isaac[4], Nathaniel[3], Nathaniel[2], William[1]) was born 9 November 1775[1] in Elizabethtown, Essex (now Union) co, NJ. The will of his grandfather Timothy Woodruff, dated 6 February 1786, proved 4 February 1799, provided 40 shillings for him when he reached age 21[2]. On 25 March 1820 he was married by Rev. John C. Rudd of St. John's Episcopal Church in Elizabeth to ELIZABETH BARHYT[1] who was born 30 March 1786 in New Jersey[1]. Seth appears in the census records in Elizabeth in 1830: 01000001-0110001[1] and in 1840: 000100001-0001001[1]. In the 1850 census in Elizabeth Seth was listed at age 74, a grocer, owning real estate worth $4500, with his wife Elizabeth B., age 63, and children Laura Horton, age 28, husband not living, and son David, age 25, a tailor[1,6].

Seth made his will on 21 August 1832, appointing his wife Elizabeth executor and giving her the use of the entire estate until she died or remarried, after which the three children were to share equally[1]. On 14 April 1856 Seth, as administrator of his brother Noah's estate made the inventory[1]. However, Noah's estate had not been finally probated when Seth died 11 February 1859 at Elizabeth at the age of 83 years, 3 months and 2 days[1]. He was buried 15 February 1859 in the Cemetery of the First Presbyterian Church, Elizabeth[1]. His estate was probated 4 March 1859, and on 6 April 1859 his widow took over as administrator to complete the probate of Noah's estate.

Elizabeth appears in the 1860 census in Elizabeth, Union co, NJ, at age 74 with property valued at $12,000[1]. Her daughter Laura E. Horton, age 38, milliner, lived with her[1]. Elizabeth died 12 October 1873[1] at the home of her son-in-law Henry Meeker Price in New Brunswick, Middlesex co, NJ[1]. She was 87 years, 6 months and 14 days old[1], and was buried in Evergreen Cemetery, New Brunswick[1].

Children:
1. 320516. Abigail Nareda, b. 16 July 1820[3]; bapt. 27 June 1824[3]; m. 1839 Henry Meeker Price[1].
2. 320517. Laura Elizabeth, b. 30 July 1822[3]; bapt. 27 June 1824[3]; m. (first) _____ Horton; m. (second) 18 May 1887 Curtis Goodwin[5]
   Children (surname Horton):[4]
   1. Frederick A.
3. 320518. David Warren, b. Apr. 1826[4]; bapt. 23 May 1830[1]; m. 4 Jan. 1854 Henrietta B. Vreeland[1]; d. 26 Oct. 1901[1].
   Children (surname Bonnell):[1]
   1. Warren.   3. Elizabeth.   5. Ann N.
   2. Edmund.   4. Jesse Vreeland. 6. Clarence E.

REFERENCES:
1. CB Database.
2. NJ Wills - Vol. IX, p. 423.
3. Gen Mag of NJ, Vol. VII, No. 2, p. 58.
4. Duncan, p. 108. Note that Duncan gives the wrong Isaac as father of Seth and his brothers.
5. *The Goodwins of Hartford, Connecticut*, by James J. Goodwin and Frank F. Starr - 1891, p. 485, abstracted and sent to me by Mary Katherine DeLong, Belvedere, CA.
6. 1850 census, Elizabeth, Essex co, NJ, abstracted by Ruth C. Duncan.

SIXTH GENERATION

1-3-1-7-1-1   D66i   CB310272

JAMES[6] BUNNELL (Stephen[5], James[4], Nathaniel[3], Nathaniel[2], William[1]) was born about 1765[1] (or about 1755[2,3]) in Essex (now Union) co, NJ. Probably with his father, he moved to a new settlement at Mays Lick in Mason co, VA (KY after 1 June 1792). James appears for the first time in the Mason co tax records in 1792 as James Bonnell, one white male[6]. He was apparently living with his father since he had no land or cattle to be taxed. Probably about this time he was married to Jennie[4] (or Mary[5]) Childers[4,5] of Virginia[4]. In 1793 he was taxed also on 4 horses or mules and 4 cattle[6]. By 1794 and again in 1795 he had 7 cows[6]. In 1796 he was also taxed on 1 black male over 16 and 196 acres of land on Turtle Creek[6]. Turtle Creek was then in Mason co, but was included in Bracken co, KY, when it was set off on 14 December 1796. The land on Turtle Creek does not appear again on the Mason co Tax Book, although James continues to be taxed in Mason co in 1797, 1799 and 1800[6]. In 1801, however, he is listed on the Delinquent Tax List, with the notation that he was living in Northwest Territory, across the Ohio River[6].

James moved to Adams co, OH, where he settled on 102.5 acres on Ohio Brush Creek in Meigs twp[7]. (There is still a Bundle Run flowing into Ohio Brush Creek in Meigs twp.) He appears on an Adams co tax list as a resident-owner in 1806[8]. He sold the land "where James Bunnell now lives" on Ohio Brush Creek to William Davis, who gave him a mortgage on 9 March 1809 secured by the property[7]. He was living in Highland co, OH, when he died before 8 February 1812, when William Noble was appointed administrator of his estate, with Samuel Harvey and John Shockley as sureties. Morgan Van Matre, Joel Drake and Israel Nordyke acted as appraisers. The first account refers to receiving a legacy from Ephraim Blackwood (sic), executor of the last will of Stephen Bunnel, dec'd[9]. The actual probate file in Highland co has disappeared. James didn't live to receive the legacy of $1.00 left to him by his father's will probated 16 February 1813. I have found no further record which could apply to him.

REFERENCES:
1. Revised Family Group Sheet compiled by Nona Bassett, Merced, CA. No references.
2. Ltr. 25 Feb. 1960 from Homer Baldwin - line of Mrs. Charles (Nettie) Glaser.
3. Original Family Group Sheet compiled by Nona Bassett. Ref: Nina O. Roberts.
4. Family record fastened in the Family Bible of Merritt Bunnell CB320362.
5. Duncan, p. 52.
6. Mason co, KY, Tax Book, 1790-1810, on LDS Film #008,400, abstracted and sent to me by Mrs. William S. George, Phoenix, AZ.
7. Adams co, OH, Deeds, abstracted and sent to me by Christine D. Kraft, Lawrence, KS.
8. *Early Ohio Tax Records*, compiled by Esther Weygandt Powell, 1971, p. 449, reference sent to me by Christine D. Kraft.
9. *Wills, Administrations, Guardianships and Adoptions of Highland County, Ohio (1805-1880)*, compiled by David N. and June N. McBride, 1957. Sent to me by Crum's Genealogy Research Team, Sinking Spring, OH.

SIXTH GENERATION

1-3-1-7-1-2   D167   CB310273

STEPHEN[6] BUNNELL (Stephen[5], James[4], Nathaniel[3], Nathaniel[2], William[1]) was born 25 June 1767[1] in Essex (now Union) co, NJ. A hand-written note fastened in the Bunnel-Swain Bible says that Stephen learned the trade of gunsmith in Philadelphia, then worked in the U. S. Armory in Cincinnati, OH[1]. He later went to Mason co, KY[1]. He appears on the tax records of Mason co with his father and his brothers Jonas and James in 1792 through 1797[2].

On 1[3] (or 3[1]) March 1795[1,3] he married Freelove Williams[1], who was born 24 February 1769[1] in Virginia[3,5]. Her father's plantation on the Potomac joined George Washington's, and she frequently saw him riding around on his plantation[5]. Her father was a slave owner, and when she married he gave her several household slaves[5]. (The tax assessment in 1797 lists 2 black males over 16 among Stephen's taxables for the first time[5].)

Stephen bought land in Mason co, KY, on 19 November 1799[3] from his brother Jonas, but they left Kentucky very soon to move to Ohio[1]. They settled in Warren co where Stephen appears with his father on the 1809 and 1810 tax lists for Franklin twp[3,4]. He bought his father's farm[5], and when his father died in 1813 his will left $1.00 to Stephen and each of his brothers. In 1820 Stephen was counted in the census in Clear Creek twp, Warren co: 110301-01101-AG1-MFG1[3]. This seems to represent a change in political boundaries rather than a physical move. He appears again in Clear Creek twp in 1830: 000100001-00000001[3]. Stephen and Freelove eventually sold the farm to their son Merritt[5], and they were counted in Merritt's household in 1840 in Clear Creek[3]. The 1850 census in Clear Creek listed Stephen age 80, born in New Jersey and his wife Freelove age 81, born in Virginia[3]. He was the owner of property valued at $26,800[3].

Freelove died 7 October 1855[1] (or 1850[5]) and Stephen died 4 May 1857[1] in Clear Creek twp. They were buried beside his parents in the old Baptist Cemetery near Ridgeville in Clear Creek twp, Warren co, OH[1]. (DeLorme Mapping Company's Atlas and Gazetteer of Ohio shows that Bunnell Hill Road still runs near Ridgeville in Clear Creek twp.)

Children:
- 1. 320360. William W., b. 1795[1]; m. 20 Aug. 1822 Olinda Ball[1,6]; d. 4 Sept. 1852[1].
    Children (surname Bunnell):[5]
    - 1. Julia Ann.
    - 2. Nominia.
    - 3. Rhodes William.
    - 4. Horace.
    - 5. Eulace.
- 2. 320361. Stephen, b. 21 June 1797[5]; m. 4 Dec. 1821 4 Dec. 1821 Lucinda Ward[5]; d. 1877[5].
    Children (surname Bunnell):[5]
    - 1. John.
    - 2. Jane.
    - 3. Samuel.
    - 4. Diana.
    - 5. Arminta.
    - 6. Olinda.
    - 7. Jackson.
    - 8. Stephen.
- 3. 320362. Merritt, b. 21 Jan. 1799[1]; m. 8 Jan. 1828 Henrietta King[1,6]; d. 27 Jan. 1890[5].

391

Children (surname Bunnell):[1,3]
1. Caroline Emma.   2. Mary Jane.

4. 320363. Mary, b. 13 Jan. 1801[5]; m. (first) 1 June 1820 Samuel Wood[3]; m. (second) Cyrus Robinson Hunter[5]; m. (third) William Chambers[5]; d. 1871[5].
Children (surname Wood):[5]
1. Julia Ann.
Children (surname Hunter):[5]
2. Cyrus Robinson.   3. William Adison.   4. Mary Jane.
Children (surname Chambers):[5]
5. Newton Aron.   6. Sarah Louisa.   7. Merritt Bunnell.

5. 320364. Elizabeth, b. 1803[5]; m. (first) George King[5]; m. (second) William Martindale, div.[5]; m. (third) _____ Bishop[5].
Children (surname Martindale):[5]
1. son, d. y.   2. Henrietta.

6. 320368. Rachel; b. 1804[5]; d. young[5].

7. 320369. Rosa, b. 1806[5]; d. young[5].

8. 320365. Julia Ann, b. 8 May 1808[5]; m. (first) 26 Sept. 1829 Nicholas Pence[5]; m. (second) 27 June 1844 Albert Gallatin Ayers[5]; d. 30 Jan. 1861[5].
Children (surname Pence):[5]
1. George Washington. 2. John Bunnell.
Children (surname Ayers):[5]
3. Samuel Day.

9. 320366. Luther Ball, b. 16 June 1810[5]; m. 30 May 1832 Esther Mendenhall[5]; d. 29 Sept. 1850[5].
Children (surname Bunnell):[5]
1. child, d. y.   3. Esther Romania.   5. Luther B.
2. child, d.y.   4. Josephine.

10. 320367. John, b. 30 May 1813[5]; m. (first) 12 Sept. 1830[5] or 11 Sept. 1831[6] Sarah Ivy Clymer[3,5,6]; m. (second) 22 Dec. 1861 Nancy Crossley[3,5]; d. 18 Feb. 1873[5].
Children (surname Bunnell)(by first wife):[5]
1. Olinda.   5. Sarah Jane.   8. Stephen Henry.
2. Luther.   6. Robert C.   9. Moses K.
3. William Marion.   7. John W.   10. Mary Ivy.
4. Julia Ann.

REFERENCES:

1. Bunnel-Swain Family Bible, A. & E. Phinney's Cooperstown, NY, 1842. Merritt Bunnel, original owner. Now in possession of Warren co, OH, Historical Society. Transcript sent to me by Mrs. Lyle Snyder, Fellsmere, FL.
2. Mason co, KY, Tax Book, 1790-1810, on LDS Film #008,400, abstracted and sent to me by Mrs. William S. George, Phoenix, AZ.
3. CB Database.
4. *Early Ohio Tax Records*, compiled by Esther Weygandt Powell, 1971, p. 449, reference sent to me by Christine D. Kraft, Lawrence, KS.
5. *Genealogy of the Bunnell Family*, by John Bunnell Pence, grandson of Stephen CB310273. Copy sent to Ruth C. Duncan by Mrs. William George.
6. *Warren County, OH, Marriage Records 1803-1834*, compiled by Willard Heiss, 1977.

1-3-1-7-1-3   D165   CB310274

JONAS[6] BUNNELL (Stephen[5], James[4], Nathaniel[3], Nathaniel[2], William[1]) was born about 1769[1] (or about 1759[2,3] or 29 Aug. 1759[4]) in Essex (now Union) co, NJ. He is said to have served in the Revolution[5] (which would preclude the 1769 date of birth). However, I can find no confirmation of this statement and do not believe it credible. In the late 1780s Jonas moved with his parents to a new settlement in Mays Lick, in Mason co, VA (KY after 1 June 1792). There, about 1790, he married (first) SARAH TOMLIN[6], who was raised in Tennessee[5]. From 1792 to 1795 Jonas appears in the Mason co Tax Book assessed on one or two horses and some cattle[7]. In 1796 and 1797 he was also assessed on 25 acres of land on Lee's Creek in Mason co[7]. In 1799 he was assessed only on three horses[7]. At this time he was preparing to leave Kentucky. He sold his land to his brother Stephen[16] and moved to Ohio.

He located first east of Cincinnati about four miles north of the Ohio River[5]. The land consisted of 104+ acres on Twelve Mile Creek in Clermont co[8]. His wife Sarah died there about 1808 leaving him with nine children, most of whom he placed with friends and relatives[5]. He appears on the Clermont co tax list on 1809 and 1810. On 15 August 1810 he married (second) ELIZABETH COLEMAN[9]. Although several sources state that his second wife was Betsey Hathaway[5], daughter of John W. Hathaway[10], and that Elizabeth Coleman was a third wife, I believe they were one person - Elizabeth (Hathaway) Coleman, widow of _____ Coleman.

On 10 April 1811 Jonas and Elizabeth sold their home on Twelve Mile Creek for $425 to John Monroe[8]. They removed north to Madison co, OH, where he bought more land on 6 July 1815[4]. His youngest child was born about 1816, but his wife Elizabeth died soon, probably in childbirth. On 8 September 1816 he married (third) in Warren co, OH, NANCY WILLIS[11]. Clark co was set off from Madison and Champagne counties on 22 December 1817. Jonas and Nancy found themselves living in the new Clark co. Jonas died intestate in Clark co in 1819[4]. Nancy Bunnell and Reuben Daniels served as administrators of his estate[4]. In 1813 Jonas received $1.00 by the terms of his father's will.

Children (by first wife):
1. 320305. William, b. 14 Oct. 1791[14]; m. 17 Aug. 1826 Mary Cassaday[12]; d. 1846[4].
    Children (surname Bunnell):[14]

1. Oliver P.	4. Mary Caroline.	6. Sarah M.
2. William C.	5. Rhoda.	7. John W.
3. Ruth Jane.		

2. 320307. John Milton, b. 11 Sept. 1794[4]; m. 19 Nov. 1815 Catherine Bunnell[12]
    1-3-1-7-8-7 CB310419; d. 28 Nov. 1862[4].
    Children (surname Bunnell):[4]

1. David N.	4. Martha J.	7. Harriet.
2. Abigail K.	5. Oliver Perry.	8. America H.
3. John Milton.	6. Mary V.	

3. 320312. Tabitha[5].

4. 320310. Elijah, b. about 1796[4]; m. 31 July 1823 Rachel Ford[12]; d. 7 Sept. 1868[15].
Children (surname Bunnell):[15]

1. Thomas Jefferson.	6. Sytha.	11. Mary C.
2. Martha.	7. William.	12. James B.
3. Eliza.	8. Sarah.	13. Amanda Jane.
4. John Wesley.	9. Squire George.	14. Edward Hazen.
5. Noah.	10. Rebecca.	

5. 320308. Sytha[5], m. 18 Dec. 1817 Samuel Hays[11].

6. 320311. Nancy, b. about 1800[14]; m. 18 Dec. 1817 Curtis Reed[13]; d. 1840[14].
Children (surname Reed):[14]

1. Esther.	5. Susan.	9. child, d. y.
2. William.	6. Mary.	10. Jefferson?
3. John.	7. Rebecca.	11. Cytha Ann.
4. America.		

7. 320306. George Esom, b. 15 Mar. 1802[5]; m. 15 May 1821 Sarah Peck[12]; d. 28 Apr. 1884[4].
Children (surname Bunnell):[14]

1. James P.	4. Archibald S.	7. Lucinda.
2. Sytha Ann.	5. Isaac.	8. John David.
3. Richard.	6. William.	9. Henry.

Did he also have sons Noah and Franc?[14]

8. 320313. Sarah[5], m. 12 Nov. 1820 Ezekiel Loud?[11]

9. 320309. America[5], m. (first) _____ Higgins[14]; m. (second) 25 Sept. 1823 Alexander G. Morgan[14].

10. 320314. Jefferson[5], probably died young.

Children (by second wife):

11. 320304, Eliza Ann, b. about 1816[14]; m. 22 Sept. 1836 Eber Pugh[14].
Children (surname Pugh):[14]

1. Sarah.	4. Peter B.	7. Mary M.
2. Leander.	5. Abram M.	8. Alice.
3. Oscar W.	6. Rebecca I.	

REFERENCES:
1. Revised Family Group Sheet compiled by Nona Bassett, Merced, CA. No references.
2. Ltr. Feb. 1960 from Homer Baldwin - line of Mrs. Charles (Nettie) Glaser.
3. Original Family Group Sheet compiled by Nona Bassett. Ref: Nina O. Roberts.
4. CB Database.
5. *History of Warren County, OHio*, W. H. Beers & Co. 1882, pp. 894, 895.
6. Bunnel-Swain Family Bible, A. & E. Phinney's Cooperstown, NY, 1842. Merritt Bunnel, original owner. Now in possession of Warren co, OH, Historical Society. Transcript sent to me by Mrs. Lyle Snyder, Fellsmere, FL.
7. Mason co, KY, Tax Book, 1790-1810, on LDS Film #008,400, abstracted and sent to me by Mrs. William S. George, Phoenix, AZ.
8. Clermont co, OH, Deeds, Bk. H7, p. 354, photocopy sent to me by Mrs. William S. George.
9. Marriage License, Jonas Bunnel to Elizabeth Coleman, photocopy sent to me by Mrs. George.

10. Duncan, p. 100.
11. *Warren County, Ohio, Marriage Records 1803-1834*, compiled by Willard Heiss, Indianapolis 1977.
13. Transcript of the marriage record of Curtis Reed & Nancy Bunnel in Warren co, OH, photocopy
    sent to me by Mrs. George.
14. Family Group Sheets compiled by Mrs. William S. George:
    Jonas Bunnell
    William Bunnell
    George Easome Bunnell
    Curtis Reed & Nancy Bunnell
    Eber Pugh & Eliza Ann Bunnell
15. Ltr. 9 July 1994 from Eileen B. Findling, Windfall, IN.
16. Mason co, KY Deeds, Bk H, p. 377 - notes gathered and sent to me by Marjorie Gibbs, Saratoga
    Springs, NY.

1-3-1-7-1-4 D66iii CB310275

BRAZILLA[6] BUNNELL (Stephen[5], James[4], Nathaniel[3], Nathaniel[2], William[1]) was born about 1771[1] (or about 1761[2,3]) in Essex (now Union) co, NJ. This name appears in several versions - Barzilla, Barzella, Berzilia, Bazilla, Buzillar, etc. According to one source, after moving to Mason co, KY, with his parents he "went back to N.J. to marry but died"[4]. I have found no reference to Brazilla in Kentucky and doubt that he ever moved there. The Bunnel-Swain Bible states succinctly, "Brazilla married in New Jersey and died there"[5]. Duncan says he "d. 9 March 1796; m. NANCY RIGGS"[6].

REFERENCES:
1. Revised Family Group Sheet compiled by Nona Bassett, Merced, CA. No references.
2. Ltr. Feb. 1960 from Homer Baldwin - line of Mrs. Charles (Nettie) Glaser.
3. Original Family Group Sheet compiled by Nona Bassett. Ref: Nina O. Roberts.
4. Bunnell genealogical notes compiled by Mable Mae McClamroch, Crawfordsville, IN.
5. Bunnel-Swain Family Bible, A.& E. Phinney's Cooperstown, NY, 1842. Merritt Bunnel, original
   owner. Now in possession of Warren co, OH, Historical Society. Transcript sent to me by
   Mrs. Lyle Snyder, Fellsmere, FL.
6. Duncan, p. 52.

1-3-1-7-1-5 D166 CB310276

DAVID[6] BUNNELL (Stephen[5], James[4], Nathaniel[3], Nathaniel[2], William[1]) was born about 1773[1] (or about 1764[2,3]) in Essex (now Union) co, NJ. While still in his teens he moved with his parents, about 1788, to Mason co, VA (KY after 1 June 1792). There, on 19 March 1796, he was married by Richard Durett to ELIZABETH PRICE[4], daughter of Veazey and Ann (Barton) Price[1]. She was born in January 1768 in Frederick co, MD. David first appeared on the tax lists of Mason co in 1797[6]. From that year through 1800 he was assessed only on horses[6]. By 1802, however, he had acquired 100 acres of land on Lee's Creek in Mason co and was assessed as well on 4 horses and 30 cattle[6]. In 1803 no cattle were listed[6]. In 1804 his assessment was on 4 horses, 100 acres on Lee's Creek and a Tavern license[6]. The Tavern license was not listed in 1806, and in 1807 David had apparently disposed of his land[6]. In 1808 and 1809 he was assessed only on horses[6].

David and his family removed to Warren co, OH, in the latter year. Like his father and his brother Stephen he is listed on the 1810 tax list of Franklin twp in Warren co[7]. In Warren co he bought two tracts of land, one of 50 acres from Christian and Catherine Null and the other of 75 acres from David Fudge[10]. In 1813 he received a bequest of $1.00 under the terms of his father's will.

David died in Warren co, OH, 10 February 1816[5] and was buried in the old Springboro Cemetery in Clear Creek twp, Warren co[5]. Letters of administration were issued to Elizabeth Bunnell, David's widow 14 February 1816[8], but the estate was not finally settled for many years. Many of the children were still minors[9]. Elizabeth Bunnell, widow, appears in the 1820 census of Clear Creek twp, Warren co, OH: 223410-21010-AG2[5]. On 6 November 1821, in Warren co, Elizabeth Bunnell married (second) her brother-in-law Nathaniel[11].

By 1824 the five oldest children were over 21 years of age. On 27 April that year Alfred, age 18, chose John Bunnel to be his guardian[12], and on 5 May "Beza" (Veazey), age 16, chose George Lowry as guardian[12]. Then on 6 November 1827, the Court of Common Pleas in Clark co, OH, appointed Nathaniel Bunnell, their uncle and step-father to be legal guardian of David's three youngest children, Nancy age 17, John age 14 and Eliza age 10[13]. The following year Nathaniel successfully petitioned the court in Warren co for permission to sell the 30% interest of his three wards in the 125 acres of land that David had owned in Warren co[10]. The older children had apparently sold their rights to "strangers" by this time and Elizabeth still owned her 1/3 dower right to the land[10].

Children:[10]
1. 320292. Ephraim, b. 22 June 1797[5]; m. 15 Mar. 1827 Martha (Biddle) Price[5,11]; d. 9 Mar. 1868[5]
   Children (surname Bunnell):[5]
   1. Alfred.   3. Harriet A.   5. Ephraim.
   2. Elizabeth.   4. Veazey Croy.   6. Martha E.
2. 320293. Barton, b. 7 Aug. 1799[14]; m. (first) 15 Feb. 1821 Ann Biddle[14]; m. (second) 3 Dec. 1829 Mary Ann Buckles[14]; d. 7 Feb. 1848[14].
   Children (surname Bunnell)(by first wife):[14]
   1. Stephen J.   2. James.
   Children (surname Bunnell)(by second wife):[14]
   3. Barton.   4. Veazey.   5. Sophia.
3. 320294. Barzilla, b. about 1801[5]; m. 14 Nov. 1821 Nancy Williams[11]; d. before 1850[5]
   Children (surname Bunnell):[5]
   1. Hannah Maria.   4. Mary E.   7. Martha J.
   2. Abner William.   5. Robert J.   8. Clarissa A.
   3. John Barton.   6. Horatio W.
4. 320300. Abraham[10], b. about 1802; m. 23 Feb. 1830 Nancy Corbret[15] (Corbett?)
5. 320295. James[10] (or Jonah[5]), b. 10 Sept. 1803[5]; probably the same person as James Bunnell CB010892.

6. 320297. Alfred, b. 19 Apr. 1807[16] (or 1806[12]); m. 15 Jan. 1829 Jane Probasco[11]; d. 1836[5].
     Children (surname Bunnell):[5]
     1. Abraham.   2. Theodore P.

7. 320298. Veazey Price, b. 6 May 1809[16] (or 1808[12]); m. 23 Sept. 1834 Eliza Ann Restine[5].

8. 320302. Nancy, b. 5 May 1810[5]; m. 3 Apr. 1835 Thomas Bunnell[5] CB320317; d. 18 Jun 1886[5].
     Children (surname Bunnell): See 1-3-1-7-1-7-3.

9. 320299. John T.[10] or Wesley[5]; b. about 1813[10]; m. (first) 16 Dec. 1841 Mary Clarinda Young[5]; m. (second) 15 Feb. 1849 Elizabeth M. Young[5]; d. before 1860[5].
     Children (surname Bunnell)(by first wife):[5]
     1. Elizabeth.
     Children (surname Bunnell)(by second wife):[5]
     2. Thomas A.

10. 320322. Eliza Ann, b. about 1816[10]; m. 2 Nov. 1836 Jacob Hanaway[15]; d. 30 March 1876[5] (or 1874[17]).
     Children (surname Hanaway):[17]

1. John C.	5. William Taylor	9. Thomas.
2. Ephraim.	6. Jacob Albert.	10. Emma Alice.
3. Stephen.	7. Mary.	
4. Nathaniel.	8. Francis Marion.	

REFERENCES:

1. Revised Family Group Sheet compiled by Nona Bassett, Merced, CA. No references.
2. Ltr. Feb. 1960 from Homer Baldwin - line of Mrs. Charles (Nettie) Glaser.
3. Original Family Group Sheet compiled by Nona Bassett. Ref: Nina O. Roberts.
4. *Kentucky Ancestors*, Vol. 3, No. 4, Apr. 1968, p. 152. Abstracted and sent to me by Marjorie Gibbbs, Saratoga Springs, NY.
5. CB Database.
6. Mason co, KY, Tax Book, 1790-1810, on LDS Film #008,400, abstracted and sent to me by Mrs. William S. George, Phoenix, AZ.
7. *Early Ohio Tax Records*, compiled by Esther Weygandt Rowell, reprinted with the Index, by Genealogical Publishing Co., p. 399, reference sent to me by John Paul Grady, Roswell, NM.
8. *Warren Co. Ohio 1803-1859 Will and Estate Records*, abstracted and sent to me by Mrs. Jane Bailey, Miamisburg, OH.
9. Warren Co, OH, CHANCERY RECORD #2 (1826-1827), abstracted and sent to me by Mrs. Jane Bailey.
10. Pleas held at Lebanon, Warren co, OH, on 27 Oct. 1828 before the judges of the Court of Common Pleas:
    "Nathaniel Bunnel Guardian, &c.
    Petition for sale of Land.
    "Be it remembered that . . . . .on the second Monday of April being the fourteenth day of the same month in the year of our Lord one thousand eight hundred and twenty eight, Nathaniel Bunnel, Guardian &c by Francis Dunlavy, Esq., his attorney filed in court here his petition for

sale of Land . . . . The petition of the undersigned guardian of John T. Bunnell, Nancy Bunnell, and Eliza Bunnell minor children and heirs of David Bunnell deceased late of the county aforesaid respectfully sheweth unto your honors that sometime about the year 1822 [sic] the said David Bunnell died intestate leaving a widow and the following children and heirs to wit Ephraim Bunnell, Morton [sic] Bunnell, Barzilla Bunnell, Abraham Bunnell, Alfred Bunnell, Vesey Bunnell, and James Bunnell and the said Nancy, John T. and Eliza the wards of your petitioner. That at the time of his death he, the said David was possessed in his own right in fee simple of and in a certain tract of land situate in the County aforesaid containing one hundred and twenty five acres being parts of sections No. 1&2 in Town two Range five between the Miami rivers as will more fully and at large appear by the abstract of two deeds made to the said David Bunnell by Christian Null and David Fudge respectively and herewith submitted, marked A. And your petitioner further shews that by the decease of their said father David your petitioners wards are each entitled to one tenth of the said tract of one hundred and twenty five acres. That the widow of said David who is still living has heretofore to at the term of this court for   had her dower legally assigned to her in the premises and that the ballance nor any part thereof has not been divided among the said heirs of David Bunnell, deceased, nor can the same bear a division in the confident opinion of your petitioner without greatly injuring the whole owing to the great number of owners and the small size of said tract and your petition further shews that the greater part of the heirs of the said David Bunnell have sold out their respective shares which are in the hands of strangers and that from the peculiar situation of the shares of your wards, they are subject to waste and trespass without afording any adequate remedy. And your petitioner would further represent that at present said land or shares of your petitioners would sell to advantage and would enable your petitioner to purchase for each a small farm or one half quarter section of wild uncultivated Land by which means their respective estates would be greatly improved. Your petitioner therefore prays that such proceedings may be had so that the estate of your wards in the premises, not including said dower, may be sold according to the Statute in sch case made and provided and your petitioner will &c. Nathaniel Bunnell, guardian of the said John T., Nancy, and Eliza Bunnell.

.

..

" . . .And now at this day, to wit; the fourth Monday of October, being the twenty seventh day of the same Month in the year of our Lord One thousand eight hundred and twenty eight comes again into Court here, the petitioner by his counsel aforesaid, to whom the aforegoing order was in manner and form as above recited, directed, who makes return of the same thus, endorsed to wit Saturday Nov. 1st 1828. In pursuance of the within order after having the within described tract of land advertised in "The Western Star" printed in Lebanon, Warren County, Ohio, and by advertisements set up in five public places as the Law directs, I offered the same at public Sale on this day at the Court house in Lebanon, between the hours of 12 A.M. and four P.M. and then and there sold the same to John Seller's the highest bidder for the sum of eight Dollars per acre. Nathaniel Bunnel guardian. And thereupon after a careful examination the court approve the proceedings of said guardian an[d] order that a deed be executed to the purchaser of the premises and that the proceeding be recorded"

11. *Warren County, OH, Marriage Records 1803-1834*, compiled by Willard Heiss, 1977.
12. *Gateway to the West*, Vol. XI 1978, p. 42, abstracted and sent to me by Ellen Dorn, Manhattan Beach, CA.
13. Probate Division, Court of Common Pleas, Clark co, OH. File A-360, filed 6 Nov. 1827, photocopy sent to me by Claude A. Bunnell.
14. Some descendants of Stephen Bunnell, b. 1731, Scotch Plains, NJ, compiled by Mable M. McClamroch, Crawfordsville, IN.
15. *INDIANA MARRIAGES 1826 TO 1850*, by Archival Vision, Inc., copyright by Liahona Research, Inc. 1994, abstracted and sent to me by Marjorie Gibbs, Saratoga Springs, NY.
16. Family Group Sheet, David Bonnell, compiled by Mrs. William S. George.
17. Ltr. 1 Apr. 1915 to John A. Biles from Mrs. F. Howell Colman, Kalamazoo, MI, daughter of Emma Alice Hathaway.

1-3-1-7-1-7   D168   CB310277

NATHANIEL[6] BUNNELL (Peg Leg) (Stephen[5], James[4], Nathaniel[3], Nathaniel[2], William[1]) was born 3 July 1778[1] in Essex (now Union) co, NJ. In the late 1780s his parents moved to Mason co, VA (KY after 1 June 1792). As a young man he was engaged in the Ohio River trade and was one of a crew who navigated a pirogue of goods from Maysville, KY, up the Scioto River to Chillicothe, OH[3]. This was said to have been the first boat load of merchandise ever landed at that point[3]. On 15 January 1800 Nathaniel was married at Maysville, Mason co, KY, by George Tarvin to ELIZABETH DONOVAN[2], a native of Kentucky[3]. He appears first on the Mason co, KY, tax records in 1800[4]. The following year he was listed as delinquent, with the notation "living in Northwest Territory[4].

Soon after his marriage he moved with his bride to Ross co, OH[3]. In 1808 Nathaniel Bunnell of Ross co paid his parents, Stephen and Mary Bunnell of Mason co, KY, $227 for 125 acres in Adams co, OH, on Ohio Brush Creek[5]. On 30 October 1808 he and his wife Elizabeth sold the same land for the same price to Jacob Platter of Adams co[5]. In 1810 Nathaniel purchased 130 acres of land in Paint twp, Ross co, OH, from Jacob Platter[6].

Nathaniel is said to have seen service in the War of 1812[3], but while still a young man a horse fell on him. His right leg was so badly injured that it had to be amputated[8]. Subsequently he learned and followed the trade of shoemaker[8]. In 1813 he received $1.00 under the terms of his father's will.

His next move was to Morefield twp, Clark co, OH, just north of Springfield, where he appears in the 1820 census: 122311-21011[7]. Clearly, his brother David's three youngest children were already living in his household. Probably Nathaniel's first wife was dead by this time and the woman of 26-45 was David's widow. If that is true it pinpoints the time of their move to Nathaniel's home in Clark co, since Elizabeth and her children had already been counted in the 1820 census in Clear Creek twp, Warren co[7]. Nathaniel and ELIZABETH (PRICE) BUNNELL, his sister-in-law, were married 6 November 1821 in Warren co, OH[9]. In 1824 Nathaniel and Elizabeth sold his land in Paint twp, Ross co to Charles White[6]. Nathaniel appears again in the 1830 census in Morefield twp: 0002300101-00201001[7]. (Records show that in 1831 he purchased half of lot 44 in Chillicothe, Ross co, OH[6].)

On 6 November 1827, in Clark co, Nathaniel was appointed legal guardian of three of his step-children, Nancy age 17, John age 14, and Eliza age 10[10]. They were the three youngest children of David and Elizabeth (Price) Bunnell. In April 1828 he applied to the court in Warren co, OH, for permission to sell the interest of his wards in 125 acres of land in Warren co which had belonged to his brother, "which would enable your petitioner to purchase for each a small farm or one half quarter section of wild uncultivated land by which means their respective estates would be greatly improved."[11]

In the fall of 1833 Nathaniel decided to move his family again, this time to Big Creek twp, Carroll co, IN. He entered his first tract of land in section 34 on 9 December 1833[3]. He probably did not settle upon it until the following spring or summer[3]. The following year this part of Carroll co was set off as White co, IN.

Sons Nathaniel and Thomas entered lands in section 27, Honey Creek twp, White co, in April 1834[3]. Thomas would soon marry his cousin and step-sister Nancy. On 16 December her brother John entered land in section 26 and sister Eliza Ann in section 33[3], presumably with the funds provided by the sale of their rights to their father's land in Warren co, OH.

Nathaniel's second wife must have died either just before or just after the move to Indiana. He was married (third) on 10 March 1835, in Monticello, White co, IN, by George A. Spencer, J. P. to NANCY BUNNELL[7], probably a widow, with two children, Thomas A. Bunnell, born in 1833, and Elizabeth Bunnell, born in 1835. She was born about 1802 in Pennsylvania, but it is not known who her first husband was. [SPECULATION: The 1860 census included Sarah Scowder age 78, born in PA, living with Nancy. When Nathaniel wrote the codicil to his will in 1847, one of the witnesses was Joshua Scowden. Nancy named one of her sons Joshua, a name not common in the Bunnell family. I suggest that Nancy's maiden name was Scowden, that Sarah was her mother and that Joshua was her brother, or possibly her father. Both Bunnell and Scowden were common names in Crawford co, PA. The only candidate for Nancy's husband I could find in Crawford co is Abraham Bonnell CB310394, son of Abraham CB300134, who wrote in his will on 27 September 1817: "5th. I give and bequeath unto my son Abraham Bonnel twenty five dollars if he should return home in three years after my decease, if not it is my will that the said twenty five dollars be paid to his daughter Julian Bonnel." This speculation is provided only to suggest a line of research.]

Nathaniel appears on a list of voters in Big Creek twp, White co, in November 1836[3] and in 1838 he was elected school examiner in White co[3]. He appears in the 1840 census in White co: 110110001-010101[7]. He wrote his will on 27 October 1845 and added a codicil on 16 June 1847:

> "In the name of God, Amen, I, Nathaniel Bunnell Senior, of the County of White and State of Indiana, being of sound mind and disposing memory, do make, ordain and publish this my last will and testament; hereby revoking and making void all former wills by me at any time heretofore made.
> "First, I direct that my be decently interred, that my funeral be conducted in a manner corresponding with my estate and situation in life. And as to such worldly estate as it has pleased God to entrust me with, I dispose of the same in the following manner to wit:-I direct, first that all my just debts and funeral expenses be paid as soon after my decease as possible out of the moneys that shall come into the hands of my executors from any portion of the estate, real or personal, and my executors are hereby authorized to sell so much of my personal estate as may be necessary for discharging my debts and funeral expenses aforesaid. And it is further my will that my estate be appraised by them of my neighbors to be selected for that purpose by my executors, and an inventory and appraisement thereof signed by said appraisers, be given my executors. I further will and direct that my beloved wife Nancy shall have the possession and control of all my property both real and personal, excepting as hereinafter may be accepted, so long as the said Nancy may remain my widow, if until my youngest child shall arrive at the age of 21 years. But in case the said Nancy should marry again, then in that case it is my will that the said Nancy, my wife, have and retain the one third of my estate, both real and personal, during her natural life, and at her decease the same property to revert

back to my now minor children, Benjamin, Samuel R., and Joshua, and in case my wife should have more children in a reasonable time after my decease, it is my will that they all share equally in my estate at the time that my youngest child shall arrive at the age of twenty one years., or in case that either or any of my now minor children should decease before the youngest arrives at the age of twenty one years, then it is my will that the others, now minor heirs, shall hold the shares of the deceased.

"I also further will, constitute and appoint John Brady and Thos. Spencer as my lawful executors. I further will that my executors counsel with the widow respecting the cultivation of the farm, and if it become necessary, I will that my executors have the authority to rent the farm to such ones as they may think best for the benefit of the widow and minor children for their support and education. I also will that the widow have the mansion house and such as the orchard garden and other necessary privileges about the house with out any restraint. I also further will that my executors have the care and oversight of my minor children, and if at any time, in their opinion, it becomes necessary to bind out any of the said for the benefit of the children, then in that case it is my will and request that my executor bind said children to some good steady farmer and to the best possible advantage and benefit of said children, whereas herein above I have appointed John Brady and Thomas Spencer executors of my last will and testament, in witness whereof, I Nathaniel Bunnell (Senior), the testator have hereunto set my hand and seal this 27th day of October 1845.   Nathaniel Bunnell Senior..

Signed, sealed, published and delivered by the above Nathaniel Bunnell Sr. as his last will and testament in the presence of us who have hereunto subscribed our names as witnesses thereto in the presence of the said testator and in the presence of each other.
Abner Bunnell   James Barnes."

"Whereas I have heretofore made and executed the within as my last will and testament on the Oct. 27th, 1845 and bequeathed all the land that I then owned to my three youngest children therein named, but finding it necessary to dispose of a portion thereof, I there revoke so much thereof as respects forty acres lying and being the S.E. quarter of the S.E. quarter of Section 7, as described within and no more. this 16th day of June 1847.
Nathaniel Bunnell

James Barnes
Joshua Scowden"
Executed Sept. 24, 1850   Ransom McConnaughhay, Clerk"
Monticello, White co, IN, Will Records, Book I. p. 63.

Note that the will mentions his beloved wife Nancy and his minor children Benjamin, Samuel R. and Joshua. None of the other children, his own or those of his wives, were mentioned in any way. He died at his farm in section 34, Big Creek twp, on 14 April 1850[3] and was buried in the Bunnell Cemetery near Reynolds, White co, IN[3]. He was a life-long member of the Methodist Episcopal Church[3].

His widow appears in the 1850 census in District 130, Whiute co, IN, with the five of her own children, ages 7 to 17[7]. In the 1860 census in Big Creek twp, White co, only Samuel and Joshua were still living with her[7]. Also, Sarah Scowder, age 78, born in PA, was a member of her household[7]. Nancy died 18 June 1886[1].

Children (by first wife):
    1. 320315. Isaac, b. 5 June 1802[12]; m. May 1826 Hannah Collins[7]; d. 26 Feb. 1847[12].
            Children (surname Bunnell):[7]

1. Dennis C.	4. Mary Emeline.	7. Edward Collins.
2. Emeline.	5. Nathaniel V.	8. Louisa Jane.
3. James.	6. Sarah A.	

    2. 320316. Stephen, b. 9 Mar. 1803[1]; m. (first) 1 Feb. 1827 Agnes (Nancy) Roberts[7];
            m. (second) 7 Sept. 1871 Martha Irvin[7]; d. 25 Apr. 1880[1].
            Children (surname Bunnell)(by first wife):[12]

1. Elizabeth Jane.	3. Thomas Nelson.	5. Rebecca A.
2. Daniel R.	4. John W.	

    3. 320317. Thomas, b. 6 Sept. 1804[1]; m. 3 Apr. 1835 Nancy Bunnell CB320302[7,12];
            d. 16 July 1870[1].
            Children (surname Bunnell):[12]

1. Eliza Ann.	3. William H.	5. Stephen.
2. John Barton.	4. Nathaniel Fletcher.	

    4. 320318. Nathaniel, b. 27 Dec. 1805[1]; m. (first) 29 Dec. 1831 Susanna Runyan[1];
            m. (second) 28 Aug. 1875 Mary A. (Bartlett)(Buchanan) McNealey[1];
            d. 4 Sept. 1891[1].
            Children (surname Bunnell)(by first wife):[1]

1. Abraham Runyan.	5. Thomas Reed.	9. Stephen M.
2. Nathaniel Wesley.	6. Sophia E.	10. Eliza.
3. Esther A.	7. Nancy Ann.	
4. John Nelson.	8. Rachel Jane.	

    5. 320319. Barzilla, b. 2 Apr. 1807[1]; m. 16 Aug. 1832[7] Sophia Bumgarner[12];
            d. 29 Dec. 1891[1]
            Children (surname Bunnell):[12]

1. Telitha Ann.	4. Sarah J.	7. Margaret C.
2. Rebecca.	5. Sophia L.	8. John A.
3. George W.	6. Susan J.	

    6. 320320. Sarah, b. 1809[1]; m. 27 Nov. 1826 William Cornell[7].

Children (by third wife):
    7. 320759. Benjamin F., b. about 1837[7]; m. 18 Oct. 1857 Sarah E. Bunnell[7].
            Children (surname Bunnell):[7]

1. Mary G.	3. Emma F.	5. Willard E.
2. Eldora.	4. Martha E.	6. Nettie V.

    8. 320760. Samuel R., b. about 1840[7]; m. 2 Apr. 1862 Ellen Turner[7];
            d. 27 Aug. 1863[7].
            Children (surname Bunnell):[7]
            1. William Frank.

    9. 320761. Joshua, b. about 1843[7]; m. 3 Dec. 1863 Sarah V. Cain[7]; d. 30 Nov. 1898[7].
            Children (surname Bunnell):[7]

1. Ina Mary.	2. Charles.	3. Emma.

REFERENCES:

1. Descendants of Stephen Bunnell CB300135 compiled by Nina Osburn Roberts and sent to me in 1967.
2. Mason co, KY, marriages, GS Film 281,849, abstracted and sent to me by Mrs. Bertha Shannon, Salem, OR.
3. *Counties of White and Pulaski, Indiana, Historical and Biographical - 1883*, photocopies of pp. 246 and 283 sent to me by Carole Flannery, Lima OH.
4. Mason co, KY, Tax Book, 1790-1810, on LDS Film #008,400, abstracted and sent to me by Mrs. William S. George, Phoenix, AZ.
5. Adms co, OH, Deeds, Bk 6, pp 393 and 435, abstracted and sent to me by Christine D. Kraft, Lawrence, KS.
6. Ltr. 9 Mar. 1922 from George W. Spencer, Recorder of Deeds, Ross co, OH, to Genevieve R. Vosburgh, Wilkinsburgh, PA, who sent a copy to John A. Biles.
7. CB Database.
8. Ltr. 19 July 1911 to John A. Biles from John R. Bunnell, great grandson of Nathaniel.
9. *Warren County, Ohio, Marriage Records 1803-1834*, compiled by Willard Heiss, Indianapolis 1977.
10. Probate Division, Court of Common Pleas, Clark co, OH. File A-360, filed 6 Nov. 1827, photocopy sent to me by Claude A. Bunnell.
11. *Warren Co. Ohio 1803-1859 Will and Estate Records*, abstracted and sent to me by Mrs. Jane Bailey, Miamisburg, OH.
12. Duncan, pp. 180, 181, 182.

1-3-1-7-3-4   D170   CB310391

JAMES[6] BONNELL (Abraham[5], James[4], Nathaniel[3], Nathaniel[2], William[1]) was born in 1772[1] in Scotch Plains, Westfield twp, Essex (now Union) co, NJ[1]. He was listed as a member of the militia in Essex co in 1793[2]. About 1794 he married (first) _____ _____, who died 20 September 1795[3] of typhoid fever at the age of about 20 years[1]. She was buried in the cemetery of the First Presbyterian Church in Elizabeth, Essex (now Union) co, NJ[3]. He was married (second) by Rev. Menzies Raynor, Rector of St. John's Protestant Episcopal Church, Elizabethtown, to PRUSSIA (TOWNLEY) STACKHOUSE[4], daughter of William and Rhoda (Price) Townley[5,6] and widow of _____ Stackhouse. They settled in the Borough of Elizabeth. Her father died in November 1801[6]. In his will she inherited one-twelfth of the value of the estate to be sold after the death of her mother[6].

On 6 March 1802 James bought a lot in Elizabeth for $550 from Abraham and Mary Cook[3]. It was bounded by the lots of John S. Townley (her brother), Elihue Britton and Jonathan Dayton[3]. On 9 May 1802 he bought an adjoining lot from John S. and Cornelia Townley for $104[3]. None of the records indicate James' occupation, but he must have had a fairly good cash flow. The mortgage records of both Essex and Morris counties show that James and Prussia borrowed money on a number of occasions, mortgaging the same lots several times as security[3].

On 7 January 1805 and again on 19 March 1807 they borrowed money secured by their lots in Elizabeth[3]. In both cases they were called residents of Elizabeth[3]. In January 1808 they sold both lots in Elizabeth to Henry Whitlock[3] and moved to Morristown, Morris co, NJ. By 15 March 1808 they were residents of Morristown, where they owned 5 acres in Morris twp which they pledged as security[3]. On 1 April 1808 they purchased a ¼-acre lot in Morristown from Jabez and Hannah Mill on which to live[3]. In August 1812 they sold the 5-acre lot and a small slice of their home lot in Morristown to John B. Johns[3].

Before 1819 James and his family left Morristown and returned to Elizabeth, where on 1 May they borrowed $250 from John M. Trumbull, using as security 37 and 5/12 perches they had acquired with 72 feet of frontage on the north side of Washington Street[8]. James' father died 5 February the next year. James and three of his brothers shared the balance of the real and personal property after legacies to several relatives were paid[3]. James must still have owned property in his home town of Westfield, for he appears on a tax listing there in 1815[7].

James Bonnel appears in the 1830 census in Elizabeth: 010030001-0000001[3]. The figures representing James and Prussia do not seem accurate as to age, and I am unable to account for the male child of 5 to 10 years. James died 5 September 1830 in Elizabeth in the 59th year of his age[3]. He had written his will on 29 June 1830 appointing his wife and his son William as executors[3]. Prussia died 21 February 1849 in Elizabeth at the age of 83[3], according to the records of the Presbyterian Church of Elizabeth.

Children (by first wife):
    1. 320915. Stephen, b. 28 May 1795[1]; m. (first) 27 Feb. 1817 Jane Dorrington
                Ashward[1]; m. (second) 22 May 1872 Eliza (Bishop) Barber[3];
                d. 28 Dec. 1877[1].
                Children (surname Bunnell)(by first wife):[1]

1. Harriet Wade.	5. Margaret Almira.	9. Samuel Pierce.
2. Jane Elizabeth.	6. Carey Judson.	10. Rachael Naomi.
3. Caroline Amelia.	7. Harriet Maria.	11. George Boardman.
4. William Harvey.	8. James Fuller.	

Children (by second wife):
    2. 320919. Nathan[9].
    3. 320918. James[9], b. about 1803[3]; d. 18 Nov. 1838[3].
    4. 320914. William[9], b. about 1804[3]; m. 10 Feb. 1835 Mary Ann Stites[3];
                d. 27 Nov. 1849[3].
                Children (surname Bonnell): [3,9]
                1. William Harper.
    5. 320917. Charles[9], b. about 1806; d. 21 Jan. 1841[3].
    6. 320916. Benjamin[9] C., b. about 1810[3]; m. _____ _____[3]; d. 2 Aug. 1849[3].

REFERENCES:
    1. Three ltrs containing information extracted by George Boardman Bunnell from a booklet of family records written by his father, Stephen Bunnell.
        Ltr. 13 Feb. 1914 George Boardman Bunnell to Mrs. Nellie Bunnell Lewis, copy sent to me by her daughter Edna Lewis Myers.
        Ltr. 8 Nov. 1954 Maud Bunnell May to Homer E. Baldwin,
        Ltr. 6 Aug. 1957 Maud Bunnell May to Mrs. Celia Fleming, copies sent to me by Homer Baldwin.

2. NJ in 1793, p. 133.
3. CB Database.
4. NJ Marriages, p. 102.
5. Duncan, p. 102.
6. NJ Wills - Vol. X, pp. 451, 452.
7. NJ Tax Lists, p. 298.
8. Essex co, NJ, Mortgages, Book N, p. 66, transcribed and sent to me by Claude A. Bunnell.
9. Ltr. 9 Mar. 1885 from William Harper Bonnell, East Boston, MA, to E. G. Bunnell, LaPorte, IN, son of Carey Judson Bunnell.

1-3-1-7-3-7   D67v   CB310394

ABRAHAM[6] BONNELL (Abraham[5], James[4], Nathaniel[3], Nathaniel[2], William[1]) was born about 1784[2] in Scotch Plains, Westfield twp, Essex (now Union) co, NJ. He may have married as a young man, since he certainly had a daughter. He left his home for parts unknown and had not been heard from for sometime when his father wrote his will in 1817. No further record has been found concerning him. The will of Abraham, Sr., dated 27 September 1817, states: "5th. I give and bequeath unto my son Abraham Bonnel twenty-five dollars if he should return home in three years after my decease, if not it is my will that the said twenty-five dollars be paid to his daughter Julian Bonnel. . . . "10th. I give to my granddaughter Julian Bonnel fifty dollars to be paid out of my moveable estate to her and to her heirs and assigns forever."

Children:
　　1. 320477. Julian.

REFERENCES:
　　1. Will of Abraham Bonnel, docket #3092, A True Copy from the Surrogate of Essex County, NJ, sent to me by Alice Weigand, Spokane, WA, 15 Feb. 1992.
　　2. CB Database.

　　Note: I wonder if he could have been the first husband of the widow Nancy Bunnell who married his cousin Nathaniel Bunnell CB310277 in Indiana as his third wife. It's a very long shot, but there are few candidates to consider. In middle age he MAY have returned to his family by joining some of his siblings in Crawford co, PA. He MAY have met and married a girl 20 years his junior, Nancy (Scowden, IF that was her maiden name). With her he MAY have moved to Indiana and died toward the end of 1834 with his second child by Nancy still unborn. This is a POSSIBLE scenario, but too fanciful for anything but as a stimulus to a line of research.

1-3-1-7-3-9   D171   CB310392

SAMUEL[6] BUNNELL (Abraham[5], James[4], Nathaniel[3], Nathaniel[2], William[1]) was born in 1781[9] in Scotch Plains, Westfield twp, Essex (now Union) co, NJ. On 5 June 1800 he married REBECCA HETFIELD[2], daughter of Daniel and Sarah (Owen) Hetfield[2]. She was born 6

June 1781 in Westfield twp[2]. On 2 March 1802 Samuel Bonnell of Westfield bought a lot in Westfield of 29 square rods for $400 from Pratt Williamson[1]. Samuel Bonnal or Bonnel appears on the tax list in Westfield in 1810, 1811, 1812, 1813 and 1820. In February 1820 Samuel's father died. Under the terms of Abraham's will Samuel shared with three of his brothers all the remaining real and personal property after the payment of bequests to several relatives[4].

In June 1830 Samuel and his family moved to Crawford co, PA, settling one mile northeast of Linesville. He appears in the 1840 census of North Shenango (now Pine) twp, Crawford co: 001100001-00000001[1]. The 1850 census of Pine twp, Crawford co, shows Samuel Bonnell, Sr., age 70 , and his wife Rebecca, age 69, living with their son Samuel, Jr., and their daughter Eliza (Bennett - sic)[1,6]. About 1854 or 1856, after the death of his wife Samuel moved with his son Ezra to Wisconsin[7], where he appears in the 1860 censu in Excelsior, P. O. Baraboo, Sauk co, at age 80, living with his son Ezra and family. The date of his death has not been found.

Children:
1. 320968. Sarah H., b. 1806[9]; m. 21 Feb. 1836 Ansel Denison[9,10].
   Children (surname Denison):[9]
   1. William Hetfield.   2. Phebe.
2. 320973. Jedekiah[9]; b. about 1807?[1]. (Is he the same person as CB010938 Jedde O. Bunnell who married Maria Calkins and had a son William Bunnell?)[1]
3. 320970. Jane, b. 1810[9]; m. Jesse Gilliland[9].
   Children (surname Gilliland):[9]
   1. Amos.   2. Sara.   3. Ezra.
4. 320971. Eliza, b. 1812[9]; never married[9], or married _____ Bennett[1].
5. 320972. Frances H., b. 21 Aug. 1814[1]; m. 21 Feb. 1836 Lewis H. Denison[10]; d. Jan. 1884[1].
   Children (surname Denison):[9]
   1. Rebecca Felicia.
6. 320391. Ezra D., b. about 1815[11]; m. (first) 23 Feb. 1839 Susan Anderson[11]; m. (second) Selinda Kennedy[6,8,11]; d. 8 Jan. 1861[11].
   Children (surname Bunnell):[1,8]
   1. Maria.   4. Frank Wayland.   7. Priscilla.
   2. Ezra Howard.   5. William F.
   3. John E.   6. Gina J.
7. 320969. Mary, b. 1818[1]; m. _____ Bennett[9].
8. 320974. Samuel, b. 6 Mar. 1821[5]; m. 30 Nov. 1850 his cousin Rebecca Hetfield[1,5]; d. 2 Mar. 1895[5].
   Children (surname Bunnell):[1]
   1. Sarah M.   3. Frazee L.   5. Daniel Lee.
   2. Malvina Hattie.   4. Ezra H.   6. Eva R.
9. 320975. Aaron W., b. 13 Apr. 1824[9]; m. 1848[1] Susan Adelia Irons[9]; d. 11 Jan. 1890[9].

Children (surname Bunnell):[1,9]

1. George Irons.   4. Theodore.   7. Malvina A.
2. Rachel R.   5. John W.
3. Martha Ann.   6. Jedekiah (Judson O.).

REFERENCES:
1. CB Database.
2. *The Descendants of Matthias Hatfield*, compiled by Abraham Hatfield, 1954, pp. 114, 115, 116. Sent to me by Mrs. Charles Gardiner, Morton, IL.
3. NJ Tax Lists, pp. 295, 299.
4. Will of Abraham Bonnell, qv.
5. *Directory of Crawford County, Pennsylvania 1879-1880*, Closson Press, Reprint 1998, p. 306, extracted and sent to me by Kathleen Cutshall, Conneaut, OH.
6. 1850 census, Pine twp, Crawford co, PA, abstracted by Ruth C. Duncan.
7. Ltr. 3 July 1911 from George Boardman Bunnell to John A. Biles. Ltr. 6 Aug. 1957 from Maud Bunnell May to her cousin Mrs. Celia Fleming.
8. 1860 census in Excelsior, Sauk co, WI, sent to me by Homer E. Baldwin.
9. Descendants of Samuel Bunnell, Sr., compiled by Homer E. Baldwin.
10. Marriages in Crawford co, PA, Newspapers, copied by Kathleen Cutshall in the Linesville, PA, Historical Society and printed in *The Bunnell/Bonnell Newsletter*, Vol. 18, No. 4, p. 68.
11. Ltr. 5 Sept. 1990 from Sharon A. Brady, San Luis Obispo, CA.

1-3-1-7-3-10   D172   CB310393

WILLIAM[6] BUNNELL (Abraham[5], James[4], Nathaniel[3], Nathaniel[2], William[1]) was born 25 December 1782[1] in Scotch Plains, Westfield twp, Essex (now Union) co, NJ. On 19 August 1805, at the First Presbyterian Church in Metuchen, Middlesex co, NJ, he married MARGARET HAND[2,3], daughter of Robert and Rachel (Whitehead) Hand[3]. She was born in 1787[2]. William appears in the tax lists in Westfield twp, Essex (now Union) co in 1810, 1811, 1812, 1813 and 1815[12].

Littell says they moved to French Creek, PA[3]. This was apparently the French Creek valley in Wayne twp, Crawford co, PA. When they moved they left behind the grave of their first son, buried in the Scotch Plains Baptist Cemetery at the age of 2 years, 10 months, and 9 days. William Bunnell was in Crawford co at least by 1819 when he was listed as one of the first members of the Baptist Church there[4]. He may have been there almost a decade earlier.

When his father died in February 1820, his will provided for William to share with three of his brothers all the real and personal property remaining after specific bequests to various family members[5]. William appears in the 1820 census in Conneaut twp, Crawford co: 31001-1101[2]. In the 1840 census he appears in Summerhill twp, Crawford co: 00101001-00010001[2]. In Summerhill twp William and his nephew Stephen Bunnell (son of his brother James) bought 100 acres of land from Samuel Shotwell[6]. Stephen later sold his share to William[6] and moved to Indiana.

On 29 April 1840 William signed his last will and testament, in which he provided for the maintenance of his wife Margaret:[6]

"In the name of God, Amen. I, William Bunnell of Summerhill Twsp, Crawford County, State of Pennsylvania, being in good health of body and of sound mind and memory (Praised be God for the same) and being desirous to settle my worldly affairs whilst I have strength and capacity, so do make and publish this my last will and testament, thereby revoking and making void all former wills by me at any time heretofore made, and first and principally I commit my soul into the hands of my Creator who gave it, and my body to the earth to be interred in the burying ground of _____ at the discretion of my executors, hereinafter named. As to such worldly estate as it has pleased God to intrust me I dispose of the same as follows:

First- all my lawful debts to be paid. Second- My wife Margaret shall have her maintenance in a good and comfortable manner on the farm where I now live during her lifetime, and further shall be provided with suitable to go about while her health and circumstances will permit. Third-I give and bequeath unto my son Freeman Bunnell the use during his life of the farm on which he lives, it being fifty four acres and a half of the east end of tract No. 742, after his death to be equally divided among his children.

Fourth-I give and bequeath unto my son Israel the west end of tract 742, containing fifty four acres and a half together with the saw mill standing on said tract, to have the use during his lifetime. After his death the widow to have her maintenance during her widowhood, and further, I give and bequeath unto my two sons Freeman and Israel fifty acres of land on tract 741 in north Shenango twsp. to be equally divided.

Fifth- I give and bequeath unto my son Uzal Bunnell 100 acres of land, it being land formerly owned by Samuel Shotwell, and by him sold to Stephen Bunnel and myself, since conveyed by Stephen Bunnell to me, on which my son Uzal now lives, he the same Uzal must pay $100. after my decease to be equally divided among my four daughters or their heirs.

Sixth- I give and bequeath unto my son, Stephen Bunnell, my farm home on which I now live containing 125 acres. My son is to maintain after my decease, his mother- my widow- as is mentioned above.

Seventh- I give and bequeath unto my son Israel one wagon or the amount of $65. to be paid by my son Stephen after my decease if I do not make it to him in my lifetime.

Eighth - I give unto my son Stephen one wagon and one horse.

Ninth- I give and bequeath unto my four daughters all my personal property after my decease to be equally divided, giving to my dau. Clarissa Ann $100. out of the avails in the first place to make her equal with the other three if I do not make it to her in my lifetime; It is understood--and let it be remembered--that my wife, after my decease, has the privilege of living with any one of her children, her support is to be as mentioned above. And further I do constitute and appoint my two sons, Uzal and Israel Bunnell my executors to this my last will and testament--Given under my hand and seal this 29th day of April 1840.   William Bunnell.
Signed in presence of
Daniel H. Vaughan
Walter Strong "

Unfortunately Margaret (Hand) Bunnell died the following year, on 20 March 1841[2]. William married (second) 14 April 1842 HANNAH GEE[4], who was born about 1805[2]. Apparently she was a recent widow with three infant sons. The twins were probably born postumously and may even have been born after her marriage to William Bunnell. The 1850 census in Summit twp, Crawford co, lists William, age 66, with real property worth $2000, Hannah, age 45, born in Vermont, and three boys, Andrew W, age 12, George H. and James H, twins, age 8. The boys were brought up with the surname Bunnell[2,8], although I suspect they were actually sons of her first husband.

William died 13 September 1852, "late of Summerhill twp" and was buried with his first wife in the cemetery of the Seeley/Old Baptist Church in Linesville, Pine twp, Crawford co. Between the time William wrote his will in 1840 and his death in 1852, death had claimed not only his wife Margaret, but also his sons Israel and Uzal, whom he had appointed executors, and three of his four daughters. However, he had never written a new will, and no provision was made for his second wife or her children. Accordingly, the 1840 will was registered in Summerhill twp on 12 January 1853[6]. It would be interesting to know how the estate was actually settled. In some families a situation like that would be a holiday for lawyers. I have no further information about Hannah (Gee) Bunnell.

Children (by first wife):
1. 320941. William D., b. 15 June 1806[9]; d. 24 Apr. 1809[9].
2.   daughter, b. about 1807/8[2]; d. between 1840 and 1852[1,6].
3. 320942. Freeman, b. 1809[4]; m. 11 Feb. 1858 Sophronia (Blaisdell) Lowell[4]; d. 3 Dec. 1864[4].
        Children (surname Burnell):[4]
        1. Charles Franklin.
4. 320944. Israel, b. about 1812, m. _____ _____; d. between 1840 and 1852[1,6].
5. 320945. Uzal, b.about 1814; m. Harriet McClure[11]; d. 30 Sept. 1845[2].
        Children (surname Bunnell):[11]
        1. William Cyrus (or Silas).   2. John McClure.   3. Mary Ellen.
6. 320946. Frances, b. 28 May 1816[2]; m. 13 Mar. 1834 James McClure[10]; d. 10 Apr. 1894[2].
        Children (surname McClure):[8]
        1. Sarepta.   2. Clarissa.   3. Margaret.
7. 320947. Stephen R., b. 18 Mar. 1819[2]; m. 1837 Hannah _____[2]; d. 28 Mar. 1895[2].
        Children (surname Bunnell):[2]
        1. Henry A.   3. Frances.   5. Charles Edward.
        2. Mary L.   4. Hiram Richmond.
8.   daughter, b. about 1820[2]; d. between 1840 and 1852[1,6].
9. 320943. Clarissa Ann, b. about 1822[2]; m. 4 Feb. 1841 George Anson Sherman[10]; d. 13 Jan. 1847[2].

Children (of second wife)(surname Bunnell):
1. 320457. Andrew W., b. 1838[8];
2. 320464. James H., b. 1842[8]; m. Luella Kite[2].
3. 320458. George H., b. 1842[8].

REFERENCES:
1. Death Record of William Bunnell, abstracted from LDS Library Film 909298, Wills, Marriages, Deaths, Crawford co, PA, 1852-1854, abstracted and sent to me by Connie Wilson, El Cerrito, CA.
2. CB Database.
3. Littell, pp. 170, 171.
4. Ltrs. 1 Nov. 1991, 21 Jan. 1992, and 15 Feb. 1992 from Mrs. Alice (Kennedy) Weigand, Spokane, WA.
5. Will of Abraham Bonnel, q.v.
6. Will of William Bunnell, Crawford co, PA, Will Book ?, p. 467, transcription sent to me by Homer E. Baldwin.

7. Obituary of Margaret (Hand) Bunnell in Crawford Democrat, 6 April 1841, photocopy sent to me by Mrs. Alice Weigand.
8. 1850 census, Crawford co, PA, abstracted by Ruth C. Duncan.
9. Gravestone Inscriptions from the Baptist Cemetery in Scotch Plains, NJ, copied by Frederick Conkling, East Orange, NJ, and sent to me by Homer E. Baldwin.
10. *The Bunnell/Bonnell Newsletter*, Vol. 18, p. 68.
11. Ltr. 22 July 1987 from Connie Wilson, El Cerrito, CA.
12. NJ Tax Lists, pp. 295, 300.

1-3-1-7-3-12 D169 CB310390

STEPHEN[6] BONNELL (Abraham[5], James[4], Nathaniel[3], Nathaniel[2], William[1]) was born about 1789[1] in Scotch Plains, Westfield twp, Essex (now Union) co, NJ. On 23 June 1811 at Belleville, Essex co, NJ, he was married (first) by Rev. John Dow to HARRIET BALL[1], daughter of Aaron and Patty (Wade) Ball of Morris co, NJ[2]. She was born about 1791[1]. Stephen appears in the tax lists of Westfield twp in 1810, 1811, 1812, 1813, 1815 and 1820[3].

Under the terms of his father's will in 1820, Stephen and Reuben Woodruff were appointed executors. In the will Stephen was bequeathed the lot of land "with the dwelling house and all the buildings thereon where I now live" in Westfield twp. Stephen also shared equally with three of his brothers in all the real and personal property remaining after the payment of various specific bequests[5].

Stephen appears in the 1830 census in Elizabeth, Essex (now Union) co, NJ: 1001121-000201[1]. His daughter Eliza was married there in August 1830[1]. Within the next few years they left New Jersey and settled in Medina, Medina co, OH, where his second daughter was married in 1835[1]. Stephen appears in the 1840 census in Medina: 00100001-0000001[1].

Their final move was made to the town of Wilna, Jefferson co, in northern New York. By 1850 he was the owner of 400 acres in Wilna[4]. His first wife, "Harriet Bonnell, wife of Deacon S." died 20 January 1849 in her 58th year[4]. She was buried in the Old State Street Cemetery, Carthage, Jefferson co, NY[4]. He married soon for a second time SARAH _____, born about 1805, a native of New York state[1]. They appear in the 1850 census in the town of Wilna, listed as Stephen, age 60, born in NJ, carpenter, wife Sarah, age 45, born in NY, also 21-year-old Carmen W. Hendrickson, farmer[1] (was he Sarah's son by a first husband?). The 1860 census in Wilna shows Stephen, age 71, farmer, with property valued at $2880, and wife Sarah, age 55[1]. Still in Wilna in 1870 the census lists Stephen, age 81, retired farmer, and wife Sarah, age 65[1].

Stephen made his will on 21 September 1871[4]. It can be found in Jefferson co Will Book 13, page 249. It names his wife Sarah and four children: John Bonnell of Worcester, MA, William H. Bonnell of Lancaster, NY, Elsa Wood of the town of Wilna, and Julia Benedict of the Province of Ontario, Canada[4]. I have not found the date of his death or that of Sarah.

Children (by first wife):
    1. 320618. Eliza Eleanor[1], m. 4 Aug. 1830 Jacob A. Wood[1].

2. 320621. Julia[1], m. 5 Aug. 1835 Judson Benedict[1].
3. 320622. John B., b. Oct. 1815[1]; m. (first) Adelia F. Randolph[1]; m. (second) 17 Sept.
   1851 Frances E. P. Whelpley[1].
   Children (surname Bonnell)(by first wife):[1]
   1. Spencer R.   2. Judson B.
   Children (surname Bonnell)(by second wife):[1]
   3. John Jacob.   6. Mary Agnes.   9. William W.
   4. Mary Agnes.   7. Susan A.   10. Williama L.
   5. Harriet F.   8. Sarah H.
4. 320645. William Henry, b. about 1826[1]; m. Sarah Ann _____[1].
   Children (surname Bonnell):[1]
   1. George.   2. Gertrude H.

REFERENCES:
   1. CB Database.
   2. Littell, pp. 32, 33.
   3. NJ Tax Lists, pp. 295, 299.
   4. Ltrs. April 1965 from Earle M. Cass, Cape Vincent, NY, to Homer E. Baldwin.
   5. Will of Abraham Bonnell, q.v.

1-3-1-7-8-2   D173   CB310414

MATTHEW[6] BUNNELL (Daniel[5], James[4], Nathaniel[3], Nathaniel[2], William[1]) was born 7 August 1785[1] in Westfield, Essex (now Union) co, NJ[2]. As a young man he moved west to Butler co, OH. On 1 December 1808, in neighboring Warren co, OH, Matthew obtained a marriage license[3] and was married on 15 December to RUTH FLORA[1], who was born 27 January 1788 in Maryland[1]. They settled in Lemon twp, in or near Middletown, Butler co, OH, where he appears in the 1820 census: 110010-40011[2]. He was a farmer. In 1812 Matthew served as a private in the First Ohio Regiment of Militia[2]. On 4 September 1813 he was mustered in to Capt. William B. Fordyce's company, First Ohio Regiment of Militia, under Colonel Henry Zumwalt[2]. He was mustered out 4 March 1814[2].

In 1828, after the birth of their nine children[2], Matthew and Ruth moved their family from Ohio to a new farm in Section 5, Jackson (now Center) twp, Clinton co, IN[4]. Here he built a log cabin[5]. The first religious meeting in the township was held in his cabin in 1829 by the Presbyterians[4], and the first school was held in a cabin on his farm the same year[4]. In 1830 a schoolhouse was built on Matthew's land[4]. The first election in the county was held in his cabin on Monday, 3 May 1830[5]. Also in 1830, Matthew donated land for a cemetery, still called the Bunnell Cemetery after much enlargement over the years[5].

Matthew Bunnel appears in the 1840 census in Clinton co: 00110001-00001001[2]. In the 1850 census of Jackson twp Matthew Bunnell is listed as 65, born in NJ, a farmer, with property valued at $5600, his wife Ruth, age 62, born in MD, son Aaron 21, born in OH, Aaron's wife Ann J., born in OH, and Aaron's son Charles, 2 months old, born in IN[2,6]. Also living with them was Henry Baum, age 14, born in IN[2].

Matthew died 6 March 1863 at Frankfort, Clinton co, IN[2]. His widow Ruth died 11 April 1870[2]. They were buried in the Bunnell Cemetery[5], the land for which he had donated many years before. The name on their gravestone is spelled BOUNEL[5], a spelling which Matthew seems to have used intermittently with BUNNELL and BONNELL, and which some of his descendants retained.

Children:
1. 320859. John F., b. 15 Sept. 1809[2]; d. 3 Sept. 1830[2,5].
2. 321029. Abigail, b. 22 Apr. 1811[2]; m. 4 Apr. 1833 Albert C. Ayers[2]; d. 27 Aug. 1842[2].
3. 320860. Daniel, b. 27 Apr. 1813[2]; d. 15 Aug. 1833[2].
4. 321030. Amy, b. 30 June 1815[2]; m. 21 Feb. 1835 Joseph C. Wallace[2]; d. 3 Sept. 1868[2]
   Children (surname Wallace):[2]
   1. John U.
5. 320856. Mary Ann, b. 12 Aug. 1817[2]; m. 27 Aug. 1836 William Crips[2]; d. 30 Mar. 1909[2].
6. 321031. Sarah Ann, b. 17 May 1819[2]; m. 21 Feb. 1839 John Berryhill[2]; d. 14 Jan. 1846[2].
7. 320857. Matthew Hugh, b. 12 Nov. 1822[2]; m. (first) 19 Sept. 1844 Mary Louise Kilgore[2]; m. (second) 27 May 1863 Elizabeth Heath[2]; d. 23 Mar. 1896[2].
   Children (surname Bounell)(by first wife):[2]
   1. Thomas Aaron.   2. India J.
   Children (surname Bounell)(by second wife):[2]
   3. William Heath.   4. Harry Matthew.   5. Emery Guy.
8. 321028. Jesse, b. 13 Apr. 1826[2]; d. 24 Aug. 1826[2].
9. 320858. Aaron, b. 11 Mar. 1828[2]; m. 27 Feb. 1849 Ann Jane Gutrey[2]; d. 14 July 1884[2].
   Children (surname Bunnell):[2]
   1. Elizabeth.   3. Edward M.   4. Eva May.
   2. Charles M.

REFERENCES:
1. Duncan, pp. 103, 104.
2. CB Database.
3. Index to Marriage and License Books, Warren co, OH, 1803-1834, sent to me by Eileen Bunnell Findling, Windfall, IN.
4. *History of Clinton County, Indiana,* Inter-State Publishing Co., 1886, pp. 598, 599, photocopies sent to me by Mrs. Max Sullivan, Delphi, IN.
5. *Frankfort Morning Times,* Sunday, 31 May 1925, and Sunday, 23 Feb. 1930, *Stories of the Town and the Country Round,* by Ed N. Thacher, photo copies sent to me by Mrs. Max Sullivan.
6. Ltr. 25 June 1996 from Mrs. Max Sullivan.

SIXTH GENERATION

1-3-1-7-8-4   CB310417

NOAH[6] BUNNELL (Daniel[5], James[4], Nathaniel[3], Nathaniel[2], William[1]) was born in April 1794[1] in Westfield twp, Essex (now Union) co, NJ[4]. While Noah was still an infant the family moved to Lexington, Fayette co, KY[2]. After a year or so they moved on to southwest Ohio, where his father met an untimely death in 1798[2]. The widowed mother settled in Warren co, OH, where Noah grew to manhood. On 15 February 1811, in Warren co, Noah chose George Harrisbarger as his guardian[1]. He served as a private in the War of 1812 under Colonel Zumwalt in the 2nd Regiment, Ohio Militia[3,4].

Noah married CATHERINE CONLEY on 18 December 1820 in Warren co[4,5]. She was born about 1800 in Maryland[3,4], daughter of James Y. Conley. In 1823 Noah was a trustee in Clear Creek twp, Warren co[6]. He was a wheelwright by trade[3]. In 1828 they removed to Clinton co, IN, where they settled on Section 8, Jackson (now Center) twp[7]. They soon moved to Owen twp, Clinton co, near the village of Jefferson, where Noah erected a log cabin and cleared the farm where he would spend the rest of his life[3]. Noah appears in the Clinton co census in 1830: 110001-110001[4] and in 1840: 0102001-0010001[4]. Noah and Catherine appear in the census in Owen twp, Clinton co, in 1850, 1860 and 1870[4]. In 1850 their youngest son Noah Livy was still with them at age 19[4]. He also appeared with his parents in 1860 at age 25 with wife Julia A., age 20[4]. Noah's occupation was listed as farmer throughout the period[4].

Noah died on his farm in Clinton co in 1871[3]. His widow died in 1875[3].

Children:
1. 321026. Harriet, b. about 1822[4]; m. 16 Jan. 1839 Henry Chaney[4]; d. before 1913[3].
2. 320225. Daniel James, b. Jan. 1824[4]; m. 3 June 1846 Mary Ann Kennard[4]; d. before 1913[3].
3. 320246. Seneca, b. about 1826[4]; m. (first) 4 Apr. 1849 Temperance Brown[4]; m. (second) 9 Sept. 1854 Amanda Crane[4]; d. before 1913[3].
   Children (surname Bunnell)(by first wife):[4]
   1. James Herbert.
   Children (surname Bunnell)(by second wife):[4]
   2. Alonzo.   5. Mary Ann.   8. Simeon.
   3. Julia E.   6. Osenia.   9. Howard Brenton.
   4. Harry Thomas.   7. Catherine.
4. 321027. Mary, b. about 1828[4]; d. before 1913[3].
5. 320250. Noah Livy, b. 20 Jan. 1834[3]; m. 7 Jan. 1857 Julia Ann Bell[3,4]; d. 9 Jan. 1920[4].
   Children (surname Bunnell):[4]
   1. Mary C.   3. Elver D.   5. Thomas C.
   2. James W.   4. William Clyde.

413

REFERENCES:

1. *Gateway to the West*, Vol. 2, by Ruth Bowers and Anita Short, 1989, p. 640, sent to me by Mary Katherine DeLong, Belvedere, CA.
2. *Genealogy and History*, 15 Dec. 1947, Washington DC, query submitted by a daughter of Thomas Aaron Bounell, copied and sent to me by Claude B. Mitchell, Muskegon, MI.
3. *History of Clinton County, IN*, by Joseph Claybaugh, 1913, p. 626, sent to me by Mrs Max Sullivan, Delphi, IN.
4. CB Database.
5. Index *to Marriage and License Books, Warren co, OH, 1803-1834*, sent to me by Eileen Bunnell Findling, Windfall, IN.
6. *History of Warren co, OH*, W. H. Beers & Co., Chicago 1882, p. 589, abstracted and sent to me by Marjorie Gibbs, Saratoga Springs, NY.
7. *History of Clinton County, IN*, Inter-State Publishing Co., Chicago, 1886, sent to me by Mrs. Max Sullivan.

1-3-1-7-8-5   D174   CB310415

SAMUEL[6] BONNELL (Daniel[5], James[4], Nathaniel[3], Nathaniel[2], William[1]) was born 25 October 1796[1] in Lexington, Fayette co, KY[2,3]. On 11 February 1811, in Warren co, OH, he chose Adam Keever as his guardian[1]. During the War of 1812 Samuel served as a fifer in Sutton's First Regiment of Ohio Militia[2]. On 20 May 1819 he was married in Butler co, OH by Rev. Matthew G. Wallace to ELIZABETH DICKEY of Amanda, Fairfield co, OH[4,5,6]. She was born about 1799 in Pennsylvania[2].

Samuel appears in the 1820 census in Middletown, Butler co, OH: 002-001-4-1[2] and in the 1830 census there: 120101-10001[2]. On 21 November 1836 he bought land in Butler co, Range 2, Tier 14, Section 15[2], apparently in Lemon twp, where he lived for the rest of his life. He appears in Lemon twp, Butler co, in the 1840 census: 2222001-0010001[2] and in the 1850[2], 1860[2] and 1870[2] census in Lemon twp, where he was a farmer[2]. He died after 1870 in Middletown, Butler co, OH[2].

Children:
1. 320925. James, b. 30 Apr. 1821[2]; d. 17 Aug. 1849[2].
2. 320926. John Carrolton, b. about 1824[2]; m. (first) 26 Jan. 1848 Mary Ann Vail[2]; m. (second) 26 June 1879 Amanda E. (_____) Fisher[2]; d. 20 Mar. 1891[2].
     Children (surname Bonnell)(by first wife):[2]
     James Vail.
3. 320927. Ferdinand, b. 14 June 1826[2]; d. 15 Aug. 1847[2].
4. 320928. Mary Ann, b. about 1828[2]; 24 Dec. 1851 John L. Reed[2].
5. 320929. William, b. 22 July 1830[2]; d. 3 Feb. 1883[2].
6. 320930. George, b. about 1832[2]; d. after 1850[2].
7. 320931. Adam, b. about 1835[2]; d. after 1850[2].

8. 320932. Daniel V., b. 16 Aug. 1837[2]; m. 31 Mar. 1870 Sarah T. Jones[2]; d. 2 July 1903[2].
   Children (surname Bonnell):[2]
   1. Edward F.   2. Charles A.   3. Mary Ann.
9. 320933. Samuel, b. May 1840[2]; d. after 1900[2].
10. 320934. Sarah Elizabeth, b. about 1843[2]; m. 10 Apr. 1864 John N. Harris[2].

REFERENCES:
1. *Gateway to the West*, Vol. 2, by Ruth Bowers and Anita Short, 1989, p. 640, sent to me by Mary Katherine DeLong, Belvedere, CA.
2. CB Database.
3. *Genealogy and History*, 15 Dec. 1947, Washington DC, query submitted by a daughter of Thomas Aaron Bounell, copied and sent to me by Claude B. Mitchell, Muskegon, MI.
4. *Ohio Marriages Recorded in County Courts Through 1820 - an Index*, by Jean Nathan - Ohio Genealogical Society, 1996, p. 114, abstracted and sent to me by Marjorie Gibbs, Saratoga Springs, NY.
5. Marriage records in the Butler co, OH, Records Office, abstracted and sent to me by Roberta W. Iiames, Springboro, OH.
6. Duncan, p. 104.

1-3-1-7-8-6   CB310418

DANIEL[6] BUNNELL (Daniel[5], James[4], Nathaniel[3], Nathaniel[2], William[1]) was born 25 October 1796[1] in Lexington, Fayette co, KY[2,3]. On 15 February 1811, in Warren co, OH, he chose George Harrisbarger as his guardian[1]. On 12 March 1818, in Xenia, Greene co, OH, he was married (first) to ALICE ALBAUGH[4] by Rev. John Sale[5]. They appear in the 1820 census: 1024-001-MFG[3] and in the 1830 census: 211211-100001[3] in Xenia, Greene co.

About 1833 Alice Bunnell died[3], and Daniel married (second) 21 January 1834, in Greene co, ALMA LAREW[5], who was born about 1804 in New York[3]. Daniel was a stonecutter, and on 27 October 1835 he was issued a patent for mills for sawing stone which he designed[3]. He and his family appear in the 1840 census: 2012001-010001[3] and the 1850[3] and 1860[3] census, all in Xenia, Greene co, where his occupation was listed as stone cutter and farmer[3]. Before the next census they moved to Camp Branch twp, P. O. Warrenton, Warren co, MO, where he continued farming[3]. The two youngest daughters were still living with Daniel and Alma when the 1870 census was taken[3]. Son George and family also appear in the 1870 census in Warrenton[3]. Daniel died 10 September 1876 in Warren co, MO[5].

Children (by first wife):
1. 320251. Samuel F., b. about 1819[5]; m. (first) 24 Sept. 1839 Eliza Conwell[5]; m. (second) 3 Feb. 1859 Sarah Jane Krone[3]; d. after 1880[3].
   Children (surname Bunnell)(by first wife):[5]
   1. Oscar Orlando.   2. Norina Marietta.   3. Huldah Alice.
   Children (surname Bunnell)(by second wife):[3]
   4. Abraham Lincoln. 6. Samuel.   8. Ray.
   5. Florence.   7. Ned.

2. 320655. Noah Thomas, b. 23 Sept. 1822[3]; m. 10 Mar. 1846 Sarah Martha Heaton[3];
    d. 31 July 1898[3]
    Children (surname Bunnell):[3]
    1. Thomas Corwin.   5. Nettie Musgrove.   9. Elmer Ellsworth.
    2. Daniel Marion.   6. George William.   10. Clara May.
    3. Martha Alice.   7. Ida Sarah.   11. Charles Vesa.
    4. John Henry.   8. Edward Fuller

3. 320261. Daniel Clayborne, b. about 1824[3]; m. 15 June 1848 Savilla Bowers[3].
4. 320271. John M., b. about 1827[3].
5. 320281. Alica A., b. about 1830[3]; m. 31 May 1850 John M. Seldomridge[3].

Children (by second wife):
    6. 320282. George H., b. 23 Dec. 1837[6]; m. 1863 Mary L. Beeman[6]; d. after 1880[3].
        Children (surname Bunnell):[3]
        1. Alma.   2. Bonnie.   3. Maude.
    7. 320283. Moses Leander, b. 8 Aug. 1840[3]; m. (first) Jan. 1868 Amelia Sweet, div.[3];
        m. (second) 2 Jan. 1871 Emma Stout, div.[3]; m. (third) 24 Oct. 1895
        Eliza Hannah (Brown) Merrill[3]; d. 28 Nov. 1914[3].
    8. 320284. Henrietta, b. about 1843[3]; d. after 1870[3].
    9. 320291. Caroline A., b. about 1848[3]; m. _____ Young[3]; d. after Mar. 1915[3].

REFERENCES:
1. *Gateway to the West*, Vol. 2, by Ruth Bowers and Anita Short, p. 640, sent to me by Mary Katherine
    DeLong, Belvedere, CA.
2. *Genealogy and History*, 15 Dec. 1947, Washington, DC, query submitted by a daughter of Thomas
    Aaron Bounell, copied and sent to me by Claude B. Mitchell, Muskegon, MI.
3. CB Database.
4. *Ohio Marriages Recorded in County Courts Through 1820 - an Index*, by Jean Nathan - Ohio
    Genealogical Society, 1996, p. 114, abstracted and sent to me by Marjorie Gibbs, Saratoga
    Springs, NY.
5. Ltr., 9 Nov. 1960, from Mary S. Maxfield, Washington, DC, great great granddaughter of Daniel
    Bunnell.
6. *The Bunnell/Bonnell Newsletter*, Vol. 13, No. 1, p. 83.

1-3-2-2-1-2   D175   CB310033

JOHN[6] BONNELL (Abraham[5], Abraham[4], Isaac[3], Nathaniel[2], William[1]) was born 16 May 1762[1]
in Bethlehem, Hunterdon co, NJ. (A number of references indicate that this John Bonnell
married Jemima Van Sycle in 1807. However, Paula Sacco has uncovered proof that the
husband of Jemima Van Sycle was a different John Bonnell, #1-3-2-2-4-2, q.v.) At age 19,
during the Revolution, he enlisted in March 1782 in the artillery regiment commanded by Col.
John Lamb, Capt. Thomas Machin's company, New York Line[2,3]. He served in this unit until
the end of the war in 1783, when he was discharged at West Point, NY[2].

After the Revolution he moved west to Virginia. Sometime between 1785 and 1796 John's father, Col. Abraham Bonnell, acquired over 2500 acres of land on the Elk River in Virginia (now WV)[5]. He deed this land to his son John[5]. Whether this was the cause or the result of John's move is not clear. On 8 May 1792, in Harrison co, VA (now WV), John was married (first) by Rev. John W. Loofborough to HANNAH SMITH[2,6]. At that time Harrison co included parts or all of 15 present counties in West Virginia. Of these, only the northern part of what is now Braxton co included any portion of the Elk River.

After about three years of marriage Hannah deserted her husband. Taking their little daughter Sarah with her she ran away with William Asa and lived with him in Cincinnati, Hamilton co, OH. Asa was drowned and she later married William Byers on 25 May 1815 in Scioto co, OH.

On 21 November 1796, in Harrison co, VA (now WV), John signed a power of attorney authorizing his friend Stephen Ruddell Wilson to sell his land on Elk River, "containing two thousand five hundred and sixty acres situate on the Cherry tree fork of Elk river by survey bearing date the first day of July in the year seventeen hundred and Eighty four (It being the same tract of land and premises which his excellency Patrick Henry Esquire Governor of the Commonwealth of Virginia by Patent bearing date the twenty seventh day of December in the year seventeen hundred and eighty five granted unto Samuel Henway in ffee, and which the said Samuel Hanway conveyed in ffee to Colonel Abraham Bonnell and from said Colo. Abraham Bonnell conveyed to me the said John Bonnell in ffee . . .[5].

John married for a second time on 18 December 1797 at New Salem[7] (Fort New Salem?), Harrison co, RHULANA FITZRANDOLPH, daughter of Samuel and Margaret (FitzRandolph) FitzRandolph[7,9]. She was born 13 March 1773 in New Jersey[7,9]. In 1798 John built a cabin in what is now the town of Pennsboro, WV, said to be the first cabin built in the present Ritchie co[4]. Although he was the first settler in that part of then Harrison co, he did not remain long[4]. Precisely where he moved is not clear. He seems to have spent the rest of his life in Harrison co, in all probability in that part of it which was set off as Doddridge co between 1840 and 1850.

On 27 September 1799 John's brother Alexander applied to the court in Hunterdon co, NJ, for the partition of lands in Bethlehem and Kingwood, Hunterdon co, late the property of their father Abraham Bonnell. The land was divided into nine portions and lots were drawn for the shares on 27 September 1800. John received two one-ninth shares, lot numbers 5 and 7[8]. John must have disposed of this land, but I have not seen any further record regarding it.

On 19 May 1818 John applied for a pension based on his service in the Continental Army[2]. The pension, $96 per year, was approved and commenced on 28 January 1819[2]. In June 1820 he testified in court relative to his pension: "I own 82 acres of land but the title is disputed, five acres of which is in cultivation and very little more can be improved. I have a claim for 452 acres of land on Hughes River, on which there is no improvement. I am not in possession. I fear I never will be. 3 cows 2 heifers, Pigs and Hogs 10, one horse, Household furniture and farming Utensils $17.00, debts due me none. I am in debt $65.00. John Bunnell. and the said John also declared as follows. I am by occupation a farmer, but affected with the Rheumatism and unable to work. I have in family residing with me, excluding myself, viz my wife aged 48 years and my children Charles aged 12 and Margaret aged 3 years, not able to earn their living.[2]

SIXTH GENERATION

John Bonnell died 1 April 1823 in Harrison co, VA[2] (now WV). His wife Rhulana was not eligible for a widow's pension since she was not married until after 1795. John's first wife, then Hannah Byers, actually drew a pension as his widow[2]. Rhulana Bonnell survived her husband by many years. Her death occurred on 6 May 1865 in Doddridge co, WV[9].

Children (by first wife):
    1. 320935. Sarah, b. 1793, m. 4 May 1812 Joseph Kester[10].

Children (by second wife):
    2. 320937. Jonathan, b. 14 July 1800[10]; m. 20 Sept. 1825 Elizabeth Maxwell[6]; d. 30 June 1885[9].
        Children (surname Bonnell):[9,10]

1. Jane.	5. Lewis.	9. Charles B.
2. John B.	6. Joshua Hill.	10. Mark W.
3. Sarah K.	7. Samuel Preston.	11. Emma H.
4. David Maxwell.	8. Nathaniel M.	

    3. 320938. Charles, b. 23 Mar. 1808[7]; m. (first) July 1829 Jane Martin[9]; m. (second) 25 June 1872 Rebecca A. Wilcox[10]; m. (third) 24 June 1877 Permelia A. Harvey[10]; d. 9 May 1898[10].
        Children (surname Bonnell)(by first wife):[9,10]

1. Elizabeth.	5. Floyd Neely.	9. Margaret.
2. Leamon Preston.	6. Nancy.	10. Almeda.
3. John B.	7. Rhulana.	11. Benjamin Franklin.
4. William Martin.	8. Jonathan.	12. Samuel Preston.

    4. 320939. Margaret, b. 1817[9]; d. young, after June 1820[9,10].

REFERENCES:
1. Family Bible of Lt. Col. Abraham Bonnell, transcript sent to me by Clement M. Bonnell III, Milford, NJ.
2. Pension File #W6222, John Bunnell, copy obtained from the National Archives and sent to me by Claude A. Bunnell
3. *New York in the Revolution*, 2nd edition, 1898, compiled by James A. Roberts, Comptroller, pp. 63, 64.
4. *Ritchie County in History and Romance*, by Minnie Kendall Lowther, 1990, pp. 115, 423.
5. Transcript of John Bonnell's Power of Attorney granted to Stephen Ruddell Wilson 21 Nov. 1796, copy sent to me by Paula Sacco, Pittsburgh, PA.
6. *Marriage Records Of Harrison County, VA (West Virginia), 1784-1851*, by Earle H. Morris, Pub. Fort Wayne (Indiana) Public Library, p. 18, abstracted and sent to me by Marjorie Gibbs, Saratoga Springs, NY.
7. Duncan, pp. 104, 105.
8. *Partitions of Land, Hunterdon co, NJ*, Book A, pp. 1-9 (Recorded 4 Oct. 1800), abstracted and sent to me by Paula Sacco.
9. Family Group Sheets, John and Rhulana (FitzRandolph) Bonnell, compiled by Paula Sacco.
10. CB Database.

SIXTH GENERATION

1-3-2-2-1-4   D176   CB310016

CLEMENT DuMONT[6] BONNELL (Abraham[5], Abraham[4], Isaac[3], Nathaniel[2], William[1]) was born 4 January 1766[1] in Bethlehem twp, Hunterdon co, NJ. About 1786 or 1787 he married RACHEL WOOLVERTON[2], daughter of Charles and Mary (Drake) Woolverton[3]. She was born 17 April 1766[1]. (Her portrait was painted by her son William C. Bonnell.[4]) Clement appears on the tax list of Hunterdon co in Bethlehem twp in 1789 and in 1790 as "Clemet Bonol".[5] In 1793 he was listed among the militia of Bethlehem twp as "Clemment Bonnel".[6] With his brother Alexander he served as administrator of his father's estate in 1797[7]. He received lots number 1 and 9 in the partition of his father's real estate in October 1800. Clement was a prominent man in his community. He was chosen freeholder of Bethlehem twp in 1798, 1800 and 1801[2]. He was a judge and member of Town Council[12]. He appears in the 1830 census in Bethlehem twp, Hunterdon co, NJ: 010110001-000000001, listed as a tavern owner[7]. They lived at the Old Bonnell Tavern at Clinton, Bethlehem twp, Hunterdon co, which he owned and operated from 1797 until his death[7] on 24 January 1836[1,13]. His wife died 16 February 1836[1]. They were buried in the Bethlehem Presbyterian Church Cemetery[13,14]. The Last Will and Testament of Clement Bonnell, dated 1 April 1834, was proved 4 February 1836, as follows:

"In the name of God Amen. I Clement Bonnell of the Township of Bethlehem in the County of Hunterdon and State of New Jersey, being of sound and disposing mind and memory, calling to mind the certainty of death and the uncertainty of the time therof, and to the end that I may be better prepared to leave this world whenever it shall please God to call me hence, do make and publish this my last will and testament in manner following:-

"First and principally I recommend my soul into the hands of Almighty God who gave it me in hopes of a free pardon and remission of all my sins through the merits of the all-atoning blood of Jesus Christ my Saviour and my body to be interred in the earth from whence it was taken in a decent and Christian-like manner at the discretion of my executor hereinafter named, in a full hope of a joyful resurrection on the last day, and as touching the worldly estate wherewith it hath pleased God to bless me I dispose of it in the following manner.

"First, I order and direct that all my just debts and funeral expenses be paid by my executor hereinafter named as soon after my decease as can be conveniently done.

"Second, I give and bequeath to my wife Rachel, her heirs and assigns my pleasure wagon and harness, one horse such as she chooseth from my stock, one cow to be selected by her from my stock of cattle, and so much of my household goods beds and bedding as she may choose to select, together with twelve hundred dollars to be paid to her by my executor as soon after my decease as the same can be conveniently collected, and if the same shall not be sufficient for her support during her lifetime, then and in that case it is my son William shall provide for her an ample support so long as she may stand in need of it, and in case she should have anything remaining at her decease I would recommend her to give it to her two daughters, all of which bequests are intended to be in lieu of her right of dower in my estate.

"Third. I give and bequeath to my daughter Mary, wife of Joseph Bowlby, her heirs and assigns, the sum of two thousand five hundred dollars, to be paid in two equal annual payments by my executor, the first of which to be paid at the expiration of one year after my decease, and the second to be paid at the expiration of two years from the time of my decease.

"Fourth. I give and bequeath to my daughter Elisabeth, wife of Daniel Carhart, her heirs and assigns, the sum of one thousand dollars to be paid her by my executor in two equal annual payments, the first to be paid at the expiration of one year from the time of my decease, and the second to be paid at the expiration of two years after the time of my decease, and I do hereby exonerate and discharge my soninlaw, Daniel Carhart and his heirs from the payment of all debts and demands due and owing to me at the time of my decease from him, the said Daniel Carhart.

"Fifth. I give and bequeath to my son Abraham, his heirs and assigns, the sum of one thousand dollars to be paid him by my said executor in two equal annual payments, the first to be paid at the expiration of one year from the time of my decease, and the second to be paid at the expiration of two years from the time of my decease, and I do hereby exonerate and discharge my son Abraham and his heirs from the payment of all debts and demands due and owing to me at the time of my decease from him, the said Abraham.

"Sixth. I give and bequeath to my son Charles W. Bonnell his heirs and assigns forever, my farm situate in the township of Bethlehem County of Hunterdon which I purchased of Jacob Anderson.

"Seventh. To my grandson, William Carhart, son of Daniel Carhart, the sum of five hundred dollars to be paid by my executor in two years after my decease. And to my grandson William Bonnell, son of Abraham Bonnell, the sum of five hundred dollars, and to my granddaughters, Catharine Bonnell, Rachel Ann Bonnell and Sarah Bonnell, daughters of my son Abraham Bonnell, the sum of two hundred dollars to each of them, the money to be paid to my grandson and granddaughters in two years after my decease.

"Eighth. All the residue of my estate, both real and personal, not hereinbefore disposed of, I give and bequeath and devise to my son William Bonnell his heirs and assigns forever.

"Ninth. And lastly I do hereby constitute and appoint my said son William Bonnell, Executor of this my last Will and testament, hereby authorizing and empowering him to do all necessary acts for the carrying the same into effect, always recommending to my said children that in case the monies due to me cannot be collected in time to meet the legacies herein specified not to enter any prosecution against my said executor for the payment of the same. Provided he uses all due and legal means for the collection of said debts.

"In testimony whereof I have to this my testament and last Will set my hand and seal this first day of April in the year of our Lord one thousand eight hundred and thirty four.

Clement Bonnell   (seal)

"Signed, sealed, published and declared by the testator to be his last will and testament in presence of us, who in the presence of said testator and each of us subscribed our names as witnesses.

A. W. Dunham

Alex. V. Bonnell

Nehemiah Dunham"[3,10]

Children:

1. 320191. Mary, b. 7 Oct. 1787[1]; m. 24 Feb. 1814 Joseph Bowlby[8]; d. 6 Feb. 1852[11].
   Children (surname Bowlby):[11]

1. Rachel.	4. Dennis.	7. Mary C.
2. Olivia M.	5. Abner Parks.	8. William.
3. Sarah.	6. Elizabeth Carhart.	9. Lydia.

2. 320192. Elizabeth, b. 3 July 1789[1]; m. 16 Feb. 1812, Daniel Carhart[8]; d. 20 Apr. 1863[13].
   Children (surname Carhart):[9]

1. Charles.	4. William.	7. Samuel.
2. Mary.	5. Asa.	8. Joseph B.
3. Abraham.	6. John.	

3. 320196. Dennis, b. 6 Aug. 1793[1]; d. 18 June 1817[1].

4. 320190. Abraham Stockton, b. 14 Sept. 1795[1]; m. (first) about 1818 Lydia Hull Beavers[13], div.[7] ; m. (second) 20 Apr. 1843 Sarah Humes Lusk[13]; d. 4. Jan. 1859[13].
   Children (surname Bonnell)(by first wife):[12]

1. Catherine Beaver.	3. William Moses.	5. Emeline.
2. Rachel Ann.	4. Sarah M.	

   Children (surname Bonnell)(by second wife):[12]

6. James L.	8. Mary K.	10. Joseph Warren.
7. Catherine L.	9. Jane Elizabeth.	11. Susan R.

5. 320194. Charles Woolverton, b. 15 June 1798[1]; m. Abigail VanDorn[14]; d. 4 May 1846[14].

Children (surname Bonnell):[14]

1. Joseph.	4. Susan V.	7. Caroline.
2. Margaret.	5. Clement.	8. Mary Carhart.
3. Sarah Ann.	6. Augustus.	

6. 320193. William C., b. 1 Feb. 1804[1]; m. 9 June 1836 Margaret Hinchman[14]; d. 12 Oct. 1865[1].

Children (surname Bonnell):[13,14]

1. Henry.	2. Clement Hinchman.

7. 320195. Rachel, b. 11 July 1807[1]; d. 16 Nov. 1807[1].

REFERENCES:

1. Transcript of the Clement DuMont Bonnell family Bible, sent to me by Clement M. Bonnell, III, Milford, NJ.
2. Bonnell, pp. X-1, 10, 11, 12.
3. Duncan, pp. 105, 106.
4. *Hunterdon Historical Newsletter*, Fall 1973, p. 5, published by Hunterdon Co. Historical Society.
5. *Hunterdon Co. NJ, Taxpayers 1778-1797*, 1990, by T.L.C. Genealogy, Miami Beach, FL, p. 20.
6. NJ in 1793, p. 196.
7. CB Database.
8. *The Revised Printing of Hunterdon County Marriages 1795-1875*, published in Cooperation With The Hunterdon County Historical Society, 1986, p. 36.
9. *Genealogy of the Carhart Family*, p. 66, copy sent to me by Clement M. Bonnell, III.
10. Last Will and Testament of Clement Bonnell. Three transcripts, one sent to me by Clement M. Bonnell, III, one printed in Duncan, p. 105, and one found in Ruth Duncan's files identified as "transcribed by Raymond Edwin Bowlby, 4324 Belle Vista Drive, St. Petersburg Beach, Florida 33706, 1978."
11. Excerpts from a manuscript *A Bowlby Family in Indiana* by Raymond Edwin Bowlby, B.A., M.A., found in Ruth Duncan's files.
12. Transcript of the Bible of Abraham Stockton Bonnell sent to John A. Biles 16 Oct. 1929 by Addie Watts Crawford, granddaughter of Abraham, together with family records compiled by Mrs. Crawford.
13. Handwritten notes compiled by Hiram E. Deats, Genealogist, Flemington, N. J., photocopied and sent to me by Clement M. Bonnell, III.
14. Bonnell family records collected and compiled by Clement M. Bonnell, III, Milford, NJ.

1-3-2-2-1-5 D177 CB310035

ALEXANDER[6] BONNELL (Abraham[5], Abraham[4], Isaac[3], Nathaniel[2], William[1]) was born 31 January 1768[1] at Bethlehem, Hunterdon co, NJ. He appears in the lists of taxpayers in Bethlehem in 1789 and 1790 as "Alexander Bonol,"[2] and in the New Jersey census of militia in 1793 in Bethlehem twp, Hunterdon co[3]. On 3 January 1793 he married CATHERINE MATTISON[4], daughter of Joseph and Catherine (Bodine) Mattison[5]. She was born 12 January 1770[4].

They settled in Flemington, Hunterdon co, where he became a prominent citizen[6]. With his brother Clement he was an administrator of his father's estate in 1797[5]. In 1799, in the absence of a will, he petitioned the court to divide his father's real estate among the heirs. A committee was appointed, the land was appraised and divided into nine parcels. By lot, each of the four surviving sons was awarded two parcels, and the children of their deceased sister Newell Godley received the remaining parcel[7]. Alexander drew lots number 2 and 3[7]. Alexander held a pew in the Presbyterian Church in Flemington[6]. He was the proprietor of Bunnell's Hotel in Flemington, from which he is said to have made $40,000[6]. Deeds on file in Hunterdon co reflect his many real estate transactions[5,7]. On 21 July 1811 Alexander was initiated into Trenton, NJ, #5 Masonic Lodge[5]. A month later he was demitted to Hiram #25 Lodge in Jersey City, NJ[5].

Alexander died 4 August 1819[1,4] in Flemington, and was interred in the cemetery of the Flemington Presbyterian Church[4]. His will, dated 20 February 1819 and probated 30 September 1819 is as follows:

"For as much as it is appointed for all men once to die, I Alexander Bonnell of Flemington in the county of Hunterdon and State of New Jersey, being weak in body but of sound and disposing mind and memory do make and publish this to be my last Will and Testament   in manner and form following to wit:

"1   My Will is and I do hereby order and direct my Executors and the survivor, to sell and dispose of all and singular my land, tenements, hereditaments and real estate whatsoever and wheresoever, whereof I am now possessed, or may die seized, at their discretion, and I do hereby authorize and empower my Executors or the survivor of them to make execute and deliver good and sufficient title or deed therefore, or for any and every part thereof, conveying the same as fully in all respects as I now hold and may die seized thereof.

"2   I give devise and bequeath unto my dear wife Catherine, the use and occupation of the house and two acres of land, in Flemington aforesaid, which Samuel L. Southard, Esq., lately conveyed to me, for and during her natural life, together with the use of two thousand dollars, to be put out on good security, and the Interest thereof to be paid, to her annually during her life. I also give to her as her own property, two hundred dollars in such house hold and kitchen furniture as she may select. All which I give to her for and in lieu of Dower.

"3   I give unto my two daughters Ten thousand three hundred dollars, to wit, unto Eliza Bonnell five thousand three hundred dollars, and unto Mary Bonnell, five thousand (including all my Bank and Bridge Stock to be taken at Par value, and the residue in money or good obligations) to be paid or transferred to them as soon after my death as possible.

"4   I give and bequeath unto my son Charles five hundred Dollars more than that which he has received to make him about equal to that which I may have advanced to my son Joseph for his education &c.

"5   I give, devise and bequeath all and singular the residue of my estate whatsoever unto my three sons, to wit, Joseph, Charles and Alexander Victor Bonnell, equally between them to have and to hold to them and their respective heirs and assigns forever.

"6   I hereby nominate and appoint my said sons Joseph and Charles Bonnell, Executors of this my last Will and Testament, with full power to carry the same into complete effect. I also appoint my said son Joseph, guardian of the person and property of my said son Alexander Victor Bonnell.

"In Witness whereof I have hereunto set my hand and seal the twentieth day of February A..D. One thousand eight hundred & nineteen.

Signed, sealed, published and
declared by the said Alexander
Bonnell to be his Testament
and last Will, in the presence   Alex Bonnell (seal)
of us
        Rich- Hooley
        W. H. Sloan
        Thos. Gordon"[8]   422

Alexander's widow Catherine appears in the 1830 census in Amwell twp, Hunterdon co: 0-00001001[5]. When the 1850 census was taken, she was living with her daughter and son-in-law, Mary and Alexander Wurts, in Raritan twp, Hunterdon co[5]. She died in Raritan twp 25 May 1854 and was buried with her husband in the Flemington Presbyterian Church cemetery[4,6].

Children:
1. 320472. Joseph, b. 1793[4,6]; d. 13 Oct. 1823[4,6].
2. 320471. Charles, b. 20 Nov. 1795[4]; m. 18 June 1817 Margaret Anderson[4];
   d. 24 Mar. 1830[4].
   Children (surname Bonnell):[4]
   1. Alexander.   3. Mary.   5. Cornelia Catherine.
   2. Ann Anderson.   4. Joseph Anderson. 6. Elizabeth Anderson.
3. 320470. William D., b. 1797[5]; d. 8 Aug. 1813[4,5].
4. 320474. Eliza Ann, b. 14 Dec. 1799[5]; m. 15 Sept. 1829 John M. Mann[5];
   d. 14 July 1851[4,5].
5. 320476. John R., b. about 1800[5]; d. 19 Feb. 1802[4,5].
6. 320475. Mary, b.14 Aug. 1805[4,5]; m. 26 May 1831 Alexander Wurts[9];
   d. 27 Mar. 1892[4,5,10].
7. 320473. Alexander Victor, b. 30 June 1809[4,5]; m. 5 Oct. 1830 Catherine Richmond[5];
   d. 13 Aug. 1872[4,5].
   Children (surname Bonnell):[4]
   1. Alexander.   3. Mary W.   4. Henry Richmond.
   2. Joanna R.

REFERENCES:
1. Family Bible of Lt. Col. Abraham Bonnell, transcription sent to me by Clement M. Bonnell, III, Milford, NJ. Printed in *the Bunnell/Bonnell Newsletter*, Vol. II, No. 2, p. 10.
2. *Hunterdon Co., NJ, Taxpayers, 1778-1797*, by T.L.C. Genealogy, Miami Beach, FL, p. 20.
3. NJ in 1793, p. 194.
4. Bonnell family records collected by Homer Deats, Genealogist, Flemington, NJ. Photocopy sent to me by Clement M. Bonnell, III.
5. CB Database.
6. Bonnell, pp. XVIII-7,8, XIX-1,2.
7. *Partitions of Land, Hunterdon co, NJ*. Book A, pp. 1-9, recorded 4 Oct. 1800. Abstract sent to me by Clement M. Bonnell, III.
8. Will of Alexander Bonnell - transcription sent to me by Clement M. Bonnell, III.
9. *The Revised Printing of Hunterdon County Marriages, 1795-1875*, published in cooperation with the Hunterdon County Historical Society, 1986, p. 36.
10. Newspaper obit, Mrs. Mary B. Wurts, photocopy sent to me by Clement M. Bonnell, III.

1-3-2-2-1-7   D178   CB310198

CHARLES FOSTER[6] BONNELL (Abraham[5], Abraham[4], Isaac[3], Nathaniel[2], William[1]) was born 13 December 1781[1,2] at the Bonnell Tavern in Bethlehem (now Union) twp, Hunterdon co, NJ. In the partition of his father's real estate in 1800, Charles drew lots 4 and 6. in 1803 he essentially traded lot 6 to his brother Alexander in exchange for lot 3[3]. On 16 December 1801, just after his twentieth birthday, he acted as a witness to the will of Nehemiah Dunham of Kingwood twp, Hunterdon co[3].

On 24 October 1818, in Hunterdon co, Charles was married by Rev. Hunt to DEBORAH LEIGH[3,6], who was born 20 August 1789[2]. Charles appears in the 1830 census: 2100001-00110001[3] and in the 1840 census: 00210001-00110001[3], both in Bethlehem twp, Hunterdon co. He kept negro slaves as servants, Silva, and Dinah, whose husband was owned by the Dunham family[4].

Deborah (Leigh) Bonnell died 18[1] (or 25[5]) January 1846[1,5], aged 57 years, 5 months, 0 days[5]. Charles died 8 December 1847[1,5], aged 65 years, 11 months, 25 days[5]. They were buried in Bethlehem Presbyterian Church Cemetery[5].

Children:
1. 320370. Eliza(beth) Ann, b. 1 Sept. 1819[1]; m. (first) 1 Oct. 1838 Joseph Stiger[6]; m. (second) 15 Mar. 1866 Aaron Dunham[6]; d. 17 Mar. 1880[4].
   Children (surname Stiger):[4]
   1. Charles B.   2. Emily A.
2. 320370. Amy[4,6] Leigh[7] (Anna[1]), b. 23 Mar. 1821[1]; m. 10 Nov.1840 Mansfield Hummer[6]; d. 31 Dec. 1894[7].
3. 320372. Samuel Leigh, b. 18 Nov. 1822[1]; m. 7 Oct. 1851 Helen Mar Carhart[7]; d. 21 Feb. 1888[7].
   Children (surname Bonnell):[4,7]
   1. Amy Hummer.   4. Charles.   6. Josephine Carhart.
   2. Alexander.   5. Elmer E.   7. Alexander Carhart
   3. Lily.
4. 320373. Alexander, b. 6 May 1825[1]; m. (first) Emily Van Sycle[7]; m. (second) Sarah R. Dumont[7]; m. (third) 4 Aug. 1879[3] Sarah Jane (Douglas)[3] Rudderson[7]; d. 30 Sept. 1886[7].
   Children (surname Bonnell)(by first wife):[7]
   1. Sarah.   4. Frank Roe.   6. Mary D.
   2. Catherine V.   5. Edith.   7. Charles Van Syckle.
   3. Alexander.
   [CB Database lists another child, Everett Bonnell (1864-187).]
5. 320374. Ichabod Leigh, b. 18 Aug. 1826[1]; m. about 1847[3] Mary E. Yard[7] d. 19 Nov. 1851[1].
   Children (surname Bonnell):[4,7]
   1. Emily C. Y.   2. Samuel L.   3. Ichabod Leigh.

6. 320375. Sarah Leigh, b. 8 Sept. 1829[1]; m. 18 Jan. 1848 Benjamin Chew Bird[7];
  d. 12 May 1896[7].
  Children (surname Bird):[7]
  1. Alexander Bonnell. 4. Mansfield Hummer. 7. Annie Leigh.
  2. Elizabeth Joanna.   5. Byron Clark.   8. Sarah Dumont.
  3. Emma.   6. Isabelle B.   9. Carrie Dunham.

REFERENCES:
1. Bible of Lt. Col. Abraham Bonnell, copied from the records in possession of the late Arthur
    Franklin Bonnell, of Whitehouse, NJ, 30 Nov. 1914 - copy sent to me by Clement M.
    Bonnell, IIII.
2. Deats, Bible of Charles Foster Bonnell.
3. CB Database.
4. Bonnell, pp. XXII-7,8,9, XXIII-3.
5. Deats, gravestones of Charles and Deborah Bonnell.
6. *The Revised Printing of Hunterdon County Marriages, 1795-1875*, published in cooperation with the
    Hunterdon County Historical Society, 1986, p.36.
7. Descendants of Charles Foster Bonnell, compiled and sent to me by Clement M. Bonnell, III,
    6 Feb. 1992.

1-3-2-2-1-8   D69viii   CB310197

ABRAHAM[6] BONNELL (Abraham[5], Abraham[4], Isaac[3], Nathaniel[2], William[1])   Only two
contemporary records appear to refer to this man. His father's family Bible lists his birth on 10
December 1783[1,2], the last of the eight children of Abraham and Elizabeth (Foster) Bonnell.
The other is the record written by Rev. John Hanna who served the Presbyterian church in
Kingwood, Alexandria and Bethlehem, Hunterdon co, NJ: "I married Abram Bonnell & Catherine Rhea
December 30, 1797 of Kingwood."[3,4]

It seems unlikely that Abraham would have been married at 14 years of age. Homer Deats in his
study of the problem questioned the year of birth[2], particularly in light of the eleven-year gap
between the sixth and seventh children of Abraham, Sr. However, the birth date in 1781 of
Charles Foster Bonnell, the seventh child, seems to be supported consistently by other records
throughout his life and death. For Abraham, Jr., to have been born earlier than 1783, it would
require that the order of births in several Bibles would have been wrong, a situation I think
improbable.

I know of no other Abraham Bonnell who could have married Catherine Rhea. Physically and
biologically the marriage would have been possible at age 14, however unusual. With no further
information to work with, only a fertile imagination could devise a story to explain it.

For all practical purposes, the question is moot, since Abraham, Jr., was apparently dead without
issue when the real estate of his father was partitioned by the court in 1799. No further record of
Catherine (Rhea) Bonnell as a widow has been found. Perhaps they were both carried off in an
epidemic.

REFERENCES:
1. Bible of Lt. Col. Abraham Bonnell, copied from the records in possession of the late Arthur Franklin Bonnell, of Whitehouse, NJ, 30 Nov. 1914 - copy sent to me by Clement M. Bonnell, III, of Milford, NJ.
2. Deats, Bible of Charles Foster Bonnell.
3. Record of marriage by Rev. John Hanna, found in the Archives in Trenton, NJ, by Clement M. Bonnell, III, and sent to me by e-mail 22 May 2002.
4. *The Revised Printing of Hunterdon County Marriages, 1795-1875*, published in cooperation with the Hunterdon County Historical Society, 1986, p. 36.

1-3-2-2-3-1   CB310064

SAMUEL[6] BUNNELL (Isaac[5], Abraham[4], Isaac[3], Nathaniel[2], William[1]) was born 22 February 1780[1,2] in Kingwood twp, Hunterdon co, NJ[3]. He moved with his parents, about 1795, to Loudoun co, VA, where he married (first) ELIZABETH DAVIS[1]. She was born in Loudoun co about 1779 or 1780[1], probably daughter of Samuel Davis. The actual marriage date has not been found, but on 29 August 1801 Samuel Davis requested the Circuit Court of Loudoun co to grant a license for the marriage of Samuel Bunnell and Elizabeth Davis[3,4].

About 1805 Samuel and his family accompanied his parents and siblings in the move to Wayne twp, Crawford co, PA. He and his father were listed as early settlers there in the county history[1]. He appears in Wayne twp in the 1810 census: 10010-20010[1]. Before 1813 Samuel and his family were living in Venango co, PA[1]. As early as 1809/10 the children of Samuel Bunnell were among those to be schooled in Venango co[1]. In 1820 he appears in the census of French Creek twp, Venango co: 01011-2111[3].

He is said to have served in the War of 1812[1]. In any case he appears on the 1823 Militia Roster of Venango co, age 42, along with his son Isaac, age 20[1].

Elizabeth (Davis) Bunnell died in Venango co on 19 December 1826 in the 47th year of her life, according to her tombstone in Sandy Cemetery, Polk, Venango co[1]. Samuel appears in the 1830 census, still in French Creek twp: 0000001-11[3]. Samuel married (second) 15 February 1831 (Mrs.?) CATHERINE CRULL, both of French Creek twp[1,3].

In 1836 Samuel was one of the defendants, with his siblings, in the suit to partition the real estate in Guernsey co, OH, left by his father. The property was sold at auction and Samuel received one-eleventh of the proceeds as his share. Venango co records show that Samuel and Catherine were involved in a number of land transactions[5]. They appear in the 1840 census in Sandy Creek twp, Venango co: 000000001-001001[3]. By 1860 they were living in Franklin borough, couty seat of Venango co, where they were listed in the census as Samuel Bundle 80, born in NJ, laborer, $500, with wife C. 71, born in PA[3].

In 1858 a law suit was filed against them for non-payment of a note they both had signed[5]. Samuel died, about 1866[5], before the final judgement was issued in 1869 against Catherine as surviving spouse[5]. Samuel was probably buried in Sandy Cemetery in Polk with his first wife, but no gravestone exists to mark his grave[5]. No record of Catherine's death has come to my attention.

Children:

1. 320478. Isaac, b. 21 Aug. 1802[6]; m. 14 Feb. 1822 Eleanor Cannon[6]; d. 7 Jan. 1883[6]
   Children (surname Bunnell):[3,6]
   1. Elizabeth. 4. Samuel. 7. Louisa.
   2. Jane. 5. Letitia. 8. Sarah Ann.
   3. Eleanor (Ellen). 6. Loretta. 9. Emeline.
2. 320468. Sarah (Sally), b. about 1804[3-census].
3. 320469. Margaret (Peggy), b. about 1805[3-census].
4. 320479. Alfred James, b. about 1806[1]; m. (first) Rachel Ann Canon (or Cannon)[1,3]; m. (second) Hannah _____; m. (third) 27 Jan. 1867 Elizabeth Ellingsworth[3]; d. 7 Aug. 1878[3].
   Children (surname Bunnell)(by first wife):[1,3]
   1. Eleanor. 4. Emily E. 6. Rachel A.
   2. Catherine. 5. Sarah J. 7. Amanda.
   3. Letitia C.
   Children (surname Bunnell)(by second wife):[1,3]
   8. Alfred James Myers.
5. daughter(?), b. 181x[3-1820 & 1830 census]
6. 320480. Emily, b. 13 Aug. 1817[2]; m. 8 Apr. 1834 James Stroble Myers[1]; d. after 1885[1].
   Children (surname Myers):[1]
   1. Samuel B. 4. Frank. 7. James B.
   2. James P. 5. Lauretta. 8. Wilbur F.
   3. Emily. 6. Ella. 9. Charles A.

REFERENCES:
1. *Bunnells of Venango Co., PA* - Rough Draft, typescript by Charlotte Blair Stewart, Windber, PA.
2. Family Group Sheet - Samuel Bunnell, compiled by Elizabeth McCulley, West Point, GA, 26 Mar.1993
3. CB Database.
4. Ltr. 29 Feb. 1996 from Office of Clerk of Circuit Court of Loudoun co, VA, to Clement M. Bonnell, III Milford, NJ.
5. Ltr. 15 Sept. 1998, from Charlotte Blair Stewart.
6. Family Group Sheet - Isaac Bunnell, compiled by Elizabeth McCulley, 26 Mar. 1993.

1-3-2-2-3-2 CB310066

JONATHAN[6] BONNELL (Isaac[5], Abraham[4], Isaac[3], Nathaniel[2], William[1]) was born 13 November 1781 in Kingwood twp, Hunterdon co, NJ[1]. About 1795 he moved with his parents to Loudoun co, VA. In 1802 he was a member of Capt. White's company, Virginia Militia[1]. On 24 December 1807, in Loudoun co, he was married by Rev. John Littlejohn to RUTH MILBURN[2], who was born in Virginia. Jonathan appears in the 1810 census in Loudoun co,

VA: 1021-001[1]. He appears on the roster of Capt. White's co, 2nd Battalion, Virginia Militia, in 1812[1]. He was removed from the roster the following year[1], after which he took his family to Guernsey co, OH, to join his parents there. He appears in the 1820 census in Jefferson twp, Guernsey co: 210010-30010[1] and in the 1830 census in Madison twp, Guernsey co: 1002101-0221001[1]. When his father died in 1834 Jonathan was appointed administrator of the estate. On 5 January 1835 he sold his one-eleventh share in 305 acres of land in Guernsey, owned by his father at his death, to his three oldest sons for $300 each[1].

Jonathan appears again in Madison twp in the 1840 census: 00101001-00112[1]. The Chancery Court in Guernsey co assessed him in March 1845 for failing to appear to settle his father's estate[1]. The 1850 census lists him in Wills twp, Guernsey co, as John Bundle 65, born in NJ, farmer, with wife Ruth 58, born in PA[1]. Their three youngest children were living with them[1].

Jonathan died 16 September 1854 in Benton twp, Monroe co, OH[1], and was buried in the United Presbyterian Cemetery in Brownsville, OH[1]. His widow Ruth appears in the 1860 census living with her daughter and son-in-law Cinderella and Francis Helm in Washington twp, Grant co, IN[1].

Children:
1. 320512. Philo P., b. 1809[1]; m. 20 Oct. 1836 Maria Heskett[1]; d. 7 June 1886[1].
   Children (surname Bonnell):[1]
   1. Mary E.   2. Benjamin F.
2. 320513. George W., b. 1812[1]; m. (first) 30 Oct. 1834 Mary Ann Cox[1]; m. (second)
   Caroline (or Carey) Anderson[1]; m. (third) by 1857 Levina _____[1];
   d. between 1860 and 1870[1].
   Children (surname Bonnell)(by second wife):[1]
   1. Ruth A.   3. Sarah J.   5. John S.
   2. Harriet E.   4. George W.   6. Vachel Thomas.
   Children (surname Bonnell)(by third wife):[1]
   7. James.   8. Philo P.
3. 320514. Theodore M., b. 8 Apr. 1813[3]; m. 18 July 1841 Margaret Elizabeth (Harris)
   Smith[1]; d. 12 Nov. 1894[3].
   Children (surname Bonnell):[1,3]
   1. William Henry.   5. John Milburn.   8. Isaac F.
   2. Nancy Jane.   6. Rebecca R.   9. Malinda C.
   3. Mary.   7. George W.   10. Benjamin Franklin.
   4. Cinderella Francis Ann.
4. 320515. Cinderella, b. 1815[1]; m. 8 July 1843 Francis N. Helm[1].
5.   daughter?, b. 1815-1820[1-1820 & 1830 census]
6.   daughter?, b. 1815-1820[1-1820 & 1830 census]
7. 320519. Julia A., b. about 1823[1].
8. 320520. Jonathan Milburn, b. 14 Nov. 1825[4,5]; m. (first) 8 Apr. 1855 Elizabeth
   Madden[5]; m. (second) 24 Nov. 1868 Mary Margaret (Morgan) Vernon)[5];
   d. 20 June 1911[4,5].

Children (surname Bonnell)(by first wife):[1,6]

1. Sylvanus. 3. Frances Josephine. 5. Scott Alonzo.
2. Maria Louise. 4. Dora (Deborah Ann). 6. Jennie.

Children (surname Bonnell)(by second wife): [1,6]

7. John Edward. 8. William Howard. 9. Hattie May.

9. 320521. Nancy, b. about 1826[1].

REFERENCES:

1. CB Database.
2. Ltr. 29 Feb. 1996 from Office of the Clerk of Circuit Court of Loudoun co, VA, to Clement M. Bonnell, Milford, NJ.
3. Ltr. 4 Feb. 1970 from Mrs. Elmer Webb, Hobbs, NM.
4. Death Certificate, Jonathan Milburn Bonnell, sent to me by Mrs. William Cole, Woodbridge, VA.
5. Obit, Jonathan Milburn Bonnell, in Sidney Times, Sidney, IL, 23 June 1911, sent to me by Mrs. William Cole.
6. Family Froup Sheets, Jonathan M. Bonnell and wives Elizabeth Madden and Mary Margaret (Morgan) Vernon, compiled and sent to me by Mrs. William Cole.

1-3-2-2-3-3 CB310065

DANIEL[6] BONNELL (Isaac[5], Abraham[4], Isaac[3], Nathaniel[2], William[1]) was born about 1785 in Kingwood twp, Hunterdon co, NJ[1]. About 1795 he moved with his parents to Loudoun co, VA. In Loudoun co on 13 November 1809 he maried NANCY THOMAS, ward of William Harned[1]. She was born about 1792[2]. Daniel appears in the 1810 census in Loudoun co, VA: 001-102[1].

In 1815 Daniel moved his family from Virginia to join his parents and most of his siblings in Guernsey co, OH[3]. In 1817 they resided in Madison twp, Guernsey co, where he had bought land from the Zanesville Military District[1]. He appears in the 1820 census in Madison twp: 200010-41020[1] and in the 1830 census in Winchester, Madison twp, Guernscy co, OH: 2300001-0222011[1]. (The town of Winchester, in the township of Madison, was laid out by Daniel's father, Isaac Bonnell. At times it was referred to as New Winchester, but ultimately its name became Winterset, the principal town in Madison twp, Guernsey co, OH.) On 5 April 1833 Daniel paid $20 to William N. and Rachel Smith for lot 14 in the town of New Winchester, Madison twp[1].

In 1834 Daniel inherited one of the eleven shares in the real estate left by his father. He sold his share on 5 January 1835 for $300 to Sarah Thomas of Wheeling, Ohio co, VA (now WV)[1]. (Was she a relative of his wife?) On 29 March 1836 Daniel filed a bill in Chancery for the April term in Guernsey co naming his mother and all of his brothers, sisters and brothers-in-law[4]. The subject of his complaint is not evident. The record indicates that the case was "continued" at each spring, summer and fall term until the May term 1841, when the Bill was "dismissed at Complainant's cost without prejudice"[4]. At the September term 1837 the record notes simply, "Death of Complainant suggested, Continued"[4].

Daniel died 16 April 1837[2] and was buried in the Winterset Cemetery in Madison twp, Guernsey co, OH[2]. His widow Nancy appears in the 1840 census in Madison twp: 01111-0011201[1], and again in the 1860 census with son Isaac and daughter Catherine[1] and in 1870 with daughter Catherine[1]. In 1860 Nancy's occupation was listed as "seamstress"[1]. She died 22 February 1874 at age 82[2] and was buried with her husband in Winterset Cemetery[2].

Children:
- 1. 320482. Helen, b. 1810[1]; m. _____ Bartholomew[3].
  - Children (surname Bartholomew):[3]
  - 1. Seabery.
- 2. 320488. Fanny, b. 1812[1]; d. 183x[1,3].
- 3. 320494. Harriet, b. about 1814[1]; m. 25 Dec. 1832 John B. Shepard[1,3].
  - Children (surname Shepard):[1]
  - 1. Elizabeth.   2. Margaret.   3. John.
- 4. 320495. Herod, b. about 1816[1]; never married[3].
- 5. 320499. Edna, b. 1819[1]; m. _____ Marks[3].
  - Children (surname Marks):[3]
  - 1. Belle.
- 6. 320504. Lindsey T., b. 1820[1]; m. 1 Nov. 1853 Emily McMurry[5,6]; d. 1890[1].
  - Children (surname Bonnell):[1]
  - 1. Laura.   2. Sarah Alice.
- 7. 320505. Catherine S., b. Mar. 1822[1]; never married[1,3].
- 8. 320506. Isaac M., b. about 1823[1]; never married[3].
- 9. 320496. Eveline Hamilton, b. 11 Jan. 1825[3] (or 11 June 1818[1]); m. 22 Apr. 1852 Charles Dwight Marcy[3]; d. 20 July 1881[1].
  - Children (surname Marcy):[3]
  - 1. Mary Almyra.   six others, died young.
- 10. 320500. Mary K.[3]; m. 4 Feb. 1847 Benjamin Clark[5,6].
  - Children (surname Clark):[3]
  - 1. Snowden.   4. Seabury.   7. Arabell.
  - 2. Troy.   5. Jennie.   8. Mina.
  - 3. Antoinette.   6. Emma.
- 11. 320510. Daniel C., b. 1827[7]; m. 21 Feb. 1854 Eliza J. Catherwood[5,6]; d. 1897[7].
  - Children (surname Bonnell):[1,3]
  - 1. Clara Ann.   4. Mary C.   7. Margaret B.
  - 2. Emma.   5. Walter L.   8. Harry F.
  - 3. James T. F.   6. Josephine.   9. Grace A.

REFERENCES:
1. CB Database.
2. *Genealogy - Ohio, The Cross Road of Our Nation*, magazine, Vol. VII, 1966, copied at the El Segundo, CA, Library and sent to me by Ellen Dorn, Manhattan Beach, CA.
3. Bonnell family history - compiled by Elizabeth May Nuttall 1887-1976, granddaughter of Evaline Hamilton (Bonnell) Marcy. Copy sent to me by Ilene Grimes, Cottage Grove, OR.
4. Bill filed in Chancery by Daniel Bonnell 29 March 1836. Photocopy of Chancery record sent to me by Claude A. Bunnell.

5. *Marriages, Guernsey County, Ohio*, abstracted and sent to me by Don Bonnell, Danville, CA, citing Marriage Records 1844-1861 - Roll 894936.
6. IGI-OH 1988, Guernsey county - Marriages.
7. Photo of gravestone of Daniel C. Bonnell, sent to me by Ralph George, San Francisco, CA.

1-3-2-2-3-5 CB310073

JOHN[6] BONNELL (Isaac[5], Abraham[4], Isaac[3], Nathaniel[2], William[1]) was born about 1788 in Kingwood twp, Hunterdon co, NJ[1]. About 1795 he moved with his parents to Loudoun co, VA. Between 1804 and 1808 the family moved again to Wayne twp, Crawford co, PA, and finally about 1813 they settled in Madison twp, Guernsey co, OH. In Guernsey co, on 28 January 1822, John married MARY McCOLLUM[2], who was born in 1800 in New Jersey[1]. He appears in the 1830 census in Madison twp: 110001-10011[1] and in the 1840 census in Wills twp, Guernsey co: 21110001- 0101001[1]. In Wills twp in 1841 he bought 144 acres of land in Section 1, Township 2, Range 2 from John Thompson for $1500[1]. In 1849 he bought an additional 165 acres adjoining from Mary Ann Campbell[1].

John and Mary appear in the 1850 census in Wills twp with all their children except Eliza Jane who had already married[1,3]. The 1860 census of Wills twp lists John 72, born in NJ, farmer, $3300 real estate, wife May 60, born in NJ, and children Charles L. 24, John N 22, and Nancy 19[1]. The 1870 census of Wills twp shows John 82, wife Mary 70 and daughter Nancy J. S. 28[1]. John probably died before 1880, but I haven't seen a record of his death or that of his wife Mary.

Children:
1. 320522. Eliza Jane, b. about 1825[1]; m. 7 June 1842 Wesley Brown[2]; d. after 1880[1]/
2. 320523. Duncan M., b. Mar. 1827[1]; m. about 1852 Elizabeth _____[4]; d. 7 Apr. 1908[1].
   Children (surname Bonnell):[1,4]
   1. John W.   3. Albert.   5. Lemuel B.
   2. Obadiah G. 4. Perry A.   6. Wesley.
3. 320524. Samuel S., b. Oct. 1830[1]; m. 8 Nov. 1855 Elizabeth Ann Bracken[2]; d. 1903[1].
   Children (surname Bonnell):[1]
   1. Francis Marion. 4. Oscar A.   7. James Clayton.
   2. John L. (or S.) 5. Caroline.   8. Alva Anson.
   3. Ida M.   6. Vinton.
4. 320525. Martha A., b. about 1833[1].
5. 320527. Charles L., b. May 1836[1]; m. 1 Jan. 1861 Martha J. Hall[2]; d. between 1900 and 1910[1].
   Children (surname Bonnell):[1]
   1. Mary Rebecca. 3. Ulysses E.   5. Dode P.
   2. Martha Ann.   4. Obadiah Lewis. three others d. bef. 1900.
6. 320535. John H., b. Sept. 1838[1]; m. 9 July 1865 Hannah Jane Thomas[2]; d. 27 Feb. 1912[5].

Children (surname Bonnell):[1]

1. Lura M.	3. Wilbert R.	5. Clementine A.
2. Viola.	4. Irena.	6. Jennie Etta.

7. 320536. Nancy J. S., b. ? (age 11 in 1850[1], 19 in 1860[1], 28 in 1870[1] and 37 in 1880[1]).

REFERENCES:
1. CB Datase.
2. IGI-OH 1988 - Guernsey co - Marriages.
3. 1850 census - Wills twp, Guernsey co, OH. John Bundle and family. Photocopy sent to me by Althea Statum, Catoosa, OK.
4. Family Group Record - Duncan and Elizabeth Bonnell, compiled and sent to me by Don and Mary Jo Bonnell, Dansville, CA.
5. Obit - John H. Bonnell, photocopy sent to me by Elmer A. Bonnell, Warroad, MN.

1-3-2-2-3-6   CB310074

WILLIAM[6] BONNELL , son of (Isaac[5], Abraham[4], Isaac[3], Nathaniel[2], William[1]) was born 18 March 1791 in Kingwood twp, Hunterdon co, NJ[1]. He was about four years old when he moved with his parents to Loudoun co, VA. When his parents moved next to Crawford co, PA, about 1805 William, in his early teens, probably moved with them. If so, he had returned to Loudoun co, VA, by the time he was 20. On the other hand he may have remained instead in Virginia with his older brothers Jonathan and Daniel.

On 31 December 1811 in Loudoun co, VA, William married (first) ANN MILBURN[2]. His brother Jonathan attested their ages.[3]. He was drafted as an orderly sergeant in Capt. Blincoe's company, Virginia militia on 23 August 1814 in Leesburg, VA, and was discharged in Baltimore, MD, on 16 September 1814[1]. William appears in the 1820 census as a farmer in French's Quarter, Fauquier co, VA: 300011-2011[3], and again in Fauquier co in the 1830 census: 2121001-011101[3].

Before 1836 he and his family had removed to Cambridge, Guernsey co, OH, where he was called a resident of the county in the petition for partition of his father's estate. At the auction of the property on 10 September 1836 William bought the two tracts of 160 acres and 145 acres for $1635 and $1765, respectively, and two lots in the Town of New Winchester for $17 and $21.50 (see court record in the article on his father Isaac.) Apparently he sold the two larger properties to William Carlisle for $3800 on 12 April 1837[3].

William's wife Ann must have died sometime in the 1830s, either before or after the move to Ohio. William appears in the 1840 census in Cambridge, Guernsey co, OH: 00111101-00001[3], when the only female in his household seems to have been his daughter Louisa. William married (second) MARGARET ROSS on 10 December 1846 in Guernsey co, OH[4]. She must have died soon after the birth of their only child. He married (third) HANNAH DIXON[1]. A true copy of the Marriage Records in the Probate Court of Guernsey co was submitted with

Hannah's pension application: "William Bonnell and Hannah Dixon. By virtue of a Marriage Licens issued from the Court of Common Please of said County I did on the 15th day of September 1850 Solemnize the Marriage of Mr. William Bonnell with Miss Hannah Dixson. Given under my hand this 5th day of October 1850.

Benjamin Waddle, Minister."[1]

The 1850 census of Cambridge twp, Guernsey co, lists William Bonnel 59 Farmer $2000, born NJ, Hannah 30, born OH, Louise 31, born VA, and Margaret 2[3].

On 18 December 1850 "William Bonnell aged fifty nine years the 18th day of March last, a resident of Cambridge township, Guernsey county," applied to obtain "the bounty land to which he may be entitled under the Act . . . . passed September 28, 1850."[1] This application was not approved[1], and on 22 March 1855 he applied again for bounty land, this time under the act passed 3 March 1855[1]. Land warrant 2246 for 160 acres was issued to him[1]. From his widow's pension application we read "the man who prosecuted and secured the land warrant for her husband before his death was Nathan Evens of Cambridge, Guernsey County, Ohio, and said land warrant was purchased from her husband by Noah Hyatt of the same place."[1]

William was a member of the Cambridge City Council in 1858, when he purchased 5 acres southeast of Cambridge for the city cemetery[3]. He died at Cambridge on 28 December 1858[1].

The widow Hannah Bonnell age 38 appears in the 1860 census in Westland twp, Guernsey co, OH, with her five children Landon 8, Leander 7, Lurie 7, Leicester 5 and Mary 2[3]. She was still in Westland twp when the census was taken in 1870[3]. She applied for a widow's pension on 11 September 1879[1]. By that time she was living in the borough of Washington, Washington co, PA, probably with her son John Leander Bonnell. Her pension, under Certificate #29485, was approved 9 April 1880 for $8.00 per month retroactive to 9 March 1878, to be paid out of the Pittsburgh, PA, Agency[1]. She moved soon from Pennsylvania to New Concord, Muskingum co, OH, where she appears in the 1880 census living with her son Landon[3]. There she remained until her death sometime in the second quarter of 1891[1].

Children (by first wife):
    1. 320537. Ludwell P., b. about 1812 or 1813[3]; m. 23 Nov. 1837 Ann Elizabeth
           Pierce[3]; d. 12 July 1864[3].
           Children (surname Bonnell):[3]

1. Louisa Adelia.	5. Thomas L.	9. Daniel Alpheus.
2. William Amos.	6. Cecilia.	10. child, d. young.
3. Hannah M.	7. Elizabeth.	
4. Herod Dallas.	8. Ludwell.	

    2. 320538. Lemuel L., b. about 1819[3]; m. 31 Mar. 1842 Maria Durrheifer[4]; d. after
           1870[3].
           Children (surname Bonnell):[3]

1. John Fletcher.	3. Charles J.	4. Thomas J.
2. Catherine A.		

    3. 320541. Louisa J., b. about 1819[3]; d. after 1880[3].
    4. 008988. Lewis W., b. about 1822[5]; m. 24 Feb. 1853 Levina A. Sunnefrank[4];
           d. after 1880[3].

Children (surname Bonnell):[3]
1. Louisa.   3. George W.   5. John F.
2. Lemuel J.   4. Theodore David.   6. Margaret E.

5. 320542. Ludlow (Ludlum), b. 1 Aug. 1825[3]; m. (first) _____ _____ [3]; m. (second) 26 June 1873 Margaret Allison[4]; d. 19 Nov. 1893[3]
Children (surname Bonnell)(by first wife):[3]
1. Charles W.
Children (surname Bonnell)(by second wife):[3]
2. Mary A.

Children (by second wife):
6. 320543. Margaret V., b. about 1848[3]; m. 19 Dec. 1870 Thomas J. Cook[3].
Children (surname Cook):[3]
1. Roxie Ellen.

Children (by third wife):
7. 320544. Landon D., b. 16 Sept. 1851[6]; m. 20 Oct. 1874 Emma L. Evitt[4]; d. 15 Aug. 1915[6].
Children (surname Bonnell):[3]
1. William H.   3. Clifford Landon.   5. Lorena.
2. Harry McKinnon.   4. Nellie.   6. May H.
8. 320546. Lurie, b. about 1853[3].
9. 320545. John Leander, b. about 1853[3]; m. 1879 Ada Wilson[3]; d. after 1920[3].
Children (surname Bonnell):[3]
1. John W.   2. child.
10. 320547. Lester (Leicester) Hooper, b. 1 Oct. 1855[3]; m. (first) 1876 Adaline L. Moore[3]; m. (second) 1898 Emma V. _____ [3]; d. 21 Mar. 1937[3].
Children (surname Bonnell)(by first wife):[3]
1. Lenora.   3. Blanche.   4. Charles C.
2. Caroline H.
Children (of second wife)(adopted - surname Bonnell):[3]
5. Edgar Kelsey.
11. 320551. Mary, b. about 1858[3]; d. after 1870[3].

NOTE: The Fauquier co, VA, Marriage Bonds 1759-1854, by Chappelear & Gott, lists the marriage of Lucinda E. Bonnel, daughter of Thomas Bonnel, to George Latham on 11 May 1829. No other record of any sort has turned up, to my knowledge, of this Thomas Bonnel. Two letters from Mrs. Carl Graves, Dover, OH, one to Ruth Duncan on 23 Sept. 1984 and one to me on 7 Sept. 1992, provide additional information about Lucinda (Bonnel) Latham. Mrs. Graves stated that her great grandfather George Washington Latham, b. 28 Jan. 1807 at Hopewell, Fauquier co, VA, married Lucinda Elizabeth Bonnel, b. 13 Nov. 1813, also of Hopewell, Fauquier co on 14 May 1829. They moved from Virginia to Ohio in 183t5. They had 12 children which Mrs. Graves named. Two of them were Laura Louida (sic) and Lemuel Lorenzo.

I wrote to Mrs. Graves and suggested that Lucinda's father might have been William Bonnell instead of Thomas. She replied that when traveling to Fauquier co she found the marriage license of Lucinda and George Latham. It was authorized by her father Thomas Bonnel. "The writing was faded and poor but we feel sure it was Thomas." "She had a brother Lloyd Bonnel, who was a minister, and possible brothers Ludlow and Charles, a printer. They settled in Coshocton County, Ohio, in 1835. To my knowledge, none of the family ever lived in Cambridge, Guernsey co, OH."

For several reasons I am reluctant to discard the possibility that Lucinda was a child of William and Ann (Milburn) Bonnell:

1. William appears in the 1820 and 1830 census of Fauquier co, VA, and Thomas does not. In fact, no other reference to a Thomas has appeared.
2. The 1820 census of Fauquier co listts 2 females under 10 in William's household. One of them was his daughter Louisa. The other could have been Lucinda. The 1820 and 1830 census in Fauquier co indicate the possibility of additional male and female children.
3. If Lucinda were William's child she would have been either the oldest or, more likely, the second child.
4. William had an odd penchant for giving his children names beginning with "L". Lucinda would fit right in.
5. Both families, William Bonnell's and George Latham's, moved from Virginia to Ohio about 1835, the Bonnells to Guernsey co and the Lathams to Coshocton co next door.
6. Ludlow (or Ludlum), the youngest son of William's first family, married his second wife in Guernsey co in 1873, but moved before 1880 to Coshocton co, OH, where he spent the rest of his life.
7. Lucinda Latham named two of her children Laura Louida (Louisa?) and Lemuel Lorenzo. If she were William's daughter, these would seem to be named after her only sister and her next younger brother.

These points are entirely circumstantial, in the face of a single document which appears to name the father as Thomas. However, I felt it should be included in the record for possible further investigation.

REFERENCES:
1. National Archives - War of 1812 Bounty Land and Pension Files - William & Hannah Bonnell, photocopy of the file sent to me by Claude A. Bunnell.
2. Ltr. 29 Feb. 1996 from Office of Clerk of Circuit Court of Loudoun co, VA, to Clement M. Bonnell, Milford, NJ.
3. CB Database.
4. IGI-OH 1988 Marriages in Guernsey co.
5. 1850 census, Guernsey co, OH, abstracted and sent to me by Don Bonnell, Danville, CA.
6. Ltr. 15 Aug. 1996 from Kathy Bonnell, St. Clairsville, OH.

SIXTH GENERATION

1-3-2-2-3-7   CB310075

JESSE[6] BONNELL (Isaac[5], Abraham[4], Isaac[3], Nathaniel[2], William[1]) was born about 1794[1], probably in Kingwood twp, Hunterdon co, NJ. With his parents he moved first to Loudoun co, VA, about 1795, then to Crawford co, PA, about 1805, and finally to Guernsey co, OH, about 1813. On 12 September 1815, in Guernsey co, Jesse was married by E. G. Lee, Justice of the Peace, to RACHEL LIEUZADER[1,3]. She was born about 1796 in Pennsylvania, daughter of Abraham and Leah (Hogue) Lieuzader[2,3]. Jesse appears in the 1820 census in Jefferson twp, Guernsey co, OH: 100010-10100[1], and in the 1830 census in Madison twp, Guernsey co: 110101-011001[1].

In 1835 Jesse sold his one-eleventh share in his deceased father's real estate to William Carlisle for $250[1]. Therefore he did not participate in the partition of the estate in 1836. He appears in the 1840 census in Center twp, Guernsey co: 0011101-0000201[1] and in the 1860 census in Perry twp, Coshocton co, OH, living with George Joy, age 58, born in OH, and his wife Sarah Joy, age 49, born in PA[1]. No information has come to my attention regarding his later life. Further research is required to fill out his life story.

Children (probably):
  1.   Angeline, b. 13 Jan. 1821[4]; m. James Allender[4]; d. Mar. 1885[4].
            Children (surname Allender):[4]
            1. Alexander.   4. John.   6. Emma.
            2. George.   5. Sanford James.   7. C. Albert.
            3. William.
  2. 036820. Simeon, b. about 1825[1]; m. Jemima Warne[1,5]; d. 23 Aug. 1893[5].
            Children (surname Bonnell):
            1. Sarah E.   4. Caroline.   7. Mary Catherine.
            2. Martha A.   5. Emily.   8. James E.
            3. Nancy Jane.   6. George W.
  3. 010140. William A., b. 8 July 1827[6,7]; m. 15 Mar. 1883 Minerva Stewart[1];
            d. 6 Oct. 1889[7].
  others??

REFERENCES:
  1. CB Database.
  2. Pension application of Leah Lieuzader, widow of Revolutionary War veteran Abraham Lieuzader, copy sent to me by Louise Graves, North Canton, OH.
  3. Family Group Sheet, Abraham Lieuzader, compiled by Louise Graves.
  4. Family Group Sheet, James Allender, compiled by Louise Graves.
  5. Will of Simeon Bonnell, photocopy sent to me by Louise Graves.
  6. Ltr. 27 July 1995 from Louise Graves.
  7. Gravestones of William A. and Minerva Bonnell in Cambridge Holiness Church Cemetery, Center, OH, copied and sent to me by Elmer A. Bonnell, Warroad, MN.

SIXTH GENERATION

1-3-2-2-3-9   CB310079

ISAAC[6] BONNELL (Isaac[5], Abraham[4], Isaac[3], Nathaniel[2], William[1]) was born 20 February 1800[1] in Loudoun co, VA[3]. About 1805 the family moved to Wayne twp, Crawford co, PA. Then about 1813 Isaac, Sr., moved his family to Guernsey co, OH. On 10 April 1826, in Ohio, Isaac, Jr., married SARAH LINDSEY[2], daughter of Samuel Lindsey[1]. She was born about 1810 in Pennsylvania[3].

Isaac appears in the 1830 census in Winchester (now Winterset), Madison twp, Guernsey co, OH: 00001-20101[3]. In 1836 he received his one-eleventh share of the proceeds when his deceased father's real estate was sold at auction. He and his wife remained in Madison twp the rest of their lives. They appear there in the 1840 census: 120001-113001[3], and in 1850[3], 1860[3], and 1870[3]. Isaac was a farmer. He died 19 December 1871 age 71. Sarah died 23 May 1873 age 62. They were buried in the Winterset Cemetery in Madison twp, Guernsey co.

Children:
1. 320560. Nancy Jane, b. about 1827[3]; m. 24 Oct. 1849 John Dugan[3].
2. 320561. Ann E., b. about 1829[3]; m. 18 Feb. 1873 James Gardner[5].
3. 320568. John M., b. 28 Jan. 1831[4]; m. 26 Jan. 1854 Elizabeth Orr[5]; d. 14 Dec. 1906[4].
   Children (surname Bonnell):[3]
1. Sarah E.	4. Ellola J.	7. Emma A.
2. Mary C.	5. Ida E.	8. Margaret May.
3. Milton Leicester.	6. Matilda G.	
4. 320569. Joseph L., b. Nov. 1833[3]; m. 6 Mar. 1856 Hannah Turkle[5]; d. after 1900[3].
   Children (surname Bonnell):[3]
1. James H.	3. Alice Violet.	5. Joseph.
2. Susan M.	4. George.	
5. 320570. Mary E., b. about 1836[3]; d. after 1870[3].
6. 320579. William H. H., b. Mar. 1838[3]; m. (first) 14 Aug. 1866 Mary Jane Tettrick[5]; m. (second) 31 Jan. 1884 Hattie A. Oliver[5]; m. (third) 10 Aug. 1892 Fannie Bird[3]; d. 8 July 1918[3].
   Children (surname Bonnell)(by first wife):[3]
1. Thomas E.	3. James W.	4. child, d. young.
2. Harry G.		
   Children (surname Bonnell)(by second wife):[3]
5. Earl Burton.	6. Frank O.
7. 320580. Priscilla A., b. 8 Apr. 1840[3]; m. 11 Feb. 1862 James Henry[5]; d. 15 Oct. 1919[3].
   Children (surname Henry):[3]
1. Mary L. (or E.).	4. William E.	6. James H.
2. Isaac E.	5. Sallie J.	7. Hattie F.
3. George H.		

8. 320583. Thomas C., b. 6 May 1841[3]; m. (first) 30 Mar. 1870 Eliza Jane Boyd[3,4,5]; m. (second) 2 Nov. 1879 Margaret Hursey[3]; d. 18 May 1928[3,4].
Children (surname Bonnell)(by first wife):[6]
1. Clarence L.   2. Thomas Austin.
Children (surname Bonnell)(by second wife):[6]
3. George Harrison.   4. Arlington Roy.
9. 320584. Sarah E., b. about 1844[3]; d. after 1870[3].
10. 320602. Martha C., b. about 1846[3]; d. after1870[3].
11. 320604. Ambrosine L., b. about 1851[3]; m. 31 Aug. 1873 David Ripley Smith[7].

REFERENCES:

1. *The Household Guide and Instructor, with Biographies, History of Guernsey Co., Ohio*, by T. F. Williams, 1882, p. 486.
2. *Marriage License. State of Ohio, Guernsey County*, Vol. A, 1810-1832, by Guernsey co Chapter, Ohio Genealogical Society 1987, p. 3.
3. CB Database.
4. *Cemeteries of Guernsey co, Ohio*, Madison twp, Vol. 9, p. 49, copy sent to me by Clement M. Bonnell, Milford, NJ.
5. IGI-OH 1988 - Guernsey co Marriages.
6. Ltr. 19 May 1990 from Dr. George H. Bonnell, Worthington, OH.
7. *The Report*, Vol. 27, No. 4, 1987, page 192, published by the Ohio Genealogical Society.

1-3-2-2-4-2 D181 CB310430

JOHN C.[6] BONNELL (John[5], Abraham[4], Isaac[3], Nathaniel[2], William[1]) was born 4 April 1778[1], probably in Bethlehem twp, Hunterdon co, NJ[2]. On 20 April 1799 his sister Mercy and her husband Obed Coalman conveyed their share of her deceased father's land in Gloucester co, NJ, to her brother John C. and sister Rachel[4]. John was married on 31 January 1807 by Rev. Holoway W. Hunt to JEMIMA VAN SYCKLE[2,3,8] of Alexandria twp, Hunterdon co[6,8]. She was born about 1787[1], daughter of Richard Van Syckle.

On 6 July 1811 John and Jemima and his sister Rachel and her husband Andrew Fleming sold to George West, Esq., of Burlington, Hunterdon co, the 100-acre tract in Gloucester co which had been willed to their father John by his father Abraham[4,5]. At the time John and Jemima lived in Alexandria twp, Hunterdon co, NJ[4]. Apparently they remained there the rest of their lives. He was chosen Freeholder in 1834, 36, 39 and 40[6].

John appears in the census in Alexandria twp in 1830: 00101001-0112001[2], and in 1840: 000020001-0012001[2]. The 1850 census in Alexandria twp lists John 72, farmer with $7000 real estate, wife Jemima 62 and daughter Hannah 30[2]. The 1860 census, still in Alexandria, lists John 82, wife Jemima 73 and daughter Hannah 46[2].

John and Jemima died in Alexandria, he on 23 June 1861 at the age of 83 years, 2 months and 19 days[1], and she on 18 February 1865, aged 79 years 3 months and 3 days[1]. They were buried in Mt. Pleasant Cemetery, Alexandria twp[1]. His will, dated 14 August 1843, was probated 8 July 1861[7].

Children:

1. 320199. Charles, b. 25 Sept. 1807[2]; m. 25 Nov. (or Sept.) 1835 Sarah M. Quick[2]; d. 20 Apr. 1893 (or 1895)[2].
   Children (surname Bonnell):[2,9]
   1. John H.   4. Theodore R.   7. Minnie (or Amanda) E.
   2. George William. 5. Charles Victor.   8. Edward Alonzo.
   3. Ralph Quick.   6. Peter A.

2. 320198. George W., b. about 1808[2]; m. 30 Oct. 1838 Sarah Beaver[3]; d. 1918[9].
   Children (surname Bonnell):[2]
   1. William.   3. Margaret J.   4. Samuel G.
   2. John G.

3. 320202. Catherine Ann, b. about 1813[2]; m. 17 June 1843 Isaac B. Manning[3]; d. 1893.

4. 320201. Hannah, b. 22 Dec. 1813[1]; d. unmarried 23 Oct. 1865[1].

5. 320200. John Runyan, b. 182x[2]; m. Ann Townsend[2].
   Children (surname Bonnell):[2]
   1. Mahlon.   2. John R.

6. 320203. Mary, b. about 1823[2]; m. Samuel M. Severs[6].
   Children (surname Severs):
   1. Abraham.   2. Frank[6] (Benjamin Franklin??).

REFERENCES:

1. Gravestones in the cemetery of Alexandria Presbyterian Church, Mt. Pleasant, Alexandria twp, NJ, copied and sent to me by Clement M. Bonnell, III, Milford, NJ.
2. CB Database.
3. *The Revised Printing of Hunterdon County Marriages 1795-1875*, published in cooperation with the Hunterdon County Historical Society, 1956, p. 36.
4. Hunterdon co, NJ, Deed Book P, p. 506, recorded 20 Mar. 1812, photocopied and sent to me by Paula Sacco, Pittsburgh, PA.
5. *The Bunnell/Bonnell Newsletter*, Vol. 1, No. 3, pp. 4, 5.
6. *Genealogy of the Bonnell Family*, by Arthur Franklin Bonnell, p. IX-6, typescript sent to me by Clement M. Bonnell, III.
7. Notes on the Bonnell family in New Jersey records compiled by Homer Deats, copied and sent to me by Jerome Hatch, Chicago, IL.
8. Hunterdon co, NJ, Marriages, Book 1, p. 115, abstracted by Clement M. Bonnell, III.
9. *Encyclopedia of Pennsylvania Biography,* Vol. 13, p. 145, by Jordan.

1-3-3-1-1-3   D179   C10098

HENRY[6] BONNELL (Jacob[5], Benjamin[4], ?Samuel[3], Nathaniel[2], William[1]) was born 28 November 1767[1] into a Quaker family living in Mendham twp, Morris co, NJ. He married

ELIZABETH SIMCOCK[4], daughter of Nathan and Charity Simcock[4]. She was born 27 April 1775[4], probably in Mendham. The date of their marriage is given as 21 October 1795 in CB Database[3], citing the Rahway Friends Meeting records in Ancestry.com. However, this marriage does not appear in the Rahway Meeting records printed in the *New ork Genealogical and Biographical Record*[1]. Book A of the Morris County, NJ, Marriage Records shows the marriage of "Henry Bonnet and Mary Simcox" on 22 April 1795 by the Rev. Isaac Price, Mt. Freedom and Mendham. Henry W. Pelch, Madison, NJ, read this entry as "Henry Bonnel" to "Mary Simeon"[6].

It seems that Henry as a young man had drifted away from his Quaker upbringing. I am inclined to believe that the record of the marriage in Morris County is the true record of his marriage even though his bride was incorrectly listed as Mary instead of Elizabeth. Then, a few months later, on 21 October 1795, Henry was dismissed from the Rahway and Plainfield Monthly Meeting[3]. On 21 March 1796 he was one of the founders of the Mendham Presbyterian Church[3] (or was this the other Henry Bonnell of Mendham 1-3-7-7-1-3 CB310283?). Henry and Elizabeth returned to their Quaker heritage and were reinstated together in the Rahway and Plainfield Monthly Meeting on 18 October 1797[3]. They remained devoted to their faith for the rest of their lives.

On 1 April 1797 Henry, with his widowed mother Mary and his sister Mercy Simcock, sold 43.33 acres of land on the bank of the Rockaway River in Roxbury (probably now Jefferson) twp, Morris co, to Israel Canfield and Jacob Losey[7]. The land had been purchased by his father Jacob shortly before his death[7].

In 1804 Henry decided that he could improve his family's situation in life by removing from Mendham to new land in western New York. Accordingly, on 10 October 1804 Henry and Elizabeth sold the 25 acres in Mendham twp which they had purchased from Henry Nichols to Thomas Dell for $300[7]. The Quaker Records of New Jersey has the following: "Removal Certificate. Bunnel, Henry and wife Elizabeth and six minor children: Mary, Mercy, Jacob, William, Charles and Elizabeth from Hardwick to Farmington, 7th of 11 month 1804"[8]. One source says that Henry "came to New York in company with Richard Dell, another Quaker [his cousin - wra], who went to the land-office a Albany and purchased a farm for both of them."[9] Henry settled his family on 55 acres in the north part of Lot 79 in the town of Junius (now Waterloo), Seneca co, NY[10]. Henry cleared the land and built his house on the west side of the highway bounding the lot[10]. He appears in the 1810 census in the twon of Junius (now part of Waterloo), Seneca co, NY: 5101-1201[3]. Some years later he sold the farm to his cousin Richard Dell and removed, about 1815, with his family to the town of Galen, Wayne co, NY, a few miles north of Junius.

The Galen Prepatory Meeting of Friends was organized in conjunction with North Junius about 1810, and in 1815 was organized into a regular monthly meeting at Junius to be held alternately in the Towns of Galen and Junius under the control of a committee from Farmington, Ontario co, NY[11]. Among the first members of the monthly meeting were . . . Richard Dell of Junius and . . . Henry Bonnell . . . of Galen[11]. In 1812 the meeting house was erected on the north side of the turnpike a quarter of a mile west of the intersection at Marengo in the town of Galen[11].

Henry appears in the 1820 census in the town of Galen: 230201-00001[3]. He died in Galen on 28 July 1829, aged 61 years and 8 months[10]. A deed dated 6 December 1833 recorded the settlement of his widow Elizabeth's dower with the heirs[10]. Under its terms, Benjamin Tripp and Mary his wife, William Bunnel and Lucretia his wife, Charles Bunnel and Deanna his wife, Henry Bunnel and Mary his wife, James Bunnel and Hannah his wife, Jacob Bunnel and Daniel M. Bunnel convey to Elizabeth Bunnel land in Galen, Wayne County, a part of Lot 72, containing 53 1/4 acres. The farm is described as bounded on the north by land of Henry Thorn; on the east by lands of James Fish; on the south by the Highway on the south line of the lot; on the west by Levi Watson's land[10]. Elizabeth Bonnel died 17 March 1849 at Galen[10].

Children:

1. 320666. Mary, b. 21 (or 29[10]) Feb. 1796[4]; m. 1 July 1819 Benjamin Tripp[12]; d. 29 July 1849[13].
   Children (surname Tripp):[4]
   1. Mercy B.   4. Priscilla.   6. Margaret G.
   2. Louisa.   5. Henry.   7. Elizabeth B.
   3. Charity W.

2. 320671. Mercy, b. 17 Dec. (or Mar.[10]) 1797[4]; d. 26 Feb. 1815[4].

3. 320681. Jacob, b. 20 Mar. 1799[3,10]; d. before Aug. 1814.

4. 320682. William, b. 5 Sept. 1800[4,10]; m. (first) 1 Sept. 1825 Lucretia Clark[12]; m. (second) 29 Oct. 1869 Antoinette Harwood[3]; d. 28 Apr. 1874[13].
   Children (by second wife):[3]
   1. Inez Josaphine.

5. 320683. Charles, b. 26 Nov. 1801[4,10]; m. 27 Sept. 1826 Deanna Dell; d. 25 (or 5[10]) Apr. 1879[13].
   Children (surname Bonnell):
   1. Rachel Dell.   3. Henry Schooley.   5. Mary T.
   2. Elizabeth S.   4. Phebe Wilson.

6. 320685. Elizabeth, b. about 1803[3].

7. 320686. Nathan, b. 28 Mar. 1805[4,10]; d. 6 Oct. 1822[4].

8. 320693. Henry, b. 14 Nov. (or Jan.[10]) 1807[4]; m. 30 Sept. 1829 Mary H. Dell[12]; d. 22 Sept.[3] 1894[13].
   Children (surname Bonnell):[4,12]
   1. Hannah S.   3. Lucretia M.   5. George Albert.
   2. William Richard.   4. Henry Harvey.

9. 320696. James, b. 8 May (or 7 Apr.[10]) 1809[4]; m. about 1831 Hannah (Dell) Dunham[4,13]; d. 4 Nov. 1836[10].
   Children (surname Bonnell):[4]
   1. Samuel A.   2. Mercy.   3. Lydia M.

10. 320700. Charity, b. 1811[12].

11. 320702. Samuel, b. 9 Apr. 1813[4]; d. 14 Sept. 1815[4].

441

12. 320703. Jacob, b. 3 Aug. 1814[4]; m. 28 May 1834 Sarah Wilson[12]; d. 7 Oct. 1887.
    Children (surname Bonnell):[12]

1. Edna S.	5. Henry.	9. Mary T.
2. Bathsheba.	6. Charles William.	10. George Harvey.
3. Ann C.	7. Amy Ann.	
4. Eliza B.	8. Margaret E.	

13. 320704. Daniel M., b. 11 May 1816[10]; d. 16 Feb. 1841[4].

REFERENCES:

1. Records of Rahway and Plainfield, NJ, Monthly Meeting of Friends, printed in *New York Genealogical and Biographical Record*, Vol. X, 1879, p. 141.
2. NJ in 1793, p. 251.
3. CB Database
4. Records of Junius Friends Monthly Meeting, Seneca and Wayne Counties, NY, published in *National Genealogical Society Quarterly*, Vol. 69, and sent to me by L. Dayl Stout, St. Clair, MI.
5. Morris County Marriage Records, published in the *Genealogical Magazine of New Jersey*, Vol. IV, No. 1, p. 30.
6. "Bonnels not associated with the Chatham and Madison branches of the family, or whose relationship is unknown," abstracted from Deed Books and other documents in Morris co, NJ, by Henry W. Pilch, Madison, NJ, and sent to me by Jerome Hatch, Chicago, IL.
7. Morris County Deeds.
8. Duncan, pp. 107, 108.
9. *Portrait and Biographical Record of Seneca and Schuyler Counties, NY*, Chapman Publishing Co., 1895, p. 449, sent to me by Claude A. Bunnell.
10. *Wills, Deeds and Ways*, by Caroline Syron Valentine, 1926, photocopy sent to me be Philip D. Lacy, New York, NY.
11. *Early History, &c, Town of Galen, Wayne Co., N.Y.*, by Wayne E. Morrison, Sr., extract sent to me by Guilbert Gates, New York, NY.
12. IGI-NY 1988.
13. Ltr. 18 July 2003 from Guilbert Gates, including gravestone inscriptions in the Quaker Cemetery, Nine Foot Road, Waterloo, NY, and the Old Quaker Cemetery at Marengo, Town of Galen, NY.

1-3-3-1-2-1   CB310110

BENJAMIN[6] BUNNELL (Benjamin[5], Benjamin[4], ?Samuel[3], Nathaniel[2], William[1]) was born in 1789 in Westfield Parish, Kings co, New Brunswick, Canada[1,2]. He married (first) SARAH DAY, daughter of John Day[2]. She was born in 1791 in New Brunswick[1,2]. Benjamin was baptized in the Anglican Church in Westfield on 28 April 1827[1]. He was a farmer. They appear in the 1851 census in Westfield, NB, Benjamin age 62, Sarah age 60, with sons Abraham 30, Isaac 25, Samuel 24, Graves 20 and William 17, also their servant Mary Doherty and her 5-year-old son James[2,5].

Sarah (Day) Bunnell died at Westfield Thursday 18 (probably November) 1858 at the age of 68 years[3]. A little over a year later, on 14 December 1859[1], Benjamin married (second) HENRIETTA[5] (HEDDY[1]) _____. She had previously been married to _____ Hay[5]. They appear in the 1861 census in Westfield with his son Charles and her three children, William,

Sarah and Jessie Hay[5]. Benjamin made his will on 2 August 1866[1]. He died at Westfield 10 August 1866[1]. His estate was probated 4 September 1866 by son Samuel and William Buchanan, administrators[1]. His widow survived him.

Children (by first wife):
1. 320711. Mary Jane (Polly), b. 1810[1]; 23 July 1831 Robert French[3].
2. 320705. Ophelia[1,2].
3. 320712. James, b. about 1814[1]; m. Feb. 1837 Mary Lingley[1]; d. 23 Aug. 1877[1,2].
4. 320713. Simeon, b. about 1817[1]; m. (first) 6 Apr. 1834 Prudence Crabb[1]; m. (second) 3 Nov. 1841 Mary Jane Stevens[1]; m. (third) 1848 Eliza Stevens[6]; d. 1 Feb. 1882[1].
    Children (surname Bonnell)(by first wife):[1]
    1. Benjamin H.
    Children (surname Bonnell)(by second wife):[1]
    2. Charlotte.   3. Mary Jane.   4. John M.
    Children (surname Bonnell)(by third wife):[6]
    5. Alfred Ludlow.   8. Frederick Simeon. 10. Charlotte.
    6. Walter.   9. Harry F.   11. Elizabeth.
    7. Freddie.
5. 320714. Benjamin, b. 1820[1]; m. 11 Apr. 1847 Mary S. Cottle; d. 3 July 1891.
    Children (surname Bunnell):[1]
    1. Sarah Elizabeth.   5. James Edward.   8. Charles H.
    2. George Woodbury. 6. Mary.   9. Ann May.
    3. Hannah.   7. Benjamin Frank. 10. Mabel.
    4. Evangeline.
6. 320715. Abraham, b. 1821[1]; m. Catherine _____ [3].
    Children (surname Bonnell):[3]
    1. Fred Wilmot.
7. 320720. Eleanor, b. 1824[1]; m. 3 Nov. 1842 William DeLong[1].
8. 320721. Isaac, b. about 1826[1]; m. 4 Mar. 1848 Martha McLean[1].
9. 320722. Samuel, b. about 1827[1].
10. 320723. Graves William, b. Oct. 1830[1]; m. 19 Sept. 1859 Hannah M. Cottle[1,4]; d. June 1868[1].
    Children (surname Bunnell):[1,4]
    1. William Albert (later Graves William).
    2. Alice M.   3. Ann A.
11. 320724. William, b. 1834[1]; m. (first) 18 Jan. 1874 Sarah Elizabeth Bunnell[1]; m. (second) Livinia _____ [1].
    Children (surname Bunnell)(by first wife):[1]
    1. Mabel.   3. Eva Louise.   4. Henry Steeves.
    2. Ida Adelia.
12. 320726. Henry, b. about 1836[1].
13. 320727. Charles, b. about 1838[1].
14. 320728. Alfred, b. 1842[1].

REFERENCES:
1. CB Database.
2. Family Group Sheet, Benjamin Bunnell and wives Sarah (Day) and Heddy, compiled and sent to me by Paul J. Bunnell, Amesbury, MA.
3. Bunnell and Bonnell references gleaned by Carole Bonnell, Spanaway, WA, in extensive research in Canadian census, church and cemetery records.
4. Ltr. 2 Nov. 1987 from William Bunnell, Concord, NH.
5. 1851 and 1861 census, Westfield Parish, New Brunswick, CAN, abstracted and sent to me by Carole Bonnell.
6. Ltr. 18 Feb. 1992 from Paul R. Bonnell, Saint Lambert, Quebec, CAN.

1-3-3-1-2-2 CB310123

JOSEPH[6] BUNNELL (Benjamin[5], Benjamin[4], ?Samuel[3], Nathaniel[2], William[1]) was born in 1790 in Westfield Parish, Kings co, New Brunswick, CAN[1,2]. On 31 May 1823, in the Anglican Church in Westfield, he married SOPHIA ELIZABETH WARD of Westfield[3]. She was born about 1802 in New Brunswick[3].

Joseph was named in his father's will dated 29 June 1827 in Westfield[1]. They appear in the 1851 census in Westfield Parish as: Joseph Bunnell, age 61; Sophia, age 57(?), James, age 26, Mary, age 17, Affey, age 12, Joseph, age 10, Eliza A., age 7, and an infant, age 1 month old[3]. They appear again in the 1861 census of Westfield: Joseph Bunnell, age 70, born in New Brunswick, farmer, Episcopal; Sophia, wife, age 59, born in New Brunswick; George, son, age 33; Afee, daughter, age 23; and Joseph, son, age 21.

Children:
1. 320736. Benjamin, b. 1824[1].
2. 320739. James, b. about 1825[3] or 1831[1].
3. 320740. Mary, b. about 1834[1,3]; m. 12 Nov. 1856 Robert Porter[3].
4. 320762. George, b. 22 Sept. 1837[1].
5. 320763. Affey, b. about 1839[3].
6. 320764. Joseph, b. about 1841[1,3].
7. 320769. Eliza Ann, b. about 1844[1,3].
8.   infant, b. 1851[3] - Was this their child?

REFERENCES:
1. CB Database.
2. Family Group Sheet, Benjamin and Sarah Bunnell, compiled and set to me by Paul J. Bunnell, Amesbury, MA.
3. Bunnell and Bonnell references gleaned by Carole Bonnell, Spanaway, WA, in extensive research in Canadian census, church and cemetery records.

1-3-3-1-2-3 CB310140

SIMEON[6] BUNNELL, son of Benjamin[5], was born about 1798 in Westfield Parish, Kings co, New Brunswick, CAN[1]. On 29 June 1827 he was listed in his father's will[1]. On 6 April 1834 he married (second?) PRUDENCE CRABB, daughter of John Crabb[2,3]. CB Database concludes that he was the Simeon Bunnell who appears in the 1870 census in Clarkston PO, Independence, Oakland co, MI[1]. Much research is needed to clarify Simeon's life history.

Children:
1. 320772. Abner Benjamin, b. June 1828[1]; m. (first) 14 Nov. 1852 Mary E. Jenkins[1]; m. (second) 14 ? 1878 Phebe Bond[1].
   Children (surname Bunnell)(by first wife):
   1. Ellen Agnes.   2. Martha.

REFERENCES:
1. CB Database.
2. Bunnell and Bonnell references gleaned by Carole Bonnell, Spanaway, WA, in extensive research in Canadian census, church and cemetery records.
3. Family Group Sheet, Benjamin and Sarah Bunnell, compiled and sent to me by Paul J. Bunnell, Amesbury, MA.

1-3-3-1-2-7 CB310141

ISAAC[6] BUNNELL (Benjamin[5], Benjamin[4], ?Samuel[3], Nathaniel[2], William[1]) was born about 1800[3] in Westfield Parish, Kings co, New Brunswick, CAN[1]. On 28 December 1831 in the Anglican Church in Westfield he married LAVINIA KIMBAL of Westfield[1,3]. His residence at the time was in Greenwich Parish[1,3]. She was born about 1810 in Westfield[1].

They appear in the 1851 census of Westfield Parish: Isaac Bunnell, 50, wife Lavinia 42, Elmira 18, Laviniua 16, Isaac 15, Affy A. 14, Mary #. 12, Solomon 10, David 9, Susan 7, Sarah E. 5, Robert 4, and Elain 2[3]. Twenty years later, in the census of 1871, Isaac 72 and Lavina 61 were living in Greenwich Parish with their son David 27 and the three youngest children Elener? 22, Deveber? 21 and Benjamin 20[3]. Isaac's will was dated 5 February 1856[1], but the date or place of his death has not come to my attention.

Children:
1. 320773. Elmira, b. about 1833[3]; m. 1854 William Parker[1].
2. 320774. Lavinia, b. about 1835[3].
3. 320776. Isaac, b. about 1836[3]; m. after 1871 Lydia C. Brown[1].
   & 002765.   Children (surname Bonnell):[1]
       1. Malcolm I.   2. Fred Herbert.
4. 320777. Affy A., b. about 1837[3].
5. 320778. Mary E., b. about 1839[3].
6. 320779. Solomon, b. about 1841[3].
7. 320795. David I., b. about 1842[3].
8. 320796. Susan, b. about 1844[3].
9. 320797. Sarah E., b. about 1846[3]. She was probably the Sarah Elizabeth Bunnell of Greenwich Parish who married William Bunnell of Westfield 1-3-3-1-2-1-13 on 18 Jan. 1874[3].

10. 320798. Robert L., b. about 1847[3].

11. 320799. Elain or Elenor, b. about 1849[3]. This is probably the Ellen Adelia Bunnell of Greenwich Parish who married James H. Parker of Westfield on 8 Feb. 1872[3].

12.   Deveber? (Could this be Deborah?), b. about 1850[3].

13.   Benjamin, b. about 1851[3].

REFERENCES:
1. CB Database.
2. Family Group Sheet, Benjamin and Sarah Bunnell, compiled and sent to me by Paul J. Bunnell, Amesbury, MA.
3. Bunnell and Bonnell references gleaned by Carole Bonnell, Spanaway, WA, in extensive research in Canadian census, church and cemetery records.

1-3-3-1-3-2 CB310150

MOSES[6] BONNELL (Aaron[5], Benjamin[4], ?Samuel[3], Nathaniel[2], William[1]) was born 3 April 1774[1,2] in Mendham, Morris co, NJ[2]. He moved with his parents to Washington co, PA, about 1788. He came back to Mendham for a year and then returned to Pennsylvania[3]. On 22 March 1798, apparently in Washington co, PA, he married HANNAH BUCKINGHAM[2], daughter of William Buckingham[4]. She was born 6 November 1775 in Welsh Tract, New Castle co, DE[2,4]. They moved to Ohio in the early years of the new century[4]. Two letters to him written by his father-in-law William Buckingham survive[1]. One dated 7 October 1804 (or possibly 1809) was addressed to him "Living near the Big Sandy Creek."[4] The other dated 26 September 1814 was addressed to "Butler Co., Farefield[5] twp, Hamilton P. O., Ohio."[4] Moses died on 7 September 1814[4], almost three weeks before the second letter was written.

Moses must have been quite ill before he died since he made his will on 30 August 1814[5]. He was only 40 years old. He appointed his beloved wife Hannah and his brother David as executors[4]. The children were not named. The estate was probated on 5 October 1814 after being appraised by Joseph Potter, Joseph McMacken and John Dixon[4]. It consisted of household goods, farm animals and farm equipment, but no land[4]. Their home in Fairfield twp, Butler co, must have been just north of the border with Hamilton co, since in his will he requested to be buried in the graveyard of the Presbyterian Church at Springfield (now Springdale), just across the line in Hamilton co[5].

After his death Hannah took her children to Montgomery, Sycamore twp, Hamilton co, to be near her brothers Levi and Enoch Buckingham, early settlers there[4]. Hannah Bunnell appears in the 1820 census in Sycamore twp: 113100-02001[5]. She died 7[4] (or 9[2]) September 1844[2,4] in Hamilton co, OH, and was buried on what is now the Fleishman Estate near Cincinnati[4].

Children:

1. 320800. Levi, b. 17 Jan. 1799[2,4]; m. 22 Sept. 1833 Elizabeth L. Hill[2,6]; d. 29 June 1874[2,4].
   Children (surname Bonnell):[4,6]

1. Henry H.	4. Hannah Jane.	7. Ann Elizabeth.
2. John Morea.	5. Catherine.	8. Amelia Maryann.
3. Aaron.	6. Mark L.	9. Frank.

2. 320801. Ann, b. 1 Sept. 1800[2,4]; d. 25 Aug. 1864[4] (or 21 Aug. 1861[2]).
3. 320809. Jane, b. 16 May 1802[2,4]; d. 9 Jan. 1850[2,4].
4. 320817. Aaron, b. 14 Feb. 1804[2,4]; m. 29 Jan. 1837 Margaret Dackey[2,4]; d. 29 Aug. 1882[2,4].
5. 320829. William B., b. 19 Oct. 1805[2,4]; m. 4 Dec. 1834 Harriet Bolser[2,4]; d. 25 Mar. 1847[4,6]
   Children (surname Bonnell):[6]

1. Moses.	3. Courtland F.	5. William Charles.
2. Henry A.	4. Ann Eliza.	6. Sarah Ellen.

6. 320831. Esther, b. 23 Dec. 1807[2,4]; d. 3 Oct. 1813[2,4].
7. 320838. Henry, b. 27 Oct. 1809[7]; m. 30 Oct. 1834 Amelia Mattox[7]; d. 25 July 1870[7].
   Children (surname Bonnell):[7]

1. William W.	5. Albert.	9. Kate.
2. Thomas.	6. Ann Elizabeth.	10. Belle.
3. Mary J.	7. Laura.	11. Margaret Alice.
4. Joseph G.	8. Helen.	

8. 320855. John, b. 18 Oct. 1811[2,4]; d. 11 Aug. 1826[2,4].
9. 320861. Elizabeth, b. 17 Apr. 1814[2,4]; d. 16 Feb. 1815[2,4].

REFERENCES:
1. The Hatfield Family Bible.
2. The Moses Bonnell Family Bible, possessed by Lola Bonnell, Cincinnati, OH, copied and sent to me by Margaret W. Cooke, Springfield, IL.
3. Ltr. 28 Nov. 1855 from Richard Brotherton to Charles Bonnell.
4. *Genealogy of Brotherton, Bonnell Families of Morris County, New Jersey, and Hamilton and Clermont Counties, Ohio*, compiled by Margaret W. Cooke.
5. *Hamilton County - Court and Other Records*, by Cummins, Vol. I, p. 19, abstracted and sent to me by Mrs. Harry Atleson, Cuyahoga Falls, OH.
6. CB Database.
7. Photocopies of the family register in the Bible of Henry Bonnel, sent to me by Marilyn Lynch, Sayre, OK.

1-3-3-1-3-3 CB310151

HENRY[6] BONNELL (Aaron[5], Benjamin[4], ?Samuel[3], Nathaniel[2], William[1]) was born 29 July 1776[1], in Mendham, Morris co, NJ. He moved with his parents to Redstone (now Washington co), PA, about 1788. As a young man he returned to Mendham and remained there for a year[2]. He did not return to his parents' home in Pennsylvania, but moved to Pelham, Lincoln co,

Ontario, CAN, with some of his Brotherton and Schooley relatives and other Quakers from the Mendham Monthly Meeting[3]. At the Pelham Monthly Meeting on 4 February 1801 he married MARGARET BURWELL of Bertie[3], daughter of Adam and Sarah Burwell[3]. He was "of Pelham" when they were married, but soon they moved to Pickering[2] on the north shore of Lake Ontario above Toronto. Here they joined the Yonge St. Monthly Meeting at Newmarket, Ontario, where the births of their children were recorded[4]. Henry was still living in 1832, when he was called the "oldest son" in the partition proceedings of his father's estate[5].

Children:
1. 320867. John, b. 31 Aug. 1803[4]; d. 26 Apr. 1825[4]
2. 320868. Moses, b. 1 May 1805[4]; m. (first) 11 ? 1829 Susan Kester[4]; m. (second) 23 Sept. 1837 Amy (Estes) Brown[4,6].
    Children (surname Bonnell)(by first wife)[4]
    1. Elizabeth.   2. William.
3. 320874. Aaron, b. 3 June 1807[4]; m. 19 Feb. 1835 Lydia Ann Pearson[6].
    Children (surname Bonnell):[6]
    1. John H.   3. Joseph Pearson.   4. Charles A.
    2. Margaret.
4. 320876. Mahlon, b. 17 May 1809[4].
5. 320877. Lewis, b. 1 Aug. 1811[4]; m. Lucy C. Williams[6].
    Children (surname Bonnell):[6]
    1. William H.   3. Ellen Lucy.   5. Jessie.
    2. Mary Elizabeth.   4. Margaret.
6. 320881. Sarah, b. 27 Dec. 1813[4].
7. 320882. Henry, b. 23 Aug. 1817[4].

REFERENCES:
1. The Hatfield Family Bible.
2. Ltr. 28 Nov. 1855 from Richard Brotherton to Charles Bonnell.
3. Marriage Records: Pelham Monthly Meeting Register, abstracted from *The Genealogical Magazine of New Jersey* by Margaret W. Cooke, Sppringfield, IL.
4. Vital records of Yonge St. Monthly Meeting (Newmarket, Ontario, CAN), abstracted and sent to me by Ellen Dorn, Alhambra, CA.
5. *Genealogy of Brotherton, Bonnell Families of Morris County, New Jersey, and Hamilton and Clermont counties, Ohio*, compiled by Margaret W. Cooke.
6. CB Database.

1-3-3-1-3-8   CB310177

BENJAMIN[6] BONNELL (Aaron[5], Benjamin[4], ?Samuel[3], Nathaniel[2], William[1]) was born 12 April 1786[1] in Mendham, Morris co, NJ. While still a small child he moved with his parents to Washington co, PA. In 1820[2] he married RACHEL MONGSMITH[1], daughter of Christian and Ann Mongsmith[1]. She was born 22 November 1803[1]. Benjamin continued to live on the family farm in West Bethlehem twp, Washington co, where he appears in the 1820 census: 00001-00101[2]. The female of 26-45 was probably his mother Ann, though her age was actually

50. He appears again in the census of West Bethlehem twp in 1830: 2200101-00001[2]. In 1831 Benjamin petitioned the county court to have his father's estate appraised and divided among the heirs[3]. The land was valued and appraised at $948.13 1/2 on 27 March 1832, but the court decided that the land could not be beneficially divided[3]. Benjamin then purchased the farm from the other heirs[3], most of whom were no longer living in Washington co. In 1833 he sold 9 acres on Tenmile Creek in West Bethlehem twp to his brother William for $100[2].

Benjamin and his family appear in the 1840 census in Clear Creek twp, Warren co, OH: 10220001-120001[2]. Benjamin died sometime within the next decade and Rachel took her family to a new home in Washington twp, Hancock co, OH, where she appears in the 1850, 1860 and 1870 census. She died 18 April 1889 at Fostoria, Seneca co, OH, probably at the home of her son Christian. She was buried in Fountain Cemetery at Fostoria.

Children:
1. 320883. Aaron, b. 13 Oct. 1820[1]; m. (first) 9 Dec. 1847 Sarah J. Wisner[2]; m. (second) 2 June 1850[2] Asenath Snyder[3]; d. 5 Jan. 1898[4].
   Children (surname Bonnell)(by second wife):[2]
   1. Benjamin Franklin. 4. Jennie. 7. Reuben Americus.
   2. John S. 5. Rulema. 8. Charles W.
   3. Sarah Jane. 6. Edwin E.
2. 320884. Christian, b. 29 June 1822[1]; m. (first) 30 Sept. 1849 Margaret Gorsuch[4]; m. (second) 5 Dec. 1875 Margaret A. Baldwin[2]; m. (third) 30 Oct. 1884 May (Newcomb) Hollopeter[2]; d. 3 Aug. 1906[2].
   Children (surname Bonnell)(by first wife):[2,4]
   1. Ella Mae. 3. Frank. 5. Nellie.
   2. Ida M. 4. Edith. 6. Susan.
3. 320894. Elizabeth, b. 9 Oct. 1824[1]; d. apparently before 1830[2].
4. 320901. Isaac, b. 26 Sept. 1826[1]; m. Mary E. _____[2].
   Children (surname Bonnell):[2]
   1. Charles Edwin. 2. Henry W.
5. 320906. Moses, b. 24 Nov. 1829[4]; m. 30 Nov. 1851 Susan Jane Parkey[4]; d. 7 Apr. 1909[4].
   Children (surname Bonnell):[2,4]
   1. Willis S. 4. Elsie. 7. Emma.
   2. Charles B. 5. Joshua Reansean. 8. Celestia.
   3. Frederick. 6. Jennie.
6. 320913. Nancy Ann, b. 1832[4]; d. after 1870[2].
7. 320920. Mary Ellen, b. 1834[4]; d. after 1850[2].
8. 320921. Barnett Whitlock, b. 8 May 1836[4]; m. (first) 11 Sept. 1859 Mary Ann Carr Gorsuch[2,4]; m. (second) 17 Apr. 1887 Mary E. Crum[2,4]; d. 11 June 1909[2,4].
   Children (surname Bonnell)(by first wife):[2,4]
   1. Jesse W. 3. Mary Ann. 4. Harry.
   2. Frank B.

9. 320922. Susan A., b. 1839[4]; d. after 1850[2].
10. 320923. Sarah Jane, b. 1842[4]; d. after 1860[2].

REFERENCES:
1. The Hatfield Family Bible.
2. CB Database.
3. *Genealogy of Brotherton, Bonnell families of Morris County, New Jersey and Hamilton and Clermont Counties, Ohio*, compiled by Margaret W. Cooke.
4. Family of Benjamin Bonnell, compiled by Hilda Tidman, San Diego, CA, found in the files of Ruth C. Duncan.

1-3-3-1-3-10   CB310188

JOHN[6] BONNELL (Aaron[5], Benjamin[4], ?Samuel[3], Nathaniel[2], William[1]) was born 29 April 1791[1] in Washington co, PA. He married in 1811[2] DEBORAH ARMSTRONG[3,6] (or ALEXANDER[2]), who was born in Ohio[3]. During their married life they moved frequently. John appears in the 1820 census in Richmond, Wayne co, IN: 10001-4001[2], in 1830 in Morgan twp, Greene co, PA: 221011-1010001[2], in 1840 in Jackson twp, Wayne co, OH: 0032101-01012001[2], and in 1850 in Ruggles twp, Ashland co, OH[2]. By 1850 John was a widower, but his youngest son William age 17 and his sister Mary Buckingham age 72 lived with him[2,4]. In the spring of 1850 John sold eighty acres of land in Section 7, Perry twp, Wood co, OH, which he had bought some time previously to James D. Buckingham, his sister Mary's son[4,5]. John died 20 October 1853 in Ruggles twp, Ashland co, OH. He was buried in Orange Cemetery, Nankin, Ashland co.

Children:
1. 320924. Mehetable, b. 16 Mar. 1812[3].
2. 320936. Anne, b. 4 Oct. 1814[3]; m. 15 Mar. 1840 Sylvester Parmenter[2].
3. 320940. Harriet, b. 7 July 1816[2]; m. 1832[2] Adam Horn[3]; d. after 1850[2,3].
   Children (surname Horn):[3]

1. Morgan.	4. Elizabeth.	6. Cephas.
2. John.	5. Maria.	7. Madison.
3. Anne.		

4. 320948. Elizabeth, b. 30 Nov. 1817[3].
5. 320949. Aaron, b. 2 Dec. 1819[3]; m. Hannah Wickery[3]; d. 8 Oct. 1884[3].
   Children (surname Bonnell):[2,3]

1. Morgan.	4. Samantha.	7. Aaron W.
2. Sarah Ann.	5. John Louis.	8. Amos L.
3. Mary.	6. Samuel	9. Frances Flora.

6. 320962. Henry, b. 6 July 1821[3]; m. (first) 27 Apr. 1845 Mary Hiles[2]; m. (second) Mary _____[2].
   Children (surname Bonnell)(by first wife):[2]
   1. Nathaniel
   Children (surname Bonnell)(by second wife):[2]

2. John.	3. Adam.	4. Flora.

7. 320963. Simeon, b. 6 Apr. 1823[3]; Jemima Warne[2]; d. 23 Aug. 1893[2]
    Children (surname Bonnell):[2]

1. Sarah E.	4. Caroline.	7. Mary Catherine.
2. Martha A.	5. Emily.	8. James E.
3. Nancy Jane.	6. George W.	

8. 320966. Joanna M., b. 16 May 1825, "Perry twp, Wood co, OH"[6]; m. 27 Feb. 1848 John Sherid Hatfield[6]; d. 1 Oct. 1886[6]
    Children (surname Hatfield):[6]

1. Job.	5. Nathan.	9. William.
2. Theodore.	6. Viola.	10. ViRena.
3. Mary C.	7. Clark.	11. Susan.
4. Evaline.	8. Charles.	

9. 320967. David, b. 18 May 1827[3].
10. 320976. John A., b. 31 Oct. 1828[3]; m. 27 Feb. 1853 Charlotte Bronson[2]; d. 10 Oct. 1892[2].
    Children (surname Bonnell):[2]

1. Charles.	2. Ida.	3. William H.

11. 320983. Eunice, b. 21 Jan. 1831[3].
12. 320984. William S., b. 21 July 1833[3]; d. after 1900[2].

REFERENCES:
1. The Hatfield Family Bible.
2. CB Database.
3. *Genealogy of Brotherton, Bonnell Families of Morris County, New Jersey and Hamilton and Clermont Counties, Ohio*, compiled by Margaret W. Cooke.
4. Ltr. 26 Dec. 1990 from Mary Burdick, Watertown, MA.
5. *Commemorative & Biographical Record of Wood County, OH*, Beers 1897, p. 1068, photocopy sent to me by Mary Burdick.
6. Family Group Sheet, John Sherid and Joanna M. (Bonnell) Hatfield, compiled by Mrs. Ruth (England) Amer, Medford, OR, owner of the Hatfield Family Bible.

1-3-3-1-3-12   CB310195

DAVID[6] BONNELL (Aaron[5], Benjamin[4], ?Samuel[3], Nathaniel[2], William[1]) was born 17 June 1795[1] in Washington co, PA. No further information has been learned about him. Whether he died in infancy or later, he was not mentioned in the legal proceedings of 1831 and 1832 to partition his father's estate. He must have been dead without issue then.

REFERENCES:
1. The Hatfield Family Bible.

1-3-3-1-3-13   CB310196

WILLIAM[6] BONNELL (Aaron[5], Benjamin[4], ?Samuel[3], Nathaniel[2], William[1]) was born 28 July 1797[1] in Washington co, PA. About 1823[2] he married REBECCA McGINNIS[2] who was born 19 June 1803 in Pennsylvania[2]. She was the daughter of John and Sarah (Clark) McGinnis[2].

They appear in the 1830 census in West Bethlehem twp, Washington co, PA: 100001-2100101[3]. On 6 Sept. 1833 William bought 9 acres on Tenmile Creek in West Bethlehem twp from his brother Benjamin for $100[3].

Before 1836 they removed to Massillon, Stark co, OH, where their sons John and George were born[3]. They remained in Ohio only a few years, and in the fall of 1838 they moved again to Pike twp, Jay co, IN[4]. There they cleared 80 acres and built a home in the dense forest about a half mile south of the present site of Collett[4]. William appears in Pike twp in the 1840 census: 3110001-002101[3] and in the 1850 census with his wife Rebecca and their children, Henry, John, George, Lewis, Mary Ellen and Susan[3]. William was called a farmer in 1850[3], but in the 1860 census of Pike twp he was listed as a shoemaker[3]. The following year they sold the original homestead and bought a home inb Section 1, Pike twp[4], where Rebecca died in 1862[4]. William subsequently sold his home in Pike twp and went to Kansas. Later he returned to Indiana, and in 1875 he died at the home of his daughter Mrs. Hannah Mays in Pike twp[4].

Children:
1. 320985. Hannah, b. 5 May 1824[5]; m. 6 Jan. 1846 Thomas Jefferson Mays[5]; d. 18 Jan. 1902[5].
    Children (surname Mays):[5]

1. John S.	4. Catharine or	6. Thomas Jefferson.
2. Rebecca.	Caroline H.	7. Hannah.
3. William Bonnel.	5. Sarah E.	8. Henry.

2. 320986. Sarah, b. 182x[5]; m. _____ Ralph[5]; d. before 1877[5].
3. 320987. Elizabeth, b.1827[3]; m. 24 Nov. 1850 Alexander Garinger[3]; d. after 1877[5].
    Children (surname Garinger):[3]

1. George.	2. Mary	others?

4. 320988. Henry, b. about 1830[3]; m. Margaretta _____ [3]; d. 6 Apr. 1863[3].
5. 320989. John M., b. 6 Apr. 1836[3]; m. 17 Apr. 1859 Susanna Jane Collins[3]; d. 19 June 1917[3].
    Children (surname Bonnell):[3]

1. Melissa Ellen.	4. John Harrison.	7. Albert W.
2. William Riley.	5. Estella Glendora.	8. Susanna I.
3. George Henry.	6. Amelia C. Rosella.	

6. 320990. George W., b. 18 Mar. 1838[3]; m. 15 June 1906 Elizabeth Jane Summerville[3]; d. 23 Apr. 1891[3].
    Children (surname Bonnell):[3]
    1. Ada M.
7. 320991. Lewis B., b. 11 May 1840[4]; m. 4 June 1868 Angeline Henry[3,4]; d. 22 Oct. 1887[3].
    Children (surname Bonnell):

1. Florence R.	3. Robert William.	5. Emeline.
2. Naomi G.	4. Clarissa H.	6. Angeline.

8. 320992. Mary Ellen, b. 1841[5]; d. about 1860 at age 19[5].
9. 320993. Susan, b. about 1844[5]; m. 8 July 1866 William J. Ralph[3]; d. before 1877[5].

10. 320994. James, b. about 1845[3]; d. in early childhood[4].
11. 320995. William, b. about 1847[3]; d. in early childhood[4].

REFERENCES:
1. The Hatfield Family Bible.
2. *The Horn Papers*, by W. F. Horn, Vol. II, p. 706, abstracted and sent to me by Mary Spies, Spokane, WA.
3. CB Database.
4. *Biographical & Historical Records of Jay County, Indiana*, Lewis Publishing Co, pp. 421 and 422, photocopies sent to me by Monty Peden, Rochester, IN.
5. Family Group Sheets, William and Rebecca Bonnel and Thomas Jefferson and Hannah Mays, compiled and sent to me by Monty Peden.

1-3-3-1-4-1   CB310199

SIMEON[6] BONNELL (Nathaniel[5], Benjamin[4], ?Samuel[3], Nathaniel[2], William[1]) was born 15 November 1783[1] in Mendham, Morris co, NJ. He is certainly the Simeon Bonnell who witnessed the wills of Mercy Brotherton in 1810 and William Brotherton in 1811 and who appears on tax lists in 1809 and 188, all in Randolph twp, Morris co, NJ[2]. He died in Randolph twp on 1 January 1814 and was buried in the cemetery of Hardwick meeting of Friends in Warren co, NJ[2].

REFERENCES:
1. Family data compiled by Mrs. Lois Tripp, Avon, NY, and sent to Homer E. Baldwin, Greensburg, PA, on 14 July 1943.
2. CB Database.
3. Ltr. 28 Nov. 1855 from Richard Brotherton to Charles Bonnell.

1-3-3-1-4-3   CB310210

WILLIAM[6] BONNELL (Nathaniel[5], Benjamin[4], ?Samuel[3], Nathaniel[2], William[1]) was born 26 January 1786[1] in Mendham, Morris co, NJ. He died some years before 1855[2].

REFERENCES:
1. Family data compiled by Mrs. Lois Tripp, Avon, NY, and sent to Homer E. Baldwin, Greensburg, PA, on 14 July 1943.
2. Ltr. 28 Nov. 1855 from Richard Brotherton to Charles Bonnell.

1-3-3-1-4-4   CB310211

DARIUS[6] BONNELL (Nathaniel[5], Benjamin[4], ?Samuel[3], Nathaniel[2], William[1] was born 13 January 1788[1] in Mendham, Morris co, NJ. He appears as a farmer in the 1820 census in Junius, Seneca co, NY: 100010-30010[3]. In the 1830 census he is listed in Waterloo, Seneca co, NY: 1001001-0110001[3]. When his father made his will early in 1833 Darius and his family were living in Rochester, Monroe co, NY, where they appear in the 1840 census: 00020001-00010001[3]. The last record we have found for him was in 1845 when he was listed as one of the next of kin in the probate of his father's estate[3]. His residence in 1845 was still in Rochester[3]. From the census records it is clear that he was married and had children but their names have not yet been found.

REFERENCES:
1. Family data compiled by Mrs. Lois Tripp, Avon, NY, and sent to Homer E. Baldwin, Greensburg, PA, on 14 July 1943.
2. Ltr. 28 Nov. 1855 from Richard Brotherton to Charles Bonnell.
3. CB Database.

1-3-3-1-4-6 CB310213

NATHANIEL[6] BONNELL (Nathaniel[5], Benjamin[4], ?Samuel[3], Nathaniel[2], William[1]) was born 22 August 1797[1] at Mendham, Morris co, NJ. He moved with his father to Junius, Seneca co, NY[2]. He is apparently the young boy living with his father there in the census of 1810[3]. On 10 February 1820 he married ELIZABETH BRUCE[1] who was born 8 July 1820[1]. They appear in the 1820 census in Junius: 000100-00100[3]. He was engaged in farming[3]. Late in the decade they moved to Boston, Erie co, NY. On 26 May 1829 Nathaniel's wife Elizabeth was dismissed from the Friends Monthly Meeting at Junius to the Monthly Meeting at Hamburgh, Erie co, NY[4]. Their son Alonzo was born at Hamburgh 12 May 1831[1,3], and daughter Margaret was born there 18 Oct. 1838[3]. By 1840 they had moved on to Sheffield, Ashtabula co, OH, where Nathaniel appears in the census: 0212001-2011001[3]. His residence was given as Sheffield, OH, in 1845 when his father's will was probated[3], and in 1852, when the death of his son Francis Marion was reported[3]. Nathaniel appears in the 1860 census in Sheffield as a carpenter, with his wife Elizabeth, son Eseck George and daughter Margaret[3]. Nathaniel, as a farmer, and Elizabeth appear in the 1870 census in Sheffield[3]. The date of his death has not yet been found.

Children:
1. 320996. Simeon, b. 1 Dec. 1820[1].
2. 320997. Asenath, b. 30 Sept. 1822[1]; m. 3 Jan. 1841 Asahel Shaw[3].
3. 320998. Aaron, b. 29 June 1824[1]; m. 25 Feb. 1851 Harriet Eugenia Spring[3]; d. 1906[3].
    Children (surname Bonnell):[3]
    1. Francis Marion.   3. William Riley.   5. Harriet Cornelia.
    2. C. (daughter).   4. Mary Belle.
4. 320999. Charlotte D., b. 11 Oct. 1826[1].
5. 321000. Ezra N., b. 29 Sept. 1828[1]; m. (first) 20 Nov. 1851 Elizabeth Large[3]; m. (second) 9 May 1867 Sarah Clink[3]; d. 12 May 1918[3]/
    Children (surname Bonnell)(by first wife):[3]
    1. Aise W.   3. Mary.   4. Martha.
    2. Christian.
    Children (surname Bonnell)(by second wife):[3]
    5. Frank K.   6. Austie J.   7. Alma A.

6. 321001. Alonzo Burlingame, b. 12 May 1831[1,3]; m. 27 Jan. 1862 Mary Marlette[1]; d. 3 July 1920[3].

Children (surname Bonnell):[1,3]

1. Elsworth Burlingame. 5. James Bruce. 9. Alonzo Bancroft.
2. Abner Romanty. 6. Evangeline Celestia. 10. George Arthur.
3. Amber Estelle. 7. Cornelia Catherine.
4. Orson Alonzo. 8. John Henry.

7. 321002. Eseck George, b. 28 Oct. 1833[1,3]; m. 1861 Caroline Celestia Shaw[3]; d. after 1900[3].

Children (surname Bonnell):[3]

1. George Omar. 4. Jay Bruce. 7. Andrew Marco.
2. Carrie May. 5. Edna Miranda. 8. Ernest Noble.
3. Casper Eri. 6. Lewis Nathaniel. 9. Wilbur Lee.

8. 321003. Cornelia Catherine, b. 21 Aug. 1837[1,3].

9. 321004. Margaret Pamelia, b. 18 Oct. 1838[1,3]; m. 6 June 1861 William Riley Spring[3]; d. 1913[3].

Children (surname Spring):[3]

1. Theda E. 2. Ethel A. others?

10. 321005. Francis Marion, b. 30 Aug. 1841[1] (or 1845[3]); d. 29 Dec. 1852[3].

REFERENCES:

1. Family data compiled by Mrs. Lois Tripp, Avon, NY, and sent to Homer E. Baldwin, Greensburg, PA, on 14 July 1943.
2. Ltr. 28 Nov. 1855 from Richard Brotherton to Charles Bonnell.
3. CB Database.
4. Records of the Junius Friends Monthly Meeting, printed in the National Genealogical Society Quarterly, p. 18.

1-3-3-1-6-1   CB310215

THOMAS[6] BONNELL (David[5], Benjamin[4], ?Samuel[3], Nathaniel[2], William[1]) was born about 1784 in Mendham, Morris co, NJ, and moved to Bedford co, PA, with his parents before 1800[1]. He is apparently the male aged 16 - 26 in David Bundle's household in the 1800 census in Londonderry twp, Bedford co, PA[2]. He removed to Nova Scotia[3].

REFERENCES:

1. Ltr. 28 Nov. 1855 from Richard Brotherton to Charles Bonnell.
2. CB Database.
3. *Descendants of David & Mary Ann Bonnell*, from Bedford County, Pennsylvania, compiled by Jeane Ansteth Kennedy, 1976-1981, p. 64.

SIXTH GENERATION

1-3-3-1-6-2   CB310214

JOHN[6] BONNELL (David[5], Benjamin[4], ?Samuel[3], Nathaniel[2], William[1]) was born 25 April 1788[1] in Mendham, Morris co, NJ. As a young boy he moved with his parents to Bedford co, PA[2], probably before 1795. He is apparently the male 10 - 16 years of age in the household of David Bundle in the 1800 census of Londonderry twp, Bedford co, PA[3].

His wife was ELIZABETH GAUMER[1]. She was born 17 August 1796[1] (or 1795 in Pennsylvania[3]). They lived in Londonderry twp, Bedford co, where John appears in the census in 1820: 10001-301[3], 1830: 1110001-112001[3], and 1840: 20111001-0211201[3]. John age 50 and Elizabeth age 50 are listed in the 1850 census in Londonderry twp, with their children David 22, Samuel 21, Catherine 20, Margaret 18, John 16, Daniel 12 and Levi 10[3]. In 1836 John and his brother Henry were appointed administrators of their father's estate[4]. In 1846 and again in 1852 John appears on the triennial tax assessment books of Londonderry twp as the owner of real property there[5].

After 1852 John and Elizabeth moved to Clarion twp, Bureau co, IL, where they appear in the 1860 census[3]. David, Margaret, John, Daniel and Levi were still living with them[3]. They appear in the 1870 census in neighboring La Moille twp, Bureau co, IL[3]. Son David, unmarried, continued to live with them[3]. Elizabeth died 19 November 1870[1] and John died 26 June 1872[1]. They were buried in Greenfield Cemetery in La Moille[1].

Children:
1. 321007. Tena (Alve Tinene[6]), b. 9 June 1814[1] (or Olver Tenia, b. 9 June 1817[3]); m. (first) 20 Sept. 1835 Daniel Shroyer[6]; m. (second) 3 Jan. 1858 Aquilla Lowe[3]; d. 27 Mar. 1873[1,3].
   Children (surname Shroyer):[3]
   1. Magdalina.   3. Andrew Jackson.   5. Daniel.
   2. Catherine.   4. Mary Ann.   6. Silas.
2. 321008. Mary (Polly), b. Aug. 1818[3]; m. (first) Frank Ennis[3]; m. (second) _____ Morgan[3]; d. 12 Dec. 1908[3].
3. 321006. Silas, b. 29 Mar. 1822[1] (or 29 Mar. 1815[3]); m. 25 Feb. 1845[6] Mary Ann Smith[1,3]; d. 22 May 1865[1,3].
   Children (surname Bonnell):[1]
   1. Edmond.   5. Shannon.   9. Alice.
   2. Benjamin.   6. Nell.   10. Irvin.
   3. Sylvester.   7. Albert.
   4. Margaret.   8. Sarah.
4. 321009. Phoebe, b. 26 Feb. 1825[7]; m. 1847 Josiah Bonnell 321019[1,3]; d. 24 Feb. 1910[7].
   Children (surname Bonnell):[1,3]
   1. Margaret.   3. John M.   4. Mary E.
   2. Ellen.

5. 321011. Samuel, b. Feb. 1827[3]; m. Mary Ann _____ [3]; d. after 1910[3].
        Children (surname Bonnell):[3]

1. Albert A.	3. Martha J.	5. Joseph.
2. Mary E.	5. Ellen.	6. John.

6. 321010. David H., b. 1828[1,3].
7.   Elizabeth, b. 20 Feb. 1829[7]; m. 1850 Jacob B. Bonnell 321018[1,3];
        d. 20 July 1904[7].
        Children (surname Bonnell):[1,3]

1. Benjamin.	5. Elizabeth Ann.	9. Melinda M.
2. Margaret Catherine.	6. Rebecca.	10. Rachel.
3. John Nicholas.	7. Daniel Howard.	
4. George Perry.	8. Nettie Mary Jane.	

8. 321012. Catherine, b. 17 June 1831[7]; m. 31 Mar. 1853 Emanuel Bonnell 321022[6];
        d. 23 Sept. 1888[7].
        Children (surname Bonnell):

1. Albert Maywood.	4. Matthew Nuval.	7. Clark Grant.
2. Elizabeth Jane.	5. Edmond Stanton.	8. Loezeta May.
3. John Henry.	6. Sherman E.	9. Charles Levert.

9. 321013. Margaret, b. 1832[3]; m. Sid Lippencott[1]; d. after 1910[3].
        Children (surname Lippencott):[1]
        1. Oscar.
10. 321014. John, b. about 1835[3]; m. 1 Mar. 1862 Lucretia Hayes[13]; d. 28 Aug. 1864[3].
        Children (surname Bonnell):[3]

1. Marshall T.	2. Anetta.

11. 321015. Daniel H., b. about 1838[3]; d. after 1860[3].
12. 321016. Levi, b. 1 June 1840[1]; m. 11 Jan. 1882 Harriet (Hayes)(Weeks) Monroe[1,3];
        d. 19 May 1917[1].
        Children (surname Bonnell):[1]

1. Scott.	2. Florence.	3. Millie.

REFERENCES:

1. *Descendants of David & Mary Ann Bonnell*, from Bedford County, Pennsylvania, compiled by Jeane Ansteth Kennedy, 1976-1981, p. 39 et seq.
2. Ltr. 28 Nov. 1855 from Richard Brotherton to Charles Bonnell.
3. CB Database.
4. Letter of administration appointing John and Henry Bonnell, photocopy sent to me by Joan Flavel, Gold Beach, OR.
5. Londonderry twp triennial tax assessment books, abstracted and sent to me by Mary B. Spies, Spokane, WA.
6. Bedford co marriage records abstracted and sent to me by Mary B. Spies.
7. Gravestone records in North Prairie Cemetery and Hills Cemetery in La Moille twp, Bureau co, IL, copied by Jeane Kennedy and sent to me by Mary B. Spies.

1-3-3-1-6-4   CB310228

HENRY[6] BONNELL David[5], Benjamin[4], ?Samuel[3], Nathaniel[2], William[1]) was born about 1795[3] in Bedford co, PA[2]. On 9 January 1821 he married MARGARET HOWARD[1] who was born about 1799[3]. He appears in the 1830 census in Londonderry twp, Bedford co, PA: 230101-001001[3] and again in Londonderry in 1840: 122001-0100001[3]. In 1841 he sold property in Bedford co as one of the administrators of his father's estate[4]. In 1846 he appears on the triennial tax assessment books of Londonderry twp[5]. When the 1850 census was taken he was living in Richland twp, Belmont co, OH, with his wife and six children[3]. On 22 November 1857 the Court of Common Pleas of Bedford co ordered the County Sheriff to seize property owned by Henry in payment of debts amounting to $136.54[6]. The property seized was a tract of land of 200 acres, about 30 acres cleared and under fence, with a cabin house and log stable with thrashing floor attached[6]. The Sheriff sold the land for $175 to William Bonnell[6] CB011979, whose relationship to this family, if any, is unknown.

Henry next appears in the 1860 census in Clarion twp, Bureau co, IL, with his wife Margaret, son Abraham, and the wife and children of his son Jacob[3]. In 1870 Henry age 75 was living in La Moille twp, Bureau co, IL, with his son Henry and his family. The dates of death of Henry and Margaret have not been found. It is said that they were both buried in the Hills Cemetery in La Moille twp[3], but they were not included in the list of Bonnell burials found by Jeane Kennedy in Hills Cemetery[7].

Children:
1. 321017. Harriet, b. 1819[3] (or 1816 or 1818[8]); m. 24 Oct. 1839 Jacob O. Hetherington[1,8]; d. 17 Apr. 1902[8].
      Children (surname Hetherington):[1,8]
      1. Sham.   5. John H.   9. daughter.
      2. Henry.   6. Abraham.   10. William.
      3. Benjamin Franklin. 7. Matilda.
      4. Jacob E.   8. Mary.
2. 321018. Jacob B., b. 3 June 1821[7]; m. 1850 Elizabeth Bonnell, his cousin[1]; d. 23 Mar. 1904[7].
      Children (surname Bonnell):[1,3]
      1. Benjamin.   5. Elizabeth Ann.   9. Melinda M.
      2. Margaret Catherine. 6. Rebecca.   10. Rachel.
      3. John Nicholas.   7. Daniel Howard.
      4. George Perry.   8. Nettie Mary Jane.
3. 321019. Josiah, b. 31 Jan. 1825[7]; m. 1847 Phoebe Bonnell[1,3] CB321009; d. 1915[7].
      Children (surname Bonnell):[1,3]
      1. Margaret.   3. John M.   4. Mary E.
      2. Ellen.
4. 321020. Henry, b. 22 Nov. 1827[1] (or 1826[3]); m. 27 Feb. 1851 Charlotte Tannyhill[3]; d. 13 Nov. 1904[1,3].
      Children (surname Bonnell):[1,3]

1. Agnes.	5. Edgar B.	9. Lora L.
2. Delila C. (or J.).	6. Samuel Dawlson.	10. Viola L.
3. Martha Ann (or C.).	7. William Condie.	11. Edridge Murry.
4. James H.	8. Jacob P.	

5. 321021. Christian, b. 4 Jan. 1829[7]; m. Suzanne Kershner[3]; d. 3 May 1893[7].
6. 321022. Emanuel, b. 10 Mar. 1831[1,3]; m. 1 Apr. 1853 Catherine Bonnell[1,3] CB321012; d. 29 June 1917[3].
   Children (surname Bonnell):

1. Albert Maywood.	4. Matthew Nuval.	7. Clark Grant.
2. Elizabeth Jane.	5. Edmond Stanton.	8. Loezeta May.
3. John Henry.	6. Sherman E.	9. Charles Levert.

7. 321023. Rachel, b. 25 May 1833[1,3]; m. 21 June 1855 William E. Boylan[3]; d. 1892[1,3].
   Children (surname Boylan):[3]

1. Mary Margaret.	3. Delilah Olinda.	4. Hannah Louisa.
2. Sarah Ann.		

8. 321024. Jesse I., b. 3 Apr. 1835[3]; m. (first) 2 Jan. 1859 Hannah M. Dean[1,3]; m. (second) 3 June 1866 Belinda Dean[3]; m. (third) 27 Nov. 1878 Sarah A. _____[3]; d. 7 Mar. 1893[3].
   Children (surname Bonnell)(by first wife):[3]
   1. Jonathan Percival.   2. Jesse Ichabod.
9. 321025. Abraham, b. 18 Dec. 1839[1,3]; m. (first) Sarah C. Bryner[3]; m. (second) 11 Oct. 1880 Ida J. Vantasell[3]; d. 18 Jan. 1915[3].
   Children (surname Bonnell)(by first wife):[3]
   1. Mabel.
   Children (surname Bonnell)(by second wife):[3]
   2. Clarence.

REFERENCES:

1. *Descendants of David & Mary Ann Bonnell*, from Bedford County, Pennsylvania, compiled by Jeane Ansteth Kennedy, 1976-1981, p. 1 et seq.
2. Ltr. 28 ov. 1855 from Richard Brotherton to Charles Bonnell.
3. CB Database.
4. Letter of administration appointing John and Henry Bonnell, photocopy sent to me by Joan Flavel, Gold Beach, OR.
5. Londonderry twp triennial tax assessment books, abstracted and sent to me by Mary B. Spies, Spokane, WA.
6. Bedford co, PA, Deed Book A-O, page 502, year 1867-8, abstracted and sent to me by Mary B. Spies.
7. Gravestone records in North Prairie Cemetery and Hills Cemetery in La Moille twp, Bureau co, IL, copied by Jeane Kennedy and sent to me by Mary B. Spies.

1-3-7-7-1-1 D182 CB310281

ITHAMER[6] BONNELL (David[5], David[4], Joseph[3], Nathaniel[2], William[1]) was born 15 January 1769[1] at Springfield, Essex (now Union) co, NJ. He married (first) about 1790[2] PHEBE ALLEN MEEKER[3], daughter of Stephen and Phebe (Allen) Meeker[3]. She was born 29

November 1773[1] at Elizabethtown, Essex (now Union) co, NJ. On 1 April 1794 Ithamer borrowed £75 from Jonas Wade secured by a mortgage on a 1 3/4 acre lot in Springfield on the north side of the main road from Elizabethtown to Morristown[2]. This was apparently the lot on which his home was situated. On 7 January 1809 he paid Abraham and Eliza Wooley $114 for 1.9 acres adjoining the rear of his home lot[2]. Ithamer made the inventory of the estate of Elijah Woodruff in 1802[4] and of the estate of Noah Searing in 1805[4]. He appears in the tax list in Springfield, Essex (now Union) co in 1813, 1814, 1820 and 1821[5].

His wife Phebe died 3 August 1821, in her 48th year[1], and was buried in the cemetery of the Presbyterian Church in Springfield beside three of her children who had predeceased her[1]. On 4 June 1826 Ithamer married (second) MARY HALSEY[2], the daughter of Isaac and Sarah (Smith) Halsey[3] and the widow of David Bryant[3]. She was born 26 October 1778 in Springfield[3]. On 14 June 1826 she was dismissed from the Presbyterian Church at Westfield, Essex (now Union) co to the church at Springfield[2]. Ithamer appears in the census of Springfield, Essex co, in 1830: 001000001-00000001[2], and in 1840: 0002000001-000100001[2].

Ithamer died 17 June 1847 in his 79th year[1] and was buried with his first wife in the Presbyterian Churchyard at Springfield[1]. His will was dated 4 August 1835 and was probated 28 June 1847[2]. His son Ithamer and son-in-law Samuel Gardner were named executors[2]. Widow Mary Bonnell appears in the 1850 census living in Rahway, Essex (now Union) co, NJ, with John A. and Mary Briant[2]. She appeared in the 1870 census in Elizabeth, Union co, at age 92[2]. She lived at 161 East Grand Street, Elizabeth[2]. Mary Bonnell died 24 April 1876 in Newark, Essex co, NJ[2], and was buried in Evergreen Cemetery, Hillside, Union co, NJ[2].

Children:
  1. 320323. Ithamer, b. 2 Jan. 1792[1]; d. before 1812[3].
  2. 320324. Stephen, b. 2 Jan. 1792[1]; d. 12 Apr. 1811[1].
  3. 320325. Harriet, b. 6 Dec. 1793[3]; d. 27 Dec. 1793 aged 5 weeks[1].
  4. 320326. Phebe Allen, b. 17 May 1797[3]; d. 29 Aug. 1797, aged 5 months[1].
  5. 320327. Phebe J. or Allen, b. 26 Aug. 1799[3]; m. 8 June 1818 Samuel H. Gardner[2];
        d. 13 Mar. 1844[3].
  6. 320328. Joanna, b. 5 Nov. 1802[3]; m. 14 May 1821 Ebenezer Miller[2];
        d. 23 Jan. 1887[3].
  7. 320329. Betsey Woodruff, b. 14 Oct. 1805[3]; d. 1805[3].
  8. 320330. David Edwin, b. 25 June 1809[3]; m. 15 Apr. 1830 Sarah Heller Conrad[2,3];
        d. 3 July 1865[2,3].
        Children (surname Bunnell):[3]
        1. Daniel Kimball.   4. George Henry.   7. Martha Jane.
        2. Stephen Ithamer.   5. Phoebe Elizabeth. 8. Alpharetta Jane.
        3. Samuel Gardner.   6. Mary Armstrong.   9. Rosetta Eve.
  9. 320331. Stephen Meeker, b. 12 Sept. 1812[3]; m. 19 July 1835 Hannah Tunis[2] (or
        Hannah Spears[3]); d. 4 Dec. 1887[3].

Children (surname Bonnell):[2]
    1. William Henry.   2. David Edward.   3. William T.
10. 320332. Ithamer Wade, b. 12 Sept. 1812[3]; m. (first) 9 Sept. 1835 Phebe Jagger[2]; m. (second) Sophronia B. _____[2]; d. 22 Feb. 1890[2].
    Children (surname Bonnell)(by first wife):[2]
    1. Emma Irene.   2. George R.   3. Bentley Jay.

REFERENCES:
1. Gen Mag of NJ, Vol. V, No. 1, p. 9.
2. CB Database.
3. Family Group Sheets, David and Temperance (Wade) Bonnell, Ithamer and Phebe Allen (Meeker) Bonnell, Ithamer and Mary (Halsey)(Bryant) Bonnell, and David Edwin and Sarah (Heller) Bonnell, compiled and sent to me by Iva Bunnell Adams, Midway, UT.
4. NJ Wills - Vol. X, pp. 390, 515.
5. NJ Tax Lists, p. 297.

1-3-7-7-1-2   D75ii   CB310282

ELIAS[6] BONNELL (David[5], David[4], Joseph[3], Nathaniel[2], William[1]) was born about 1770 in Springfield, Essex (now Union) co, NJ[1]. About 1793[2] he married MARY WILKENSON who was born about 1774[3]. They lived in Mendham, Morris co, NJ. The deed and mortgage books of Morris co include several references to the real estate transactions of Elias and Mary Bonnell[2]. A thorough study of these would be useful to any descendants interested in knowing more about their life history. Their home was probably in the Randolph section of Mendham, since Elias appears in the Randolph tax lists after 1806[2], the year that Randolph was set up as a separate township. Elias died 12 May 1826[3]. Mary died 30 January 1837[3]. They were buried in the cemetery at Mt. Freedom, Randolph twp[3].

Children:
1. 320384. Aaron C., b. May 1794[2]; m. 1819 Phebe Allen Meeker[2]; d. 2 May 1855[2].
    Children (surname Bonnell):[2]
    1. Mary Crane.   4. Aaron Ogden.   6. Phebe Elizabeth.
    2. Amanda.   5. Elias.   7. Phebe Asenath.
    3. Stephen Meeker.
2. 320385. Sarah C., b. 179x[2]; m. 24 Sept. 1818 Jacob Parmer[2].
3. 320386. Charlotte, b. about 1800[2].
4. 320388. James Wilkinson, b. about 1802[3]; d. 6 June 1831, age 29[3].
5. 320387. Elizabeth, b. 29 June 1807[2]; d. June 1864[2].
6. 320389. Harriet, b. about 1810[2]; m. 9 Oct. 1833 Thomas J. Colley[2].
7. 320390. Esther D., b. about 1817[3]; d. 3 Sept. 1842[3].

REFERENCES:
1. Family Group Sheet - David and Temperance (Wade) Bonnell. See p.
2. CB Database.
3. Cemetery description books, Morris Co, NJ, Vol. II, p. 55, Mt. Freedom Cemetery, abstracted in the New Jersey Historical Society, Newark, NJ, and sent to me by Jerome Hatch, Chicago, IL.

1-3-7-7-1-3   D75iii   CB310283

HENRY[6] BUNNELL (David[5], David[4], Joseph[3], Nathaniel[2], William[1]) was born 15 October 1772 at Springfield, Essex (now Union) co, NJ[1]. On 1 April 1792[1], at Mendham, Morris co, NJ, he was married by Rev. Mr. Baldwin of Rockaway to PHEBE BONNELL, daughter of Nathaniel and Anne (Cozad) Bonnell[1,2]. She was born 18 July 1772[1]. They lived at Mendham where their first seven children were born[1]. Henry appears in the listing of the militia of Mendham twp in 1793[3]. On 16 February 1798 Henry borrowed £55 until September 1799 from Benjamin Nichols of Bridgewater, NJ, secured by a mortgage on 25 acres in Mendham[4].

About 1805 Henry moved his family from New Jersey to western New York, first stopping in Wolcott, Wayne co, NY, near Lake Ontario. Here his son Nathaniel was born in 1806[1]. They did not remain in Wolcott long; by 1810 they had removed to Mentz, Cayuga co, where their last three children were born[1]. Henry "Bummel" appears in the 1810 census of Mentz ("near Conquest", the next town to the north): 2101-1301[4]. In Mentz Henry appears in the 1820 census: 110101-00201[4], in the 1830 census: 00001001-00001001[4], and in the 1840 census: 000010001-000001001[4]. Henry's wife Phebe died at Mentz 15 June 1845[1]. She was buried in Pine Hill Cemetery in Throop[5] (the next town south of Mentz), Cayuga co, NY.

The 1850 census found Henry living with his daughter Temperance and her husband Elias Root in Mentz. Henry and his family were members of the Baptist Church. On 29 February 1852 the Baptist Church of Rose, Wayne co, NY, wrote letters of transfer for Henry and his daughter Phebe Ann[6], and on 5 March 1853 they were received into the Baptist Church of Pike, Wyoming co, NY, by letter of transfer[6]. Here they joined his son Henry George and wife Eliza who had settled in Pike in1850[6]. Son Henry George died 22 Nov. 1857 at Pike[6], and Henry was dismissed from the Baptist Church at Pike in November 1858[6]. This is probably when he moved to Oswego, Oswego co, NY, to live with his son Nathaniel. He appears as a "retired gentleman" in Nathaniel's household in the 1860 census in Oswego[4]. He died in Oswego on 15 April 1864[1].

Children:
1. 320844. Rhoda, b. 31 Jan. 1793[1]; d. 1800[1].
2. 320845. Sarah (Sally), b. 7 sept. 1794[1]; m. 1810 Noah Hatch[7]; d. 15 Feb. 1840[7].
   Children (surname Hatch):[7]
1. Ezra.	6. Cordelia.	11. Jerome Bonaparte.
2. Eccellan.	7. Timothy.	12. Odell.
3. Jane A.	8. Susan M.	13. George Frederick.
4. Henry B.	9. Nathaniel William.	14. Frances C.
5. Elizabeth.	10. Oliver Warren.	15. Edwin.
		16. Sarah Bunnell.
3. 320846. Joseph, b. 17 Aug. 1796[1]; m. Ann Cooper[1]; d. 7 Feb. 1877[1].
   Children (surname Bunnell):[8]
   1. Sibbel Jane.
4. 320847. Nancy, b. 26 July 1798[1]; m. David Verplank[4].

5. 320848. Phebe Ann, b. 26 Aug. 1800[1]; d. 15 Feb. 1854[6].
6. 320849. David, b. 5 June 1802[1]; d. in infancy[1].
7. 320850. Temperance Wade, b. 9 Feb. 1804[1]; m. Elias P. Root[1]; d. 1 Feb. 1871[1].
8. 320851. Nathaniel, b. 14 Oct. 1806[1]; m. Anna _____[4]; d. July 1888[1].
       Children (surname Bunnell):[4]
       1. James A.
9. 320852. Henry George, b. 29 Apr. 1810[1,4]; m. 14 Oct. 1842 Eliza Loomis[4];
       d. 22 Nov. 1857[6].
       Children (surname Bunnell):[4]
       1. Lyman H.   3. George Chapin.   4. Nellie E.
       2. Asahel Cooley.
10. 320853. Ithamer, b. 11 Dec. 1812[1]; d. Jan. 1873[1].
11. 320854. Stephen, b. 5 June 1815[1]; d. in infancy[1].

REFERENCES:
1. Family Group Sheet - Henry and Phebe (Bonnell) Bonnell, compiled by Viola Bunnell Kuhni and sent to me by Jerome Hatch, Chicago, IL.
2. *Wood's Newark Gazette*, 26 July 1792, photocopy sent to me by Jerome Hatch.
3. NJ in 1793, p. 251.
4. CB Database.
5. Family Group Sheet - Henry and Phebe (Bonnell) Bonnell, compiled and sent to me by Jerome Hatch (tentative record).
6. Bunnell/Bonnell Newsletter, Vol. 18, No. 4, p. 70.
7. Family Group Sheet - Noah and Sarah (Bunnell) Hatch, compiled and sent to me by Jerome Hatch.
8. Bunnell/Bonnell Newsletter, Vol. 5, No. 1, p. 8.

1-3-7-7-1-5   D183   CB310285

LUTHER[6] BONNELL (David[5], David[4], Joseph[3], Nathaniel[2], William[1]) was born 8 September 1775 in Springfield, Essex (now Union) co, NJ[1]. He appears as a member of the militia of Mendham twp, Morris co, NJ, in 1793[2]. He married SARAH WOODRUFF[1], who was born about 1780[3]. Their marriage took place by 1795 when they appear in the Session records of the Presbyterian Church of Madison, Morris co, NJ[3]. They lived at Springfield until August 1810, when they sold their house and lot in Springfield to Jonas Wade for $500[3]. They purchased a tract of over 100 acres in Morristown, Morris co from Drake Ludlow for $1300[3] and gave Ludlow and 8-year mortgage for $1300 secured by the property[3]. In 1820 he bought a public house in Morristown from Nathaniel Bull and advertised for custom[3]. Apparently he paid for it with a mortgage for $3825 from the State Bank at Morris co[3].

Luther appears in the 1830 census in Morris twp, Morris co: 01002011-1011101[3]. He died 30 April 1838 at the age of 64[3]. His widow Sarah appears in the 1840 census in Newark, Essex co, NJ: 010041-10203101[3], and again in Newark in the 1850 census at age 70 living with her daughter Abigail and husband William Utter[3].

Children:

1. 320507. Jane, b. about 1800[3]; m. 23 Sept. 1819 James Andress[5].
2. 320508. Abigail, b. about 1814[3]; m. 17 May 1836 William T. Utter[3].
3. 320509. Eliza M., b. about 1818[3].

REFERENCES:
1. Family Group Sheet, David and Temperance (Wade) Bonnell. See p. 190.
2. NJ in 1793, p. 253.
3. CB Database.
4. 1830 census, NJ, reel #82.
5. Registers - Minutes and History of the First Presbyterian Church of Morristown, NJ, 1742 to 1891, abstracted and sent to me by Homer E. Baldwin, Greensburg, PA.

1-3-7-7-1-6   D75vi   CB310286

STEPHEN C.[6] BONNELL (David[5], David[4], Joseph[3], Nathaniel[2], William[1]) was born in 1777 at Springfield, Essex (now Union) co, NJ[1]. He died 15 September 1864[1]. Although he is sometimes said to have married Sarah Simpson on 19 July 1806[1], this marriage really belongs to 1-3-1-2-7-1-1, D330, CB320393, Stephen Carter Bonnell.

REFERENCES:
1. Family Group Sheet - David and Temperance (Wade) Bonnell. See p. 190.

1-3-7-7-1-7   D184   CB310287

DAVID[6] BONNELL (David[5], David[4], Joseph[3], Nathaniel[2], William[1]) was born 25 April 1779 at Springfield, Essex (now Union) co, NJ[1]. On 17 October 1799 he was married (first) by Rev. Amzi Armstrong to ANN McELRATH, both listed as residents of Mendham, Morris co, NJ[2]. She was born 17 October 1777 at Morristown, Morris co, NJ[3], the daughter of Andrew and Abigail (Cozad) McIlrath[3]. On 9 August 1803 "David Bonal and Anna his wife" sold to David Wood for $262.50 a tract of land in Morris twp, Morris co, "it being the place wheron the said Bonal now lives."[4] It was probably at this time that their move to the west began. It is possible that they lived for a while somewhere in Pennsylvania since the 1850 census says that their daughter Electa was born about 1806 in Pennsylvania[5,9].

Before 1810 they had moved to Euclid, Cuyahoga co, OH, where David is listed on the tax rolls in 1810, 1811, 1814 and 1819[5]. He appears on the 1820 census in Euclid: 21001-1121[5]. We find his name also on "A list of the inhabitants of the township of Euclid above the age of 21 years" for the year 1823. David appears again in Euclid in the 1830 census: 00111001-111001[5].

Ann (McIlroth) Bonnell died 1 March 1839 in Elyria twp, Lorain co, OH. Later that year, on 22 December 1839, David married (second) MARY (_____) HALL[7], who was born about 1780 in Rhode Island[5]. David Bunnell appears in the 1840 census in Elyria twp, Lorain co, OH:

SIXTH GENERATION

000000001-00010001[5]. David age 71 and Mary age 70 appear in the 1850 census in Wadsworth, Medina co, OH[5]. Her daughter, Sarah Hall, age 33, lived with them[5].

David died 24 June 1854[3] in Oberlin, Lorain co, OH[5]. His widow Mary appears in the 1860 census in Medina, Medina co, OH, living with William and Electa Hall (probably her son and daughter-in-law.)[5]. She died in Medina 28 August 1861 at age 81 and was buried in Windfall Cemetery, Granger twp, Medina co[8].

Children (by first wife):
1. 320376. Isabelle, b. 15 July 1800; m. 29 Sept. 1823 James Palmer[7]; d. 1858.
2. 320378. Joanna, b. 22 July 1803[3]; m. 21 Dec. 1820 Joseph Ward Pimlot; d. 4 Apr. 1844[3].
   Children (surname Pimlot):[3]
   1. David Stanton.   4. Nancy Melissa.   6. Thomas Wellington.
   2. Clark Gordon.   5. Orpha.   7. Cary Doan.
   3. Bella.
3. 320842. Electa., b. about 1806[5]; m. 26 May 1827 Matthias Rush[5]; d. 1876[5].
   Children (surname Rush):[9]
   1. Sanford.   2. Martha A.   3. Maria Jane.
4. 320380. Ithamer Wade, b. 22 July 1808[10]; m. 16 Aug. 1830 Margaret Ann Wood[5,7]; d. 19 Sept. 1872[10].
   Children (surname Bonnell):[5]
   1. Stephen.   3. Martha Ann.   4. David Ward.
   2. Henry McIlrath.
5. 320381. Stephen Byram, b. 16 Sept. 1811[11]; d. 23 July 1816[10].
6. 320382. Ezra Graves, b. 1 May 1813[11]; m. 23 Feb. 1839 Susan Ann Anderson[7]; d. 6 July 1873[5].
   Children (surname Bonnell):[5]
   1. Edwin R.   3. Thomas Corwin.   5. William B.
   2. James B.   4. Captain Walker.
7. 320383. Angelina, b. 20 Oct. 1816[11]; m. A. Hait[10]; d. 1851[10].
8. 320840. David Newell, b. 6 June 1819[11].
9. 320841. Mary Elizabeth, b. 28 Nov. 1824[11]; m. 28 Mar. 1847 Alfred Gillette[7]; d. 1881[10].
10. 320843. Martha Abigail, b. 23 Jan. 1826[10]; bapt. 6 Aug. 1826[11]; d. young[10].

REFERENCES:
1. Family Group Sheet, David and Temperance (Wade) Bonnell. See p. 190.
2. Gen Mag of NJ, Vol. IV, No. 2, p. 89.
3. The Bonnell descent of Mrs. Leo Salters, Harper, KS, compiled and sent to me by Mrs. Salters.
4. Morris co, NJ, Deeds, Deed Book I, p. 509.
5. CB Database.
6. *The Report*, Ohio Genealogical Society, Vol. 28, No. 3, p. 154.
7. IGI-OH, 1988.

8. Gravestone of Mary Bonnell, wife of David, copied in Granger twp, Medina co, OH, and sent to me by Neal L. Gardner, Canal Fulton, OH.
9. 1850 census, East Cleveland, Cuyahoga co, OH, abstracted and sent to me by Kim Milillo, Oneonta, NY.
10. Family Group Sheet, David and Anna (McIlrath) Bonnell, compiled and sent to me by Jerome Hatch, Chicago, IL.
11. *Bunnell/Bonnell Newsletter*, Vol. 16, No. 4, p. 68. Births in the Records of the 1st Presbyterian Church, East Cleveland, OH.

1-3-7-7-1-9   D186   CB310289

WILLIAM[6] BONNELL David[5], David[4], Joseph[3], Nathaniel[2], William[1]) was born in Springfield, Essex (now Union) co, NJ[1]. The only authority we have for the existence of this person is the research conducted by Iva Bunnell Adams and her family. It seems clear that every record ascribed to this William should properly be assigned to William Bonnell 1-3-7-7-2-8 CB310380, son of Nathaniel. David Bonnell certainly could have had a son William, but if so we know nothing further about him. I am inclined to believe that this is simply an error, and that he did not exist.

REFERENCES:
1. Family Group Sheet, David and Temperance (Wade) Bonnell. See p. 190.

1-3-7-7-2-3   CB320374

HENRY[6] BONNELL (Nathaniel[5], David[4], Joseph[3], Nathaniel[2], William[1]) was born in 1777 or 1778 in Mendham, Morris co, NJ[1]. No further information regarding this man has come to my attention. He may have died in childhood.

REFERENCES:
1. Clark record.

1-3-7-7-2-4   CB310377

NATHANIEL[6] BONNELL (Nathaniel[5], David[4], Joseph[3], Nathaniel[2], William[1)] was born 26 August 1782[1] at Mendham, Morris co, NJ. On 8 September 1802 he was married (first) by Rev. Matthew Laure Perrine of Madison, NJ, to MARY STURGES[1,2]. Nathaniel was of Mendham and Mary was of Morristown[2]. On 4 April 1814 Mary was confirmed in the Madison Presbyterian Church[1] and in the same year was dismissed to the Morristown Presbyterian Church[1]. She died 30 June 1838, aged 53 years, 4 months and 16 days[1]. She was buried in the Presbyterian Church Cemetery at Madison, Morris co[1].

Nathaniel, "of Green Village," Morris co, married (second) CHARITY MILLER, daughter of James and Anna (Collard) Miller of New Vernon, Morris co[3]. They appear in the 1850 census in Morris twp, Morris co: Nathaniel 67, a tailor and wife Charity 53[4]. They appear in the 1860 census in Morristown, Morris co: Nathaniel 77, a tailor and wife Charity 65[4]. Nathaniel died 7 April 1867, aged 84 years, 7 months and 11 days[1]. He was buried with his first wife Mary in the Presbyterian Church Cemetery at Madison[1].

Children (by first wife):
    1. 320138. Carman T., b. about 1803[4]; m. 13 June 1825 Matilda Lazer[4]; d. 23 Oct. 1883[4].
        Children (surname Bonnell):[4]

1. Sarah A.	4. Phebe A.	7. Henry H.
2. Nathaniel.	5. Oliver L.	8. Nelson C.
3. Jane A.	6. John T.	9. Samuel Morgan.

    2. 320377. Mary, b. about 1805[4].
    3. 320379. Abigail, b. about 1806[4].
    4. 320405. Barnabus C., b. about 1808[4]; m. Eliza J. _____ [4]; d. after 1870[4].
        Children (surname Bunnell):[4]

1. Sarah Eliza.	3. John S.	5. Harriet.
2. Eliza J.	4. Mary.	

    5. 320421. Nathaniel, b. about 1810[4]; m. Adeline _____ [4].
        Children (surname Bonnell):[4]

1. daughter.	3. George.	4. Charles l.
2. Sarah.		

    6. 320481. Emeline, b. about 1814[4]; m. _____ Trowbridge[4].
    7. 320442. Robert G., b. 21 July 1819[1]; m. Mary A. _____ [4]; d. 25 Oct 1871[1]
    8. 320454. Martha A., b. about 1824[4].

Children (by second wife):
    9. 006911. ?Eli, b. about 1848[6]; m. (second) 29 mar. 1883 Katy Parcells[6].

REFERENCES:
    1. Madison Church Records, p. 26.
    2. Gen Mag of NJ, Vol. IV, No. 3, p. 127.
    3. Littell, p. 367.
    4. CB Database.
    5. Clark record.
    6. *Bunnell/Bonnell Newsletter*, Vol. 13, No. 4, p. 140. New Jersey Marriages 1878-1900, abstracted by Claude A. Bunnell.

1-3-7-7-2-5 CB310378

DAVID THOMPSON[6] BONNELL (Nathaniel[5], David[4], Joseph[3], Nathaniel[2], William[1]) was born 17 October 1783[1] in Mendham, Morris co, NJ[2]. He married 29 March 1802 MASSA CLARK[3], daughter of Rev. Henry and Mary (Smith) Clark[4]. She was born 26 October 1783[4]. They lived in the northern part of Mendham twp which was set off in 1806 as the town of Randolph. The deed books of Morris county record a number of David's real estate transactions[2]. A deed dated 13 march 1812 records the purchase from his father for $100 a 7.2-acre tract "adjoining his new house"[2]. David died at Randolph in 1829[1,3]. Massa survived him until 1853[3].

Children:

    1. 320977. Charles Pickney, b. 5 May 1802[5]; m. 26 June 1830 Jane Garrabrant[5]; d. 10 Dec. 1876[5].
        Children (surname Bonnell):[5]

1. John W.	5. Cornelius Matthew.	8. Octavius.
2. Charles H.	6. Winfield Scott.	9. Sarah Jane.
3. William T.	7. Edward G.	10. David Thompson.
4. Aaron H.		

    2. 320978. Henry C., b. 28 July 1804[2]; m. 22 Sept. 1827 Mary Doland[2]; d. 20 feb. 1890[2].
        Children (surname Bonnell):[2]

1. Sarah.	4. Jane C.	7. David T.
2. Marinda.	5. Catherine D.	8. George Wesley.
3. Elizabeth Doland.	6. Mary Ann.	

    3. 320979. John Adams, b. 21 Dec. 1806[6]; m. 1827 Sarah M. Wyckoff[6]; d. 9 July 1880[6].
        Children (surname Bonnell):[2,6]

1. Jessie.	4. William Polison.	7. George Winsor.
2. Elizabeth C.	5. Martha Turner.	8. Marinda.
3. David T.	6. Mary Evalina.	9. Sarah J.

    4. 320980. Aaron H., b. 21 Dec. 1806[2]; m. 7 Oct. 1829 Elizabeth Wallen[2]; d. 3 Oct. 1885[2].
        Children (surname Bonnell):[2]

1. Frances W.	4. John Summerfield.	6. John Hancock Brown
2. Marinda.	5. Henry Clark.	7. Zennetta.
3. Charles M.		

    5. 320981. Marinda A., b. 6 Apr. 1809[2]; m. Daniel Millen[2]; d. 11 Oct. 1880[2].
    6. 320982. Lawrence, b. 1810[1].
    7.   child, d. young[3].
    8.   child, d. young[3].
    9.   child, d. young[3].

REFERENCES:
    1. Descendants of William Bunnell, compiled and sent to me be Ann Skidmore, Madison, VA.
    2. CB Database.
    3. Children of Nathaniel and Anne (Cozad) Bonnell, compiled by Virginia Carroll, Cleveland, OH, and sent to me by Jerome Hatch, Chicago, IL.
    4. Clark record.
    5. Family Group Sheet compiled and sent to me by H. Russell Bonnell, Logan, UT, citing the Bible records of Charles Pickney and Jane (Garrabrant) Bonnell owned by a granddaughter, Mrs. Kitty Bonnell Neuner, Fargo, ND.
    6. The Descendants of John Adams Bonnell, compiled and sent to me by Richard Lesser, Montville, NJ.

1-3-7-7-2-6   CB310379

AARON PITNEY[6] BONNELL (Nathaniel[5], David[4], Joseph[3], Nathaniel[2], William[1]) was born in September 1784 at Mendham, Morris co, NJ[1,2]. About 1810[2] he married JANE JOHNSTONE[1,2], daughter of James and Betsey (Wolsey) Johnstone[1,2]. She was born 21 February 1791[1,2] in Virginia[2]. On 17 December 1811 Aaron, a resident of Randolph twp, Morris co, bought 3 parcels of land in Randolph twp from his father Nathaniel[3]. Nine months later, on 7 September 1812 he sold all three parcels to Jacob Drake, his brother-in-law, and others[3].

In 1814 Aaron and his family moved to Euclid, Cuyahoga co, OH[2]. He appears in the census in Euclid in 1820: 30001-0001[3] and again in 1830: 2110001-120000101[3]. In 1833 they removed to Monee twp, Will co, IL, where they remained a few years, then moved on to southern Illinois[3]. Jane (Johnstone) Bonnell died 8 August 1841[2]. Aaron appears at age 64 in the 1850 census in Casey, Clark co, IL, living with his daughter Lucy and her husband Seth P. Cooper[3]. He died 14 March 1860[2].

Children:
1. 320830. James Nelson, b. 8 Dec. 1812[1]; m. 14 Mar. 1848 Elvira Johnston[3]; d. 15 Feb. 1862[1].
    Children (surname Bonnell):[3]
    1. Sarah Amelia.
2. 320832. Job Doan, b. 23 Mar. 1816[1,2]; m. 4 Sept. 1839 Ursula Ann Jackson[2]; d. 15 Nov. 1878[5].
    Children (surname Bonnelle):[2]
    1. Helen Adelaide.   3. Emma Charlotte.   5. Ella Louise.
    2. George Frederick.   4. Frank Jackson.   6. Emma Lunettie.
3. 320833. Hannibal Louis, b. 8 Mar. 1821[1,4]; m. 9 Mar. 1845 Olive Amanda Phillips[4]; d. 11 Oct. 1882[1,4].
    Children (surname Bonnell):[4]
    1. Elizabeth J.   5. Dyantha Safford.   9. William C.
    2. child, d. young. 6. Anna Minnesota.   10. Alta Belle.
    3. Mary A.   7. Aaron Lee.   11. Lucy Almira.
    4. Adelbert H.   8. Lewis Fremont.   12. Frederick Nelson.
4. 320835. Lucy A., b. 8 Nov. 1822[1]; m. 16 Apr. 1843 Seth P. Cooper[3]; d. 17 Mar. 1898[3].
5. 320834. Eliza A., b. 8 Nov. 1822[1]; m. 10 Oct. 1842 Oakley A. Phillips[3].
6. 320836. William A., b. 12 June 1825[1]; d. Oct. 1847[1].
7. 320837. Mary Jane, b. 10 Jan. 1828[1]; m. 30 Mar. 1852 William Cooper[3].

REFERENCES:
1. Family Group Sheet, Aaron Pitney and Jane (Johnstone) Bonnell. Notation attached: "Copy sent by V. Kuhni to J. Hatch - 1986. Data reportedly compiled by Rosetta Bunnell Halliday (V. Kuhni's great aunt) about 1900-10. Data reported checked and verified by LDS (Mormon) "researcher" Mildred L. Bennett 1950-60. J. Hatch." Copy sent to me by Jerome Hatch, Chicago, IL.

2. Genealogical Notes, compiled by Frank Jackson Bonnelle, photocopy sent to me by William J. Foley, Hackettstown, NJ.
3. CB Database.
4. Family Group Sheet, Hannibal and Olive Amanda (Phillips) Bonnell, compiled and sent to me by Jerome Hatch.
5. Death certificate, Joab Doan Bonnell, photocopy sent to me by William J. Foley.

1-3-7-7-2-8   D186   CB310380

WILLIAM[6] BONNELL (Nathaniel[5], David[4], Joseph[3], Nathaniel[2], William[1]) was born 3 August 1788[1] at Mendham, Morris co, NJ. On 20 April 1811 "Mr. William Bonnel of Randolph" was married to "Miss ELIZABETH CONGER" of Mendham by Rev. Henry Clark at Mendham[2,3]. She was born 1 May 1794[1]. William and Elizabeth bought land in Mendham from Nathaniel Clark and Stephen Losee for $270 on 13 February 1819[3]. On 14 January 1830 he bought from John and Abraham Byram a 9.5-acre parcel in Mendham twp, for which he paid $140[3]. William appears in the census in Mendham in 1830: 1102001-001101[3] and in 1840: 01100001-0000001[3].

William died 14 July 1845[1] and was buried in the cemetery at Mt. Freedom, Randolph twp, Morris co[1]. His widow Elizabeth appears in the 1850 census of Mendham at age 56, with her children Elizabeth, Jane and Charles[3]. She died 4 June 1882[1] and was buried beside her husband[1].

Children:
1. 320624. Jacob Drake, b. about 1812[3]; m. Margaret _____[3]; d. 27 Feb. 1892[3].
   Children (surname Bonnell):[3]
   1. Ruth.   3. George C.   4. Sarah L.
   2. Caroline.
2. 320625. Elizabeth, b. about 1814[3]; d. after 1850[3].
3. 320626. Aaron, b. 1815[3]; m. 10 Jan. 1839 Catherine Roff[3]; d. 27 Nov. 1891[3].
   Children (surname Bonnell):[3]
   1. Mary E.   4. Henry Elias.   7. Charles Stephen.
   2. Aaron Edward.   5. Catherine M.   8. Sarah Jane.
   3. Phebe Ann.   6. Ellen Caroline.
4. 320627. Jane P., b. about 1820[3]; d. after 1850[3].
5. 320623. Phebe, b. 182x[3].
6. 320628. William, b. about 1823[3]; m. 6 July 1850 Frances Lefler[3]; d. 28 Feb. 1873[3].
7. 320629. Squire Lewis, b. about 1830[3]; m. Harriet Ann Milligan[3]; d. 26 Mar. 1887[3].
   Children (surname Bonnell):[3]
   1. Elmira.   4. Ann L.   6. Harriet.
   2. Elizabeth Clythenie   5. Charles Squire.   7. Laura Dell.
   3. Florence L.
8. 320630. Charles F., b. about 1832[3]; d. 23 Feb. 1854[3].

REFERENCES:
1. Gravestones in Mt. Freedom Cemetery copied from cemetery description books (Morris co, Vol. II) in the NJ Historical Society at Newark, NJ, by Jerome Hatch, Chicago, IL.
2. Morris co Marriages 1798-1849 *from The Palladium of Liberty*, abstracted and sent to me by Jerome Hatch.
3. CB Database.
4. Clark record.

1-3-7-7-8-3   D187   CB310385

OLIVER[6] BONNELL (William[5], David[4], Joseph[3], Nathaniel[2], William[1]) was born 28 March 1795 on the old Bonnell homestead at Connecticut Farms, Essex (now Union) co, NJ[1]. He early learned the trde of shoemaker, which he followed more or less during his life[1]. On 28 October 1822, at Connecticut Farms, he was married by Rev. S. Thompson, to PHEBE ROBINSON WINANS[1,3,4], daughter of Joshua and Sarah (Robinson) Winans[1]. By the terms of his father's will, Oliver received a half interest in his father's salt meadow. He settled on a portion of his father's estate and followed his chosen occupation of farming in a small way[1]. In the census of 20 March 1829, he was the owner of twelve acres of good land at Connecticut Farms[1]. He erected a cider mill on his property, where large quantities of cider were manufactured annually[1].

Oliver appears in the census of Union twp, Essex (now Union) co, NJ in 1830: 100001-000101[3] and in 1840: 0110001-0010001[3]. He was a man much respected in his community[1], serving at least once as freeholder of the township[2]. He was a staunch Whig in politics[1]. He and his wife were both members of the Connecticut Farms Presbyterian Church[1]. For a number of years he was engaged in custom mattress and cushion making, his two sons assisting in this work[1]. At the same time he was actively involved in his brother's rope manufacturing, selling the products of the rope walk in the local markets[1]. Oliver age 55 and Phebe age 56 appear in the 1850 census in Union twp with their sons David 24 and Elias 19[7]. Also in their household were Caroline Anderson age 23 and Mary Leber age 2[7].

Oliver died intestate 5 April 1855, aged 60 years and 7 days[5,6] and was buried in the Connecticut Farms Presbyterian Church Cemetery[5,6]. Letters of administration were granted to his two sons to administer the estate, which amounted to $3,013.85[1]. The inventory of his estate included shoes, upper and sole leather, grain, sheep, cattle and horse, curled hair, a horsepower cider and presses, farm implements and outstanding notes due his estate[1]. His widow Phebe died 1 June 1856 in her 62nd year[5,6] and was buried with her husband[5,6].

Children:
1. 320465. David Oliver, b. 19 Nov. 1827[1]; m. 29 Apr. 1857 Nancy Maxwell
   Winans[1,3]; d. 6 Feb. 1903[1,3].
   Children (surname Bonnell):[1]
   1. Oliver.   3. Elias Herbert.   4. Mabel.
   2. Nathan Winans.

2. 320466. Elias Mooney, b. 2 Oct. 1831[1]; m. 21 May 1854 Elizabeth Potter[1];
d. 1 Sept. 1894[1,3,6]
Children (surname Bonnell):[1]
1. Anna Winans.   2. Lizzie Burtis.   3. Walter Sherwood.

REFERENCES:
1. Amer Families - Long Island, pp. 63, 64, 68.
2. *History of Union and Middlesex Counties, New Jersey*, by W. Woodford Clayton, 1882, p. 378.
3. CB Database.
4. Marriage records of the Connecticut Farms Presbyterian Church, abstracted by Jerome Hatch, Chicago, IL.
5. Burial records of the Connecticut Farms Presbyterian Church, abstracted by Jerome Hatch.
6. Connecticut Farms Cemetery Inscriptions, published in *New Jersey Historical Society Proceedings*, New Series - Vol. 9, p. 171, copy sent to me by Jerome Hatch.
7. 1850 U. S. Census, Union twp, Essex co, NJ, abstracted by Ruth C. Duncan.

1-3-7-7-8-5 D188 CB310387

WILLIAM JONES[6] BONNELL (William[5], David[4], Joseph[3], Nathaniel[2], William[1]) was born 17 March 1808 at Connecticut Farms, Essex (now Union) co, NJ[1]. While still in his minority he joined his father and brother in the duties of the farm and the manufacture of shoes and rope[1]. The rope industry became a business of considerable importance[1]. Much of the flax used in its manufacture was raised on the farm or in the immediate vicinity[1]. The rope walk, a building of one hundred or more feet in length, was situated at the rear of the homestead[1]. Small ropes were mostly made for rigging to small vessels at Elizabethport, also clotheslines, holsters, and rigging for tackle blocks[1]. On the death of his father William came into possession of the homestead and rope works[1]. He continued in the manufacture of rope and shoes for many years, his brother Oliver selling the products in the nearby markets[1]. He was also engaged at carpentering in the neightborhood, and was the sexton of the old Connecticut Farms Presbyterian Church and cemetery[1].

On 1 March 1832 William was married by Rev. Stephen Thompson to MARGARET REID[1,2,3], daughter of William and Abigail (Sayre) Reid[1]. She was born 27 October 1810[1]. William appears in the 1840 census in Union twp, Essex (now Union) co, NJ: 0000001-100001001[3]. The 1850 census of Union twp lists William J. 42, wife Margaret 40, daughter Scharlotte J. 11 and sons William H. 9 and Joseph R. 1[5]. Levi Warner 23, schoolteacher, also lived in their household[5]. They were members of the Connecticut Farms Church[1].

William died 22 January 1856[1,6] and was buried in the Connecticut Farms cemetery[1,6]. Margaret died 8 February 1857[1,6] and was buried with her husband. Margaret was the residual legatee of her mother-in-law's estate, but did not survive her.

Children:
1. 320459. William Jones, b. 17 Mar. 1833[1]; d. 27 July 1839[6].

2. 320461. Charlotte Isabelle, b. 29 June 1836[1]; m. 8 June 1864 Ulysse Savage[2].
   Children (surname Savage):[1]
   1. William J.   2. Charles G.   3. Margaret.

3. 320462. William Henry, b. 27 Nov. 1840[1]; m. 10 Mar. 1872 Susan Budd Vervalen[1];
   d. 6 Sept. 1915[3].
   Children (surname Bonnell):[1]
   1. Edith M.   3. Grace Budd.   5. Nellie L.
   2. William Joseph.   4. Susie Reid.

4. 320460. Joseph, b. 17 May 1845[1]; 14 Sept. 1845[1,6].

5. 320463. Joseph Reid, b. 5 Dec. 1848[1]; m. (first) 3 Oct. 1871 Elizabeth Coit Harris[1];
   m. (second) 10 Oct. 1882 Rosalie Prairie Cox[3]; d. 8 July 1918[3].
   Children (surname Bonnell)(by first wife):[1]
   1. Walter Harris.   2. Herbert Ralph.
   Children (surname Bonnell)(by second wife):[1]
   3. Maude May.   5. Ruth Estelle.   7. Harrison Freemont.
   4. Charles Joseph.   6. Clarence Reid.

REFERENCES:

1. Amer Families - Long Island, pp. 63, 64.

2. Marriage records of the Connecticut Farms Presbyterian Church, abstracted by Jerome Hatch, Chicago, IL.

3. CB Database.

4. Littell, p. 438.

5. 1850 U.S. Census, Union twp, Essex co, NJ, abstracted by Ruth C. Duncan.

6. Connecticut Farms Cemetery Inscriptions, published in *New Jersey Historical Society Proceedings*, New Series - Vol. 9, p. 170, copy sent to me by Jerome Hatch.

Key to Reference Notes

*marks complete publications in my personal library.

Adams - FGS
> Family Group Sheets prepared by Iva Bunnell Adams, Midway, UT, and sent to me by her in 1962.

Amer Fam - Long Island
> *American Families of Historic Lineage - Long Island Edition* (in 2 volumes) issued under the Editorial Supervision of William S. Pelletreau, A.M., member of the New York Historical Society and John Howard Brown. Published by National Americana Society, New York (no date).

Andrews
> *The Ancestors and Descendants of Havilah and Dorcas Gale Bunnell,* compiled by Adele Andrews, Norwalk, OH, 1935.

Banta
> *The Lineage of Theodore Melvin Banta of New York,* extracted from the C. C. Gardner file folders in the New Jersey Historical Society, Newark, NJ, and sent to me by W. Jerome Hatch, Chicago, IL.

Barbour
> Barbour Collection of Vital Records, Connecticut State Library, Hartford, CT, researched by Mrs. Clarence Bunnell, Winsted, CT.

Bassette
> *One Bassett Family in America,* by Buell B. Bassette, 1926.

Beardsley
> *Beardsley Genealogy,* by Nellie Beardsley Holt, 1951.

Biles Letters
> Letters sent to genealogist John Addison Biles, Homets Ferry, PA, 1880s to 1920s.

Biles Manuscript
> *The Bunnell Family* - manuscript compiled by John Addison Biles, Homets Ferry, PA, about 1926.

Bonnell
> *Genealogy of the Bonnell Family,* by Arthur Franklin Bonnell, 1880, copy sent to me by Clement M. Bonnell III.

Bunnell/Bonnell Newsletter
> *The Bunnell/Bonnell Newsletter,* first ten volumes published by William R. Austin, Laceyville, PA, 1987-1996, and succeeding volumes published by Carole Bonnell, Spanaway, WA, 1997-2002; and by Charles & Patricia Bunnell, Fairglade, TN, 2003 to the present.

Bunnell Homestead
> *A Door to the Past, The Nathaniel Bunnell Homestead,* brochure of the Elizabethtown Historical Foundation.

Bunnell Sketch
> *A Sketch of The History of the Race of Bunnells,* by Nehemiah Beardsley Bunnell, 1890.

Carroll - notes
> Bonnell family notes compiled by Rose McIlrath Carroll and sent to me by W. Jerome Hatch, Chicago, IL, in 1987.

Key to Reference Notes

CB Database

     Bunnell, Bonnell, Burnell, etc., Database, compiled by Claude A. Bunnell, Ocean City, NJ, and Longboat Key, FL, accessible on the internet at *http://bunnellbonnellburnellfamily.com.*

CBR NE PA

     Commemorative Biographical Record of Northeastern Pennsylvania, 1900, published by J. H. Beers & Co.

Census 1790

     Heads of Families, 1790 Census of the United States.

Chatham

     Chatham at the Crossing of the Fishawack, by John T. Cunningham, ©1967, Chatham Historical Society, Chatham, NJ.

Chatham at War

     A Village at War, Chatham, New Jersey, and the American Revolution, by Donald Wallace White, ©1979, Associated University Presses, Inc.

Cheshire

     History of Cheshire, Connecticut, from 1694 to 1840, by Joseph P. Beach, 1912.

Clark record

     A Record of the Lands and Past Descendants of Henry and Ann Clark who settled on the head branches of Whippany River, collected and arranged by Henry Spencer Clark, April 1909.

Colonial NJ

     Documents Relating to the Colonial History of New Jersey, Vol. I, 1631-1684, edited by William A. Whitehead, 1880.

Conkling

     Ancestry of David Oliver Bonnel, compiled by F. M. Conkling, East Orange, NJ.

Cornwall Cem

     Gravestone Inscriptions in the Cornwall Cemetery, Cornwall, CT, copied by Mrs. Clarence H. Bunnell, Winsted, CT.

CT Farms Cem Inscriptions

     Connecticut Farms Cemetery Inscriptions, published in *New Jersey Historical Society   Proceedings - New Series,* Vol. 9 (1924).

CT Farms Cem Inscriptions - 2

     Tombstone Inscriptions from Connecticut Farms Presbyterian Church Graveyard, copied and sent to me by W. Jerome Hatch, Chicago, IL.

CT Farms Church records

     Photocopies of the records of the Connecticut Farms, NJ, Presbyterian Church and Cemetery, sent to me by Clement M. Bonnell III, Milford, NJ.

476

Key to Reference Notes

CT Historical Society - VIII

Rolls and Lists of Connecticut Men in the Revolution, 1775-1783, Vol. VIII in the Collections of the Connecticut Historical Society, 1901, reduced photocopy by Stemmons Publishing.

CT Historical Society - IX

Rolls of Connecticut Men in the French and Indian War, 1755-1762, Vol. I, 1755-1757, Vol. IX in the Collections of The Connecticut Historical Society, 1903, reduced photocopy by Stemmons Publishing.

CT Historical Society - X

Rolls of Connecticut Men in the French and Indian War, 1755-1762, Vol. II, 1758-1762, Vol. X in the Collections of The Connecticut Historical Society, 1905, reprint 1994 by Heritage Books, Inc.

CT Historical Society - XII

Lists and Returns of Connecticut Men in the Revolution, 1775-1783, Vol. XII in the Collections of The Connecticut Historical Society, 1909, reprint 1995 by Heritage Books, Inc.

Cutter - CT

Genealogical and Family History of the State of Connecticut, William Richard Cutter et al., editors, Vols. I - IV, 1911, published by Lewis Historical Publishing Company.

Cutter - NE

New England Families, by William Richard Cutter, Vols. I through IV, 1913, reprint 1994 by Clearfield Company.

Danbury

Land and Probate Records of Danbury, CT, copied by William R. Austin.

DAR

DAR Lineage Books, published by the Daughters of the American Revolution.

Day

Day Unto Day, The Day Family in America, by Margery Day Hanson, 1978.

Deats

Genealogical Notes on the Bonnell Family compiled by Hiram E. Deats, copied and sent to me by Clement M. Bonnell III, Milford, NJ.

Derby

History of the Old Town of Derby, Connecticut, 1642-1880, by Samuel Orcutt and Ambrose Beardsley, 1880.

Dexter

New Haven Town Records, 1649-1662, Vol. I, of the Ancient Records Series of the New Haven Historical Society, edited by Franklin Bowditch Dexter.

Duncan

William Bunnell and His Descendants, by Ruth Cost Duncan, ©1986.

Durie

The Kakiat Patent in Bergen County, N.J., by Howard I. Durie, 1970.

Key to Reference Notes

Elizabeth, NJ, Cemeteries
> *Inscriptions on Tombstones and Monuments in the Burying Grounds of the First Presbyterian Church and St. John's Church at Elizabeth, N.J., 1664-1892,* by Wheeler and Halsey, 1892.

Essex co, NJ, Deeds
> Essex co, NJ, Deeds - copied and sent to me by Claude A. Bunnell.

Essex co, NJ, Mortgages
> Essex co, NJ, Mortgages - copied and sent to me by Claude A. Bunnell.

Fairfield - Jacobus
> *History and Genealogy of Families of Old Fairfield,* by Donald Lines Jacobus, 1930-1932, reprint 1976 by Genealogical Publishing Co., Inc.

Fern Bonnell
> *Genealogy of the Sylvanus Branch of the Bonnel Family,* written by Albert Bonnell, 1638-1904, appended to *A Brief Record of the Descendants of James Harvey and Rachel Ann Bonnell, 1811-1950,* written by Fern E. Bonnell, 1950.

Gen Mag of NJ
> *Genealogical Magazine of New Jersey* (*most issues cited).

Gibby
> *Genealogy of the Bonnell Family as it pertains to Edgar Marsh Gibby and his Descendants,* by Edgar Marsh Gibby.

Gillen
> *Ancestry and Posterity of Fred Elmer Bunnell,* by Lolita Bunnell Gillen, 1986.

Gray - FGS
> Family Group Sheets prepared by Vera E. Williams Gray and sent to me by W. Jerome Hatch in 1986.

Hale, House
> *Hale, House and Related Families,* by D. L. Jacobus and E. F. Waterman, ©1952, by The Connecticut Historical Society.

Hamilton co, OH
> *History of Hamilton County, Ohio,* compiled by Henry Allen Ford and Mrs. Kate B. Ford, 1881.

Hoagland
> *Twigs From Family Trees,* by Edward Coolbaugh Hoagland, Towanda, PA, 1961.

Holley - tax records
> *Analysis of Tax Records of Mendham and Randolph Townships, Morris co, NJ,* prepared and sent to me by Sharon Holley in 1988.

Hotten
> *The Original Lists of Persons of Quality; Emigrants; etc. Who Went from Great Britain To the American Plantations 1600-1700,* edited by John Camden Hotten, 1874.

Hunterdon co, NJ
> *Hunterdon County, NJ, Taxpayers, 1778-1797,* by T.L.C. Genealogy, 1990, sent to me by Robert Dils, Dolores, CO.

Key to Reference Notes

IGI
>International Genealogical Index, 1988 Update, sent to me by Geneva Draper, Pocatello, ID, and W. Jerome Hatch, Chicago, IL.

Jayne
>*Jayne History,* compiled by Lillian Jayne Dull and Ruth Jayne Hardy, 1960.

Lines
>Notebook of Bishop Edwin S. Lines, owned and transcribed by Judith Bruce, Monument, CO.

Littell
>*Genealogies of the First Settlers of Passaic Valley (And Vicinity),* by John Littell, 1852, reduced photocopy by Stemmons Publishing

Lynch
>*The Bonnell/Bunnill Family, William Bunnil and His Sons*, compiled by Marilyn Ward Lynch, Henderson, NV, July 1990.

Madison Church Records
>*Madison, New Jersey, Presbyterian Church Vital Records, 1747-1900,* by Viola E. Shaw and Barbara S. Parker, ©1982 by The Presbyterian Church of Madison, copy given to me by Claude A. Bunnell.

Mass Bay Records
>*Records of the Governor and Company of Massachusetts Bay,* edited by N. B. Shurtleff, 6 vols., 1853.

Minisink
>*Minisink Valley Reformed Dutch Church Records, 1716-1830,* Vol. V in the Collections of The New York Genealogical and Biographical Society, 1913, reprint 1992 by Heritage Books, Inc.

Monnette
>*First Settlers of Piscataway and Woodbridge, NJ,* by Orra Eugene Monnette, 1931, furnished to me by Ruth C. Duncan, West Simsbury, CT.

Morris co, NJ, Deeds
>Morris co, NJ, Deeds - photocopied and sent to me by Claude A. Bunnell.

Morris co, NJ, Mortgages
>Morris co, NJ, Mortgages - photocopied and sent to me by Claude A. Bunnell.

Morris Gen Soc
>Morris Area Genealogical Society.

Morristown Church Records
>*History of the First Presbyterian Church, Morristown, NJ, part I, Records of Trustees and Session, From 1742-1882,* extract sent to me by Thomas A. Hill, Austintown, OH.

Mt Freedom Church Records
>Records of Mount Freedom Presbyterian Church, Randolph, Morris co, NJ, photocopies sent to me by W. Jerome Hatch and Sharon Holley.

Murray
>*Bunnell and Allied Families,* by Joan England Murray, 1990.

479

NEHGR

The New England Historical and Genealogical Register.

New Haven Colony Records

Records of the Colony and Plantation of New Haven, from 1638 to 1649, by Charles J. Hoadly, M.A., 1857.

New Haven History

History of the Colony of New Haven to its Absorption into Connecticut, Vol. I and II, by Edward E. Atwater, 1902, reprint 1989 by Heritage Books, inc.

New Haven Deeds

New Haven Land Records, copied and sent to me by Ruth C. Duncan.

New Haven Hist Society

Papers of the New Haven Historical Society, researched by Ruth C. Duncan.

New Haven - Jacobus

Families of Ancient New Haven, compiled by Donald Lines Jacobus, 1923-1932, reprint 1981 by Genealogical Publishing Co., Inc.

New Haven Newspapers

Genealogical Data From Colonial New Haven Newspapers, compiled by Kenneth Scott and Rosanne Conway, 1979, published by Genealogical Publishing Co., Inc.

New Haven Superior Court

Records of New Haven Superior Court, researched by Ruth C. Duncan.

New Milford Deeds

New Milford, CT, Land Records, copied and sent to me by Ruth C. Duncan.

New Milford History

History of the Towns of New Milford and Bridgewater, Conn., 1702-1882, by Samuel Orcutt, 1882.

NHVR

Vital Records of New Haven, Conn. to 1850.

NJ Burial Grounds

Old Burial Grounds of New Jersey, by Janice Kohl Sarapin. Extract sent to me by Marguerite LaFlesh, Montville, NJ.

NJ Collections

Historical Collections of the State of New Jersey, Containing Geographical Descriptions of Every Township in the State, by John W. Barber and Henry Howe, 1845, reprint 1990 by Heritage Books, Inc.

NJ Colonial Documents

New Jersey Colonial Documents, Vol. XIV, Journal of the Governor and Council.

NJ Conveyances

Colonial Conveyances: Provinces of East and West New Jersey 1664-1794, by Crestview Lawyers Service, 1974, extract sent to me by Claude A. Bunnell.

Key to Reference Notes

NJ Genesis

The New Jersey Genesis, Harold A. Sonn, editor & publisher, Springfield, NJ.

NJ Hist Soc

The Proceedings of the New Jersey Historical Society.

NJ in 1793

New Jersey in 1793, by James S. Norton, 1973.

NJ Marriages

New Jersey Marriage Records, 1665-1800, by William Nelson, originally published as *Archives of the State of New Jersey,* First Series, Vol. XXII, 1900, reprint 1982 by Genealogical Publishing Co., Inc.

NJ Tax Lists

New Jersey Tax Lists 1772-1822, Vol. 1, Ronald U. Jackson, Editor. © 1981 by Jacksonian Enterprises, Inc., published by Accelerated Indexing Systems, Inc., extracts sent to me by Claude A. Bunnell.

NJ Wills - Vol. I

Documents Relating to the Colonial History of the State of New Jersey, Vol. XXIII, Calendar of New Jersey Wills, Vol. I, 1670-1730, by William Nelson, 1901, reprint 1994 by Heritage Books, Inc.

NJ Wills - Vol. II

Documents Relating to the Colonial History of the State of New Jersey, First Series, Vol. XXX, Calendar of New Jersey Wills, Vol. II, 1730-1750, by William Nelson and A. Van Doren Honeyman, 1918, reprint 1994 by Heritage Books, Inc.

NJ Wills - Vol. III

Documents relating to the Colonial History of the State of New Jersey, First Series, Vol. XXXII, Calendar of New Jersey Wills, Vol. III, 1751-1760, by A. Van Doren Honeyman, 1924, reprint by Heritage Books, Inc.

NJ Wills - Vol. IV

Documents Relating to the Colonial History of the State of New Jersey, First Series, Vol. XXXIII, Calendar of New Jersey Wills, Vol. IV, 1761-1770, by A. Van Doren Honeyman, 1928, reprint 1997 by Family Line Publications, Westminster, MD.

NJ Wills - Vol. V

Documents Relating to the Colonial History of the State of New Jersey, First Series, Vol. XXXIV, Calendar of New Jersey Wills, Vol. V, 1771-1780, by A. Van Doren Honeyman, 1931, reprint 1997 by Family Line Publications.

NJ Wills - Vol. VI

Documents Relating to the Colonial History of the State of New Jersey, First Series, Vol. XXXV, Calendar of New Jersey Wills, Vol. VI, 1781-1785, by Elmer T. Hutchinson, reprint 2002 by Willow Bend Books.

NJ Wills - Vol. VII

Documents Relating to the Colonial History of the State of New Jersey, First Series, Vol. XXXVI, Calendar of New Jersey Wills, Vol. VII, 1786-1790, by Elmer T. Hutchinson, reprint 2002 by Willow Bend Books.

NJ Wills - Vol. VIII

Documents Relating to the Colonial History of the State of New Jersey, First Series, Vol. XXXVII, Calendar of New Jersey Wills, Vol. VIII, 1791-1795, by Elmer T. Hutchinson, reprint 2002 by Willow Bend Books.

NJ Wills - Vol. IX

Documents Relating to the Colonial History of the State of New Jersey, First Series, Vol. XXXVIII, Calendar of New Jersey Wills, Vol. IX, 1796-1800, by Elmer T. Hutchinson, reprint 2002 by Willow Bend Books.

NJ Wills - Vol. XI

Documents Relating to the Colonial History of the State of New Jersey, First Series, Vol. XL, Calendar of New Jersey Wills, Vol XI, 1806-1809, by Elmer T. Hutchinson, reprint 2002 by Willow Bend Books.

Nutmegger

The Connecticut Nutmegger, published by the Connecticut Society of Genealogists, Inc.

NY Gazetteer

Historical and Statistical Gazetteer of New York State, by J. H. French, 1860.

NYGBR

The New York Genealogical and Biographical Record.

NY Marriages

Marriage Index of New York, compiled by Nancie Davis, West Columbia, SC.

Raywalt

The Ancestors and Descendants of Harold Albert Mitchell, by James Raywalt, 1997.

Redding

Manual of the Congregational Church of Redding, CT, 1896.

Rev War - CT

The Record of Connecticut Men of the Military and Naval Service During the War of The Revolution, 1775-1783, edited by Henry P. Johnston, 1889, reprint 1997 for Clearfield Company, Inc., by Genealogical Publishing Co., Inc.

Rev War - NJ - 1

Official Register of the Officers and Men of New Jersey in the Revolutionary War, by William S. Stryker, 1872, reprint 1993 by Heritage Books, Inc.

Rev War - NJ - 2

New Jersey in the Revolution 1763-1783, by Larry R. Gerlach, 1975, in the research papers of Ruth Cost Duncan.

Rev War - NY

New York in The Revolution as Colony and State, Second Edition, by James A. Roberts.

Rev War pension appl.

Photocopy of Revolutionary War pension application in the National Archives, copied and sent to me by Claude A. Bunnell.

Key to Reference Notes

Snell

History of Sussex and Warren Counties, N.J., compiled by James P. Snell, 1881, reprint 1981 by Genealogical Researchers, Washington, NJ.

Stocker

Centennial History of Susquehanna County, PA, by Rhamanthus M. Stocker, Philadelphia, 1887, reprint 1974 by the Susquehanna County Historical Society and Regional Publishing Co, Baltimore, MD.

Thayer

As We Were, The Story of Old Elizabethtown, by Theodore Thayer, Vol. XIII in The Collections of The New Jersey Historical Society, ©1964.

Tioga Gazetteer

Historical Gazetteer of Tioga County, New York, 1785-1888, by W. B. Gay.

Tioga NY History

History of Tioga, Chemung, Tompkins & Schuyler Counties, New York, Philadelphia: Everts & Ensign - 1879.

Union & Middlesex co, NJ Hist

History of Union & Middlesex Counties, NJ, editec by W. Woodford Clayton, 1882. Published by Everts & Peck, Philadelphia. Extracts sent to me by Homer Baldwin, Greensburg, PA.

Virkus

The Abridged Compendium of American Genealogy, by Frederick Adams Virkus, 7 volumes, 1925-42.

Wade, Bonnell & Crane Bible

Bible Records and Wills, Boudinot Chapter DAR, Elizabeth, NJ. Wade, Bonnell & Crane Bible. Records from Bible owned by Helen Bertha Crane, 220 South Broad St., Elizabeth, NJ. Copied by Evelyn Leary Ogden. Copied and sent to me by Homer E. Baldwin in 1959.

Wallingford

History of Wallingford, Connecticut, 1670 -1870, by Charles Henry Stanley Davis, 1870, reprint 1998 by Heritage Books, Inc.

War of 1812

Records of Connecticut Men Who Served in The Regular Army and the Militia in the War of 1812, Henry P. Johnston, editor, 1889.

Wayne PA History

History of Wayne, Pike and Monroe Counties, Pennsylvania, by Alfred Mathews, Philadelphia: R. T. Peck & Co. - 1886.

Winans

Family of John & Susannah Melyn Winans, by Alice Winans Egy Woolley, 1987.

Woodbury

History of Ancient Woodbury, CT, by William Cothren, 1879, reprint 1992, by Heritage Books, Inc.

Woodruff

Woodruff Chronicles, A Genealogy, Vol. II, compiled by Ceylon Newton Woodruff and Maurine R. Herod, 1971. Sent to me by Ellen Dorn, Alhambra, CA, 8 June 1989.

When I was ready to prepare the Index which follows, I ran into a serious snag. The computer program I used to prepare the index for the first edition would not work on my current computer - one of the hazards of our constantly improving technology. When I was unable to find another indexing program, I followed my usual problem-solving technique - I called my son. It's amazing what the next generation knows that this one does not. Bill's response was "no problem". All I had to do was type all the names into a file and he could easily put it into a format just like that of the first edition. Presto! You owe this Index to the talents of my elder son William R. Austin, Jr., to whom I am extremely grateful for this latest rescue.

The Index includes every name which occurs in the text itself, beginning on page 27. It does not include names which appear in the References at the end of each article. Also, a name which appears more than once on a page is recorded only once in the Index, even if two different persons are intended. Be sure to check the entire page if you are looking up a particular individual.

- A -

ABERNATHY
Abigail, 125
Beulah (Beach), 125
Enos, 125
Samuel, 71
ACKERMAN
Albert, 144
Rachel (Bonnell), 144
Rachel (Van Winkle), 144
ADAMS
Andrew, 272
Cinderella, 340
Cinderella (Bunnell), 340
Ellen, 340
Iva (Bunnell), 190
Iva Bunnell, 466
John, 339
John M., 340
Lazarus, 86
Martha Ann, 340
Mary Ann, 340
Sam, 106
William, 339
William Clifford, 340
ADKINS
Daniel, 271
AIKE
Tunis, 86
ALBAUGH
Alice, 415
ALBRIGHT
Mary (Bonnell), 186
Solomon, 186
ALCOTT
Hannah, 238
ALEXANDER
Deborah, 450
ALLEN
Aaron, 81
Abigail, 81
Abigail (Bonnell), 81
David, 81
Elizabeth, 146
Isabelle M., 347
Jacob, 146
Mary, 366
Nathaniel Bonnel, 81
Parmalee, 107
Phebe, 459
Samuel, 81, 150
Uriah, 81
ALLENDER
Alexander, 436
Angeline (Bonnell), 436
C. Albert, 436
Emma, 436
George, 436
James, 436
John, 436
Sanford James, 436
William, 436
ALLING
Ebenezer, 301
Patty (Bunnell), 301

ALLISON
M. F., 306
Margaret, 434
ALVORD
Anna, 290
Anna (Bow), 290
Anna (Lucas), 290
Clarissa, 290
Thomas, 290
AMERINE
Henry, 185
AMERY
Alba (Bunnell), 337
Joseph W., 337
Permelia C., 337
ANDERSON
Caroline, 428, 471
Jacob, 420
Margaret, 423
Rachel V. (Bonnell), 365
Robert, 365
Susan, 406
Susan Ann, 465
ANDRESS
James, 464
Jane (Bonnell), 464
ANDREWS
Abel, 129
Abigail, 204
Adele, 106, 108, 225
Esther, 273
Mary (Clark), 354
Roxanna (Blakeslee), 129
Roxanna (Bunnell), 129
Samuel, 50
William, 50
Zenas, 134
ANDRUS
Ellen A. (Bunnell), 355
ARMSTRONG
Amzi, 464
Deborah, 450
Eleanor (Bunnell), 220
Milton, 220
ARNOLD
Benedict, 177
James, 131
Jonathan, 68
ASA
William, 417
ASHLEY
Lydia (Doolittle), 283
Olive, 283
Samuel, 283
ASHWARD
Jane Dorrington, 404
ATWATER
Eunice (Newton), 129
Hannah (Hotchkiss), 131
Jonathan, 75
Moses, 129
Naomi, 131
Rhoda, 285
Russell, 319, 320
Sarah, 129
Stephen, 131

ATWOOD
Anna, 322
AUGUR
Daniel P., 297
Hannah (_____), 297
John, 126
Puah, 126
Rachel (Barnes), 126
AUSTIN
Moses, 154
AVERILL
Elisha, 327
Elisha P., 330
Fitch, 330
Frances, 330
Frances B., 328
Gertrude V., 327
Harriet, 329
Harriet (Bunnell), 330
Selden, 328, 330
Talma, 328, 330
AVERY
Achsah (Bunnell), 129
Anson D., 129
Harriet Currance, 129
Humphrey, 129
AYERS
Abigail (Bunnell), 412
Albert C., 412
Albert Gallatin, 392
Julia Ann (Bunnell), 392
Julia Ann (Pence), 392
Samuel Day, 392
AYLESWORTH
Almira, 351

- B -

BABBIT
John M., 363
Julia, 363
Julia (Bonnell), 363
Nancy Day, 363
BABCOCK
Fanny (_____), 329
Pliny F., 329
BABLET
Ticphena, 203
BACON
Bacon, 266
Jacob, 105
John L., 266
Margaret (Bonnell), 266
Mary L., 266
Sarah, 266
William B., 266
BAHM
John, 92
BAILEY
Amanda (Bunnell), 287
Charles, 220
Gilbert, 220
Horace, 139
Howard, 220
Nathaniel, 287
Polly (Bunnell), 139

BAILEY
Rose, 287
Sarah E. (Bunnell), 220
Wayland, 220
William, 220
BAILIE
Henry, 164
BAKER
James, 343
Mary, 343
Mary (Parker), 343
Miller, 195
BALDWIN
Abigail (_____), 63
Arthur Cameron, 239
Ashbel, 207
Charles B., 239
David, 96, 97
Edwin Franklin, 258
Frances, 238
Frances Eveline, 239
Grace D., 203
Homer E., 159
Jeduthan, 364
John, 124
Jonathan, 119
Luna, 261
Lydia, 124
Margaret A., 449
Margery (Tyler), 124
Mehitable, 63
Moses, 188
Obadiah, 63
Reuben, 336
Roxanna (Bunnell), 238
Roxanna J. (Bunnell), 239
Samuel, 295
Temperance, 202
Thaddeus, 206
Thomas, 63
BALL
Aaron, 410
Anna (Bunnell, 313
Edwin L., 313
Esther (Osborn), 189
Eunice, 187
Harriet, 363, 410
Mehitable, 313
Nathaniel, 187, 189
Olinda, 391
Patty (Wade), 410
Puah, 189
Rachel, 357
Zina, 313
BALLENTINE
Eliza H., 376
Elizabeth (Bonnell), 376
Elizabeth (Bryant), 376
John, 376
BANNATYNE
Ann, 224
Archibald, 224
Elizabeth (Bunnell), 224
James, 224
John W., 224
Lydia, 224

485

BANNATYNE
Mary, 224
Robert W., 224
Savannah, 224
BARBER
Eliza (Bishop), 404
BARDWELL
Frances Elizabeth, 225
BARHYT
Elizabeth, 389
BARKALOW
Eleanor (or Lanah), 97
Herman, 98
Jacques, 97
Jane (_____), 97
BARKER
Lucy, 247
BARLOW
Margaret Maria, 326
BARNES
Amos, 272
Amzi I., 139
Eliza, 346
Elizabeth (Bunnell), 208
James, 401
Jesse, 132
Johanna, 70
Laura (Bradley), 139
Laura (Bunnell), 139
Lucy (Bunnell), 132
Martin, 125
Mindwell (Dibble), 70
Nathan, 169
Rachel, 126
Rebecca (Bunnell), 125
Thomas, 70
Willard, 208
BARNS
Lucy (Perkins), 208
BARNUM
Hannah (Bunnell), 48
John, 104
Nathan, 48
BARRY
Catherine, 98
Eunice, 216
Hester (Bryant), 98, 100
James, 98, 100
BARTHOLOMEW
Andrew, 69
Helen (Bonnell), 430
Seabery, 430
Timothy, 126
BARTLETT
Mary A., 402
BARTON
Ann, 395
_____, 396
BARTRON
Aaron, 101
Ann, 101
Benjamin Bunnell, 101
Daniel, 101
Elizabeth, 101
Esther, 101
Mary, 101

BARTRON
Moses, 101
Rebecca (Bunnell), 101
Sarah, 101
BASSETT
John R., 202
BATEMAN
John, 362
BATES
Abigail (Hine), 204
Benjamin, 204
Betty, 204
Elihu, 204
Mary O. (Bunnell), 307
Rhoda, 285
William, 307
BAUM
Henry, 411
BAXTER
Beula, 249, 252
Margaret, 268
Simeon Barton, 268
BAYLES
Minerva Ellen, 289
BEACH
Abigail, 94
Beulah, 125
Burrage, 134, 338
Jabez, 94
James, 94
Jerusha (Bonnell), 94
Joanna, 94, 114
John, 94
Joseph, 94
Martha (Clark), 76
Samuel, 94
Susan, 94
Thankful, 76
William, 76, 94
BEARDSLEY
Anna, 106
Gideon, 108
Mary, 106, 108
Mercy (Jackson), 106, 108
Obadiah, 106, 108
BEAVER
Sarah, 439
BEAVERS
Joseph, 163
Lydia Hull, 420
BEDFORD
Anne (Bonnell), 106
Anne (Bunnell), 106, 107
Jonathan, 106
Stephen, 106, 107, 362, 363
BEECH
Burrage, 135
Richard, 54
BEECHER
Abigail, 132
Mary Jane, 354
BEEMAN
Mary L., 416
BEERS
Joseph D., 303

BEHME
Margaret, 104, 106, 107
BELES
Samuel, 38
BELL
Julia Ann, 413
BENEDICT
Judson, 411
Julia (Bonnell), 410, 411
BENHAM
Adah, 76
Adna, 76
Amos, 76
Betsey, 76
Ebenezer, 273, 274
Elizabeth (Bunnell), 76
Esther (Andrews), 273
Esther (Bunnell), 76
George, 76
Isaac, 76
Jared, 76
Joel, 273
Joseph, 51, 76, 134
Mariel, 273
Mary (Brooks), 51
Mary (Bunnell), 51
Mary Ann, 76
Ransom, 76
Samuel, 76
Thomas, 76
BENNETT
Eliza (Bunnell), 406
Mary (Bunnell), 406
Tome, 204
BENSLEY
Anna, 98
Daniel, 98, 212
Eleanor, 98
Elizabeth, 98
Gershom, 98
Henry, 98
John, 98
Martha (Bunnell), 212
Mary (Bunnell), 98
Mary Ann, 98
Sarah, 98
William Rushton, 98
BENTON
Alvira (Bunnell), 299
James, 299
BERGET
Charlotte (Bunnell), 141
BERGSTRESER
Anna C., 216
BERKELEY
John, 44
BERRY
Divan, 123
BERRYHILL
John, 412
Sarah Ann (Bunnell), 412
BIDDLE
Ann, 396
Martha, 396
BIGELOW
John, 140

BILES
Aaron, 225
Albert Sidney, 225
Anna Eliza, 225
Elmore Llewellyn, 225
Emily Amanda, 225
Helen Marr, 225
Jacob Monroe, 225
Jacob Place, 225
James Monroe, 225
John, 65, 121, 278, 302, 308
John A., 102, 112, 139, 351
John Addison, 99, 225
Martin Luther, 225
Mary, 225
Mary (Bunnell), 225
Sarah, 225
BILLS
Thomas, 183
BIRD
Alexander Bonnell, 425
Amasa, 253
Amasa S., 113
Amasa T., 254
Annie Leigh, 425
Benjamin Chew, 425
Byron Clark, 425
Carrie Dunham, 425
Edward, 239
Elizabeth Joanna, 425
Ella E., 239
Emma, 425
Fannie, 437
Ida L., 239
Isabelle B., 425
James Bunnell, 239
James Humphrey, 239
John L., 113
Lucinda (Bunnell), 239
Mansfield Hummer, 425
Omeigh, 239
Orin J., 239
Oscar M., 239
Rebecca (Bunnell), 113
Sarah, 239
Sarah Dumont, 425
Sarah Leigh (Bonnell), 425
William, 239
BISHOP
Abraham, 159
Eliza, 404
Elizabeth (Bunnell), 392
Elizabeth (King), 392
Elizabeth (Martindale), 392
James, 159
Mary, 159
Moses, 159
Rachel, 159
Susanna (Bishop), 159
BLACKFORD
Abigail, 84
Abigail (Bonnell), 83, 84
Benjamin, 84
Ephraim, 156, 157, 161
Frances (Leforge), 155
Isaiah, 84

BONNELL

Charles William, 442
Charles Woolverton, 421
Charlotte, 357, 375, 377, 387, 443, 461
Charlotte (Bronson), 451
Charlotte (Tannyhill), 458
Charlotte D., 454
Charlotte Isabelle, 473
Chloe, 148, 379
Christian, 449, 454, 459
Cinderella, 428
Cinderella Francis Ann, 428
Clara Ann, 430
Clarence, 459
Clarence E., 389
Clarence L., 438
Clarence Reid, 473
Clarissa, 264
Clarissa (Canfield), 375
Clarissa Angeline, 371
Clarissa H., 452
Clark, 365, 368, 369
Clark Grant, 457, 459
Clark O., 386
Clel, 386
Clement, 164, 421
Clement DuMont, 419, 420, 422
Clement Hinchman, 421
Clement duMont, 165
Clementine A., 432
Clifford Landon, 434
Cornelia Catherine, 423, 455
Cornelia P., 382
Cornelius Matthew, 468
Courtland F., 447
Daniel, 83, 84, 158, 160, 161, 169, 263, 264, 265, 267, 429, 430, 432, 456
Daniel Alpheus, 433
Daniel C., 430
Daniel H., 457
Daniel Howard, 457, 458
Daniel Losey, 380
Daniel M., 441, 442
Daniel V., 415
Darius, 183, 184, 453
David, 61, 82, 88, 92, 93, 106, 150, 152, 153, 180, 181, 185, 186, 190, 191, 192, 197, 198, 382, 387, 388, 446, 451, 456, 464, 465, 466
David Daniel, 267
David Edward, 461
David Elias, 190
David H., 382, 457
David Maxwell, 418
David Newell, 465
David Oliverf, 471
David T., 468
David Thompson, 193, 467, 468
David W., 371, 388
David Ward, 373, 465
David Warren, 389
Deanna (Dell), 441
Deborah (Alexander), 450

BONNELL

Deborah (Armstrong), 450
Deborah (Leigh), 424
Deborah Ann, 429
Delia Emily, 366
Delila C. or J., 459
Dennis, 420
Doctor Watts, 90, 187, 188
Dode P., 431
Dora, 429
Duncan M., 431
Dyantha Safford, 469
Earl Burton, 437
Edgar B., 459
Edgar Kelsey, 434
Edith, 424, 449
Edith M., 473
Edmond, 456
Edmond Stanton, 457, 459
Edmund, 389
Edna, 430
Edna Miranda, 455
Edna S., 442
Edridge Murry., 459
Edward Alonzo, 439
Edward C., 383
Edward F., 415
Edward G., 468
Edward N., 373
Edwin, 366, 382
Edwin E., 449
Edwin R., 386, 465
Elam Williams, 357
Eleanor, 150, 151, 152, 178, 181
Eleanor (_____), 88
Eleanor Ann, 179
Eleazer, 91, 92
Electa, 382, 464, 465
Eli, 467
Eli Phillips, 371
Elias, 150, 191, 381, 382, 461, 471
Elias Freeman, 382
Elias Herbert, 471
Elias Mooney, 472
Elijah, 359, 363
Elijah Day, 363
Elijah W., 375
Elisabeth, 419
Eliza, 357, 377, 386, 422
Eliza (Stevens), 443
Eliza (Wright), 371
Eliza Ann, 423
Eliza B., 442
Eliza C. (Fink), 385
Eliza Day, 380
Eliza Eleanor, 410
Eliza J. (Catherwood), 430
Eliza Jane, 431
Eliza Jane (Boyd), 438
Eliza M., 464
Eliza M. (Pittman), 386
Eliza(beth) Ann, 424

BONNELL

Elizabeth, 81, 147, 159, 160, 181, 191, 192, 266, 267, 360, 370, 373, 377, 380, 383, 389, 418, 420, 433, 440, 441, 443, 447, 448, 449, 450, 452, 457, 458, 461, 470
Elizabeth (Allen), 146
Elizabeth (Barhyt), 389
Elizabeth (Bleakney), 265, 266
Elizabeth (Bonnell), 457, 458
Elizabeth (Bruce), 454
Elizabeth (Bryant), 376
Elizabeth (Conger), 470
Elizabeth (Crane), 359, 360
Elizabeth (Dickey), 414
Elizabeth (Foster), 162, 164, 425
Elizabeth (Hatfield), 56
Elizabeth (Jones), 92, 93
Elizabeth (Large), 454
Elizabeth (Likens), 183
Elizabeth (Maxwell), 418
Elizabeth (Orr), 437
Elizabeth (Potter), 472
Elizabeth (Simcock), 440, 441
Elizabeth (Wallen), 468
Elizabeth (_____), 56, 431
Elizabeth Anderson, 423
Elizabeth Ann, 457, 458
Elizabeth Ann (Bracken), 431
Elizabeth C., 468
Elizabeth Clythenie, 470
Elizabeth Coit (Harris), 473
Elizabeth D. (Walker), 373
Elizabeth Doland, 468
Elizabeth J., 469
Elizabeth Jane, 457, 459
Elizabeth Jane (Summerville), 452
Elizabeth L. (Hill), 447
Elizabeth S., 441
Ella Mae, 449
Ellen, 456, 457, 458
Ellen Caroline, 470
Ellen Lucy, 448
Ellis, 373
Ellola J., 437
Elmer E., 424
Elmira, 470
Eloise, 267
Elsa, 410
Elsie, 449
Elsworth Burlingame, 455
Elvira (Johnston), 469
Emanuel, 457, 459
Emeline, 420, 452, 467
Emily, 436, 451
Emily (McMurry), 430
Emily (Van Sycle), 424
Emily C. Y., 424
Emily I., 371
Emma, 373, 430, 449
Emma A., 437
Emma H., 386, 418
Emma Irene, 461

BONNELL

Emma L. (Evitt), 434
Emma V. (_____), 434
Emmaline, 373
Enoch, 147, 148, 378, 379, 380, 381
Enos, 356, 357, 378
Enos Johnson, 357
Ernest Noble, 455
Eseck George, 454, 455
Estella Glendora, 452
Esther, 160, 447
Esther D., 461
Eunice, 378, 451
Eunice (Ball), 187, 188
Evangeline Celestia, 455
Eveline Hamilton, 430
Everett, 424
Ezra, 378
Ezra Graves, 465
Ezra N., 454
Fannie (Bird), 437
Fanny, 430
Fanny (Hand), 384
Ferdinand, 414
Flora, 450
Florence, 457
Florence L., 470
Florence R., 452
Floyd Neely, 418
Frances, 383
Frances "Annie", 265
Frances (Lefler), 470
Frances E. P. (Whelpley), 411
Frances Flora, 450
Frances Josephine, 429
Frances W., 468
Francis, 383
Francis Marion, 431, 454, 455
Frank, 447, 449
Frank B., 449
Frank K., 454
Frank O., 437
Frank Roe, 424
Frank S., 386
Fred Wilmot, 443
Freddie, 443
Frederick, 449
Frederick John, 265
Frederick Nelson, 469
Frederick Simeon, 443
George, 377, 411, 414, 437, 467
George Albert, 441
George Arthur, 455
George C., 470
George Harrison, 438
George Harvey, 442
George Henry, 452
George Omar, 455
George Perry, 457, 458
George R., 461
George W., 267, 428, 434, 436, 439, 451, 452
George Washington, 386
George Wesley, 468

BONNELL

George William, 439
George Winsor, 468
Gershom, 103, 241
Gertrude H., 411
Gilbert, 374, 375, 378
Gouverneur, 377
Grace A., 430
Grace Budd, 473
H. Russell, 166
Hanna (Thompson), 93
Hannah, 53, 82, 91, 150, 152, 192, 193, 266, 382, 438, 439, 452
Hannah (Buckingham), 446
Hannah (Dell), 441
Hannah (Dixon), 432
Hannah (Dixson), 433
Hannah (Dunham), 441
Hannah (Smith), 417
Hannah (Spears), 460
Hannah (Thompson), 92, 192
Hannah (Tunis), 460
Hannah (Turkle), 437
Hannah (Ward), 355, 357
Hannah (Wickery), 450
Hannah Elizabeth, 268
Hannah Jane, 447
Hannah Jane (Thomas), 431
Hannah M., 433
Hannah M. (Dean), 459
Hannah Parcel, 382
Hannah S., 441
Hannibal Louis, 469
Harold, 106
Harold A., 267
Harriet, 357, 384, 430, 450, 458, 460, 461, 470
Harriet (Ball), 363, 410
Harriet (Bolser), 447
Harriet (Hayes), 457
Harriet (Monroe), 457
Harriet Ann (Milligan), 470
Harriet Cornelia, 454
Harriet E., 428
Harriet Eugenia (Spring), 454
Harriet F., 411
Harriet N., 382
Harriet Newel, 380
Harriett, 373
Harrison Freemont, 473
Harry, 449
Harry F., 430, 443
Harry G., 437
Harry McKinnon, 434
Harvey S., 386
Hattie A. (Oliver), 437
Hattie May, 429
Helen, 430, 447
Helen Mar (Carhart), 424
Helen R., 373
Henrietta B. (Vreeland), 389
Henrietta Frances, 383

BONNELL

Henry, 176, 181, 183, 186, 191, 192, 366, 421, 439, 440, 441, 442, 447, 448, 450, 452, 456, 458, 466
Henry A., 447
Henry Allen, 267
Henry C., 468
Henry Clark, 468
Henry Elias, 470
Henry H., 447, 467
Henry Harvey, 441
Henry McIlrath, 465
Henry Richmond, 423
Henry Schooley, 441
Henry W., 382, 449
Herbert Ralph, 473
Herod, 430
Herod Dallas, 433
Hetty Jemima, 268
Huldah, 373
Ichabod, 150, 383
Ichabod Leigh, 424
Ida, 386, 451
Ida E., 437
Ida J. (Vantasell), 459
Ida M., 431, 449
Inez Josphine, 441
Irena, 432
Irvin, 456
Isaac, 45, 53, 54, 55, 56, 57, 58, 60, 82, 84, 85, 86, 106, 153, 154, 167, 168, 169, 178, 179, 265, 266, 267, 429, 437, 449
Isaac Bleakney, 267
Isaac F., 428
Isaac M., 430
Isaac W., 267
Isabelle, 465
Israel, 149, 150, 151, 384
Ithamer, 190, 191, 459, 460
Ithamer Wade, 461, 465
Jacob, 57, 86, 87, 88, 147, 167, 176, 183, 377, 378, 379, 380, 440, 441, 442
Jacob B., 457, 458
Jacob Drake, 470
Jacob P., 459
James, 53, 55, 83, 150, 151, 158, 159, 181, 381, 383, 390, 403, 404, 414, 428, 441, 453
James B., 465
James Bruce, 455
James Clayton, 431
James E., 436, 451
James H., 437, 459
James Harvey, 386
James L., 420
James M., 382
James Nelson, 469
James T. F., 430
James Vail, 414
James W., 437
James Wilkinson, 461

BONNELL

Jane, 46, 80, 144, 147, 357, 360, 366, 371, 373, 377, 418, 447, 464
Jane (Garrabrant), 468
Jane (Jenkins), 158, 159
Jane (Johnstone), 469
Jane (Martin), 418
Jane A., 467
Jane Bruen, 363
Jane C., 468
Jane Caroline, 380
Jane Day, 357
Jane Elizabeth, 420
Jane M., 373
Jane P., 470
Janet T. (Tait), 265
Jay Bruce, 455
Jayne, 360
Jemima, 84, 267
Jemima (Fowlie), 267
Jemima (Van Syckle), 438, 439
Jemima (Van Sycle), 416
Jemima (Warne), 436, 451
Jemima Filinda (Kierstead), 268
Jennie, 429, 449
Jennie Etta, 432
Jennie M., 265
Jeremiah, 165
Jerusha, 94, 266
Jesse, 169, 436
Jesse I., 459
Jesse Ichabod, 459
Jesse Vreeland, 389
Jesse W., 449
Jessie, 448, 468
Joanna, 61, 83, 91, 144, 196, 360, 363, 460, 465
Joanna (Miller), 80
Joanna (Woodruff), 374, 375
Joanna Day, 357
Joanna M., 451
Joanna Minerva, 363
Joanna Price, 382
Joanna R., 423
Job, 378
Job Clark, 386
Joel, 150, 383
Joel Murton, 383
Johannah, 150, 151, 370
John, 57, 81, 85, 86, 87, 90, 143, 144, 146, 148, 149, 150, 151, 165, 169, 175, 181, 185, 186, 187, 264, 265, 356, 359, 361, 362, 363, 377, 381, 383, 384, 410, 416, 417, 418, 431, 438, 447, 448, 450, 456, 457
John A., 451
John Adams, 468
John B., 266, 411, 418
John Ball, 357
John C., 175, 438, 439
John Calvin, 386
John Carrolton, 414
John Edward, 429

BONNELL

John F., 434
John Fletcher, 433
John G., 439
John H., 431, 439, 448
John Hancock Brown, 468
John Harrison, 452
John Henry, 455, 457, 459
John Jacob, 411
John K., 360
John L. or S., 431
John Leander, 433, 434
John Louis, 450
John M., 437, 443, 452, 456, 458
John Milburn, 428
John Morea, 447
John Nicholas, 457, 458
John Noe, 373
John P., 382
John R., 423, 439
John Runyan, 439
John S., 428, 449
John Sherwood, 266, 267
John Summerfield, 468
John T., 467
John W., 431, 434, 468
John Wichliff, 386
Jonathan, 147, 151, 168, 169, 373, 376, 377, 381, 383, 418, 427, 428, 432
Jonathan Crane, 372, 373
Jonathan Elmer, 380
Jonathan Milburn, 428
Jonathan Percival, 459
Jonathan R., 360
Joseph, 46, 53, 54, 56, 59, 60, 61, 89, 90, 91, 93, 94, 178, 179, 187, 188, 189, 193, 194, 195, 265, 421, 422, 423, 437, 457, 473
Joseph Anderson, 423
Joseph G., 447
Joseph L., 437
Joseph Pearson, 448
Joseph R., 198, 472
Joseph Reid, 473
Joseph Warren, 420
Josephine, 430
Josephine Carhart, 424
Joshua Hill, 418
Joshua Reansean, 449
Josiah, 456, 458
Judson B., 411
Julia, 363, 373, 410, 411
Julia A., 428
Julia Ann, 387
Julia Ann (Croll), 386
Julian, 158, 159, 405
Justice Johnston, 267
Justus, 268
Justus Johnston, 267
Justus Sherwood, 268
Kate, 447
Katy (Parcells), 467
Keator (Kate), 366

BONNELL
Wilda Ann, 268
William, 57, 82, 87, 93, 94,
    147, 148, 153, 158, 159, 160,
    169, 181, 184, 191, 193, 196,
    197, 198, 265, 377, 378, 379,
    380, 381, 387, 404, 414, 420,
    432, 433, 435, 439, 440, 441,
    448, 449, 450, 451, 452, 453,
    458, 466, 470
William A., 436, 469
William Amos, 433
William B., 447, 465
William C., 419, 421, 469
William Charles, 447
William Condie, 459
William D., 423
William F., 379
William Francis, 380
William H., 198, 410, 434, 448,
    451, 472
William H. H., 437
William Harper, 404
William Harvey, 386
William Henry, 411, 428, 461,
    473
William Howard, 429
William J., 197
William Jones, 198, 472
William Joseph, 473
William Martin, 418
William Moses, 420
William Polison, 468
William Richard, 441
William Riley, 452, 454
William S., 451
William T., 461, 468
William W., 371, 411, 447
Williama L., 411
Willie, 380
Willis S., 449
Winfield Scott, 468
Zennetta, 468
BONNELLE
Ella Louise, 469
Emma Charlotte, 469
Emma Lunettie, 469
Frank Jackson, 469
George Frederick, 469
Helen Adelaide, 469
Job Doan, 469
Ursula Ann (Jackson), 469
BONNILL
Catherine (_____), 167
BOSTWICK
Abigail, 48
Ebenezer, 48
Edmund, 48
Gershom, 48
Hannah, 48
Isaac, 48
John, 47
Rebecca, 48
Rebecca (Bunnell), 48
Robert, 48

BOTSFORD
Elizabeth (Watkins), 208
Ruth, 208
Samuel, 208
BOTTUME
Josephine, 344
BOUGHTON
Francis, 67
Hannah (Bunnell), 67
BOUNELL
Elizabeth (Heath), 412
Emery Guy, 412
Harry Matthew, 412
India J., 412
Mary Louise (Kilgore), 412
Matthew Hugh, 412
Thomas Aaron, 412
William Heath, 412
BOW
Anna, 290
BOWDISH
William, 184
BOWEN
Frances Augusta (Bunnell), 270
Peter L. Bowen, 270
BOWERS
Savilla, 416
BOWLBY
Abner Parks, 420
Dennis, 420
Elizabeth Carhart, 420
Joseph, 419, 420
Lydia, 420
Mary (Bonnell), 419, 420
Mary C., 420
Olivia M., 420
Rachel, 420
Sarah, 420
William, 420
BOYD
Eliza Jane, 438
John, 212
BOYDEN
Samuel, 321
BOYLAN
Delilah Olinda, 459
Hannah Louisa, 459
Mary Margaret, 459
Rachel (Bonnell), 459
Sarah Ann, 459
William E., 459
BRACKEN
Elizabeth Ann, 431
BRADLEY
Abraham, 49
Andrew, 124
Griffin, 112
John Andrew, 124
Laura (Bunnell), 139
Leverett, 134
Lydia (_____), 338
Mabel (Thompson), 112
Maria C., 317
Mary (Bunnell), 124
Mary Josephine, 299
Mary Minerva (Bunnell), 299

BRADLEY
Rachel, 112
Seth, 299
Seth Thomas, 299
Stephen Rowe, 131
Wyllis, 139
BRADY
John, 401
BRAGG
Harriet Vivian, 355
BRANDIN
Antoinette Amelia, 122
Henry Pierre, 122
Jane Elizabeth, 122
Jerusha (Bunnell), 122, 305,
    307
Mary Jerusha, 122
Pierre Elizabeth, 122
BRANT
Benjamin, 357
Bonnel R., 357
Elliet Constantine, 357
Joseph, 333
Laura Adeline, 357
Lavenda Josephine, 357
Margaretta, 357
Prussia (Bonnell), 357
Sarah, 357
Sofronia, 357
BRATCHER
Austin, 27
BRAY
Asa, 136, 138, 271
BRIANT
John A., 460
Mary (_____), 460
BRIDGE
Elizabeth (Bunnell), 132
George A., 132
George J., 132
S. Dickerson, 132
BRINK
Benjamin, 65
James, 65
Leonora (Smith), 212
Mary, 65
Rachel, 214
Rachel (Bunnell), 65
BRISTOL
Amos, 301
Daniel, 68
Esther, 68
Esther (Sperry), 68
Thankful, 301
Thankful (Tuttle), 301
BRITTON
Elihue, 403
BROADWELL
David, 55, 83
Hannah (Bonnell), 54, 55, 83
Jacob G., 195
John, 55
Josiah, 143
Lydia, 55
Margaret, 55
Rachel, 55

BROADWELL
Richard, 55, 83
Sarah, 55, 83
Susan (_____), 195
William, 54
BROCKELBANK
John, 325
BROCKLEBANK
John, 322, 323
BRONSON
Charlotte, 451
Elijah, 78
Giles, 78
Isaac, 123
Lois (Bunnell), 78
Lucy, 78
BROOKS
Chauncy, 274
David, 71, 72
Ebenezer, 72
Ebenezer Bunnel, 71
Flavilla, 218
Henry, 115
Homer, 363
Joanna (Bonnell), 363
Jonathan, 71
Lucy, 363
Martha, 134
Martha (Hotchkiss), 50
Mary, 50, 280
Mehitabel (Bunnell), 115
Mehitabel (Royce), 115
Sarah (Bunnell), 71, 72
Thomas, 50, 78
BROTHERTON
Ann, 180
Henry, 180
Mercy, 180, 453
Mercy (Schooley), 180
Richard, 88, 180, 185
William, 180, 453
BROUK
Abia (Bunnell), 248, 250
Nicholas, 250
BROWN
Abner, 144
Amy (Estes), 448
Catherine, 254
Eliza Hannah, 416
Eliza Jane (Bonnell), 431
Elizabeth E. (Penoyer), 326
Ellathea (_____), 331
Harriet (_____), 353
Horace H., 353
Ignatius, 156
Jane (Bonnell), 144
Jerusha (Bunnell), 262
Jerusha (Hutchinson), 262
Lydia C., 445
Mary Ann, 266
Temperance, 413
Thomas, 197
Titus, 262
Wesley, 431
BROWNELL
Sarah, 83

493

BUNNELL

Cora McCoy, 304
Cora R., 215
Cordelia Waterman, 304
Cornelia, 215, 296, 320, 321
Cornelia (Kennedy, 333
Cornelia (Sterling), 304
Cornelia (Stone), 245
Cornelia Jane, 245, 349
Cornelius, 345
Cornelius Keator, 276
Crandall, 263
Crandall J., 263
Currance (_____), 210
Currance Meranda, 214
Cynthia, 207, 208
Cynthia (Huntington), 261
Cynthia Anne (Vose), 344, 345
Cyrus Brooks, 308
Cyrus Robinson, 137, 348
Damaris, 74
Damaris Blake, 343
Damarris, 248
Daniel, 69, 110, 111, 113, 114,
135, 212, 221, 222, 263, 271,
272, 273, 274, 275, 298, 412,
415
Daniel Clayborne, 416
Daniel Cooley, 239
Daniel Foote, 315
Daniel James, 413
Daniel Kimball, 460
Daniel Lee, 406
Daniel Marion, 416
Daniel Milton, 292
Daniel R., 402
Daniel Robert, 292
Daniel Virgil, 310
Darwin Hart, 355
David, 76, 96, 98, 128, 155,
156, 157, 208, 209, 210, 214,
216, 218, 222, 223, 318, 395,
396, 399, 463
David Edwin, 460
David Hume, 217
David I., 445
David King, 244
David L., 208
David Lorenzo, 276
David M., 275, 276
David Montgomery, 219
David N., 393
David Porter, 270
David R., 292
David S., 220
David Sterling, 304
David W., 348
Deborah (Harrington), 321
Deborah (King), 307
Deborah (_____), 339
Deborah Ann (Grieves), 345
Delia, 218, 277, 313
Delia Ann, 313
Deliverance, 49, 70, 296
Demarris, 250
Dennis, 135, 311, 343

BUNNELL

Dennis A., 311
Dennis C., 402
Dennis D., 311
Dennis Dowd, 122, 308, 311,
312
Derrick Tem Broeck, 307
Desire, 50, 51, 71, 72, 74,
75, 124, 128
Desire (Peck), 49, 50
Desire (_____), 123
Deveber, 445
Diana, 391
Diantha (Fitch), 303
Diantha F., 303
Diantha Fitch, 304, 309
Dinah, 285
Dinah (Tubbs), 285
Dolly, 354
Dolly W., 355
Dorcas (Gale), 256
Dotha Ann, 245
Douglas, 250
Doyle Adelbert, 223
Durham, 291
Durham P., 292
Dwight Henry, 247
Ebenezer, 29, 30, 43, 50, 51,
71, 72, 75, 122, 129, 309,
310, 318
Ebenezer Bradley, 244
Edgar B., 223
Edgar Edward, 283
Edgar G., 247
Edmund, 137, 237, 347
Edmund H., 211
Edmund Riley, 347
Edson, 317
Edward, 307, 347
Edward B., 220
Edward Collins, 402
Edward Elmer, 219
Edward Fuller, 416
Edward Hazen, 394
Edward M., 412
Edward Richmond, 279
Edward Russell, 299
Edward Salmon, 257
Edward Samuel, 246
Edwin, 288
Edwin C., 288
Edwin Fairbanks, 262
Edwin H., 279
Effie Maria, 333
Egbert, 252
Elain, 445, 446
Eldora, 402
Eleanor, 212, 217, 219, 220,
233, 238, 239, 427, 443
Eleanor (Barkalow), 97, 98
Eleanor (Cannon), 427
Eleanor (Ellen), 427
Eleanor (Fox), 102
Eleanor (Place), 231, 232
Eleanor (Russell), 238
Eleanor Gertrude, 233

BUNNELL

Eleanor Roena, 225
Eleazer, 337
Electa (Stone), 273
Elener, 445
Elenor, 446
Elethia Ellen, 292
Elfrida, 353
Eli, 283
Eliab, 133, 336, 337, 338
Eliab Mullican, 338
Eliab Mullican\, 337
Elias, 130, 311, 332
Elijah, 105, 245, 247, 250,
251, 252, 394
Elinor (Rhodes), 205
Elisha Sherman, 280
Eliza, 279, 290, 302, 327, 352,
353, 394, 396, 402, 406
Eliza (Barber), 404
Eliza (Barnes), 346, 347
Eliza (Bishop), 404
Eliza (Conwell), 415
Eliza (Durand), 311
Eliza (Hinman), 205
Eliza (Livermore), 215
Eliza (Loomis), 463
Eliza (Smith), 353
Eliza (Ward), 308
Eliza (_____), 462
Eliza A., 249
Eliza A. (_____), 244
Eliza Ann, 222, 273, 330, 394,
397, 399, 400, 402, 444
Eliza Ann (Restine), 397
Eliza Hannah (Brown), 416
Eliza Hannah (Merrill), 416
Eliza J., 467
Eliza J. (_____), 467
Eliza R. (VanCampen), 221
Eliza Rebecca (Overfield), 237
Eliza S. (Rogers), 321
Elizabeth, 66, 67, 76, 100,
109, 130, 132, 208, 211, 214,
221, 224, 232, 264, 317, 326,
335, 337, 345, 392, 396, 397,
400, 412, 427
Elizabeth (Betsy), 277
Elizabeth (Bunnell), 396, 399
Elizabeth (Coleman), 393
Elizabeth (Donovan), 399
Elizabeth (Ellingsworth), 427
Elizabeth (France), 217
Elizabeth (Garess), 217
Elizabeth (Gillett), 272, 273
Elizabeth (Grannis), 300
Elizabeth (Hathaway), 393
Elizabeth (Meyer), 318
Elizabeth (Post), 38
Elizabeth (Preston), 75
Elizabeth (Price), 395, 396,
399
Elizabeth (Robinson), 281
Elizabeth (Sperry), 38
Elizabeth (Way), 258, 259, 260
Elizabeth (Wilber), 341

BUNNELL

Elizabeth (_____), 318, 342
Elizabeth A., 300
Elizabeth Ann, 95, 210
Elizabeth Ann (Wetmore), 257
Elizabeth B., 244
Elizabeth D., 213
Elizabeth E. (Brown), 326
Elizabeth E. (Penoyer), 326
Elizabeth Fuller (Leeman), 334
Elizabeth Jane, 402
Elizabeth Jerusha, 307
Elizabeth M., 247, 261
Elizabeth M. (Young), 397
Elizabeth May, 342
Elizur, 126, 127, 317
Ella, 225
Ella P., 318
Ellen, 212, 249
Ellen (Turner), 402
Ellen A., 354, 355
Ellen Adelia, 446
Ellen Agnes, 445
Ellen Augusta, 257
Ellen F., 316
Ellen R., 309
Ellery J., 219
Ellery Pike, 219
Elliott Augustus, 299
Elmer, 261
Elmer Ellsworth, 289, 416
Elmer Sumner, 237
Elmira, 445
Elmira Juliet (Stone), 245
Elmira Juliet (Wright), 245
Elmore D., 276
Elovin, 279
Elver D., 413
Elvira Jane, 282
Elvira Lydia, 276
Elwood, 287
Ematury (Emma T.), 223
Emeline, 287, 296, 348, 402,
427
Emeline B., 214
Emeline M., 208
Emilie, 285
Emilie Amelia, 345
Emilinda, 249
Emily, 245, 256, 427
Emily C. (Jacob), 301
Emily E., 427
Emily Jane, 348
Emma, 264, 402
Emma (Graves), 263
Emma (Major), 237
Emma (Sprague), 263
Emma (Stout), 416
Emma (or Amy), 263
Emma Delphine, 233
Emma E., 289
Emma F., 402
Emma Harriet, 217
Emma Pease, 283
Emma R., 239
Emmonds, 105, 252

BUNNELL

Mary (Blackford), 155
Mary (Brooks), 50, 51, 280
Mary (Bunnell), 211, 219
Mary (Cassaday), 393
Mary (Childers), 390
Mary (Clark), 354
Mary (Daniels), 155
Mary (Dyer), 255
Mary (Harding), 224
Mary (Hendrick), 78
Mary (Hitchcock), 133, 134, 338
Mary (Holdren), 65, 100
Mary (Horton), 299
Mary (Kimberly), 118
Mary (Lingley), 443
Mary (Lockwood), 209
Mary (Lucy)(Pierpont, 298
Mary (Montgomery), 299
Mary (Nihart), 216
Mary (Ozier), 222
Mary (Phelps), 326
Mary (Place), 223, 224
Mary (Polly), 139, 289
Mary (Polly)(Cook), 289
Mary (Polly)(Lockwood), 210
Mary (Polly)(Rogers), 296
Mary (Pratt), 250, 251
Mary (Smith), 347
Mary (Taylor), 330
Mary (Twitchell), 202
Mary (Worthley), 279
Mary (_____), 154, 156, 399
Mary A., 214, 289, 340
Mary A. (Bartlett), 402
Mary A. (Graham), 310
Mary A. (McNealey), 402
Mary A. (_____), 203, 292
Mary Abigail (Harrison), 298
Mary Amanda, 280
Mary Amelia, 310
Mary Ann, 202, 233, 247, 263, 292, 298, 412, 413
Mary Ann (Buckles), 396
Mary Ann (Butler), 276
Mary Ann (Hall), 245
Mary Ann (Harvey), 326
Mary Ann (Hull), 217
Mary Ann (Kennard), 413
Mary Ann (Leighton), 279
Mary Ann (Luce), 233
Mary Ann (Smith), 202
Mary Ann (_____), 326
Mary Ann Phoebe (Caulder), 283
Mary Armstrong, 460
Mary Atwater, 334
Mary Augusta, 219
Mary C., 394, 413
Mary Caroline, 393
Mary Clarinda (Young), 397
Mary E., 208, 219, 300, 396, 445
Mary E. (Jenkins), 445
Mary Elizabeth, 208, 217, 223, 233

BUNNELL

Mary Ellen, 351, 409
Mary Emeline, 215, 402
Mary Esther, 244
Mary Etta, 353
Mary Eva (Ozier), 221, 222
Mary Evaline, 276
Mary F., 344
Mary Frances, 225
Mary G., 402
Mary Hull, 330
Mary Ivy, 392
Mary J., 249, 316, 340
Mary Jane, 213, 215, 246, 326, 337, 392, 443
Mary Jane (Beecher), 354
Mary Jane (Wakeley), 238
Mary Jerusha, 309
Mary Josephine, 299
Mary K., 310
Mary L., 273, 409
Mary L. (Beeman), 416
Mary L. (Lanterman), 217
Mary L. (Somers), 301
Mary L. (Wedmore), 301
Mary Louisa, 298
Mary Louise (Matthews), 349
Mary Lucretia, 255
Mary M., 216
Mary Mae (Everett), 214
Mary Maria (Warner), 351
Mary Minerva, 299
Mary O., 307
Mary Ophelia, 307
Mary Phoebe, 217
Mary Pierson, 334
Mary R. (_____), 139
Mary S., 347
Mary S. (Cottle), 443
Mary Sophia, 298
Mary V., 393
Mary W., 262, 282
Maryette, 207
Matilda, 245
Matilda (Desnoyer), 270
Matilda (Moses), 285
Matilda Ann, 310
Matthew, 411, 412
Maude, 416
Medora Ann, 317
Mehitabel, 64, 96, 115
Mehitabel (Royce), 114, 115
Mehitable (Baldwin), 63, 64
Mehitable (Clark), 287
Melinda Emeline (Watts), 283
Melissa, 345
Melvina Inez, 224
Mercia (Markham), 269
Mercy, 64, 321
Merriam, 71
Merrit, 287
Merrit F., 208
Merritt, 391
Michael W., 213
Miles, 114, 135, 249, 252, 339, 340

BUNNELL

Milla, 281
Mina E., 215
Minerva, 218, 335, 336
Minerva Ellen (Bayles), 289
Minerva L.(Lucinda), 292
Minerva Stevens, 336
Minerva T., 219
Minneowah, 270
Minnie, 270, 345
Minnie Alzara, 237
Minnie H., 355
Minnie Josephine, 225
Miriam, 72, 77
Molly (_____), 246
Morris, 219
Morris B., 223
Morris W., 219
Moses, 328
Moses Atwater, 130, 319, 320, 321
Moses K., 392
Moses Leander, 416
Mullikin, Mary J., 337
Munson, 318
Myron, 247, 250
Myron Clark, 255
Myron L., 254
Myron Leete, 254
Nabby, 133, 336
Nancy, 241, 285, 292, 321, 336, 394, 396, 397, 399, 400, 462
Nancy (Bunnell), 397, 400, 401, 402
Nancy (Corbret), 396
Nancy (Crossley), 392
Nancy (Riggs), 395
Nancy (Williams), 396
Nancy (Willis), 393
Nancy (_____), 405
Nancy Ann, 207, 402
Nancy Belle, 239
Nancy E., 215
Nancy Elizabeth, 301
Nancy Eloiza, 210
Nancy G. (Young), 340
Nancy Judson (Harmon), 321
Nancy McAdams (Little), 223
Nancy Woodruff, 296
Naomi, 132
Naomi (Atwater), 131
Nathan, 96, 210
Nathan T., 211
Nathaniel, 28, 29, 30, 39, 43, 45, 47, 49, 50, 51, 67, 68, 69, 71, 75, 99, 100, 109, 110, 115, 116, 119, 120, 121, 125, 126, 127, 128, 156, 157, 262, 284, 301, 302, 307, 308, 313, 315, 317, 396, 399, 400, 401, 402, 405, 462, 463
Nathaniel Fletcher, 402
Nathaniel Perkins, 282
Nathaniel Pomeroy, 214
Nathaniel V., 402
Nathaniel Wesley, 402

BUNNELL

Ned, 415
Nehemiah, 217, 258, 259, 260
Nehemiah Beardsley, 261
Nellie, 310, 340
Nellie E., 463
Nellie F., 316
Nelson George, 224
Neoma (_____), 287
Nettie, 249
Nettie Arnold, 237
Nettie Musgrove, 416
Nettie S., 307
Nettie V., 402
Nicholas S., 237
Noah, 67, 106, 108, 109, 112, 252, 253, 256, 257, 258, 394, 413
Noah Livy, 413
Noah Thomas, 416
Nominia, 391
Nora, 345
Norina Marietta, 415
Norris W., 274
Octavia, 318, 319
Olinda, 391, 392
Olinda (Ball), 391
Olive, 286, 300
Olive (Ashley), 283
Olive Elvina, 281, 282
Olive Maria, 296
Oliver, 117, 221, 307
Oliver B., 316
Oliver Blakeslee, 300
Oliver Hamlin, 219
Oliver P., 393
Oliver Perry, 393
Olivia Eliza, 300
Ophelia, 443
Orilla, 128
Orin, 210
Orlando Ephraim, 282
Orlando S., 220
Orpha Ofelia, 258, 260
Orpheus, 328, 329, 330
Orrel, 271
Orren V., 332
Orrin Nelson, 283
Orville Mortimer, 214
Oscar, 287, 312
Oscar E., 219
Oscar H., 345
Oscar Orlando, 415
Oscar Palmer, 247
Osenia, 413
Parmelia, 287
Parmelia (Bunnell), 287
Parmineas, 50, 51, 73, 74, 122
Parthena, 218, 219
Parthenia, 219
Parthenia (Bunnell), 218
Patience, 50, 51, 110, 128
Patience (Miles), 47
Patience (Smith), 128
Patience (Wheeler), 47
Patience (_____), 128, 349

BUNNELL

Patty, 301
Patty (Blakeslee), 300
Patty (Blakeslee), 299
Paul, 107, 177
Pauline S., 237
Permelia, 286
Permelia (Bunnell), 286
Permelia C. (Amery), 337
Perrin S., 223
Peter DeWitt, 217
Peter S., 277
Phebe, 114, 124, 125
Phebe (Bond), 445
Phebe (Bonnell), 462
Phebe (Durand), 354
Phebe (Goodale), 352
Phebe Ann, 462, 463
Phebe Emmeline, 257
Philema, 125
Philemon B., 96, 208
Philena (_____), 204
Phileta, 285
Philip, 120, 278, 279
Philip Doodridge, 279
Philome (Hull), 330, 331
Phoebe, 233
Phoebe (Edith)(Gaines), 205
Phoebe (Gameford), 221
Phoebe Elizabeth, 460
Polly, 107, 209, 274, 281, 299, 324, 325, 326
Polly (Hill), 273
Polly (Hyatt), 280
Polly (Pringle), 350
Polly Esther, 108, 109
Porter, 237
Potter, 296
Priscilla, 406
Prudence (Crabb), 445
Puah (Bunnell), 126
Puah (_____), 314
Purcilla, 216
Rachael Naomi, 404
Rachel, 39, 50, 51, 65, 71, 74, 113, 129, 221, 392
Rachel (Bradley), 112
Rachel (Brink), 214
Rachel (Curtis), 73, 74
Rachel (Ford), 394
Rachel (Grannis), 128
Rachel (Hill), 287
Rachel A., 211, 340, 427
Rachel Ann (Canon), 427
Rachel Jane, 402
Rachel R., 407
Rachel Sophronia, 286
Raphael, 137, 344
Ray, 415
Rebecca, 38, 39, 48, 50, 51, 67, 71, 101, 109, 113, 125, 128, 223, 394, 402
Rebecca (Hetfield), 405, 406
Rebecca (Mallory), 37, 38
Rebecca (Place), 225
Rebecca (_____), 252

BUNNELL

Rebecca A., 402
Rebecca Hannah, 66
Rebecca Keeler, 237
Rebecca S. (Longley), 351
Rebeckah (Rice), 283
Rejoicy, 292
Renus, 202
Reuben, 76, 95, 130, 132, 133, 134, 201, 202, 203, 285, 330, 331, 336, 338
Reuben A., 320, 321
Reuben Ashman, 321
Reuben W., 337
Rheu Emma, 257
Rhoda, 117, 156, 157, 277, 285, 393, 462
Rhoda (Atwater), 285
Rhoda (Bates), 285
Rhoda (Elton), 201
Rhoda (Hotchkiss), 285
Rhoda (_____), 279, 280
Rhoda Bateman, 346
Rhodes William, 391
Richard, 202, 337, 394
Richard M., 252
Robert, 216, 445
Robert C., 337, 392
Robert Elwell, 224
Robert Franklin, 321
Robert Gabriel, 216
Robert J., 396
Robert L., 446
Robert Oscar, 246
Robert Robinson, 281
Rockwell, 218
Rodney, 135, 341, 342
Roena (Griswold), 245
Roland C., 337
Romanta A., 286
Rosa, 392
Rosalia F. (or B.), 283
Rosalie (Cardinal), 349
Rosanah (Kelley), 307
Rosanna (Kimberly), 296
Rosanna (Woodruff), 286
Rose May, 239
Rosetta (Bogue, 352
Rosetta A., 292
Rosetta Eve, 460
Roxanna, 129, 208, 238
Roxanna J., 239
Roxce Blish, 306
Roxey (Simons), 207
Roxy (Dunning), 202
Rubena, 220
Rufus, 121, 303, 304, 307, 310
Rufus Parker, 307
Rufus William, 304
Russell, 137, 285, 348
Russell Reynolds, 299
Ruth, 49, 114, 115, 278, 279, 287
Ruth (Botsford), 208
Ruth (Flora), 411, 412
Ruth (Francis), 140

BUNNELL

Ruth (McDuffee), 282
Ruth (Plumb), 49
Ruth (Smith), 95
Ruth (Tuller), 142
Ruth Amy, 133
Ruth Ann, 203
Ruth Ann (Parker), 331
Ruth Jane, 393
Ruth L., 254
Ruth Leete, 255
Salina, 256, 257
Sallie Mariah (Newton), 219
Sally, 107, 141, 278, 279
Sally (Peck), 290
Sally (Sarah A.), 238
Sally (Seeley), 302
Sally (Stanley), 344
Sally (Thorpe), 316
Sally (Todd), 315
Sally (_____), 320
Sally Ann, 340, 345
Sally Ann (Chamberlain), 283
Salmon, 108, 256, 257
Salmon B., 254
Salmon Beardsley, 109, 253, 254, 255, 256
Samantha, 238, 345
Samuel, 73, 76, 118, 133, 134, 138, 263, 296, 297, 298, 300, 342, 349, 350, 391, 405, 406, 415, 426, 427, 442, 443
Samuel Augustus, 297, 298, 299
Samuel Carter, 246
Samuel Corey, 217
Samuel F., 415
Samuel Ford, 215
Samuel Gardner, 460
Samuel Gilbert, 244
Samuel H., 280
Samuel M., 298
Samuel Pierce, 404
Samuel Preston, 134, 338
Samuel R., 401, 402
Samuel Rose, 313
Samuel S., 205
Samuel W., 250
Sarah, 71, 72, 79, 102, 109, 114, 129, 137, 207, 222, 225, 247, 264, 280, 304, 317, 320, 321, 333, 348, 394, 402, 427, 462
Sarah (Atwater), 129, 130
Sarah (Bird), 239
Sarah (Buckingham), 204
Sarah (Day), 442
Sarah (Dorman), 206
Sarah (Haight), 304
Sarah (Hill), 205
Sarah (Kellogg), 240
Sarah (Kyser), 345
Sarah (Mallory), 79
Sarah (Morse), 347
Sarah (Parsons), 109
Sarah (Peck), 394
Sarah (Pickwick), 348

BUNNELL

Sarah (Quick), 332
Sarah (Sackett), 203
Sarah (Smith), 292, 297
Sarah (Stanley), 345
Sarah (Tomlin), 393
Sarah (Weir), 333
Sarah (_____), 249, 331
Sarah A., 276, 279, 402
Sarah A. (Hart), 308
Sarah A. (Smith), 270
Sarah A. J., 208
Sarah Amelia, 348
Sarah Ann, 216, 244, 326, 412, 427
Sarah Ann (Little), 224
Sarah C., 276, 292, 343
Sarah Caroline, 217
Sarah Cornelia, 333
Sarah Crittenton, 321
Sarah E., 217, 220, 292, 402, 445
Sarah E. (Bunnell), 402
Sarah Eliza, 215, 467
Sarah Elizabeth, 217, 223, 292, 443, 445
Sarah Elizabeth (Bunnell), 443, 445
Sarah Ellen, 213, 299
Sarah Emma, 220
Sarah H., 244, 406
Sarah Heller (Conrad), 460
Sarah Ivy (Clymer), 392
Sarah J., 402, 427
Sarah J. (Sawyer), 214
Sarah Jane, 208, 219, 249, 261, 287, 347, 392
Sarah Jane (Krone), 415
Sarah L., 269, 347
Sarah L. Ozier, 237
Sarah Lecta, 130
Sarah M., 237, 393, 406
Sarah Mallory, 142
Sarah Maria, 277
Sarah Martha (Heaton), 416
Sarah Matilda (McCoy), 304
Sarah Melissa, 215
Sarah P., 214
Sarah P. (_____), 292
Sarah S., 317
Sarah St. John, 334
Sarah V. (Cain), 402
Savanna Evaline, 224
Savannah, 224, 225
Savilla (Bowers), 416
Sebah, 109, 256, 257, 258, 259, 260
Selina, 296
Selinda (Kennedy), 406
Selleck J., 301
Seneca, 413
Seth, 114, 115, 278
Seth A., 282, 283
Seth Alva, 284
Seth Keeney, 237
Severn, 289

FRENCH
Jane, 30
Lydia, 30
Lydia (Bunnell), 30
Mary, 30
Mary Jane (Bunnell), 443
Robert, 443
Samuel, 30
Susannah, 30
FRIEND
Anna, 147
Elizabeth, 147
Elizabeth (Bonnell), 147
Gabriel, 147
Jacob, 147
John, 147
Jonathan, 147
Joseph, 147
Keziah, 147
Rebecca, 147
Sarah Anne, 147
FRITT
Diantha Fitch (Bunnell), 309
Edward, 309
Edward Cyrus, 309
Elizabeth Ann, 309
Henry Lincoln, 309
Leslie, 309
FROST
William, 111, 263
FUDGE
David, 396
FULLER
Betsey (Bunnell), 351
Charles, 255
Charles B., 201
Daniel, 351
Hannah, 201
James, 255
Lucius, 201
Rhoda (_____), 201
Rhoda B., 201
Ruth Leete (Bunnell), 255

- G -

GAGLES
Chancy, 274
GAINES
Phoebe (Edith), 205
GALE
Dorcas, 255
Noah, 255
Phebe (Mead), 255
GAMEFORD
Phoebe, 221
GARDNER
Abigail (Allen), 81
Abigail (Bonnell), 81
Ann E. (Bonnell), 437
James, 437
Joseph, 191
Phebe J. (Bonnell), 460
Samuel H., 460
Sarah (Bonnell), 191
Thomas, 81

GARESS
Elizabeth, 217
GARINGER
Alexander, 452
Elizabeth (Bonnell), 452
George, 452
Mary, 452
GARRABRANT
Jane, 468
GAUMER
Elizabeth, 456
GAY
Almeda, 232
Amanda, 232
Ansel, 232
Armina A., 232
Calvin S., 232
Charles, 232
Eleanor, 232
Eleanor B., 232
Elizabeth (Bunnell), 232
Emily, 232
Fisher, 117
George, 232
Harriet, 232
James P., 232
John B., 232
Lorenzo D., 232
Mary, 232
Savannah, 232
Solomon, 232
Solomon Bunnell, 232
Treadway, 232
GAYLORD
Allen, 116
Asaph, 115
Chauncey, 114, 115
Chloe, 115
Eber, 115
Hannah, 115
Jesse, 115
Joel, 116
Joseph, 116
Levi, 115
Linus, 116
Lydia, 116
Nathaniel, 116
Orrin, 115
Royce, 115
Ruth, 116
Ruth (Bunnell), 114, 115
Samuel, 291
Susanna (Bunnell), 116
GEE
Hannah (_____), 408
GIBITS
Mary (Bunnell), 351
GILBERT
Esther, 242
Eunice, 280
Samuel, 243
Thomas, 132
GILCHRIST
Catharine, 250
GILLEN
Jo, 210

GILLEN
Lolita (Bunnell), 63
GILLETT
Elizabeth, 272
GILLETTE
Alfred, 465
Charles H., 257
Edward Augustus, 257
Ellen, 257
Henriette G., 257
Hiram, 257
Mary Elizabeth (Bonnell), 465
Oscar S., 257
Salina (Bunnell), 257
GILLILAND
Amos, 406
Ezra, 406
Jane (Bunnell), 406
Jesse, 406
Nancy, 366
Sara, 406
GILMAN
Laurentine, 321
GLYNN
Maria, 317
GODDARD
Catherine, 264
Crandal, 264
Daniel, 264
Daniel Wager, 264
Elizabeth, 264
Emma (Bunnell), 264
John Calvin, 264
LeBaron, 264
Mary Ann, 264
Titus, 264
Wealthy, 264
Willard, 264
GODFREY
Ebenezer, 243
Silliman, 243
GODLEY
Benjamin, 166
Jacob, 166
Joseph, 165
Mahlon, 165
Mary, 165
Newell, 164
Newell (Bonnell), 165, 422
Sarah, 165
GOLD
John, 43
GOODALE
Anna, 352
Phebe, 352
Polly, 352
GOODSELL
Mary, 295
GOODWIN
Curtis, 389
Laura Elizabeth (Bonnell), 389
Laura Elizabeth (Horton), 389
GOODYEAR
Stephen, 29
GORDIN
Joseph, 163

GORDON
Thos., 422
GORSUCH
Margaret, 449
Mary Ann Carr, 449
GRAHAM
Bunnell, Luanna, 349
Catherine (Bunnell), 349
Luther, 349
Lydia, 350, 351
Mary A., 310
GRANGER
Gideon, 324
GRANNIS
Amy, 118
Anson, 300
Anson Smith, 300
Beda, 51
Caleb, 51, 128
Charles L., 290
David L., 301
Eldad, 51
Elihu, 118
Elizabeth, 300
Esther, 51
Esther Maria, 300
Eunice, 118
George S., 300
Henry Horace, 138
Julia Katherine (Bunnell), 138
Julia Katherine (Stedman), 138
Lois (Bunnell), 300
Margaret Louise, 300
Mary, 51
Mary (Bunnell), 118
Medad, 51
Olive, 118
Parmineas Bunnell, 51
Patience, 51
Patience (Bunnell), 51, 128
Polly, 118
Rachel, 51, 128
Russell, 138
Sarah, 118
Simeon, 51
Smith, 300
Stephen, 138
Wealthy, 118
GRAVES
Amanda, 264
Carl, 434
Elizabeth, 264
Elizabeth (Bunnell), 264
Emma, 263
Helen, 264
John, 264
LeBaron, 264
Louise (_____), 434
Mary, 264
William, 264
GRAY
Angela Evaline, 267
Esther Jane, 267
Howard D., 267
Jemima, 267
Johnston, 267

511

MCGINNIS
Sarah (Clark), 451
MCGREGOR
Blanche Louise, 266
Daniel Smith, 266
Eleanor Jane, 266
Eliza Miles, 266
Esther, 266
Isaac Bonnell, 266
John, 266
Lois Parker, 266
Mary, 266
Mary (Bonnell), 266
Sarah Ann, 266
MCKAY
Elizabeth, 78
MCKINNEY
David, 163
MCLEAN
Betsey E., 203
Fergus, 156, 157
Margaret Eliza, 265
Martha, 265, 443
Mary, 264
MCLEOD
Jerusha (Bunnell), 111
John, 111
William, 263
MCMACKEN
Joseph, 446
MCMURRY
Emily, 430
MCNEALEY
Mary A. (Buchanan), 402
Mary A.(Bartlett), 402
MCNEIL
Daniel, 320
Sally (_____), 320
MEAD
Britania, 250
Phebe, 255
Spencer, 210
MEADE
Giles, 374
MEEKER
Caleb, 375
Charity (_____), 375
Isaac, 375
Joseph, 58, 385
Jotham, 158
Mary (_____), 385
Phebe (Allen), 459
Phebe Allen, 459, 461
Stephen, 459
MELENDY
Fidelia, 256
MELYN
Isaac, 43
Maria, 56
MENDENHALL
Esther, 392
MERRIAM
Charles Andrew, 347
Desire (Bunnell), 72
Ichabod, 72
James Elliot, 353

MERRIAM
Jane Ellen (Bunnell), 353
Levi, 346
Rhoda Bateman (Bunnell), 346
Walter Henry, 347
MERRICK
Jonathan, 70
MERRILL
Eliza Hannah (Brown), 416
MERRIMAN
Katherine, 138
Katherine (Wright), 138
Lent, 138
MERWIN
Deborah, 75
John, 47
METCALK
Hiram, 329
MEYER
Elizabeth, 318
Jacob, 318
MILBURN
Ann, 432
Ruth, 427
MILES
John, 38
Patience (Wheeler), 47
Stephen, 47
MILL
Hannah (_____), 404
Jabez, 404
MILLEDGE
Thomas, 176
MILLEN
Daniel, 468
Marinda A., 468
MILLER
Abigail (Abernathy), 125
Abigail (Bunnell), 125
Anna (Collard), 466
Caleb S., 197
Charity, 466
Ebenezer, 460
Elisha, 125
Elizabeth (Riggs), 80
Elyath, 241
George, 186
Hannah (Bonnell), 357
Hannah (Ward), 357
Isaac, 159
James, 466
Joanna, 80
Joanna (Bonnell), 460
Luke, 145
Mary, 372
Moses, 357
Rachel (Bonnell), 145
Samuel, 80
Sophronia A., 288
Timothy, 195
MILLIGAN
Harriet Ann, 470
MILLS
Daniel, 176
Mercy (Bonnell), 176
Mercy (Simcock), 176

MILVEN
William, 388
MINGLE
Marcy, 216
MINTURN
Abigail (Bonnell), 147
Allen, 147
Barton, 147
Bunnel, 147
George, 147
Jacob, 147
Jane, 147
Phebe, 147
Sarah, 147
MIRES
Jacob, 266
Jerusha (Bonnell), 266
MITCHELL
Eunice (Bunnell), 282
Jane Eliza (Bunnell), 342
John, 282
Joseph, 339
Joseph E., 340
Mary (Bunnell), 339
Mary A. (Bunnell), 340
Mary H., 340
Walter, 282
MIX
Anna (Bunnell), 39
Jabez, 39
Nathaniel, 39
Stephen, 39
Timothy, 79
MOFFARD
Jesse, 54
MONGSMITH
Ann (_____), 448
Christian, 448
Rachel, 448
MONK
George, 345
George William, 345
Sally Ann (Bunnell), 345
MONROE
Harriet (Weeks), 457
MONTFORD
Charlotte (Bunnell), 269
Charlotte (Smith), 269
James Lester, 269
MONTGOMERY
Mary, 299
MOORE
Aaron, 181
Adaline L., 434
Ann, 181
Eleanor (Bonnell), 181
Elizabeth, 162
Esther, 181
Eunice, 181
John D., 367
Narcissa, 181
Thomas, 181
William, 181
MOREHOUSE
Anna, 207

MOREY
Jacob, 212
Leonora (Bunnell), 212
MORGAN
Alexander G., 394
America (Bunnell), 394
America (Higgins), 394
Ephraim, 367
Jemima (_____), 69
John, 184
Joseph, 69
Mary (Bonnell), 456
Mary (Ennis), 456
Mary Margaret, 428
Zillah M., 308
MORRELL
Calvin, 145
Jacob, 150, 384
Rhoda (Bonnell), 145
Sarah Ann, 380
MORRIS
Abigail (Bonnell), 54, 55
Hannah (Bonnell), 193
John, 59, 87
Lewis, 59
Reuben, 193
Thomas, 37
MORROW
James, 355
MORSE
Harry, 128
Lydia B. (Bunnell), 128
Orilla (Bunnell), 128
Sarah, 347
Titus, 134
William, 128
MORTON
Abigail (Bonnell), 370
Anna Maria, 370
James T., 370
William, 370
MOSES
Matilda, 285
MOSHER
Isaac, 184
Lois, 252
MOSS
Anson, 129
Chloe, 129
David, 133
Eunice (Bunnell), 133
Eunice (Rowe), 133
Jedediah, 134
Jesse, 129
Obed, 128, 129
Sarah (Bunnell), 129
MOTT
Catherine (Bunnell), 351
Israel, 351
MOUTHROP
Elias, 308
MUCHMORE
David, 94
Jerusha (Beach), 94
Jerusha (Bonnell), 94

REED
Jefferson, 394
John, 394
John L., 414
Mary, 394
Mary Ann (Bonnell), 414
Nancy (Bunnell), 394
Rebecca, 394
Susan, 394
William, 168, 394
REGNIER
Pierre (or Peter), 362
REID
Abigail (Sayre), 472
Margaret, 472
William, 472
RESTINE
Eliza Ann, 397
RHEA
Catherine, 425
RHODE
John, 79
RHODES
Elinor, 205
RICE
Bela, 115
Bela Fitch, 115
Mehitabel (Bunnell), 115
Olive, 281
Rebeckah, 283
RICH
Ella Jane, 306
Fanny, 306
George Bunnell, 306
James, 306
James A., 306
Mary, 306
Roxce Blish (Bunnell), 306
Thomas, 306
Virgil Bunnell, 306
RICHMOND
Catherine, 423
RIGGS
Elias, 357
Elizabeth, 80
Joseph, 80
Nancy, 395
Rebecca (Dodd), 60
Samuel, 60
Zophar, 192
RILEY
Christopher, 350
ROBBINS
E. S., 321
Elizabeth (_____), 346
Royal, 346
ROBERTS
Agnes (Nancy), 402
Samuel, 81
Sarah (Bonnell), 81
ROBERTSON
Jane M., 336
William B., 337
ROBESON
Margaret, 360

ROBINSON
Abigail, 360
Elizabeth, 281
John, 258
Josiah, 323, 325
Sarah, 471
William, 84, 350
ROCKHILL
John, 165
John C., 164
ROFF
Catherine, 470
ROGERS
Eliza S., 321
Mary (Polly), 296
ROOT
Elias, 462
Elias P., 463
Elizabeth, 303
Erastus, 303
Temperance (Bunnell), 462
Temperance Wade (Bunnell), 463
RORAPAUGH
Antoinette E. (Bunnell), 307
Bert J., 307
Charles, 307
Fred, 307
ROSCOE
Grace (Gridley), 166
ROSE
Amariah, 126, 127
Betsey (Bunnell), 126, 127
Frances A., 313
Rose (Bunnell), 317
Samuel, 57
ROSS
Andrew, 193
Lucinda (_____), 385
Margaret, 432
ROSSEAU
John B., 333
ROSSETER
Mary, 69
Stephen, 69
ROWE
Abigail (Beecher), 132
Eunice, 132
Joseph, 132
ROYCE
Abel, 114
Amy, 69
Benedict, 69
Dimon, 69
Esther, 69
Esther (Bunnell), 69
Evan, 119
Joanna (Beach), 114
John, 69
Lois, 119
Mehitabel, 114
Rachel (Parker), 119
Silas, 69
RUDD
John C., 389
RUDDERSON
Sarah Jane (Douglas), 424

RUNYAN
Susanna, 402
RUSH
Electa (Bonnell), 465
Maria Jane, 465
Martha A., 465
Matthias, 465
Sanford, 465
RUSSEL
Luther, 157
RUSSELL
Adaline E., 239
Alban, 238
Eleanor, 238
Hannah (Alcott), 238
Hannah (Hartwell), 238
Isaac, 252
Laura, 302
Louisa, 238

- S -

SACCO
Paula, 416
SACKETT
Jonathan, 203
Sarah, 203
SAFFORD
Hester A. (Bunnell), 238
Laban L., 238
Landis Barton, 238
Sarah E., 238
SAGE
Aaron, 346
Maria Barnes (Bunnell), 346
SALE
John, 415
SALISBURY
Russell D., 326
Susan (Bunnell), 326
SALLAE
John, 189
Puah (Ball), 189
Puah (Bonnell), 189
SAMPSON
Abraham, 379
Chloe (Bonnell), 379
SAMSON
Aaron Smith, 148
Abraham, 148
Aminda, 148
Anne Mariah, 148
Chloe (Bonnell), 148
David, 91
Elizabeth Shaver, 148
Enoch Nelson, 148
Hannah (Bonnell), 91
Julia, 148
Mary Malvina, 148
Nancy Bonnel, 148
Sally, 148
Wickliff Condit, 148
Zebra (Sabra), 148
SANDERS
Cyrus, 380
David, 380

SANDERS
Frank, 380
Jane Caroline (Bonnell), 380
Rodman, 380
William, 380
SANFORD
Caroline, 247
Content (_____), 246
Desire (Bunnell), 51
Hannah, 51
Joseph, 246
Lois, 51
Miriam, 51
Thomas, 51
Titus, 51
William, 51
SAVAGE
Charles G., 473
Charlotte Isabelle (Bonnell), 473
Margaret, 473
Ulysse, 473
William J., 473
SAWYER
Sarah J., 214
SAYER
Ezekial, 151
Sally (Bonnell), 151
SAYRE
Abigail, 472
Catherine, 152
David B., 152
David Brown, 380
Edward, 386
Electa, 152
Eliza, 386
Eliza (Bonnell), 386
Elizabeth Bonnell, 380
Emily Brown, 380
Ezekiel, 152
George, 380
George Townly, 386
John Edgar, 152
John Francis, 380
Lewis, 152
Mary Caroline, 380
Nancy Doty (Bonnell), 380
Sally (Bonnell), 152
Sally Day, 152
Sarah Day, 382
Sarah Doty, 380
Sylvanus Bonnel, 386
Theodore, 386
Theodore Lyman, 386
William, 380
SCHOFIELD
Lydia Ann, 219
SCHOOLEY
Elizabeth (Bonnell), 181
Elizabeth (French), 176
Mary, 166, 176
Mercy, 180
William, 176, 181
SCOTT
Elias, 201, 202
Eunice, 201

515

TOOLEY
Clara Beaumont, 245
Dotha Ann (Bunnell), 245
Emma Josephine, 245
Jane E., 245
Joseph, 245
Joseph H., 245
Martha Dallas, 245
Nettie, 245
TOWNLEY
Charles, 195
Cornelia (_____), 403
David E., 357
Effingham, 357
Elizabeth, 357
Enos, 357
Enos Baldwin, 357
Hannah Mariah, 357
Joanna, 357
John, 91
John S., 403
Phebe (Bonnell), 91
Prussia, 403
Rhoda (Price), 403
Richard, 189
Sally (Bunnell), 357
Stephen, 195
William, 403
TOWNSEND
Ann, 439
TRACEY
Mary J., 290
Sheldon H., 290
TREADWELL
John, 274
TRIPP
Benjamin, 441
Charity W., 441
Charles, 183, 184
Daniel, 184
Elizabeth, 184
Elizabeth B., 441
George, 184
Henry, 441
Louisa, 441
Margaret G., 441
Mary (Bonnell), 441
Mercy B., 441
Pamelia (Bonnell), 183, 184
Perthania (Bonnell), 183, 184
Priscilla, 441
Simeon, 184
Uriah, 184
Zina, 183, 184
TROWBRIDGE
Abigail, 79
Emeline (Bonnell), 467
Thomas, 37
TRUMAN
Lyman, 213
TRUMBULL
John M., 404
TUBBS
Dinah, 285
Edward, 353
Jane (_____), 353

TUCKER
Nathaniel, 92
TULLER
Ruth, 142
TUNIS
Hannah, 460
TURKLE
Hannah, 437
TURN
John, 212
TURNER
Ellen, 402
TUTTLE
Candace, 290
Freelove, 131
Maria B., 208
Moses, 131
Sybil (Thomas), 131
Thankful, 301
Timothy, 50
TWITCHELL
Elizabeth (Tomlinson), 202
Joseph, 202
Mary, 202
TYLER
Adelaide, 307
Canfield, 307
Elizabeth Jerusha (Bunnell),
    307
Elmer, 307
Hannah, 205
Henry, 127
Leroy, 307
Lucy (Bunnell), 126, 127, 317
Malachi Stent, 127
Malichi S., 126
Margery, 124

- U -

UNDERHILL
Amy, 378
Caleb, 378
Margaret (Bonnell), 378
UPSON
Benjamin, 349
Luanna (Bunnell), 349
Theodotia, 285
UTTER
Abigail (Bonnell), 463, 464
William, 463
William T., 464

- V -

VAIL
Anna, 263
Betsey (Bunnell), 256
Betsey Caroline (Bunnell), 257
Eleanor G., 257
Elizabeth H., 257
Mary (Bonnell), 161
Mary Ann, 414
Merton W., 257
Moses B., 257
Orissa T., 257

VAIL
Shobal, 161
VALENTINE
Betsey (Bunnell), 261
Louise, 345
Marca, 261
Milo, 261
Nathaniel, 261
Obadiah, 356
VANCAMPEN
Eliza R., 221
VANDORN
Abigail, 421
VANVOORHIS
Elias W., 141
VAN ARSDALE
Jacob, 374
VAN BENTHUYSEN
Keziah Keturah, 343
VAN BLARCOM
Henry, 194
VAN MATRE
Morgan, 390
VAN RENNSSELAER
Anna Maria (Bunnell), 270
Stephen H., 270
VAN SYCKLE
Jemima, 438
Richard, 438
VAN SYCLE
Emily, 424
Jemima, 416
VAN WINKLE
Johannes, 143
Magdalene (Speer), 143
Rachel, 143
VANDERPOEL
Ambrose Ely, 355
VANDERVECK
Ann Eliza, 354
VANTASELL
Ida J., 459
VARICK
Richard, 361, 362
VAUGHAN
Daniel H., 408
Edward, 59
VERMILYA
Dwight, 331
Jane, 331
John, 331
Marietta, 331
Mary (Bunnell), 331
William J., 331
VERNON
Mary Margaret (Morgan), 428
VERPLANK
David, 462
Nancy (Bunnell), 462
VERVALEN
Susan Budd, 473
VOSE
Caroline (Lowrey), 288
Cynthia Anne, 344, 345
VREELAND
Henrietta B., 389

- W -

WADDLE
Benjamin, 433
WADE
Daniel, 190
David, 93
Elizabeth (_____), 190
James W., 198
James Wilson, 196
Joanna (Bonnell), 196
Jonas, 195, 460, 463
Patience, 196
Patty, 410
Robert, 195
Temperance, 190
WADHAMS
Noah, 276
WADSWORTH
James, 74, 119, 270
WAKELEY
Mary Jane, 238
WALKER
Abraham, 382
Electa (Bonnell), 382
Elizabeth D., 373
Miller, 188
Rhoda, 382
WALLACE
Amy (Bunnell), 412
Ann, 181
Anna (Bonnell), 181
Edward, 181
John, 181
John U., 412
Joseph C., 412
Mary, 181
Matthew G., 414
Richard, 181
Thomas, 181
William, 181
WALLEN
Elizabeth, 468
WALTER
Julian Ann, 213
Samuel, 188
WALTERS
John, 264
Lucy (Bunnell), 264
WALTON
Mark, 176
WANAMAKER
James H., 267
Jemima (Bonnell), 267
WARD
Aaron Montgomery, 81
Andrew, 326
Chester B., 326
David, 355
Eleanor (Bonnell), 151, 152
Eliza, 308
Elizabeth, 81
Elizabeth (Bonnell), 81
Enos, 152
Hannah, 355
Hannah (Farrand), 355